MODERN COMPUTER HARDWARE COURSE

REVISED AND UPDATED EDITION

By
Manahar Lotia
Pradeep Nair
Payal Lotia

www.bpbonline.com

REPRINT 2026
SECOND REVISED & UPDATED EDITION 2011
FIRST EDITION 2006

ISBN: 978-81-8333-167-8

Distributors:

BPB PUBLICATIONS
20, Ansari Road, Darya Ganj
New Delhi-110002
Ph: 23254990/23254991

DECCAN AGENCIES
4-3-329, Bank Street,
Hyderabad-500195
Ph: 24756967/24756400

MICRO MEDIA
Shop No. 5, Mahendra Chambers,
150 DN Rd. Next to Capital Cinema,
V.T. (C.S.T.) Station, MUMBAI-400 001
Ph: 22078296/22078297

To View Complete BPB Publications Catalogue Scan the QR Code:

Published by Manish Jain for BPB Publications, 20 Ansari Road, Darya Ganj, New Delhi-110002 and Printed by Manipal Technologies Limited, Manipal

www.bpbonline.com

Table of Contents

6 - Motherboard Installation

11 - Floppy Disk & Disk Drive

13 - Networking

14 - Understanding Internet

15 - Make Your Own Computer

18 - Computer Virus

Introduction to Computer

Computers have become a vital part of our life. In our day to day life, in each and every field we come across some use of computer, be it in our working place or at our home.

This chapter introduces you to the computer and the way computer works. Different parts of the computer and how they work is also covered in this chapter.

Later, we take a look at the various parts that together make the modern day computer, various input/output devices, storage devices etc.

What is a Computer?

A computer is basically an electronic device which converts unorganized facts or data into some meaningful information.

This conversion is done under the control of set of instructions which is known as computer programs. People who make these programs are called computer programmers. This chapter starts with the definition of the terms Hardware & Software, two of the most common and at the same time confusing terms used in the computer field.

Hardware & Software

"Hardware" is a term used to describe the physical components of the computer, any computer part that you can see or touch, such as the computer monitor, keyboard, mouse etc. is hardware. Any accessory or device connected to the computer, such as the printer is also hardware.

To make these hardware components work, software is required. "Software" is a set of instructions, provided to the computer to carry out the job required by user.

For example, if you want the computer to print salary slip of an employee, you will require a computer and a printer as hardware and at the same time you will also require a software that will instruct the computer about

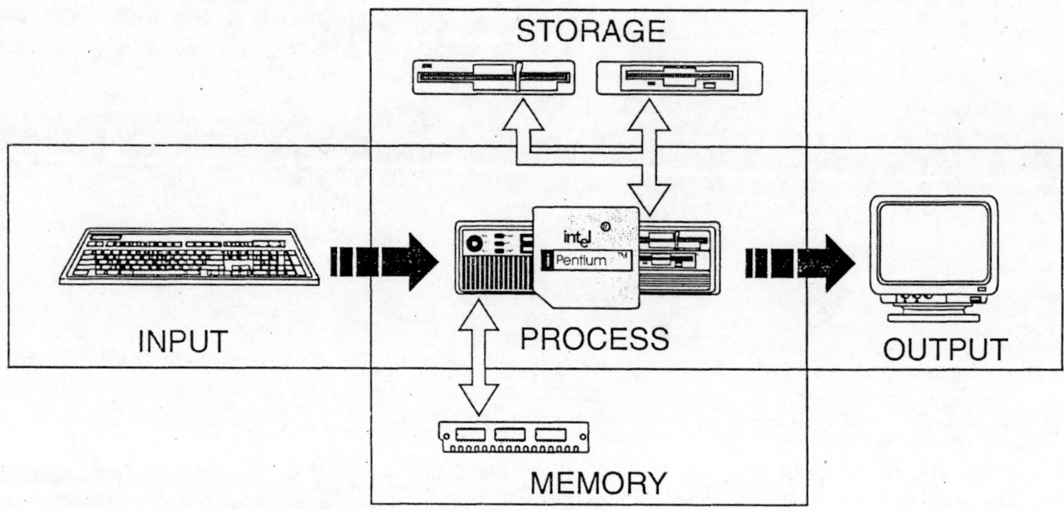

Fig. 1-1 : Concept of Input/Process/Output.

- from where to get the basic information required to calculate the salary,
- how to calculate the salary and
- how to print the calculated salary slip.

Without software the computer hardware is like a dead machine, it will be of no use.

To further understand the hardware, software concept, let us see the hardware and software in the audio system. In audio system, the cassette player, speakers, microphone etc. are hardware, even the audio cassette is a hardware, because you can see and touch it, but the songs recorded on the audio cassette, without which the complete hardware (audio system) will be of no use, is the software.

By hearing the recorded songs, you can realize that the software is there but, you cannot touch or see it.

In this same manner, when you get some software on a floppy disk or a CD-ROM disc, the floppy disk or the CD-ROM itself is hardware, but the program, the set of instructions stored on the floppy disk or the CD-ROM is software.

Other than the hardware and the software, two more wares are commonly used in the computer field, they are "firmware" and "humanware"

"Firmware" is software permanently stored inside the computer.

"Humanware", "Peopleware" or "Liveware" are the name given to the people who work with the computer, such as the computer programmers, system analyst, computer operators etc.

Input, Process, Output

Now that we know the computer system needs hardware and software to work. Let us see, how the computer does a job, such as printing of a pay-slip.

To print a pay-slip, computer needs a software, giving step by step instruction to print the pay-slip. Further, it requires the basic data, such as the employee's name, basic salary, earnings, deductions etc., required to calculate and print the pay-slip.

Using an input device, a keyboard, these basic data items are fed to the computer and are stored in some storage device such as a hard disk drive.

The input device keyboard converts the information we type at the keyboard into proper format for the computer to be able to work with them.

The brain of the computer (CPU, Central Processing Unit inside the computer) carries out step by step instructions given by the software.

By following these instructions and using the data stored in the storage device, CPU calculate and print the pay-slip. The final information such as the gross salary, gross deduction, net salary etc. are stored in the storage device for any future reference.

Finally, software instructs the computer to output the calculated information onto some output device such as on a monitor or a printer. The output device converts these information into a proper format that we can understand.

Basic Computer System

Figure 1-3 shows a basic computer system. As you can see in this figure a basic computer configuration consists of the Monitor, Main System Unit, Keyboard and a Mouse.

Initially, Mouse was not part of the basic computer configuration, but as the use of Windows and other graphical interface increased, mouse has become a part of the basic computer system configuration.

Main System Unit

It contains all major components of the computer. It contains the CPU (Central Processing Unit, Brain of the computer) and the RAM (Random Access Memory, memory of the computer), on an electronic circuit board known as the "Motherboard".

It also contains storage devices such as floppy disk drive, hard disk drive etc. Power supply which provides clean electrical power to the computer is also located inside this system unit.

The front side and back side of this system unit has many indicators, switches and connectors for various purpose, which we shall explain later.

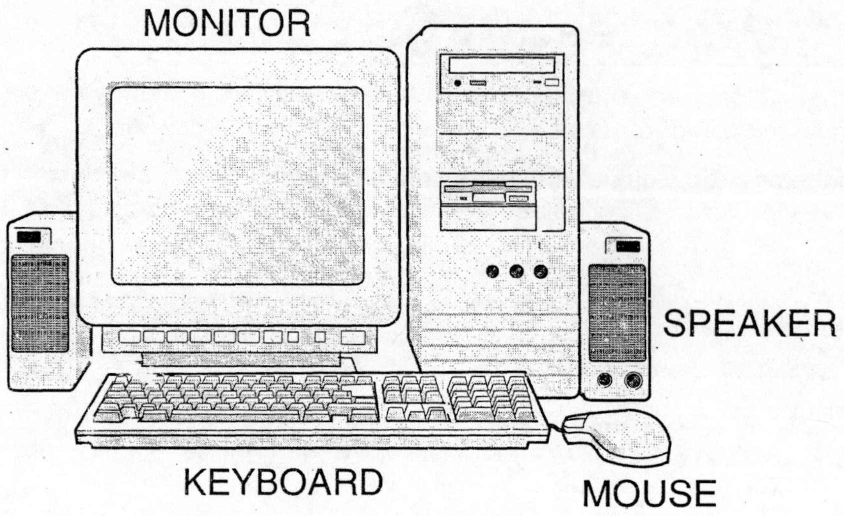

Fig. 1-2 : Basic Computer System.

The Monitor

It is most common output device used with a computer. This is a TV like device that display information send to it by the computer. A monitor can display text, as well as graphic images in multi-color or single colour, based on whether the monitor being used is a color monitor or a monochrome (single color) monitor.

The Keyboard & Mouse

These are two of the most common input devices used with the computer. Initially the keyboard was the only input device, but as the use of Windows and Windows like other graphical interface based software increased, the mouse has become an integral part of the computer.

Other than these basic/minimum devices required to use the computer, one must also have some device to get the computer output on the paper. For this a "Printer" is used.

One can use a device called "Modem" to connect the computer to a number of different computers anywhere in the world, using the "Internet", world wide network of computers.

A "Scanner" can be used to feed any existing image, photograph, drawings etc. into the computer.

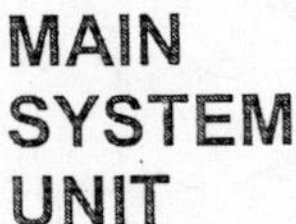

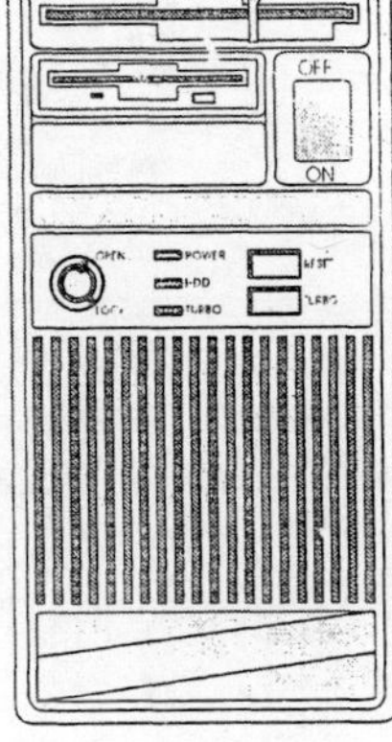

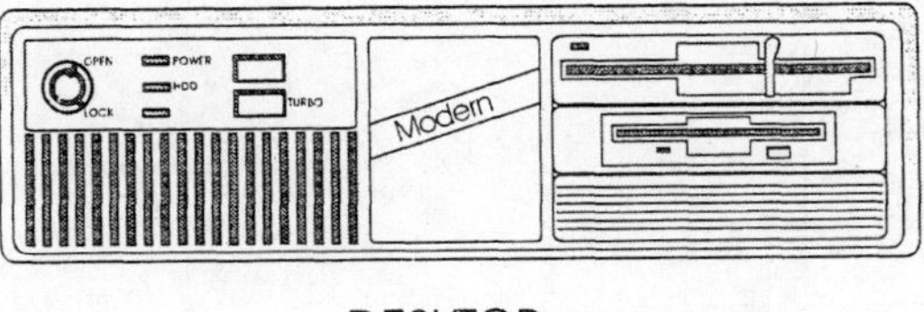

DESKTOP TOWER

Fig. 1-3 : Two types of Main System Unit.

Main System Unit

Let us now take a closer look at the main system unit of the computer. The main system unit of a computer is available in basically two different styles

- Desktop and
- Tower

The initial Personal Computer (PC) had desktop style case, but currently the tower style case is more common with the PCs. The tower style cases based on its height is available in full size, normal size and mini size.

Front of Main System Unit

The front side of the main system unit, whether it is desktop style or tower style case, contains many different switches and indicators, let us see what they are and what is their use.

Indicators

The front side of the main system unit has many indicators to indicate different activities being done by the computer. Most of these indicators are LEDs (Light Emitting Diodes) that emit red, yellow or green light to indicate different activity.

Power

This LED indicates the power on position of the computer.

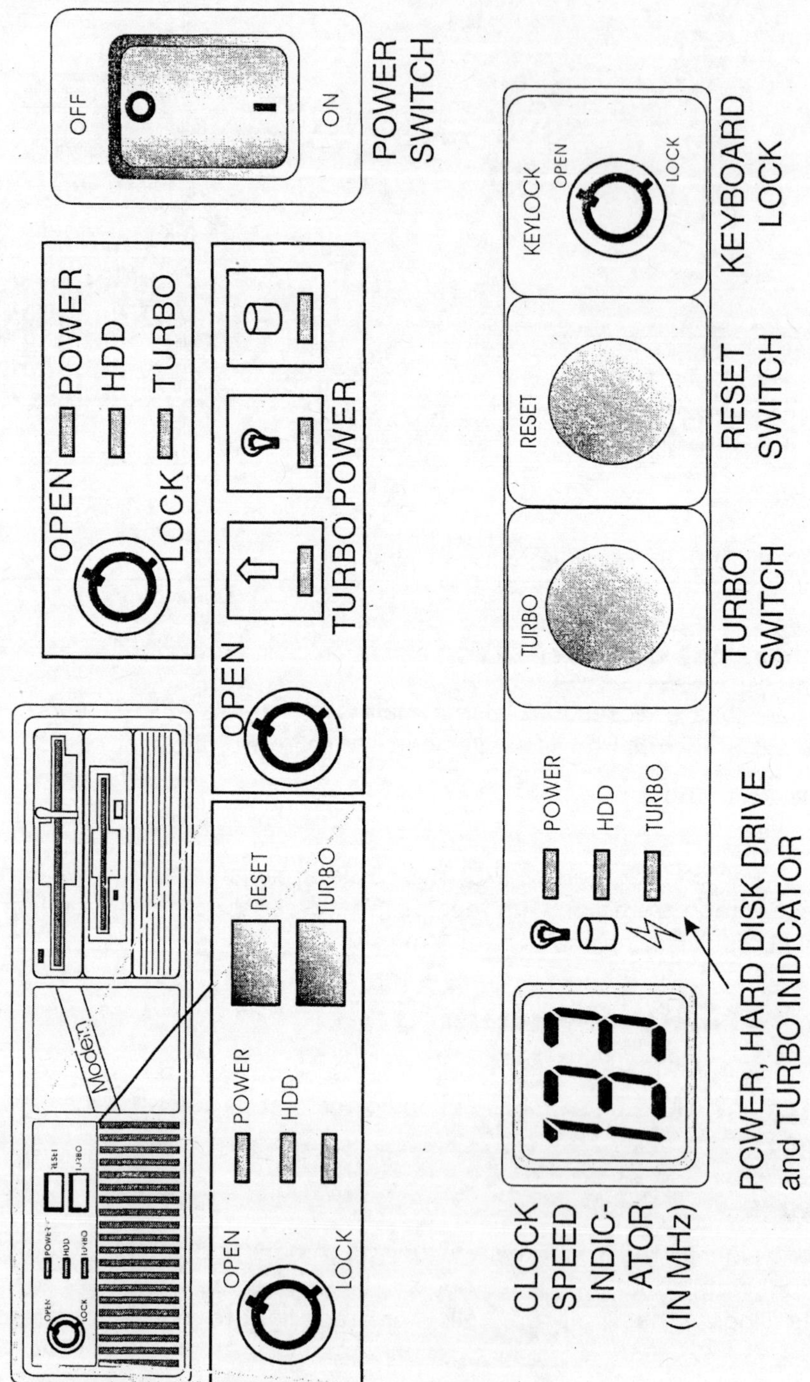

Fig. 1-4 : Various switches and indicators on the front-panel.

HDD access

This LED indicates that the storage device, Hard Disk Drives is doing a read or write operation.

Turbo

When this LED is on, it indicates that the computer is working in fast, turbo mode. Non-turbo mode is also known as "compatibility mode".

In current generation of computers this indicator is no longer used.

Speed

This is a 2/3 digit indicator to show the current speed of the computer. This speed is shown in MHz (Mega Hertz).

The speed shown on this indicator is not the real speed of the computer. When the computer is assembled, this indicator can be setup to show any speed by the person assembling the computer. So, one should not take the speed displayed by this indicator very seriously.

In current generation of computers this indicator is no longer used.

Switches

With the indicators, the front panel of the system unit also contain many switches to control the system.

Turbo

This switch is used to change the computers speed from high speed turbo mode to normal mode or from normal mode to turbo mode.

In turbo mode the turbo indicator will be on and the speed indicator will show higher MHz speed. When computer works in slow speed "normal mode" the turbo LED will be off and the speed indicator will show a slower MHz speed.

In current generation computers this switch is no longer provided.

Reset

This switch provides an option to restart the computer without switching off the power supply of the system. Pressing of this switch will restart the computer.

This switch can be used when the computer is not responding to keyboard.

Power On/Off

Desktop style computer case provide the power on/off switch on the back side of the computer, on the power supply itself. But, the tower model computers provide the power on/off switch on the front panel of the computer.

This switch is used to turn the power supply on/off.

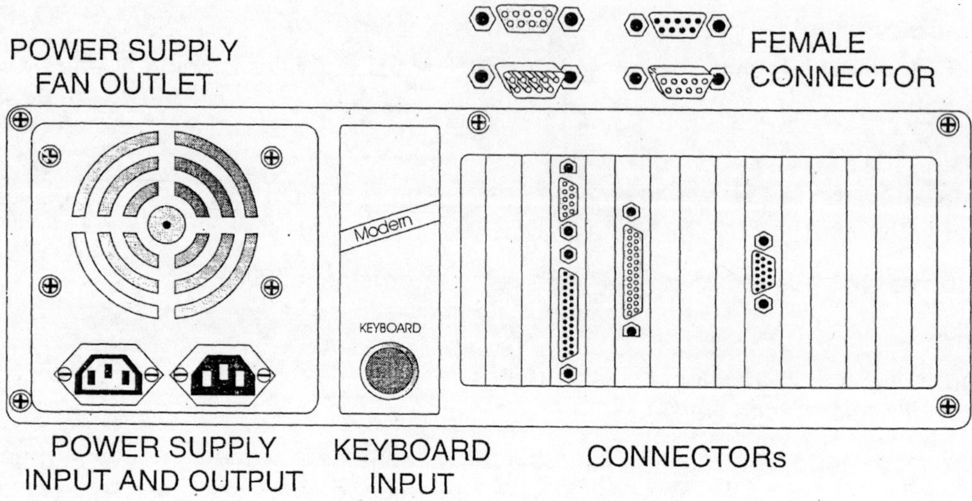

Fig. 1-5 : Various Sockets at the back of Computer System.

Keyboard Lock (Keylock)

A keyboard lock is provided in most of the computer to stop computer access by unauthorized persons. When this lock is off the keyboard will not function.

Many computers also lock the system units cover when this lock is on, so that nobody can open the cover and override the lock.

In current generation computers this lock is no longer provided.

Back of Main System Unit

The back of the main system unit, whether it is desktop or tower style contains many different connectors. Let us see them, what they are and what is their use.

Male/Female Connectors

Male connectors are connectors with pins on them and female connectors are connector with holes on them.

Power In Socket

This male socket is used to connect the power supply cable from the AC mains power supply to the computer system.

Power Out Socket

This female socket is provided on the back of the system unit to provide power supply to the monitor.

Monitor can be connected to this power output, or can be directly connected to the AC mains power supply. This depends on the type of the power connector provided on the monitor.

Power Supply Fan Outlet

The power supply, inside the main system unit, has a fan to remove the hot air generated by various components inside the unit. This fan also helps to re-circulate the outside cool air inside the system unit.

The outlet for this fan is provided at the back side of the main system unit.

Keyboard Connector

A round opening is provided on the back of the main system unit to connect the keyboard to the computer. The actual keyboard connector is little inside, on the motherboard. One can see the connector from this opening.

Peripheral Connectors

The backside of the main system unit provide connectors for the different input/output devices used with the computer. These devices are also known as peripherals.

There are different connectors for the monitor, mouse, printer, audio etc.

Inside the Main System Unit

Let us now see the components inside the main system unit.

Motherboard

The main component inside the main system unit is the motherboard. This is the biggest electronic circuit board inside the computer system, on which many other board are attached.

The boards that attach to the motherboard are known as daughterboard or expansion board.

The motherboard contains many important components, such as

- the CPU (computer's brain)
- RAM & ROM (computers memory)
- many support chips for the CPU and
- Expansion Slots to Connect Peripheral.

CPU

CPU or the Central Processing Unit is the brain of the computer. All the mathematical operations such as addition, subtraction etc. and the logical process such as comparing of two values are done by the CPU.

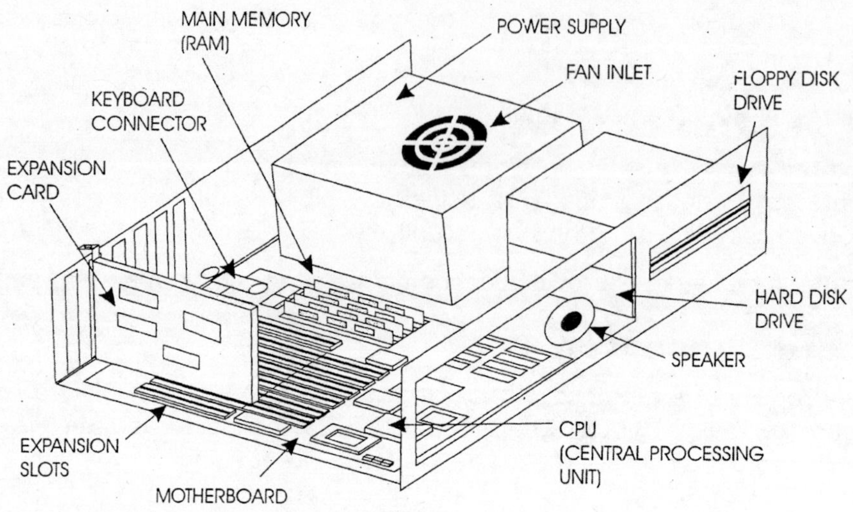

Fig. 1-6 : Inside the Main System Unit.

The CPU is also known as Microprocessor.

Memory (RAM & ROM)

For any mathematical or logical operation, CPU requires some memory. This memory is used to store the initial values, intermediate results and the final results, during any operation.

CPU Support Chips

With the CPU and the memory, motherboard also contain some support chips or ICs. These chips help the CPU in carrying out its various activities.

Some of the common support chips are DMA Controller, Interrupt Controller, Keyboard Controller, Timer etc.

Chipset

Current motherboards provide different functions provided by the support chips on a set of chips (ICs) known as chipset. These chipsets are made by various motherboard manufacturers, such as Intel, Opti, Via etc.

Expansion Slots to Connect Peripheral

The motherboard contains many expansion slots, long narrow connector towards the back of the computer. On these slots different expansion cards can be connected to attach various peripherals devices to the computer.

These expansion slots provide path to devices connected to them to communicate with the CPU and memory on the motherboard.

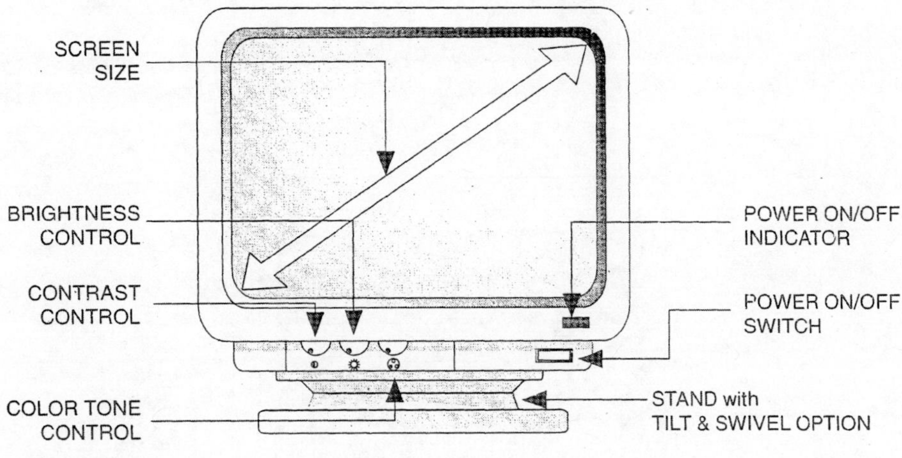

Fig. 1-7 : Monitor

Storage Device

Main system unit also contain the storage devices. These devices are used by the computer to store various information.

Some storage devices such as floppy disk and hard disk work on the principal of electromagnetism, currently storage devices that use light (laser beam) to read/write data on optical disc are becoming popular, these discs are known as CD-ROM (Compact Disc-Read Only Memory) disc.

Some of the common storage devices are

- Floppy Disk Drive
- Hard Disk Drive and
- CD-ROM/DVD Drive

Power Supply

Power Supply is the heart of the computer system. Like the human heart pumping blood to different parts of the body, the power supply provides various parts of the computer with clean DC power supply to keep the computer alive and functioning

The power supply converts high voltage AC power from the AC mains supply to DC power required by the computer.

The power supplies are rated in watts, currently power supplies of 260 or higher wattage are common.

A fan assembly is provided in the power supply to keep the computer cool, if this fan fails, the computer may overheat and start giving intermittent problems or may completely stop working.

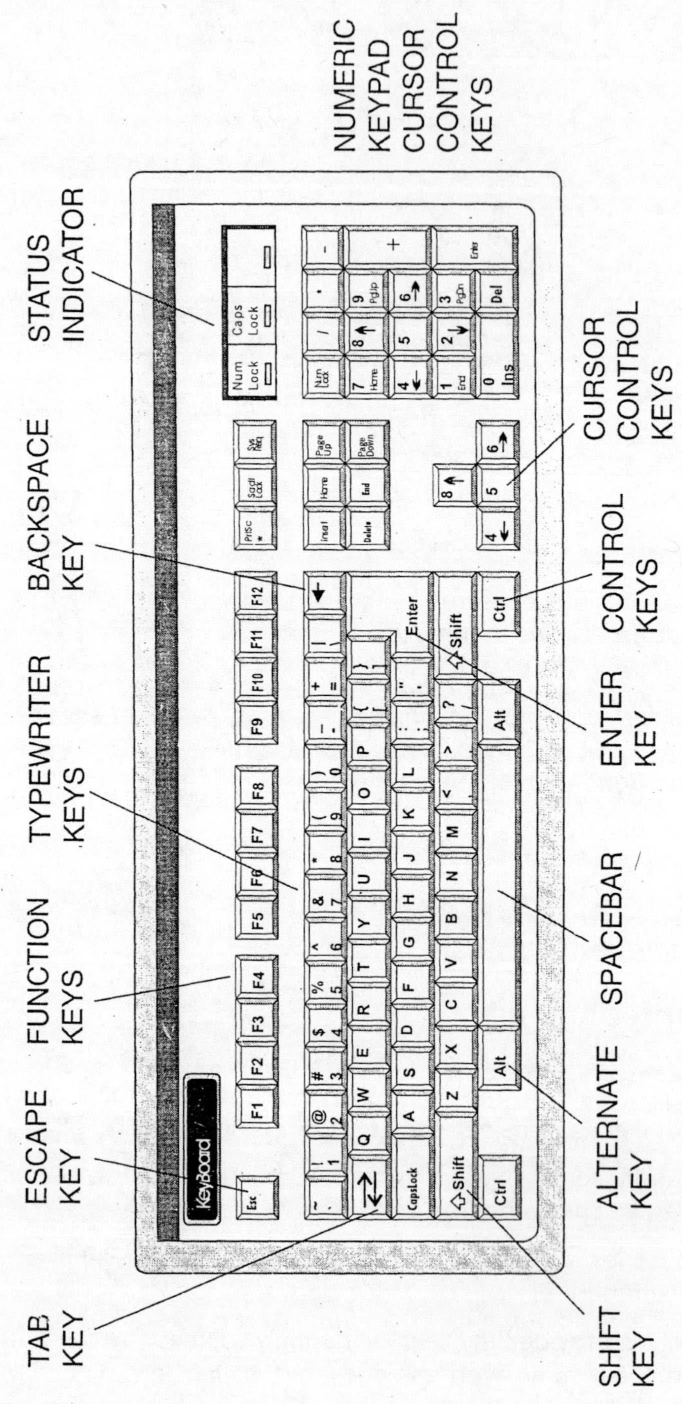

Fig. 1-8 : Keyboard.

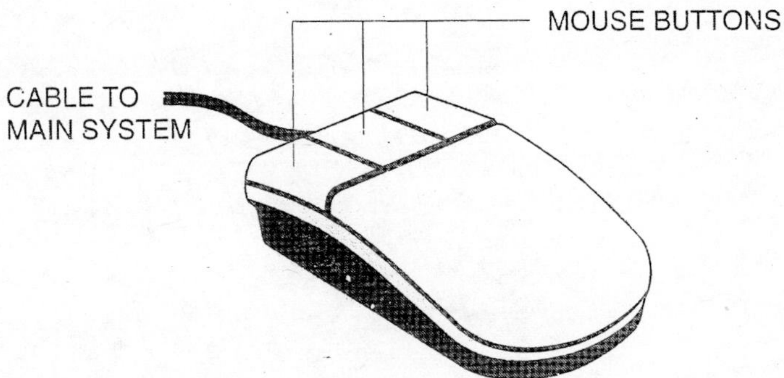

Fig. 1-9 : Mouse.

Monitor

Monitor or the VDU (Visual Display Unit) is a television like output device. It is used to show the result of processing done by the computer. Monitor can be used to show text, numbers, or graphic image such as a charts, graphs, figures etc.

The monitor is available in many different sizes. Size of monitor is measured diagonally, a common monitor size is 15 inch, for designing and desk top publishing (DTP) purposes 17 inch or bigger monitor is preferred.

Keyboard

Keyboard is the main input device for computer. Format of computer keyboard is similar to the typewriter keyboard so that a traditional typist can use the computer keyboard without any trouble.

Mouse

A mouse is basically a pointing device about the size of palm. It rolls on a small ball and has one or more buttons on the top. When the user rolls the mouse across a flat surface, the screen "cursor" (a blinking underline) or mouse pointer moves in the direction of the mouse's movement.

The "Mouse" is basically made for Graphical User Interface applications, but, compared to choosing an option using the cursor control keys, using a mouse is more natural, even in the text based environment.

The mouse can never replace the keyboard, but it can supplement the keyboard by doing tasks such as moving the cursor and pointing to on-screen objects, tasks for which the cursor movement arrow keys are ill-suited.

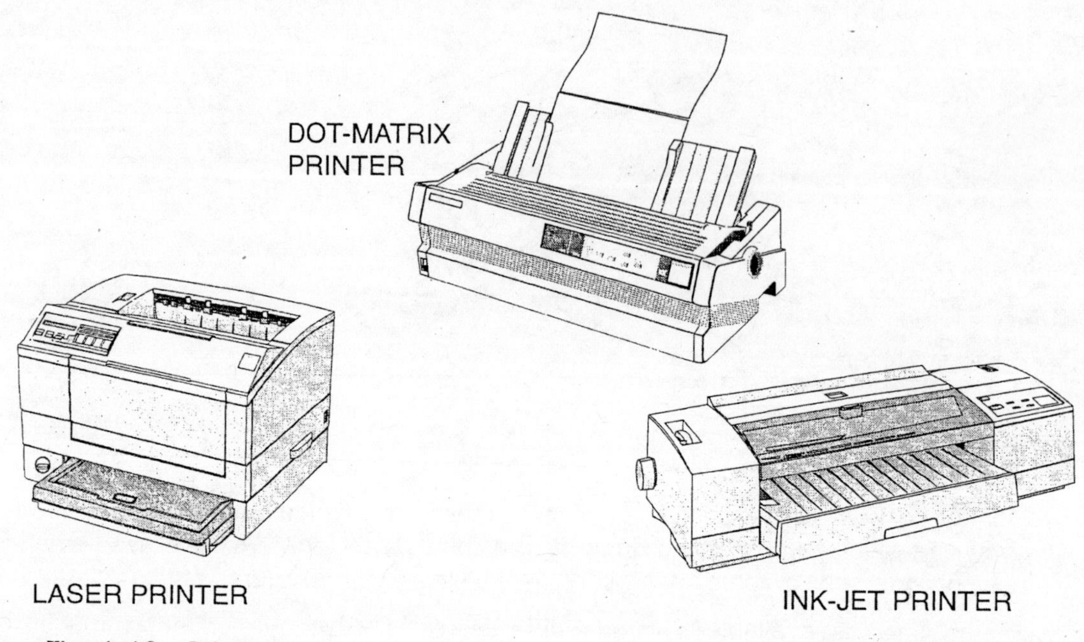

Fig. 1-10 : Printers.

Printer

Printers are output devices, they are used to get the computer output on a paper, envelop, OHP transparency sheet etc. Output produced by printer is known as "hard copy", because these outputs are permanent compared to the information displayed on the monitor, which is known as "soft copy".

Three types of printers are commonly used with the personal computer (PC). They are

- Dot-matrix
- Ink-jet
- Laser

The quality of a printed output is measured in the number of dots printed by the printer, in per square inch of area. This is known is DPI (Dots Per Inch) value.

Dot-Matrix printers have lowest DPI value, laser and ink-jet printers are available for 300 and more DPI value.

Modem

The modem is a device which allows you to connect your computer to any other computer, anywhere else in the word using a telephone line.

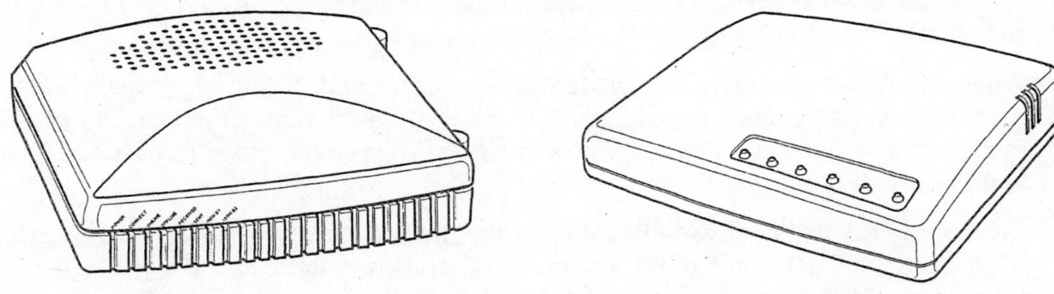

Fig. 1-11 : Modem.

This allows you to communicate with the connected person, transfer data, copy software/programs from the connected computer, sent and receive mail using e-mail etc.

Currently, the modem can also be used to sent and receives fax, for this you can use modem as a fax devices. To connect to the Internet or the WWW (World Wide Web), one requires a modem.

The modem is available as

- Internal Modem and
- External Modem

How Modem Works?

Modems is a device that allows us to connect two computer using normal telephone line. The sending computer's modem modulates the digital signal from computer into analog signal required for transmission over the telephone line.

At the receiving end, the incoming analog signal is given to the modem. This modem demodulates the analog signal back into digital signal and gives this signal to the computer.

Let us see how a modem works.

When the computer is switched on and is ready to transmit data it sends a Data Terminal Ready (DTR) signal to the modem. When the modem is ready to receive data or instruction from the computer, it sends a Data Set Ready (DSR) signal to the computer. Both these signals must be present before the next step can happen.

Next, the computer sends a command to the modem to go "Off Hook", i.e. to open communication with the phone line. Next, the computer issues a command to modem to dial a phone number.

These commands are given via "Transmit Data TxD" line. The modem acknowledges receipt of these command by replaying to the computer on the "Receive Data RxD" line.

When the remote modem, the modem at the other end of line responds, the local modem sends a special greeting tone to the remote modem, to inform the remote modem that it is being called by another modem. The remote modem responds with a higher pitched tone.

Once a communication is established between the two modems, local modem sends a "Carrier Detect" CD signal to the computer. Carrier is a steady tone signal of a fixed frequency, which is later modulated by modem to transmit the data.

Next, the two modems enter a process known as "Handshake". This process decides how the two modems are going to communicate with each other. Various things decided during this process are

- The number of bits used to represent data,
- Number of bits used to indicate start and end of data,
- Use of parity bit for error checking/correction,
- Transmission speed, transmission protocol, compression method etc. Being used

If the two modems, local and remote do not use the same settings then they will wind up sending characters that will not make sense, or they may completely refuse to communicate with each other.

Once the handshake is done, the computer sends a Request To Send (RTS) signal to the local modem. This signal asks the modem if the modem is free to receive data from the computer.

If the modem is not busy, then the modem will send a Clear To Send (CTS) signal to the computer. Once the computer receives this CTS signal from the modem, the computer will send the data to be transmitted to the modem.

If the modem cannot transmit the data, as fast as it is received from the computer, then the modem will drop the CTS signal to the computer, this will stop any further data from the computer. Computer will stop data transmission to the modem until it receives CTS signal.

Data received by the local modem is transmitted as different frequency sound signal to the remote modem, The remote modem converts these series of tones back into digital signal and gives it to the computer, it is connected to.

Once the data transmission is over, modem sends a break communication command. If the connection is broken by remote system, the local modem will drop the Carrier Detect (CD) signal.

This will inform the local computer that the communication is broken.

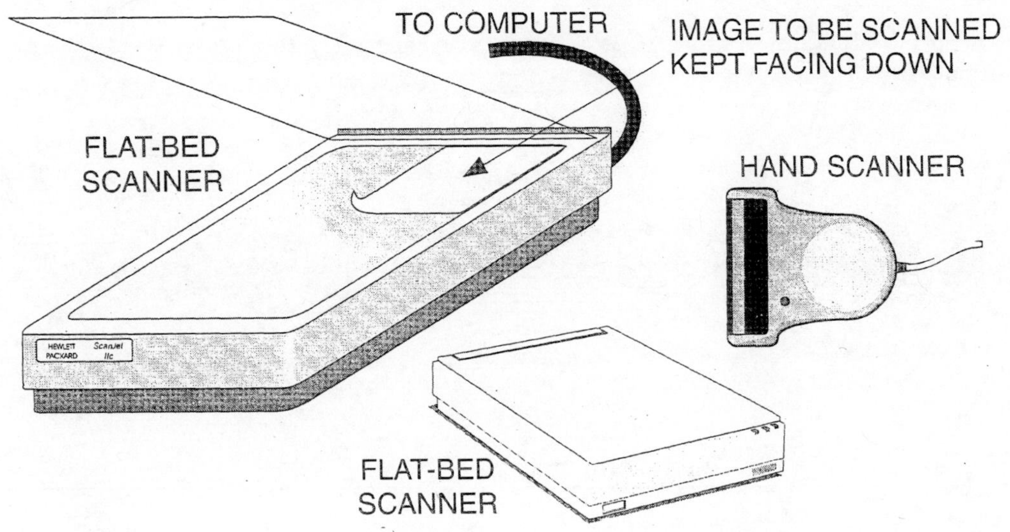

Fig. 1-12 : Scanner.

Let us now see the meaning of some of the indicator lights given on a modem's front panel.

Abbr.	Meaning
RD	Receive Data,this light flickers each time data is transferred from the modem to the computer. This indicates that modem is receiving data from the remote computer.
SD	Send Data, this light flickers each time data is transferred from the computer to the modem. This indicates that you are sending data to remote computer.
TR	Terminal Ready, this indicator glows when the modem detects DTR signal from computer. This informs that the computer is ready.
MR	Modem Ready, this indicator glows when the modem is ready for operation.
CD	Carrier Detect, this indicator glows when the modem detects a carrier signal. In indicates that the modem has established connection with the remote modem.This light goes out only when one of the modem hangs up and the carrier signal is dropped.
OH	Off Hook, this indicator glows when the modem takes the control of the phone line. This is equivalent to taking the phone receiver off hook.
HS	High Speed, when this indicator glows, it indicates that the modem is currently operating at its highest possible speed.
AA	Auto Answer, when this light glows it indicates that the modem is in Auto Answer mode. In this mode modem will automatically answer any incoming calls. This facility allows unattended access to the computer from remote modem.

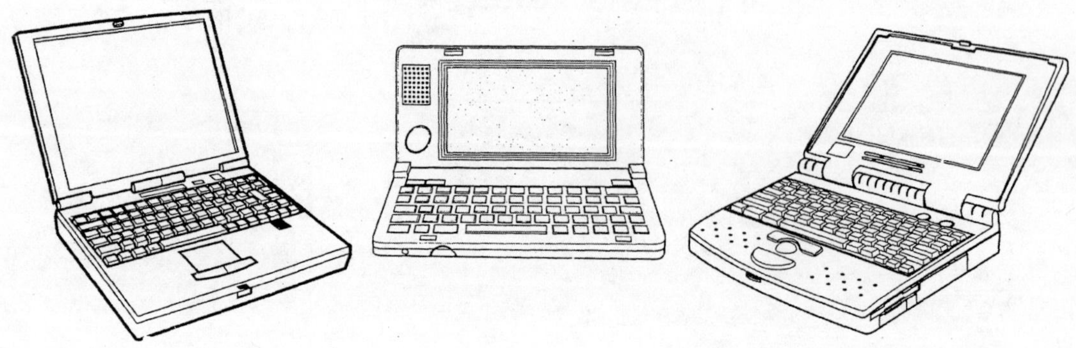

Fig. 1-13 : Portable, Laptop Computers.

Scanner

Scanner is used to input a photograph or any other existing drawing, sketch etc. into the computer.

The scanner is a photocopier like device, which scans the image put onto it and sends the image into the computer. Once the image is scanned into the computer, you can manipulate the image using graphic manipulation software such as Corel Photopaint, Adobe Photoshop etc.

Laptop/Notebook/Portable Computer

A laptop or notebook computer is a portable computer that is entirely self-contained. In a portable computer, a single package includes main processor, memory, the display system, the keyboard, mouse, and a set of batteries.

All laptop PCs have flat-panel display systems because they can fit in the computer case and also their power requirement is very small compared to standard picture tube based display.

These flat-panel display can operate from rechargeable batteries. Common flat-panel displays used with the portable computer are LCD display and Gas Plasma display.

Almost all notebook computers use a design known as "Clamshell Design". In this design, the display screen folds flat atop the keyboard, this design is good to protect both the screen and keyboard while traveling with the notebook.

Like a clamshell, the two parts of computer are hinged together at the rear.

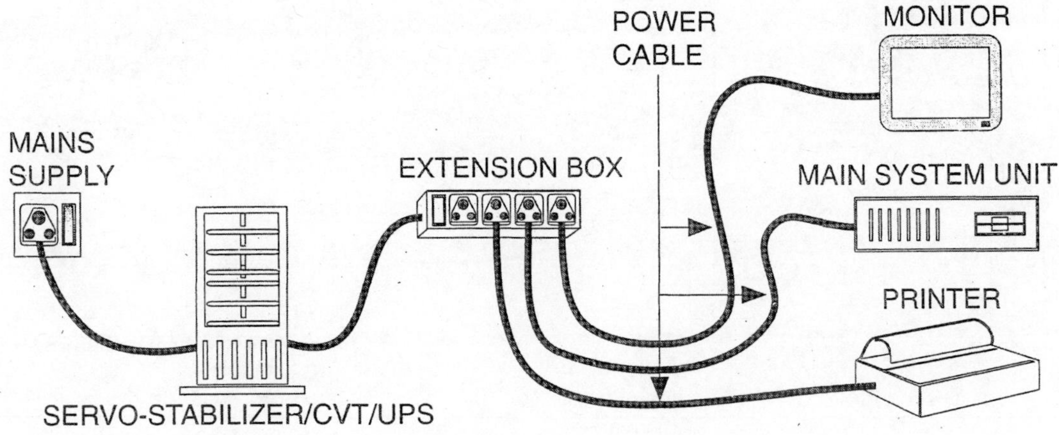

Fig. 1-15 : Connecting various devices to A/C mains supply.

Different portable computers are classified according to their size and weight. Some of them are

- Laptop
- Notebook and
- PalmTop and PDA (Personal Digital Assistant)

The laptop is heaviest portable computer and PDA is the lightest portable computer.

Regular computer expansion cards are too heavy and use too much power to use them in portable computers. Instead, a visiting card size expansion slot and card is used in these computers.

This card is known as PCMCIA cards. The term PCMCIA stands for Personal Computer Memory Card International Association.

These cards are available in type-I, type-II and type-III formats.

- The type-I cards are 3.3mm thick and can be used in all the three type slots. Type-I card is used for memory cards and software application cards.

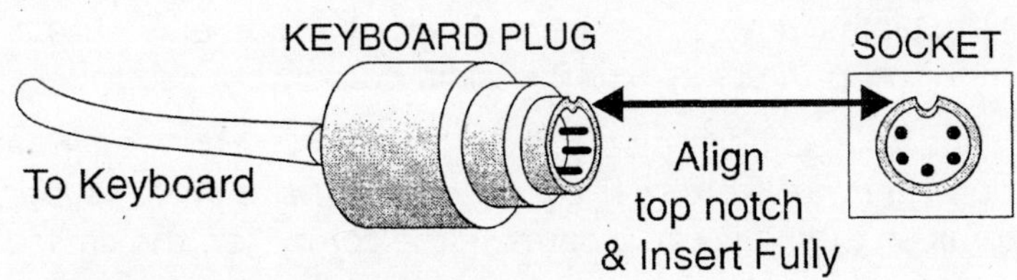

Fig. 1-14 : Keyboard Socket and Connector.

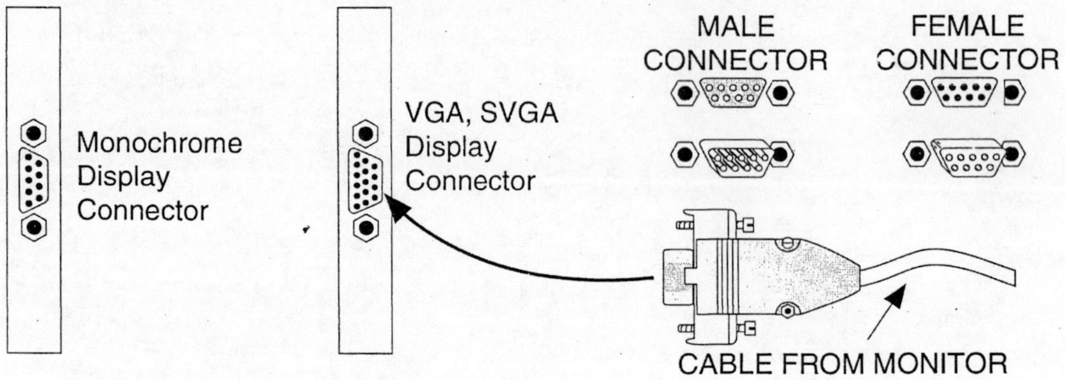

Fig. 1-16 : Monitor Socket and Connector.

- Type-II cards are 5mm thick and can be used in type II and III expansion slots. Type-II card is used for modem & fax cards, LAN cards and all type-I use.
- Type-III cards are 10.5mm thick and can be used in only type-III slots. Type-III card is used for miniature hard disk drives and for all type-I & II use.

Most of the portable computers use special low power processors to conserve the power. These computers also use data compression to increase the storage capacity of the hard disk drive to store more data in a small capacity drive.

One shortcoming of these computers is their price, these computers cost almost double compared to desktop computers of same capacity.

Using the Computer

After looking at the various parts that make a computer, let us see how to connects those parts together and how to start using the computer.

Let us start with how to connect different devices to the main computer system.

Connecting Different Devices

This section explains how to connect different input and output devices such as keyboard, monitor, printers etc. to the main computer system.

Remember that connecting or disconnecting any device to the computer must be done in the computer and device power off condition. If the power supply to the device or the computer is on then this could damage the computer, the device being connected, or both.

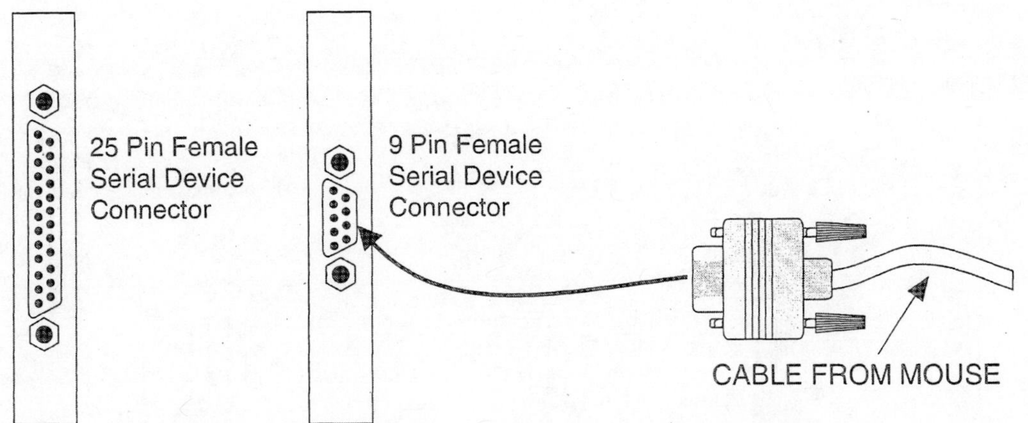

Fig. 1-17 : 9-pin and 25-pin Mouse Connector for Serial Mouse.

Power Cable

To provide power to the computer, a power conditioning device such as stabilizer, CVT (Constant Voltage Transformer) or UPS (Un-interruptible Power Supply) is first connected to the AC mains supply.

The UPS is the best power conditioning device, as it takes care of almost all power problems such as spike (very high over-voltage that lasts for less than a millisecond), surges (over-voltage that lasts for few milliseconds to a second), under-voltage, brown-out, black-out, over-voltage etc. The UPS also provides backup power to the computer in case of any power failure.

The output from this power conditioning device is given to an extension box, to which different devices are connected.

Based on the type of the power connector provided on the monitor, a monitor can be connected to the output on the power supply of the computer or it can be connected to the extension box.

Monitor

After connecting power cable of the monitor into the computer's power supply or into the power extension box, another cable known as data cable from the monitor needs to be connected to the computer system.

9-Pin female or 15-Pin female D-Shell socket at the back of system unit is used to connect monitor to the computer system.

- The 9-pin socket is used to connect Monochrome, HGA (Hercules Graphic Adapter), CGA, EGA or Dual display (which supports both HGA & CGA) monitors to the computer system.

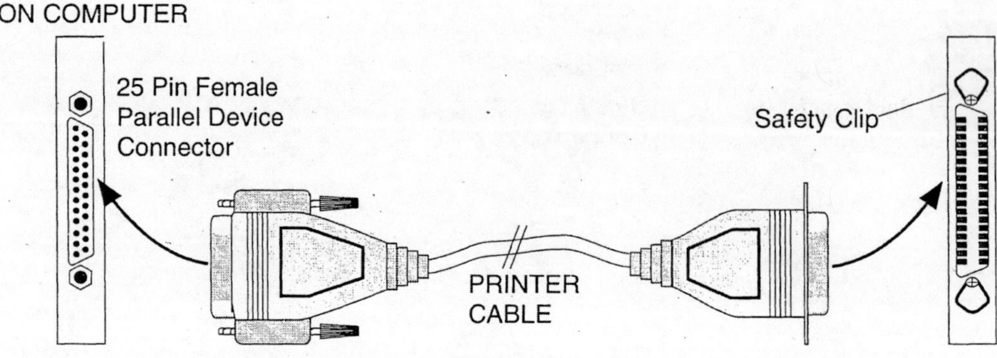

Fig. 1-18 : Printer Connector.

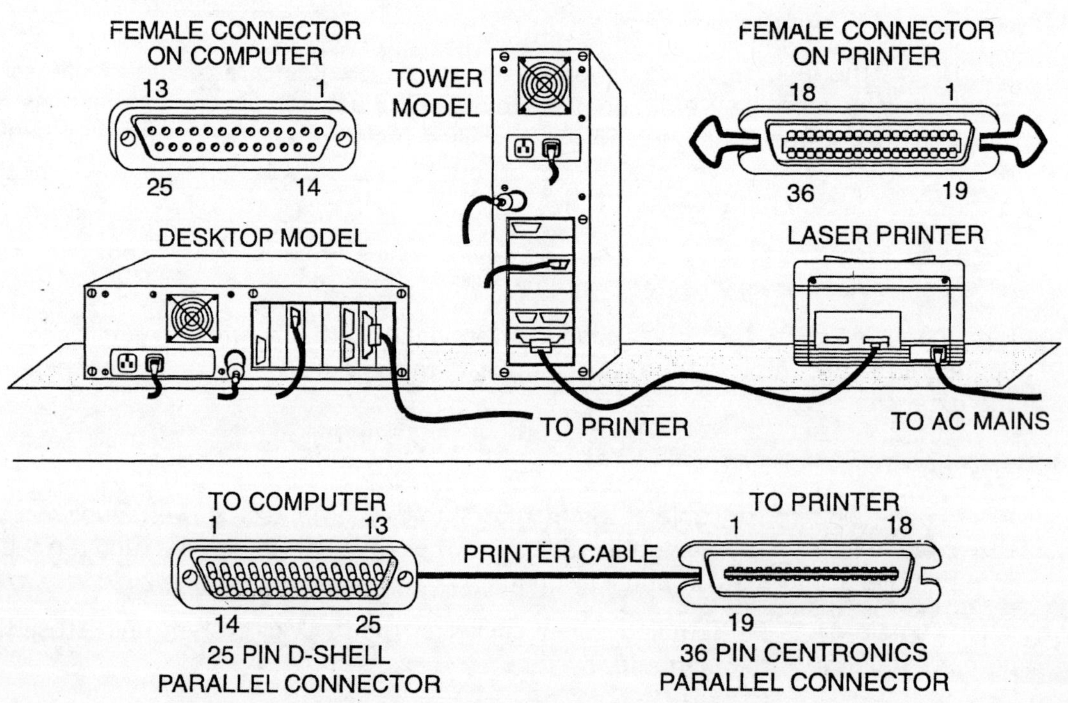

Fig. 1-19 : Connecting Printer to Computer System.

- The 15-pin socket is used to connect currently available VGA or SVGA monitor to the computer system.

Keyboard

The keyboard is connected to the small round opening provided at the back of the main system unit.

When connecting the keyboard to this socket make sure that a small notch on the socket and on the keyboard connector are properly aligned, otherwise the pins of the keyboard connector will not align with the holes provided on the socket.

Once the connector and socket are properly aligned, insert the keyboard connector fully into the socket.

Currently many keyboards come with USB, PS/2 Mini-DIN or Wireless connectors. Check the connector provided with the keyboard and attach to proper socket on the main system unit.

Mouse

A mouse is connected to the serial port socket provided at the back of the main system unit. Generally, the computer has two serial ports COM1 and COM2 (COM stands for COMmunication Port).

Most of the software provided with the mouse can automatically detect the serial port at which the mouse is connected.

Currently many mouse come with USB, PS/2 or Wireless connectors. Check the connector provided on the mouse and attach to proper socket on the main system unit.

Printer

Printer is connected to the 25-pin female D-Shell socket provided at the back of the main system unit. Socket for serial device is a 25-pin male D-Shell socket.

Cable for connecting printer to the computer has a 25-pin male D-Shell connector at one end and has a special type of connector known as Centronics Connector at the other end.

The 25-pin male D-type connector on printer cable is connected to the 25-pin female D-type socket on the main system unit and the other end of the cable with Centronics connection is connected to the Centronics socket on the printer.

Currently many printers come with USB, and Wireless connection. Check the socket provided on the printer and connect to the proper socket on the main system unit.

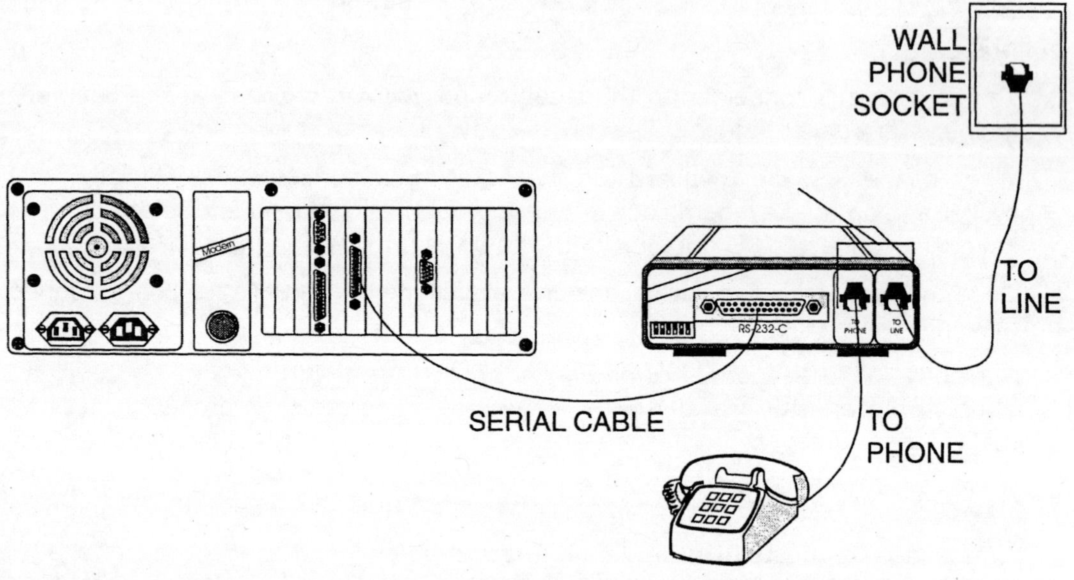

Fig. 1-20 : Connecting Modem to Computer and Telephone Line.

Speaker/Microphone

Speaker and Microphone are connected to the output provided at the back of the sound board. Back of the sound board contain jacks for connecting the microphone and a set of speakers.

Using proper cable, speaker output can be connected to an audio amplifier, or home stereo system to produce high volume sound output.

Modem

If you are using an external modem, then connect the modem to the serial port on the computer unit.

If you are using an internal modem then no serial connection is required. The internal modem comes as an expansion card and is directly connected inside the computer to one of the expansion slots.

If you want to use the same telephone line for normal voice communication as well as for the data communication then connect the modem to the telephone line and a telephone instrument can be connected to the line out provided on the modem.

Connect a RJ-11 cable to the phone socket provided on the wall, connect other end of this cable to the line socket provided on the modem.

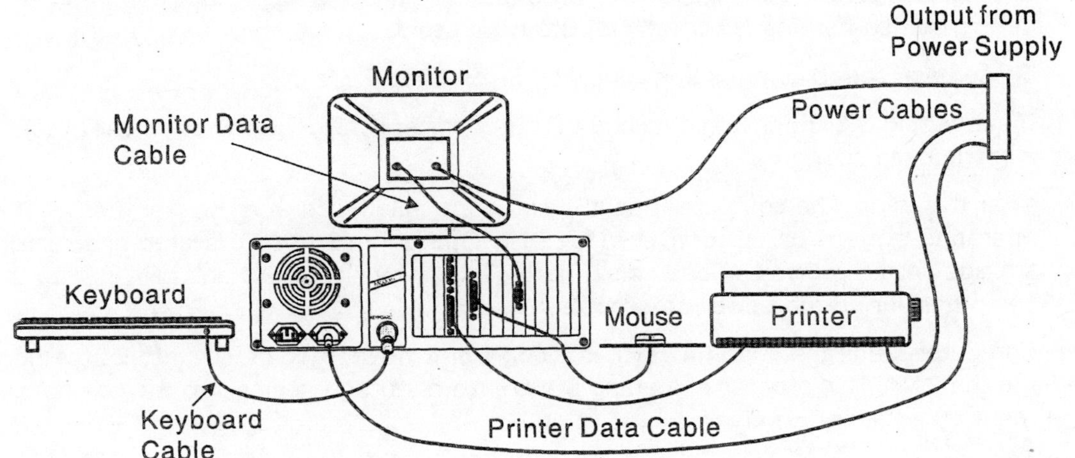

Fig. 1-21 : Various Devices Connected to Computer System and Power Supply.

One end of another RJ-11 cable should be connected to the phone socket provided on the modem and the other end of this cable can be connected to a telephone instrument.

This allows same line to be used for voice as well as data communication.

If you are using an external modem, then connect the power supply provided with the modem to the power socket.

Starting the Computer

Once all the required devices are properly connected to the main computer unit, you can switch on the computer. Start the computer by first switching on the AC mains switch, power conditioning device (UPS, stabilizer etc.) switch and the power-on switch provided on the front panel or the back of the main system unit.

Turn on the monitor, turn on the printer, the external modem, and the speaker if you require their service.

When the main unit is turned on you will hear the main unit power supply fan's rotation sound. After some time the computer will produce a single beep sound to indicate that all its parts are working properly.

Before producing this beep sound, computer does a POST (Power On Self Test) operation. During POST, computer checks most of its parts to make sure that they are working normally.

During the POST, if the computer finds that a part is not working as expected, then it will display some error message or produces some combination of beep sounds to inform that something is wrong with the computer.

These beep sound combinations is called Error-Beep Codes.

If everything is all right with the computer then, after POST, the computer will produce a single beep sound.

After this beep, the computer needs a software called Operating System (OS). This operating system or OS or DOS (for Disk Operating System) is stored on some storage device such as a floppy disk, hard disk drive or CD-ROM and provided to the computer during the power on process.

Computer reads the operating system (OS) from the storage device into its memory i.e. the RAM. This process of loading the OS from storage device into the computer's memory is called "Booting of the Computer".

This booting process is repeated whenever the computer is switched on, because every time power supply to the computer is switched off, the information stored in the computer's memory (RAM) is lost.

Some of the OS available in the market are, MS-DOS, Unix, Linux, MS-Windows, OS/2, DR DOS etc. Out of these Operating Systems the Windows developed by Microsoft Corporation is most common operating system in the PC environment.

Starting with MS-DOS

Let us see how to start a computer with MS-DOS. Based on whether the computer has a hard disk drive or not, this process is done in two different ways.

Without Hard Disk Drive

If your computer does not contain a hard disk drive, then it must have a floppy disk drive to boot the system.

To boot the system, keep a floppy disk that contains the MS-DOS (known as DOS Floppy, Boot Floppy or System Floppy) into the first drive (drive A:) and close the drive door.

Switch on the system, after some time the computer will start copying the OS from the floppy disk into the computers memory (RAM).

The computer will then display "starting MS-DOS" message on the screen. Once the OS is transferred into the computers memory, DOS will take control of the computer and you will see the DOS prompt A:\> on the screen.

```
A:\>
```

Now you can start using the computer.

Once the DOS prompt comes on the screen, you can use DOS commands to communicate with the computer. When you are at the DOS prompt, computer will recognize DOS commands.

With Hard Disk Drive

If your computer has a bootable hard disk drive then every time you switch on the computer, you will not be required to place a DOS or Boot floppy disk into A: drive.

When switched on, computer will copy the OS from the hard disk drive into its memory (RAM) and make the OS active.

When booting the system from a hard disk drive make sure that the door of all floppy disk drives are open, otherwise if you have a floppy disk without the OS in the floppy disk A: and if the door of the drive A: is close then because the computer can not find the OS in that floppy disk, computer will suspend the booting process with some error message such as

```
Non-system disk or disk error
replace the disk and press any key
```

If your hard disk drive is not bootable then you will be required to provide a bootable floppy every time the computer is switched on.

Starting With Windows 95/98

If your computer has Windows 95 or Windows 98 installed on the hard disk drive then you need to boot the machine from the hard disk drive itself.

When using Windows, booting from a floppy disk will take you to the DOS prompt, not to the Windows operating system.

When the Windows is started from the hard disk drive, after sometime, "Starting Windows 95" or "Starting Windows 98" message appears on the screen.

Next, depending on the software setup with Windows, a log on screen may appear. If this screen comes on then type in the user name and password, at appropriate places and press enter key.

After the enter key is pressed, the Windows is loaded into computers memory and the control of computer is handed over to the Windows.

After Windows is loaded, Windows task-bar and Start button will appear on the screen. At this stage one can start using the computer.

OTHER TITLES OF INTEREST

Fundamentals of **Cyber Security**
ISBN: 9789386551559

Cybersecurity Fundamentals
ISBN: 9789390684731

Mastering Network Forensics
ISBN: 9789355516916

Practical Digital Forensics
ISBN: 9789355511454

Modern Cybersecurity Strategies for Enterprises
ISBN: 9789355513137

Modern Cybersecurity Practices
ISBN: 9789389328257

Python for **Cybersecurity** Cookbook
ISBN: 9789355513809

Fundamentals of **Information Security**
ISBN: 9789389328400

Cybercrime and Preventive Measures
ISBN: 9789390684526

Zero Trust Security
ISBN: 9789355512512

Practical Cyber Threat Intelligence
ISBN: 9789355510297

Cyber Safety for Everyone
ISBN: 9789391392567

AWS All-in-one Security Guide
ISBN: 9789355510327

Cryptography and **Network Security**
ISBN: 9789389328660

Secure Chains
ISBN: 9789389328653

My Data My Privacy My Choice
ISBN: 9789389845181

Motherboard

Motherboard is the most important component in any personal computer. It contains almost every important parts of the computer system.

Normally, the motherboard contains the CPU or the brain of the computer, memory (ROM, RAM etc.) and support circuits to make the computer work.

Motherboard also contains many Expansion Slots on which you can connect various circuit boards. These circuit boards are used to connect different devices such as monitor, printer, scanner etc. with the computer.

This main board is called the motherboard because all other circuit boards, inside the computer, are attached to this board i.e. it is the mother of all boards.

As this main board is called the motherboard, all other boards that attach to it are called "daughterboard".

Sometimes the size of the daughterboard could be bigger than the size of the motherboard. But, most of the time motherboard is the largest circuit board inside a personal computer.

Motherboard contains

- CPU (Microprocessor),
- Co-Processor (optional),
- CMOS Memory,
- Real Time Clock (RTC) circuit,
- Memory (ROM and RAM),
- BIOS,
- Support Chips/Chipset to help CPU to deal with Input/Output, Interrupts, DMA etc.,
- Expansion Slots

On the Motherboard Printed Circuit Board (PCB), the components are placed and connected with the help of thin copper tracks. Motherboard PCB contains many such tracks to make electrical connection between different parts of the system.

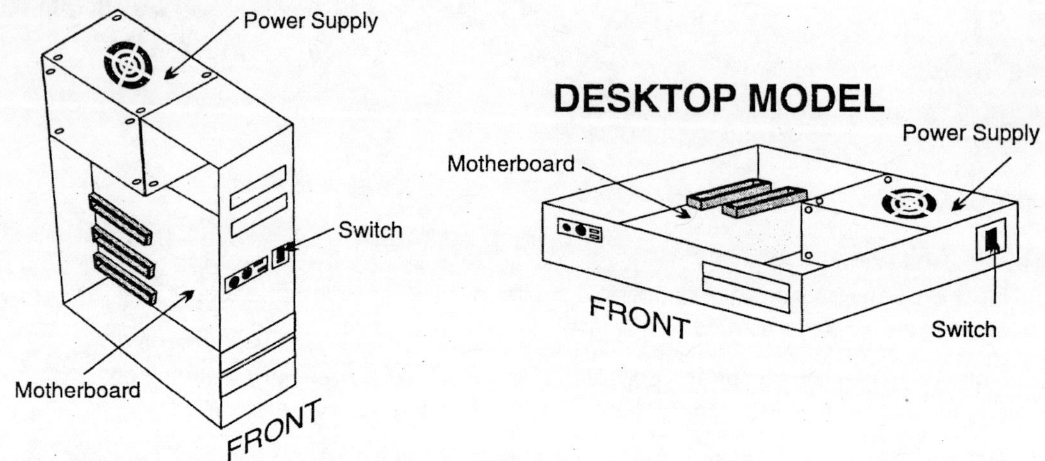

Fig. 2-1 : Position of Motherboard inside Tower and Desktop Model.

Generally these tracks are very fine, and hence one should never put excessive pressure on the board while inserting or removing cards or chips, if the board bends excessively, these tracks could develop small hairline cracks.

Once a track is broken, because of the multiple layers of tracks, it is almost impossible to trace the broken area and repair it.

When evaluating the quality of the motherboard one should consider

- The thickness of the board. Most cheaper boards are quite thin and they cannot withstand careless handling or frequent insertion and removal of the expansion cards.
- The quality of the soldering. The soldered joints of a good motherboard should be bright not foggy.

Position of the Motherboard

Insidethe main system unit, position of the motherboard depends on the model/type of the cabinet being used.

Inside a Tower model cabinet, the motherboard is attached to one side of the system box, normally it is placed just below the power supply.

On a Desktop model cabinet, the motherboard is placed at the base of the system box, next to the power supply.

Motherboard is connected to the cabinet with about 1/2 inch high plastic spacer in between the board and the cabinet at various places.

This protects the components on the motherboard from touching the cabinet's bottom metal surface and short circuiting themselves.

BUS

What is Bus?

Bus is an electronic road along which signals are send from one part of the computer to another.

Thin lines you see on the Motherboard are the buses that take data, address, contro signals and power from one place to another on the motherboard.

Depending on their use, bus is divided into three major types

- Data bus
- Address bus
- Control bus

When someone talks about the bus, without specifying its type, then most probably he is talking about the data bus.

- The data bus is used to move data from one place to another. The number of the data lines provided in the bus is very important factor that determines the speed of this data transfer.
- The address bus is used to select a particular memory location to read or write the data. Maximum memory that CPU can address depends on the size of its Address Bus.
  Addressable locations = $2^{\text{(total address lines)}}$
  if you have 3 address lines total addressable locations will be $2^3 = 8$. 32 bit PCI Local bus uses 32 address lines and it can address 2^{32} = 4,294,967,296 different locations or 4096 Mega Bytes of memory.
- The control bus is used to send control and timing signals between various parts of the computer.

Motherboard Components

Motherboard comprises of following components

CPU (Main Processor)

The main component of any motherboard is the main processor chip which controls the inner functions of the system. The Central Processing Unit (CPU) functions as the brain of PC.

CPU is usually inserted into the socket and is not soldered onto the motherboard, this makes its replacement, in case of any problem, or for upgrade, very easy.

Some of the common CPU chips are Intel 8088, 8086, 80286, 80386, 80486, Pentium, Pentium MMX, Pentium-II, Pentium-III, Pentium-4 etc.

Coprocessor

What is a Coprocessor?

Coprocessor is a special purpose microprocessor which is used to speed up main processor by taking over some of the main processor's work.

Most common type of coprocessor is a math coprocessor. A math coprocessor helps main processor in performing mathematical calculations.

Older system had special socket on the motherboard for coprocessor, but the current generation of CPU's have math coprocessor built inside them so they do not require any coprocessor.

CMOS Memory

In old IBM XT or compatible system, BIOS with the help of jumpers detected about the components on the computer system.

IBM AT and higher systems do not use these jumpers, instead they use a small CMOS memory with battery backup to store the system configuration, date, time etc.

Here CMOS stands for the "Complementary Metal Oxide Semiconductor" technology.

This CMOS memory receives power from a battery accompanying it, this battery helps it retains the information stored in it, even when the system is switched off.

When an AT or higher system is switched on, BIOS matches the information stored inside the CMOS with the components connected to the system and if it finds some mismatch or error the BIOS displays some error message, explaining the problem.

Real Time Clock Circuit

Real Time Clock (RTC) circuit keeps the computer time/date up-to-date. With the help of a battery and CMOS memory, this circuit maintains correct date and time even when the mains AC supply to the computer is switched off.

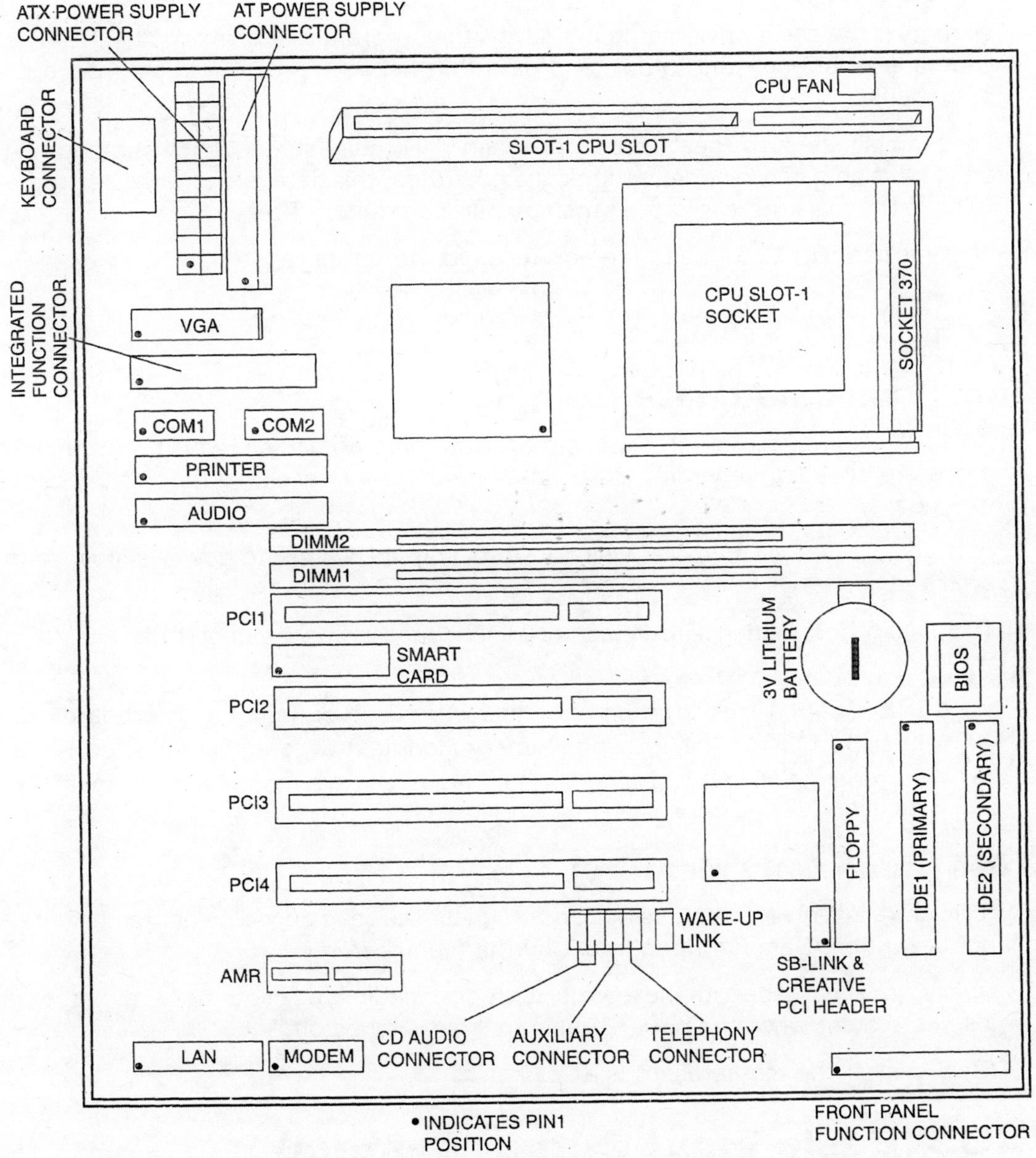

Fig. 2-2 : A Common Motherboard.

Memory

What is Memory?

Memory is the place where computer stores the program (set of instruction telling the computer what you want to do), and data that help the program in carrying out its operations.

For example, a marks sheet printing program will require student's roll number, name and marks obtained in various subjects etc. as data, this data, along with the program to print the marksheet is kept in the computer's memory (RAM).

There is basically two type of memory used in the computer

- RAM
- ROM

RAM (Random Access Memory)

RAM or Random Access Memory is a read/write type of memory which is used by the processor to keep program, data and intermediate results during the program executions.

It is volatile type of memory, which lose its content when the power supply to it is switched off.

The physical installation of RAM memory on the motherboard can take place in various ways:

- DIP (Dual In-line Pin) memory chips were used on initial motherboards
- later the SIMM (Single Inline Memory Modules) became common
- currently DIMM (Dual Inline Memory Modules) are most common memory module.

ROM (Read Only Memory)

ROM or Read Only Memory, as its name suggest is a read only type of memory. It can not be written. Data is written into it by the manufacturer.

One major advantage with the ROM is, it is non-volatile type of memory i.e. it does not lose its content when the power supply to it is switched off.

BIOS chip on the motherboard is a ROM chip.

BIOS (Basic Input Output System)

What is BIOS?

BIOS is an abbreviation of Basic Input Output System. It is one of the most important program stored inside the computer. It is a firmware, as it is stored in the ROM, . .

BIOS program lets your application program and the hardware such as floppy disk, hard disk, video adapter etc. communicate with each other.

It is pronounced "bye-os".

The BIOS also contains a program called Power-On-Self-Test or POST. This POST program checks the motherboard and other devices connected to the computer during the system power-on.

BIOS program are available from Award, Phoenix, American Megatrends Inc. (AMI) etc. various manufacturers.

Support Chips/Chipsets

Apart from the processor chip and the memory, motherboard also contains many controller chips and other devices which binds everything together.

A typical system requires Interrupt controller, DMA Controller, Timer chip, Clock chip, Bus controller chip, I/O peripheral interface chip etc. to make the computer work as a complete unit.

Modern developments in electronics have made it possible to produce very large scale integrated circuits (VLSIC), and now just two or three of these VLSIC chips can do the work which were previously performed by dozens of different chips.

These set of VLSIC chips are called "Chipsets".

A typical chipset contains in two or three VLSIC chips all the support logic required by the processor to function as a complete system.

Many of chipset maker include support for serial/parallel ports, floppy and hard disk controllers, USB support, modem support, LAN and audio support, and display adapter on their chipsets.

Expansion Slots

What is Expansion Slot?

The expansion slots are long thin connectors on the motherboard, near the backside of the computer.

Expansion slot is the backbone of the computer. When you want to add a new device to your computer-other than what is on the motherboard-you need an expansion slot.

Different expansion cards are connected to the motherboard through the data, address and control lines/buses on these slots.

Depending on the width and the technology, expansion slots can be divided into following categories

- 8-bit ISA

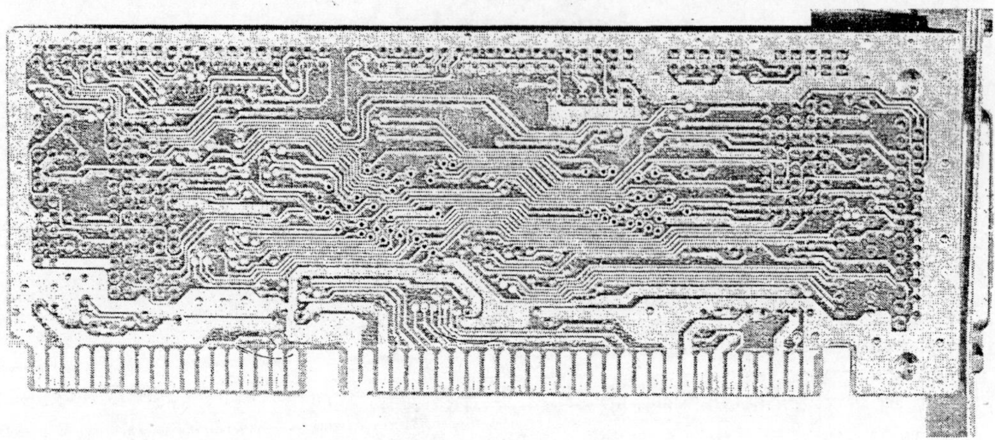

Fig. 2-3 : 16-Bit ISA Expansion Card.

- 16-bit ISA
- MCA
- EISA
- VESA Local Bus or VL Bus
- PCI Local Bus
- AGP

Modern Pentium based motherboards manufacturers stopped using ISA slots, they provide only PCI slots.

The 8-Bit ISA

ISA stands for Industry Standard Architecture, and this is the first and the most common bus architecture for the PCs.

This bus is also referred to as "Classic AT Bus". This connection contains 8-bit data line, 20-bit address line, and power and control lines.

This type of adapters have total 62 contacts at the bottom of the adapter card, i.e. 31 contacts on both sides of the card.

The main disadvantage of this bus is, whenever a new device is connected to this bus, many jumper and DIP switch settings are required.

The 16-Bit ISA

Because of the 16-bit data line available in the 80286 processor (used in the AT machines), AT motherboard's are equipped with 16-bit ISA bus.

When designing these 16-bit ISA slots, IBM had added another 36 new connector (i.e. 18 on each side) slots to the existing 8 bit ISA slots.

This makes the existing 8-bit ISA cards compatible with 16-bit ISA slots.

MCA

MCA or "Micro Channel Architecture" bus technology is based on a completely new bus design introduced by the IBM for their PS/2 range of machines.

The MCA never became a popular bus architecture because of two main reasons.

- First reason is that MCA was not compatible with the existing ISA technology, it required completely new expansion cards.

  All your existing ISA cards will become useless when you upgrade from an ISA motherboard to MCA motherboard.
- The second reason is, IBM had made the earlier 8-bit and 16-bit ISA bus system as an Open System, i.e. anybody could make and sell ISA cards.

  The MCA architecture was made a Proprietary System by the IBM, and they allowed only a few manufacturer to make MCA adapters and charged high license fee from them.

  This made the MCA adapters very expensive compared to the ISA cards.

Two new concept introduced with the MCA is now being used by many other newer bus technologies such as PCI etc., they are

- Auto configure
- Bus mastering

Auto Configure

This allow the user to connect any device to the MCA bus without worrying about the IRQ, INTerrupt and DMA channel setup problems.

Devices connected to these buses automatically configure themselves according to the other devices existing in the system.

This is another name for the Plug-and-Play.

Bus Mastering

Bus mastering allows the peripheral device to take the control of the bus from the CPU for a short time.

Using this facility the device can transmit or receive large blocks of data in a short burst modes.

EISA

EISA or Extended Industry Standard Architecture, is a bus architecture created by a group of nine computer manufacturers in response to the MCA bus design by the IBM.

One big plus point in favor of the EISA is that even though it is a 32 bit bus technology, it is fully compatible with the 8 bit ISA and 16 bit ISA adapters.

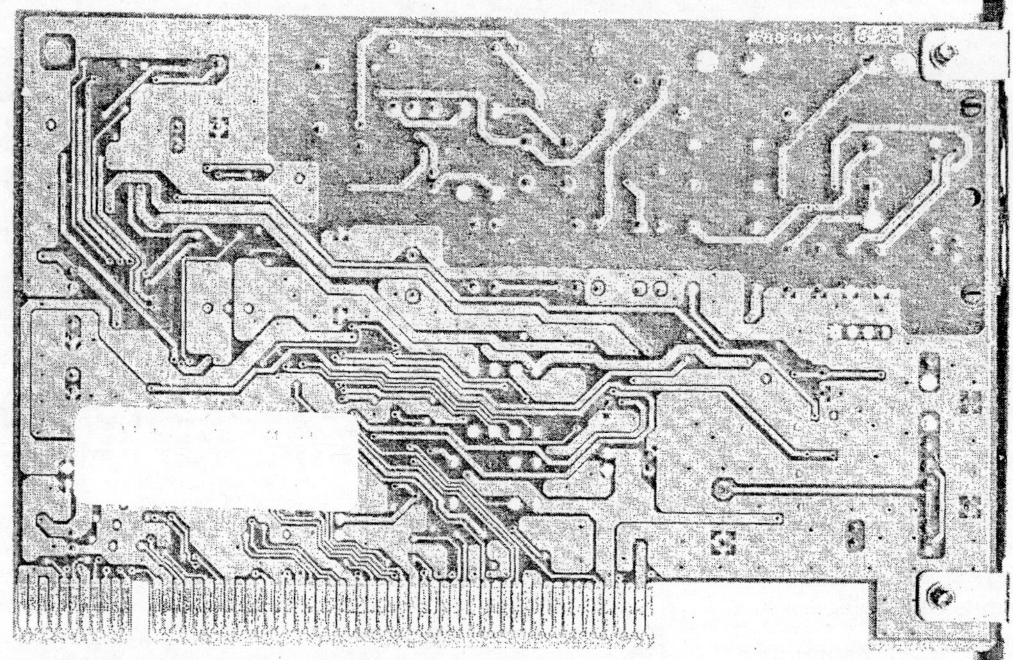

Fig. 2-4 : PCI Expansion Card.

Like the MCA architecture, the EISA technology allows "bus mastering" and "auto configure" options.

Local Bus

One major drawback of the ISA or even the EISA bus is they do not allow the devices connected to them to communicate with the CPU at the maximum speed that the CPU can offer.

If you have a motherboard with 33-MHz CPU and your expansion slot is a 8-MHz, 16-bit ISA slot, than the device such as video or the hard disk connected to this slot, can not operate at its full capability.

This situation is somewhat like trying to send the water coming in a 6 inch diameter pipe through a 1 inch pipe.

A local bus slot allows the device connected to it to communicate with the CPU at the speed, the CPU is capable of.

There are many local bus design in the market. Most of the proprietary designs from one manufacturer will not work with the card from other manufacturers.

VESA Local Bus / VL Bus

VESA stands for Video Electronics Standard Association, which is an association of video adapters and monitor manufacturers to standardize the PC video specifications.

Two main use of the Local bus slot is for connecting

- the Video adapter and
- the Hard disk drive adapter,

as these two devices requires very fast access by the CPU.

The maximum speed limit for the VL Bus specification is 33MHz without any wait state. The VL Bus can move data between the processor and the video or any other device connected to the VL Bus at the 32 bit data at a time.

The maximum throughput of the VL Bus is rated to be about 130 Mega bytes per second, which is about 16 times faster than ISA.

The VESA standard specify that at a time not more than 3 VL Bus devices should be connected to the motherboard. This is done to avoid putting too much load on these buses, which will slow them down.

PCI Local Bus

VL Bus was the best option for a 486 machine, when Intel introduced the Pentium CPU, with the 64 bit data path and 60-200 MHz speed, the VL Bus could not take complete advantage of these improvements.

The VL Bus had the limitation of 32-bit path and 33MHz maximum speed.

To overcome these limitations Intel provided a completely different local bus specification called PCI or Peripheral Component Interconnect. With the Pentium processor the PCI is standard local bus.

PCI supports 130 megabyte per second bandwidth, and it takes full advantage of the 64-bit data path of the Pentium processor.

PCI originally operated at 33-MHz using a 32-bit-wide path. Currently, PCI Extended, or PCI-X provides for 64-bit transfers at a speed of 133-MHz for 1-Gbps (gigabits per second) transfer rate.

AGP

AGP or Accelerated Graphics Port is a high speed bus for the display boards. Some of the features of AGP bus are

- If allows the video board to use system memory (RAM), as video memory.
- It is four to eight times faster than the PCI.

AGP slot on the motherboard can be easily distinguished because it is slightly offset from the other PCI slots, is usually darker in colour.

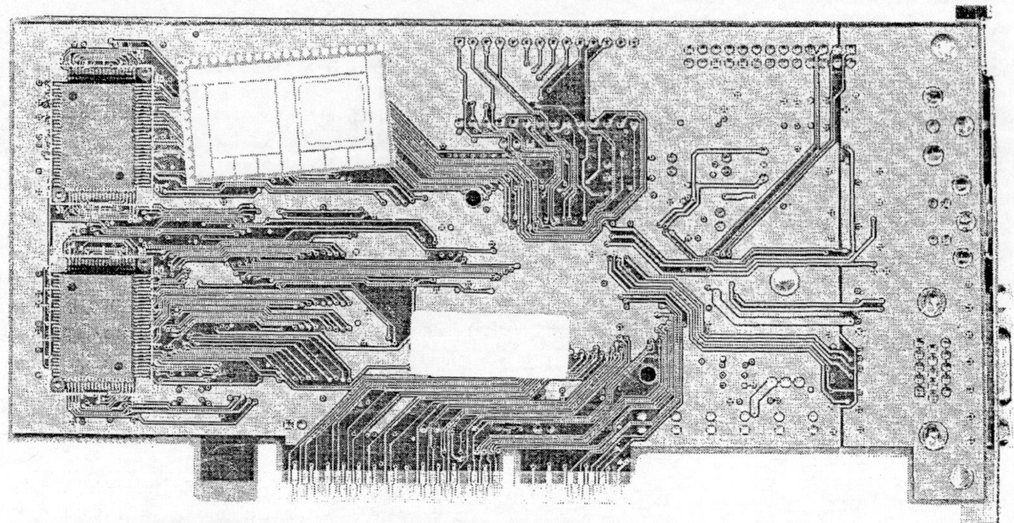

Fig. 2-5 : AGP Card.

As this slot is used only for display card, motherboards have only one AGP slot. When the AGP first came in the market its speed was 1X, now latest P4 systems offer 8X AGP slots.

Support Circuits on Motherboard

The computer cannot work on just microprocessor and memory alone, other than these, it needs some support circuits. Some of the circuits required for the working of the computer are Interrupt Control, DMA (Direct Memory Access) Control, and the Timing Control.

A fully functional computer will also require circuits for keyboard interfacing, display interfacing, storage device such as floppy disk, hard disk drive interfacing etc.

A standard motherboard contains Main Processor, Math Coprocessor, Memory, Interrupt Controller, DMA Controller, Timer, Keyboard Interfacing Circuitry and some other Support Circuits.

Processor, coprocessor and memory is already covered in previous sections, let us look at the interrupt controller, DMA controller and timer circuitry in this section.

Interrupt

What is an Interrupt?

Interrupt is one of the most common method for an external device to communicate with the processor (CPU).

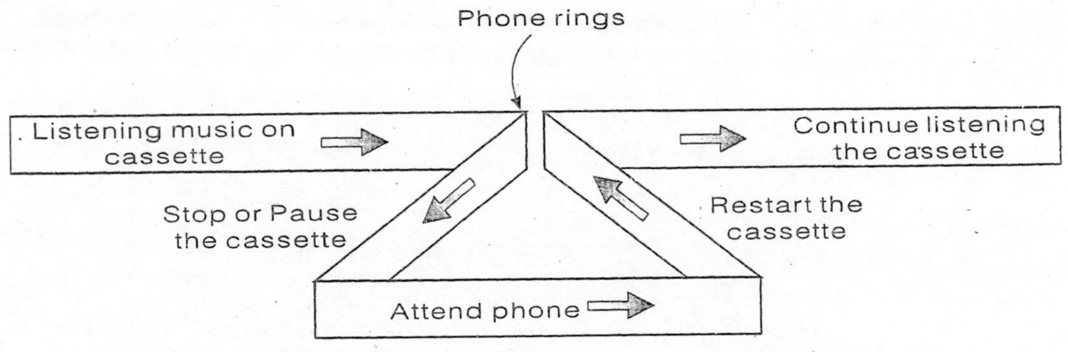

Fig. 2-6 : Concept of Interrupt.

The interrupting device generates an interrupt signal to the processor to stop processor's normal function and provide service to the interrupting device.

The Concept of Interrupt

You are sitting at home, listening to some music on your audio system and the phone rings. As you do not want to miss any part of the music, you stop or pause the audio system and attend the phone.

Once the conversation is over, you restart the audio system and continue the music from the point it was paused.

In the above example you should consider two points

- first - you are not checking the phone every now and then to see if someone wants to talk to you
- second - before attending the phone you have stopped/paused the music, so you can continue to listen without missing any part of it.

Somewhat similar to this situation, when the computer is performing some work, the external devices connected to the CPU, such as keyboard, mouse etc. gain the CPU's attention using one of the following method:

- The computer can go and check each and every device connected to it to see if any of them needs its service.

  This method of device interfacing is called "Polling". This method has two major drawbacks:

  - First- the CPU will be wasting most of its time checking if any device wants its service.
  - Second- If a device asks for CPU's attention when the CPU is busy with some other important work then the request of that device may go unnoticed and the device may not get CPU's attention.

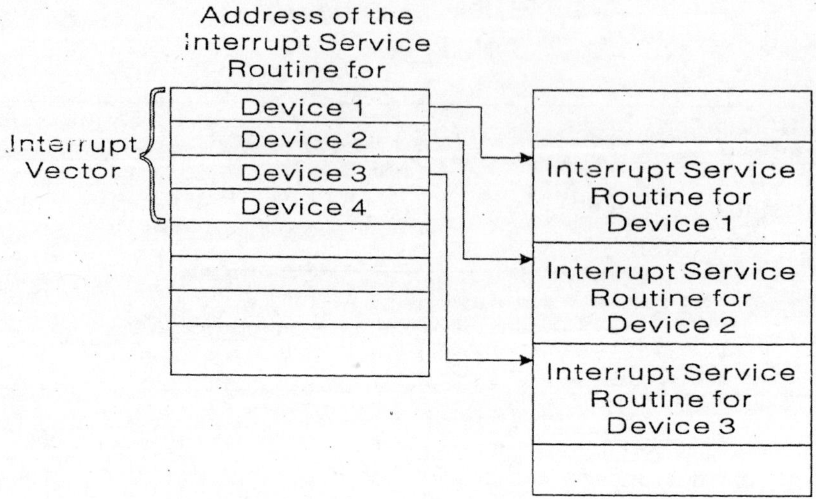

Fig. 2-7 : Interrupt Service Routine.

- In the second situation, similar to the ringing of the phone bell, when a device needs the processor's attention, device issues an interrupt to the processor.

  When the processor receives the interrupt it suspends its current job and takes care of the interrupting device.

  Once the interrupted device is taken care of, the processor goes back to the old job that it had been doing.

  This second option is called an "Interrupt" because the external device is interrupting the processor (whatever work the processor was doing) to get its attention.

  When the processor receives an interrupt signal it suspends everything and runs an "Interrupt Service Routine".

Interrupt Service Routine

What is Interrupt Service Routine?

Interrupt Service Routines are special programs that is invoked when an interrupt occurs. Each device attached to the processor will have a specific service routine in the computers memory.

A special table called Interrupt Vector Table, maintains a list of addresses for these routines.

Whenever the processor is interrupted by any device, the processor stops the execution of the current program and jumps to the interrupt service routine of the interrupted device.

Interrupt Address Vector

Address of interrupt service routine for an interrupted device can be found out by reading the Interrupt Address Vector.

In the Interrupt Address Vector, a set of addresses are stored in the memory location 0000:0000 onwards, these addresses point to the Interrupt Service Routines for different interrupt numbers.

Each vector is made up of four bytes, two byte for 16 bit segment value and two byte for 16 bit address value.

The interrupt vector for interrupt 0 is stored at the address 0000:0000, interrupt vector for interrupt 1 it is stored at 0000:0004 and so on.

The Interrupt Service Routine contains enough logic to take care of the requirements of the interrupted device.

Direct Memory Access (DMA)

What is DMA?

DMA is an abbreviation of Direct Memory Access. It is a method of transferring information directly from fast storage device such as a hard disk or from an adapter into memory, or vice versa.

During this DMA process, the information does not pass through the processor.

As the processor is not involved in the transfer, the DMA operation is usually very fast.

When a large volume of data is to be transmitted between the processor and an external device, routing them through the processor is a very slow process.

- For example, if it is a transfer of data from the memory to the disk drive, then in this process the processor will read a byte from the memory and send it to the disk.
- This process is repeated number of times until all the bytes that is to be copied to the disk is transferred to the disk.
- This reading from memory and writing to the external device byte by byte is a very slow process and this whole process slows down fast I/O devices such as floppy disk drive, hard disk, scanner etc.

Direct Memory Access or the DMA is a method used by the computer designers to overcome this problem.

An additional device called DMA Controller is placed between the I/O device and Memory for DMA operation.

This controller takes control of the system bus from the CPU, and it generates appropriate signals to do the required data transfer, without the CPU's intervention.

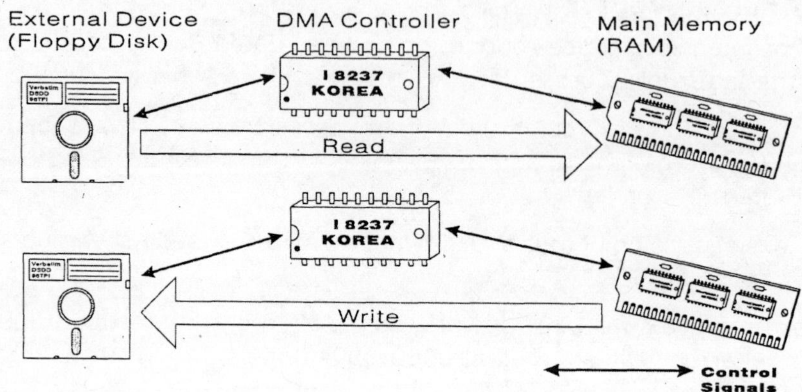

Fig. 2-8 : Memory Read/Write under DMA control.

Bus Mastering

DMA is a good option for high speed data transfer between peripherals and memory and from memory to peripheral, without CPU's intervention.

But, if one wants to transfer data from one peripheral to another peripheral, it would require two DMA operations, first peripheral to memory and then from memory to second peripheral.

Using bus mastering transfer method, system can bypass, CPU as well as the memory and data can be directly transferred from one peripheral to another peripheral.

Timing Circuits

Clock Generator

The Computer system needs some type of signal to coordinate its various activities. Without a proper synchronization signal all the components of the computer may start working on their own and the complete system may go out of control.

As you might have watched the military march, all their movements are coordinated on the drum beat. Without the drum beat each man may start a different movement and the complete march may end up as a mob.

As the drumbeat of the march, the clock signal is used by the computer to make its different parts work in harmony.

Inside the computer a clock generator provides the timing signal to control different components of the system.

A computer's output depends on the speed at which it can work and that speed depends on the clock speed of the system.

The clock speed of any system is measured in hertz (Hz) or cycles per second, which is a unit of frequency. A more common unit of the clock speed is the Mega Hertz (MHz) or One million cycles per second.

The original PC used a clock frequency of 4.77MHz, whereas nowadays 3000MHz (3GHz-Giga Hertz) and above clock speed based Pentium processors are common.

Timers

The Timer and the clock circuits are used for two different functions.

The clock circuit is used by the computer to provide timing signals to different components of the computer system, to make the complete system work in a proper and organized manner.

On the other hand a timer is used for completely different purpose, the timers used in the PC are programmable and they are used to generate different pulses at some predefined fixed frequency.

The timer used in the PC has three outputs.

- The first output Timer 0 is used to generate the interrupt 8, which is used by the computer to update its internal time and date value.
  This interrupt takes place 18.2 times in a second.
- The second output timer 1 is used to generate the refresh signal for the DRAM memory chip used as the main memory in the computer.
  This output is programmed by the BIOS at the system startup time to refresh the DRAM at a fixed frequency
- The third output Timer 2 is used to generate sound on the PC speaker. The speaker can be made to generate different sound by making its cone move in and out or vibrate at the required frequency.

Real Time Clock (RTC)

The PC, whenever switched on, asked for the current date and time. If you do not type current date or time value then the date is taken as 1 January 1980 and the time is taken as midnight 12 O Clock.

To solve this problem, AT and later machines used a battery backed clock circuit called Real Time Clock (RTC), which could keep the system clock running even when the AC mains power is switched off.

The RTC chip uses CMOS technology to make its power consumption very low. A good, high quality battery can keep the entire content of CMOS for many years.

This RTC chip contains some battery backed CMOS RAM memory which is used to store the machine's configuration information.

This configuration information contains information such as number and type of drives and hard disk, display type, total installed memory size and various other information.

Information stored here can be set using the BIOS setup option.

Chipsets

In early PCs, support circuits for main processor were constructed from a variety of small, general purpose ICs each with a specific function, such as DMA controller, Interrupt controller etc.

As PCs became increasingly popular, semiconductor firms combined many of these support functions into a set of Integrated Circuits. This set of ICs are called Chipsets.

What is Chipset?

All the diverse support functions inside a PC were integrated into a few VLSI components individually termed Application-Specific Integrated Circuits or ASICs, these ASICs are collectively called Chipset.

Common Intel Chipsets

Intel 810 Chipset

The Intel 810 chipset lowers overall costs of the motherboard while delivering new technologies and features to the Celeron processor-powered PC. This chipset enhances the performance of the Intel Celeron and Intel Pentium III processor-based PCs.

Intel 810 chipset provides next-generation features and great graphics performance at a lower cost. Richer 2D and 3D graphics are optimized using second-generation Intel Graphics Technology.

Features

This chipset contains following components

- 82810 Graphics Memory Controller Hub in 421 Ball Grid Array (BGA) package
- 82801 Integrated Controller Hub in 241 Ball Grid Array (BGA) package.

Following table lists various features of the Intel 810 chipset, it also lists the benefits of these features.

FEATURES	BENEFITS
Intel Hub Architecture	Increased I/O performance allows better concurrency for richer multimedia applications
Integrated graphics/AC'97 controller	System cost savings, more flexibility and better audio quality

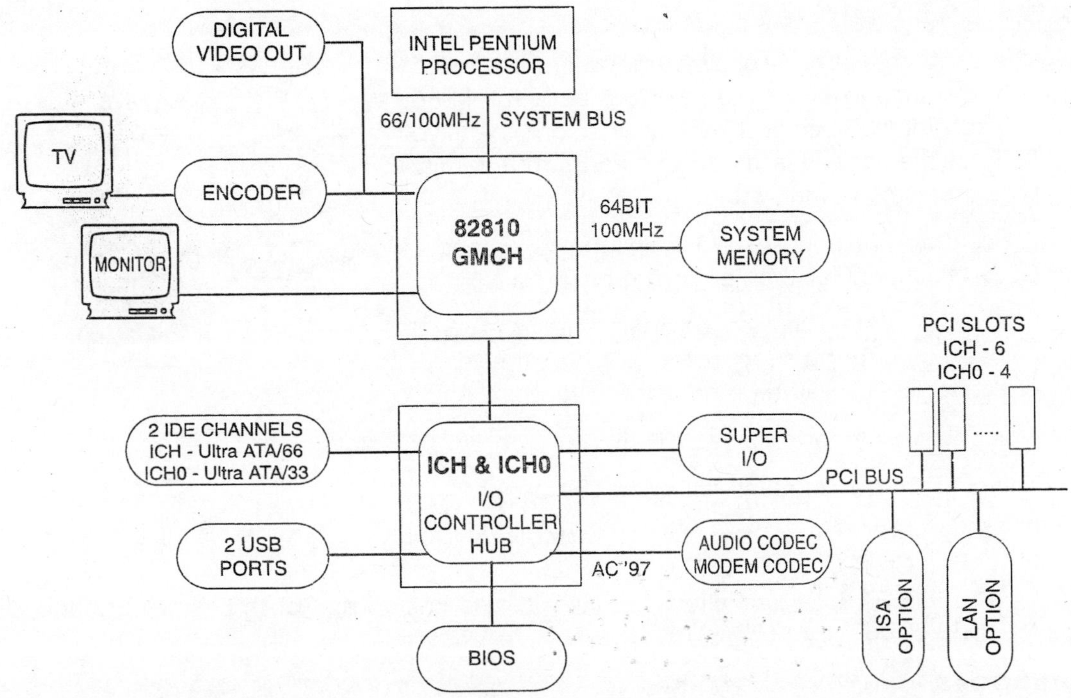

Fig. 2-9 : Intel 810 Chipset Block Diagram.

FEATURES	BENEFITS
Intel 3D graphics with Direct AGP	Vivid 2D and 3D graphics, system cost savings, efficient use of system memory for graphics, O/S and applications
Optional 4MB of dedicated display cache video memory	Enables SKU differentiation with increased 3D graphics performance improvement over Direct AGP
Low-power sleep modes	Energy Savings
One software driver code base	More stable platform, higher quality graphics, reduced OEM support costs
Digital Video Out port	Allows connection of traditional TV or new digital flat panel displays; compatible with DVI specification
Soft DVD MPEG-2 playback with Hardware Motion Compensation	Lifelike video and audio
66 and 100-MHz System Bus capable	Flexibility for performance headroom when used with Intel Celeron and Pentium processors
2 USB ports Plug and Play	Multiple Intel 810 chipset SKUs for performance and value PC price points Lower platform and manufacturing costs with single motherboard design

Intel 845 Chipset

The Pentium 4 processor was originally introduced with the support of the high-performance Intel 850 chipset. Intel 850 chipset required use of expensive RDRAM memory, this made the Pentium 4 family face problems in marketing.

Later, Intel introduced 845 chipset with cheaper SDRAM support for the Pentium 4 processor.

The Intel 845 Chipset complements the 850 chipset, by offering support for high-volume, cost-effective PC133 SDRAM memory for Pentium 4 processor systems.

This chipset supports up to 3GB memory on 3 DIMM slots.

This 845 chipset contains following components

- 82845 Memory Controller Hub (MCH, also known as North Bridge) Flip Chip Ball Grid Array (FCBGA)
- 82801BA I/O Controller Hub (ICH2, also known as South Bridge) Enhanced Ball Grid Array (EBGA)

Features

The 845 chipset was designed with the following features to deliver a compelling solution for both corporate and consumer market segments.

FEATURES	BENIFITS
400 MHz System Bus	Increased system bandwidth for greater system responsiveness and seamless user interaction
256 bit Internal data paths	4x the internal data transfer capability over previous generations
Intel Hub Architecture	Dedicated data paths to deliver maximum bandwidth for I/O intensive applications
PC133 SDRAM	High-volume and cost-effective memory technology
AGP4X interface	High-bandwidth interface for high-quality 2D, 3D, and video streams
LAN Connect Interface	Multiple networking options taking advantage of Intel SingleDriver technology
Alert on LAN 1.0	Emits an alert in case of software failures or system intrusion, even when the O/S is not present or the system is suspended
Dual USB controllers	Two controllers for four ports, delivering a total USB bandwidth of 24 Mbps
Ultra ATA/100	Takes advantage of the latest industry innovations in HDD features and performance

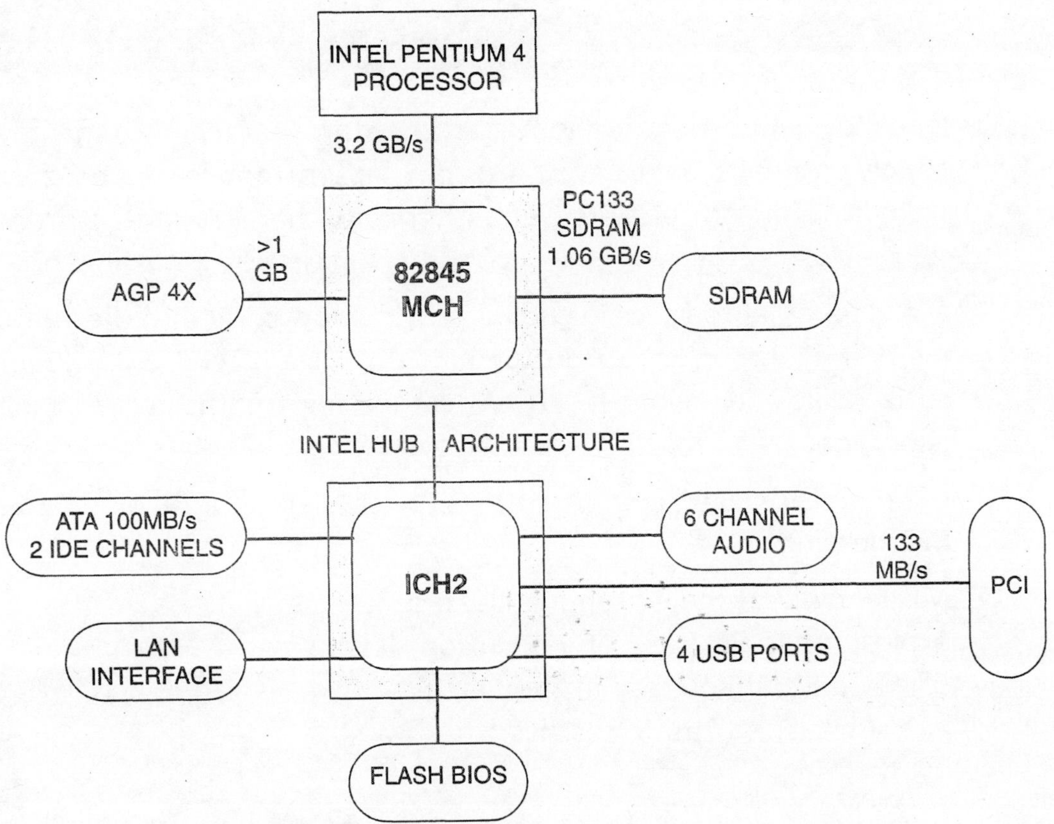

Fig. 2-10 : Intel 845 Chipset Block Diagram.

FEATURES	BENIFITS
Intel Application Accelerator	Software that helps accelerate boot time and application launch times
AC'97 Controller	Excellent audio quality, with up to six channels for full surround sound capability including a simultaneous modem connection
Communications and Network Riser (CNR) card	Allows flexibility for multiple configurations on a single card to extend USB, LAN, and audio
Low-Power sleep mode	Energy savings

Out of Box Knowledge

- One may get an electric shock if an adaptor is attached to the power supply cord fails. So, to avoid this buy laptop/mobile and its charger from authorised dealers, unauthorised chargers are extremely dangerous.
- Many times laptop suck in cooling air (the flow of air into the laptop is disturbed) through their bottoms. If they are placed on an uneven surface like bed, pillow. It causes overheating and thus may result in explosion.
- If laptop is plugged in all the times for charging may explode due to overheating.
- Mishandling of the laptop may lead to its explosion as in case if you drop it somewhere, its battery alignment may get disturbed and results in overheating.
- In hot and humid environment, there are chances of short-circuit that causes overheating and thus explosion of laptop.
- Try to change a laptop battery if it is old with new one and if it is not possible to replace, then remove the battery and run the laptop on direct power supply. 
- If you are away on a vacation, do not forget to remove the battery and keep it in a dry place.

Processor & Coprocessor

The main processor or the CPU (Central Processing Unit) of a computer system is located on the Motherboard. CPU is the brain of the computer, it does all the arithmetic and logic operations such as adding two numbers, comparing two values etc.

All the IBM and IBM compatible Personal computers use microprocessor designed and produced by the Intel Corporation. Some IBM compatible computer manufacturers use Intel compatible processor made by some other manufacturer such as Chips & Technology, Advanced Micro Devices (AMD) and Cyrix etc.

Some Common Processors (CPUs)

8088/8086

8088 processor was the first CPU used in the IBM PC computers, its clock speed was 4.77MHz and it had 8-bit external data bus.

Event though this CPU had 8-bit data bus it is called a 16-bit CPU because of its internal 16-bit registers and data path.

The 8088 chip comes in a 40-pin DIP package (Dual Inline Package), which is a rectangular size plastic package with 20-pins on each sides.

8088 has 20-bit address lines using which it can access 1 Mega Byte (MB) of memory locations. 8086 CPU is the full version of the 8088 chip, full in the sense that the 8086 has both internal as well as external 16-bit data path.

80286

After the 8088/8086 chips next important processor is the 80286 which introduced many new computing technologies. This chip was backward compatible with the 8086/8088 chips.

286 chip was first used with the IBM PC-AT computers, here AT stands for Advanced Technology. 80286 chip working at 6 MHz gave five times more throughput than the 8088 chip working at the 4.77 MHz speed.

With the 286 CPU a new mode of working was introduced for the PC computer, The 286 CPU can work in the

- Real Mode and
- Protected Mode.

In the real mode the 286 works just like the 8088/8086 CPU, it can execute any program written for the 8088 CPU without any modification.

In the protected mode the CPU behave in a completely different manner, in this mode the CPU can take the full advantage of its internal designs. In this mode the CPU can address 1 gigabyte of virtual memory.

286 was the first CPU introduced with the multitasking capability, in which multiple programs could run in the computers memory at the same time.

80386

80386 is a 32-bit processor, which was made specially for the high speed operations. The 386 CPU can also execute in protected mode and real mode like the 286 processor.

The 386 CPU could go from real to protected and from protected to real mode under the control of the software without the need for a hardware reset.

In addition to these two modes, 386 introduced a new mode called "virtual real mode", this mode is used by many multitasking software such as windows 3.1, OS/2 etc. In this mode the CPU can run many real mode (8088/8086) software simultaneously in the system.

80486

The Intel 80486 processor has many new ideas introduced with this chip. Some very important things about this chip is that

- It has a built-in math-coprocessor
- It has a 8KB of internal cache memory.
- It also has internal and external 32 bit data bus

It's 32-bit address bus can address 4 gigabyte of physical memory and 64 terabyte of virtual memory. The 486 is the first CPU with the math coprocessor built in the processor.

The 486 is available in the speed range from the 20MHz to 50MHz.

Modern Microprocessors

Pentium/P5/80586

Pentium, P5, 80586 or 586 is the next processor from the Intel.

Intel could not copyright numeric name such as 80586, so they decided to call their next processor "Pentium". This word Pentium comes from the Greek word pente, which means five.

Pentium Processor with MMX Technology

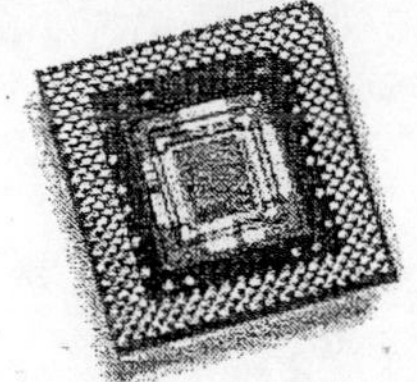

Pentium MMX processor offers higher performance compared to the original Pentium processor. MMX stands for Multimedia Extension.

Some of the features of the pentium MMX processor are:

- 10-20% more performance on current software.
- Over 60% faster on Intel Media Benchmark.
- Micro-architectural enhancements over the original Pentium processor
- Full support of Intel MMX media enhancement technology
- Doubled code and data caches to 16K each
- Improved branch prediction
- Enhanced pipeline
- Deeper write buffers

Pentium-MMX is fully compatible with all software written for the Intel 386, 486 and Pentium processor.

Features

- 64-bit data bus
- Multiprocessor Interrupt Controller on-chip
- Performance monitoring and execution tracing
- Power management features
- A Superscalar Architecture capable of executing two integer instructions in parallel in a single clock.
- A Pipelined Floating-Point Unit (FPU) for supporting the 32 and 64-bit formats specified in the IEEE standard 754, as well as an 80-bit format.
- FPU is capable of executing two floating-point instructions in a single clock.
- The FPU is object-code compatible with the Intel486 DX and Intel 487 SX, Intel 387 DX, and Intel 387 SX math coprocessors.

- Many instructions microcoded in earlier x86 processors are now hardwired for increased performance.
- Bus control signals for maintaining cache consistency in multiprocessor systems.
- Multiprocessor Interrupt Controller on-chip, enabling low-cost symmetric multiprocessing.
- Dual Processor mode which provides a performance boost for applications running under advanced 32-bit operating systems.
- Hardware support for Virtual Interrupts provided through the Virtual Interrupt Flag (VIF) and Virtual Interrupt Pending (VIP) bits.
- CPU identification for providing family, model, stepping and feature information with the CPUID instruction.
- Error Detection of internal devices and the external bus interface provided through Parity Protection and a Machine Check Exception (MCE). Hardware support is also provided to verify bus cycle completion.

Celeron Processor

The Intel Celeron processor offers great performance at an exceptional value for today's applications.

The Intel Celeron processor at speeds ranging from 600 MHz to 1.20 GHz expand Intel processing performance into the value-priced PC market segment.

Features

- Available at speeds ranging from 600 MHz to above 1.20 GHz.
- 100 MHz multi-transaction processor system bus on Intel Celeron processors at 800 MHz and greater frequencies.
- 66 MHz multi-transaction processor system bus on Intel Celeron processors at 766 MHz and below.
- Dynamic Execution technology.
- Includes Intel MMX Multimedia Enhancement Technology.
- Intel Streaming SIMD Extensions.
- 32 Kbytes (16 Kbyte/16 Kbyte) Level 1 cache.
- 128 Kbytes integrated Level 2 cache on frequencies from 600 MHz to 1.10 GHz.
- 256 Kbytes integrated Level 2 cache on 1.20 GHz frequency.
- Intel Chipset support is determined by processor frequency.
- Fully compatible with existing Intel Architecture-based software.

Pentium II Processor

The Pentium II processor at 450 MHz, Intel's high performance desktop processor, integrates the best attributes of the P6 micro-architecture processors plus Intel's MMX media enhancement technology.

The Intel Pentium II processors deliver excellent performance for all PC software and are fully compatible with existing DOS and Windows based software.

Software designed for Intel's MMX technology unleashes the full multimedia capabilities of these processors including full-screen, full-motion video, enhanced color, and realistic graphics.

Systems based on Pentium II processors also include the latest features to simplify system management.

Features

- Available in speeds from 233 MHz up to 450 MHz.
- Utilizes Intel's 0.25 micron manufacturing process for increased processor core frequencies and reduced power consumption.
- Includes MMX media enhancement technology.
- Dual Independent Bus (DIB) architecture increases bandwidth and performance over single-bus processors.
- 450, 400, and 350 MHz versions improve system bandwidth and performance by increasing the system bus speed from 66 to 100 MHz.
- The Intel 440BX AGP set enables the 100 MHz system bus to increase peak processor data transfers to the rest of the system by 50%.
- Single Edge Contact (SEC) cartridge packaging technology delivers high-performance processing and bus technology to mainstream systems.
- 32K (16K/16K) non-blocking, level-one cache provides fast access to heavily used data. 512K unified, non-blocking, level-two cache.
- 450, 400, and 350 MHz versions support memory cacheability for up to 4GB of addressable memory space.
- Enables scaleable systems to be expanded to two processors and 64GB of physical memory.
- Includes data integrity and reliability features such as Error Correction Code (ECC), Fault Analysis, Recovery, and Functional Redundancy Checking for both system and L2 cache buses.

Pentium III (P3) Processor

The Intel Pentium III processor is a top performer for mainstream business and consumer desktops.

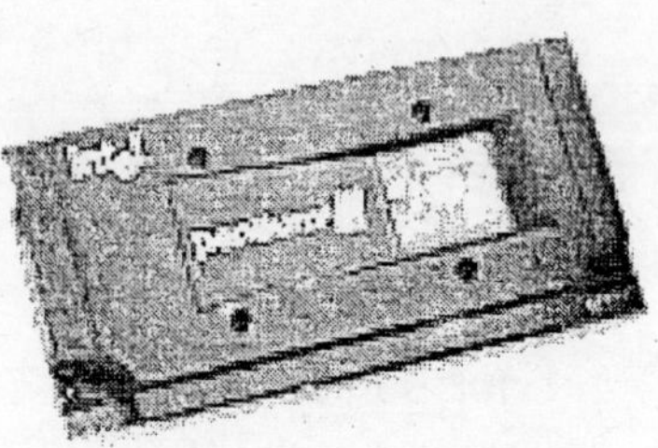

The Pentium III processor provides the power to handle today's information overload, with the versatility and compatibility to manage a broad range of applications in your e-Business or e-Home environment.

Features

- The Pentium III Processor is available at speeds ranging from 450 MHz to 1.2 GHz
- Versions available with either a 133 MHz or a 100 MHz system bus.
- Versions that incorporate 256 KB Advanced Transfer Cache (on-die, full-speed level 2 (L2) cache with Error Correcting Code (ECC) or versions that incorporate a discrete, half-speed, 256 KB in package L2 cache with ECC.
- Versions that incorporate Data Prefetch Logic (DPL), which anticipates the data needed by the application and pre-loads it into the Advance Transfer Cache, designed to further increase the processor and application performance.
- 32 KB (16 KB/16 KB) non-blocking, level 1 (L1) cache.
- P6 Dynamic Execution micro-architecture including multiple branch prediction, data flow analysis and speculative execution.
- Internet Streaming SIMD Extensions, consisting of 70 instructions that enable advanced imaging, 3D streaming audio and video, speech recognition and an enhanced Internet experience.
- Intel MMX media enhancement technology.
- Dual Independent Bus (DIB) architecture increases bandwidth and performance over single-bus processors.
- Memory cacheability up to 4 GB of addressable memory space and system memory scaleability up to 64 GB of physical memory.
- Both dual-processor capable and uni-processor only versions.
- Data integrity and reliability features such as Error Correction Code, Fault Analysis and Recovery for both system and L2 cache buses.
- Versions based upon Intel's 0.13, 0.18 and 0.25 micron manufacturing processes for increased processor core frequencies and reduced power consumption.
- Fully compatible with existing Intel Architecture-based software.

Pentium 4 (P4) Processor

The Intel Pentium 4 processor, Intel's most advanced, most powerful processor, is based on the new Intel NetBurst micro-architecture.

This processor is designed to deliver performance across applications and usage where end users can truly appreciate and experience the performance.

These applications include Internet audio and streaming video, image processing, video content creation, speech, 3D, CAD, games, multimedia, and multi-tasking user environments.

Features

- The Intel Pentium 4 is available at speeds ranging from 1.30 to 3.6 GHz.
- The Intel Pentium 4 is available in PGA-423 and uPGA-478 form factors.
- Featuring the new Intel NetBurst micro-architecture.
- Supported by the Intel 850/845 chipset.
- Fully compatible with existing Intel Architecture-based software.
- Internet Streaming SIMD Extensions.
- Intel MMX media enhancement technology.
- Memory cacheability up to 4 GB of addressable memory space and system memory scaleability up to 64 GB of physical memory.
- Support for uni-processor designs.
- Based upon Intel's 0.18 micron manufacturing process.
- This processor is binary compatible with previous generation of Intel processors.

Intel Xeon Processor

The Intel Xeon processor is ideal for compute intensive and heavy workload applications that require floating point performance and the intense use of graphics for design.

The Intel Xeon processor features a 400 MHz front side bus, dual channel RDRAM memory and the Intel 860 chipset.

This provides the bandwidth and performance throughput to deliver streaming audio/video and online collaboration.

Features

- The Intel Xeon processor is available at speeds 1.40 GHz and higher.
- Featuring the new Intel NetBurst micro-architecture.

- Supported by the Intel 860 chipset.
- Fully compatible with existing Intel Architecture-based software.
- Internet Streaming SIMD Extensions 2.
- Memory cacheability up to 4 GB of addressable memory space.
- System memory scaleability up to 64 GB of physical memory.
- Support for dual-processor designs.
- Based upon Intel's 0.18 micron manufacturing process.

Future Processors

In near future processors based on IA-32 architecture will continue to provide ever-increasing performance for the desktop, mobile, workstation, and server market segments.

Intel Itanium Processor

Intel's Itanium brand processor will deliver world class performance, scaleability, availability, reliability, and full IA-32 binary compatibility for high-end servers and workstations.

The Intel Itanium processor family will coexist with future IA-32 processors to enable a complete range of Intel Architecture solutions.

Intel processors based upon new micro-architecture, and designed for speeds well above 1 GHz as well as for new levels of performance will be able to power today's most demanding applications as well as those emerging applications for the Internet economy.

Pentium 4 Xeon Processor

is Intel's most advanced, most powerful processor for server and workstation market segments and delivers the performance headroom and scaleability for the demanding requirements of E-business.

The Intel Pentium 4 Xeon processor is available in versions that support up to 2-way processing for the entry to midrange markets as well as versions that support multiprocessing (2-Way and greater) for the midrange to high-end markets.

The Pentium 4 Xeon processor uses Internet Streaming SIMD Extensions to speed display of rich media types and enhances the performance of streaming media applications and memory-intensive applications.

Front Side Bus (FSB)

Front Side Bus or FSB or System Bus is the microprocessor's link to the rest of the computer system. The FSB speed is the maximum speed at which the microprocessor can send data to other circuits in the computer.

Initially the microprocessors operated at 66MHz system bus speed, but slowly this speed increased to 100MHz, 133MHz, and up to 800MHz. Currently many motherboard manufacturers are offering P4 motherboard with 800MHz FSB.

With the P4 microprocessor Intel introduced a new concept called "quad-pumping". In this, Intel forces four data bits on the bus in each clock cycle of the system bus.

This makes a quad-pumped system bus operating at 100MHz to move 400Mb of data per second.

Performance of FSB is also described in "bandwidth". Bandwidth is the total number of bytes that can move through the bus in one second. Data bus of all current processor are 64-bit wide. By multiplying the clock speed of the bus with its bus width will give us the bus bandwidth.

For example, a 100MHz system bus will have 800MBps (Mega bytes per second) bandwidth. A 600MHz system bus will have 4800MBps bandwidth.

This FSB speed is locked to the microprocessor clock speed to optimize the transfer rate between the bus and the microprocessor.

AMD Microprocessor

So far we looked into the Intel microprocessor. Intel microprocessor were the first choice with most of the PC compatible computer manufacturers, but slowly some new companies such as AMD are providing cheaper and better alternative to the Intel microprocessor.

Athlon

Athlon is answer to the Intel Pentium III chip by the AMD. Technically Athlon is even better than the Pentium III chip.

Athlon chip has floating point units specially for the multimedia and gaming applications. It also supports the MMX and "3D Now" instruction sets.

It has both primary cache (L1) and secondary cache (L2) on-chip for improving its performance. Primary cache is of 128K and secondary cache size is 256K.

It has an 43-bit wide address bus, which can address up to 8TB of memory.

With time AMD has introduced several variants of the Athlon microprocessor some of them are :

- Basic Athlon
- Athlon 4
- Athlon XP
- Athlon MP

Athlon 4 is basically the same basic Athlon with a new name, Athlon XP was introduced by AMD with the introduction of Windows XP. According the AMD, Athlon XP is better suited to run Windows XP operating system.

Athlon MP is specially made for servers and multiprocessing applications.

Duron

AMD's Duron is a lower priced version of the Athlon processor. Duron is placed against the Intel Celeron processor.

Its basic architecture math the Athlon processor, but it has smaller L1 and L2 cache memory. It has 128K L1 and 64K L2 cache memory.

Also, Duron's FSB speed is limited to 200MHz.

PC Processor Specification - At a Glance

Processor	Register Size-bit	Data Bus-bit	Address Bus-bit	Int. Cache	Int. FPU	Max. Memory	Trans. Used
8088	16	8	20	No	No	1MB	29,000
8086	16	16	20	No	No	1MB	29,000
286	16	16	24	No	No	16MB	130,000
386SX	32	16	24	No	No	16MB	275,000
386SL	32	16	24	*	No	16MB	855,000
386DX	32	32	32	No	No	4GB	275,000
486SX	32	32	32	8K	No	4GB	1,185,000
486DX	32	32	32	8K	Yes	4GB	1,200,000
486DX2	32	32	32	8K	Yes	4GB	1,100,000
586	32	64	32	8K Data 8K Instr	Yes	4GB	3,100,000
P6	32	64	36	8K Data 8K Instr	Yes	64GB	5,500,000

Memory

Computer has many use, it can be used to solve a mathematical problem, to type a letter, to draw some graphic etc., for all these applications you have to execute some program or set of instructions.

Before executing the program, it is stored into the computers memory and from the memory, computer takes program instructions one by one and execute them.

The data required to operate on or the result after the program is executed are also kept in the computer's memory-before transferring them onto some other permanent storage device or an output device.

The computer memory can be of two types based on the whether the memory is inside the computer or it is an external storage device.

- Primary Memory
- Secondary Memory

Primary Memory

The main memory or the memory on the motherboard is called the primary memory.

This primary memory can be further divided into following types

- RAM
- ROM

RAM is a type of memory which is used by the computer to store temporary values, programs etc.

RAM is a Volatile Memory. The volatile memory is a memory which loses its content when the power supply to the memory is switched off.

Any information in the RAM is transferred to some permanent storage device such as floppy disk, hard disk or CD-ROM before switching off the computer.

ROM is nonvolatile memory. Nonvolatile memory is a permanent memory, which does not lose its contents even when the power supply is switched off.

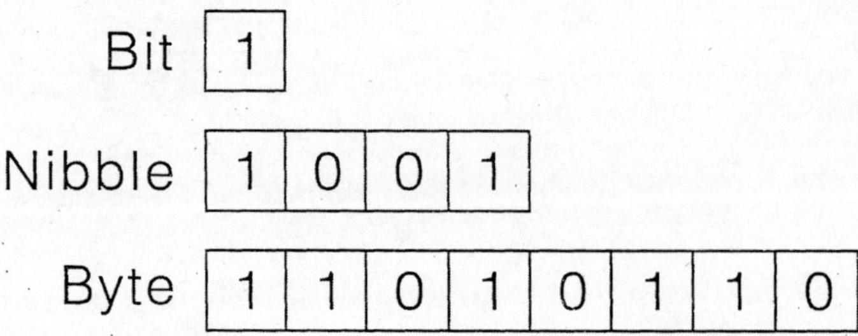

Fig. 4-1 : Bit, Byte and Nibble

A Nonvolatile memory such as ROM is used inside the computer to keep permanent information such as boot program which is required each time the machine is switched on.

Secondary Memory

Secondary memory is not a memory in conventional terms, it is actually the storage device used to store the program or the data. Floppy disk, hard disk, CD-ROM etc. are examples of secondary memory.

Because of its size, secondary memory is also called mass storage device.

Bits & Byte

Bit or Binary Digit i.e. number 0 and number 1 are the most basic information that one can store inside the computer.

A single bit can be stored inside the computer using a capacitor, using a bistable multivibrator such as flip-flops, using the transistor as a switch, or by using a relay etc.

As a single bit alone does not provide much information, a combination of these bits are used to convey different information.

When two bits are used they can be combined in four different ways 00, 01, 10, and 11 and each combination can convey a different information.

A combination of 4 bit, called a "nibble" and is used to store information inside the calculators, as the 4 bit can have $2^4 = 16$ different combinations, it is enough to convey 10 different digits (0 to 9) and some additional information such as decimal point etc.

The computer can manipulate characters as well as numbers, so a combination of 8 bits (called a "byte") is used inside the computer to store different characters.

A combination of 8 bits can have $2^8 = 256$ different combinations, which is enough to convey all the alphabet, lower case, upper case, numbers, and various special text and graphic symbols used by the computer.

Different combination of 0s and 1s of these 8 bits is used to store different information inside the computer's memory. For example

```
01000001 is used to store character "A"
00110001 is used to store the number "1"
```

Inside the computer one byte or 8-bits can store one character, a character can be any alphabet, number or special symbols such as @, #, $, * etc.

- Combination of 1000 byte is called a Kilo Byte (1 KB)
- Combination of 1000 KB is called a Mega Byte (1 MB)
- Combination of 1000 MB is called a Giga Byte (1 GB)
- Combination of 1000 GB is called a Tera Byte (1 TB)
- Combination of 1000 TB is called a Peta Byte (1 PB)
- Combination of 1000 PB is called a Exa Byte (1 EB).

RAM

RAM or Random Access Memory is the main memory inside the computer. It is used to store program, data and results.

It is called Random access because this memory is organized in such a way that any part of the memory can be accessed without serially going through all the previous memory locations.

A better term to describe the RAM would be Read/Write Memory. One can read the information stored inside the RAM as well as write or store information into it.

Two common RAM are

- DRAM (Dynamic RAM)
- SRAM (Static RAM)

Dynamic RAM (DRAM)

A dynamic RAM (DRAM) is cost wise cheaper than the static RAM (SRAM), and it is the main reason of using the DRAM as the main memory.

DRAM utilizes capacitors to store information, so the problem with the DRAM is once data is stored into it, it can't retain the data for long unless the data is refreshed periodically.

Refreshing of a DRAM memory is done by rewriting the entire content of the memory every few millisecond. For this a special refresh circuitry is used.

Unless the DRAM is refreshed every few millisecond it loses its content.

Static RAM (SRAM)

Unlike the DRAM, SRAM memory retains the information stored inside it, as long as the power supply is provided to the SRAM chip.

One need not refresh the information stored in the SRAM.

Because the SRAM does not require any refresh circuits, the circuitry required to interface SRAM is very simple compared to the interface circuitry for the DRAM chips. Also, the SRAM is much faster than the DRAM.

SRAM generally use flip-flops to store the information.

ROM

ROM or Read Only Memory, as its name suggest, is a memory that can be read only, one cannot write any information into it.

ROM is a nonvolatile memory, it does not lose its content when the power supply is cut off.

Like RAM, ROM is also random access memory i.e. one can directly access any part of the ROM without serially going through the complete ROM.

Information is stored into the ROM by the manufacturers. Based on the method used to write into the ROM, ROM can be classified into following types:

Mask ROM

A mask ROM is the basic ROM chip. In this type of chips the information is fabricated into the chip at the time of manufacturing itself.

Number of chips to be manufactured should be very high when this type of ROM is made, to justify the high investment required in their making.

PROM

PROM or Programmable Read Only Memory is the ROM memory with a small difference.

At the time of manufacturing, this chip is made as a blank ROM chip and later using special PROM programmers the information is stored into them.

Once some information is stored into the PROM by "burning" the information into it, it becomes a ROM.

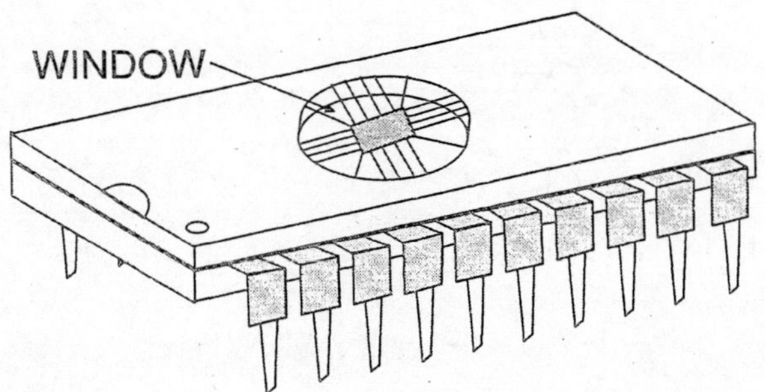

Fig. 4-2 : EPROM Chip.

EPROM

EPROM or Erasable PROM, is a PROM but with an option to erase its content if user wants to change the information stored into it.

EPROM is easily distinguishable from other chips because of a small window in the middle of this chip. This window is covered with a transparent quartz glass.

Through this window, ultraviolet light can be shined on the EPROM to erase its content. Once the EPROM is erased it can be reprogrammed or rewritten using the EPROM programmer.

After the EPROM is programmed the top window should be closed with some opaque label, because the sun rays which contains the ultra violet light can slowly erase its content.

EEPROM

EEPROM or Electrically Erasable PROM (pronounced "ee ee prom" or "double e prom") is another type of EPROM.

The difference between an EPROM and EEPROM is in the way its content is erased.

In an EPROM the content is erased by shining ultraviolet rays through the window directly to the circuits, whereas in the EEPROM the content is removed by using electricity.

Flash Memory

A new type of EEPROM that can be erased and reprogrammed using the normal operating voltage found inside the PC is called flash memory.

The flash memory has the same limitation as the EEPROM, it can be erased and programmed only for a fixed number of times and it must be erased and programmed in blocks.

Odd Parity System

Byte	Parity	Byte	Parity
1 1 0 1 0 1 1 0	0	1 1 0 1 0 1 1 1	1

Total number of 1's including the parity bit should be an odd number

Even Parity System

Byte	Parity	Byte	Parity
1 1 0 0 0 1 1 0	0	1 1 0 1 0 1 0 1	1

Total number of 1's including the parity bit should be an even number

Fig. 4-3 : Odd and Even Parity.

Parity

What is Parity?

Parity is a method used by the Memory Management Unit (MMU) to find if any error has happened when writing or reading the information stored into the memory.

Parity checking involves adding one extra bit to each byte of information in order to make the total number of ones (1s) in the byte odd or even.

In this method one additional parity bit is generated by the processor and stored with each byte during the memory write process and during the read process the state of this additional bit will inform the processor if the byte information is correct or has some error.

If because of some read or write error more than one bit changes its state then this method will not be useful to find the error.

Based on the parity generation method, two types of parity error checking method is used

- Odd Parity
- Even Parity

In the odd parity system, the number of bits that are 1, should be an odd number such as 1, 3, 5, etc. (including the parity bit).

In the even parity system, the number of ones including the parity bit should be an even number such as 2, 4, 6 etc. (including the parity bit).

ECC Memory

As we add more and more memory, the chance of data corruption due to even one bit going wrong increases. A computer with parity checking memory can only detect the error and shutdown the system, it cannot take any corrective steps.

However, an Error Correction Code (ECC) memory can automatically detect and correct memory errors using special algorithms.

To use ECC memory, motherboard must have this option. When ECC memory is installed on such systems, the motherboard will detect and configure the system to use it.

In a 168-pin DIMM, 64-bit variety is without ECC and 72-bit variety is with ECC, so if one wants ECC facility, one should buy 72-bit DIMM.

Physical Memory Organization

Initially the memory used inside the computer came in as separate DIP chips and earlier PCs were designed with sockets on their motherboard to accept these chips.

With the introduction of 32 bit processors 386, 486 and Pentium etc. the number of chips required on motherboard became unmanageable.

This has lead to the concept of memory modules. The memory module is a set of RAM chip on a single plug-in circuit board.

The memory modules are available in the following packing

- DIP (Dual Inline Package)
- SIPP (Single In-line Pin Package)
- SIMM (Single In-line Memory Modules)
- DIMM (Dual In-line Memory Modules)

DIP (Dual Inline Package)

DIP or Dual Inline Package was used to be the most common packing for the memory chips, it resembles a small flat, rectangle box with metal legs on both sides.

The memory chip introduced with the first PC could store only 16Kbits of information each. Later with the AT machines 256Kbit chips were introduced.

SIPP (Single In-line Pin Package)

SIPP or Single Inline Pin Package contains pins at the bottom to connect them into the memory socket on the motherboard.

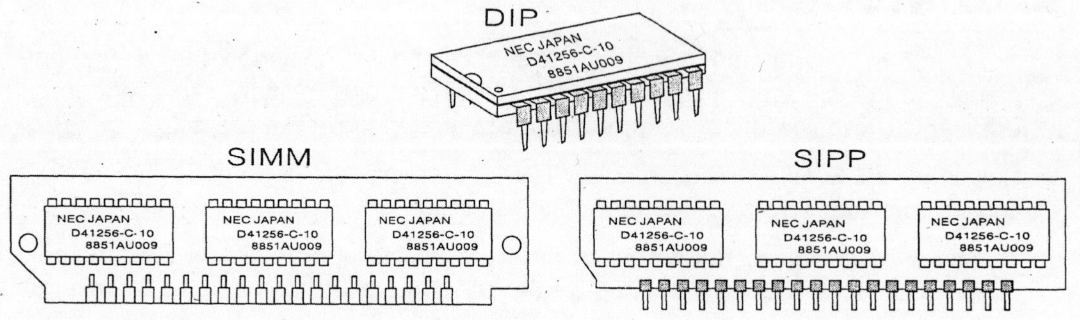

Fig. 4-4 : Physical Memory Organization.

Most of the time these SIPPs are directly soldered onto the mother board rather then inserting them into the socket.

To remove a SIPP module, one can just pull the SIPP module from both sides using even force and remove it from the socket.

To insert a SIPP module into it's socket, first place the module in proper orientation on the socket and slowly press both sides down using even force, this should fix the module into the socket.

SIMM (Single Inline Memory Module)

SIMM or Single Inline Memory Module is a number of memory chips soldered onto a small expansion board. The edge connector of this expansion board is plugged into a special SIMM sockets on the motherboard.

This design allows the memory to be added and removed from the computer without the risk of destroying it.

Just like the discrete memory chips, the memory modules also come in different capacities.

Inserting and removing the SIMM module in the socket is very easy, if you know how to do it.

- The SIMM is hold in the place by two metal or plastic clips on the both sides.
- Two latching holes in the module is also fixed on small round tabs on the socket.
- To remove the module, move the clips away from the module and push the module out of the tab, this will free the module, now pull it out.
- To insert the module place it on the socket and press from both ends until the tab is in the latching hole and the clips have locket the SIMM into the socket.

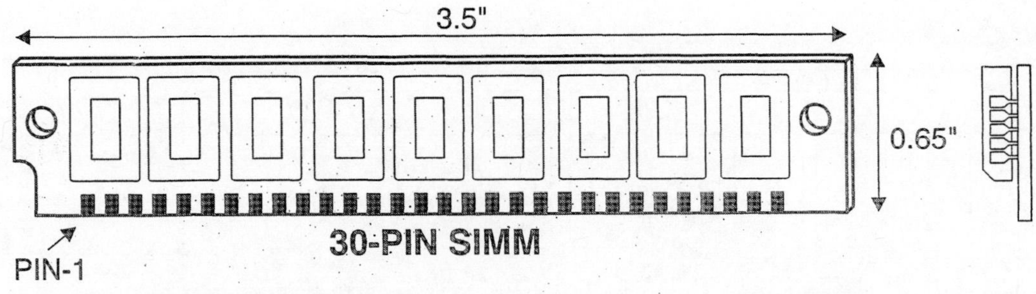

Fig. 4-5 : 30-Pin SIMM.

- One should be very careful about the orientation of the SIMM when inserting them into the socket. Many sockets have key tab to prevent the module from inserting reverse.

30-pin SIMM

30-pin SIMM is the first SIMM introduced with the PC system. The 30-pin SIMM measures about 3.5 inches wide and an inch tall.

30-pin SIMMs use one byte-wide data buses, you need multiple SIMMs to make a single memory bank with most microprocessors. PCs with 16-bit data buses (based on the 286 and 386SX microprocessors) will require two 30-pin SIMMs per bank.

PCs with 32-bit data buses (such as 386DX and 486 PCs) require four 30-pin SIMMs per memory bank. PCs with 64-bit data buses (such as the Pentium) would require eight 30-pin SIMMs per memory bank.

Using eight 30-pin SIMMs per memory bank is almost as ungainly as using discrete memory chips. This resulted in 30-pin SIMMs getting replaced with 72-pin SIMM modules.

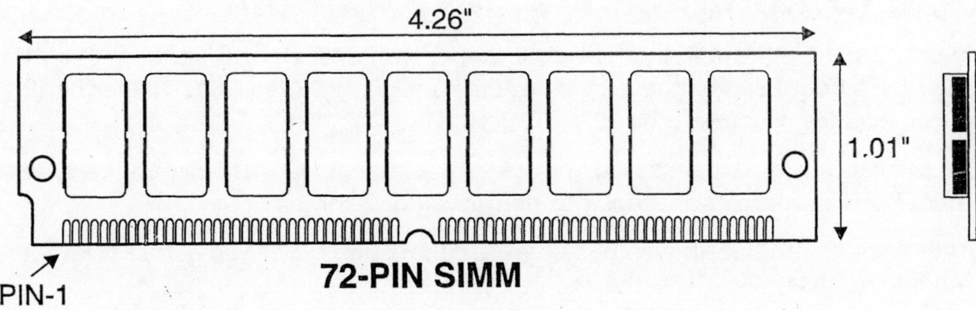

Fig. 4-6 : 72-Pin SIMM.

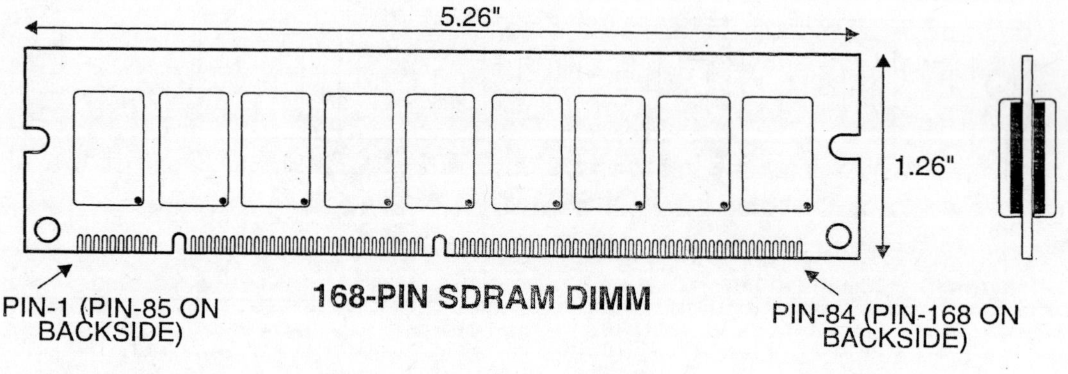

Fig. 4-7 : 168-Pin SDRAM DIMM.

72-pin SIMM

Compared to using individual memory chips, using 30-pin SIMMs were a big improvement, but with the introduction of new processors with wider data buses a new SIMM with more pins to accommodate wider data buses was required.

This lead IBM to introduce 72-pin SIMMs, its 72-pin could pack four byte-wide banks on a single module.

72-pin SIMM incorporates several interlocks to prevent you from plugging in the wrong style of SIMM or sliding in at improper orientation.

The notch in the center of the SIMM edge connector prevents one from accidentally sliding a 30-pin SIMM into a 72-pin socket.

Modules may have components on either one or two sides. To achieve higher capacities, 72-pin SIMMs are often double-sided. That is, they place chips on both sides of board.

DIMM (Dual Inline Memory Module)

Even 72-pin SIMMs fall short when it comes to Pentium and Pentium Pro PCs. With their 64-bit data buses, these chips would require two 72-pin SIMMs per bank, just as 486 machines required four 30-pin SIMMs.

To provide easier expansion for newer 64-bit machines, memory makers developed modules with more connections to permit wider addressing.

The resulting modules have 168 separate connections, arrayed across two sides of the module, a design that created the first Dual In-line Memory Modules.

Two rows of edge connectors, one on each side of the module, are divided into three groups with short gaps between. The first group runs from pin 1 to pin 10; the second

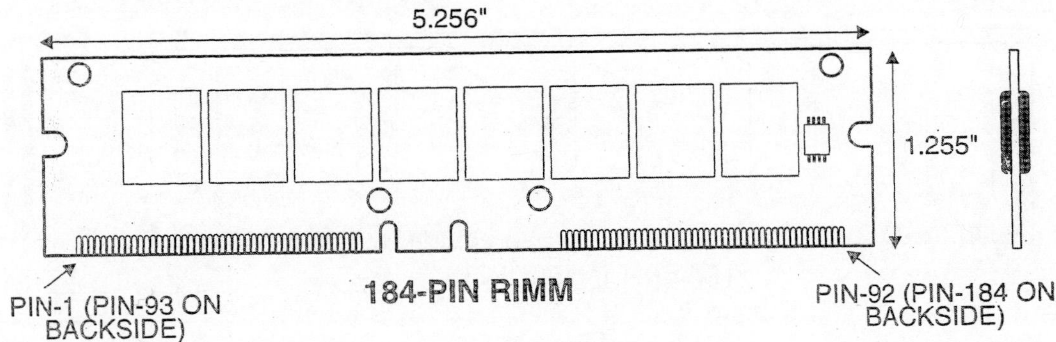

Fig. 4-8 : 184-Pin RIMM.

group from pin 11 to pin 40; and the third group from pin 41 to pin 84. Pin 85 is opposite pin 1.

Notches in the edge connector of the DIMM prevent one from sliding smaller SIMMs with fewer connections into a DIMM socket.

Instead of a notch on the side of the DIMM, the asymmetrical arrangement of the notches on the DIMM prevent its unintentional improper insertion into its socket.

Some DIMMs have holes to allow you to latch the modules into their sockets, although some DIMMs lack these holes.

To accommodate the larger edge connectors and provide greater storage capacity, DIMMs are physically large, about 5.25 inches wide and typically one inch tall.

As with 72-pin SIMMs, 168-pin DIMMs include electrical provisions for telling your PC the speed rating of the module. The module connector provides eight pins for signaling this information.

RIMM (Rambus Inline Memory Module)

When Intel introduced Pentium 4 microprocessor, they wanted a very fast memory for it and there choice was RDRAM or Rambus DRAM memory.

Instead of using SIMM or DIMM, RDRAM comes in a special 184-pin RIMM, i.e: Rambus Inline Memory Module.

RIMM can not be used on the motherboards not designed for Rambus memory. Currently only Pentium 4 motherboard based on Intel 850 chipset supports RIMM.

Even after its high speed operation, RIMM was not asuccess, the main reason behind its limited success was its cost, RIMM is very costly memory modules. Which makes people reluctant to buy this memory module.

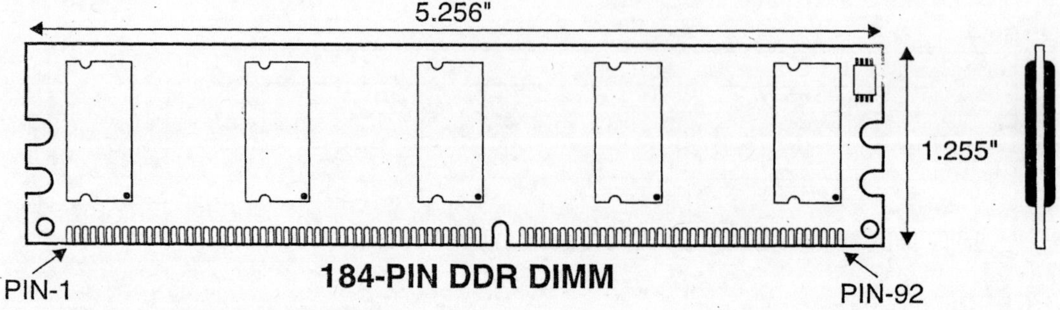

Fig. 4-9 : 184-Pin DDR DIMM.

Because of faster speed, SIMM generates more heat, an aluminum casing, called heat spreader, covers the module to protect the chips from overheating.

DDR DIMM

A much cheaper Double Data Rate (DDR) SDRAM provides speed almost equal to the RDRAM. DDR SDRAM doubles the rate at which SDRAM process data.

DDR SDRAM is costlier than standard SDRAM but it is much cheaper than the RDRAM. This resulted in most of the Pentium 4 based system going for DDR DIMM, instead of going for costlier RIMM.

DDR DIMM use a connector with 184-pins. This connector contains a single notch near the center of the connector.

Memory Speed

The speed of a memory chips is always shown in nano second or ns which is one billionth of a second, PC memory speed vary from 40 to 80 nano second.

1 ns = .000000001 second, so, the lower the nano second value the faster is the chip i.e. a 20 ns chip is faster than a 30 ns chip.

When installing a memory chip or memory module one should be very careful about the speed of the chip being used. Mixing chips of different speed may give problem and the machine may not work properly.

Most of the time the memory speed is displayed on the packing of the chip as a part of the chips part number. Sometimes this may be shown separately as -12 or -7 etc. and sometimes it may be difficult to distinguish the speed value from the part number.

Motherboard Memory Capacity

The memory capacity of the motherboard depends on the CPU, chipset being used and on the motherboard design.

If a CPU can address 4 gigabyte of memory, it does not mean that the motherboard using that CPU can address 4 gigabyte on the motherboard.

A 486 or Pentium based computer has the capability to address 4 gigabyte of memory, but if you look at the cost of the SIMM memory module then it is unlikely that someone will put 4 gigabyte of memory in his computer.

Nowadays, many motherboards come with a capacity to add up to 2GB on the motherboard.

If the motherboard does not have a capacity to install as much memory you need, then you have two options

- get a new motherboard
- use memory expansion boards that plug into the expansion slots.

Some motherboards have an address limitation i.e. they do not access memory beyond a certain limit, may be beyond 16 MB or 32MB etc. on this type of motherboards adding memory beyond this limit will not have any use, you may have to go for a new motherboard.

Extended (XMS) Memory

Extended Memory is the memory beyond the 1 MB limit, any memory available after the 1 MB memory is called extended memory.

The 8088/8086 cannot address memory beyond 1 MB, the extended memory is available in the 286 and later processor based computers only.

The extended memory is not much useful for the DOS users because the DOS does not know how to use this memory, for a DOS user this memory can be used only as disk cache or RAM disk.

For the Windows user this memory is very useful as these operating systems can use this extended memory and any program specifically written for these environment can use the extended memory available in the computer system.

Memory Speed Improvements

The overall speed or the throughput of the computer can be increased by increasing the speed of the RAM or by using concepts like Cache, Shadow memory etc.

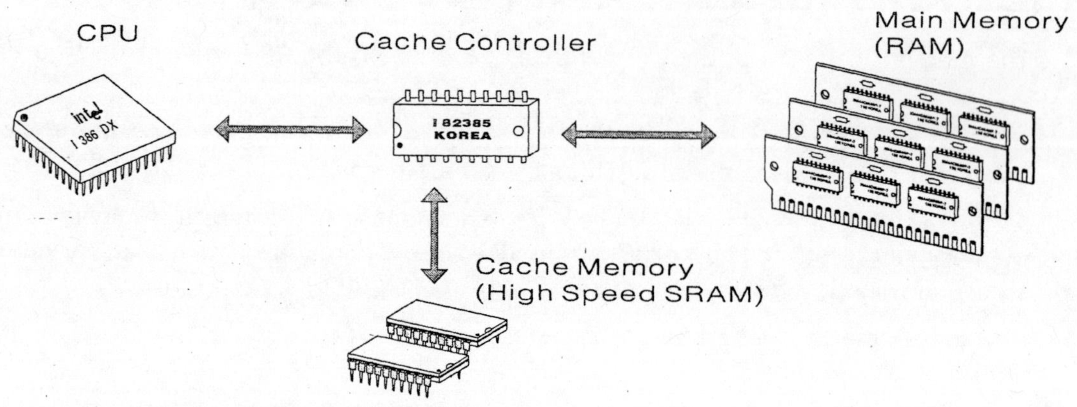

Fig. 4-10 : Cache Memory Concept.

Cache Memory

With each new model of the processor, the processor's speed is on the increase, but the speed of the memory chip has not increased much compared to the processor speed.

High speed RAM chips are available in the market but they are very costly to be used as the main memory.

This makes the CPU to wait for the result from memory, after any memory read or write command is given. Once the slow memory finishes the read or write operation then only the processor can continue with the next job.

Cache (pronounced "cash") memory is a very small amount of very high speed memory used in between the main memory (RAM) and the processor.

The high speed memory used for the cache purpose is very costly that is the reason it is not used as the main memory of the computer.

The information frequently required by the processor is kept in the cache memory by a cache controller. This cache controller always tries to make sure that the data required by the processor in the next memory access is available in the cache memory.

This improves the speed of the computer very much because if the required data is in the cache memory it is made available to the CPU without any wait state.

The performance of the cache depends on the

- speed and size of the cache memory and
- the logic used to read the data around the memory area read by the CPU.

When the required data is available in the cache it is called a hit and if the required data is not available in the cache memory it is called a miss.

Internal Cache

The internal cache is internal to the processor i.e. it is a part of the same chip as the processor. This cache is also known as primary cache or L1 cache.

This cache is sometimes divided into different types based on the function, such as data cache and instruction cache. This further increases the performance of the cache system.

External Cache

External cache is a separate high speed memory in between the processor and the main memory which is controlled by a cache controller.

This cache is also known as the secondary cache, second level cache or the L2 cache.

This cache is called the external cache because it is external to the main processor but in the recent processors, Intel has put this cache within the processor itself, inside the same packing.

Shadow Memory

What is Shadow Memory?

In 80386 and later processor copying the content of the slow BIOS ROM into faster system RAM is known as shadow memory. It is also known as shadow RAM or shadow ROM.

By copying the ROMs contents into empty area of the RAM and by redirecting any ROM read request to the RAM, the read operation can be made faster.

The RAM memory is about three to five times faster than the ROM memory.

This is called Shadow Memory because the RAM memory contains exact copy or the shadow of the ROM.

The shadow memory provides an improvement in the computer speed by providing fast response to the ROM request .

Some software that works directly with the hardware, bypassing the BIOS ROM, will not gain any speed improvement by using the shadow memory. This option has no effect in the Windows environment, as Windows directly communicates with the hardware.

The shadow ROM option is provided in most of the BIOS Setup option.

Upgrading / Adding Memory

Upgrading of the memory can be done by installing faster and higher capacity memory. To install new memory you have to decide about the type, capacity and the speed of the memory you want to install in the motherboard.

When installing new memory in your computer the steps that you should follow is explained next.

SIMM

SIMM is easier to upgrade compared to the discrete memory chips. SIMM can be removed and installed any number of times without any difficulty.

Removing SIMM

- To remove a SIMM switch off the computer and remove the power cord.
- Remove the cover of the computer and locate the SIMMs.
- The SIMM is hold in the place using clips on both the sides of the SIMM module, To remove the SIMM you need to push these clips slightly out.
- Once the module becomes free from the clip, push it out of the tab onto which the hole of the module is connected.
- Once the module comes out of the hole you can lift it out.
- Once the SIMM is removed from the board put it in some safe place.
- When handling the SIMM do not touch the edge connectors, the oil from the hand can make the connectors bad.

Adding SIMM

- Locate the empty socket where you want to install the SIMM, now position the SIMM at some angle on the empty SIMM socket.
- Make sure that the orientation of the SIMM is correct and is edge connector is placed properly on the socket.
- Most of the SIMM module contain a notch on one side so that they cannot be inserted in wrong orientation.
- Once the SIMM is placed properly into the slot gently push it into straight position, which should lock it in using two clips on both the sides
- Never force the SIMM module into the slot, if excessive force is required then you are doing something wrong.
- Two tabs on the socket should go into the two holes on the SIMM module.
- Repeat above steps for all the SIMMs that you want to connect.
- Once all the SIMMs are placed into the socket double-check all the SIMM modules that they are placed properly into the socket.
- Check the unit by switching it on before closing the main cover.
- Most of the BIOS automatically detect the correct memory size.

DIMM

Process for upgrading a DIMM is same as explained above. Only difference is in the process used to remove/insert the DIMM into the socket.

- To remove the DIMM, you need to push chip holder tabs at both ends slightly out, away from the slot. This will lift the DIMM out of the slot.
- To install the DIMM, vertically lower the DIMM into the slot in proper orientation and gently push down. The chip holder tabs should move up and lock the DIMM.

Some Common Memory Errors

You install some new memory, and the machine is switched on. On switching on computer stops with some error beep of error message on screen.

You may get the following error

Wrong Memory Size

- If the machine shows wrong memory size error on switching on, it could be due to
  - It could be due to wrong CMOS setup information.
  - Run the setup program and change the RAM size to correct value and reboot the computer.

The memory module installed is not being recognized by the computer

- The reason behind this could be improper installation of the module
  - the card may not be seated properly in the slot
  - some memory chip on the module may be not working properly i.e. it may be defective.
  - Connector on the motherboard may be faulty.

Parity Error

- One very common reason behind this error is a bad memory chip, or a chip not being seated properly.
- This error could also be due to insufficient capacity of the power supply. In this situation the computer may work fine until a disk access is required, when a disk access occurs the power supply to the RAM chips may get reduced and the parity error may happen.
- A power supply with a bad power to the computer or some device near the computer which is generating some electrical noise can also sometimes generate the parity error.

The BIOS

BIOS or the Basic Input Output System, is a set of programs stored inside a ROM chip and put on the Motherboard. The main job of the program stored into this ROM is as it's name suggest is to provide the computer user with a set of standard routines to take care of input/output from different input, output and storage devices connected to the computer.

This BIOS ROM is always available in the computer, so any user program can access these routines for their input/output requirements.

The first PC BIOS was made by the IBM for their PC range of computer. The BIOS program being the copyright property of the IBM corp., PC compatible makers use the BIOS made by AMI, Award, Phoenix etc.

BIOS Basics

What is the BIOS?

BIOS is the acronym for Basic Input Output System and it is pronounced "bye-os". It is a program stored inside a PROM chip on your computer.

This program lets your operating system and application programs communicate with computer hardware and peripheral devices such as floppy disk, hard disk, printer, display adapter etc.

Reading the keystroke, displaying on the screen, reading/writing of the serial & parallel port, reading/writing to and from the floppy & hard disk etc. is done under the control of the BIOS.

The BIOS is a set of instructions or software stored inside a PROM (Programmable Read Only Memory), PROM is a hardware, so a BIOS is not a complete software nor a complete hardware that is the reason a new name "firmware" is used to describe the BIOS.

The term "firmware" is used to describe a software stored in read only memory.

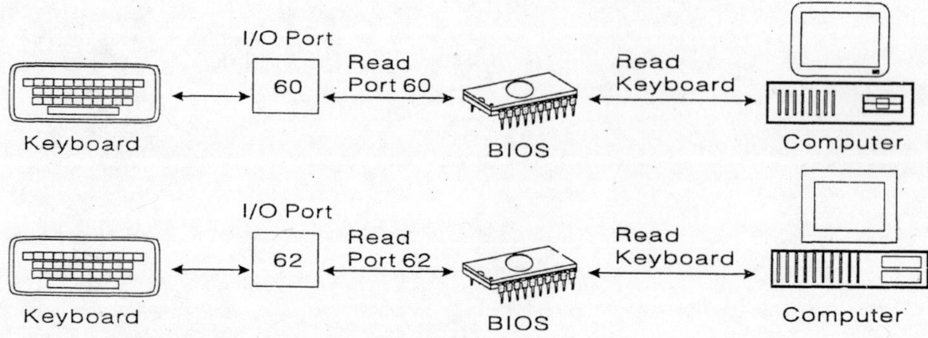

Fig. 5-1 : Different BIOS for Different Computer.

When the user program asks the BIOS to read the keyboard it is the job of the BIOS to read the keyboard in a proper manner, so as the data from the keyboard can be made available to the user program.

If you have two different computers, one having keyboard connection at I/O port 60 and the other having keyboard connection at I/O port 62, you don't have to purchase a different program for each of them.

Your program can just give the "read keyboard" command to the BIOS and it will be the job of the BIOS to read proper I/O port:

- port 60 on the first computer and
- port 62 on the second computer.

PC-BIOS Communication

The computer or user program and the BIOS communicates with each other using something called interrupts.

Whenever the computer has to request for some information to the BIOS, computer generates an interrupt, and the BIOS will carry out a specific work such as reading the keyboard or displaying something on screen etc. according to the interrupt number.

These interrupts are software interrupts and are different from the hardware interrupt generated by some devices to communicate to the CPU.

Just like a hardware interrupt, when a software interrupt is received by the processor, the processor stops whatever it was doing and takes care of the interrupt.

When an interrupt is received, the BIOS will search the interrupt vector table (IVT) for the address of the program that should provide the required service to the interrupting program.

Once the address is found, BIOS starts execution of the interrupt service routine- a program that provides the requested service to the interrupting program. After finishing the interrupt service routine the BIOS will return back to the old process that has initiated or called the interrupt routine.

The Interrupt vector table is located at the lowest RAM memory address that is at the address 0000 at segment 0000 and contains 4 byte for each interrupt number.

This Interrupt Vector Table (IVT) is loaded from the BIOS ROM to the RAM at the time of system startup.

Loading the address from the ROM to the RAM is done so that if the user wants to change the interrupt service routine provided by the BIOS, he can do so by changing the routine's address in the RAM vector table.

Other BIOS Functions

Other than the input/output function explained so far the BIOS contains two more modules

- Power on self test and
- Bootstrap loader

POST (Power On Self Test)

What is POST?

This is an abbreviation of Power On Self Test. It is a set of diagnostic programs loaded from the BIOS ROM during the system power on time.

This program ensures that in a computer all the major system components are present and are working properly.

This POST program checks the processor, memory, support circuits and other devices connected to the computer when the computer is first powered on.

If this routine finds any error or fault during this POST, the error is informed to the user as an error beep or as some error message on the screen.

Some errors called nonfatal errors allow user to continue, whereas fatal errors will not allow the POST to continue until the problem is rectified.

Once the POST routine is executed successfully, BIOS goes to the boot process.

Bootstrap Loader

After the POST routine, BIOS continues with a program called bootstrap loader.

It is the job of bootstrap loader to load the Operating System (OS) from the floppy disk, hard disk or CD-ROM into the computers main memory (RAM).

Unless the boot process is completed successfully i.e. the OS is copied from storage device to the main memory, user cannot use the computer.

A successful transfer of the OS into the RAM or the boot process is indicated by displaying the DOS prompt such as A:\> or C:\> on the computer monitor.

If you have Windows 95/98/ME etc. installed into your system then instead of the DOS prompt, you will directly go to the Windows screen.

Upgrading BIOS

You may want to upgrade your existing BIOS, if it does not support the device you want to use in your system.

Some old BIOS do not have support for 2.88MB 3.5 inch floppy drives, 20GB HDD, booting from CD-ROM etc. In this conditions you have two options

- Either you can buy a new BIOS or
- You can modify your existing BIOS.

Buying a new BIOS and installing it into your system is an easy approach compared to the modification of the existing BIOS. You will need some additional hardware devices and a thorough knowledge of hardware and software to modify your existing BIOS.

BIOS Modification

Other than the BIOS upgrade you can also do the BIOS modification, if you have proper hardware and software knowledge and EPROM programming device.

Using these devices you can make any change to the existing BIOS code, you can change the system start up message being displayed, or the error codes displayed etc.

Copying BIOS

Before making any change in the existing BIOS it is always safe to make a backup copy of your old BIOS code, this will help you if something goes wrong during the modification.

The EPROM programmers can read from the EPROM and write to the disk file, this facility can be used to make a disk backup of your BIOS code. You can also copy the disk backup file to an empty EPROM.

Flash BIOS

A ROM based BIOS cannot be changed without going through the long process explained above and requires additional devices to program it.

A new type of BIOS chip is gaining popularity with the new systems. This new BIOS is called "Flash BIOS".

"Flash BIOS" is a particular type of EEPROM (Electrically Erasable Programmable Read Only Memory) chip that can be erased and programmed in the system itself.

Using a Flash BIOS in a system allows the manufacturer to upgrade or modify the existing BIOS code by sending an upgrade on a disk to the users.

The user can then download the content of the floppy to the Flash BIOS.

Normally all the Flash BIOS based system have some type of hardware write protection to the Flash BIOS, otherwise a virus program may change or destroy the BIOS code and make the system crash.

This write protection uses some type of switch or jumper on the motherboard.

Flash BIOS Upgrade

To update Flash BIOS, two files are required,

- a binary file containing actual BIOS code and
- a Flash BIOS upgrade utility program.

When the BIOS upgrade utility program is executed the motherboard circuitry required to write to the BIOS chips is activated, and the binary file containing the BIOS code is transferred to the flash BIOS chip.

To upgrade a flash BIOS, download these files from the motherboard manufacturer's website. Once you have these files ready, upgrade the BIOS as follows:

- If your motherboard has a Flash BIOS jumper that protects the BIOS from being changed or overwritten, change the setting to allow flashing BIOS.
- Generally computer must be running in a real-mode DOS environment, not the DOS window of Windows NT or Windows 95/98. For this create a new formatted DOS system floppy diskette.
- Copy the downloaded files to the newly formatted system diskette.
- Turn off computer and insert the newly formatted DOS diskette in your computer's diskette drive.
- You might need to run the BIOS setup utility and change the boot priority to make your computer to boot from the floppy diskette drive first.
- At the DOS prompt (A:\), after your computer has booted, type in the program filename and press Enter.
- In the opening dialog box, type in the filename of the new BIOS code and follow the onscreen directions to flash the BIOS.
- When the installation is complete, remove the floppy diskette from the diskette drive and restart your computer.
- If the motherboard has a Flash BIOS jumper, reset the jumper to protect the newly installed BIOS from being overwritten.

```
AMIBIOS HIFLEX SETUP UTILITY - VERSION 1.21
(C)1998 Americal Megatrends, Inc. All Rights Reserved

Standard CMOS Setup
Advanced CMOS Setup
Advanced Chipset Setup
Power Management Setup
PCI/Plug and Play Setup
Peripheral Setup
CPU Configuration Setup
Hardware Monitor Setup
Auto-Detect Hard Disks
Change User Password
Change Supervisor Password
Change Language Setting
Auto Configuration with Optimal Settings
Auto Configuration with Fail Safe Settings
Save Settings and Exit
Exit Without Saving

Standard CMOS Setup for changing time, date, hard disk type, etc.
ESC:Exit    ⇧⇩:Sel   F2/F3:Color   F10:Save & Exit
```

Fig. 5-2 : AMIBIOS Setup Main Menu.

BIOS Setup

The BIOS ROM or the Basic Input Output System has an on-screen system configuration setup utility program.

The setup facility provided by different make of BIOS differ. In this section we shall cover one of the most popular BIOS, i.e. the American Megatrends Inc. (AMI) BIOS.

Most of the setup facility provided on this BIOS could be found on majority of the other BIOS available in the market

When a system is switched on, after the successful completion of the POST routines, the following message appears on the screen.

"Hit <DEL>, If you want to run SETUP"

If you intend to change the already existing configuration of your system or if you are configuring a new system, press the DEL key on the keyboard.

Sometimes this message is disabled using the option provided in the BIOS Setup, if it is disabled, you can press the "Del" key just after the POST memory test is completed.

After you press the "DEL" key, BIOS Setup Main Menu screen will appear on the monitor. Sometimes this BIOS Setup is protected with a password, and if you do not remember the password, then to enter the setup screen you must reset the BIOS.

To reset the BIOS and remove password, you have two options:

- either you can use the BIOS reset jumper provided on your motherboard, check the manual of your PC or motherboard for "Clear CMOS Memory" jumper setting.
- or you can remove the CMOS Setup battery and allow ten minutes for the residual power in the CMOS to drain away. Then, reconnect or reinstall the battery.

Once the BIOS Setup Main Menu appears, in this menu you can move up/down to different options by pressing the up and down arrow keys.

The selected option will appear in reverse color and a helpline about the selected option will be displayed at the bottom of the menu.

F2/F3 keys can be used to change the foreground/background color. F10 key can be pressed to save the changes made in the setup and to exit to the boot process.

Pressing "ESC" key will continue with the boot process without saving the changes made in the setup.

Let us now see a brief description of various options given in this BIOS Setup Main Menu.

AMIBIOS Setup

Standard CMOS Setup

Sets time, date, Hard Disk type, types of Floppy Drive, Monitor type, and if Keyboard is installed.

Advanced CMOS Setup

Sets Typematic Rate and Delay, Above 1 MB Memory Test, Memory Test Tick Sound, Hit <Del> Message Display, System Boot Up Sequence, and many others options.

Advanced Chipset Setup

Sets chipset-specific options and features.

Power Management Setup

Controls power conservation options

PCI/PnP Setup

Sets options related to PCI bus and Plug and Play options.

```
                 AMIBIOS SETUP - STANDARD CMOS SETUP
        (C)1998 Americal Megatrends, Inc. All Rights Reserved

Date (mm/dd/yyyy): Mon Aug 16,2002                  Base Memory: 0 KB
Time (hh/mm/ss)   : 17:34:44                        Extd Memory: 0 KB

Floppy Drive A:    1.44MB 3½
Floppy Drive A:    Not Installed
                                                    LBA  Blk  PIO  32Bit
             Type           Size  Cyln  Head WPcom Sec Mode Mode Mode Mode
Pri Master : Auto                                                   On
Pri Slave  : Auto                                                   On
Sec Master : Auto                                                   On
Sec Slave  : Auto                                                   On

Boot Sector Virus Protection   Disabled

    Available Options:                            ESC:Exit    ↑↓:Sel
   ➤Disabled                                       PgUp/PgDn:Modify
    Enabled                                        F1:Help F2/F3:Color
```

Fig. 5-3 : Standard CMOS Setup.

Peripheral Setup

Controls I/O Controller-related options.

CPU Configuration Setup

This option selects the type of CPU installed in the motherboard.

The settings are Auto (AMIBIOS automatically determines the CPU type.)

Standard CMOS Setup

Select the Standard CMOS Setup from the AMIBIOS Setup Main Menu. Various options in this Standard Setup are described below.

Floppy Drive A: and B:

Move the cursor to these fields and select the floppy type. The settings are

- 360 KB 5 1/4 inch
- 1.2 MB 5 1/4 inch
- 720 KB 3 1/2 inch
- 2.88 MB 3 1/2 inch

```
AMIBIOS SETUP - CPU CONFIGURATION SETUP
(C)1998 Americal Megatrends, Inc. All Rights Reserved

CPU Type                      Pentium III     Available Options:
CPU Speed                     600MHz
System Clock Over Clocking    Disabled        >Disabled
                                               75MHz
                                               83.3MHz
                                               100.3MHz
                                               103MHz
                                               105MHz
                                               110MHz
                                               112MHz
                                               115MHz

                                              Option Comment:

                                              Warning: Overclocking may
                                              cause system instability,
                                              Note: If system hangs reboot
                                              the system to enter setup
```

Fig. 5-4 : CPU Configuration Setup.

Primary Master/Primary Slave/Secondary Master/Secondary Slave

Select these options to configure the drive named in the option. Select Auto Detect IDE to let AMIBIOS automatically configure the drive.

- A screen with a list of drive parameters appears.
- Click on OK to configure the drive.

Type	How to Configure
SCSI	Select Type. Select Not Installed to the drive parameter screen. The SCSI drivers provided by the SCSI manufacturer should allow you to configure the SCSI drive.
IDE	Select Type. Select Auto to let AMIBIOS determine the parameters. Click on OK when AMIBIOS displays the drive parameters. Select LBA Mode. Select On if the drive has a capacity greater than 540 MB. Select Block Mode. Select On to allow block mode data transfers. Select 32-Bit Mode. Select On to allow 32-bit data transfers. Select the PIO Mode. It is best to select Auto to allow AMIBIOS to determine the PIO mode. If you select a PIO mode that is not supported by the IDE drive. The drive will not work properly. If you are absolutely certain that you know the drive's PIO mode. Select PIO mode 0-4, as appropriate.

Type	How to Configure
CD-ROM	Select Type. Select CD-ROM. Click on OK when AMIBIOS displays the drive parameters.
Standard MFM	Select Type. You must know the drive parameters. Select the drive type that exactly matches your drive's parameters.
Non-Standard MFM	Select Type. If the drive parameters do not match the drive parameters listed for drive types 1 - 46, select User and enter the correct hard disk drive parameters.

Entering Drive Parameters

Parameter	Description
Type	The number for a drive with certain identification parameters.
Cylinders	The number of cylinders in the disk drive.
Heads	The number of heads.
Write Precompensation	The actual physical size of a sector gets progressively smaller as the track diameter diminishes. Yet each sector must still hold 512 bytes. Write precompensation circuitry on the hard disk compensates for the physical difference in sector size by boosting the write current for sectors on inner tracks. This parameter is the track number on the disk surface where write precompensation begins.
Landing Zone	This number is the cylinder location where the heads normally park when the system is shut down.
Sectors	Sectors is the smallest unit of storage on a disk. It is usually 512 bytes in size.
Capacity	The formatted capacity of the drive is the number of heads times the number of cylinders times the number of sectors per track times 512 (bytes per sector). Heads x Cylinders x Sectors/track x 512

CPU Configuration Setup

The system BIOS is capable to detect the CPU type. The user is only required to select the CPU speed.

In addition, overclocking option is provided for advanced users who prefer to run the CPU over the specified clock frequency

Advanced CMOS Setup

Quick Boot

Set this option to Enabled to instruct AMIBIOS to boot quickly when the computer is powered on.

```
            AMIBIOS SETUP - ADVANCED CMOS SETUP
   (C)1998 Americal Megatrends, Inc. All Rights Reserved

Quick Boot                      Enabled      Available Options:
1st Boot Device                 Floppy        >Disabled
2nd Boot Device                 IDE 0          Enabled
3rd Boot Device                 CDROM
Try Other Boot Devices          Yes
Initial Display Mode            BIOS
Display Mode at Add-On ROM Init Force BIOS
Floppy Access Control           Read-Write
Hard Disk Access Control        Read-Write
S.M.A.R.T. for Hard Disks       Enabled
BootUp Num-Lock                 On
Floppy Drive Swap               Disabled
Floppy Drive Seek               Disabled
PS/2 Mouse Support              Enabled
Primary Display                 VGA/EGA
Password Check                  Setup
Boot To OS/2 > 64MB             No
CPU Serial Number               Disabled      Esc:Exit  ↑↓:Sel
L1 Cache                        WriteBack     PgUp/PgDn:Modify
L2 Cache                        WriteBack     F1:Help F2/F3:Color
```

Fig. 5-5 : Advanced CMOS Setup.

1st Boot Device

This option sets the type of device for the first boot drives that the AMIBIOS attempts to boot from after AMIBIOS POST completes.

The settings are Disabled, Network, Optical, SCSI, CD-ROM, IDE-0, IDE-1, IDE-2 or IDE-3.

The Optimal and Fail-Safe default settings are IDE-0.

2nd Boot Device

This option sets the type of device for the second boot drives that the AMIBIOS attempts to boot from after AMIBIOS POST completes.

The settings are Disabled, Floppy or IDE-0.

The Optimal and Fail-Safe default settings are Floppy.

3rd Boot Device

This option sets the type of device for the third boot drives that the AMIBIOS attempts to boot from after AMIBIOS POST completes.

The settings are Disabled, CD-ROM or IDE-0.

The Optimal and Fail-Safe default settings are CD-ROM.

Try Other Boot Devices

Set this option to Yes to instruct AMIBIOS to attempt to boot from any other drive in the system if it cannot find a boot drive among the drives specified in the 1st Boot Device, 2nd Boot Device, 3rd Boot Device options.

Initial Display Mode

Set this option to BIOS for initial display mode by BIOS.

Settings are BIOS or Silent.

Display Mode at add-on ROM Nit

Set the display mode at add-on ROM Nit.

Settings are Force or Keep Current.

Floppy Access Control

This option specifies the Read/Write access that is set when booting from a floppy drive.

The settings are Read/Write or Read-Only.

The Optimal and Fail-Safe default settings are Read/Write.

Hard Disk Access Control

This option specifies the Read/Write access that is set when booting from a hard disk drive.

The settings are Read/Write or Read-Only.

The Optimal and Fail-Safe default settings are Read/Write.

S.M.A.R.T. For Hard Disks

Set this option to Enable to permit AMIBIOS to use the SMART (System Management and Reporting Technologies) protocol for reporting server system information over a network. The settings are Enabled/Disabled.

The Optimal and Fail-Safe default settings are Disabled.

Boot Up Num Lock

Set the option to Off to turn the Num Lock Key off when the computer boots up so you can use the arrow keys on both the numeric keypad and the keyboard.

The settings are On or Off. The default settings are On.

PS/2 Mouse Support

Set this option to enable AMIBIOS support for a PS/2 mouse.

The settings are Enabled or Disabled.

The Optimal and Fail-Safe default settings are Enabled.

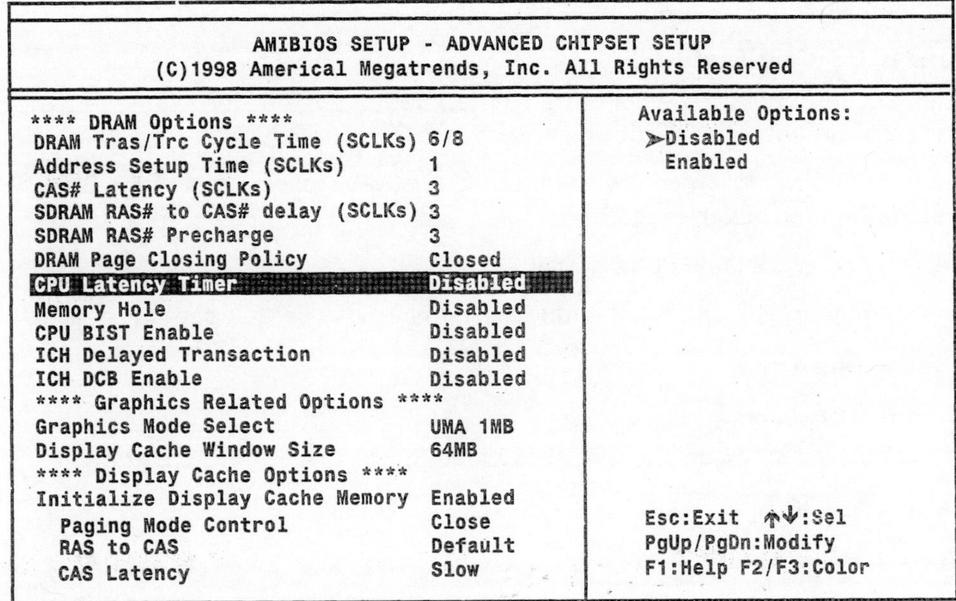
```
AMIBIOS SETUP - ADVANCED CHIPSET SETUP
(C)1998 Americal Megatrends, Inc. All Rights Reserved

**** DRAM Options ****                           Available Options:
DRAM Tras/Trc Cycle Time (SCLKs) 6/8              >Disabled
Address Setup Time (SCLKs)       1                 Enabled
CAS# Latency (SCLKs)             3
SDRAM RAS# to CAS# delay (SCLKs) 3
SDRAM RAS# Precharge             3
DRAM Page Closing Policy         Closed
CPU Latency Timer                Disabled
Memory Hole                      Disabled
CPU BIST Enable                  Disabled
ICH Delayed Transaction          Disabled
ICH DCB Enable                   Disabled
**** Graphics Related Options ****
Graphics Mode Select             UMA 1MB
Display Cache Window Size        64MB
**** Display Cache Options ****
Initialize Display Cache Memory  Enabled
  Paging Mode Control            Close           Esc:Exit  ↑↓:Sel
  RAS to CAS                     Default         PgUp/PgDn:Modify
  CAS Latency                    Slow            F1:Help F2/F3:Color
```

Fig. 5-6 : Advanced Chipset Setup.

Primary Display

This option configures the type of monitor attached to the computer.

The settings are Mono, CGA 40x25, CGA 80x25, VGA/EGA or Absent.

The Optimal and Fail-Safe default settings are VGA/EGA.

Password Check

This option enables password checking when system boots up or when AMIBIOS Setup is run.

Settings are Setup or Always.

Boot To OS/2>64MB

Set this option to Enabled if running OS/2 operating system and using more than 64 MB of system memory on the motherboard.

The settings are Enabled or Disabled.

The Optimal and Fail-Safe default settings are Disabled.

CPU Serial Number

Set this option to Enabled to display the CPU Serial Number.

The settings are Enabled or Disabled.

The Optimal and Fail-Safe default settings are Disabled.

System BIOS Cacheable

When set to Enabled, the contents of the F0000h system memory segment can be read from or written to cache memory.

The contents of this memory segment are always copied from the BIOS ROM to System RAM for faster execution.

The settings are Enabled or Disabled.

The Optimal default setting is Enabled. The Fail-Safe default setting is Disabled.

C000,16K Shadow

C400,16K Shadow

The options specify how the 32 KB of Video ROM at C0000h is treated.

The settings are:

Setting	Description
Disabled	The contents of the video ROM are not copied to RAM.
Enabled	The contents of the video ROM area from C0000h - C7FFFh are copied (shadowed) from ROM to RAM for faster execution.
Cached	The contents of the video ROM area from C0000h - C7FFFh are copied from ROM to RAM and can be written to or read from cache memory.

C800, 16K Shadow

CC00, 16K Shadow

D000, 16K Shadow

D400, 16K Shadow

D800, 16K Shadow

DC00, 16K Shadow

These options enable shadowing of the contents of the ROM area named in the option. The ROM area not used by ISA adapter cards is allocated to PCI adapter cards. The settings are:

Setting	Description
Disabled	The contents of the video ROM are not copied to RAM.
Enabled	The contents of the video ROM area from C000h - C7FFFh are copied (shadowed) from ROM to RAM for faster execution.
Cached	The contents of the Video ROM area from C0000h - C7FFFh are copied from ROM to RAM and can be written to or read from cache memory

Advanced Chipset Setup

Choose Advanced Chipset Setup on the AMIBIOS Setup Main Menu, all Chipset Setup options are then displayed.

DRAM Tras/Trc Cycle time <SCLKs>

This option specifies the length of the DRAM TRAS/TRC Cycle time.

The settings are 5/7 or 6/8.

The Optimal and Fail-Safe default settings are 5/7.

Address Setup Time <SCLKs>

This option specifies the address setup time.

The settings are Auto (BIOS automatically decide the optimal delay) or Manual.

The Optimal and Fail-Safe default settings are Auto.

CAS# Latency <SCLKs>

This option sets the latency period for the CAS signal.

The settings are 2 CLKs or 3 CLKs.

The Optimal and Fail-Safe default settings are 3 CLKs.

SDRAM RAS# To CAS# delay <SCLKs>

This option specifies the length of the delay inserted between the RAS and CAS signals of the DRAM system memory access cycle.

The settings are 2 CLKs or 3 CLKs.

The Optimal and Fail-Safe default settings are 3 CLKs.

SDRAM RAS# Precharge

This option specifies the length of the RAS precharge part of the DRAM system memory access cycle when DRAM system memory is installed in this computer.

The settings are 3 CLKs, 2 CLKs or Auto.

The Optimal and Fail-Safe default setting is 3 CLKs.

DRAM Page closing Policy

This option sets the DRAM Page closing Policy.

The settings are Closed or Open.

CPU Latency Timer

This option specifies the latency for the Timer.

The settings are Disabled or Enabled.

The Optimal and Faii-Safe default settings are Disabled.

Memory Hole

This option specifies the location of an area of memory that cannot be addressed on the PCI bus.

The settings are Disabled, 15 MB-16 MB.

The Optimal and Fail-Safe default settings are Disabled.

CPU BIST Enable

This option specifies the CPU BIST settings.

The settings are Disabled or Enabled.

The Optimal and Fail-Safe default settings are Disabled.

ICH Delayed Transaction

This option specifies the ICH Delay Transaction settings.

The settings are Disabled or Enabled.

The Optimal and Fail-Safe default settings are Disabled.

ICH DCB Enable

This option specifies the ICH DCB Enable settings.

The settings are Disabled or Enabled.

The Optimal and Fail-Safe default settings are Disabled.

Graphic Mode Select

This option specifies the Graphics Mode settings.

The settings are UMA 1MB or UMA 512KB.

The Optimal and Fail-Safe default settings are UMA 1MB.

Display Cache Window Size

This option specifies the Display Windows Size.

The settings are 64MB or 32MB.

The Optimal and Fail-Safe default settings are 64MB.

Initialize Display Cache Memory

This option specifies the Initialize Display Cache Memory.

The settings are Enable or Disable.

The Optimal and Fail-Safe default settings are Enabled.

```
AMIBIOS SETUP - PCI / PLUG AND PLAY SETUP
(C)1998 Americal Megatrends, Inc. All Rights Reserved

Plug and Play Aware O/S           No             Available Options:
Clear NVRAM                       No              ➢No
PCI Latency Timer (PCI Clocks)    64               Yes
Primary Graphics Adapter          Add-on VGA
VBU Load                          No
PCI VGA Palette Snoop             Disabled
PCI IDE BusMaster                 Disabled
DMA Channel 0                     PnP
DMA Channel 1                     PnP
DMA Channel 3                     PnP
DMA Channel 5                     PnP
DMA Channel 6                     PnP
DMA Channel 7                     PnP
IRQ3                              PCI/PnP
IRQ4                              PCI/PnP
IRQ5                              PCI/PnP
IRQ7                              PCI/PnP
IRQ9                              PCI/PnP        Esc:Exit  ↑↓:Sel
IRQ10                             PCI/PnP        PgUp/PgDn:Modify
IRQ11                             PCI/PnP        F1:Help F2/F3:Color
```

Fig. 5-7 : PCI/PnP Setup.

Paging Mode Control

This option specifies the control of Paging Mode.

The settings are CLOSE or OPEN.

The Optimal and Fail-Safe default settings are CLOSE.

RAS-to-CAS

This option specifies the RAS-to-CAS Settings.

The settings are Default or Override.

The Optimal and Fail-Safe default settings are Default.

CAS Latency

This option specifies the CAS Latency Settings.

The settings are Slow or Fast.

The Optimal and Fail-Safe default settings are Slow.

RAS Timing

This option specifies the RAS Timing Settings.

The settings are Slow or Fast.

The Optimal and Fail-Safe default settings are Slow.

RAS Recharge Timing

This option specifies the RAS Precharge Timing.

The settings are Slow or Fast.

The Optimal and Fail-Safe default settings are Slow.

PCI/PnP Setup

Choose PCI Plug and Play Setup from the AMIBIOS Setup Main Screen to display the PCI and Plug and Play Setup options, described below.

Plug and Play Aware O/S

Set this option to Yes to inform AMIBIOS Setup that the operating system can handle Plug and Play (PnP) devices.

The settings are No or Yes.

The Optimal and Fail-Safe default settings are No

PCI Latency Timer (PCI Clocks)

This option specifies the Latency Timing (in PCI clocks) for PCI devices installed in the PCI expansion slots.

The settings are 32, 64. 96, 128, 160, 192, 224 or 248.

The Optimal and Fail-Safe default settings are 64

Primary Graphics Adapter

This option is set to choose Onboard VGA or add-on VGA.

VBU Load

The options are No or Yes.

PCI VGA Palette Snoop

When this option is set to Enabled, multiple VGA devices operating on different buses can handle data from the CPU on each set of palette registers on every video device.

Bit 5 of the command register in the PCI device configuration space is the VGA Palette Snoop bit (0 is disabled).

VGA palette

Snoop Bit	Description
Disabled	Data read and written by the CPU is only directed to the PCI VGA device's palette registers.

Snoop Bit	Description
Enabled	Data read and written by the CPU is directed to the both the PCI VGA device's palette registers and ISA VGA device palette registers, permitting the palette registers of both devices to be identical.

PCI IDE Bus Master

Set this option to Enabled to specify that the IDE controller on the PCI bus has bus-mastering capability.

The settings are Disabled or Enabled.

The Optimal and Fail-Safe default settings are Disabled.

DMA Channel O, DMA Channel 1, DMA Channel 3, DMA Channel 5, DMA Channel 6, DMA Channel 7

These options allow you to specify the bus type used by each DMA channel.

The settings are PnP or ISA/EISA.

The Optimal and Fail-Safe default settings are PnP.

IRQ3, IRQ4, IRQ5, IRQ7, IRQ9, IRQ10, IRQ11, IRQ12, IRQ14, IRQ15

These options specify the bus that the specified IRQ line is used on.

These options allow you to reserve IRQs for legacy ISA adapter cards.

These options determine if AMIBIOS should remove an IRQ from the pool of available IRQs passed to devices that are configurable by the system BIOS.

- The available IRQ pool is determined by reading the ESCD NVRAM.
- If more IRQs must be removed from the pool, the end user can use these options to reserve the IRQ by assigning an ISA/EISA setting to it.
- Onboard I/O is configured by AMIBIOS.
- All IRQs used by onboard I/O are configured as PCI/PnP.
- IRQ12 only appears if the Mouse Support option in Advanced Setup is set to Disabled.
- IRQ14 and 15 will not be available if the onboard PCI IDE is enabled.
- If all IRQs are set to ISA/EISA and IRQ14 and 15 are allocated to the onboard PCI IDE, IRQ9 will still be available for PCI and PnP devices, because at least one IRQ must be available for PCI and PnP devices.

The settings are ISA/EISA or PCI/PnP.

The Optimal and Fail-Safe default settings are PCI/PnP.

Reserved Memory Size

This option specifies the size of the memory area reserved for legacy ISA adapter cards.

```
                 AMIBIOS SETUP - POWER MANAGEMENT SETUP
        (C)1998 Americal Megatrends, Inc. All Rights Reserved

 ******* ACPI Options *******                       | Available Options:
ACPI Aware O/S                      Yes             |  ➤No
InstantOn PC                        Disabled        |   Yes
 ******* Wakeup Events *******                      |
Power Button Function               On/Off          |
Keyboard Power On                   Disabled        |
   Wakeup String                    N/A             |
PS/2 Mouse Power On                 Disabled        |
Wakeup on Modem Ring                Disabled        |
PCI Device/LAN Wakeup               Disabled        |
RTC Alarm Resume From Soft Off      Disabled        |
 ******* RTC Alarm Date *******                     |
     Date                           15              |
     Hour                           12              |
     Minute                         30              |
     Second                         30              |
 ******* Power Management *******                   |
Power Management/APM                Enabled         | Esc:Exit  ↑↓:Sel
Video Power Down Mode               Suspend         | PgUp/PgDn:Modify
Hard Disk Power Down Mode           Stand By        | F1:Help F2/F3:Color
```

Fig. 5-8 : Power Management Setup.

The settings are Disabled, 16K, 32K, or 64K.

The Optimal and Fail- Safe default settings are Disabled.

Reserved Memory Address

This option specifies the beginning address (in hex) of the reserved memory area.

The specified ROM memory area is reserved for use by legacy ISA adapter cards. This option does not appear if the Reserved Memory Size option is set to Disabled.

The settings are N/A.

The Optimal and Fail-Safe settings are N/A.

Power Management Setup

The AMIBIOS Setup options described in this section are selected by choosing Power Management Setup from the AMIBIOS Setup Main Menu.

Power Management/APM

Set this option to Enabled to enable the chipset power management and APM (Advanced Power Management) features.

The settings are Enabled or Disabled.

The Optimal and Fail-Safe default settings are Disabled.

Power Button Function

This option specifies how the power button mounted externally on the computer cabinet is used.

The settings are:

Setting	Description
On/Off	Pushing the power button turns the computer on or off
Suspend	Pushing the Power button places the computer in Suspend mode or Full On Power Mode.

InstantON PC

Set this option to Enabled to enable AMIBIOS support for the Intel InstantON specification.

The settings are Enabled or Disabled.

The Optimal and Fail-Safe default settings are Disabled.

Video Power Down Mode

This option specifies the power state that the video subsystem enters when AMIBIOS places it in a Power Saving State after the specified period of display inactivity has expired.

The settings are Standby, Suspend or Disabled.

The Optimal and Fail-Safe default settings are Disabled.

Hard Disk Power Down Mode

This option specifies the power conserving state that the hard disk drive enters after the specified period of hard drive inactivity has expired.

The settings are Disabled, Standby, or Suspend.

The Optimal and Fail-Safe default settings are Disabled.

Hard Disk Timeout

This option specifies the length of a period of hard disk drive inactivity.

When this length of time expires, the computer enters power-conserving state specified in the Hard Disk Power Down Mode Option; see previous option.

The settings are Disabled, 1 min. (minute), 2 min., 3 min., 4 min., 5 min., 6 min., 7 min., 8 min., 9 min., 10 min., 11 min., 12 min., 13 min., 14 min. and 15 min.

The Optimal and Fail-Safe default settings are Disabled.

Standby/Suspend Timer Unit

This option specifies the unit of time used for the Standby and Suspend timeout periods.

The settings are 4 msec., 4 sec, 32 sec, or 4 min.

The Optimal and Fail-Safe default settings are 4 min.

Standby Timeout

This option specifies the length of a period of system inactivity while in Full Power On state. When this length of time expires, the computer enters Standby Power state.

The settings are Disabled, 4 msec, 8 msec, 12 msec, 16 msec, up to 508 msec, in increments of 4 msec.

The Optimal and Fail-Safe default settings are Disabled.

Suspend Timeout

This option specifies the length of a period of system inactivity while in Standby state. When this length of time expires, the computer enters Suspend Power state.

The settings are Disabled, 4 msec, 8 msec, 12 msec, 16 msec, up to 508 msec, in increments of 4 msec.

The Optimal and Fail-Safe default settings are Disabled.

Throttle Slow Clock Ratio

This option specifies the Throttle Slow Clock Ratio.

The settings are 87.5%, 75.0%, 62.5%, 50.0%, 37.5%, 25.0%, 12.5%.

The Optimal and Fail-Safe default settings are 50.0%.

Keyboard & PS/2 Mouse Access	Option: Monitor or Ignore
FDC/LPT/COM Ports Access	Option: Monitor or Ignore
SB & MSS Audio Ports Access	Option: Monitor or Ignore
MIDI parts Access	Option: Monitor or Ignore
ADLIB Ports Access	Option: Monitor or Ignore
Primary/Secondary, Master/Slave IDE Access	Option: Monitor or Ignore
PIRQ [A]-[D] IRQ Active	Option: Monitor or Ignore
System Thermal	Option: Monitor or Ignore

Keyboard Wakeup A& PS/2 Mouse Wakeup Guide

These features enable using Keyboard or PS/2 Mouse to wakeup the system

```
AMIBIOS SETUP - PERIPHERAL SETUP
(C)1998 Americal Megatrends, Inc. All Rights Reserved

Onboard USB Controller          Enabled       Available Options:
  USB Keyb Legacy Support       Disabled        Disabled
OnBoard IDE                     Both          ➤ Enabled
OnBoard 3D Audio                Enabled
OnBoard Game Port               200
OnBoard FDC                     Enabled
OnBoard Serial Port1            3F8/COM1
OnBoard Serial Port2            Auto
Ir Function                     Disabled
  Ir Duplex Mode                N/A
OnBoard Parallel Port           378
  Parallel Port Mode            Normal
  Parallel Port IRQ             7
  Parallel Port DMA             N/A
OnBoard Midi Port               Disabled
  Midi IRQ Select               9
                                              Esc:Exit  ↑↓:Sel
                                              PgUp/PgDn:Modify
                                              F1:Help F2/F3:Color
```

Fig. 5-9 : Peripheral Setup.

Keyboard Wake-Up Setup

1. Boot Up System
2. Press DEL to enter CMOS
3. Select Power Management Setup
4. Enable Keyboard Power On
5. Select Wakeup String & Press Enter

Wakeup String

The Screen shows "Enter new keyboard wakeup string:"

- Press <Enter> <Enter> to set default as Right Shift Key (R Shift)
- Enter a Wakeup String for Keyboard Wakeup, for example, `Modern`.

How to wakeup using Keyboard or PS/2 Mouse?

Keyboard Wakeup

- Select Shut Down
- Press "Right Shift" or type the wake-up string (e.g.. `Modern`) & Press "Enter"

Mouse Wakeup

- In Windows 98
- Select Shut Down
- Double Click Left Mouse Button

Peripheral Setup

Peripheral Setup options are displayed by choosing Peripheral Setup form the AMIBIOS Setup Main Menu.

All Peripheral Setup options are described here.

USB Function

Set this option to Enabled to enable USB (Universal Serial Bus) support.

The settings are Enabled or Disabled.

USB Keyboard/Mouse Legacy Support

Set this option to Enabled to enable support for older keyboards and mouse devices if the USB Function option is set to Enabled.

The settings are Enabled or Disabled.

On board 3D Audio

Set this option to Enabled to enable the onboard 3D Audio.

The settings are Enabled or Disabled.

On board Game Port

Set this option to Enabled to enable the onboard Game Port.

The settings are 200, 208 or Disabled.

Onboard IDE

This option specifies the IDE channel used by the onboard IDE controller.

The settings are Disabled, Primary, or Secondary.

Onboard Floppy Controller

Set this option to Enabled to enable the floppy drive controller on the motherboard.

The settings are Auto (AMIBIOS automatically determines if the floppy controller should be enabled), Enabled or Disabled.

Onboard Serial Port 1

This option specifies the base I/O port address of Serial Port 1.

The settings are Auto (AMIBIOS automatically determines the correct base I/O port address), Disabled, 3F8h, 2F8h, 2E8h, or 3E8h.

The Optimal and Fail-Safe default settings are Auto.

Onboard Serial Port 2

This option specifies the base I/O port address of Serial Port 2.

The settings are Auto (AMIBIOS automatically determines the correct base I/O port address), Disabled, 3F8h, 2F8h, 2E8h, or 3EBh.

The Optimal and Fail-Safe default settings are Auto.

IR Mode

This option specifies the type of infrared devices supported by the system.

This option appears if the Onboard Serial Port is not set to Auto or disabled.

The settings are Encoded or Non-Encoded. There are no default settings.

IR Duplex Mode

This option specifies type of duplexing used for infrared on serial port 2.

This option only appears if the Onboard Serial Port option is not set to Auto or Disabled.

The settings are Half or Full. There are no default settings.

IR Transmitter

This option specifies the type of transmission used by the infrared devices attached to serial port 2.

This option only appears if the Onboard Serial Port option is not set to Auto or Disabled.

The settings are 1.6 uS or 3/16 Baud. There are no default settings.

Onboard Parallel Port

This option specifies the base I/O port address of the parallel port on the motherboard. The settings are Disabled, 378h, 278h or 3BCh. The Optimal default setting is 378h.

Parallel Port Mode

This option specifies the parallel port mode.

The Optimal default setting is Normal. The Fail-Safe default setting is Disabled.

The available settings are:

Setting	Description
Normal	The normal parallel port mode is used.
Bi-Dir	Use this setting to support Bi-directional transfers on the parallel port.

Setting	Description
EPP	The parallel port can be used with devices that adhere in the Enhanced Parallel Port (EPP) specification. ECP uses the DMA protocol to achieve data transfer rates up to 2.5 Megabits per second. ECP provides symmetric bi-directional communication.

EPP Version

This option specifies the Enhanced Parallel Port specification version number that is used in the system.

This option only appears if the Parallel Port Mode option is set to EPP.

The settings are 1.7 or 1.9.

There are no Optimal and Fail-Safe default settings because the default setting for the Parallel Port Mode option is not EPP.

Parallel Port DMA Channel

This option is only available if the setting for the Parallel Port Mode option is ECP.

This option sets the DMA channel used by the Parallel Port.

The settings are DMA Channel O, 1 or 3.

The Optimal and Fail-Safe default settings are not provided.

Parallel Port IRQ

This option specifies the IRQ used by the Parallel Port.

The settings are Auto, IRQ 5, or IRQ 7.

The Optimal and Fail-Safe default settings are Auto.

Onboard Midi Port

Set this option to Enabled to enable the onboard Game Port.

The settings are 200, 208 or Disabled.

Motherboard Installation

Pentium 4 (P4) Motherboard

In this section we shall see how to install a motherboard designed for Pentium 4 processor.

This board has four 2.5V memory module sockets that support RIMMs containing Direct Rambus DRAM (RDRAM) devices.

This board supports the following memory features:

- Maximum of 32 Direct Rambus devices per channel
- Memory Configuration from 128MB (minimum) to 2GB (maximum) using 128 Mbit or 256 Mbit technology
- PC600 or PC800 compliant RDRAM
- Single or Double sided RIMM modules
- Serial Presence Detect (SPD) memory
- ECC or Non-ECC support

When installing this board, failure to use an ATX 12V power supply, or not connecting both additional power supply leads to the board may result in damage to the board.

Motherboard Installation

Always disconnect the power supply from the AC mains before you connect, disconnect, install or remove any board component. Failure to do this could result in damage to the equipment.

Some circuitry on the Motherboard can continue to operate even when the front panel power switch is off.

Installing AGP Card Retention Mechanism

If you want to use an AGP card with retention notch, as shown in the figure, with this motherboard then install the Retention Mechanism (RM) on the motherboard.

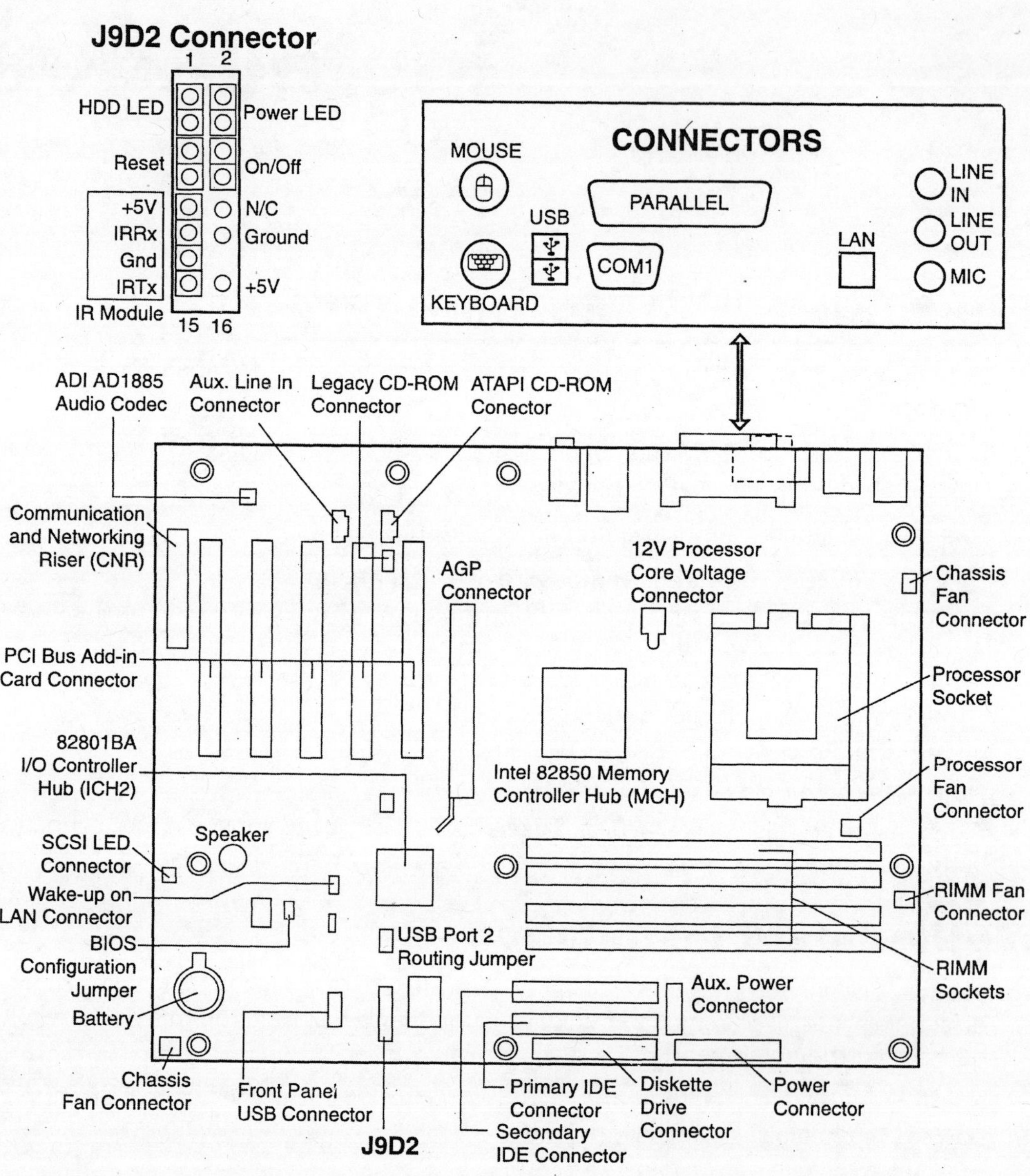

Fig. 6-1 : Motherboard Using Intel D850GB/D850GBAL Desktop Board.

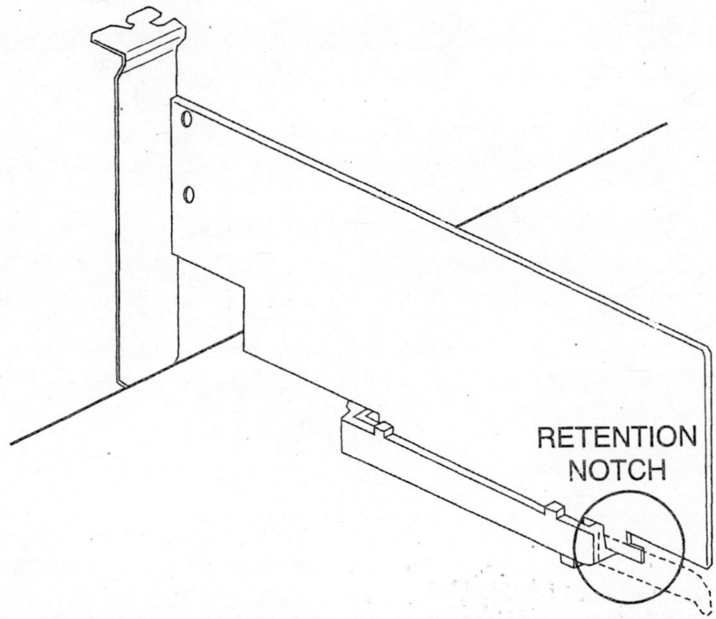

Fig. 6-2 : AGP Card Retention Notch.

Using the RM with an unnotched card may impair video operation.

The RM encloses the motherboard's AGP connector and stabilizes the AGP card.

To install the RM, place the Motherboard (component side up) on a flat, supportive surface, preferable on the anti-static bag in which the board was shipped in.

Follow the steps given below to attach the RM to the AGP connector on the Motherboard.

- Locate the AGP connector on the motherboard. Note that the screen printing on the Motherboard (C) shows the correct final position of the lever (D) on the RM.
- Position the RM over the AGP connector.
- Push the lever end of the RM in the direction of the arrow until the two rearmost tabs (E) spread over the end of the AGP connector.
- Push the free end of the RM over the other end of the AGP connector and press down evenly on both ends of the RM until all four tabs click underneath the AGP connector.

Do not apply unnecessary pressure to avoid damaging the board.

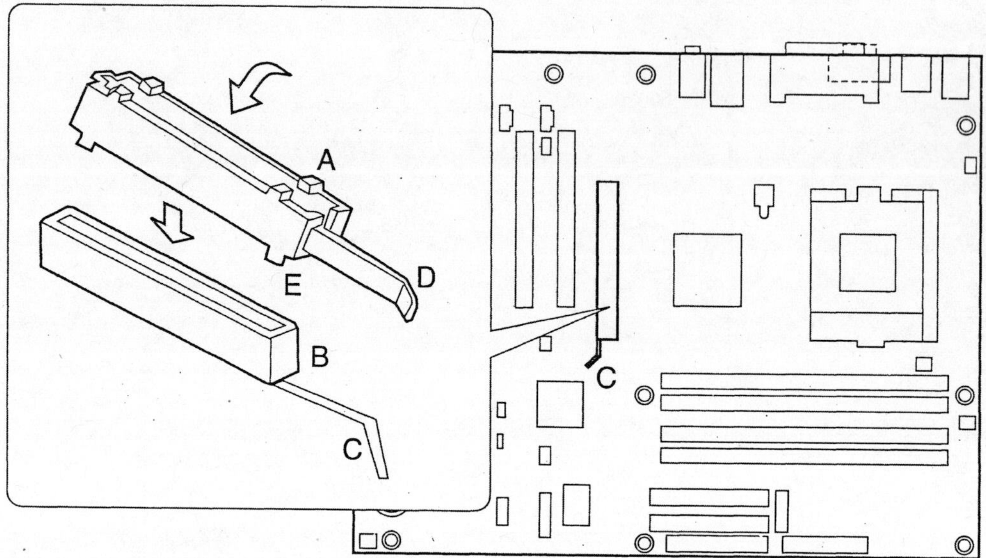

Fig. 6-3 : Installing Retention Mechanism to AGP Connector.

Installing the I/O Shield

This Motherboard comes with an I/O shield to block radio frequency transmissions, necessary to pass the Emissions (EMI) certification testing.

It also protects internal components from dust and foreign objects, and promotes correct airflow inside the chassis.

Install the I/O shield before installing the board in the chassis.

Place the shield inside the chassis as shown in the figure. Press the shield into place so that it fits tightly and securely.

Installing the Motherboard

Secure the motherboard to the standoff provided on the chassis. Insert screws in the mounting holes as shown in the figure.

Do not install the four screws around the processor socket at this time.

Before installing the motherboard to the chassis make sure that the chassis supports the Pentium 4 processor.

You can find out this by verifying that the standoffs for the processor retention mechanism are in the correct position on the chassis.

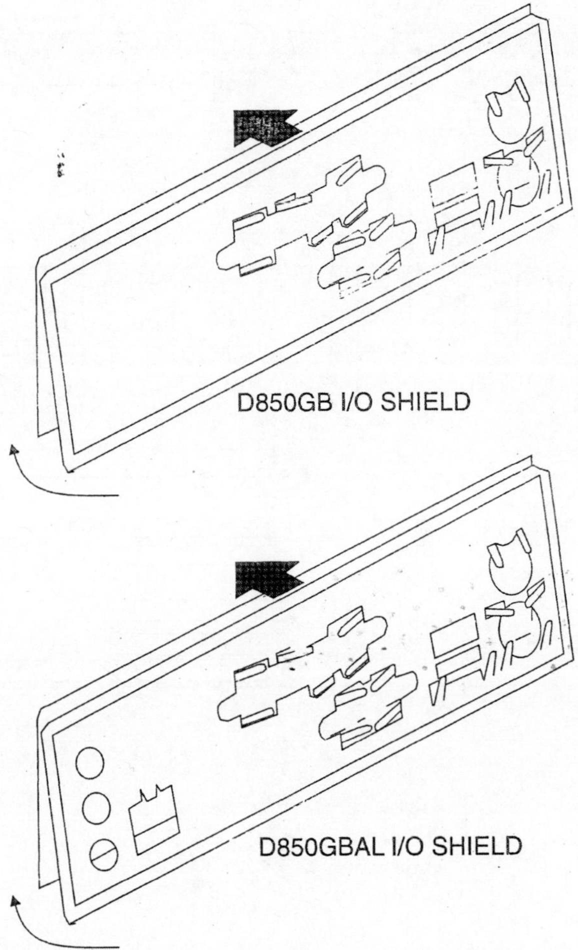

Fig. 6-4 : Installing I/O Shield.

Installing the Processor Retention Mechanisms

Processor Retention Mechanisms are secured to the Motherboard with four screws provided with the chassis. Location of the processor Retention Mechanism (RM) holes is shown in the figure.

To install the RM, place the RM on the board by aligning the holes in the RM with the holes in the motherboard.

Using the screws provided with the chassis, install the RM into the four holes on the chassis.

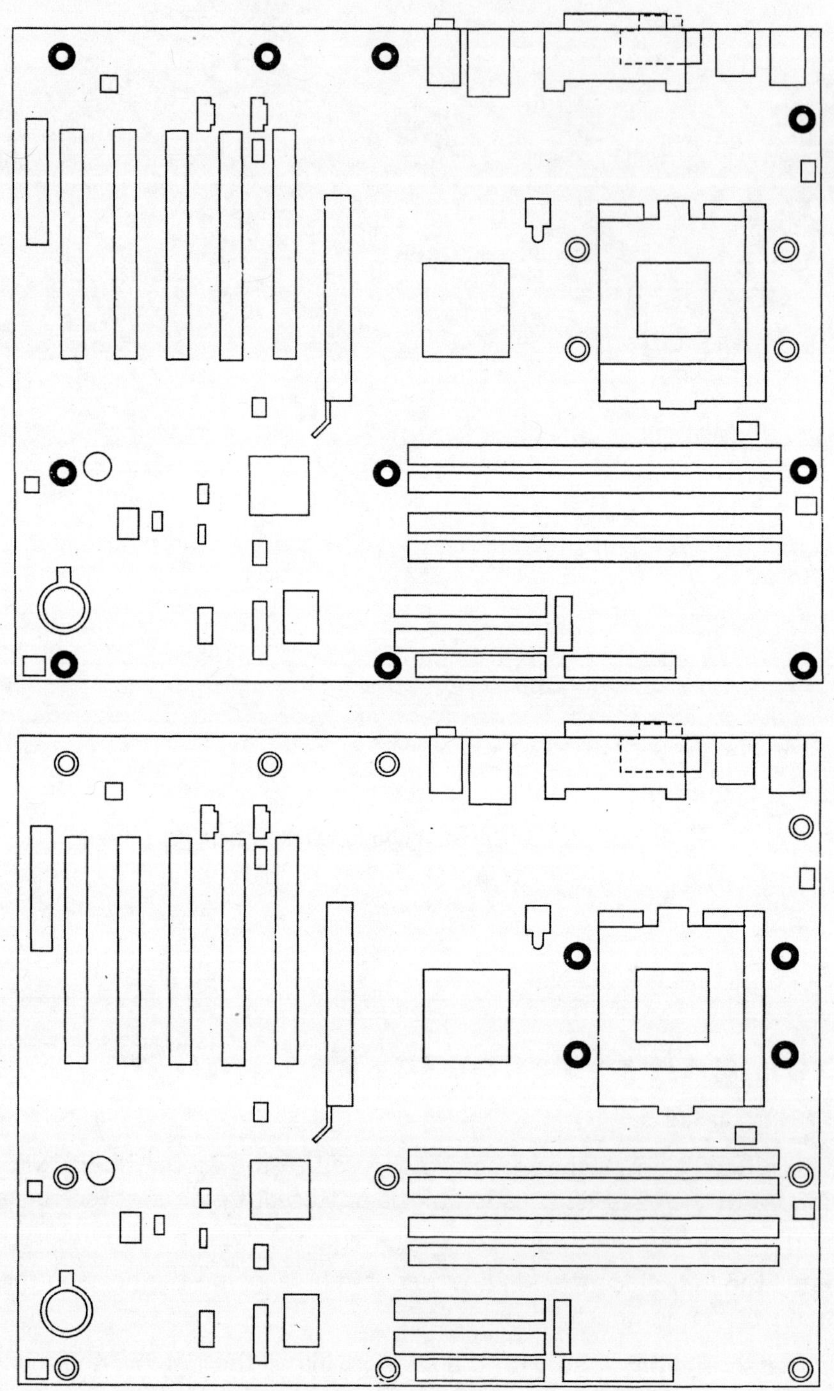

Fig. 6-5 : Installing Motherboard.

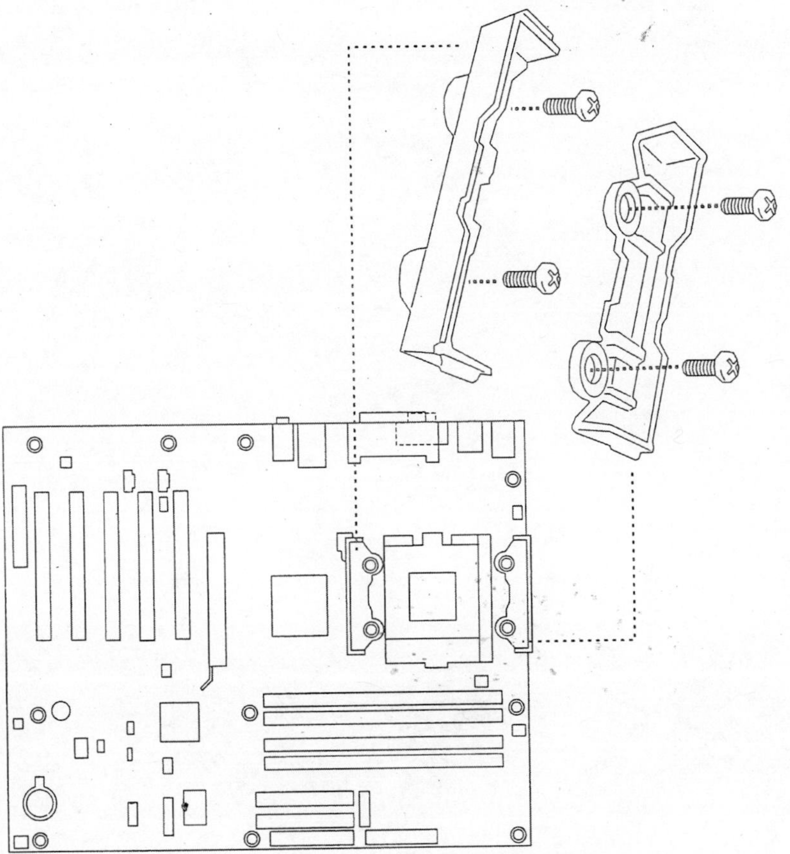

Fig. 6-6 : Installing Processor Retention Mechanism.

Installing the Processor

To install the processor, lift the processor socket lever, place the processor into the socket so that the first pin (pin A) of the processor is aligned with the first pin location on the Motherboard.

Lower the lever back to its original position.

Applying Thermal Grease to the Processor

After placing the processor into the socket apply about half of the thermal grease from the thermal grease syringe to the center of the processor surface.

Thermal grease syringe is generally included in the processor package.

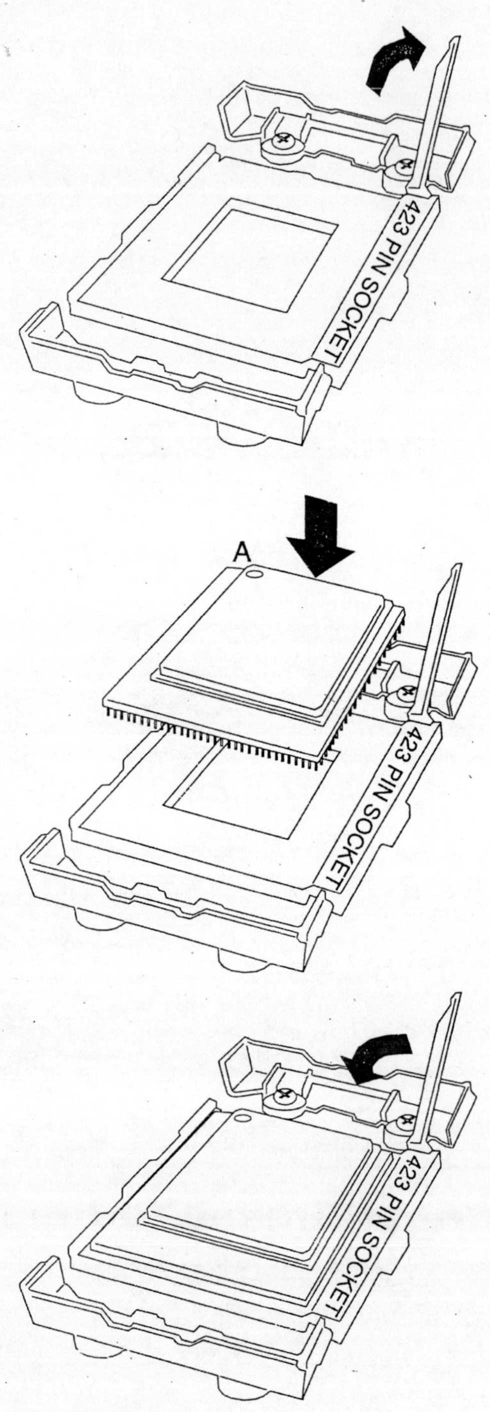

Fig. 6-7: Installing the Processor.

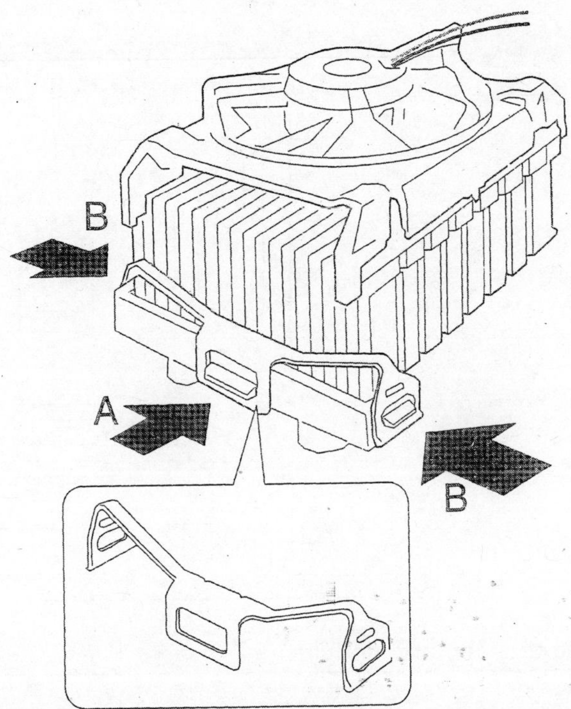

Fig. 6-8 : Installing the Fan Heatsink Clips.

Installing the Processor Fan Heatsink

Place the fan heatsink on top of the processor so that the fan cable is facing the right edge of the board.

Installing the Fan Heatsink Clips

Once the Fan Heatsink is securely placed on the processor, secure it using the Fan Heatsink clips.

Install the clips by attaching the opening at both ends of the clip (B) to the tabs on the Retention Mechanism (RM).

Then connect the side clip (A) to the RM until you hear a click sound.

Repeat this procedure on the opposite side of the fan heatsink.

Installing the Memory Modules

This board uses RIMM memory modules. Install the RIMMs into bank 0 first. If you want to leave the Bank 1 empty then insert a Continuity RIMM (CRIMM) in the bank 1.

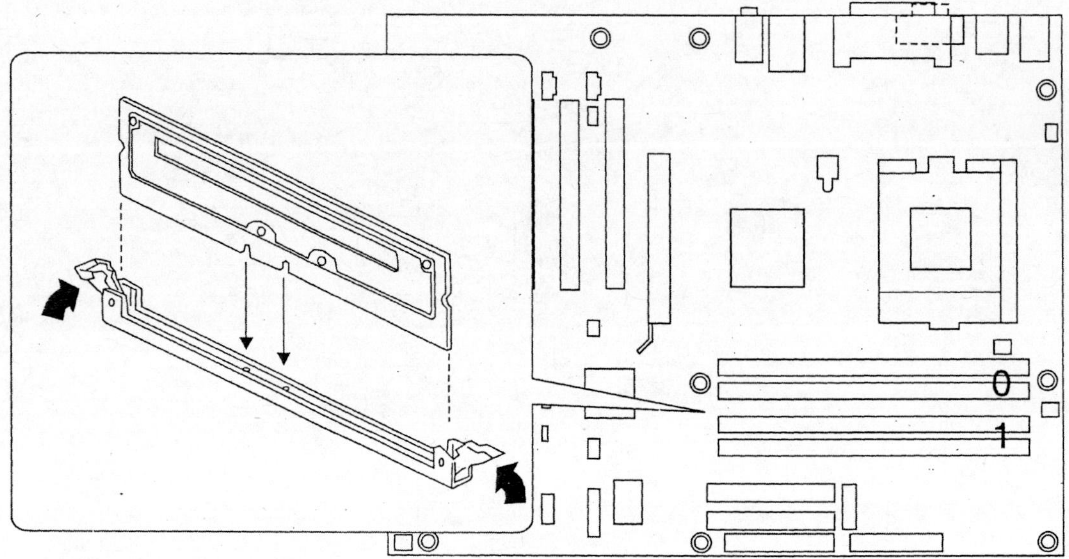

Fig. 6-9 : Installing the Memory Modules.

Failing to do this may result in Boot Failure.

To install RIMM, high insertion force is required, use caution to prevent the Motherboard from flexing.

RIMMs must be installed in identical pairs, same speed, and density.

If memory is to be installed in bank 1, then the RIMM module to be installed must be identical in size and density to each other and must match the speed of the RIMM module in bank 0.

The RIMM modules in bank 0 and bank 1 need not match in size.

For example, if bank 0 has two 128MB RIMMs of PC800 RDRAM, then bank 1 would also require PC800 RDRAM, however size of RIMM module could be 64MB or 128MB.

Connecting the Fans

This Motherboard has four points to connect the fans. If you are installing a processor with an active fan heatsink, then connect the processor's fan cable to the board connector next to the CPU socket.

Connect the chassis fan cables to a separate fan connector provided on the motherboard.

Installing an AGP Card

This motherboard supports only 1.5V AGP cards.

To install an AGP card with a retention notch:

- Place the AGP card in the AGP connector
- Press down on the card until it is completely seated in the connector and the card retention notch snaps into place below the RM.
- Secure the card's metal bracket to the chassis back panel with screw.

The Battery

The battery inside the PC keeps the clock working when the main power supply to the system is switched off, so that the next time when you switch on the system you will get correct time and date.

This battery also provides power to the CMOS memory that keeps the setup information about the system.

Usually this battery lasts for many years, when it eventually fails, your system will lose the setup information saved in the CMOS RAM and also the Real Time Clock (RTC) of your system will stop showing correct time.

In this condition, every time you switch on the system, you will have to run the setup and feed proper setup information, otherwise the machine will not work properly.

Also, every time you need to feed the correct time and date to the system, to allow the system to show correct time and date as long as machine is on.

When the battery inside your system fails you need to replace it with another working battery of the same size and type.

To replace battery

- Switch off the system and remove the power supply cable.
- Remove the main system unit's cover.
- Remove the battery from the holder and slide in a new battery of the same size and type in the holder.
- Make sure that it is in correct orientation.
- Once the battery is replaced, close the cover, switch on the system and run the setup to configure the system.

Presently 3V, CR-2030 Lithium battery is commonly used in most of the motherboards.

Connectors on the Motherboard

Several connectors are provided on the motherboard to connect external Reset switch, Power-on LED, Speaker etc. to the system.

When you remove any lead, always remember to note the position and orientation of each of them as some of them are orientation sensitive and will not work when connected in wrong orientation.

Let us see some of these connectors.

External Battery Connector

Pin Number	Function
1	Battery (+6V DC Input)
2	No Connection
3	Ground
4	Ground

On IBM AT and compatibles, CMOS RAM data is maintained by battery on the motherboard itself and hence do not require any external connection.

Optional Keyboard Connector

Pin Number	Function
1	Keyboard Clock
2	Keyboard Data
3	No Connection
4	Ground
5	+5V

Keyboard connector is a five-pin DIN socket placed towards the rear right hand side of the motherboard.

Power Connector

AT Power Supply

J10	J11
Power Good	Ground
+5V	Ground
+12V	-5V

J10	J11
-12V	+5V
Ground	+5V
Ground	+5V

Power is fed to motherboard from two 6-way non-reversible connectors.

In case you are unsure about which way these two connectors go, always remember that the black wires (ground) of connector J10 and J11 are placed together when connecting them to the motherboard.

ATX Power Supply

Pin Number	Function	Pin Number	Function
1	+3.3V	11	+3.3V
2	+3.3V	12	-12V
3	Ground	13	Ground
4	+5V	14	PWR ON
5	Ground	15	Ground
6	+5V	16	Ground
7	Ground	17	Ground
8	PWR GOOD	18	-5V
9	+5V SB	19	+5V
10	+12V	20	+5V

Keylock and Power-on LED Connector

Pin Number	Function
1	LED+
2	NO CONNECTION
3	LED-
4	KEYLOCK
5	KEYLOCK GROUND

The LED is connected to pin-1 and 3, the keyboard lock switch is connected to pin-4 and 5.

Speaker Connector

Pin Number	Function
1	+5V

Pin Number	Function
2	Ground
3	Ground
4	SPKR

The loudspeaker is connected by a four-way socket. Only the outer two pins (1 and 4) are used. The loudspeaker is not orientation sensitive and hence it does not matter which way it is connected.

Turbo Mode Selection

Switch Position	System Clock Speed
Open	Turbo
Close	Non-Turbo

"Turbo" switch is nonstandard, so its pin assignments may vary. If you are not sure of its connections, consult the system manual, a wrong connection is unlikely to cause any harm.

Turbo Mode LED Connector

Pin Number	
1	LED-
2	LED+

This LED is orientation-sensitive and will light only if connected properly.

Reset Connector

Switch Position	Function
Close	Reset the system
Open	Normal Operation

The reset button uses a two-pin connector in which pin 1 is the reset line and pin 2 is ground. These two pins are linked when the switch is depressed. The polarization of this switch is unimportant.

Infra-Red (IR) Connector

Pin Number	Function
1	VCC +5V

Pin Number	Function
2	No Connection
3	IrRx Infrared Receive
4	Ground
5	IrTx Infrared Transmit

This connector provides connection for HP HSDL-1000 compatible infrared (IrDA) transmitter/receiver.

Front Panel Function Connector

Pin		Function	Pin		Function
1	Key Lock	Power LED	14	IDE LED	Ground
2		No Connection	15		IDE LED
3		Ground	16		No connection
4		Key Lock	17	SW On	GV VR
5		Ground	18		Push On
6	Ext SMI	No Connection	19	Sleep LED	Standby 5V
7		Ext. SMI	20		VCC
8		Ground	21		Sleep LED
9		No Connection	22	Reset	Ground
10	Speaker	Speaker	23		Reset
11		No Connection	24		No Connection
12		Ground	25	Turbo LED	VCC
13		Vcc	26		Ground

This connector integrates all system front-panel functions into one single 26-pin connector.

CPU Fan Connector

Pin Number	Function
1	No Connection
2	+12V
3	Ground

CPU fan connector provides +12V DC supply to the CPU cooling fan. This fan is attached on top of the heatsink element.

CD Audio Input Connector

Pin Number	Function
1	Left Channel Audio
2	Ground
3	Ground
4	Right Channel Audio

Auxiliary Input Connector

Pin Number	Function
1	Left Channel Audio
2	Ground
3	Ground
4	Right Channel Audio

Telephony Input Connector

Pin Number	Function
1	Phone
2	Ground
3	Ground
4	Mono

Integrated Function Connector

Pin		Function	Pin		Function
1	USB1	USB +5Volt	11	USB2	USB +5Volt
2		USB Port1 -	12		USB Port2 -
3		USB port1 +	13		USB Port2 +
4		Ground	14		Ground
5		No Connection	15		No Connection
6	PS/2 Mouse	PS/2 Data	16	Infrared	+5V
7		PS/2 Clock	17		No Connection
8		Ground	18		IR Receive
9		No Connection	19		Ground
10		+5V	20		IR Transmit

Keeping CPU Cool

Most of the modern CPUs such as 486, Pentium etc. are made of a large number of transistors. When these processor work, specially the high speed version of these chips, DX2, DX4 etc., they generate a lot of heat.

This heat generated by the CPU should be dissipated faster than the heat is generated, otherwise the heat buildup will destroy the chip.

Most probably the system will crash before the processor is permanently destroyed.

To cool the CPU, the power supply used with these high speed processor must have heavy duty fan, to suck in and circulate the cool air inside the system box.

Other than this the CPU is also fitted with a heat sink or a combination of heat sink and a small fan assembly.

A heat sink is a heat conducting metal piece usually made from aluminum with a lot of fins on top, when attached on top of the CPU, they absorb the heat from the CPU and radiate it away.

A heat sink is a "Passive Cooling System" as it does not require any additional power, but when this is not enough an "Active Cooling System" i.e. heat sink with fan is used.

The fan will blow a greater volume of air over the heat sink to dissipate the heat absorbed by it.

Motherboard Troubleshooting

In this section we shall look at the error message displayed by the BIOS during the system startup. These error messages are conveyed to us either as error beep signals or as error message displayed on the monitor.

Motherboard Problems

When switched on, if the system produces error beeps or shows POST error message.

- Check for perfect seating of socketed chips such as Memory chips, SIMM modules, BIOS and keyboard controller, CPU etc.
- Temporarily remove nonessential cards from the Motherboard.
- If the problem is solved, replace cards one by one and each time check for correct operation, this will help to locate the actual faulty device.
- If there is intermittent crashing/stopping of system, determine the circumstances and check whether the crashing of system occurs only when a specific software is executed.
- Remove unnecessary memory resident programs and device drivers.

- Check for various card conflicts like IRQs, input/output ports, DMA channels and memory locations. Reconfigure in case any such conflict is located.
- Remove and reseat expansion cards and interconnecting cables.
- Run diagnostic utilities for identifying any hardware problem.
- Try reducing the speed of processor or the bus clock.

BIOS Error Beep Codes

The following error messages are conveyed through a number of short beeps; you can always identify the error by counting the number of short beeps.

All errors listed, with the exception of number 8, are fatal errors.

No. of Beeps	Error
1	Refresh Failure - The memory refresh circuitry of the Motherboard is faulty.
2	Parity Error - A parity error was detected in the base memory (the first block of 64 KB) of the system.
3	Base 64 KB Memory Failure - A memory failure occurred in the base memory i.e. within the first 64 KB of memory.
4	Timer Not Operational - Timer #1 on the system board has failed to function properly.
5	Processor Error - The CPU (Central Processor Unit) on the system board has generated an error.
6	8042 - Gate A20 Failure - The keyboard controller (8042) contains the Gate A20 switch which allows the CPU to operate in virtual mode. This error message means that the BIOS is not able to switch the CPU into protected mode.
7	Processor Exception Interrupt Error - The CPU on the motherboard has generated an exception interrupt.
8	Display Memory Read/Write Error - The system video adapter is either missing or its memory is faulty. This is not a fatal error.
9	ROM Checksum Error - The BIOS ROM checksum value does not match the value encoded in the BIOS.
10	CMOS Shutdown Register Read/Write Error - The shutdown register for the CMOS memory has failed.

BIOS nonfatal Error Messages

If a nonfatal error occurs during the POST routine, each time the system is powered on, the error message will appear on the screen in the following format:

```
ERROR Message Line 1
ERROR Message Line 2
Press <F1> to RESUME
```

Note down the error message and press the <F1> key to continue with the bootup procedure.

NOTE:

If the "Wait for <F1> If Any Error" option in the Advanced CMOS Setup portion of the BIOS SETUP PROGRAM has been set to "disabled", the "Press <F1> to RESUME" prompt will not appear on the third line.

For most of the error messages, generally there is no ERROR Message Line 2.

Generally, for those messages containing a line 2 ERROR Message, the line 2 text will be "RUN SETUP UTILITY". Pressing the <F1> key will invoke the BIOS SETUP PROGRAM.

A description of some common error messages appears below.

1. CH-2 Timer Error
   Most AT standard system boards include two timers. An error with timer #1 is a fatal error. This error message indicates an error with timer #2.
2. INTR #1 Error
   Some problem with the interrupt channel #1.
3. INTR #2 Error
   Some error with the interrupt channel #2.
4. CMOS Battery State Low
   There is a battery in your system which is used for storing the CMOS values.
   This battery appears to be low in power and needs to be replaced.
5. CMOS Checksum Failure
   After the CMOS values are saved, a checksum value is generated to provide for error checking.
   If the previous value is different from the value currently read, this error message appears.
   To correct this error, you should run the BIOS SETUP Program.
6. CMOS System Options Not Set
   The values stored in the CMOS are either corrupt or nonexistent.
   Run the BIOS SETUP Program to correct this error.
7. CMOS Display Type Mismatch
   The type of video stored in CMOS does not match with the type detected by the BIOS.
   Run the BIOS SETUP Program to correct this error.
8. Display Switch Not Proper
   Some systems require that a video switch/jumper on the motherboard be set to either color or monochrome, depending on the type of video you are using.
   To correct this situation, set the switch properly. (Remember to shut down the system first.)
   Set the switch to color for CGA, EGA, VGA, PGA and to monochrome for other display.
9. Keyboard Is Locked...Unlock It
   The keyboard lock on the system is engaged. The system must be unlocked to continue the boot up procedure.

10. Keyboard Error
The BIOS has encountered a timing problem with the keyboard. Make sure you have a main BIOS compatible Keyboard BIOS installed in your system.
You may also set the "Keyboard" option in the BIOS SETUP Program's Standard CMOS Setup option to "Not Installed" which will cause the BIOS to skip the keyboard ¯OST routines.

11. KB/Interface Error
The BIOS has found an error with the keyboard connector on the system board.

12. CMOS Memory Size Mismatch
If the BIOS finds the amount of memory on your system board to be different from the amount stored in CMOS, this error message is generated.
Run the BIOS SETUP Program to correct this error.

13. FDD Controller Failure
The BIOS is not able to communicate with the floppy disk drive controller. Check all appropriate connections after the system is powered off.

14. HDD Controller Failure
The BIOS is not able to communicate with the hard disk drive controller.
Check all appropriate connections after the system is powered down. Also check the drive type in the CMOS setup.

15. C: Drive Error
The BIOS is not receiving any response from hard disk drive C:. It may be necessary to run the Hard Disk Utility to correct this problem.
Also, check the type of hard disk selected in the Standard CMOS Setup of the BIOS SETUP program.

16. D: Drive Error
The same error has occurred with hard drive D:. Follow the procedures in Error #15 to correct this situation.

17. C: Drive Failure
The BIOS cannot get any response from the hard disk drive C:. It may be necessary to replace the hard disk.

18. D: Drive Failure
The same error as #17 has occurred with hard drive D:.

19. CMOS Time & Date Not Set
Run the Standard CMOS Setup of the BIOS SETUP Program to set the date and time.

20. Cache Memory Bad, Do Not Enable Cache
The BIOS has found the cache memory of the motherboard to be defective.

21. 8042 Gate-A20 Error
The gate-A20 portion of the keyboard controller (8042) has failed to operate correctly.
The 8042 chip should be replaced.

22. Address Line Short
An error has occurred in the address decoding circuitry of the motherboard.

23. DMA #2 Error
An error has occurred with the second DMA channel on the motherboard.

24. DMA #1 Error
An error has occurred with the first DMA channel on the motherboard.

25. DMA Error
An error has occurred with the DMA controller on the mother board.

26. No ROM BASIC
This error occurs when a proper bootable sector cannot be found on either the floppy diskette drive A: or the hard disk drive C:.
The BIOS will try at this point to run ROM BASIC and this error message will be generated when the BIOS does not find it.

27. Diskette Boot Failure
The diskette used to boot-up in floppy drive A: is corrupted, you cannot use it to boot-up the system.
Use another boot diskette and follow the instructions on the screen.

28. Invalid Boot Diskette
The BIOS can read the diskette in floppy drive A:, but it cannot boot-up the system with it.
Use another boot diskette and follow the instructions on the screen.

29. On Board Parity Error
The BIOS has encountered a parity error with some memory installed on the system board.
The message will appear as follows:

```
ON BOARD PARITY ERROR
ADDR (HEX) = (XXXX)
```

Where XXXX is the address (in hexadecimal) at which the error has occurred.
"On Board" means that this memory is part of the memory attached directly to the system board.

30. Off Board Parity Error
The BIOS has encountered a parity error with some memory installed in an I/O (BUS) slot.
The message will appear as follows:

```
OFF BOARD PARITY ERROR
ADDR (HEX) = (XXXX)
```

Where XXXX is the address (in hexadecimal) at which the error has occurred.
"Off Board" means that it is part of the memory installed via an expansion card in an I/O (BUS) slot.

31. Parity Error ????
The BIOS has encountered a parity error with some memory in the system, but it is not able to determine the address of the error.
Memory diagnostic software, such as AMIDIAG or QAPLUS etc., can be used to find and correct memory problems.

OTHER TITLES OF INTEREST

ARTIFICIAL INTELLIGENCE
ISBN: 9789388511070

Artificial Intelligence for Managers
ISBN: 9789389898385

Demystifying **Artificial Intelligence**
ISBN: 9789389898705

Artificial Intelligence for All
ISBN: 9789389328509

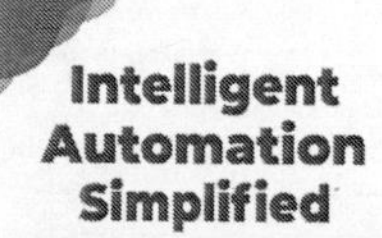

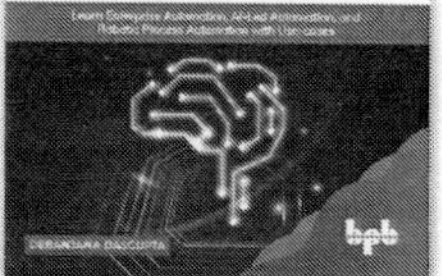

Intelligent Automation Simplified
ISBN: 9789391392543

Hands-On **Artificial Intelligence** for **Android**
ISBN: 9789355510242

Artificial Intelligence Meets **Augmented Reality**
ISBN: 9789388511339

No-Code Artificial Intelligence
ISBN: 9789355513496

Microsoft Azure AI: A Beginner's Guide
ISBN: 9789355510518

Think AI
ISBN: 9789355513199

Artificial Intelligence & **Deep Learning** for Decision Makers
ISBN: 9789389328684

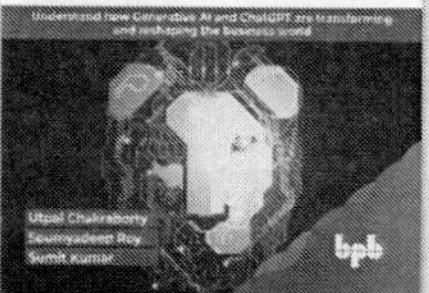

Rise of **Generative AI** & **ChatGPT**
ISBN: 9789355517982

Learning Google Cloud Vertex AI
ISBN: 9789355515353

Hyperautomation with **Generative AI**
ISBN: 9789355518590

Learn AI with **Python**
ISBN: 9789391392611

Pythonic AI
ISBN: 9789355515919

Keyboard

To communicate with the computer system we require some kind of input device and output device. Input device is used to feed data into the computer system and output device is required by the computer to communicate the result to the user.

Keyboard Switch

One of the main component of any keyboard is the key switch. These switches convert our typing action into proper signal for the keyboard interface, so that the interface will know that a key is being depressed.

Different technology used to make these switches are

- Membrane Switch
- Mechanical Switch
- Rubber Dome Switch

Membrane Switch

A membrane keyboard is a multi-layer plastic or rubber assembly which is commonly used as keyboard in video game machines, calculators, medical instruments, cash registers etc.

In this keyboard, two rubber or plastic sheet are used as row conductor sheet and column conductor sheet. These row and column sheet are separated by another sheet with holes at the keytop positions.

When the keytop is pressed, it forces the row conductor sheet through the hole to touch the column conductor sheet.

When the row lines on the row conductor sheet touch the column line on the column conductor sheet, key contact is made. This is interpreted by the keyboard interface as key closure.

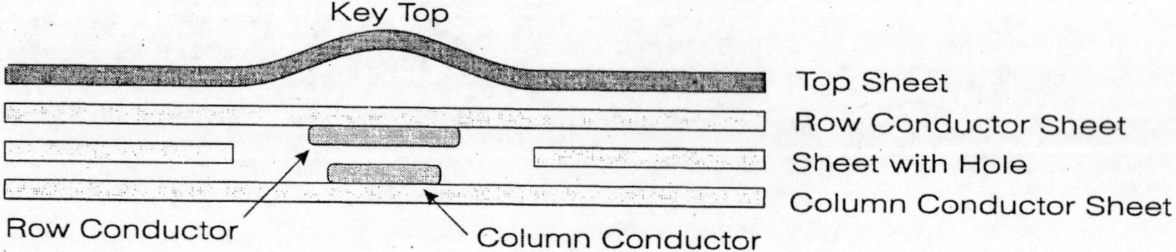

Fig. 7-1 : Membrane Type Keyboard Switch.

Mechanical Switch

Various types of mechanical switches are used to make the keyboard, the basic theory behind these switches are same. In this type of switches, two metal pieces or contacts are kept in open position and moved into close position when the switch is depressed.

When the switch is in normal position the contact is open, when the switch is pushed, the contact closes, and this closure is sensed by the keyboard interface.

As this type of switches require physical contact for proper working, after some use these contact becomes oxidized or dirty and switch starts giving problem.

Most of the quality manufacturers provide gold plating on switch contacts to improve the switch's lifespan.

Rubber Dome Switch

In this type of keys a rubber like synthetic is moulded to form a dome like shape, this dome like rubber structure keeps the key in up position.

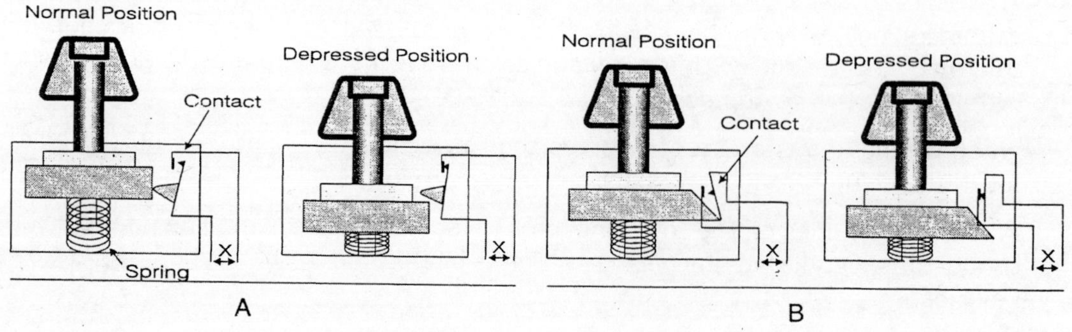

Fig. 7-2 : Mechanical Type Keyboard Switch.

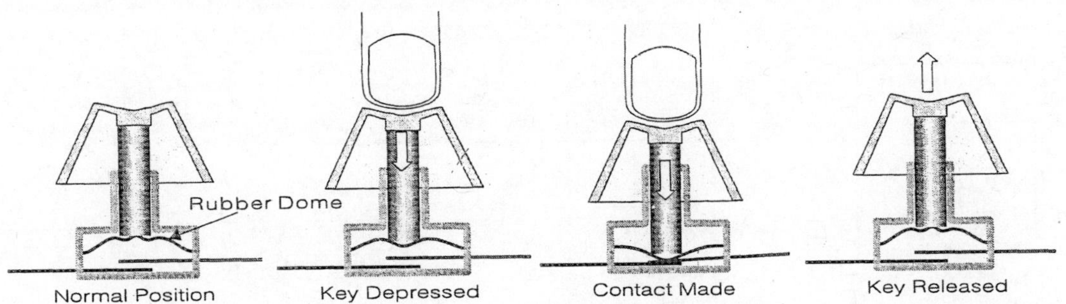

Fig. 7-3 : Rubber Dome Switch.

When the key is pressed, dome collapses and a small tab of carbon or some other conductive material inside the dome completes the circuit.

Once the pressure from the keys is released, the rubber dome goes back to its normal shape, with it pushing the key into normal up position and breaking the contact.

This design is currently used in many inexpensive, lightweight keyboards.

One drawback of this keyboard is, with time as the rubber loses its elasticity, the keys becomes stiff.

Now that we have looked at some of the technologies used in the making of the keyboard switches let us look at how these switches are used to make a working keyboard.

Keyboard Organization

The most common organization of the keyboard is as shown in the figure 7-4. As shown in this figure the key switches are arranged in a matrix of row and columns.

This matrix organization saves a lot of complication and additional circuits required for directly connecting each key to a separate sensing circuit.

In this method each key switch has a corresponding row and column number associated to it. When the switch is closed, the row and column sensor senses the switch closure.

Scanning

The process of finding out which key is being pressed by reading the row and column value is called "Keyboard Scanning". The word "scanning" is used here because the interfacing circuitry scans each row and column one by one to find out the key switch being pressed.

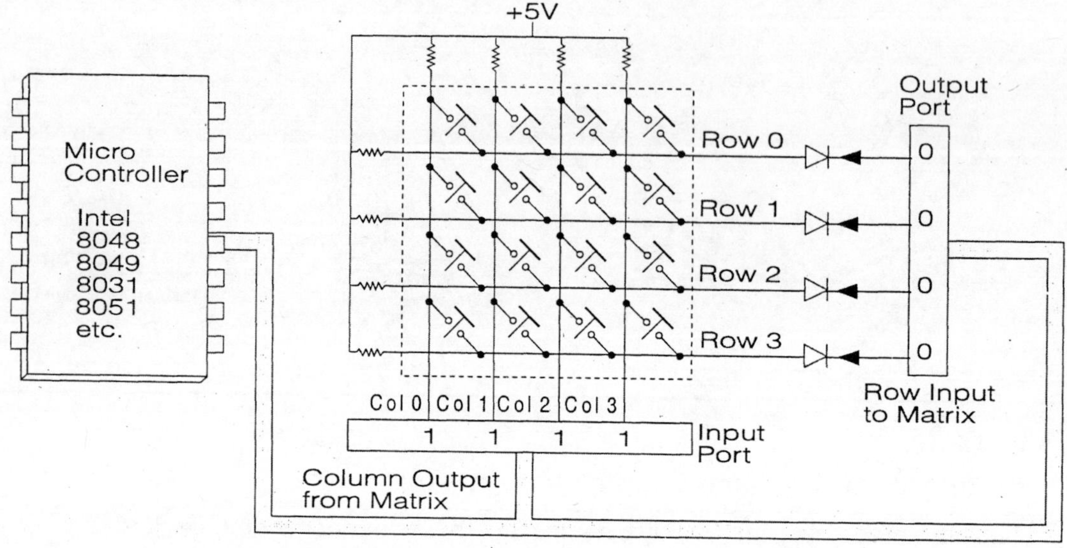

Fig. 7-4 : Keyboard Scanning.

This complete process of keyboard scanning can be divided into the following steps.

- First value 0 is output to all the row lines and the column lines are read over and over until all the columns show 1 or high value. This is done to insure that all the keys are in open position before trying to read a key press. If any of the switch is in close position that column will show value 0.
- Once all the columns are 1, the column values are again checked until one of the column shows a 0 or low value. This indicates that a key has been pressed. After a small delay of around 20 ms the columns values are again checked. This rechecking is done to insure that actually a key has been pressed and the low value is not some noise pulse.
- If the column is still 0 or low it indicates that a key has been pressed.
- Next step is to find out which key is being pressed. To find out which key is being pressed, initially the first row is kept 0 and all other rows are made 1. Then all the columns are checked one by one for a low value. If no column is found with a low values this indicates that the pressed key is not in the first row.
- Now make the second row 0 and all other rows 1 or high and scan all the columns for a low value. This process of making a row 0 and checking all the columns for a 0 value is repeated until a low or 0 values in a row produce a low or 0 value in one of the columns.
- If the second column key of the second row is pressed, this will give you a low or 0 value at the second column, when the second row is made 0.

The value at the row input and column output at the time of key press detection can be send as the scan code of the key being pressed to the keyboard interface for further processing.

In our example the value of the row at the time of key press detection is 1011 and column is 1101, or we can say that the scan code of the key being pressed is "10111101".

Encoding

We have seen that the keyboard sends a scan code to the processor to inform about the pressing of a key on the keyboard. This scan code has nothing to do with the characters printed on top of the key switches, it completely depends on the position of the keys on the keyboard.

Once the scan code is send to the processor, it is the job of the processor to convert this scan code into some meaningful format such as ASCII Code (American Standard Code for Information Interchange).

Make/Break Code

Keyboard sends different scan code for the pressing of the key and for the release of the key. The code send by the keyboard to the computer when you press a key is called "Make Code" and the code send when you release the key is called "Break Code".

As the keyboard sends a different code for the make and for the break, one can keep track of the position of "Shift", "Alt", "Ctrl" etc. keys whose up or down position change the way other keys are interpreted by the computer.

Keyboard Type

Many different type of keyboards are used with the IBM PC computers. With each new model of the PC such as PC-XT, PC-AT etc., IBM introduced a new type of keyboard. Currently Window/Internet/Multimedia ready keyboards are being used as industry standard by most of the computer manufacturers.

Original PC/PC-XT Keyboard

The original PC/PC-XT keyboard layout had a lot of shortcomings such as the position and size of "Enter" and "Shift" keys. Also, on this keyboard many keys were marked with arrows instead of the word describing them such as the "Tab" or the "Enter" keys.

Another major disadvantage of this keyboard is that there were no indicators to provide information about the status of the three toggle keys- Num Lock, Scroll Lock

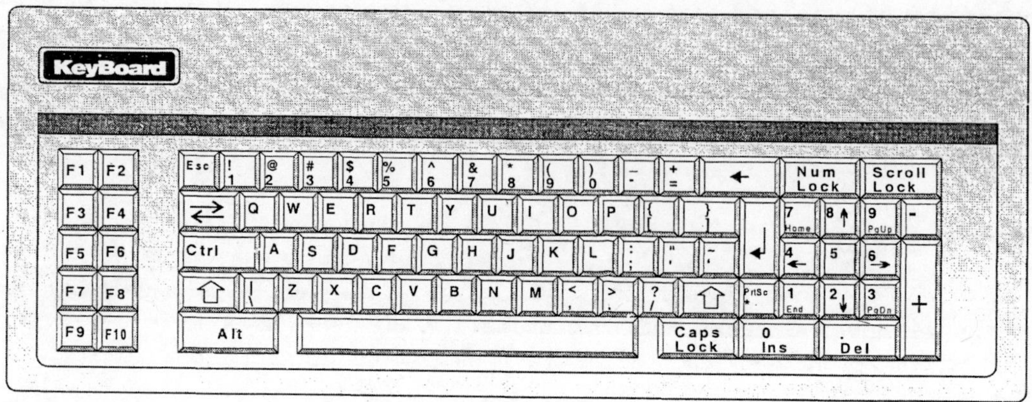

Fig. 7-5 : PC/PC-XT Keyboard Layout.

and Caps Lock, this lead to many touch typist typing small letters instead of the capital letters, or using the cursor control instead of typing numbers etc.

This keyboard has total 83 keys so it is also called as 83-key keyboard.

PC-AT Keyboard

The PC-AT keyboard was an improvements over the original PC/PC-XT keyboard. IBM tried to solve most of the problems associated with the original PC/PC-XT keyboard with the introduction of this new keyboard with their PC-AT range of machines.

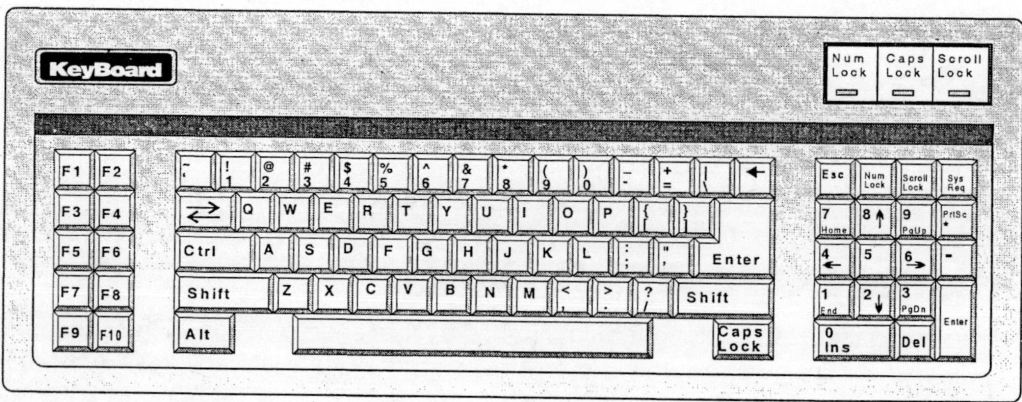

Fig. 7-6 : PC-AT Keyboard Layout.

In this keyboard there are indicators to show the status of the three toggle keys. The numeric keypad is moved away from the alphabet key area for easy access during the numeric data entry.

The size of the "Enter" key is also increased and the word "Enter" is printed on its keytop. Most of the keys that were indicated only with arrow symbols were also indicated with words describing them.

Changes in the electrical connection of this keyboard made this keyboard incompatible with the old PC and PC-XT machines.

The connectors of the PC/PC-XT keyboard and that of the PC-AT keyboards are same but a PC/PC-XT keyboard will not work with PC-AT machines and a PC-AT keyboard will not work with a PC/PC-XT machine.

Many old keyboards provide a XT/AT or 8088/80286 switch on the keyboard to configure the keyboard to be used with PC/PC-XT (8088/8086) machine or PC-AT (80286) machine.

One drawback of PC-AT keyboard was it shared the same keys for the cursor movement and numeric keypads, this made it difficult to use these keys in spreadsheet programs such as Microsoft Excel, where one needs to move the pointer as well as enter numbers.

This keyboard has total 84 keys so sometimes it is also referred as 84-key keyboard.

Enhanced PC-AT Keyboard

Sometime after the introduction of the PC-AT keyboard, IBM made one more change into the keyboard layout and introduced an enhanced PC-AT keyboard layout.

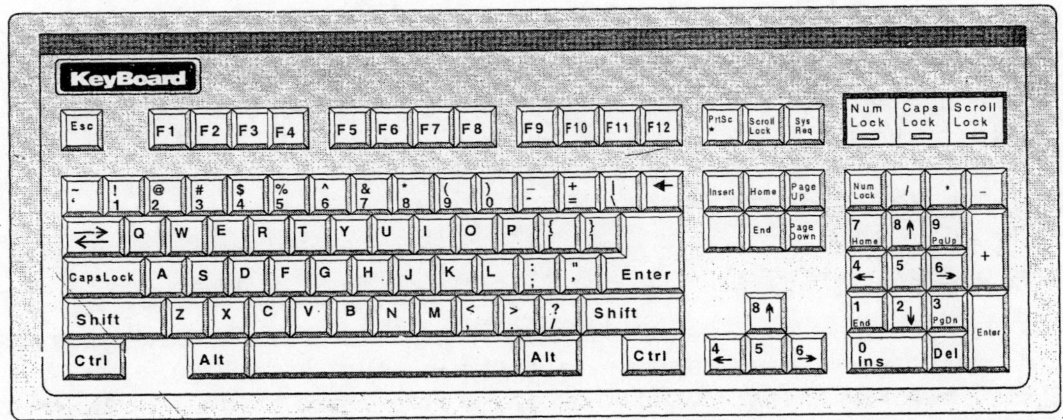

Fig. 7-7 : Enhanced PC-AT Keyboard Layout.

One major enhancement in this layout is moving of function keys to the top of the keyboard and providing additional cursor control keypads.

In this layout, all the ten function keys were moved to the top of the keyboard, and two more keys F11 and F12 were added.

Moving the cursor movement keys to a different pad, makes it easy to use this keyboard with spreadsheet programs. This layout also provided duplicate CTRL and ALT keys on both sides of the space bar for easy access.

This keyboard has total 101 keys so sometimes it is also referred as 101-keys keyboard.

Currently many variations of this enhanced PC-AT layout is available in the market, many new keys for Window, MultiMedia and Internet operation are added to this layout.

The key layout of the enhanced PC-AT 101-key keyboard can be divided into the following sections:

Typewriter or Alphabet Keys

Alphabet keys are arranged in the center of the keyboard. The arrangement of the alphabets are same as it is on a standard typewriter.

This arrangement is called "QWERTY" arrangement of the keys because the first six letters on the top row of the alphabet keys are Q, W, E, R, T and Y.

Other than the alphabets, some punctuation symbols such as , ; . ? ! etc. are also provided on the keyboard. Some of these punctuation symbols can be used when the key is pressed with the shift key.

Numeric Keys

Number are provided on the top of alphabet area and on the right corner of the keyboard. The numeric keypad on the extreme right of the keyboard can be used to enter numbers when the "Num Lock" indicator is on, otherwise these keys are used for cursor movement.

Cursor Movement Key

Cursor is a blinking underline or block on the screen which shows where the next character being typed will appear.

Cursor movement keys are provided between alphabet and the numeric keypad area. In this area one upside-down T-type key arrangement is provided for the cursor movement keys and two rows of three keys each is provided for Insert, Delete, Home, End, Page Up and Page Down keys.

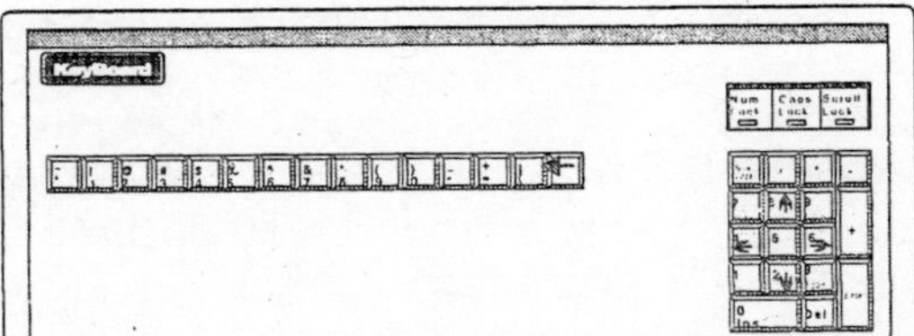

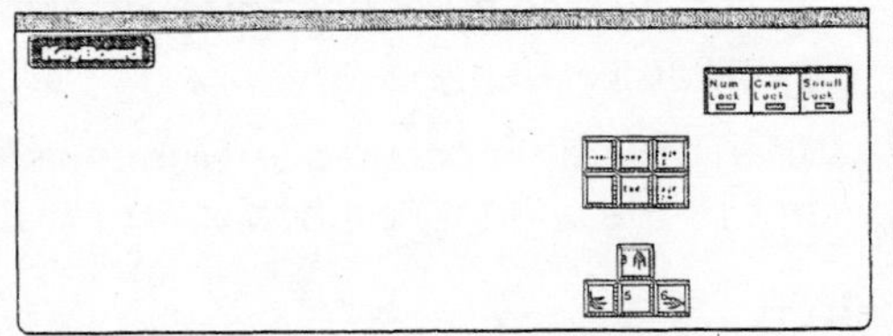

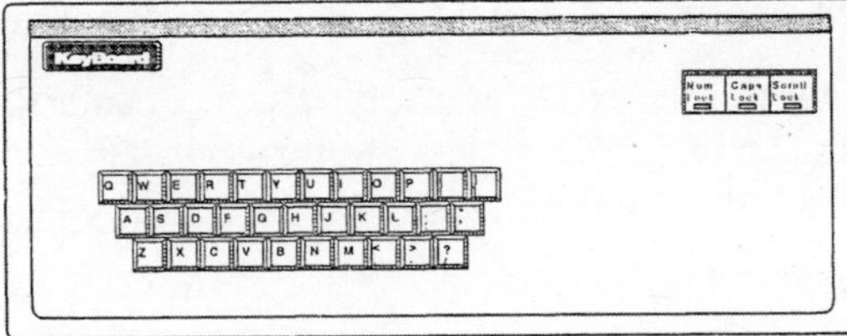

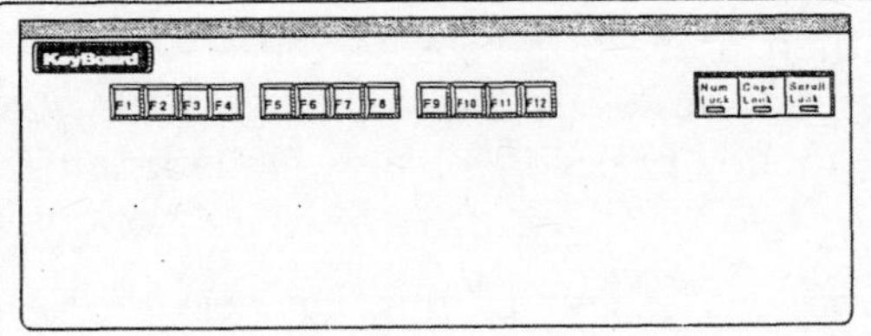

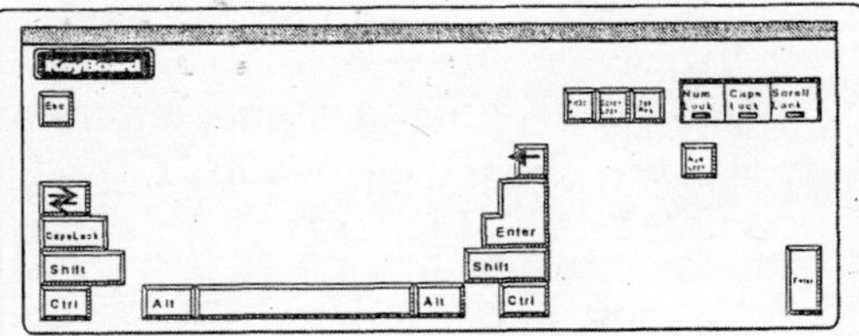

Fig. 7-8 : Various Sections of PC-AT Keyboard.

These keys are dedicated for cursor movement only, they cannot be used for numeric data entry. Keys on the numeric pad can be used for entering numbers as well as for the cursor movements.

Function Keys

Function keys F1 to F12 are spaced in group of four on the topmost area of the keyboard. These keys are user defined i.e. they do not have a fixed purpose and the user or various software assign different function to these keys.

Special Purpose Keys

Other than the above mentioned keys, computer keyboard contains many special keys that are used for some specific jobs. These keys are:

Print Screen (Prt Scr)

This key labeled "Print Screen" or "Prt Scr" or "Print Scrn" is used to get a printout of the screen display. When this key is pressed the entire content of the screen is send to the printer.

When this key is pressed in "Windows" environment, the screen image is captured and sent to the window clipboard, from where one can insert them into any document.

Shift

Two shift keys on each side of the alphabet area is used to get capital letters when the Caps Lock is off , when the Caps Lock is on this key is used to get small letters.

This key can also be used to get !@#$%^& etc. symbols on the top of some keys.

For example, if you want to type "$" symbols then press and hold down the "Shift" key then press and release the number 4 on the top row. This will give you "$" symbols on the screen. Once the "Shift" key is released keyboard will return to normal state.

Caps Lock

This key is called a toggle key because pressing this key toggles or changes the keyboard from one state to another. Unlike the shift key one need not keep it pressed.

If the keyboard is in small letter mode then press and release this key once, the keyboard will go into capital letters mode and the "Caps Lock" LED on the keyboard will glow. Once you are in "Caps Lock" mode, pressing of any alphabet key will generate capital letters.

When the keyboard is in "Caps Lock" mode pressing of this key will toggle the keyboard back to normal mode. This will also switch off the "Caps Lock" LED on the keyboard. In this normal mode pressing any alphabet on the keyboard will give small letters.

One cannot get !@#$ etc. symbol in this mode without pressing the Shift keys.

Num Lock

This Num Lock key is another toggle key. This key is used to toggle the state of the numeric keypad provided on the right side of the keyboard.

When the keypad is in numeric mode, pressing of "Num Lock" key will toggle it to cursor control mode and switch off the "Num Lock" LED. In this cursor control mode pressing of any key on the numeric keypad will move the cursor.

Pressing this "Num Lock" key once again will switch the keyboard back to numeric mode and the "Num Lock" LED will turn on. In this numeric mode pressing of any key on the numeric keypad will produce a number.

Scroll Lock

This is the third and final toggle key on the PC-AT 101-key keyboard. Pressing of this key toggles the keyboard into "Scroll Lock" mode and the "Scroll Lock" LED is switched on.

Pressing of this key once again returns the keyboard into normal mode and the "Scroll Lock" LED is switched off.

This key has not much of use, some spread sheet programs use this key to scroll the entire spreadsheet around.

Ctrl

CTRL or Control key is a shift like key that can be used with other keys for different purposes. For example, in WordPad, after some text is selected, if you press and Hold down the CTRL key, then if you press B, the selected text will become bold.

Pressing of any key with the Control key is indicated as CTRL+Key or Ctrl-Key or as ^Key, for example pressing the K key when the Control key is down is shown as Ctrl+K or Ctrl-K or ^K.

Alt

Alt or Alternate key is another shift like key that can be used to change the way different keys are interpreted by the computer.

For example, after you press and Hold down the ALT key, if you press S key, most of the software interpret this as an indication that you want to save something.

Tab

The Tab key on the keyboard generates a specific ASCII code that can be interpreted by different programs in different ways.

Most of the word processing software move the cursor five or eight spaces to the right when this key is pressed. Windows use this key to move around in a set of given options.

Enter/Return

This is one of the most useful key on the keyboard. When entering any value into the computer, pressing of this key informs the computer that you have finished typing and the computer can start processing the input data.

Some keyboards have "Enter" key some have "Return" key and some keyboards use symbol "↵" to show this key on the keyboard.

Keyboard contains two Enter keys, one in the alphabet typing area and another on the numeric keypad.

Pause

This key as the name suggests can be pressed to suspend any operation being done by the computer. Most of the time this key is used to stop fast multi-page display on the screen. Pressing of some other key will release the computer from this pause mode.

Break

Break key by itself does nothing but when pressed with the CTRL key, this key can be used to stop programs in the middle of their execution. The difference between Pause and Break key is pause key is used to temporarily stop or suspend the operation, whereas the break key is used to permanently stop the program execution.

On most of the keyboard this key is shared with the Pause key or with Scroll Lock key.

Ctrl+Alt+Del

When the computer is not responding to any key on the keyboard, a combination of the Ctrl and Alt and the Delete key can be used to restart the computer.

First the Ctrl key is pressed and held down, next the Alt key is pressed and held down, while holding these two keys down, the third key Delete is pressed and then all the three keys are released.

This key combination is called a "Soft Reset" or "Warm Boot". If this soft reset does not restart the system then one need to press the Reset key on the front panel, or one can switch off the system and restart after waiting for about ten seconds.

Sys Rq

This key was added to the keyboard by the IBM to use the keyboard with some multi-user future version of DOS. But that version is still awaited and this key has not much of use in the current DOS or the Windows environment.

Esc

The Esc or the Escape key as the name suggest is used in most of the software to escape from the situation one is in.

For example, suppose you have given the command to print 100 copies of some document to a word processor and then you want to stop after printing ten copies, in this situation you can press the Esc key after the printer has printed ten copies of the letter.

Back Space

This key is a back arrow key "←" located at the top right corner of the alphabet area.

This key as the name suggest is used to move the cursor one character to the back i.e. to the left, and delete the character at that position.

For example, if the cursor is under the letter "P" in the word "BACKSPACE", then pressing of the backspace key will delete the character at the left i.e. the letter "S" and move the cursor one character to the left.

Troubleshooting

Most of the problem faced in keyboard operation can be divided into two categories

- complete non-operation of the keyboard and
- broken or stuck keys

First problem could be either because of a broken connection between the keyboard and the system or because of some problem in the keyboard or the main system itself.

If you find that your keyboard is not working then to see if the problem is with the keyboard or the main system you can try a different working keyboard on your system.

If the new keyboard is also not working then the problem most probably is with the main system. If the new keyboard is working properly then the problem is with your old keyboard. You can also try your old keyboard on some other machine to make sure that the fault is really with the keyboard.

When the keyboard of a system is not working then some of the points that must be checked are:

- Some old keyboards have a small switch at their bottom side to select the operating mode of the keyboard. Using this switch one can select either XT (8088/8086) or AT (80286) operating mode.

  If this switch is in the wrong position then the keyboard will not function and this will generate a POST error message during the system starting time.
- Many old computers have a keyboard lock on the front panel. This lock disables the keyboard. Forgetting to unlock this lock, or not properly unlocking this could be one reason of the keyboard not working.

  Another problem could be the connector from lock to the motherboard coming loose at the lock or the motherboard side.
- The keyboard socket on the motherboard-into which the keyboard is plugged- is often one of the reason of keyboard failure.

  This socket sometimes become loose and may not connect properly with the keyboard. A loose socket may give intermittent problems in the keyboard operation.
- Check the connection between the socket and the motherboard. Check for any loose solder on motherboard.
- Check the keyboard cable. Open the keyboard, remove the cable and using a Multi-meter test each wire for continuity and cross-connection. If some fault is found then replace the cable.

Sometimes, you may find that a set of keys are not working, this is most probably the result of some problem with the row decode or the column decode logic inside the keyboard.

- Check the keyboard's main circuit board for any broken lines, dry soldering, loose contact etc., this problem may require replacement of the keyboard.
- This could also be caused by some problem with the keyboard driver software being used.

One very common keyboard problem is one or more keys getting stuck or broken. Keyboard with a broken or stuck keyswitch can be rectified by replacing the broken key with a new working keyswitch.

- Finding a new keyswitch of the same type is more difficult than replacing the switch. One should always keep the keyboards beyond repair to be used for spare parts.
  - If you can not find a spare keyswitch of the type being used in your keyboard then the only option left would be to remove some working switch from the keyboard, you can remove a key that has very little use such as Scroll Lock, F11 or F12 etc. keys or you can remove one of those keys which are provided in pair such as the additional Alt or Ctrl key.
  - To replace a keyswitch one need to first open the keyboard and desolder the faulty keyswitch. Number of the switch's contact to the keyboards main board depends on the switch being used, some switches are connected to the main board using only two contacts whereas some are connected using as much as six contacts.
  - One can unsolder the faulty switch using a soldering iron and desoldering braid or a solder sucker. Once the switch becomes loose remove it from the circuit board.
  - Solder the new switch in place of the faulty switch and try the keyboard on a working machine.

If the problem is of keys being sticky or difficult to press then the problem is most likely caused by accumulation of dirt inside the keyboard switches.

- This can be rectified by a proper cleaning of the keyboard and the key switches.

Disassembly, Cleaning and Reassembly

Disassembling or opening of the keyboard is a very easy procedure.

- First switch off the system, disconnect the keyboard from the system and keep the keyboard upside down on a clean surface.
- Look around for a series of small screws on the base plate and undo these carefully, note down where each screw goes, this is important if the screws are of different lengths and sizes.
- If there are no screws then the two halves of the keyboard are generally held together with snap fit clips which can be loosened with a screwdriver.

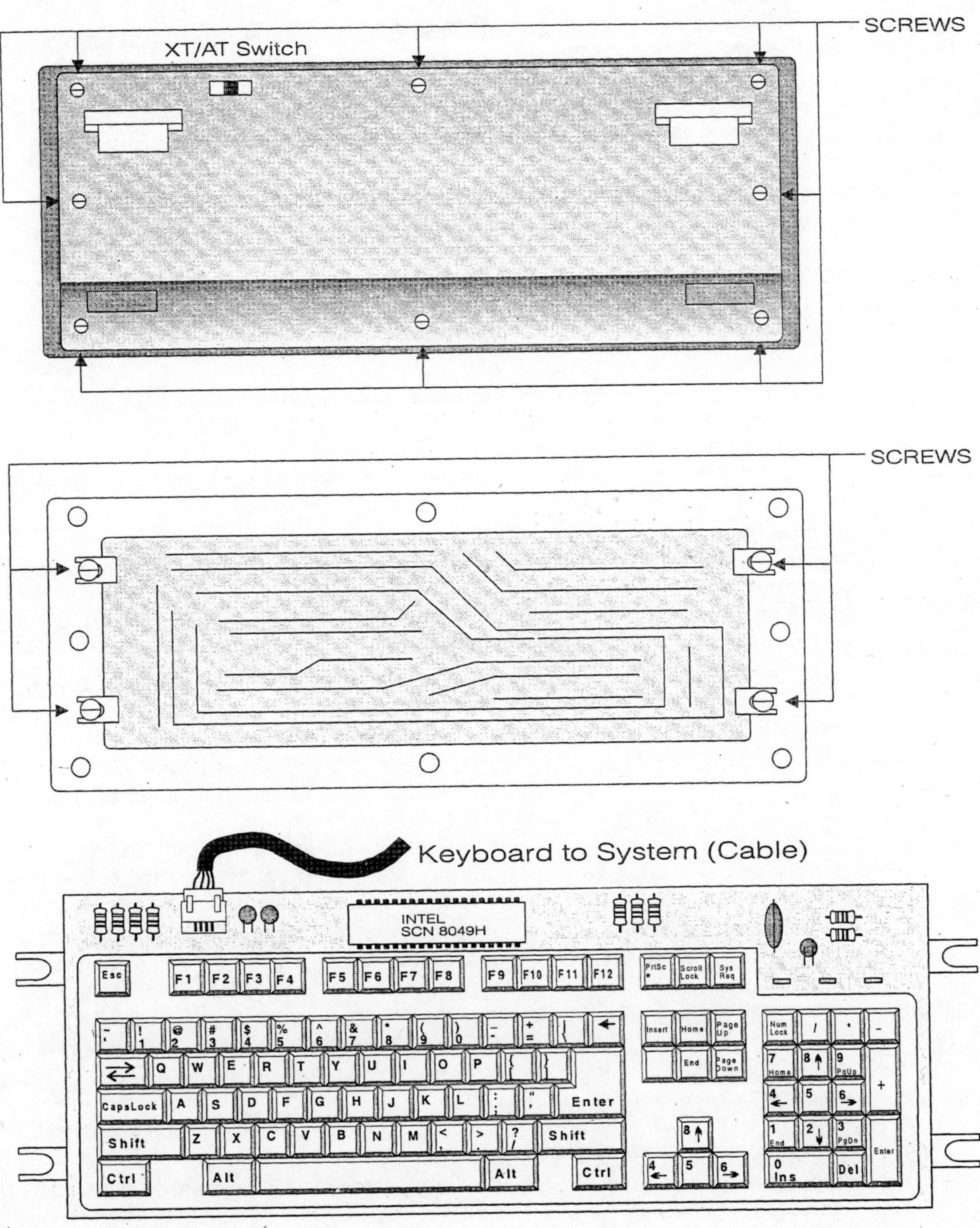

Fig. 7-9 : Opening a Keyboard.

- Once the screws or clips are removed, the keyboard circuit board and the keys can be removed from their frame. Be very careful and note exactly how the frame fits so that you can reassemble it without any trouble.
- Sometimes, some screws are hidden behind rubber leg or manufacturers name plate/sticker etc. provided on the backplate of the keyboard, look for it if you find that the cover is not coming loose even after opening all the screws.
- Once the keyboard circuit board is removed you can clean the plastic top and bottom cover using some mild soap or detergent and lukewarm water. You can also remove the keytops and clean them with detergent and water, this will make you keyboard look completely new.
- Before removing the keytops you should have some diagram of your keyboard layout ready or later it will be difficult to remember which keytop goes where.
- Cleaning of cover and keytops will make your keyboard look new but to make it work as new you need to first blow away the dust from the keyboard and the keys using a mini vacuum cleaner, you can also shake out the dust and clean the dirt between the keyswitches using some soft brush.
- Once all the loose bits are removed, check that all the keys are working smoothly and if not, loosen them by lubricating with a couple of drops of iso-propanol on the key shaft and by pressing the key a number of times. Do not use any oil based lubricant, as it will attract dust and after sometimes key will become inoperable.
- If the keyboard contains a key which does not work then the solution will depend upon the type of keyboard being used.
  - If the keyboard is a mechanical keyboard with a pair of contacts then non-working of the switch may be due to accumulation of dirt on the contacts. To rectify this problem try little contact cleaner down the key stem into the key switch and press the key very vigorously a number of times, clean dissolved dirt from the shaft and apply more cleaner if necessary. Check with a multimeter if the key is making contact. Replace the keycap and reassemble the case, if you have a working keyswitch.
  - If your keyboard has capacitive switches then dismantle the backplate by taking out all the tiny screws and then wipe clean the inner surface and all the key contacts with iso-propanol. Once the contacts are cleaned re-assemble the unit, taking care not to get your fingerprints over the circuit board. This is a time consuming job but it works and you may save the cost of a new keyboard.
- Temporarily re-assemble the keyboard and connect to the main system to check its operation. If problems such as stuck or non-active keys persist, then more lubricating or cleaning is required.
- If liquid such as tea or coffee has been spilled on the keyboard, switch off the system immediately and disconnect the keyboard from the main system. Now you first objective should be to wash the liquid away before it dries.

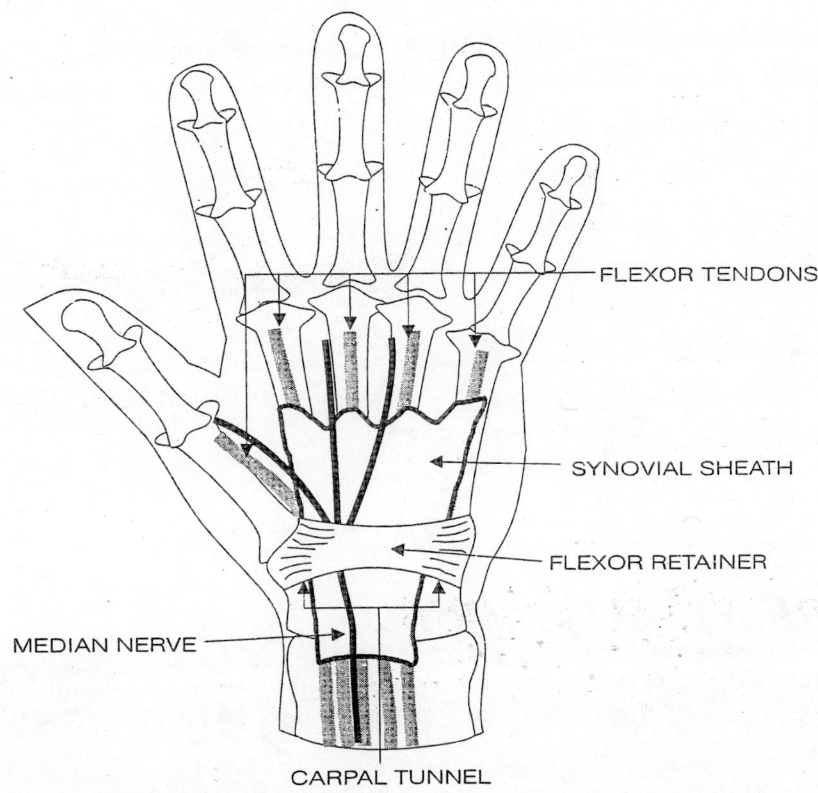

Fig. 7-10 : Carpal Tunnel Syndrome.

Once the keyboard is clean, turn it upside down over a towel in a warm and dry place. Leave it there for 2-3 days, as water that seeps inside the keyswitches will take some time to evaporate.

- Reassembly of the keyboard is the reverse of dismantling it. Replace the keytops, checking for correct position and free movement of all the keys. Check that all the cables are attached to the proper connectors. Finally reassemble the top and bottom cover.

If your keyboard problem is not solved even after all the above procedures then there may be some problem with the electronic circuit of the keyboard which controls the keyboard's activities.

If this is your problem then instead of trying to repair the old keyboard, go for a new one, new keyboards are available very cheap. You can keep your old keyboard for spare keytop or keyswitch requirement in the future.

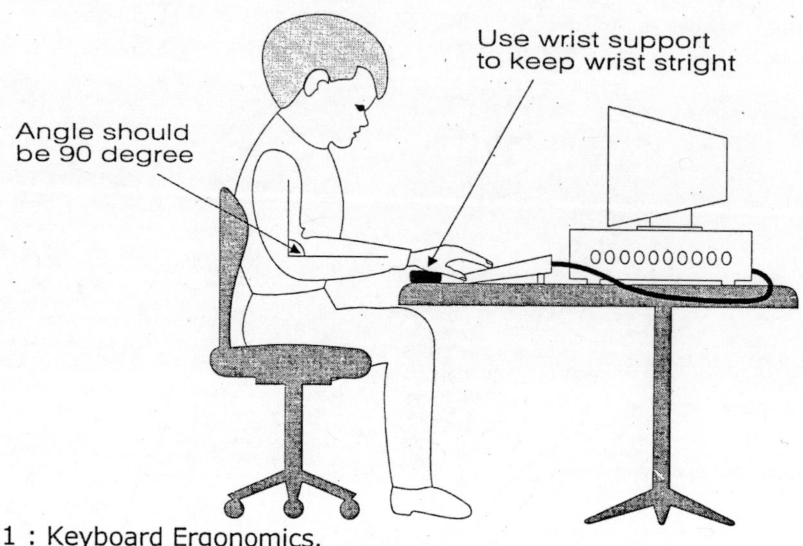

Fig. 7-11 : Keyboard Ergonomics.

Keyboard Ergonomic

"Ergonomic" word is used to describe the design and use of a product in such a way that it can be used most efficiently with maximum comfort and minimum risk of any injury.

Many ergonomic keyboards are in the market which claims to increase keyboarding comfort and decrease the risk of hand injury such as "Carpal Tunnel Syndrome". The basic designs of these ergonomic keyboards focus on moving the hands further apart (straight with the shoulders) and keeping the wrists straight.

Some of the points that one should be careful during the typing to avoid injury include

- The wrist should not be bent outward in the direction of the little finger.Try to keep your wrists straight while typing.
- The hands and arms should not be angled together in front of the body, they should be kept at the shoulder width.
- The wrist should not be bent down such that the fingers are lower than the wrist joint.
- The wrist should not be bent up and back such that the fingers are higher than the wrist joint.
- Adjust your chair height so that as you type, your elbows are at the same height as your wrists.
- Resting your wrists is very important. If you have enough room, rest your wrists on the desk as you type. Better still get special contoured wrist-rest pads, which attach to the front of the keyboard.
- Every hour, rest your hands and wrists for about five minutes.

Mouse

So far we have looked at the keyboard, one of the most common input device used in the computer field. Even though the keyboard is the most common input device, for many first time computer users it is the biggest barriers in using the computer i.e. learning to use the keyboard takes time for a new computer user.

Using keyboard commands (such as pressing Ctrl+K+S on the keyboard for saving a file) to carry out different works by the computer is difficult to remember and understand even for many experienced users.

This problem made engineers at the Xerox Corporation's Palo Alto Research Center (PARC) to develop a completely different method for software operation. This concept was first explored by Douglas C. Engelbert of the Stanford Research Center.

His concept was of a pointing device, that a computer user could move on his desktop-causing a corresponding cursor movement on the screen-to select different options on the screen.

Because of its shape and taillike cable, this device was named "Mouse".

Apple Computers were the first to make the mouse a standard feature in their Macintosh range of computers. Initially IBM Corp. rejected this idea as a child's toy, but later as the popularity of Macintosh increased and as more and more Graphical User Interface (GUI) software such as "Windows" etc. appeared, IBM made "Mouse" a standard part of their PCs, as well.

Mouse is basically a pointing device about the size of a palm. It rolls on a small ball and has one or more buttons on the top. When the user rolls the mouse across a flat surface, the screen cursor moves in the direction of the mouse movement.

For example, if the user rolls the mouse forward and left, the screen cursor also moves up left on the screen. Because the cursor follows the user's hand movement, the user has a better idea of pointing at something on the screen.

Positioning the cursor using a mouse is much more easier for the non-typists or the first time computer users, rather than pressing different combination of keys for doing the same.

The mouse can never replace the keyboard, but it can supplement the keyboard by doing tasks such as moving and pointing to on-screen objects, tasks for which the cursor movement arrow keys are ill-suited.

Mouse Type

Based on the technology used to detect the mouse movement and the method used to transfer the mouse information to the computer, mouse can be divided into different categories.

Based on the technology used to detect the mouse movement, mouse can be divided into following categories:

- Mechanical
- Opto-Mechanical
- Optical

Based on the method used to interface or to connect the mouse to the main computer system, mouse can be divided into following categories:

- serial port mouse
- A bus connection mouse
- PS/2 port mouse
- USB port mouse
- Wireless mouse

Mouse can also be divided into different category based on the number of buttons provided on them, basically there are three types of mouse based on this

- Single Button
- Double Button
- Three Button

Mechanical Mouse

A mechanical mouse works by the mechanical action of its various parts. When this mouse is rolled across a flat surface different rollers inside the mouse move and generate electric signals.

These signals are given to the computer and computer converts them into proper action on the screen. Let us see this whole process in detail:

- As a mechanical mouse is moved across a flat surface, a ball (made of rubber or rubber covering over a steel ball) protruding from the underside of the mouse and touching the surface, starts to rotate in the direction of the movement.

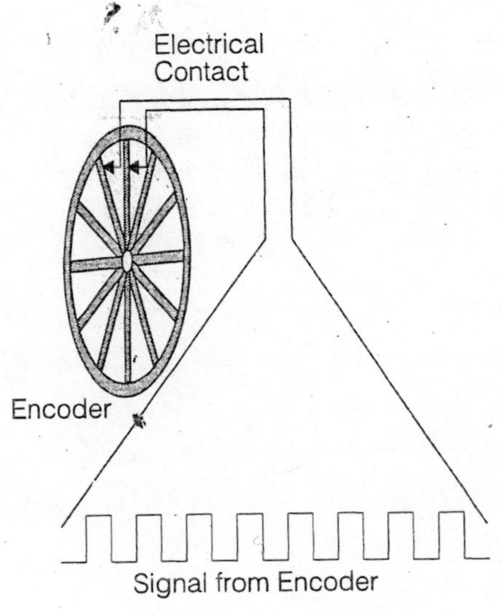

Fig. 8-1 : Inside Mechanical Mouse.

- As the ball rotates, inside the mouse, it touches and turns two rollers touching the ball. These rollers are mounted at a 90-degree angle to each other.
- One roller is used for the back-and-forth movements of the mouse, which correspond to vertical movements of the cursor on screen. The other roller is used for sideways movements, which correspond to horizontal movement of the cursor on the screen.
- Each roller is attached to an encoder, which is a wheel like structure. As the rollers turns, these encoders rotate with them. Two pairs of contact bars touch the small metal contact points provided on the rims of each of these encoders.
- Each time a contact bar touches a point, an electrical signal is generated. The number of these signals indicates how many points the contact bars have touched. As the mouse is moved farther away, more signals are generated.
- The direction in which the mouse is moving can be found out by finding the number of signals from these two vertical and horizontal rollers.
- The signal generated by these rollers are sent serially to the PC over the mouse's taillike cable. The mouse driver software converts these signals into the distance, direction, and speed necessary to move the screen cursor.
- Pressing of mouse buttons sends signal to the PC. Based on which button is pressed, how many times the button is pressed and the position of the cursor at the time of the pressing the button, the mouse driver software performs the task you want to accomplish.

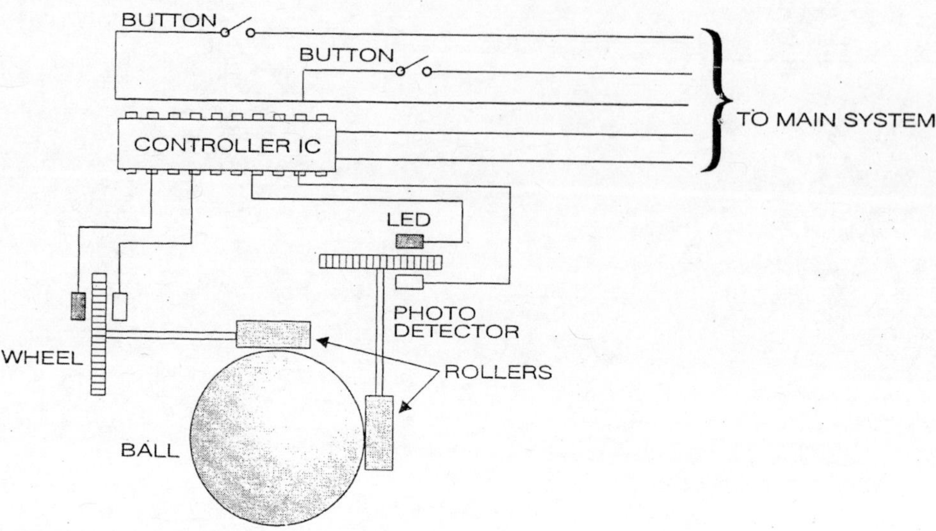

Fig. 8-2 : Inside Opto-Mechanical Mouse.

Opto-Mechanical Mouse

Basic construction of the Opto-Mechanical mouse is same as that of the mechanical mouse. Only difference is in the sensing circuit used to detect the movement of the mouse.

In a mechanical mouse a decoder is used to detect the distance mouse is moved on the tabletop, whereas in a opto-mechanical mouse a combination of LED (Light Emitting Diode) and Photo detectors is used to sense the distance traveled by the mouse.

Let us see how an Opto-Mechanical mouse works.

- When the mouse is moved, the ball at the bottom of the mouse moves and it turns two separate rollers fixed at 90 degree to each other.
- One of these rollers is associated with back-and-forth movement of the mouse, i.e., vertical movement of the cursor on the screen. The other roller is associated with the side-to-side movement of the mouse, i.e., the horizontal movement of the cursor on the screen.
- Each roller is further connected with a wheel. These wheels are rotated by the corresponding movement of the rollers.
- There are small openings on the rim of each wheel. As the wheel rotates, a pair of LED and Photo detectors detect the number of openings passed between them.
- The number of signals generated indicates the number of openings in the rim of wheel passed, i.e., the more is the number of signals, the farther has been the mouse moved.

- These signals are passed to the PC through the wire connecting mouse to the main system. The PC, in turn, passes them to the mouse driver software which then converts them into distance, direction and speed for the movement of the screen cursor.
- Depressing any of the mouse button, produces a signal. Depending upon the button being pressed, number of times the button being pressed and the present location of the mouse pointer on the screen, the software accomplishes the task desired by the user.

Optical Mouse

Optical - Old Design

In optical mouse, instead of the customary ball and rollers, a light source and photo-detector is used with a special mouse pad.

- When the optical mouse is moved on this special pad, light from the light source gets reflected from the pad and special photo-detectors inside the mouse detect the horizontal and vertical movement based on the reflected light.
- Depressing any of the mouse button also produces a signal which is passed to the PC and the PC passes it to the mouse driver software.
- Depending upon the button being pressed, number of times the button being pressed and the present location of the mouse pointer on the screen, the software accomplish the task desired by the user.

Optical - New Design

Current Optical Mouse design differs from the original design in many ways. The new optical mouse is a small computer in itself. It contains a full pattern-recognition hardware/software in its digital processor IC.

This pattern-recognition capability allows the new optical mouse to be used on any surface without the need to use any special mouse pad.

As the mouse is moved, it compares the image of its current position with the image of the previous position stored in its memory. The difference between two images inform about the direction, the mouse is moved.

This new optical mouse contains three basic parts

- LED to illuminate the surface on which the mouse is used.
- A Sensor made of Photo-Detector Array, basically a small video comera to detect the pattern on the surface.
- Digital Signal Processor (DSP) for pattern recognition purpose.

Let us see the working principle of this optical mouse.

- A LED at the mouse bottom side shines a bright, focused light at the surface on which mouse is placed. This light is kept very close to the

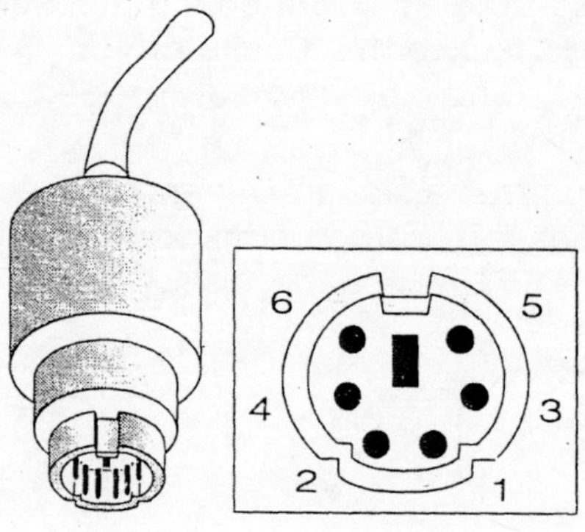

6 Pin Mouse Port Connector

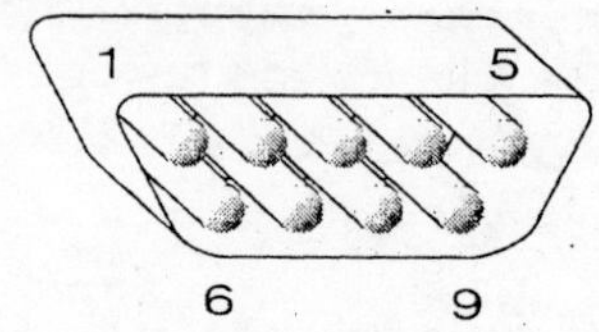

9 Pin - D Type Male Serial Connector

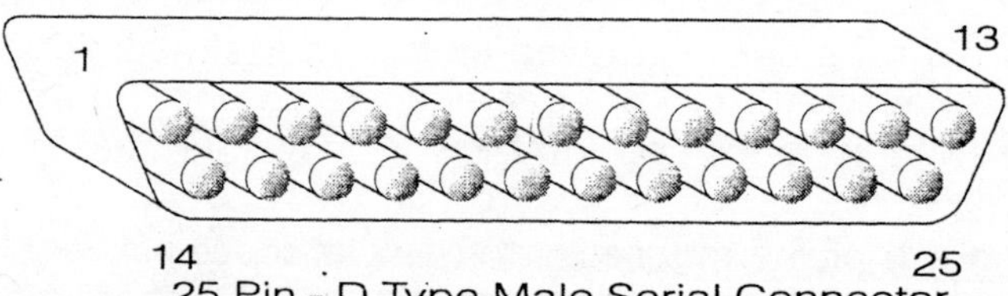

25 Pin - D Type Male Serial Connector

Fig. 8-3 : Various Connectors/Sockets for Mouse.

surface and directed at an angle to create a pattern of dark and light areas even on a apparently smooth surface.

- Sensor detects the pattern created by the LED on the work surface.
- This sensor contains a lens and photo-detector arrays. The lens is used to focus pattern on the photo-detector array. Photo-detector array is a matrix of light sensitive CMOS elements.
- DSP samples the output of the sensor several thousand times per seconds. Each sample is compared with the previous sample to detect the direction and extend of change in the mouse postion comparted to the last position.
- Based on the information from the DSP, mouse informs about the new position to the computer and computer moves on screen mouse pointer to the new position.

An optical mouse can sample at a rate of 1500 to about 6000 images per second.

As this mouse has no moving parts, it does not require frequent maintenance and does not easily wear out.

One drawback of this mouse is it may not work on a surface which is highly reflective or contains no visible detail such as a glass surface. Sometime highly repetitive pattern such as offset printed screens also confuse the pattern recognition system of this mouse.

Connecting Mouse

A mouse can be connected to computer system in one of the following ways:

- Using a serial port
- A bus connection
- PS/2 mouse port
- USB port
- Wireless

Let us see these different types of mouse connections in some detail

Serial Mouse

A serial port is the most common method of connecting a mouse. A serial mouse is connected to either COM1 or COM2, i.e. to any one of the available serial port on the computer.

Connecting a serial mouse is very easy as one need to just plug in the connector attached to the mouse wire to the vacant serial port on the computer.

Sometimes, one need to configure the mouse driver to specify the COM port used for the mouse, but most of the new mouse driver software can automatically sense the port to which the mouse is connected and auto-configure themselves.

Bus Mouse

Difference between a bus mouse and a serial mouse is, a serial mouse is connected to a serial port, whereas the bus mouse is connected to a special card made just for the mouse.

This special mouse adapter board is installed into the PC's expansion slot and then the mouse is connected to the connector provided at the back.

PS/2 Port Mouse

Now a days, many computers come equipped with special mouse port for connecting the mouse. This method is similar to the bus mouse approach except that the mouse control circuitry is directly built into the motherboard of the PC and not connected as a separate card.

This type of mouse is called PS/2 mouse because these connector are common with IBM's PS/2 range of computers.

USB Mouse

The USB port can be used to connect a mouse. As the mouse is not required during power on/bootup process, no special BIOS is required for handling USB mouse.

Hardware installation of the USB mouse requires just plugging in the mouse to the USB port.

Wireless Mouse

In this type of mouse, everything is similar to the conventional mouse except that no cable is used to connect the mouse to the computer system.

Basically there are two types of wireless mouse

- Infrared Wireless Mouse
- Radio-controlled Wireless Mouse

The infrared mouse communicates with the receiving unit connected to the main system unit using infrared light. As the infrared light can not pass through objects, this requires an infrared mouse to be in direct line of sight with the receiving unit connected to the main system.

When the radio-controlled wireless mouse is moved, radio signals are transmitted by it to a special receiver unit connected to the main system. The radio signal received by the receiver is sent to the computer as any normal mouse signal received through the cable is sent.

As the radio signal can pass through objects, the radio-controlled mouse need not be in line of sight with the receiving unit.

In case, more than one wireless mouse is being used at one place, they use different radio frequencies, so one need not worry about signal from one mouse getting disturbed by the signal from another mouse.

Most of the Infrared Wireless Mouse and Radio-contrloled Wireless Mouse require the mouse to be within six feet of the receiving unit.

Mouse Resolution

The resolution of a mouse is measured in Points Per Inch (PPI). when you move your mouse, the mouse generates electronic signals and sends them to the computer. The higher a mouse's resolution, the more signals the mouse generates as you move it.

It is the resolution of the mouse which relates the movement of the mouse cursor on the screen with the actual movement of the mouse on tabletop. For a long time the resolution of mouse was fixed at 200 PPI. Most of the mouse available today can have a resolution of 800 or even 1200 PPI.

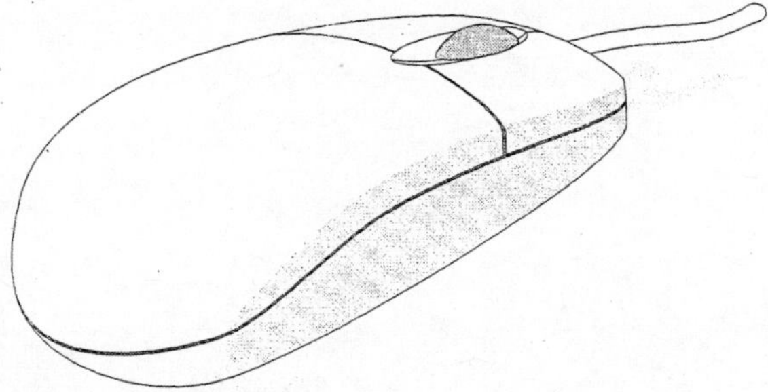

Fig. 8-4 : Scroll/Wheel Mouse.

The advantage of having a higher resolution is that the actual movement of the mouse is not required to be as much as to obtain the corresponding movement of the mouse cursor on screen. Mouse resolution, therefore, corresponds to mouse speed, not its precision.

Some mouse manufacturers use the term "Mickey" for denoting the mouse resolution. This term comes from the name of the cartoon character "Mickey Mouse" created by Walt Disney. Generally speaking, one Mickey is equivalent to 1/200th of an inch.

Scroll Mouse/Wheel Mouse

When Microsoft introduced a new mouse, intellimouse, they added a small rubber wheel between the two pushbuttons. This wheel allowed mouse user to scroll the screen without clicking on the Windows side scroll bars.

Because of the wheels and because of the its use in scrolling the screen, a mouse with scroll wheel is known as "Scroll Mouse" or "Wheel Mouse"

This wheel is generally made from textured rubbor, to give your finger a better grip. Inside the mousc this wheel is connected to a rotary motion sensor. This sensor could be of mechanical, optical or magnetic type.

Some mechanical resistance is added to the wheel to stop it from free spin.

A scroll mouse could be of optical or mechanical type.

Using a Mouse

To use a mouse one needs keep the mouse on a mouse pad on top of the table and hold it with the base of your palm resting on the table and index and middle finger kept on each button of a two button mouse.

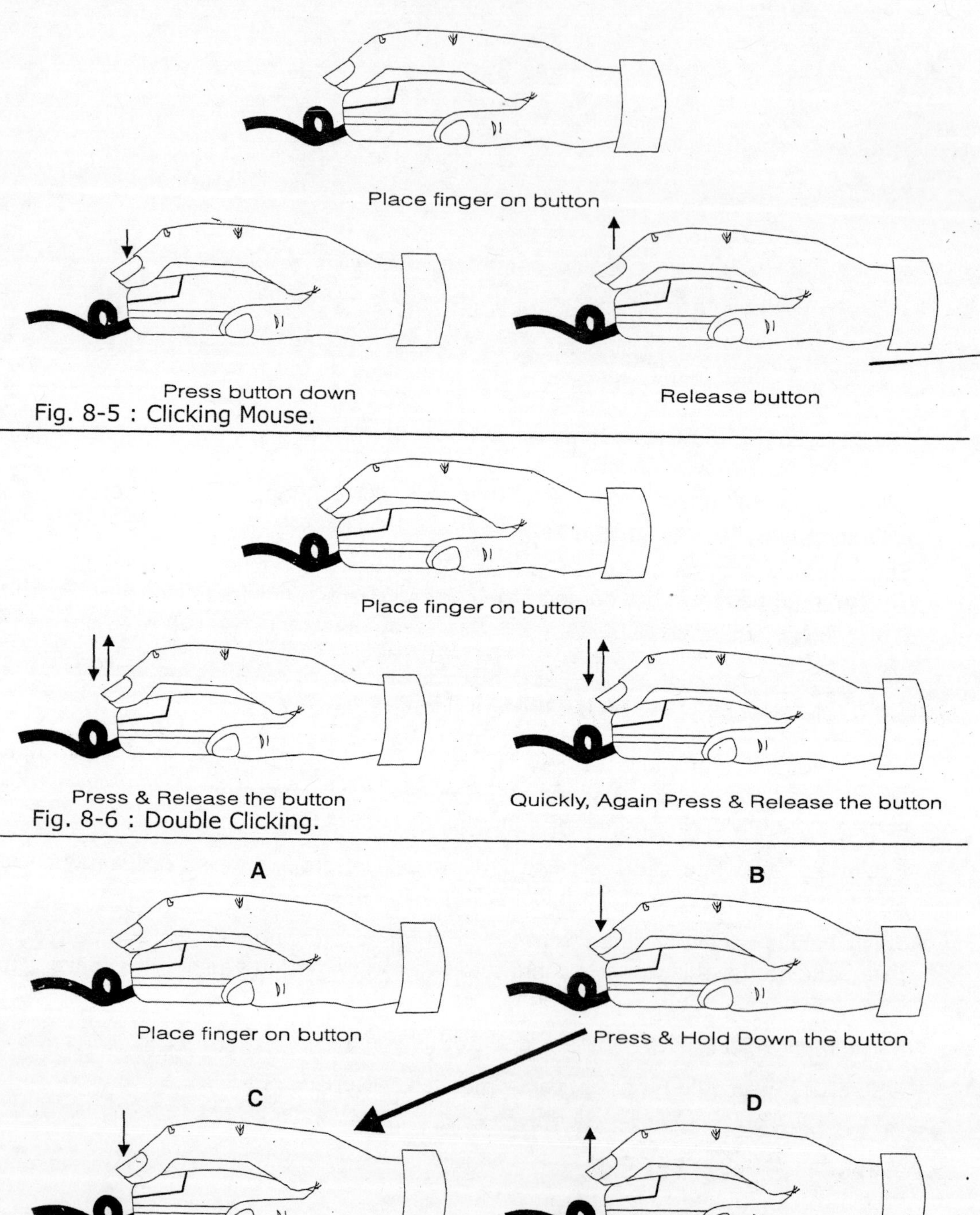

Fig. 8-5 : Clicking Mouse.

Fig. 8-6 : Double Clicking.

Fig. 8-7 : Drag and Drop.

Holding the mouse in this position you can move the mouse on the pad in the direction you want the mouse pointer on the screen to move. If you want the screen point to move up then move the mouse up, if you want the screen pointer to move left then move the mouse to the left etc.

To use a mouse one should also know what the terms click, double click and drag/drop means. Let us see what these terms refer to.

Clicking

Clicking a mouse is used to select some option or object from the screen. To click a mouse one need to move the mouse pointer to appropriate place on the screen (this is called pointing) and press and release the mouse button quickly.

Double Clicking

Double Clicking a mouse is done to start some action on the selected item. Double clicking is equal to pressing of the "Enter" key once some option is selected.

Double clicking is done by pressing and releasing the mouse button twice in quick succession. This should be done without moving the mouse pointer from the selected object.

Drag/Drop

Dragging is used to move an object selected with the mouse pointer from one place to another place on the screen.

To drag an object, first the mouse pointer is moved to the required object, next the mouse button is pressed and hold down. In this mouse button down condition, mouse is moved to a new position. This is called dragging.

Finally, when the on screen object is at the required position, mouse button is released. Releasing the object at this new position is known as dropping the object.

Mouse Installation

Installing a mouse is very easy, in this section we shall look at how to install a serial mouse.

Whenever one installs a new mouse or changes the old mouse one must make appropriate change in the mouse driver.

Serial Mouse

A serial mouse is a mouse that connects to one of serial ports, such as COM1 or COM2 on your computer. This is one of the most simple and commonly used mouse.

To replace or to install a serial mouse, perform these steps

- First of all check if you have a spare serial port for the mouse. If you do not have a spare serial port, then you need to first install a serial interface board or a multi I/O board into your computer.

If you have a spare serial port or if you are replacing an already available serial mouse then perform the following steps

- Power off the PC's main system unit.
- Remove the existing mouse by removing the mouse from the serial port.
- Select the serial port into which you want to install a new mouse, connect the new mouse into the port. Sometime you may require 9 to 25 pin or 25 to 9 pin convertor to connect the mouse to the available serial port.
- Power on your system, update your mouse driver and other software as necessary. Test the mouse.

Troubleshooting Mouse

If you experience problems with your mouse, the problem could be because of the mouse, mouse driver software, the application software you are using, cables or the main system itself. So, before you throw away your mouse, try the following troubleshooting techniques:

- Make sure the mouse cable is correctly connected to its port.
- Turn your PC's system unit power off and back on and see if the error disappears.
- If you have a second mouse available, turn off your PC's power and connect the new mouse. Power the PC back on to see if the error disappears.
- Try the mouse on some other system where a mouse of the same type is working without any trouble.
- Some software do not support mouse. Try mouse with a program that is known to support the mouse.
- Make sure the mouse device driver being used is correct one and is setup correctly.
- If the mouse is a serial mouse, try using a second serial port. You might need to update the mouse device driver to use the second serial port.
- If you are using a bus mouse, make sure that the mouse adapter card is properly seated in its expansion slot.

Some Other Common Problems

The mouse works with some software but not with some others.

Many software programs require that you configure them or reinstall them to take advantage of a mouse. Consult the documentation of the program to find the steps necessary to make the program work with your mouse.

The mouse works in only one direction, up-down or left-right.

This problem could be due to wrong software setup or could be due to one set of roller or sensors not working properly.

If the problem is software related then trying the mouse with some other software or on some other machine should make the mouse behave properly. If the mouse starts to work properly, then reinstall or reconfigure the program with problem.

If the problem is hardware related then open the mouse and clean it properly. Check if the problem has disappeared.

Mouse Stopped responding to its buttons.

Most mouse button are miniature push type buttons used in most of the electronic device such as VCR, VCP etc, so, if you have a mouse with unresponsive buttons then open the mouse and check the button type, get same type of button from some electronic spare shop.

Remove old button by desoldering it and solder the new button in place of it. If same type of button is not available then you can exchange a working button which is not used, such as the middle button in a three button mouse, with the non-working button.

Mouse movement seems bumpy, irregular, uneven.

This problem is most likely due to accumulation of dust inside the mouse, on mouse ball and rollers. Clean the mouse properly as explained earlier.

This could also be due to wrong setup of the mouse driver software, if the cleaning does not solve your problem then check the mouse configuration and different settings such as vertical speed, horizontal speed, acceleration, mouse type etc. settings.

Cleaning the Mouse

A mouse needs to be cleaned periodically to get a trouble free service. This is required because when the ball rolls over a mouse pad or some other surface it picks up dirt from the desk or the pad. Slowly this dirt gets packed onto the ball and the rollers inside the mouse.

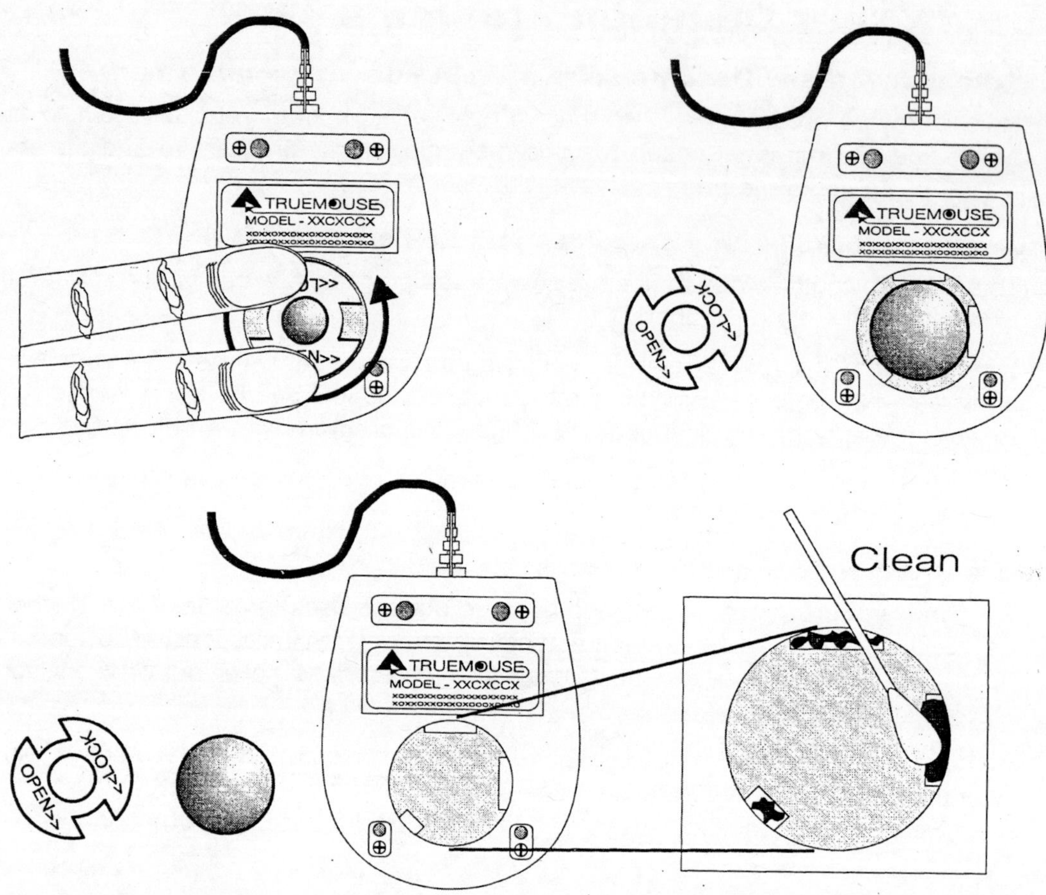

Fig. 8-8 : Cleaning Mouse.

As the the accumulation of dirt increases, mouse start to behave erratically, it may not seem as responsive as it once was, mouse action starts to feels "lumpy", even when it is rolled on a clean surface. All these symptoms indicate that the mouse needs to be cleaned.

To clean your mouse, switch off the system and disconnect the mouse from the PC. Turn the mouse over and open the cover holding the rubber ball inside the case. To open the cover you need to rotate or move the cover in the direction shown with arrow for "open".

Once the cover is removed, take out the rubber ball and clean it with lukewarm water and mild detergent and dry with a lint-free cloth. Make sure not to scratch the ball surface. Next, blow out any dust that may reside in the mouse ball's container.

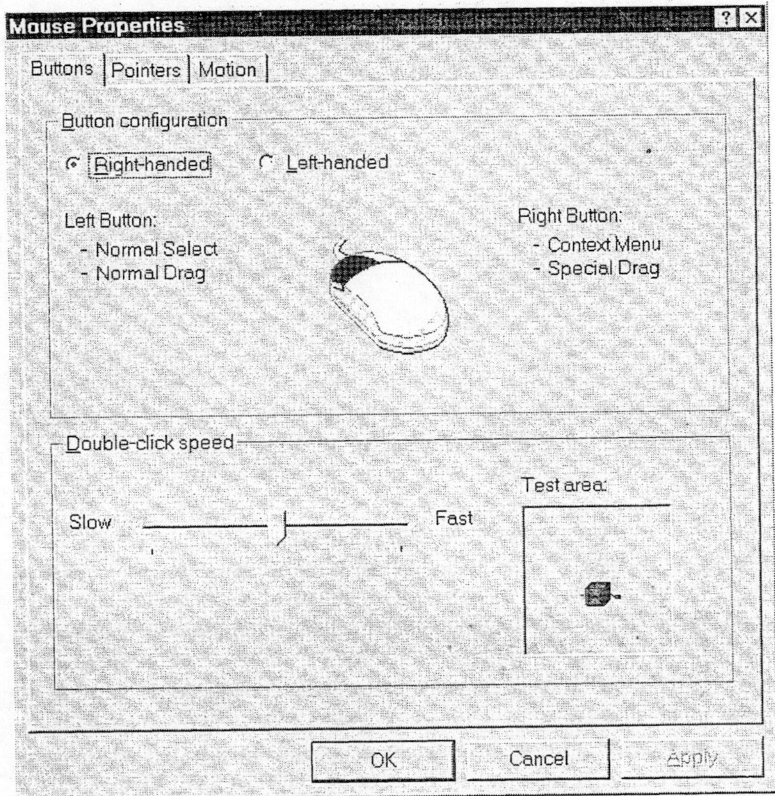

Fig. 8-9 : Swapping Mouse Buttons.

If you look inside the cavity where the ball sits, you can see little rollers against which the ball sits. Clean it with a cotton swab or soft toothpick, if necessary use alcohol on the cotton bud for a better cleaning.

Rotate and clean all the rollers completely. Blow out any particles that may have fallen in while cleaning the rollers. Wait for some time before replacing the rubber ball in, so that the cleaned surface becomes dry.

Place the clean ball back into the mouse and secure the cover.

Connect the mouse again with the PC after making sure that the mouse is moving freely.

Once a week or once in two weeks- depending on the environment in which you use the mouse- cleaning of the mouse will provide a long and trouble free service to you.

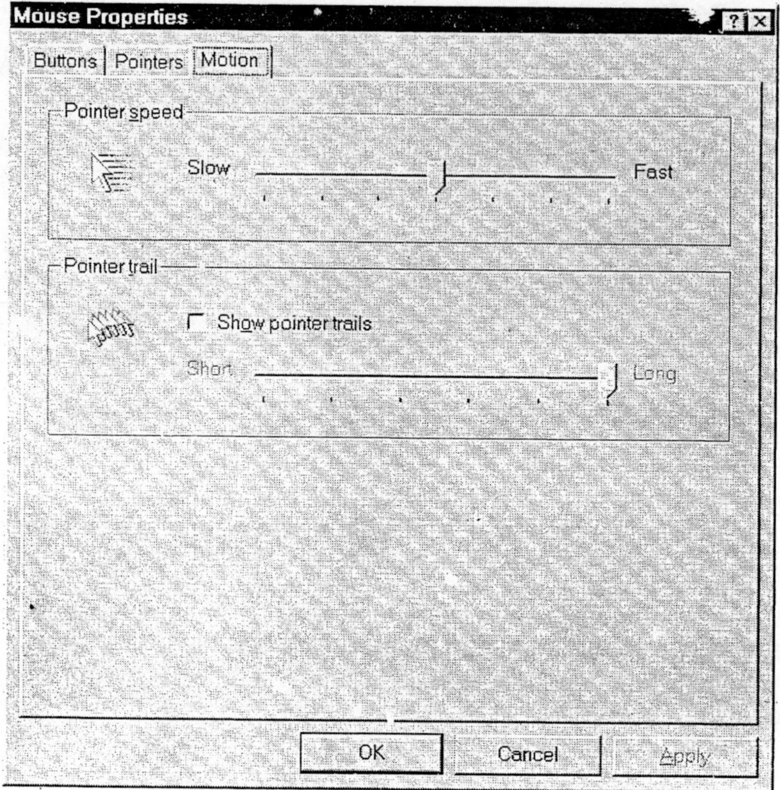

Fig. 8-10 : Changing Mouse Pointer Movement Speed.

Swapping Mouse Buttons

By default, mouse normally come configured for right-handed users. Many software programs, however, let you switch the mouse buttons. If you are using Windows, for example, you can switch the mouse buttons using the Control Panel Mouse Properties dialog box.

Open the "Mouse Properties" dialog box by clicking Start, pointing to Settings, clicking Control Panel, and then double-clicking Mouse.

In the "Button configuration" option click "Right-handed" or "Left-handed".

This will make the left mouse button act as right button and the right button as left. Remember, that this setting will be effective only for the software running under Windows.

Using the "Pointer Speed" option under "Motion" tab one can change the speed at which the mouse pointer moves on the screen.

Alternate Input Devices

In previous section we have looked at two most common input devices, first one- the keyboard- is used for entering text and number into the computer system and the second device- the mouse- is mainly used as a pointing or drawing device, it is used to move a pointer around the screen and is mainly used with Graphical User Interfaces (GUIs) such as Microsoft Windows.

Other than these two devices many other input devices are available for different type of applications. Some of these devices are useful in places where you may want to use a mouse but may not have enough table space to use it, some are better than mouse for drawing purpose, some other device may be useful to convert existing engineering drawings into the computer format etc.

In this chapter we shall look at some of these alternate input devices.

Trackball

Basically the trackball looks like a mouse turned upside down but it is a completely new device which is based on the mouse technology.

Trackball removes the space problem faced in using the mouse, to keep and to move around the mouse one needs some space on the tabletop. With a trackball one needs only the space to keep the trackball, no space is required to move the trackball around.

With a trackball the screen pointer is moved by manipulating the ball with the thumb or fingers. one can click on the buttons with the other fingers.

Trackballs use the same driver software as mouse and most of them are compatible to the Microsoft mouse. Just like the mouse, the trackball is also available in two and three button type.

Currently optical trackball is gaining in popularity. Like the old optical mouse design, the ball of optical trackball contain faint lines which help the optical sensor inside the trackball to detect ball movement.

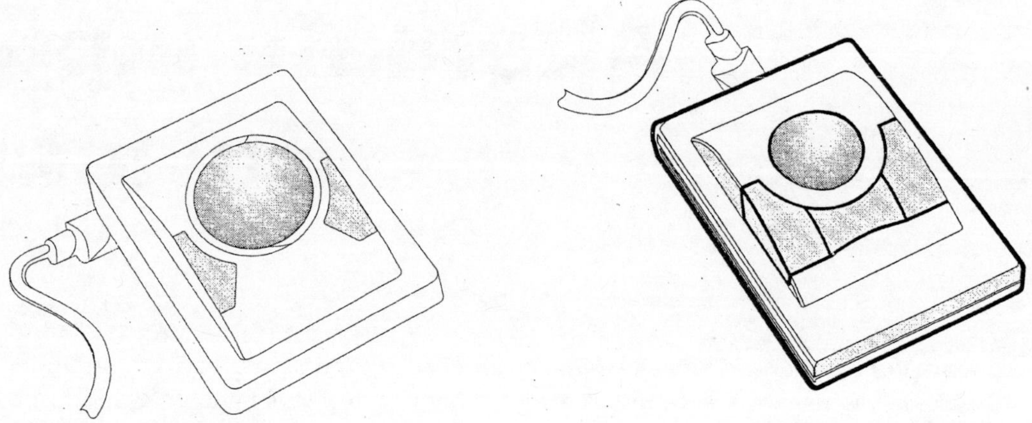

Fig. 9-1 : Trackball.

Optical trackball require less maintenance, when they get dirty remove the ball and clean the optical sensor with cotton dampened with plain water or lens cleaner liquid.

Almost all trackballs connect to the computer in the same ways as one connects a mouse. Trackballs require an expansion slot or a free serial port for connecting them to the computer.

Graphics Tablet (Digitizer/Digitizing Tablet)

A mouse or a trackball is made for the pointing purpose i.e. to point at some object on the screen and to initiate some action, they can also be used for some simple drawing purpose. But, if you try to make your signature into "Paintbrush", "Coreldraw" or some other drawing package using a mouse or a trackball, you will find that, even after a lot of practice, you can not get the exact shape into the computer.

A different input device called "Graphic Tablet" (also called a Digitizer, or a Digitizing Tablet) can be used for doing fine drawing works and for image manipulation application.

A graphic tablet with a Pen (also called a Stylus) is used for the artistic work, such as drawing or manipulating graphics image on the screen. Graphic tablet with another device called Puck (also called a Cursor) is used for drafting work, like entering engineering drawing into the computer from a set of plans.

The kind of work is to be done determines which device, pen or puck, you should choose with the graphic tablet.

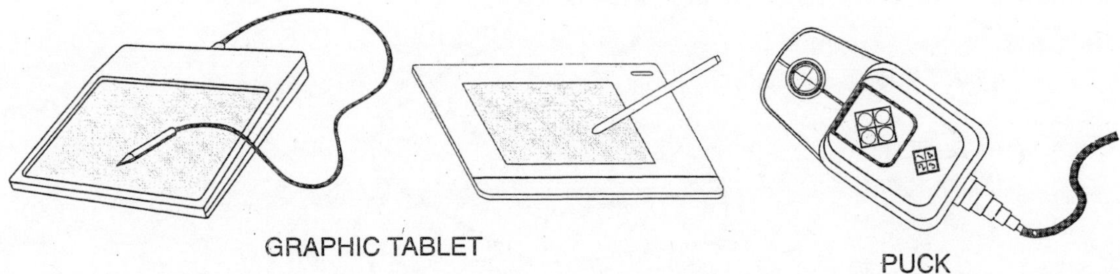

Fig. 9-2 : Graphic Tablet.

Both Pens and Pucks come with or without cords. A cordless Pen or Puck gives the user greater freedom of movement and it allows one to switch between the two devices just by picking one up and keeping the other down.

Pen or Stylus

A Pen or Stylus, looks and feels just like an ordinary pen. One can hold this pen like a regular pen and use all the artistic strokes and gestures on the graphics tablet to draw image on the screen. The image on the screen is drawn based on pen strokes you apply on the graphic tablet.

Nowadays some high-end pressure-sensitive Pens are available which can change the way the drawing software interprets your Pen movements. If the drawing software has been written to take advantage of the differences in pressure, then like a real pen you can press harder on the graphic tablet with this Pen to get a darker image on the screen.

Puck or Cursor

A puck or cursor is more suited for Computer Aided Design/Drafting (CAD) and engineering applications such as for transferring data from a set of building plans into the computer. For this one need to put the plan over the graphic tablet, position the puck's cross-hair over a point on the plans and click a button to enter that point in the computer. Point by point, the complete plan is transferred to the computer.

When the puck is moved over the surface of the tablet, Sensors in the tablet and the puck can tell the computer exactly where the puck is at any given time and the current co-ordinates are sent to the computer when a button on the puck is pressed.

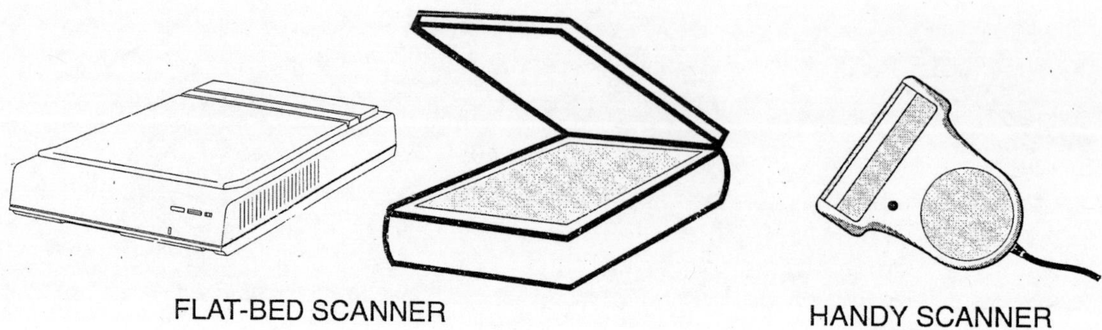

Fig. 9-3 : Scanners - Flat-Bed and Hand-Held.

A puck can have from 1 to 16 buttons, these buttons can be programmed to send different commands to the computer.

Before buying a Graphic Tablet one should always verify that the application software one wants to use (such as the Autocad etc.) with the Graphics Tablet supports all the feature provided in the Tablet.

Scanners

So far we have looked at various input devices, Keyboard, Mouse, Trackball, Graphic Tablet etc. Input devices Keyboard is most suited for entering and editing text data, Mouse and Trackball are best suited as pointing devices in Graphical User Interface such as Windows and Graphics Tablet is best suited for entering freehand and engineering drawing into the computer.

If you have some existing photograph and if you want to transfer it into the computer, none of the above device are useful for this purpose, you need another input device called "Scanner" for this purpose.

Scanners are the best choice for getting existing graphical images such as photograph, logo etc. into the computer. Using a scanner one can quickly and easily bring existing images into the computer.

Once these images are scanned and brought into the computer one can include them into documents or edit them with image editing software such as "Paintbrush", "Corel Photopaint", "Adobe Photoshop" etc.

A scanner is also useful for OCR (Optical Character Recognition) work. Using OCR software one can scan existing text documents into the computer and then convert them into a format that word processing software such as "Microsoft Word" can edit.

The scanner is also useful with the fax cards in your system. A fax cards does not have any facility to get existing documents into the computer, one can use the scanner to scan and get the documents into the computer, which can then be faxed using the fax card.

Before adding a scanner to existing system one should make sure that the system is capable of handling the requirements of the scanner. First you would require a lot of hard disk space to store the scanned images, a simple black & white image may need around 100 kilobytes and a single full color high-quality, high-resolution scanned color image may require many megabytes (around 80) of hard disk space.

One would also require a high quality display system to view and manipulate scanned images. Similarly, if one is planning to do OCR work then for the computational requirement one needs atleast an entry level Pentium based system.

Scanner Type

Depending on the type of image that a scanner can scan and store into the computer scanner are divided into three categories i.e. Black & White, Gray Scale and Color. The scanner can also be divided into following two categories Hand Held and Flatbed based on their working method.

Let us see about these different scanners.

Black & White, Grayscale and Color

A black & white scanner as its name suggests scans any image as a combination of black and white color, there is no shades of gray or colour, this type of scanner is good for scanning line drawing or sketches etc.

A gray scale scanners is best suited to scan photographs, as these scanners can scan and store photograph as different shades of gray. One needs a color scanner to scan and store color diagrams or photographs into the computer.

Currently very inexpensive colour scanners are available, so one should go for a flatbed colour scanner.

Most color scanners today support up to 16.7 million colors (true color) which is also called 24-bit or true color. A scanner scans any images as a series of separate dots, each of which can be either black or white or have a level of gray or a color.

A scanner should be able to recognize minimum 300 of these dots per inch, this number of dots per inch (DPI) is called resolution of the scanner, better scanners have a resolution of 1200DPI or more.

Hand Held and Flatbed Scanner

A hand-held type of scanner is less expansive and less capable. It is used to scan small figures into the computer. With a hand-held scanner one would require some practice for moving the scanner over the surface of the document or image.

Another type of scanner Flatbed scanners are costly, but are very easy to use and give good quality scanned image.

Working of Hand-held Scanner

Hand-held scanners are typically limited by the size of the image they can scan-usually the width is limited to about 4 to 6 inches and the height depending on the scan resolution could be a bit longer than this.

Because of their size limitations, these hand-held scanners are best suited for scanning small images, small photographs, logos, signatures etc.

- When you press the scan button on a typical hand-held scanner, a light-emitting diode (LED) illuminates the image beneath the scanner. An angled mirror directly above the scanner's window reflects this image onto a lens in the back of the scanner.
- The lens focuses a single line of the image onto a Charge Coupled Device (CCD), The CCD contains a row of light detectors, as the light shines onto these detectors, each detect the amount of light as a voltage level.
- The voltages generated by these CCDs are sent to an analog-to-digital (A-D) converter. In a grayscale scanner, the converter assigns 8 bits to each pixel, which translates into 256 levels of gray in the final digitized image. The A-D converter on a monochrome scanner assigns only 1 bit per pixel, either on or off, representing, black or white.
- As the hand moves the scanner, a rubber roller- the main purpose of which is to keep the scanner's path straight- also rotate a slotted disk.
- As the disk turns, a light shines through the slits and is detected by a photosensor on the other side of the disk. The sensor sends a signal to the A-D converter.
- This signal tells the converter to send the line of bits generated by the converter to your PC. After which the converter clears the data and is ready to receive a new stream of voltage from the next line of the image.

Working of Flatbed Scanner

Flatbed scanner (also known as a page scanner) look and work somewhat like a photocopier. One need to simply lay an image or page of text face down on the flatbed scanner and then issue a command to scan the page.

Because the page stays stationary and the mechanism inside the flatbed scanner move over the image, the scans from a flatbed scanner tend to be less distorted than the image available from a handheld scanner. For a high-quality scan, one should always choose a flatbed scanner.

- A light source illuminates a piece of paper placed face down against a glass window above the scanning mechanism.
- A motor moves the scan head beneath the page. As it moves, the scan head captures light reflected from individual areas of the page.
- The light from the page is reflected through a system of mirrors A lens focuses the beams of light onto light-sensitive diodes that translate the amount of light into electrical current.
- The more light that's reflected, the greater the voltage of the current. Blank or white spaces reflect more light than black or colored letters or images.
- An analog-to-digital (A-D) converter converts each analog reading of voltage as a digital pixel representing the scanned area. In a grayscale scanner, the converter assigns 8 bits to each pixel, which translates into 256 levels of gray in the final digitized image. The A-D converter on a monochrome scanner stores only 1 bit per pixel, either on or off, representing, black or white.
- If the scanner is a color scanner then the scan head makes three passes under the images and the light on each pass is directed through a red, green or blue filter before it strikes the original image.
- In some colour scanners, the scanning head makes single pass by rotating each of the red, green and blue filter in front of the light source in turn.
- The reflected signal from these pass are converted into digital information and stored to represent red, green and blue color value of the scanned area on the page.
- This digital information is sent to the computer, where the data is stored in a format on which a graphics program or an Optical Character Recognition (OCR) program can work.

Connecting Scanners to Your PC

A scanner can be connected to the PC in many ways

- using proprietary interface provided by the scanner manufacturer
- using general purpose SCSI (Small Computer System Interface) host adapter
- using Parallel connector
- using USB connector

Connect the scanner to the proper interface and run the setup program provided with the scanner. Most of these setup program install the scanner for the Window and OCR use. They also install some image editing software.

OCR Software

If you think that once a page full of text is scanned and stored into the computer, you can edit or spell check them using some word processing program, then it is a mistake. Because when you scan an image into your PC, it's stored as a group of dots with different colors or levels of gray. The computer doesn't have a clue about what information it contains.

With a word processor, your computer stores each letter/character as a single byte of information. When your computer scans an image, it just stores patterns of dots.

For the computer to translate the pattern of dots that happen to contain text into something that you can load into your word processor, you need an OCR (Optical Character Recognition) program. These programs use sophisticated techniques to recognize patterns of dots as letters and words and to save them as letters that your word processor can recognize and manipulate.

These software are sometimes provided free with the scanner or one can separately purchase them.

Optical Character Recognition Process

The OCR software after reading the bitmap created by the scanner maps the white space on the page. This enables the software to recognize number of columns, paragraphs, headlines and graphics on the page.

- In its first pass at converting images to text, the software tries to match each character in the bitmap through a pixel-by-pixel comparison to different character image that the program holds in memory.
- The characters that remain unrecognized go through a more intensive and time-consuming process called feature extraction. In this method the OCR software calculates the text's x-height i.e the height of a font's lowercase x, and analyzes each character's combination of straight lines, curves and bowls i.e. hollow areas within loops, as in o or b etc. With the recognition of each new character further recognition of the same character becomes easy and the recognition speed increases.
- If these two processes can not decipher a character, OCR programs take two approaches for the remaining characters. Some OCR programs label the unrecognized characters with a distinctive character- such as @, $ etc. and quit. One can use the search facility provided in a word processor to find these distinctive character and correct the word manually.
- Some OCR programs may also display a magnified bitmap on screen and ask you to press the character needed.
- Still some other OCR programs go through a special spell checking to search and locate possible alternatives for words that contain unrecognized characters. A spelling checker recognizes some common OCR errors such as the difference between the number 5 and the letter S or the letter cl and letter d and corrects them.

Most OCR programs have an option of saving the converted document into a file format recognized by popular word processors or spreadsheets package. They can also save these documents as an ASCII file.

Twain

Initially each scanner used its own proprietary command set to interface with the CPU. This resulted in the user being able to use only the software provided by the scanner manufacturer to scan an image.

To solve this problem, the scanner industry has developed a software interface standard known as "Twain", this allowed any software following the twain standard to be able to communicate with any scanner supporting the twain standard.

This made the scanning consistent across different applications. The same screen that control scanner in Corel Photo-Paint will appear on the Adobe PhotoShop.

Twain is a software interface standard which provides standard set of functions to any software for controlling various features of a scanner.

To use Twain interface, both the scanner as well as the software being used should be Twain compatible.

Digital Camera

Digital camera can be used to capture any image and to save them on storage device such as hard disk, CD-ROM, etc. these images can be posted on the web or printed on a colour ink-jet printer.

Some common digital camera are

- Digital Still camera
- Digital Video camera.
- Web Camera

Digital Still Camera

Digital still camera look like the older film based camera. To use it one need to look through the view-finder, set the image, and push a button to take the picture.

Currently most of the digital still camera provide high resolution images which can be printed to 8 inch x 10 inch size without any lose of image quality.

Depending on the memory available to the camera, one can store from a dozen to hundreds of image into it. Most of these camera have additional features such a 2X to 10X zoom, facility to capture video clip, option to record audio etc.

One can connect the digital still camera to the computer and use it to capture moving images, this camera can also be used as web camera.

Fig. 9-4 : Digital Camera.

Digital Video Camera

Digital Video Camera is used to capture moving images digitally. They provide an image capture rate of around 30 frames per second. Resolution of this camera is lower than the resolution of digital still camera. Most of the digital video camera provides 30 frames per second video at VGA mode, i.e. 640 x 480 pixels.

Most of the digital video camera provide zoom upto 30X. They can be used as a digital still camera, they can also be used as a web camera.

Web Camera

A web camera is basically a low-end digital video camera with low resolution and fixed focus lens. This camera is suited for webcasting, video messaging etc. applications.

One can use the web camera to make low-grade movies and capture still images.

Image Sensor

Image sensor is the heart of the digital camera. It is the job of the image sensor to capture the light falling on it and convert the light into electrical signal, which can then be converted into digital data to store as the captured image

An array of CCD or Charge Coupled Device elements are used as image sensing device in most of these digital cameras. Some manufacturer use CMOS sensors for this purpose.

Image Storage

Most of the digital camera use flash memory to store the captured image. This memory is available in the form of removable memory cards. Generally the digital

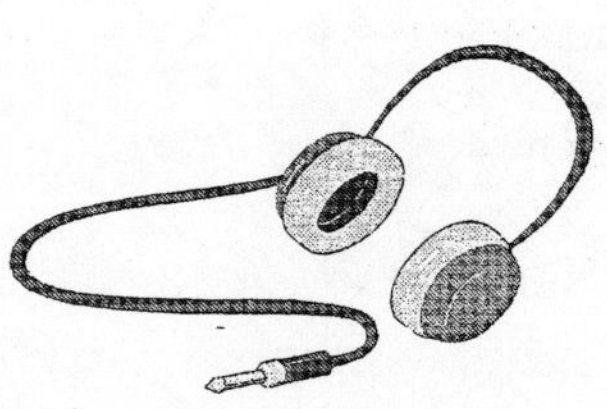 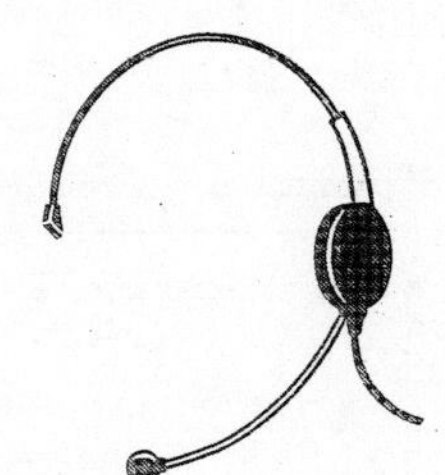 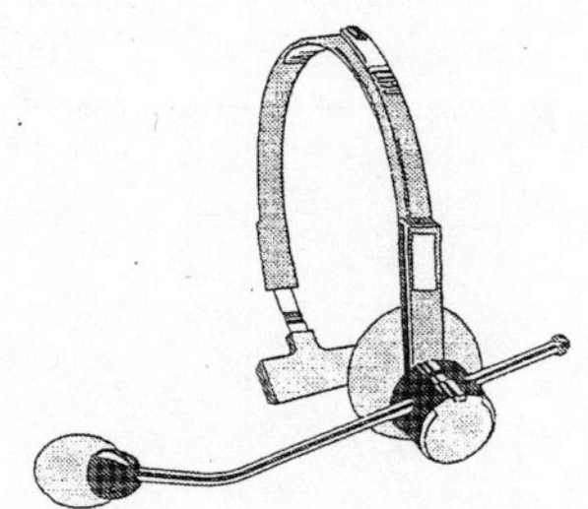

Fig. 9-5 : Headsets for Voice Input.

camera have option of storing the image in two or more quality level. Lower quality level allows more image to be stored in same memory size.

Voice Input

Almost all the science fiction movies such as Star Trek, Star Wars etc. contain talking computers where the user need to just tell the computer his or her requirement and within seconds the computer gives the reply.

Intelligent conversations as shown in these movies with a computer is currently not a possibility, but it is possible to have devices that can understand and respond to simple words.

For example, one can highlight a sentence with the mouse and say the word "delete" so the computer delete the highlighted word from the text, or by issuing voice command, such as "copy", "move" or "print" one should be able to copy, move or print selected file.

The whole process of listening to voice command and then determining what the speaker wants may seem easy for us humans, but for a computer it is a very complicated process.

Currently devices that take dictation, so that you can say memos rather than type them on the keyboard are easily available. As the machine power increase and software improve this voice input technology will come in common use.

Touchpad

Touchpads are pointing device for the notebook computers. Initially trackball was used as pointing device with the notebook computers. After the introduction of touchpad, almost all notebook manufacturer has switched to touchpad as their choice for pointing device.

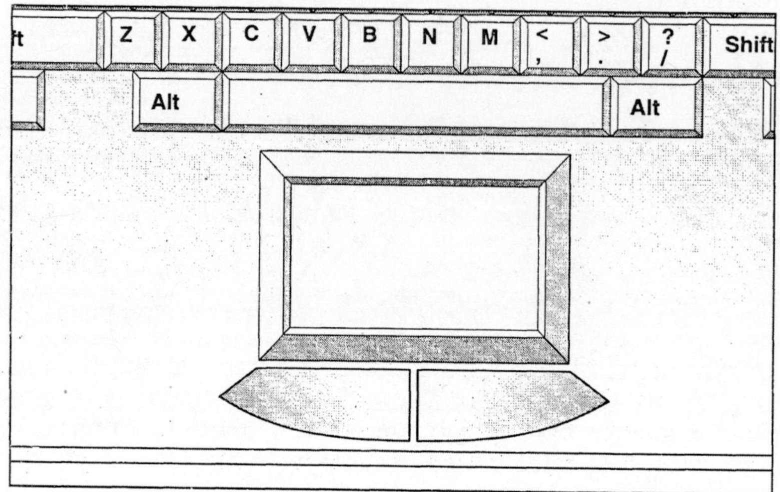

Fig. 9-6 : Touchpad below Spacebar on a Notebook Computer Keyboard.

Touchpad is used by moving ones finger on the pad surface. The finger movement on the pad surface is converted into mouse pointer's movement on the monitor.

A touchpad is a printed circuit board (PCB), top of which holds a pattern of conductive sensor lines etched into place. A layer of myler covers this top of the board to protect it and to give the finger a place for smooth movement.

As the touchpad is completely sealed, it is safe from any environmental contamination such as dust, water etc.

When the finger is placed on the pad, the pad detects location of the finger by detecting the electrical capacitance of finger.

As the finger attracts a small static electrical charge, it cause small current to flow in the circuitry of the touchpad. Electronics of the touchpad detects this small current from two adjacent edges of the pad.

This makes the touchpad circuitry to be able to detect the position of the finger. By following the changes in the current, touchpad can detect the movement of the finger across the pad.

The touchpad is generally placed just below the spacebar on the keyboard. This allows a touch-typist to use his thumb to operate the touchpad without lifting his fingers from the home row.

Hard Disk Drive

Today Hard Disk Drives are the most common storage device used with the computer system. The hard disk drive is also known as Hard Disk, Hard Drive, Fixed Disk Drive or Winchester Disk Drive.

The hard disk drive is used to store data and programs permanently inside the computer. The information stored in the hard disk drive does not get erased when the power supply to the computer is switched off.

Information is stored in the hard drive using the same magnetic recording method, which is used to store songs on an audiotape or movies on videotape. The audio or video tape does not lose its content when the power supply given to the audio or video recorder is switched off, same way the hard drive also retains the information stored in it, even when the power supply to the hard drive is switched off.

Before starting about the Hard Disk Drives, let us see how the magnetic recording on the disk surface takes place:

Magnetic Recording

Data is stored inside the computer in the form of Binary Digits or bits and based on the value of this bit, a 0 or a 1, the magnetic particles on the disk surface is recorded in NS (North, South) or SN (South, North) orientation.

When you buy a new hard disk, the magnetic particles of the coating on the disk surface are in a random orientation.

Data is recorded on this surface by making these random magnetic particles orient in some predefined order in NS or SN orientation.

Data Recording

The magnetic recording on the disk surface is done by a magnetic read/write head, which is similar to the read/record head of an audio/video tape recorder.

The read/write head of the disk drive is an electromagnet whose polarity can be switched by changing the direction of the electric current through it.

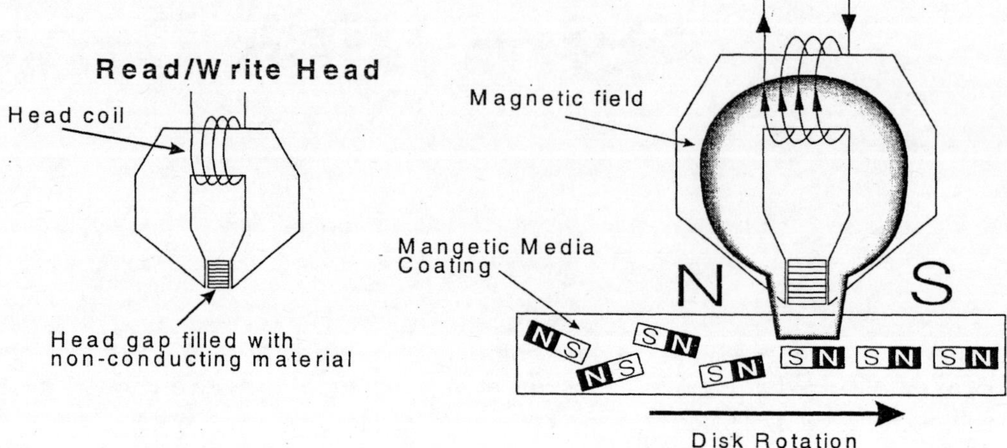

Fig. 10-1 : Data Recording by Read/Write Head.

Hard disk drive head is basically a U-shaped conductive piece of material, which is wrapped with a coil of conductor wire.

A small gap in the section of the head that touches the disk surface is used to concentrated the generated magnetic flux to the surface of the disk. Normally, this gap is filled with a nonmagnetic material, such as glass or ceramic.

When current is passed through the coil, a magnetic field is generated on the head. This magnetic field aligns the polarity of the magnetic particles on the disk media.

The polarity of magnetic particles on the disk media will depend on the direction of the magnetic field and the direction of the magnetic field will depend on the direction of the flow of current through the head coil.

By changing the direction of flow of current through the head coil, magnetic particles on the disk can be arranged in NS or SN orientation.

Reading from a Disk Surface

When reading any information from the disk surface, the principles of the induced current on a conductor wire due to the change of magnetic field is at work.

According to this principle, any change in magnetic field across a coil of conductor wire produce current through the coil. This produced current is called an "induced current", because there is no direct connection between the magnet and the coil.

The current is induced because of the relative motion of the magnet with respect to the coil.

This property of the magnet and coil to generate induced current is used to read the information stored on the disk surface.

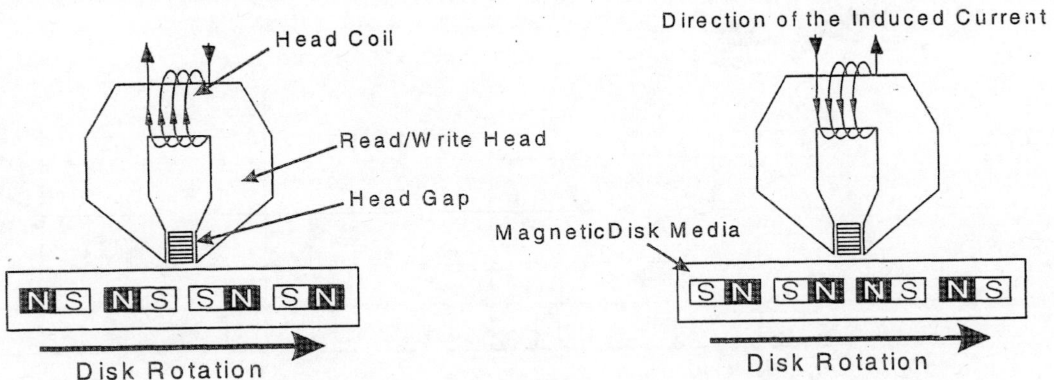

Fig. 10-2 : Data Reading by Read/Write Head.

When the read/write head passes over the surface of the disk, an electric pulse is induced in the read/write head circuitry for each change in the orientation of the magnetic particle on the disk surface.

The state of this electric pulse tells the read/write head whether the information on the disk surface is a 0 or a 1.

Current is produced on the head only if there is a change in the direction of the magnetic particle on the disk surface, if all the magnetic particles of the disk surface are oriented in the same direction then there will not be any current produced on the read/write head of the drive.

If bit 1 is stored as NS and bit 0 is stored as SN, then 1101 will be stored as NS NS SN NS magnetic flux on the disk surface. When this data is read back, it will produce signal on the read/write head at only two places.

In this method, without any additional information just by seeing two pulses it is very difficult to predict what is the data stored at that location.

To overcome this problem, an additional signal is stored with each data bit. This signal is called clock signal. This clock signal is always stored before the data bit.

This clock bit is always stored in the opposite orientation of the data bit preceding it, so there will always be a current or pulse generation for the clock signal because of the flux reversal of the magnetism.

After the clock bit, if the data is 1 then the next bit i.e. the data bit is oriented in the reverse direction compared to the clock bit, if the data bit is 0 then the next bit, i.e. the data bit is oriented in the same direction as the clock bit.

When the data is 0, i.e. if the clock bit and the data bit orientation are same then there will not be any data pulse and no current generation on the read/write head. When the

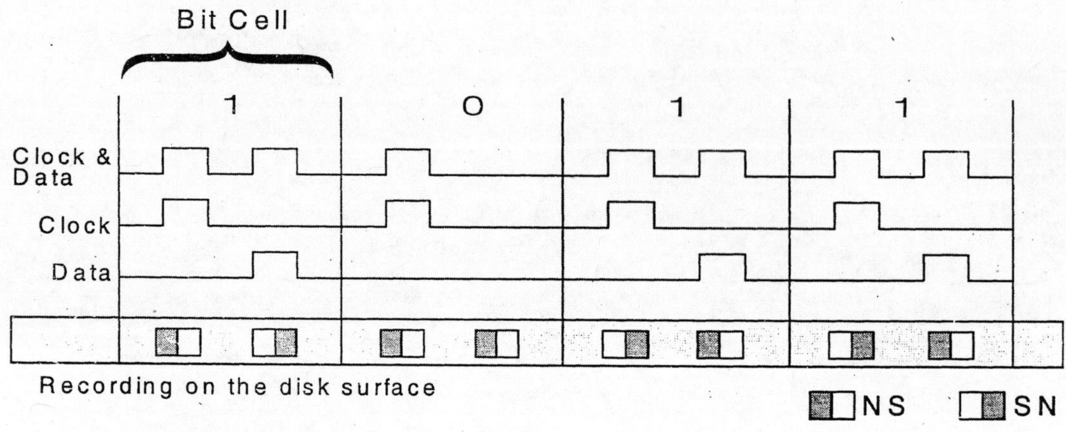

Fig. 10-3 : FM Encoding.

data is 1, i.e. if the clock bit and the data bit orientation are not same then there will be a data pulse on the read/write head.

To increase the storage density of the recording medium most of the recording or encoding schemes try to limit the number of clock pulses to the very minimum.

Data Encoding Method

When the data is received from a serial digital circuit, it is in a format known as NRZ or Non-Return to Zero. This is the most common format of data output by a parallel to serial shift register.

In this format a pulse is used to store the binary digit 1 and no pulse or a blank is used to store binary digit 0. However, this format is not compatible with the magnetic recording method used to store data on the disk surface.

The reason is the read/write coil will not produce any induced voltage when the head is moved parallel to a non-changing field of magnetic flux.

The only time a current will be induced in the head (in a read operation) is when a change in the orientation of the magnetic particle is encountered i.e. on a transition from "NS" to "SN" or from "SN" to "NS".

If all the binary 1's are stored as "NS" magnetic particle on the disk surface then during the time intervals when the head is passing over a series of 1s, no voltage will be induced. This could lead to problem as the synchronization between the interfacing circuitry and the incoming data, which is read from the disk, could be lost.

After some time the disk interfacing circuitry will not be able to tell when a bit has started and when it has ended.

A very easy solution to this problem as we have seen would be to record a clock signal with the data signal for synchronization purposes.

As writing a clock bit with each data bit would require double space for the data storage, another alternative method, which is normally used in the disk storage method, is to encode the date that is to be written to the disk.

This encoding is normally done using some data encoding technique from which the clock synchronization information can be separated, without any loss of the data information.

Three most common encoding methods are:

- FM encoding method
- MFM encoding method
- RLL encoding method

Let use see these data encoding methods in detail.

FM Encoding Scheme

FM or Frequency Modulation was the original data-encoding scheme used for storing the data on the magnetic recording surface.

This method of data encoding is also known as the "single density recording", as this method was used to write to the single density floppy diskettes. This method was popular in the 1970s and is no longer used today.

In this method, a clock signal is put with every data signal on the recording surface. This clock signal is used for synchronizing the read operation, as there will always be a clock signal, whether the data signal is there or not.

Let us see one example, suppose you want to store the binary digit 1011 on a magnetic recording media using the FM recording technique. In this FM method of data recording a 1 bit is stored as two pulses (one clock pulse and one data pulse), and a 0 bit is stored as a one pulse and one gap or no pulse (1 clock pulse and one "no pulse" to show that it is a 0 bit).

- A binary digit 1 is stored as two pulses (PP)
- A binary digit 0 is stored as one pulse and one "no pulse" (PN)

A clock pulse and data pulse together is called a "bit cell", as they represent one bit of information.

For example, a binary number 1011 will be stored as

```
PP PN PP PP
```

A pulse is recorded on the recording medium as a change in the direction of the magnetic field from the last magnetic field and a "no pulse" is recorded as no change in the direction of the magnetic field from the last magnetic field, i.e. if the last magnetic field was NS then a pulse or bit 1 is recorded as SN, and a no pulse or a 0 is recorded as NS.

For example 1011 or PP PN PP PP will be stored as

```
NSSN NSNS SNNS SNNS
```

When using the FM encoding technique, the synchronization signal will always be available for the disk read operations.

FM method of data recording is also known as (0,1) Run Length Limited (RLL) recording. The reason behind this name is, in a series or in a running length the minimum number of 0s is zero, i.e. you can have two pulses next to each other without any 0 or "no pulse" in between and the maximum number of 0s is one, i.e. you will never have more than one position without a 0 or "no pulse" signal.

MFM Encoding Scheme

More data can be stored on the same surface or the data storage density can be increased, if the number of pulses required to store the data can be minimized.

When minimizing the pulses, one should be careful that the number of no pulses together should not be very long, otherwise the disk controller may go out of synchronization with the data.

The MFM (Modified frequency modulation) method of data storage, by reducing the number of pulses, is able to store more data without any data and synchronization loss.

In MFM recording the 0s and 1s are encoded as given below

- 1 is always stored as a no pulse, and a pulse (NP)
- 0, when preceded by another 0, is stored as a pulse, and no pulse (PN)
- 0, when preceded by a 1, is stored as two no pulses (NN)

If you store 1001 on the disk surface using the MFM storage method, it would be stored as

```
NP NN PN NP
```

As you can see, this requires only three pulses in MFM method, let us store the same data using the FM method of data recording

```
PP PN PN PP
```

Total six pulses are required to store the same data using the FM method.

In this MFM method of data recording the minimum number of 0s together is one and the maximum number of 0s is three, this is a (1,3) RLL, Run Length Limited data recording, i.e. in MFM recording there will always be at least one "no pulse" signal i.e. two pulses will never come together, and the maximum number of positions without any pulse will never be more than three.

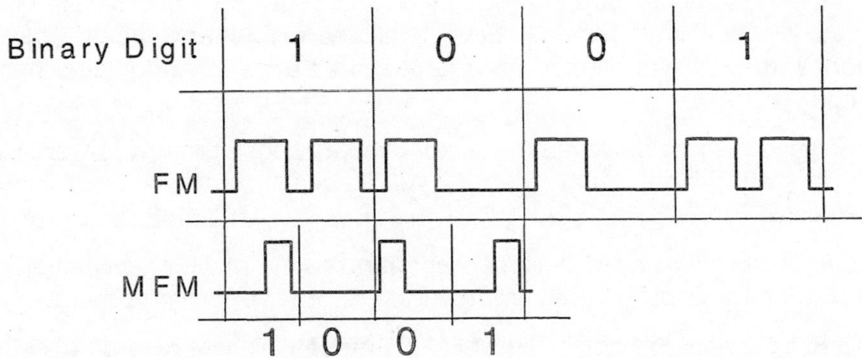

Fig. 10-4 : FM and MFM Encoding.

This guarantee of at least one "no pulse" between the pulses and the number of pulses required to store the data being less than the FM encoding scheme made the MFM scheme write the pulses closer together, denser on the disk surface, compared to the FM data recording.

In overall effect of this scheme was a recording in double the density of the FM recording. MFM recording is used for the Double Density (DD) and High Density (HD) floppy disk recording, older hard disk drives also used this MFM recording method.

The advantage of MFM over FM is on the average fewer pulses are required to read or write in MFM.

This makes it possible to record data at a higher density using MFM as opposed to FM. The MFM technique will allow twice as many bits to be stored in a given length of disk space as FM.

The disadvantage of MFM is that the circuitry required to encode and decode the data is more complex.

RLL Encoding Scheme

The RLL encoding or the Run Length Limited encoding is the most common encoding scheme used in the hard disk storage. This encoding scheme can be more accurately called as 2,7 RLL encoding because in this scheme in a series or in a running length the minimum number of 0s next to each other is two, and the maximum number of 0s together can not be more than seven.

The RLL encoding scheme can store 50 percent more information than MFM encoding scheme on a given surface and it can store three times as much information as the FM encoding scheme.

The Run Length Limited name comes from the minimum number (Run Length) and maximum number (Run Limit) of "no pulse" values allowed between two pulses.

Many different schemes of different Length and Limit have been tried, but only two schemes 2,7 RLL and 1,7 RLL have achieved popularity. As we have already mentioned, the FM scheme can be referred to as 0,1 RLL and MFM scheme can be referred as 1,3 RLL.

Initially the RLL encoding scheme was not used, because the drives were not capable enough to store the data in RLL density. As the quality of the drives improved use of RLL increased.

As the RLL encoding stores data denser than the FM or MFM encoding, it provides much faster data transfer rate compared to the other encoding schemes.

The 2,7 RLL provides very high-density (1.5 times MFM) data recording, but it is not as reliable as the 1,7 RLL which provides 1.27 times the MFM density. This makes most of the drive manufacturers to use the 1,7 RLL for their hard disk drives.

For the RLL encoding, an encoder/decoder (Endec) table is used to find the pulse signal to be used for different data bit groups. Thousands of different translation tables are possible for the 2,7 RLL encoder, as an example let us see the Endec table used by the IBM to convert bit information to the pulse signal.

Data Bit	Pulse Encoding
10	NPNN
11	PNNN
000	NNNPNN
010	PNNPNN
011	NNPNNN
0010	NNPNNPNN
0011	NNNNPNNN

You can check in the above table that for any combination of 0s and 1s there will not be less than two "no pulse" situation and at the same time there will not be more than seven "no pulse" situation next to each other at a time.

If you study this table then you might think that this table does not contain enough information to encode all the possible bit combination, for example, if you want to encode a byte 10001100 to proper RLL pulse signal then the

- Bit 10 can be encoded as NPNN
- Bit 0011 can be encoded as NNNNPNNN

Finally, when you look in the table, you will find that there is no information given about how to convert the remaining bit 00.

In this type of situation, one must remember that the RLL controller is not used to encode single byte of information, instead it converts the entire collection of bytes to be sent to the hard drive.

The controller includes bit from the next byte to complete a bit combination that can be encoded. In the above example if the next byte is 10110011, then by adding the first two bit of this byte to the previous bit combination 00, we will get a bit combination given in the table.

00 from last byte, and 10 from this byte will give 0010 which can be converted to NNPNNPNN.

If the last byte of the data contain a bit combination that is not given in the table then the controller adds the excess bits required to encode the byte, and encodes it. During the decoding, the excess bit is removed from the byte.

To store 10001111 using different data encoding schemes, you need

- PP-PN-PN-PN-PP-PP-PP-PP, i.e. total 13 pulses in FM scheme
- NP-NN-PN-PN-NP-NP-NP-NP, i.e. total 7 pulses in MFM scheme and
- NPNN-NNNNPNNN-PNNN, i.e. total 3 pulses in 2,7 RLL scheme

As you can see in the above comparison when the FM scheme requires 13 pulses to store a byte, the MFM requires only 7 pulses and for the same byte 2,7 RLL requires only 3 pulses.

As the number of pulse required to store the data using RLL encoding is very less compared to other encoding schemes, one can increase the clock rate three times of FM or 1.5 times of MFM when writing the RLL data onto the disk.

Even with increased clock rate, the physical maximum and minimum distance between the any two pulses on the disk surface will remain almost same on all the three encoding schemes. This is possible because of the different number of pulses required in different schemes.

In other word, we can say that although the data storage density of the RLL is more than the data density of other schemes, the actual pulse density on the disk surface remains same. Only when these pulses are decoded one get more data from RLL encoded storage, compared to other schemes.

Hard Disk Drive

In the last section, you saw how the magnetic data recording takes place on a disk surface. In this section we will study about the construction of a typical Hard Disk Drive, its different parts, what are their jobs and different types of these parts used in the drive construction.

Hard Disk Drive Components

Let us see the different parts of a hard-disk drive. Hard disk drive is available in many different capacity and size, but the basic component inside them are almost same.

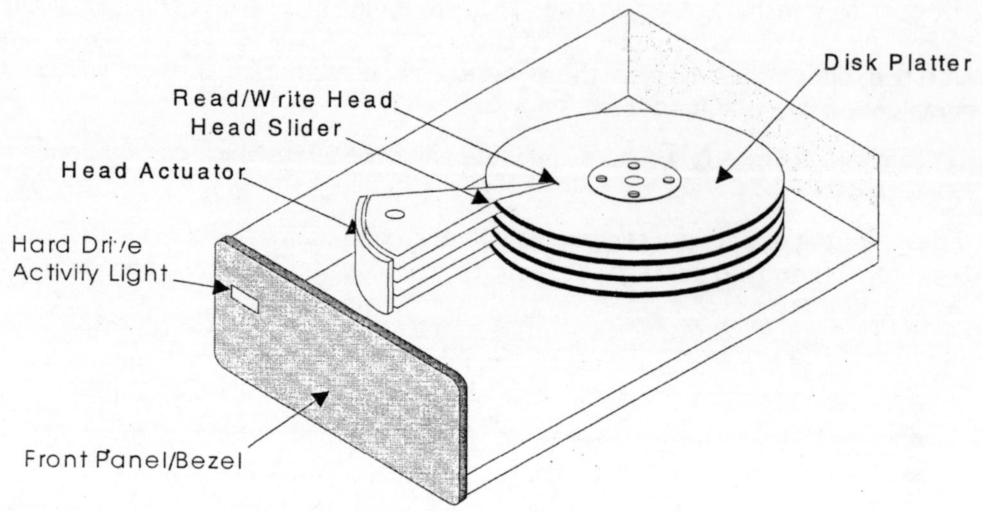

Fig. 10-5 : Components of Hard Disk Drive.

A typical hard disk drive contains the following components:

- Disk Platter
- Read/Write Head
- Head Arm/Head Slider
- Head Actuator Mechanism
- Spindle Motor
- Logic Board
- Air Filter
- Bezel
- Cable & Connectors

Disk Platter

Hard disk drive contains a number of platters, or the circular shaped disks on which the information is magnetically recorded.

The platter size (i.e. the diameter) is called the form-factor of the hard drive, and one refers the hard drive size by its platter's diameter. There were many different platter sizes in use, some of the common platter sizes are:

- 5.25 inch, (actually 5.12 inch)
- 3.5 inch, (actually 3.74 inch)
- 2.5 inch
- 1 1/8 inch
- 1 1/3 inch

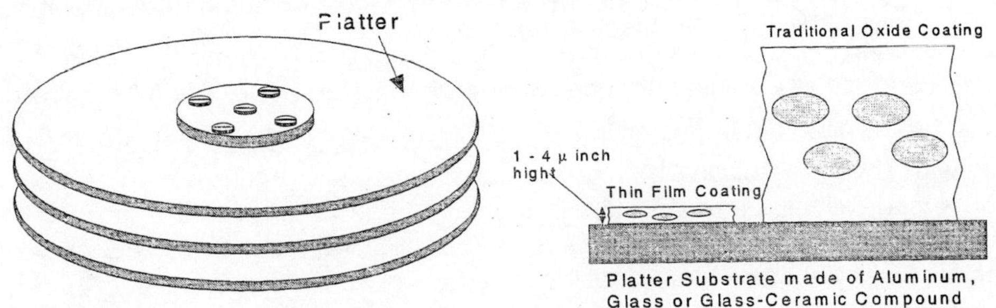

Fig. 10-6 : Disk Platter and Media Coating.

The 3 1/2 inch size platter is currently most common with the Personal Computers, and the 2 1/2 inch is common in the portable/laptop computers.

The latest 1 1/3 inch drives are very small, almost the wristwatch size, these drives are very rugged and available in the 1GB or more storage capacity.

Number of platters on the hard disk drive can be as low as 1 and as high as 10 or more, 2 or 3 platter drives are most common.

These platters were made from aluminum alloy because of their strength and light weight. Being a metal, the aluminum is not thermally stable i.e. they expand and contract with the change in the temperature.

This has lead the drive manufacturers to use glass and glass-ceramic compound as platter on their drives, glass and glass-ceramic platter allows the drive to be smaller with higher storage density.

In 3 1/2 inch and 2 1/2 inch hard drives almost all the drives are made using the glass or glass-ceramic platter.

The material using which the platter is made is called the substrate of the disk, on this substrate the magnetizable media (oxide of some ferrous material) is coated. This media coating stores information magnetically.

In current hard disk drives, oxide coating is replaced with thin-film magnetic coating. In thin-film magnetic coating, a very microscopically thin layer of pure metal, or compound of metal is bound on the platter surface.

This-film media allows higher density recording and is many times tougher than the oxide coating.

Read/Write Head

Read/write head is used to write any information on the disk surface and to read the written data, without any data loss. A hard disk drive contains one read/write head for each side of its platter. For example if a drive contains 3 platters then total six read/write head will be used to read/write the top & bottom sides of each platter.

All the head used in a disk drive system are connected together and moved in and out on the disk surface as a single unit, one cannot move different head in different order.

Inside the hard disk, when the disk is at rest i.e. not spinning, the head is in direct contact with the disk surface. As the disk starts to spin, because of its very high rotation speed, air pressure develops under the head. This pressure lifts the head from the disk surface and the head starts to float on an air cushion, 3 to 5 micro inch (millionth of inch) above from the disk surface.

Hard disk drives use two types of read/write head technology:

- Inductive and
- Magneto-Resistive

Inductive Read/Write Head

In an inductive read/write head, the disk drive circuits sends a current through the read/write head coil which induces a magnetic field in the core and alters the orientation of the magnetic particles on the nearby platter.

To read the information stored on the disk surface, when the head is moved over the platter, magnetic fields of the particles on the platter slightly magnetize the core which, in turn, induces a small voltage in the coil.

The circuits on the disk drive detects the small voltage in the coil and interprets them as data.

Current read/write heads use a thin layer of copper deposited in coil form as a film. This type of head is called thin-film heads. This technology allows finer, lower-mass coils that are easier and less expensive to make.

Magneto-Resistive Head

This is a new technology. This head works by measuring the change in electrical resistance that a magnetic field causes in some materials.

The disk drive circuit sends a small current through the magneto-resistive material and measures the change in voltage across the head, when the resistance of the head goes up, the voltage goes down.

The magneto-resistive material is usually an alloy of iron and nickel.

This technology can be used to read the signal stored on the disk surface, it cannot be used to write on the disk surface.

So, a magneto-resistive head will have another inductive head for writing operation.

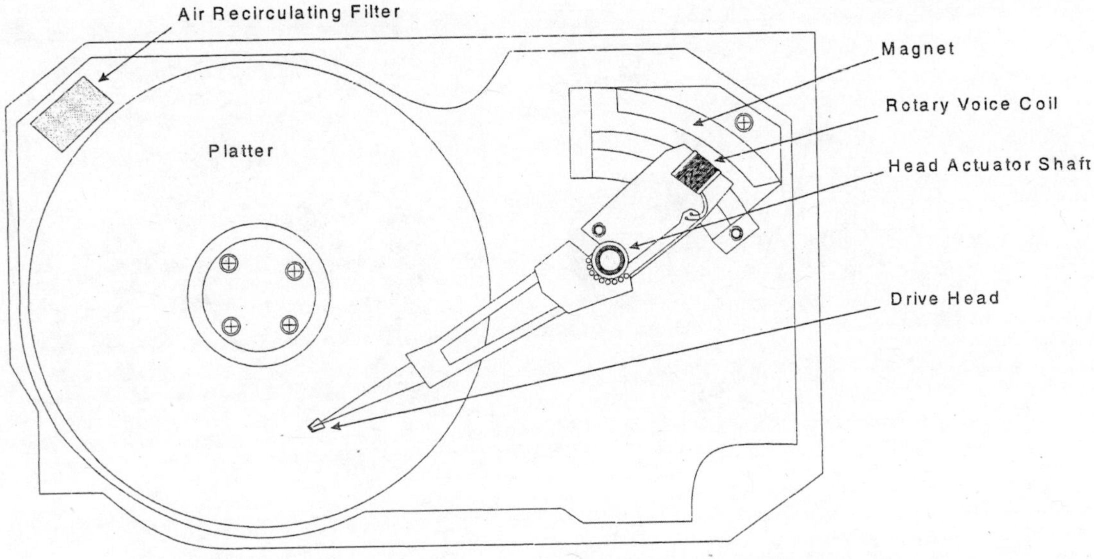

Fig. 10-7 : Drive Head and Other Internal Components.

Head Arm/Head Slider

The arm on which the read/write head of the disk drive is located is called the head slider. These sliders are made in a catamaran sailboat shape.

A small size slider has many advantages, such as the lower weight allows for faster acceleration and deceleration which makes the disk access faster.

Disk drive manufacturers provide special textured patterns on the head slider surface to keep the slider at a constant height from the disk surface, during the disk operation.

Spindle Motor

Spindle motor is the main motor which rotates the hard disk drive's platters. It is called the spindle motor because this motor is directly connected to the spindle on which the platters are connected.

This motor works on a feedback loop to automatically adjust the disk's rotation speed. A hard disk platters rotates at around 3,600 to 7,200 RPM (Rotations Per Minute) or more.

On some of the new drives, the spindle motor is directly built into the platter hub, inside the sealed assembly. The advantage of this design is, more platters can be used on the same height disk drive, as the spindle motor does not take any additional vertical space.

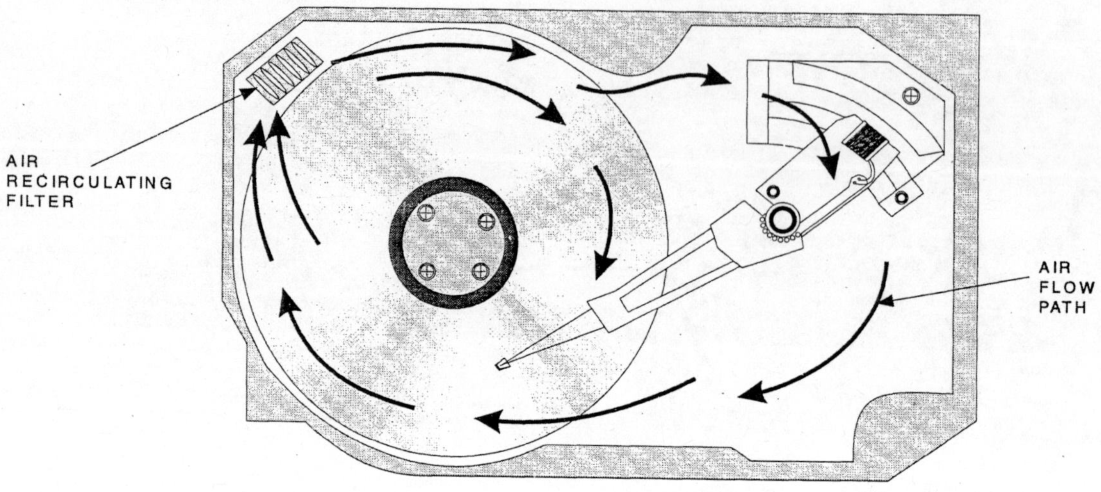

Fig. 10-8 : Air Circulation inside the Hard Disk Drive.

Logic Board

The hard disk also contains a logic board to control different parts of the hard disk drive. This logic board is also used to interface the hard disk drive with the computer.

A hard disk drive may contain more than one, logic boards.

Many a time the hard disk failure is due to the failure of this logic board, a power problem or some other problem may destroy the logic board on the hard disk drive. On this type of disk if the mechanical parts are in good condition then one can bring the drive to life by just replacing the dead logic board with a new board of the same type.

Air Filter

Most of the people think that inside the hard disk drive there is vacuum. But this is not true, the hard disk drive will not work in a vacuum condition, because the read/write head needs air to float on the disk surface.

Most of the hard disk drive will have two air filters, one is called recirculating air filter and the second is called breather filter.

- The recirculating air filter is used to filter any particles dislodged from inside the drive such as scrap of disk media, removed by the read/write head during the disk operation. This filter does not circulate the external air to the inside of the disk drive.
- The breather filter or the barometric filter is the only connection of the inside of the hard disk drive with the outside environment, as the name

suggests this filter is used to equalize the external air pressure and the pressure inside the hard disk drive.

The air filter for breather filter is made with such fine holes that particles bigger than about 10 micro inch cannot enter inside the drive through it.

Bezel/Front Faceplate

Bezel is the front faceplate provided on most of the hard disk drives. Nowadays, as most of the hard disk are connected internally, and is hidden behind the PC system's cover, the faceplate or the bezel is not needed. Most of the hard disk drive today come without a bezel.

Cable & Connectors

Cables and connectors are used to connect the hard disk drive to the main computer system. Almost all hard disk drive contains connectors for

- Data/Control Interface connector
- Power connector

Other than these two connectors one separate connector for the power ground is also provided on most of the hard disk drives.

The data/control cable is the most important part of the hard disk drive and PC interfacing. Most of the hard disk drive interface such as the IDE or the SCSI use only one cable for the data as well as control signal, some other PC to hard disk drive interface such as the ST-506, or the ESDI etc. use separate cable for data and the control signal.

The power connector used on the hard disk drive is same as the connector used for the floppy disk drive, it has four pins that provide 5 volt, 12 volt and ground signal to the disk drive.

Head Actuator Mechanism

The read/write head of the hard disk drive is moved on the platter using different mechanism, this is referred as Head Actuator Mechanism. Two different Head Actuator Mechanisms are

- Stepper Motor Actuator
- Voice Coil Actuator

The head actuator is one of the most important part of the hard drive, because different characteristic of the hard disk drive such as its read/write speed, accuracy, reliability etc., depends on the head actuator mechanism used in that drive.

Let us compare different characteristics of the hard disk drive using these actuator mechanisms

Characteristic	Stepper Motor Actuator	Voice Coil Actuator
Access Speed	Slow	Fast
Reliability	Poor	Very Good
Automatic Head Parking	Usually No	Yes
Temperature Sensitive	Yes	No
Periodic Maintenance	Low Level Formatting	No
Positionally Sensitive	Yes	No

As you can see in the above table, a stepper motor actuator based hard disk drive is inferior to the voice coil actuator based hard disk drive.

Stepper Motor Actuator

A stepper motor is a motor that rotates in steps, when you rotate an ordinary motor, it will turn any angle of rotation, but a stepper motor turns a fixed angle with each step. The smallest fixed angle that a stepper motor rotates with each pulse is called a "detent".

With each electrical pulse received, a stepper motor turns in a predefined angle.

One can recognize a stepper motor in the power off position by spinning it by hand, when spin in power off position, its movement will not be smooth, instead you will feel it move in small jumps.

The stepper motor is connected to the read/write head actuator using the following two method

- Split metal band mechanism
- Rack-and-pinion gear mechanism

These mechanism are used to convert the rotational motion of the stepper motor into the in-and-out motion required to move the read/write head over the disk surface.

Split Metal Band Mechanism

The split metal band mechanism uses two band made of special steel alloys, to convert the rotation of the stepper motor into the linear motion required to move the head over the disk surface.

One end of the band is coiled on the spindle of the stepper motor and the other end is connected to the head rack.

As the spindle rotates one band uncoils from the spindle and the other band coils around the spindle, making the head rack to move; moving the head with it; in-out on the disk surface.

A metal band mechanism finds a particular information on the disk surface by rotating the stepper motor to move the read/write head to that particular location where data is located.

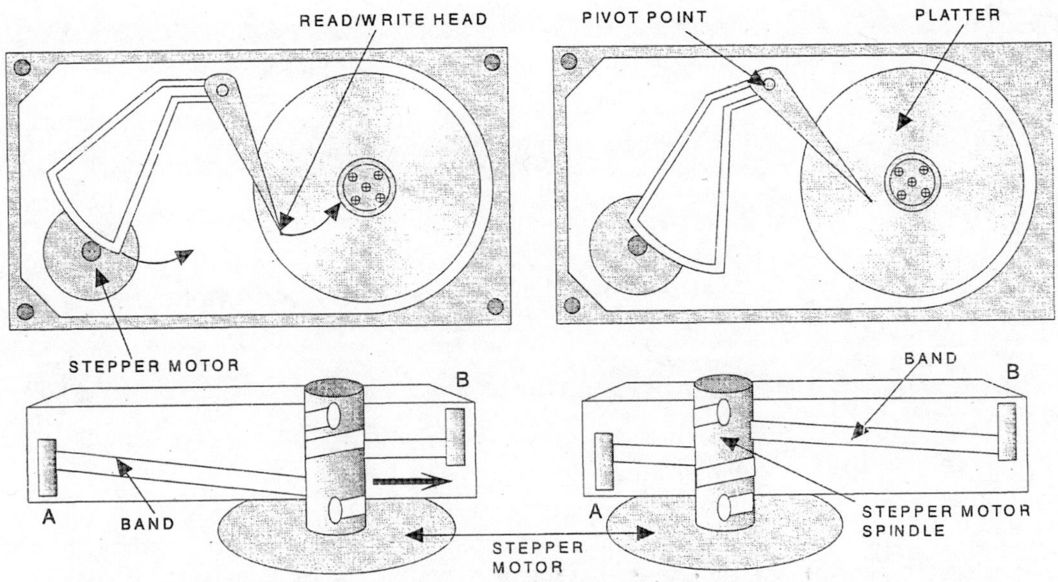

Fig. 10-9 : Split Metal Band Head Actuator Mechanism.

If the data is located on the 50th cylinder, then the stepper motor is rotated by 50 detends, this will move the read/write head to the 50th cylinder, and the head can read information from it.

One problem with this type of system is with time the bands may stretch, and the positioning systems accuracy may reduce.

The change in the head positioning can also occur due to the thermal expansion of the platter, head actuator assembly etc. This is the reason why some hard disks show error when cold and later after keeping on for some time, start working without any trouble.

To solve this problem the stepper band based hard disk drive requires periodic low level formatting. This will write the cylinder/sector address at the new position on platter surface.

Rack-and-Pinion Gear mechanism

Rack-and-pinion gear mechanism used to drive the read/write head is not as common as the Split metal band mechanism.

In this mechanism a pinion gear is provided on the spindle of the stepper motor, as the motor turns it will also rotate the gear. As this pinion gear rotates it moves a rack gear in and out.

The rack gear is connected to the read/write head assembly, so the in and out movement of the rack gear will make the head to move in and out on the disk surface.

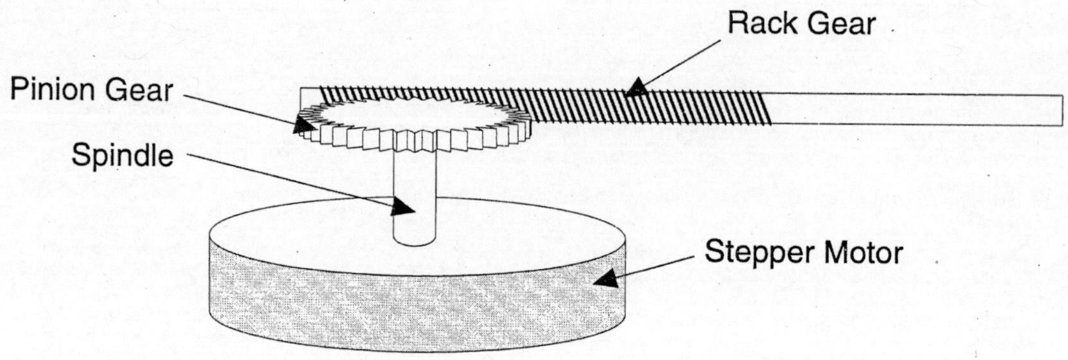

Fig. 10-10 : Rack-and-Pinion Gear Mechanism.

This rack-and-pinion assembly is slightly better than the Split metal band mechanism, because it provides better thermal stability.

One problem with this system is, with time as the gears deteriorate, the wear will increase play in the gears. This will slowly make the complete actuator system useless.

Voice Coil Actuator

Voice coil actuator is used to solve most of the problem associated with the stepper motor head actuator system.

The name "voice coil" is used for this system because the basic principle behind this system is taken from the voice coil used inside a typical audio speaker.

In a voice coil based head actuator mechanism the electromagnetic coil is connected to the head rack and placed near a stationary permanent magnet. There is no direct contact between the magnet and the coil. As the coil is given current, magnetic field will be generated in the coil

This magnetic force will make the coil to move away from or towards the permanent magnet. As the coil moves it will move the read/write head over the disk surface.

This type of system is more efficient and very quick compared to the stepper motor actuators, it is also much quieter.

The voice coils system that uses a rotatory arm to move the read/write head is called the rotary voice coil actuator.

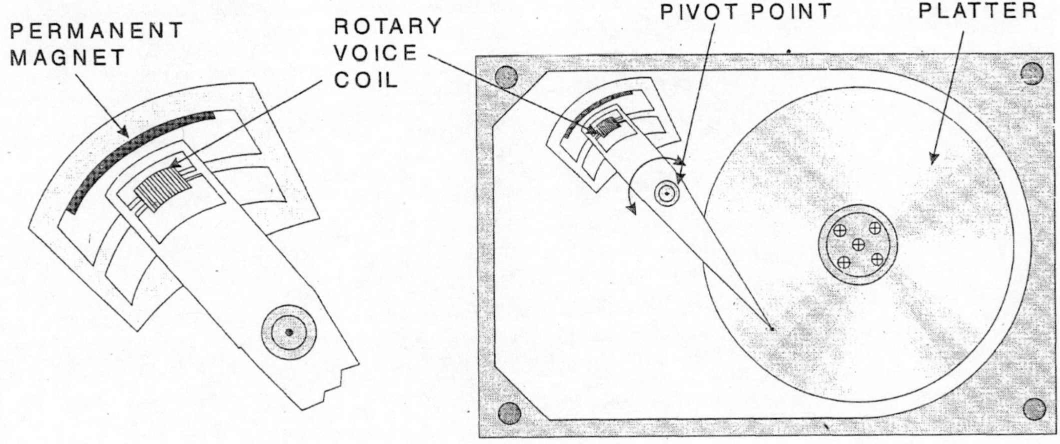

Fig. 10-11 : Voice Coil Actuator.

Head Positioning of a Voice Coil Based System

The voice coil based hard disk drives use a special information previously written on the disk surface to locate any place.

This special index information on the disk surface is called "servo". This servo information is written on the disk surface during the disk manufacturing.

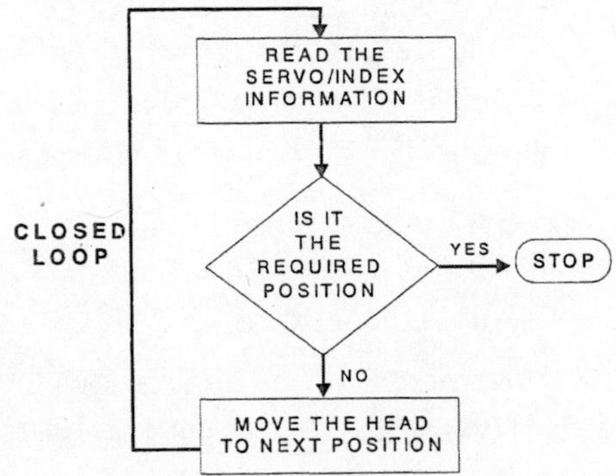

Voice coil actuators use this servo information as an index to accurately move the read/write head to any required location.

This servo based system is often called closed loop, servo controlled system.

It is called a closed system because it works on a closed loop to correctly position the head, the information about the current position of the head is used to move the head to the new position. Again the next position is checked and the head is moved. this process is repeated, as a loop, until the head reaches correct position.

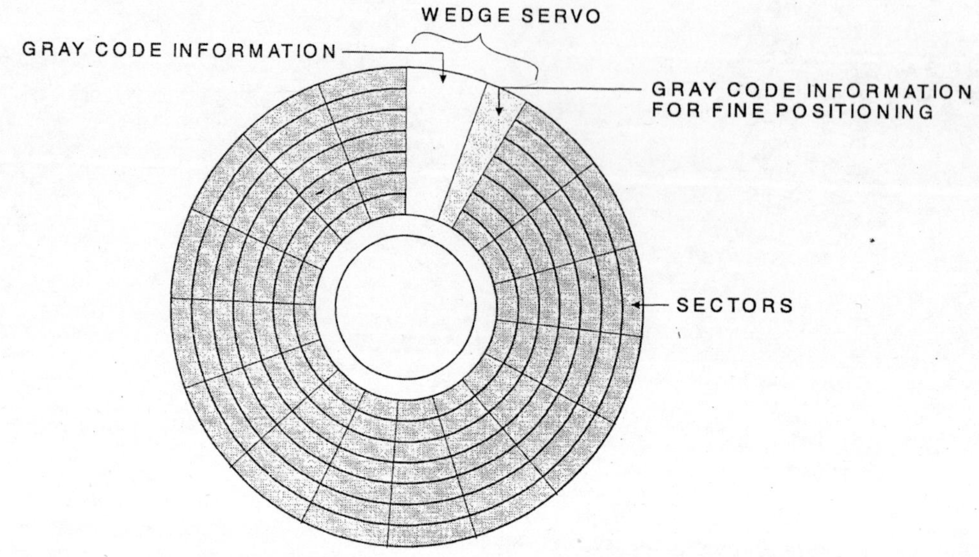

Fig. 10-12 : Wedge Servo.

This type of drives do not require frequent low level formatting to correct the relative position of the information on the disk surface with respect to the head position, as required by the stepper based hard disk drives.

As we have already mentioned the servo information is written on the disk surface during the disk manufacturing itself, there are basically three different types of servo information used to control the voice coil based head positioning system.

They are

- Wedge Servo
- Embedded Servo
- Dedicated Servo

Most people think that a low level formatting of the servo based (especially IDE) drives, destroys the servo information and makes the hard disk unusable.

It is a wrong idea because the disk drive electronic is made in such a way that the servo information cannot be overwritten without using the special Servo-writer.

Wedge Servo

Wedge servo appears in a wedge like shape on the disk surface. In drives using wedge servo, the servo information is written in the pre-index gap, i.e. the gap between the end and beginning of the track.

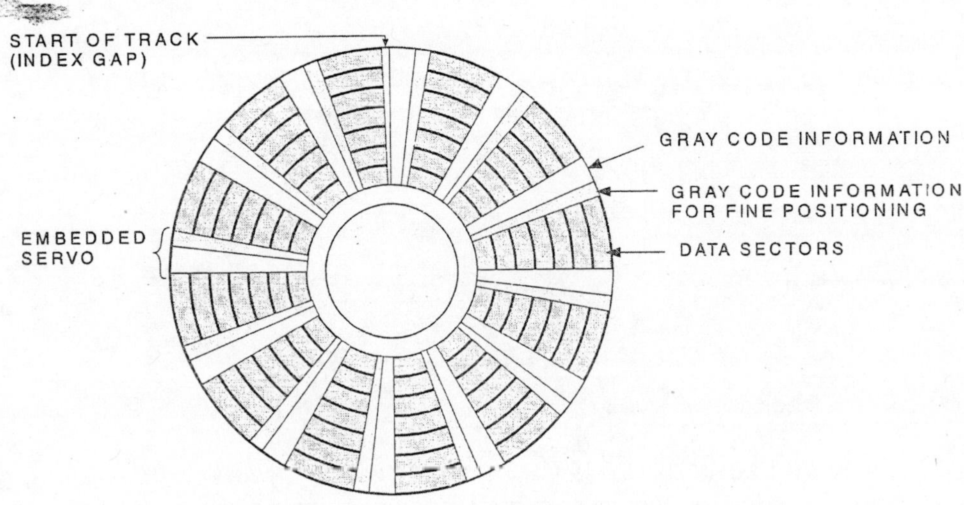

Fig. 10-13 : Embedded Servo.

Most of the controller can be used without any problem with the wedge servo based disk drives, but some controller may require to be specially configured to work with these drives.

One problem with the wedge servo based hard disk drive is the servo information appears only once per rotation. If a head is looking for some information on the hard disk drive, then the drive needs several rotations for the head to properly find the required information. This problem made the hard disk manufacturers to look for a new type of servo design i.e. the embedded servo design.

Embedded Servo

In the embedded servo design the servo information is kept at the beginning of each sector. Whereas, in the normal wedge servo design the servo information was kept at the beginning of the track only.

This design allows the head positioning system to receive the current position many times in a single rotation, this allows the head positioning to be more precise and faster compared to the wedge servo design.

This system gives the positioning information a number of times per rotation of the disk platter, but it would be even better if the servo information is always present to the head positioning circuit, for this dedicated servo design is used.

Dedicated Servo

In the dedicated servo system one side of one platter is exclusively used for the servo information. The name "dedicated" comes from the fact that one side of the platter and one read/write head is completely dedicated for the servo operation, it is not used for any other purpose.

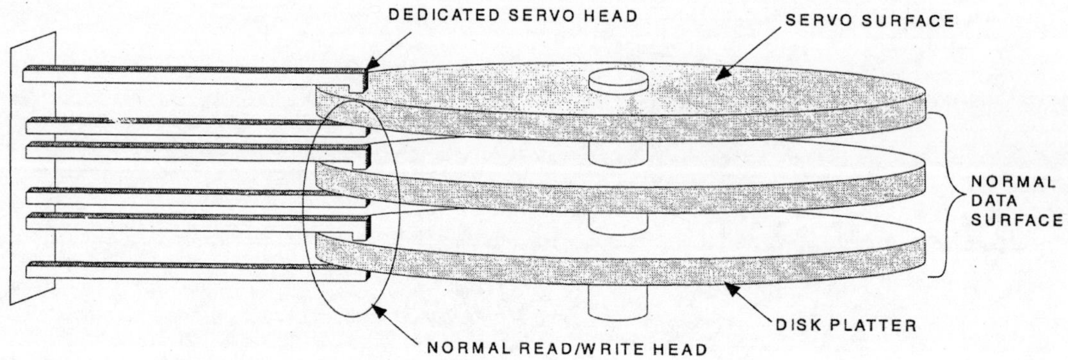

Fig. 10-14 : Dedicated Servo.

As the head on the servo side is not made for normal read/write operation, no low level format program or controller can change or remove the servo information from this platter.

One can recognize the dedicated servo based hard disk by the odd number of read/write heads. As one side of a platter is used for storing servo information, that side is reduced from the actual usable sides, one may find a dedicated servo based hard disk drive with 7, 9, 15 etc. odd number of heads.

Today most of the high capacity, high speed hard disk drives use the dedicated servo design for head positioning, because this design makes the servo information available to the positioning circuit all the time. It allows best positional accuracy at the highest possible speed.

Hard Disk Features

This section covers different characteristics of the hard disk drive, such as the size, capacity, interleave, head skew, cylinder skew, etc.

Most of the characteristics given in this section depends on the hard disk drive, but some of these properties also depend on the hard disk drive controller used to connect the drive to the main computer system.

Form Factor

Drives are available in many different widths and height. The Form Factor is a basic unit of measurement of the size of the drive. Drives with platter width of 5.25 inch and 3.5 inch are called 5.25 inch form factor and 3.5 inch form factor drive.

Storage Capacity

Storage capacity of a hard disk drive can be very confusing thing. For example, you may see a hard disk advertised as having 301MB capacity, with the following characteristic

- 1024 cylinder, 16 heads, 36 sectors and 512 bytes per sector.

On entering these values in the BIOS setup you will find that BIOS is showing the hard disk capacity as 288MB, now where the extra 13MB is gone.

This missing MB is due to the way hard disk storage capacity is specified in different manner by different manufacturers.

A hard disk capacity can be expressed in the following ways

- Unformatted storage capacity in millions of bytes
- Formatted storage capacity in millions of bytes
- Unformatted storage capacity in megabytes
- Formatted storage capacity in megabytes

The difference between millions of byte and megabyte will become clear if we look at the last example once more. As we have said that the hard disk drive is advertised as having 301MB storage capacity. Let use see how this figure is reached.

1024 x 16 x 36 x 512 = 301,989,888 bytes or approximately 301 millions of byte, is the storage capacity of the hard drive. This same 301,989,888 when converted into megabyte by dividing it twice with 1024 will give 288.

Now it may be clear that the manufacturer has mentioned storage capacity in millions of byte in the advertisement and the BIOS has reported the storage capacity in megabyte. Therefore, a 301 Million-Byte drive is also a 288-Megabyte drive.

Industry standard method to indicate the unit of measure is "M" is used to indicate millions of byte, and "Meg" is used to indicate megabyte. The last drives storage capacity can be written as 301M or 288Meg.

Unformatted capacity of the drives is normally 19 percent higher than their formatted capacity, so same hard disks can be advertised as having following capacities

- Formatted Capacity - 301M
- Formatted Capacity - 288Meg
- Unformatted Capacity - 358M
- Unformatted capacity - 343Meg

All the above values are correct, so one must be careful when comparing hard disk by different manufacturer that their actual storage capacity is according to your requirement.

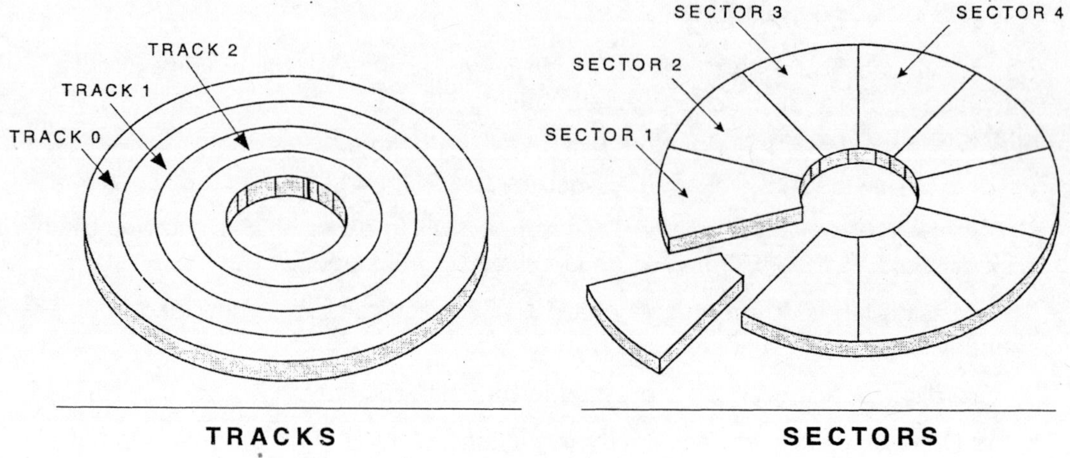

Fig. 10-15 : Tracks and Sectors on a Hard Disk Drive.

Disk Geometry

The hard disk drive stores data as magnetic information on its surface. If the data is stored continuously one next to another, then at the time of retrieval one will have to scan the entire hard disk to find the required data.

To arrange the data properly on the disk surface, the disk surface it divided into different sections called head/side, tracks, sectors, cylinders etc.

When some information is written on the disk surface the computers writes it on some specific side on some specific tracks and sectors. This value of side, track and sectors are saved in an index like place called directory and FAT (File Allocation Table).

When the data is required, the computer looks at the entry in the directory and FAT for the side, track and sector where the data is stored. From this information, computer can get the stored data without any trouble.

Sides or Heads

We have already specified that a hard disk drive can contain many platters, or disks. Each side of these disk can be used for read and write purpose. For example, if a hard disk drive has three platters then the drive will have total six sides.

Each side will have a separate read/write head to read and write information on that side. All these heads are connected to a single head rack, which makes these read/write heads to move together over different parts of the disk drive.

When specifying the head number the first head is specified as head 0, next as head 1 then head 2, head 3 etc.

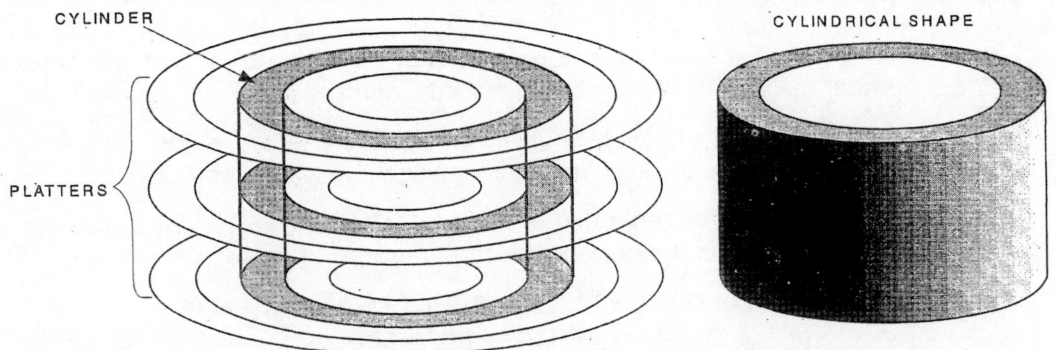

Fig. 10-16 : Cylindrical Shape Made of Same Tracks on Different Platters.

Track

Each side of the hard disk drives platter's surface is divided into concentric circles called tracks. These tracks are not visible marks on the disk surface instead these are magnetic information written during the formatting of the hard disk drive.

The outermost track is given track number 0 and the next track is 1, next track 2 and so on, the innermost track will have the highest number.

Cylinder

On a hard disk drive which has more than one platter, same tracks of different platters form an imaginary cylinder like structure.

When data is stored on the hard disk drive, it is stored cylinder by cylinder, i.e. first all the tracks on a cylinder is written, once the cylinder becomes full the read/write head moves to the next cylinder and writes balance data to the next cylinder.

A track usually refers to one part of the cylinder i.e. track is on one side of the platter whereas, a cylinder is combination of all the tracks having same value.

Sector

A track is a very big area to store the data, normally a track can hold more than 5,000 bytes of data. When one is storing small amount of data then having a minimum storage area with 5,000 byte capacity will be a wastage.

This has led to dividing of the tracks or cylinders into number of sectors. Like a track, the sectors are also not visible on the hard disk surface. During the formatting of the hard disk, the formatting program divides the disk surface into different sector by writing magnetic pattern on the disk surface.

Different capacity of hard disk drive divide the track into different number of sectors.

When it comes to the number of bytes that can be stored in a sector, as a standard, almost all drives store 512 bytes of data per sector.

We saw that the side number or the head number starts with 0, and the track or cylinder number also starts with 0, but the sector number always starts with 1.

If one knows the number of sides, track, and sectors per track value of a hard disk drive then one can easily calculate the total storage capacity of the drive.

Let use see the same drive mentioned previously, it had 6 sides, 1024 tracks and 37 sectors per track. Let us first calculate the total number of sectors

```
Total sectors =  total sides x total tracks per sides
                 x total sectors per track
Total sectors =  6 x 1024 x 37
Total sectors =  227,328
```

We know that the storage capacity of one sector is 512 bytes, so the storage capacity of the 227,328 sectors will be

```
Total storage capacity =     227,328 x 512 bytes
Total storage capacity =     116,391,936 bytes or
                             116.4 M (million byte) or
                             111 Meg (megabyte).
```

Interleave

If the sectors on the hard disk drive are numbered sequentially from 1 to the maximum number of sectors available, then the disk read operation will be very slow.

Let us see why, when the hard disk drive is given an instruction to read the complete track, i.e. sectors 1, 2, 3... . After receiving this instruction, the drive starts reading when the read/write head reaches sector 1.

After reading the sector 1, the drive sends this data to the controller. The controller checks that the data has no errors (its CRC or ECC code is correct). During this, the disk is continuously rotating.

As the disk is continuously spinning during all this process, by the time controller gets the data, checks it for error and pass it to the requested program, the read/write head passes over the 2nd sector.

Now when the read 2nd sector instruction is given to the head, head is siting over the 3rd or 4th sector. To read the 2nd sector the disk will require one complete rotation.

Therefore, if we put the sectors in serial order one after the other then during the read process we will always miss the subsequent sectors. For each subsequent sector, the drive will require an unnecessary complete rotation. This will make the hard disk read process very slow.

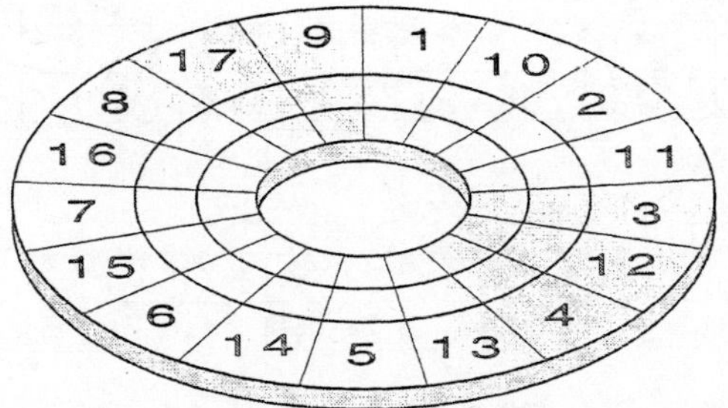

1:2 Interleave

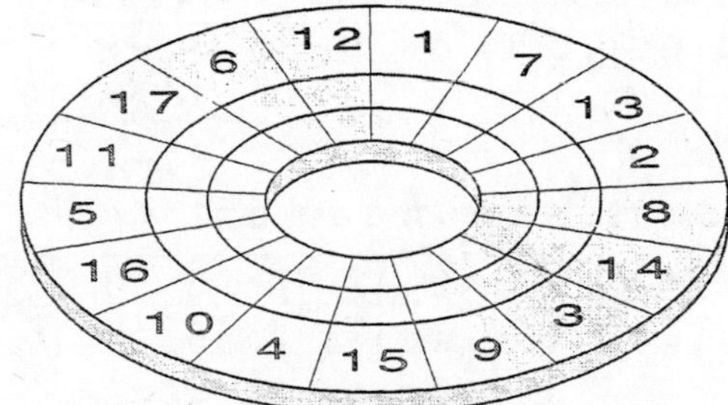

1:3 Interleave

Fig. 10-17 : Sector Number Order with 1:2 and 1:3 Interleave.

A very easy solution to this problem, is to put the 2nd sector at the 3rd or 4th position then the 2nd sector will be at the correct position when the read 2nd sector instruction is received by the read/write head. This will save the unnecessary disk rotation after each sector read.

During the low level formatting of the hard disk drive, one can leave a gap of one or more sectors in between the consecutive sectors to take care of this problem.

Numbering the sectors out of order with leaving a gap of one or more sectors in the sector numbering is called interleaving.

Depending on the speed of the system and the hard disk drive one can follow 1:2 or 1:3 or any other interleave scheme. An interleave of 1:2 means that the next serially numbered sectored is two sectors away from the current sector.

Currently the interleave is not an issue because most of the current system can support the speed required for 1:1 interleave i.e. no interleave and the IDE and SCSI drives, which are most common hard disk types used today, both of them have controller built in the drive itself and can easily support 1:1 interleave.

Skew

In the last section we saw that most of the current hard disk drives and controllers are capable of 1:1 interleave or it can be said that they do not require any interleave.

However, even on these drive and controller combination the head skew and cylinder/track skew is a very important issue. Let us see what is this skew.

Head Skew

When the drive is reading information on the disk surface. It first starts to read the information on the Cylinder 0, Head 0, Sector 1. Next, it reads all the information on the remaining sectors on the same cylinder, until the last sector is reached.

Sector arrangement without head skew

Head 0	1	2	3	4	5	6	7	8	9	10	11	12	13	14	15	16	17
Head 1	1	2	3	4	5	6	7	8	9	10	11	12	13	14	15	16	17

Sector arrangement with 1:1 head skew

Head 0	1	2	3	4	5	6	7	8	9	10	11	12	13	14	15	16	17
Head 1	17	1	2	3	4	5	6	7	8	9	10	11	12	13	14	15	16

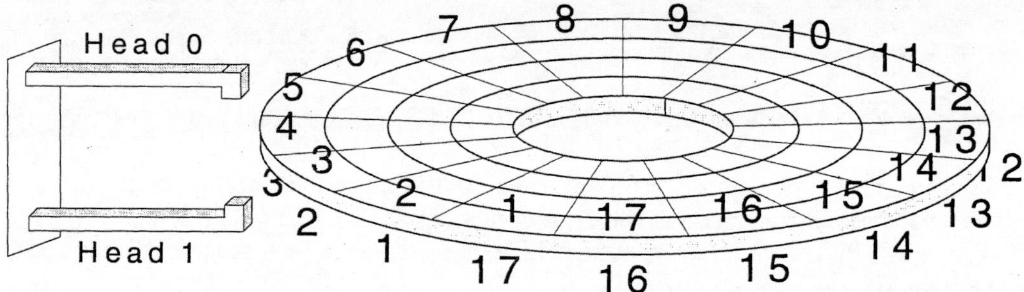

Fig. 10-18 : Sector Arrangement with 0 and 1:1 Head Skew.

Once the last sector of the cylinder is reached, the drive will have two options, one is to read the data from the next cylinder or read the data from same cylinder but under the next head.

To read the data from the next cylinder, drive will need to move the read/write head to the next position, whereas to read data under the next head, only the head need to be switched.

Switching the head is much more faster than moving the head to the next cylinder, so the drive designers have decided that after the drive finishes reading all the sectors from cylinder 0, head 0, the drive must start reading from cylinder 0, head 1, then once all the sectors of the head 1 finishes, it should start reading cylinder 0, head 2 and so on until the data under the last head is read.

After reading the data under the last head, the drive will move to cylinder 1. In cylinder 1 again the drive will start reading all the sectors from cylinder 1, head 0, then cylinder 1, head 1, then cylinder 1, head 2 and so on until the data under the last head is read.

In a normal sector arrangement, without any skewing of the sectors, let us see what happens when the multi-head reading takes place.

As explained above, the read/write head will first reads all the sectors from the head 0 and then the hard disk controller will give a command to the drive to switch to head 1 and continue the reading process.

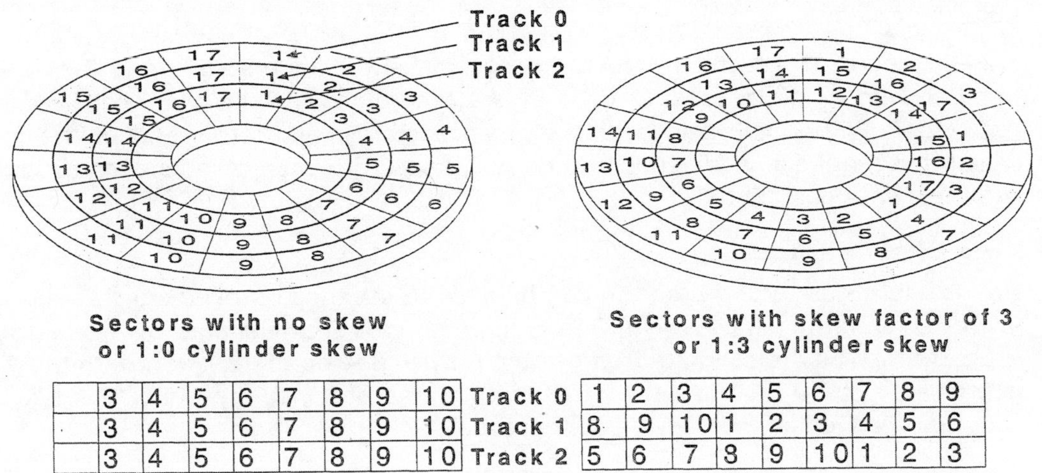

	3	4	5	6	7	8	9	10	Track 0	1	2	3	4	5	6	7	8	9
	3	4	5	6	7	8	9	10	Track 1	8	9	10	1	2	3	4	5	6
	3	4	5	6	7	8	9	10	Track 2	5	6	7	8	9	10	1	2	3

Fig. 10-19 : Sector Arrangement with 0 and 1:3 Cylinder Skew.

In sector arrangement without any skewing, the same numbered sectors are directly under and over each other. After finishing reading of all the sectors from head 0, by the time controller issue command to switch to head 1 and head switching takes place, the sector 1 will pass by the head 1, i.e. by the time head 1 is ready to read, it will be over the sector 2 or 3, but not over the sector 1.

As the sector 1 has passed by the head, the drive will need to wait for one full rotation of the disk, to start reading from sector 1.

This problem will waste one full rotation of the disk with each change of the read/write head. The solution for this problem is head skewing. Head skew is the change or offset in the sector numbering in tracks under adjacent heads of the same cylinder. This head skewing takes care of the delay incurred in head switching when data is read continuous from one head to the next head.

When head skewing is used i.e. when the sectors on the cylinders of the adjacent heads are offset by 1 or more number, continuous read/write operation across the head, without wasting any disk rotation can take place.

Cylinder Skew

Just as a head switching requires some time, the moving of the read/write head from one cylinder to the next also takes some time. In fact, moving of the head from one cylinder to the next cylinder takes more time than the time required for the head switching.

Because of this, the cylinder skew value is always larger than the head skew value.

As explained before, the cylinder skew is an offset in the sector numbering in the two adjacent cylinders.

This shifting of the sector numbers in the adjacent cylinders will bring the sector number 1 under the read write head by the time drive and the controller becomes ready for it. Without this shifting or skewing of sectors in adjacent cylinders, the drive will always require an additional rotation of the disk with each cylinder change during the read/write operation.

Setting Skew Factors

Any low level-formatting program can be used to set these skew factors during the low level formatting of the drive. One such program is Disk Manager by the Ontrack. Program such as the Calibrate from Norton utilities do not directly work with the disk controller, instead they use the BIOS to communicate with the drive, this type of programs cannot set the skew factors properly.

IDE and SCSI drives are low level formatted by the manufacture and set to the optimum skew factors so they do not require any change in these values. Low level formatting of these drives with some new value will actually slow down these drives.

On IDE and SCSI drives using zone bit recording, one cannot change the head and cylinder skew values. On these drives these values are fully protected from the format operation, no formatting can change the skew values on these hard disk drives.

Zone Bit Recording

So far, all the drives we saw had same number of sectors in their outer cylinder as well as in the inner cylinder. If you look at the drive platter then you can easily see that the outer track or cylinder has much more area compared to the inner track of the disk drive.

Using the same number of sectors in the outer as well as inner track of the drive is a waste of the storage capacity of the disk drive. The outer tracks because of its larger circumference can easily hold 50 percent more data compared to the inner tracks.

A new recording method called Zone Bit Recording is used by the current high capacity IDE and SCSI hard disk drives to store more number of sectors in the outer tracks compared to the number of sectors in the inner tracks.

This method is called zone bit recording, because in this method the hard disk platter is divided into a number of different zone, and each zone will have a fixed number of sectors per track. The outermost zone will have maximum number of sectors per track and the innermost zone will have minimum number of sectors per track.

The controller used with the drive using the zone bit recording has one additional job of converting the odd number of sectors per track in different zone into a standard number of sectors per track.

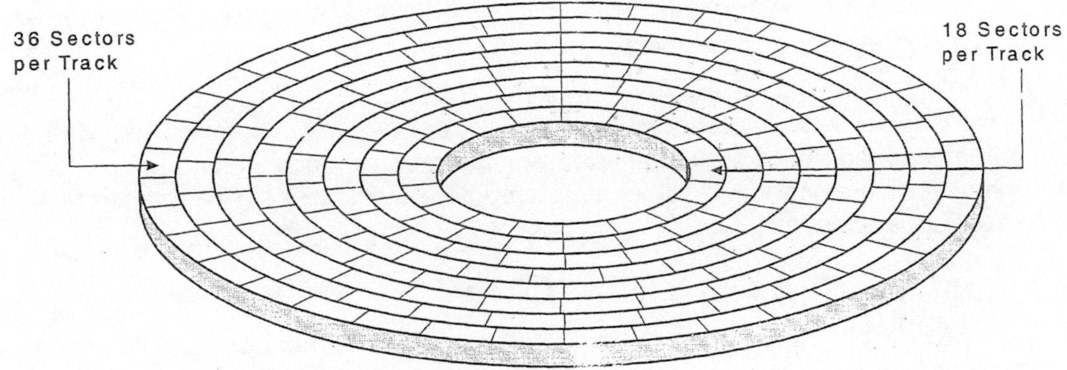

Fig. 10-20 : Normal and Zone Bit Recording.

This is required because the BIOS and the DOS requires that the number of sectors per track be a constant value. The BIOS and DOS can not work with a disk drive having different number of sectors per track, so it is the job of the hard disk controller to translate the different number of sectors on the zone bit recorded hard disk drive's track into a constant number of track. This is called "Sector Translation Scheme".

This recording method is also known as "Multiple Zone Recording".

Disk Geometry Translation

Sector Translation

When the hard disk drive uses zone bit recording, it needs some kind of sector translation method to inform constant number of sectors per track to the BIOS.

Sector translation is also used when the storage capacity of the hard disk drive is very high. Most of the BIOS have a limitation of maximum 1024 cylinders, i.e. one cannot use a hard disk drive with more than 1024 cylinders. However, most of these BIOS allow up to 256 heads per drive.

This has made many manufacturers to specify a hard disk drive with more than 1024 tracks, as drive with less than 1024 track but with more than the actual number of heads. The hard disk controller internally translates this logical track and head value into actual physical track and head value when a disk read/write operation is required.

For example, if a hard disk drive has 2000 cylinder and 4 heads, then this will be treated by BIOS as a hard disk drive with 1000 cylinders with 8 heads. A disk geometry translation scheme will take care that the drive must read data from proper cylinder and head.

It will be the job of the hard disk controller to do this translation from the physical to logical and logical to physical values.

During the setup of the hard disk drive, most of the drive that support the sector translation will accept any drive parameters (track, head etc. number), as long as the total capacity of the specified parameter is equal to the actual capacity of the drive.

Once a parameter is specified and the hard disk drive is formatted with that parameter, then the specified parameter cannot be changed without reformatting of the drive as the operating system has stored data on the disk surface according to the specified parameter.

Logical Block Addressing (LBA)

On the drives using the zone bit recording, because the number of sectors per track are not fixed, one cannot directly convert the head and track values as explained in the "sector translation".

The drives using zone bit recording have variable number of sectors in their different tracks. If one goes through the technical catalog of these drives, one will not find the sectors per track information in them. However, the BIOS or the DOS requires the drive to have a constant number of sectors per track.

This is achieved by some kind of sector translation scheme by the controller on the hard disk drive. The controller will convert the odd disk geometry of the hard disk drive into proper values that the BIOS can use.

Now if the value send by the controller is such that it cannot be used by the BIOS because of higher number of tracks or any other reason then another translation of these values are required.

For example, if you are using a zone bit recorded drive with around 1 GB (Gigabyte) storage capacity and the drives geometry given by the disk controller to the BIOS is 2000 tracks, 16 head, 63 sectors per track.

In this drive the value of the head, sectors per track, can be easily used by the BIOS but the value of the number of track (2000) can not be accepted by most of the BIOS, so the drive and controller together need to do another translation of these translated track, head and sector values.

This second translation of the translated track, head and sector values is called logical block addressing or LBA. The LBA rearranges these track, head and sector values in such a way that the BIOS can use them without any problem.

This drive can be specified as 1000 track, 32 heads, 63 sectors per track hard disk drive. Now these values are acceptable to the BIOS and BIOS will work with the drive without any problem.

Only the controller and the drive need to do two translation of the track, head and sector values send to them. First translation will take care of the logical block addressing and the second translation will convert the fixed sector values into actual variable sector on the disk drive.

Most of the drives automatically takes care of the LBA scheme used by the controller, but some drives require jumper setting to inform them that LBA is being used.

LBA is very useful when you want to use high capacity hard disk drives with high number of tracks.

Reduced Write Current Cylinder

We know that on a normal hard disk drive which is not using the zone bit recording, the size of the inner sectors are smaller than the size of outer sectors.

Even if the size of the inner sector are smaller, they contain same number of data bytes. This makes the storage density of the inner tracks more than the density of the outer tracks,

If electric current used to write data on the inner surface of the hard disk drive is same as the current used to write data on the outer tracks, then the magnetic domain generated by this current will be too large for the given density and they will overlap into each other.

This problem will make the data written on the disk surface unreadable.

To solve this problem on the drives not using zone bit recording, one can specify the reduced write current cylinder. The read/write circuitry of the hard disk drive will reduce the write current when writing on the specified cylinder and all the cylinders that are inside the given cylinder towards the center of the disk drive.

The outer cylinders will be written using the normal write current.

Write Pre-Compensation

Like the reduced write current, the write pre-compensation is also useful for the drives using the standard track, sector format. Drives using the zone bit recording do not require any write precompensation.

We know that the hard disk drive write information on the disk surface by magnetizing the surface of the disk platter. The magnetic particles used to write on the disk surface have north and south poles. It is a known fact that like pole repel each other and opposite poles attract each other.

In the outer surface of the hard disk drive platter, the magnetic particles are far apart to be affected by the attraction and repulsion of the magnetic particles.

In the inner tracks of the disk drive the density of the magnetic particles are very high and adjacent particles start to attract or repel each other. This attraction and repulsion force will change the information written on the disk.

To compensate for this shift of the data particles due to the attraction and repulsion, the drive can write the data further apart or closer than the required position.

The particles will slowly shift to the required position because of the attraction and repulsion between them. This process of writing the data closer or farther to compensate for the attraction and repulsion of the magnetic particles is called write precompensation.

The cylinder from which this pre-compensation is started is called write pre-compensation cylinder. All the cylinders that are towards the center of the drive, starting from the specified cylinder the pre-compensation value will be used during the writing of the data particles.

Seek Time

To read any data on the hard disk drive first the read/write head needs to be moved to the required cylinder. Once the head reaches the required cylinder, the disk is rotated until the required data reach under the read/write head. After this, the drive starts reading the data.

The time required to move the read/write head to the required cylinder is known as seek time. Because the drive contains a number of cylinders, a seek from track 0 to track 100 will take much more time compared to a seek from track 0 to track 10. This makes the hard disk manufacturers to use a "Average Seek Time" in their comparative statements.

This seek time is measured in ms (milli seconds). Hard disk drives with 10ms to 100ms average seek time is available in the market.

Rotational Latency Period

The rotational latency period is the time required for the required data to rotate under the read/write head, after the read/write head is moved to the required cylinder.

Like the seek timing the latency period is also calculated as average rotational latency period. This is done because after the seek, if the head is just over the required data then no rotational delay would occur, but if the required data has just passed under the head then the head will need to wait for the data to make a full rotation and come under the head.

The "average rotational latency period" is calculated by finding out the time required for the drive to make half revolution.

If a hard disk drive rotates at the speed of 7200 Rotations Per Minute (RPM) then one rotation will take 1/7200 of a minute or 60/7200 of a second.

This speed of 60/7200 seconds is for one rotation, the half rotation will require only half of this time i.e. 4.166 milli second (ms).

Access Time

Access time is the total time required by a hard disk drive to find the requested data or we can say that the access time is the time required by the hard disk drive to move the read/write head to the requested data after a read or write command is received from the CPU/Controller.

Access time is the total of seek time and the rotational latency period.

```
Access Time = Seek Time + Rotational Latency Period.
```

This time is also measured in milliseconds (ms), initial hard disk drives had an average access time of 40 ms but currently most of the drives have 15 ms or better access time. Some of the faster SCSI drives can provide 10 ms or better access time.

One requires a faster access speed hard disk drive to read/write data faster, but the overall performance of the drive will also depend on the data transfer rate of the drive/controller combination being used.

Data Transfer Rate

Data transfer rate is the most important figure that one should consider when comparing two different hard disk drive systems. But most of the time this figure is not given in the hard disk drive advertisements because the data transfer rate does not depend only on the hard disk drive, it also depends on the configuration of the system, the controller being used etc.

The transfer rate is measured in megabytes per second or kilobytes per second. Initial drives were able to provide a data transfer speed less than 1 megabytes per second, the current high speed SCSI drives can provide 10 megabytes per second or more data transfer speed.

Currently fast ATA-2 types of hard disk drives have very high data transfer speed. Newer versions of the Fast-Wide SCSI specification supports data transfer rate of 40 megabytes per seconds.

Buffer Size

Many of the hard disk drives provide some kind of data buffer in them. This buffer works somewhat like the external cache memory being used to improve the performance of the hard disk drive.

Most of the time this buffer memory is a part of the drive controller. This buffer memory is used to temporarily store the data being read, before sending the data to the CPU. The main reason of use of this buffer is the speed difference between the CPU and the hard disk drive.

Current generation of hard disk drives contain 2GB to 8GB cache memory.

One can use external software based disk cache to improve drive's performance.

Head Parking

The read/write head of the hard disk drive floats on an air cushion during the normal operation of the drive. When the drive is stopped, the rotation of the platter will slow, this will make the airflow to slowly deplete and the head will move downwards and land on the disk surface.

By the time platter completely stops, the read/write head will skid many linear feet distance on the disk platter surface.

This same process is again repeated when the drive is switched on, the read/write head will again skid on the disk surface for many rotations of the platter, until proper rotation speed is achieved and the air cushion forms to lift the head from the disk surface.

This skidding of the head on the disk surface takes place on whichever track the head was, when the drive was switched on/off. This skidding of the head on the disk surface could damage the disk surface and the data stored on the disk.

This problem has lead to moving of the read/write head to some safe area on the disk surface before switching off the drive.

Most of the time the innermost track of the drive is not used for any data storage and the head is moved to this track before the drive is switched off.

This process of moving of the read/write head to some safe area is called "parking the head" or "head parking". This head parking is done with the help of some program that move the head to the safe area.

Older drive required special software to move the read/write head to the safe area before switching off the system, current generation of hard disk drives have "Automatic-park-and-lock" function.

This function automatically moves the read/write head to a safe area when the power supply to these drives is switched off. Also, in case of some impact or shock, a latch prevents the head from moving out from this parking zone.

The area where the read/write head is moved for parking is called "Landing Zone". In most of the drives this area is on the innermost cylinder of the drive.

Hard Disk Drive Interfacing

This section deals with the interfacing of the hard disk drive with the main computer system. This interfacing can be studied from two different point of view, one is hardware interfacing which deals with the controller card, cable, connector etc. used to connect the hard disk drive to the main computer system and the other is software interfacing which deals with the way different software interact with the hard disk drive.

In this section, we look into the hardware aspect of the interfacing.

To connect a hard disk drive to the computer system, first a hard disk drive controller is connected to the I/O bus or I/O slot on the motherboard and later the hard disk drive is connected to this controller card.

Most of the new drives have the controller built in the drive itself so they do not require a controller to connect them to the main system, but they require some kind of interface to connect the drive to the I/O bus on the motherboard.

Currently, most of the motherboard contain the interface required to connect hard disk drive directly to them. In this type of system, one can connect the cable from the hard disk drive directly to the connector provided on the motherboard.

In this section, we will look at the IDE interface, used to connect a hard disk drive to the motherboard. IDE interface is called system level interface, as it contains the controller circuit in the drive itself.

Some other interface available to connect a hard disk drive to the computer system are:

- ST-506/412
- ESDI
- EIDE
- SCSI

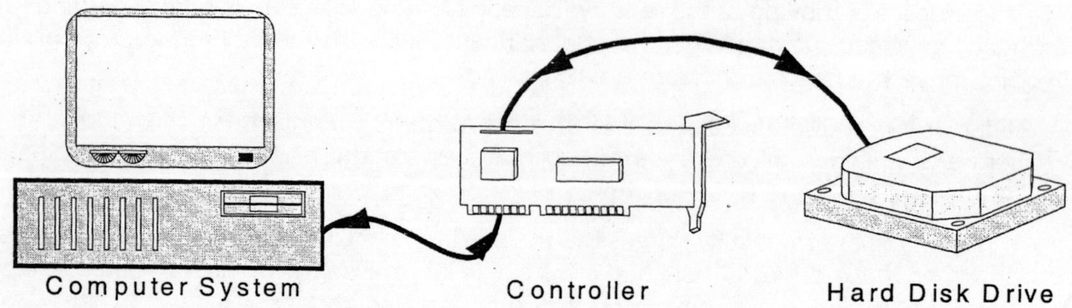

Fig. 10-21 : Host Computer and Hard Disk Drive Interfacing.

IDE

IDE or Integrated Drive Electronics stands for any drive that has controller integrated (built) with the drive. Around 1986, Compaq (computer manufacturer) wanted to improve the ST-506/412 drive used in their system, for this they approached a hard disk drive manufacturer company called Western Digital (WD).

Together they realized that one of the biggest problem with the ST-506/412 interface was its controller being away from the drive. As the distance between the controller and the drive increased, chance of data corruption increased.

This has lead the WD to put the controller directly on the drives, removing the need for using long cables to connect them. This design made the complete system more reliable, allowing IDE drive manufacturer's to put 30 or more sectors per track on these drives.

Another advantage because of putting the controller and the drive in one unit is reduced cost, these IDE drives cost much less than separate drive controller combination.

As the controller is embedded on these drives, the IDE drive is sometimes also known as "embedded controller drive".

Because the controller is on the drive itself, IDE drive/controller combination could be directly connected to the I/O bus slot on the motherboard.

Currently most of the motherboards come with connector for IDE drives, one can directly connect the IDE drive to this connector using a 40-wire cable.

The motherboard supporting the IDE connector does not contain any hard disk controller circuit, the controller is on the drive itself, the connector on the motherboard only provides a connection to connect the hard disk drive to the I/O bus of the computer.

There are basically three different IDE interface in use, their specification is based on the type of the system bus for which they are made, the interfaces are:

Signal	Pin	Pin	Signal
Drive Reset	1	2	Ground
Data Bit 7	3	4	Data Bit 8
Data Bit 6	5	6	Data Bit 9
Data Bit 5	7	8	Data Bit 10
Data Bit 4	9	10	Data Bit 11
Data Bit 3	11	12	Data Bit 12
Data Bit 2	13	14	Data Bit 13
Data Bit 1	15	16	Data Bit 14
Data Bit 0	17	18	Data Bit 15
Ground	19	20	Key (Pin Removed)
DMA Request	21	22	Ground
I/O Write	23	24	Ground
I/O Read	25	26	Ground
I/O Channel Ready	27	28	Spindle Sync/Cable Select
DMA Acknowledge	29	30	Ground
Interrupt Request	31	32	16 bit I/O
Drive Address Bus 1	33	34	Passed Diagnostic
Drive Address Bus 0	35	36	Drive Address Bus 2
Drive Chip Select 0	37	38	Drive Chip Select 1
Drive Active/ Slave Present	39	40	Ground

Fig. 10-22 : ATA-IDE Connector Pin Configuration.

- AT Attachment IDE also known as ATA IDE (16 bit) Works with 16 bit ISA and EISA buses
- XT IDE (8 bit) Works with 8 bit XT class ISA bus
- MCA IDE (16 bit, Micro channel architecture based) Works with MCA based systems

ATA IDE

ATA IDE is the default IDE drive, if someone talks about IDE drive, without specifying the drive type, then most probably he is referring to the ATA IDE drive.

The ATA IDE interface was based on the WD1003 controller used by the original IBM AT systems. This made the BIOS provided on the AT systems to support the ATA IDE drives without any problem.

Other then the basic functions provided by the system BIOS such as seek, read, write etc. the IDE interface provides many new commands to improve the capability of this interface.

Only the ATA IDE interface was standardized, the other XT IDE and MCA IDE was never standardized.

ATA Cable/Connector

ATA IDE interface use 40-pin pin-connector (also called header type connector). Pin 20 of this connector is removed and corresponding pin is plugged on the cable connector to prevent reverse connection.

A 40-line, ribbon cable no longer than 18 inch is used to carry the signal from IDE drive/controller unit to the connector on the motherboard.

Let use see different signals present on these connectors.

Drive Reset (pin 1)

This signal causes the drive to return to its power on state. This signal is used to initialize the hard disk drive when the system is switched on. Activating this signal during any activity will cancel that activity and return the drive to power on state.

Ground (pin 2, 19, 22, 24, 26, 30, 40)

These ground pins are scattered among the signal pins to give some isolation to the signals from each other.

Data (pin 3 - 18)

Sixteen pins, pin number 3 to 18 are used to carry 16 bit data from the drive to the system and system to the drives. Odd numbered eight pins of this sequence can be used for 8-bit data transfer.

Key Pin (pin 20)

This pin is used as key pin for proper cable orientation. On the connector, this pin is removed and on the cable, the hole for pin 20 is plugged off. This prevents reverse insertion of the cable on the connector.

DMA Request (pin 21) & DMA Acknowledge (pin 29)

Normally ATA IDE interface transfer data in 16 bits, but this interface also allows DMA data transfer method.

During the DMA read this pin is used by the drive to inform to the host computer that it is ready to transfer data in DMA mode. The computer acknowledge that it is ready to accept data using the DMA Acknowledge signal on pin 29.

If the host computer cannot accept all the data at once, then it removes the DMA Acknowledge signal until it is ready to accept more.

In the DMA write the host PC uses pin 29 DMA Acknowledge to inform to the drive that data is available, and the drive uses DMA Request pin 21 as handshaking signal to control the flow of data.

During the DMA operation the I/O read/write signal is used to indicate in which direction the data should flow, it should be read or written.

I/O Write (pin 23) & I/O Read (pin 25)

During the data transfer the falling edge of the i/o write signal on pin 23 is used to indicate that the data on the bus can be written on the disk and the falling edge of the i/o read signal on pin 25 indicates to the host computer that the data bus contains valid data after a disk read operation.

I/O Channel Ready (pin 27)

This signal is used by the disk drive to inform to the host computer that the drive is not ready to transfer data, i.e. it cannot read or write.

Normally this signal is high, the drive makes it low when the drive is not ready for a data transfer request.

Spindle Sync/Cable Select (pin 28)

This signal is used to make the hard disk drive spindle spin synchronously when the drive is being used in a drive array. This signal is also used to make the drive to be identified as master or slave using the cable, instead of using the jumper on the drive. The use of this pin is decided by the manufacturer during the installation.

In the spindle synchronization mode the master drive generates a periodic pulse and the slave drive use this pulse to lock its spin with the master drive.

In the Cable Select mode supplying a ground to the pin-28 make the drive to act as a master (drive 0) and leaving the connection open makes the drive act as a slave drive (drive 1).

This master/slave arrangement requires special cable arrangement. This is normally achieved using a "Y" cable arrangement, where the IDE bus connector is put in the middle and the drives are put on each end of the cable.

The drive which is master will have the CSEL line (line 28) connected and the drive which is slave will have the CSEL line (line 28) open, by removing the conductor wire or making some cut in the conductor.

Interrupt Request (pin 31)

This line is used by the ATA IDE drive to get immediate attention of the processor on host computer.

The use of this line depends on the data transfer mode being used. In programmed transfer mode, this line is used at the beginning of each block of data to be transferred to interrupt the processor. In the DMA transfer mode, this interrupt is used to inform about the end of the DMA operation.

16 Bit I/O (pin 32)

This signal is used to inform whether the read and write operation is of 8 bit data or 16 bit data. A high value on this line indicates 16-bit data transfer.

Drive Address Bus 0, 1, 2 (pin 35, 33, 36) & Chip Select Signal 0, 1 (pin 37, 38)

These lines are used to select a particular register from the two groups of registers. The resisters on the interface are divided into two groups, Control Block Registers and Command Block Registers.

The chip select signal is used to select a particular group of register. When the signal on the chip select 0 is activated it selects Control Block Register, when the signal on the chip select 1 is activated it selects the Command Block Registers.

The chip select signal along with the I/O write signal (pin 23) is used to select a register for the read or write operation. When the I/O write signal is high the register that accept data/command from the host computer is active, when the I/O read signal (pin 25) is high, the register that indicates drive status is selected.

Once a register is selected, its content is available on the data bus.

Once the control block register or command block register is selected using the chip select 0 and 1 line, Drive address bus 0 to 3 are used to select a particular register from these block of registers.

The ATA IDE interface has three control block registers (two read and one write) and fourteen-command block registers (seven read and seven write).

Write command block registers are used to select active drive, head, track, starting sector and number of sectors for read or write operation, the read command block register are used to know which drive, head, track, sector are being scanned, these registers also provide status and error information during a drive operation.

In ATA IDE interface the number of bit allocated for head, track and sectors per track puts a limit of 16 head, 65,536 track, 256 sectors per track on any drive. A drive with these values and 512 bytes per sector storage capacity can store up to 128 GB (Gigabyte) of data. However, because the BIOS in most of the PC are incapable to handle more than 1024 track, the maximum storage of an ATA IDE drive is limited to two GB (Gigabyte).

Passed Diagnostic (pin 34)

This Passed Diagnostic line is used by the slave drive to indicate to its host that the drive is running a diagnostic routine.

The word "passed" in the "passed diagnostic" does not mean that the slave drive has successfully passed the diagnostic test, rather it refer to the diagnostic results being passed to the host computer system.

The instruction to execute diagnostic routine and the result after the diagnostic are passed through the register of ATA interface.

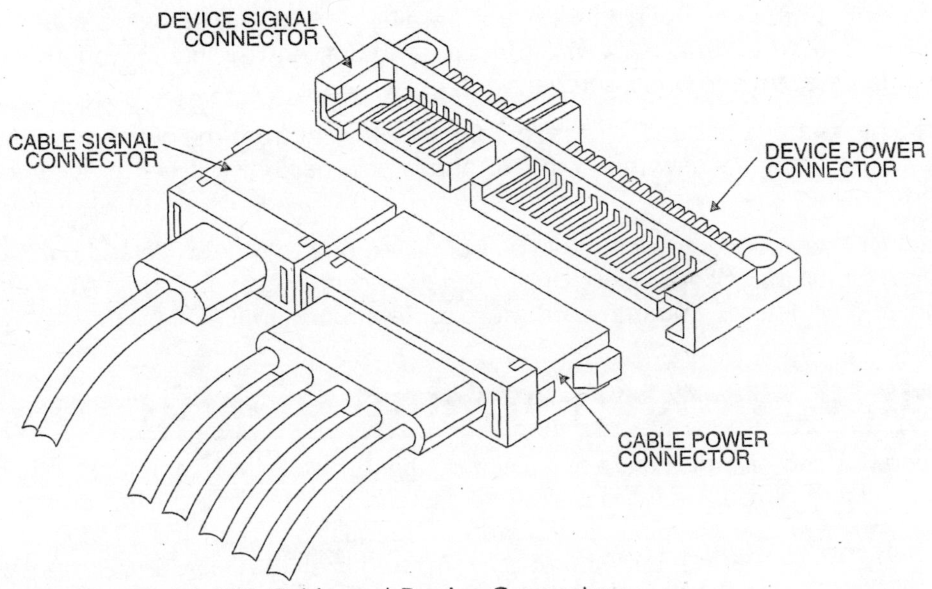

Fig. 10-23 : Serial ATA Cable and Device Connectors.

Drive Active/Slave Present (pin 39)

This is a dual-purpose time multiplexed signal, during the power on initialization process this line is used to indicate whether a slave drive is present. Once the initialization is over this line is used by the drive to indicate that it is active.

Serial ATA

ATA is an old interface, after the introduction of ATA, its designers have tried various tricks to make it faster/better with each new faster/better hard disk drives. Today's ATA interface is around 25 times faster than the first ATA.

But, this improvements cannot continue as the ATA is reaching its limit. So, Intel, with several drive manufacturers have announced a new ATA interface standard known as "Serial ATA" or SATA.

As the name suggests this new ATA interface is a serial interface. Current ATA is parallel interface, it uses 16 data channels at a time. Serial ATA will use only one data channel, but it will operate at a very high speed, to provide better throughput than the parallel ATA interface.

Initial specification for serial ATA talks about 150MBps transfer rate, which is only 10 percent better than the current top speed of parallel ATA interface.

But, there is very little chance of parallel ATA speed getting doubled, whereas the serial ATA speed could be increased to 300MBps and 600MBps in the near future.

Serial ATA is fully compatible with the parallel ATA at the software level, a drive connected to the serial ATA will function without any problem with the current operating system and other software.

At the hardware level serial ATA is completely different from the old parallel interface, one would require a new motherboard and a new hard disk drive to use serial ATA interface.

Serial ATA device requires only two pair of wires, one to the device and one from the device, for full duplex operation. Only one device connects to one serial ATA port, so to connect four devices, motherboard must contain four serial ATA ports.

Logical Working of Hard Disk Drive

A good working hard disk drive and a compatible controller will complete the hardware or machinery part of the hard disk drive system, but to make this hardware system work you require the support of software. The most basic software required for this job is the BIOS (Basic Input Output System) and the OS (Operating System).

Without proper support from BIOS and the OS one will not be able to use a hard disk drive with the computer system.

What is OS?

The hard disk drive controller is a hardware interface between the computer and the hard disk drive and the OS is a software interface between the user and the computer.

The OS or the Operating System is a set of software that acts as an interface between the hardware or the machinery part of the computer and the user program. Some of the job of the OS is to manage the computer's memory efficiently, read the keyboard, display information on the screen, manage the disk read and write operation etc.

It is the job of the OS to take care of how the data is stored in different storage devices such as hard disk drive, floppy disk drive etc., OS also takes care of what type of disk format should be used to write the data.

An operating system gives a common platform to all the programs, so that the data stored by one program can be read by any other program on the same operating system.

An operating system also give the tool to copy a file, delete those files that are no longer required, format a disk to make it usable with the DOS, display or print a file etc.

An OS or Operating System does not directly talk to the hardware or the devices connected to your computer, there is one more layer of program called BIOS between the OS and the hardware.

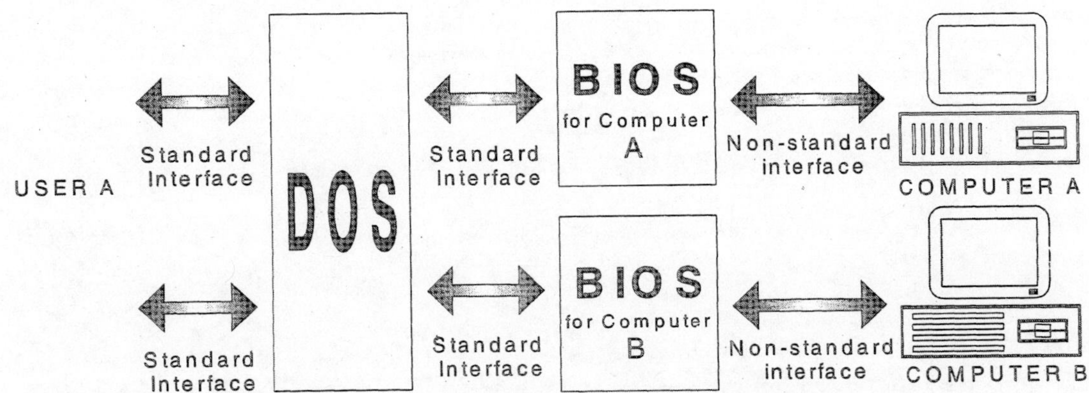

Fig. 10-24 : OS and BIOS as an Interface Between Computer and User.

What is BIOS?

BIOS or the "Basic Input Output System" is a program or firmware (software on a ROM-Read Only Memory chip) on the motherboard or the main board of the computer.

Main job of this BIOS program is to provide a standard interface between the hardware or the devices connected to the computer (keyboard, monitor, hard disk drive etc.) and the OS.

Any instruction given by the user program, first goes to the OS, OS sends this to the BIOS and BIOS gets the work done by the computer. The result is send by the BIOS to the OS and OS gives the result to the user program.

OS and BIOS talk with each other using something called an interrupt and the BIOS talks with the computer using these same interrupts.

Track and Sector

A technical understanding of the way OS maintains information on the hard disks will be useful to understand the general principle behind the hard disk storage.

To read/write any information on the disk and to allow all programs to use a standard disk interface, OS uses a fixed disk format.

From the OS point of view, data on the hard disks is arranged in tracks and sectors. Tracks are narrow concentric circles that go around the disk and sectors are pie-shaped slices of the disk.

Tracks are sometimes called cylinder, because when a tracks of different platters are kept together they form a cylinder like shape.

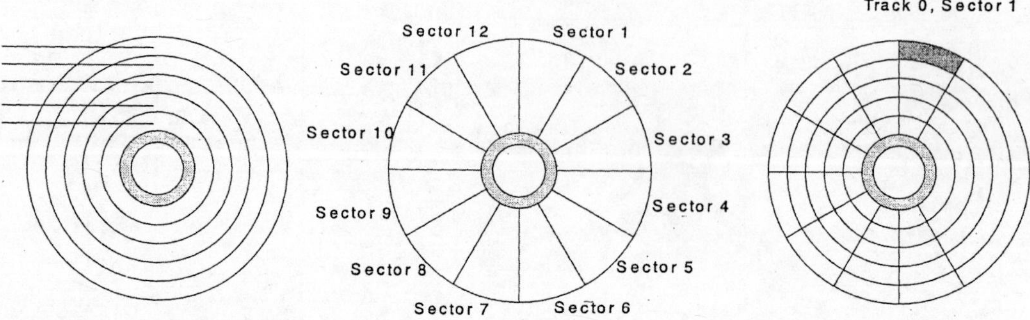

Fig. 10-25 : Tracks and Sectors.

Format of Disk

A new hard disk can be used for various operating systems, provided they are appropriately formatted. Formatting is the process of preparing the blank hard disk for a particular operating system.

Formatting a hard disk puts special magnetic marks of tracks and sectors, on the hard disk surface. When a new hard disk is bought, it is just like a plain sheet of paper with no information. By formatting the disk, OS adds the track and sector information to the disk surface, these are magnetic information written on the disk media, one cannot see it on the disk surface.

Formatting a new disk is like adding lines on a blank paper so that you will be able to properly write on it.

Different operating systems format the disk in different ways, this is the reason a hard disk formatted for an Apple machine cannot be read by an IBM machine.

One thing you should remember about the track/sector number is the first track or the cylinder number is always taken as 0, whereas the first sector number is always taken as 1.

When a disk is formatted, other than writing track and sector address, formatting also puts some information that OS needs to maintain the data storage on the disk. Such as directory, FAT etc.

Cluster

When OS writes some information on the hard disk, it does not allocate the space sector wise, instead it uses a new unit of storage called "cluster".

Clusters are the minimum space allocated by the DOS when storing any information on the disk. Even to store only one byte long information on the disk requires minimum one cluster area on the disk surface. If one cluster can store 512 bytes of information then to store 513 bytes you will require two clusters.

A cluster can be made of one or more sectors, it depends on the disk type being used. As a cluster can be made of more than one sector, using clusters as the allocation unit reduce the size of the File Allocation Table (FAT) that DOS uses to keep track of the used and empty disk space.

We have already told you that cylinder or track number starts from 0 and the first sector number is always taken as 1, one more thing you should remember is that the first cluster number is always taken as 2.

Clusters are used to allocate the storage area for the data area only, FAT and directory areas are not allocates according to the cluster size.

Default Cluster Sizes for different Volumes sizes

Volume size	FAT16 cluster	FAT32 cluster	NTFS cluster
7 MB–16 MB	2 KB	Not supported	512 bytes
17 MB–32 MB	512 bytes	Not supported	512 bytes
33 MB–64 MB	1 KB	512 bytes	512 bytes
65 MB–128 MB	2 KB	1 KB	512 bytes
129 MB–256 MB	4 KB	2 KB	512 bytes
257 MB–512 MB	8 KB	4 KB	512 bytes
513 MB–1,024 MB	16 KB	4 KB	1 KB
1,025 MB–2 GB	32 KB	4 KB	2 KB
2 GB–4 GB	64 KB	4 KB	4 KB
4 GB–8 GB	Not supported	4 KB	4 KB
8 GB–16 GB	Not supported	8 KB	4 KB
16 GB–32 GB	Not supported	16 KB	4 KB
32 GB–2 TB	Not supported	Not supported	4 KB

Absolute Sector & Relative Sector

Unlike the sector number used in a floppy disk drive, on a hard disk drive, two different sector numbers are used. One of them is called "absolute sector number", which is the real physical sector number and the other is called "relative sector number", this is the sector number used by OS.

Absolute sector number is specified as three-dimensional address, by specifying side or head number, cylinder number and the sector number to be accessed. Whereas the relative sector number is specified as a single dimensional value by just specifying the

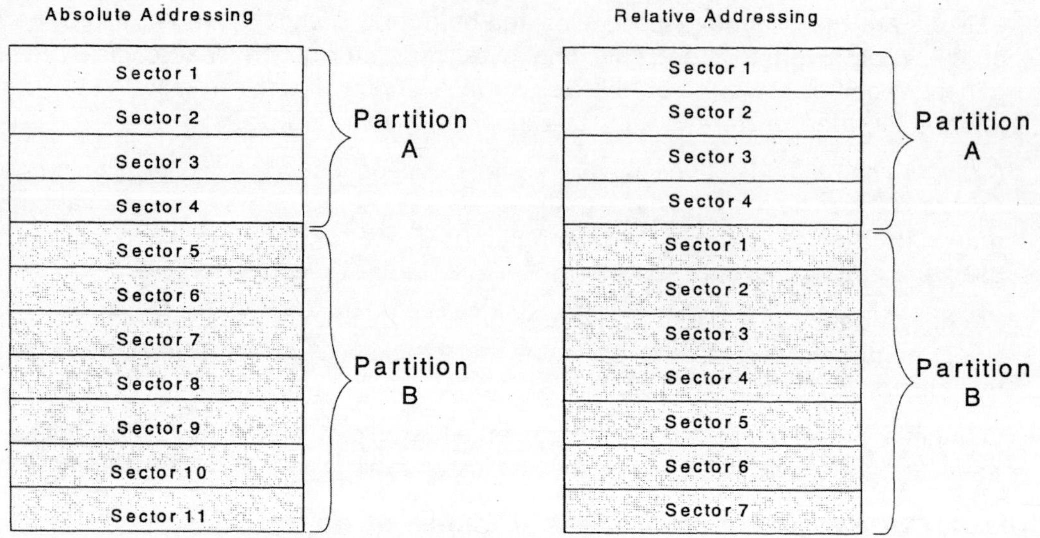

Fig. 10-26 : Absolute Sector and Relative Sector.

sector number. It will be the job of the BIOS to convert this single dimensional sector number specified by the OS into real three-dimensional address.

The relative sector address is called relative, because in relative addressing, the sector number 1 is not taken from the beginning of the hard disk drive, instead it is taken relative to the beginning of different partitions on the hard disk drive.

Partition

Partitioning is a new concept introduced by IBM when they launched the 10MB hard disk drives. At that time the 10MB hard disk was considered very big storage area and they decided to use it for two different operating systems, DOS and XENIX, by dividing the drive into two logical parts or volumes. One part devoted for each operating system. Partition is also known as volume.

This partitioning was necessary because the DOS and XENIX operating system used different file formats and both operating systems could not coexist on a single drive.

The partitioning of hard disk is required even if the hard disk is to be used as a single volume disk or for a single operating system.

DOS/Window program FDISK.EXE is used to partition a hard disk drive. One should not experiment with this command because any change in existing partition will destroy the data stored on the hard disk drive.

One problem with big size partition is wastage of space, let us see how this happens. The following table shows cluster size for different size hard disk drives.

Size of Logical Drive (in MB)	Cluster Size (in KB)
0 - 15	4
16 - 127	2
128 - 255	4
256 - 511	8
512 - 1023	16
1024 - 2047	32
2048 - 4095	64

As you can see in the above table, if you have a 100MB partition then the cluster (i.e. the minimum allocation size) will be only 2K, whereas if the partition size is 4000MB then the cluster size will be 64KB.

In these two partitions if you store a lot of small size files i.e. file that are less than 2K, then on the first partition each of them will occupy 2K of hard disk space but on the 4000MB partition each less than 2K file will require 64KB.

Let us see the storage area wasted on both the partitions after you store 500 files each having size less than 2K.

On 100MB partition 500 files will require

```
500 x 2K = 1000Kbyte = around 1MB of space
```

The same 500 files on 4000MB partition will require

```
500 x 64K (minimum cluster size) = 32000KB = around 32MB of space
```

So, you can see, having large size partition requires about 32 times more space for storing same files, compared to having smaller size partitions.

The information about number of partition, their size, starting and ending sector etc. are stored at the beginning of the hard disk drive, before start of any partition. This area is called Master Boot Record (MBR) or Partition Table record area.

Logical Structure of a Hard Disk Drive

Next section explains various parts of the logical structure of a hard disk drive. It is the job of the DOS FDISK and FORMAT command to create these logical areas on the disk drive.

FDISK command creates Master Boot Record (MBR) and FORMAT command creates DOS Boot Record (DBR), FAT area, Root Directory area and the empty data area.

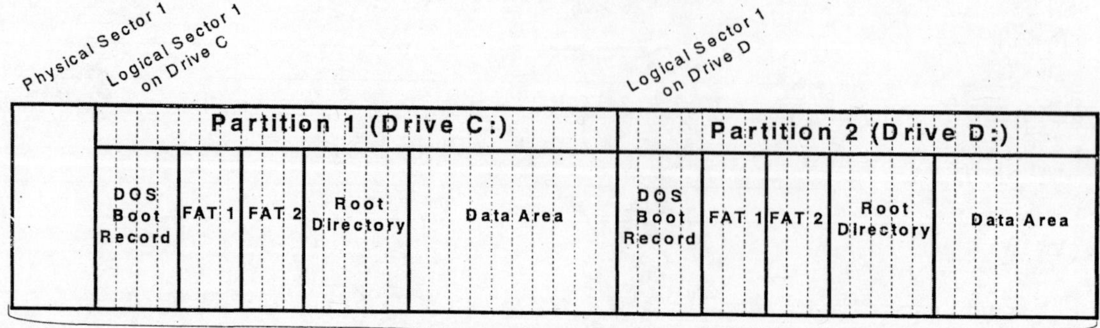

Fig. 10-27 : Logical Structure of Hard Disk Drive.

Master Boot Record (MBR) / Partition Table Record

The MBR or Master Boot Record contains a small program to load and start the active/bootable partition. This area also contains information about all four primary partitions on the hard disk drive, their starting sector, ending sector, size etc. in a format known as "partition table record".

The master boot record is always located at the cylinder 0, head 0 sector 1 and the partition boot sector are located at the beginning of each partition volume.

The maximum number of all type of partitions together allowed by DOS is 24, even if you have more than one physical hard disk drive, the total number of partitions in all the drives cannot exceed 24.

This limitation comes from the fact that DOS uses a single upper case alphabet to name a partition, the first partition is given the name C and the last partition is given upper case letter Z, so from C to Z only 24 letter are available for assigning to the partitions.

DOS Boot Record (DBR) / DOS Boot Sector

First logical sector of each partition contain a volume boot sector. On DOS partition the hard disk drive contains a DOS Boot Record (DBR) or DOS Boot Sector. The job of the DBR is to load the operating system (OS) from the hard disk drive into the computer's main memory and give the system's control to the loaded OS.

For this purpose the DBR contains a small program, this program is executed by the master boot record (MBR) program. It is the job of this Boot program to look for the two program files IO.SYS and MSDOS.SYS on the root directory of the partition.

IO.SYS and MSDOS.SYS are two hidden system program files on MS-DOS operating system provided with IBM compatible systems. These hidden program files are not displayed when DIR command is used to view the directory.

If these programs are available then the boot program on the MBR first loads the IO.SYS and gives the machine's control to this program.

Next, the IO.SYS program loads the MSDOS.SYS program and the COMMAND.COM program, this complete process is called "booting" of the computer.

If the IO.SYS and MSDOS.SYS programs are not available in the directory then following message is displayed

"Non-System disk or disk error, Press any key to continue"

This DBR also contains some important information about the disk geometry such as the number of bytes per sector, sectors per cluster, number of FATs, maximum number of root directory entry etc. This data area is called media parameter block, disk parameter block or BIOS parameter block (BPB).

The disk parameter block is very important data area for DOS, it helps the DOS to find the location of FAT and some other important values. Putting wrong information here or corrupting these values make booting from the hard disk drive impossible.

DBR is created by running the DOS program FORMAT. This program can be executed from a DOS disk.

The sector on which DBR resides becomes logical sector 1 of that particular partition for the OS. First DBR is usually located at the physical location cylinder 0, head 1, sector 1.

Root Directory

After MBR, DBR and FAT, comes root directory. This is a table of contents of the information stored on the hard disk drive.

The number of files that one can store on the root directory depends on the FAT type being used, with 12-bit FAT, it is limited to 128 entries, if one tries to store 129th file DOS will display a "file creation error". When 16-bit FAT is used, one can have total 512 entries in the root directory.

This does not mean that with 16-bit FAT one is limited to storing only 512 files on the hard disk drive. One can use sub-directories to store any number of files limited only by the size of the drive.

If the drive is a MS-DOS bootable hard disk drive then root directory contains IO.SYS and MSDOS.SYS .

The directory area keeps the information about the file name, date and time of file creation, file attribute, file size and which cluster is the first cluster of the particular file.

This directory entry is linked with the FAT entry. Once the DOS has the starting cluster value of any file from the Directory, the DOS can find out the complete file using the FAT.

Data Area

After the root directory ends, the data area starts. The data area contains the actual data stored on the disk surface.

DOS uses cluster number 2 for the first sector of the data area, i.e. cluster number starts from 2.

When formatting a hard disk drive the FORMAT command does not destroy or overwrite the data on the data area. The FORMAT command only removes the directory entry and FAT entries, it does not touch the actual data area.

This makes the recovery of accidentally formatted hard disk drive possible, which is not possible in case of accidentally formatted floppy disk.

Installing/Upgrading Hard Disk Drive (Hardware Perspective)

This section will provide you with a detailed description of how to install a new hard disk drive and how to upgrade your existing hard disk drive. The installation and upgrading is covered from the hardware point of view in this section, the software part of installation is covered in the next section.

Removing Old Hard Disk Drive

Once you have decided to purchase a new hard disk drive in place of the existing drive, then you have two options, one is to remove the existing hard disk drive, and connect the new drive in place of the old drive or you can connect the new drive with the existing drive.

If you decide to remove the existing drive then the step by step process to remove the drive is explained next.

One very important point before removing the existing drive is, if the existing drive is not autoparking type then it should be parked using proper head parking software such as SHIPDISK, PARK etc.

Once the old drive is parked, proceed as follows

- Switch off the power to the system, remove the power cable from the mains and remove the system unit's cover.

- Locate the drive and remove the data/control and power cable connections from the drive. While removing the data/control cable note down the orientation of the cable for proper reinstallation.
- When removing the cables remember to pull at the connector not the cables, pulling the cable may make the cable become loose from the connector.
- Most of the current drive which are of IDE type may contains only one data/control cable, but some old ST506/412 based drives may have two separate cables for data and control signal from the drive controller.
- Remove the mounting screws from the drive. Most of the drives are mounted on the system unit by using two screws on each side. Sometimes the screw is also connected from the bottom side to fix the drive to the mounting bay.
- Some AT-style cases may have mounting rails on the drive, with screws on either side of the drive's faceplate. On this type of mounting, the drive can be removed by sliding it towards the front and removing from the rails. Once the drive is removed, remove the mounting rails and set them in some safe place for installing in the new drive.
- If the drive is of 3.5 inch form factor, and if it is mounted on a 5.25 inch drive bay, then it may be mounted using special angle brackets. Remove these angle brackets and keep at some safe place, they may be required to install the new drive.
- Keep the drive at some safe place.

If you're removing drive C from a two drive configuration and leaving the drive D as the main bootable drive then you need to change the jumpers on the D drive to make it the master drive.

Installing a Hard Disk Drive

Installing a hard disk in a system is not difficult process but there is a vast choice of types and sizes of drives available so treat these instructions only as a guide.

- First of all collect all the parts required for installing the drives. You need cables, screws, mounting rails etc.
- Check that the power supply has extra connector for connecting drive.
- Both ST-506/412 and ESDI hard drive and the floppy drives use 34-line cables, but the two types are not interchangeable.

Let use see the procedure for installing a hard disk drive.

- Turn off the power and remove the power cable from the wall socket. Remove the system unit's cover.
- Remove the bay's blanking plate if you are installing a drive that has a bezel.

- Check the settings of jumpers on the drive to ensure that, it is properly setup. Check the position of the drive select jumper, master/slave jumper etc.
- Note down the defect list printed on a label attached to the outside of the drive. Keep it for future reference. It will not be accessible once you have installed the drive inside the machine. Also, note the location of pin-1 of the connectors on the drives logic board. It is also hard to see after installation.
- Attach the mounting rails to the sides of the drive, if appropriate, then slide it into the drive bay.
- Attach the data/control cable to the controller card, and then attach it to the back of the drive. Be sure the striped edge (edge with read color) of the ribbon cable goes to the side of the connector where pin-1 is. Attach the power supply cable.
- Insert and tighten the mounting screws. Make sure that they do not dig into the casing of the hard disk.
- Connect the HDD LED indicator connector to the appropriate pins on your controller card or HDD, if you wish to use that LED to note hard drive activity.
- Power up the system. Update the CMOS RAM configuration by entering BIOS setup. You must boot from a diskette or CD-ROM if you have inserted a new unformatted C drive.
- If BIOS detects the drive then replace the system unit cover.

Partition the new drive using FDISK and then format using the FORMAT, use the /S switch if it is to serve as a boot drive. This process is explained in following sections.

Installing a Second Drive

Installing to a second hard-disk drive is one of the most common upgrade. This is the reason almost all Hard Disk controllers are designed to handle two drives.

Adding a second drive is a simple process, buy the drive, plus any additional cables and then you install it, just as you install the 1st drive.

- Check that the data/control cable used with your current drive has an additional connector for a second hard disk drive, also check the length of the cable. To be safe get a dual-drive data/control cable when you buy your second hard disk drive.
- Get another pair of mounting rails and screws for your new drive. Check that the power supply has a free connector, If not then buy a "Y" splitter.

Let us see the steps required to install a second drive.

- Turn off the power and remove the power cable from the socket. Remove the system unit cover.
- Set the jumpers on the new drive, so that it's recognized as the master or slave drive by the computer.

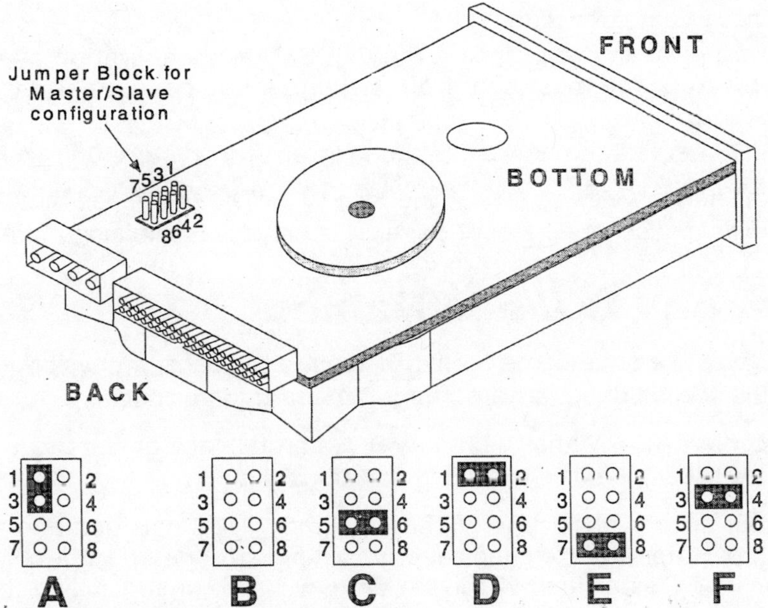

- A – Default position of the jumper.
- A & B – This jumper setting is used when the drive is a master drive. If a slave drive exist then the slave is an ATA compatible drive., or no slave drive is present.
- C – This jumper setting is used when the drive is a master drive and a slave drive exist but the slave is not an ATA compatible drive.
- D – This jumper setting is used when the drive is a master drive and a slave drive is present which uses PDIAG signal.
- E – This jumper setting is used when the drive is a slave drive and the master drive is an ATA compatible drive.
- F – Master/Slave is decided by the cable.

Fig. 10-28 : Master/Slave Setting.

- If required then attach the mounting rails to the new drive. Slide the drive into position. If you're installing an internal drive, slide into place from inside the case. External hard drives should be pushed in from the front of the computer case.
- Attach the data/control cable to the controller card/motherboard, and then attach it to the back of the drive. Be sure the striped edge (edge with read color) of the ribbon cable goes to the pin-1 of the connector.
- Attach the power supply cable to the drive. If your power supply does not have enough connectors then use a "Y" splitter.
- After connecting the data/control and power cable, slide the drive all the way into the bay. Insert and tighten the mounting screws. Make sure that they do not dig into the casing of the hard disk.

- Recheck your connections.
- Power up the system. Update the CMOS RAM configuration by entering into BIOS setup. You must boot from diskette if you have made the new drive a master drive.
- If BIOS detects the new drive then replace the system unit cover.

Partition the new drive using FDISK and then DOS FORMAT it, use the /S switch, if it is master drives and serve as a boot drive. This process is explained later.

How Second Drive is Named

The DOS gives the drive name (C:,D:,E: etc.) to the second physical drive based on whether the second drive has a primary DOS partition or not.

If your first physical drive has a primary DOS partition and an extended DOS partition with one logical drive in the extended partition. Then

- If your second physical drive has a primary DOS partition and an extended DOS partition with one logical drive in the extended partition. Then the primary DOS partition of the 1st drive will be named C:, and the primary DOS partition of the 2nd drive will be named D:.
  After this, the logical drive in the extended partition of the 1st drive will be named E: and then finally the logical drive in the extended partition of the 2nd drive will be named F:.
  Therefore, you will have drive name C: and E: on the 1st physical drive and the drive name D: and F: on the 2nd physical drive.
- If your second drive has no primary DOS partition, but has an extended DOS partition with two logical drives in the extended partition. Then the primary DOS partition of the 1st drive will be named C:, and the logical drive in the extended partition of the 1st drive will be named D:.
  After this, the logical drive in the extended partition of the 2nd drive will be named E: and then finally the 2nd logical drive in the extended partition of the 2nd drive will be named F:.
  So, you will have drive name C: and D: on the 1st physical drive and the drive name E: and F: on the 2nd physical drive.

Installing/Upgrading Hard Disk Drive (Software Perspective)

In the last section you saw how to install/upgrade a hard disk drive system, how to remove the old drive, add a new drive and add a second drive.

But, the hard disk drive upgrade will not be over by just connecting a new drive, once the new drive is added, the drive and the system needs to be properly setup/configured to make them work together. This section deals with this part of the upgrading.

After connecting a hard disk drive to the system, the user cannot straight away start using the hard disk drive. Properly connecting a new drive is only a small part of the complete hard disk upgrade job.

Once the hardware upgrade of the hard disk drive is over, one needs to setup the drive and the system to make them work together. The setup mainly consist of initialization, partitioning and formatting of the hard disk drive.

Therefore, to use a new hard disk drive in a system you need to carry out the following procedures

- Setup/Configure the system.
- Initialize/Low level format the drive. This step is optional for IDE and SCSI drives
- Partition the drive (using DOS FDISK command)
- High level format the drive (using DOS FORMAT command)

In next sections we shall see what are these steps and how to carry them out.

Setup/Configuration

Hardware setup i.e. setting up of different jumpers etc. on the hard disk drive and the main system for the hard disk drive upgrade is covered in the previous section. In this section we shall cover the system setup using the BIOS.

IBM AT-286 and later systems such as 386, 486, PENTIUM etc. contain a battery backed RAM (CMOS RAM) to store the system configuration. The system stores complete configuration information into this memory and the BIOS takes this information during the system power-on time to test and initialize the devices connected to the system.

The information about the drives connected to the system is also stored into this CMOS RAM memory. After the upgrade, if you forget to change the information in the CMOS RAM then the data in the CMOS RAM and the actual drive connected to the system will not match and the POST process will stop with some error message such as "Invalid configuration information" or "HDD Failure" etc.

This message could be different depending on the make of the BIOS.

To correct this problem you need to run the BIOS setup and feed in the correct parameters about the new drive.

Most of the systems allow pressing a key or combination of keys to go to the BIOS CMOS setup program during the system power on time.

Some common keys for this purpose are

- Delete or Del key,
- Escape or Esc key,
- F1 or F10 key,

The key or key combination to be pressed depends on the BIOS being used in the system.

Once you are into the BIOS Setup program you need to choose something called "Standard CMOS setup". This option will provide facility to define most of the hardware connected to your system.

In this standard CMOS setup, you need to select the hard disk drive type from a drive type table. The drive type is selected by matching the number of cylinder, head and sector and write precompensation and landing zone value of the hard disk drive to the value given in the drive type table.

If no drive in the table is 100% matching to your hard disk drive's parameters then select a user defined hard disk type in their drive type table. This allows the user to type the actual cylinder, head, write pre-compensation, sector and landing zone value of the drive directly into the CMOS drive parameter setup.

Once drive parameters values of the new hard disk drive is typed into the CMOS Setup program, you need to save these values and restart the system.

Most of the current BIOS contain an options called "Auto-Detect Hard Disks", on the main menu. Selecting this option will automatically configure the BIOS with drives connected at primary and secondary channels.

This completes informing the system about the new drive. The next step is partitioning the new drive.

If after selecting "Auto-Detect Hard Disks" option the new hard disk drives are not detected by the BIOS then there is some hardware problem with the hard disk drive, check the data/power cable, drive jumper setting etc.

Drive Partitioning

Once the drive is detected by the BIOS, next step is to partition the drive. Partitioning was basically done for two purposes

- To have more than one operating system on the same drive
  For example, you could put DOS and UNIX on the same hard drive.
- To have more than one logical drive
  This helps to keep your files organized and File Allocation Table (FAT) failure of one drive will not make the complete data on the hard disk corrupt.

One point you must remember is even if you want to use the complete drive for one operating system, or if you want to use the complete drive as one logical drive, you must partition the drive.

When a disk is partitioned the partition program FDISK writes a MBR or Master Boot Record in the first physical sector i.e. at the cylinder 0, head 0, sector 1.

This MBR sector contains a small program to load operating system from the bootable partition and also it contains a partition table, giving information about the different partitions on the hard disk drive, their starting cylinder, head and sector and ending cylinder, head and sector locations.

This partition table also indicates to the ROM BIOS which partition is bootable, so that the BIOS can load proper operating system.

On a single hard disk drive, one can have minimum 1 partition and maximum 24 partitions. This minimum and maximum number is given for the total number of partitions on all the hard disk drives physically installed on the system.

Let us now see how one can partition a hard disk drive.

FDISK

FDISK is the DOS utility program that is used to partition a hard disk drive. After low-level formatting a new or old hard disk drive, you must run the DOS program FDISK to properly partition the newly formatted hard disk.

Without FDISKing the drive you will not be able to use the drive to read/write any information. You must run the FDISK program and partition the drive, whether you want to use the entire drive as single partition or want to have multiple partitions on the drive.

Even if the drive was low-level formatted at the factory you must run the FDISK utility and partition the drive before doing high-level formatting and using the drive.

The FDISK program can be used for the following

- Creating a primary DOS partition
- Creating an extended DOS partition
- Creating logical drives in extended partition.
- Setting a partition to active (bootable)
- Deleting a partition
- Displaying partition data
- Selecting a hard disk drive for partitioning, when more than one hard disks drive is installed.

How to Partition and Format Hard Disk Drive

Before doing this, make sure that your hard disk drive is empty, as the following steps will permanently delete all of the data on that hard disk drive.

To partition hard disk drive, run the FDISK command.

- Insert the Startup disk/CD in the drive, restart your computer.
- In the BIOS setup make sure that boot from floppy disk or CD-ROM is selected.

- When the Microsoft Windows 98 Startup menu is displayed, select the "Start computer without CD-ROM support" menu option, and then press ENTER.
- At a command prompt, type FDISK, and then press ENTER.
- If your hard disk is larger than 512 MB, you receive the following message

```
Your computer has a disk larger than 512 MB. This version of
Windows includes improved support for large disks, resulting in
more efficient use of disk space on large drives, and allowing
disks over 2 GB to be formatted as a single drive.
IMPORTANT: If you enable large disk support and create any new
drives on this disk, you will not be able to access the new
drive(s) using other operating systems, including some versions
of Windows 95 and Windows NT, as well as earlier versions of
Windows and MS-DOS. In addition, disk utilities that were not
designated explicitly for the FAT32 file system will not be able
to work with this disk. If you need to access this disk with
other operating systems or older disk utilities, do not enable
large drive support.
Do you wish to enable large disk support? Y
```

- Press Y and then press ENTER. Pressing N will give you FAT16 file system.
- After you press ENTER, the following Fdisk Options menu is displayed.

```
--------------------------------------------------------------------
                    Microsoft Windows 98
                 Fixed Disk Setup Program
          (C)Copyright Microsoft Corp. 1983-1998

                       FDISK Options

   Current fixed disk drive: 1

   Choose one of the following:

   1. Create DOS partition or Logical DOS Drive
   2. Set active partition
   3. Delete partition or Logical DOS Drive
   4. Display partition information
   5. Change current fixed disk drive

   Enter choice: [1]

   Press ESC to exit FDISK
--------------------------------------------------------------------
```

- Option 5 is available only if you have two physical hard disks installed.
- Press 1 to select the "Create DOS partition or Logical DOS Drive" menu option, and then press **ENTER**.
- After you press ENTER, the following Fdisk Options menu is displayed.

```
------------------------------------------------------------------
            Create DOS Partition or Logical DOS Drive

    Current fixed disk drive: 1

    Choose one of the following:

    1. Create Primary DOS Partition
    2. Create Extended DOS Partition
    3. Create Logical DOS Drive(s) in the Extended DOS Partition

    Enter choice: [1]

    Press ESC to return to FDISK Options
------------------------------------------------------------------
```

- In this menu, Press 1 to select the "Create Primary DOS Partition" menu option, and then press **ENTER**.
- After you press ENTER, you receive the following message:

```
------------------------------------------------------------------
                  Create Primary DOS Partition

  Current fixed disk drive: 1

  Do you wish to use the maximum available size for a Primary DOS
  Partition and make the partition active (Y/N).............?[Y]

  Press ESC to return to FDISK Options
------------------------------------------------------------------
```

- After you receive this message
  - If you want all of the space on the hard disk to be assigned to drive C, press **Y**, and then press **ENTER**. Press **ESC**, and then again press **ESC** to quit the Fdisk tool and return to command prompt.
  - If you want to customize the size of the partitions, press **N**, and then press **ENTER**.
- A dialog box is displayed in which you can type the size that you want for the primary partition in MB or percent of disk space. For computers that are running either Windows 98 or Windows Me, make the primary partition at

least 500 MB in size. Type the size of the partition that you want to create, and then press **ENTER**.

- Press **ESC** to return to the Options menu.
- To assign drive letters to the additional space on the hard disk, press 1, and then press **ENTER**.
- Press 2 to select the "Create Extended DOS Partition" menu option, and then press **ENTER**.
  You receive a dialog box that displays the maximum space available for the extended partition. You can adjust the size of the partition or use the default size. Type the amount of space that you want, press **ENTER**, and then press **ESC**.
  The "Create Logical DOS Drive(s) in the Extended DOS Partition" menu is displayed. This is the menu that you can use to assign the remaining hard disk space to the additional drive letters. Type the amount of space that you want to assign to the next drive letter in the "Enter logical drive size in Mbytes or percent of disk space (%)" box, and then press **ENTER**.
- A table that lists the drive letter that you created and the amount of space on that drive is displayed. If there is free space available on the hard disk, it is displayed near the bottom of the table. Repeat previous step until you receive the following message.
  All available space in the Extended DOS Partition is assigned to local drives.
- After you receive this message, press **ESC** to return to the Options menu.
- To activate the partition from which you plan to boot (usually drive C), press 2 to select the "Set active partition" menu option, and then press **ENTER**.
- When you receive the following message, press 1, and then press **ENTER**:
  Enter the number of the partition you want to make active.
- Press **ESC**, and then press **ESC** to quit the **FDISK** and return to a command prompt.

Once the hard disk drive is partitioned, you must restart the computer to activate the currently partitioned information.

Fdisk Does Not Recognize Full Size of Hard Disks Larger than 64 GB

When you use Fdisk.exe to partition a hard disk that is larger than 64 GB (64 gigabytes) in size, Fdisk does not report the correct size of the hard disk.

The size that Fdisk reports is the full size of the hard disk minus 64 GB. For example, if the physical drive is 70.3 GB in size, Fdisk reports the drive as being 6.3 GB in size.

A supported fix is now available from Microsoft, To resolve this problem immediately, download the fix from Microsoft web site.

http://support.microsoft.com/

How to Format a Hard Disk

After you created the partitions, to use the newly created partition, you must format those partitions.

- Restart your computer with the Startup disk/CD in the drive.
- Select the "Start computer without CD-ROM support" menu option when the Windows 98 Startup menu is displayed.
- When a command prompt is displayed, type
  `FORMAT C:/S`
- and then press **ENTER**.
- This command transfers the system files and should only be used when you format bootable drive C (or your "active" drive).

  For all other partitions, type
  `FORMAT drive:`

  where drive: is the letter of the partition that you want to format.
- If you receive a "Bad command" or "Bad file name" error message, you may need to extract the FORMAT.COM tool to your boot disk. To do this, type the following command at a command prompt, and then press ENTER.
  `EXTRACT EBD.CAB FORMAT.COM`
- After the FORMAT.COM tool is extracted to your boot disk, type
  `FORMAT C:/S`

  at command prompt to format your bootable partition, or type
  `FORMAT drive:`

  if you want to format a partition that is not your bootable partition.
- When you have successfully run the FORMAT.COM tool, you receive the following message:
  `WARNING, ALL DATA ON NON-REMOVABLE DISK DRIVE C: WILL BE LOST!`

  `Proceed with Format?`
- Press `Y`, and then press **ENTER** to format drive C.
- After the format process is finished, you receive the following message.
  `Volume label (11 characters, ENTER for none)?`
- This is an optional feature that you can use to give a name to the drive. You can either type an 11-character name for the drive, or you can leave it blank by pressing **ENTER**.

Now, your hard disk drive is ready for job, partitioned and formatted. You can remove Startup disk/CD from the drive, and boot from the hard disk drive.

Before using the computer, you need to install some operating system into the newly prepared hard disk drive.

FORMAT Displays Size of Partitions or Logical Drives Larger Than 64 GB Incorrectly.

When you use FORMAT.COM to format a partition or logical drive that is larger than 64 gigabytes (64 GB) in size, FORMAT.COM does not report the correct size of the drive being formatted at the beginning of the format process.

However, as the formatting process progresses, the entire drive is formatted, and the correct formatted size is displayed when the operation is finished.

This is a display only problem, the drive is formatted to its full size. This problem does not occur if you format the drive from within Windows Explorer.

The initial, incorrect size that Format reports is drive size - 64 GB. For example, if a partition or logical drive is 70.3 GB in size, Format initially reports the drive as being 6.3 GB in size.

Alternative to New Drive

If one wants to increase the disk access speed or increase the storage space then before going for a new drive try the following software based alternatives.

Speed Improvement

Defragmenting the Drive

After some use, if you feel that your drive has started getting slow. DOS or Windows programs and data files started taking much more time to load compared to when the drive was new, then most probably this could be due to fragmentation problem.

On a disk drive any information is stored in clusters, when all the clusters of a file is stored in consecutive sectors then it is not fragmented. But, when the clusters are scattered across the disk then the file or the disk is said to be fragmented.

It takes the read/write head longer to read a file scattered across the disk surface, this makes a fragmented file takes longer to load compared to unfragmented file.

This problem of fragmentation can be solved by using software utilities such as Speedisk from the Norton Utilities, or PCTool Utilities by Central Point, a shareware program called Disk OrGanizer (DOG) or one can use the Disk Defragmenter utility provided with the Windows.

You can start Disk Defragmenter in Windows by

- clicking on Start, pointing to Programs, pointing to Accessories, pointing to System Tools, and then clicking Disk Defragmenter.
- In the Select Drive dialog box, specify the drive that requires defragmentation.
- Click the Settings button if you want to do any of the following:

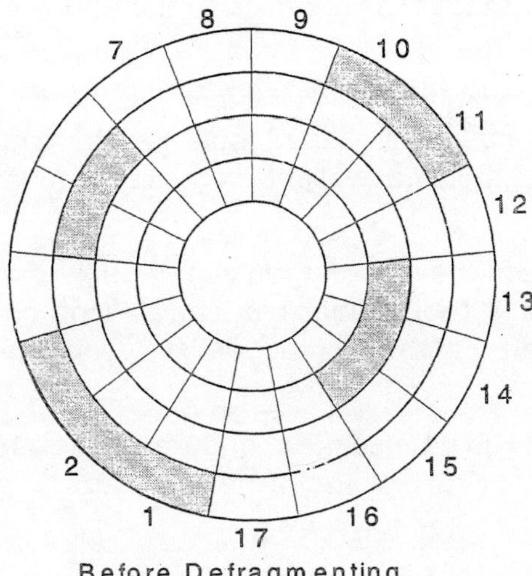

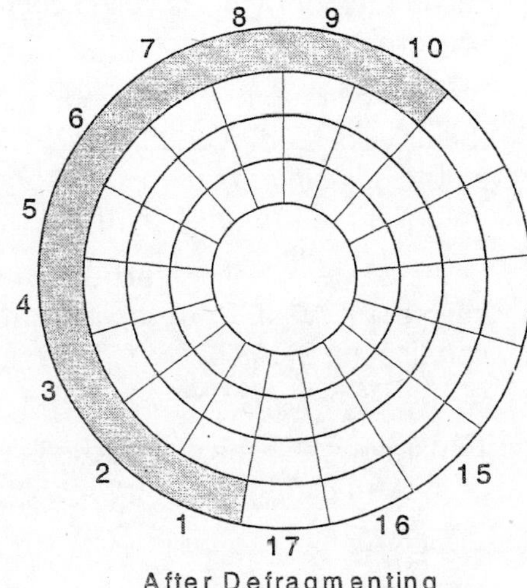

Fig. 10-29 : Defragmenting Hard Disk Drive.

- Rearrange program files so they start faster.
- Check the drive for errors.
- Choose the above options for this session only or for all sessions.

■ Click OK.

These utilities are called defragmenter and they read and rewrite the files on the disk to reorder them so that each file is once again stored contiguously on the disk surface and can be read much more efficiently by the hard disk drive.

Depending on the frequency of creating/editing/deleting of the files on the hard disk drive one can defragment the drive once a week or once a month to keep the files in one place.

Using a Disk Caching Software

If the defragmenting of the drive does not make much difference in the speed of the disk access then using a software based disk cache will surely improve the disk performance very much.

Let us see what a disk cache is. First, you must remember that it is pronounced "cash" not "catch."

A disk cache is part of the system's main memory (RAM), which is used by the cache software to store the frequently accessed information from the disk drive. Whenever a disk access occur, the cache software reads the area around the read data and keeps it into the cache memory.

When the next read instruction is issued, the cache software checks the cache memory first to see if the required data is there, if the required data is found in the cache memory (this is called cache hit), then the data is provided to the CPU without requiring any disk access.

If the required data is not found in the cache memory (called a cache miss) then only the drive is read. A good cache software uses intelligent guess about the data required by the drive in next read command and makes the data available in the cache memory before a read request by the disk drive.

There are many good cache utilities available in the market, you can use any of them such as NCACHE from the Norton Utilities, or PCTool Utilities by Central Point, or one can use the SMARTDRV.EXE program provided with the current version (version 6.xx) of the DOS or MS-Windows.

In Windows 98, the disk cache is dynamic. You do not need to configure its size as part of system configuration. Windows automatically takes care of the cache size.

Using BIOS Setup

Most of the current BIOS have some option to improve the disk access speed when they are used with IDE drives. These facilities are

- Enabling the IDE prefetch read buffer
- Enabling the IDE block mode

Enabling these two options will improve the disk access speed of the IDE drives.

Increasing Storage Space

Whatever be the size of your hard disk drive, it is filled up very fast. It does not matter if you have 20MB, 200MB or 2000MB hard disk drive, after some time you will find that the space is not enough for everything that you want to store.

As the cost of hard disk drive continue to drop and faster, higher capacity drives come in the market, one can replace his/her existing hard disk drive with higher capacity drive. One can also add a new drive to the existing drive to increase the overall storage capacity.

You can increase the existing storage capacity of your hard disk drive without investing in a new drive by using

- a disk compression utility or
- a file compression utility

File compression utility can be used to compress the files that is not frequently needed.

Disk Compression

Disk compression methods works by compressing the data that is stored on the disk drive at the time of writing of the data and when this data is read, the data is again expanded to its original form.

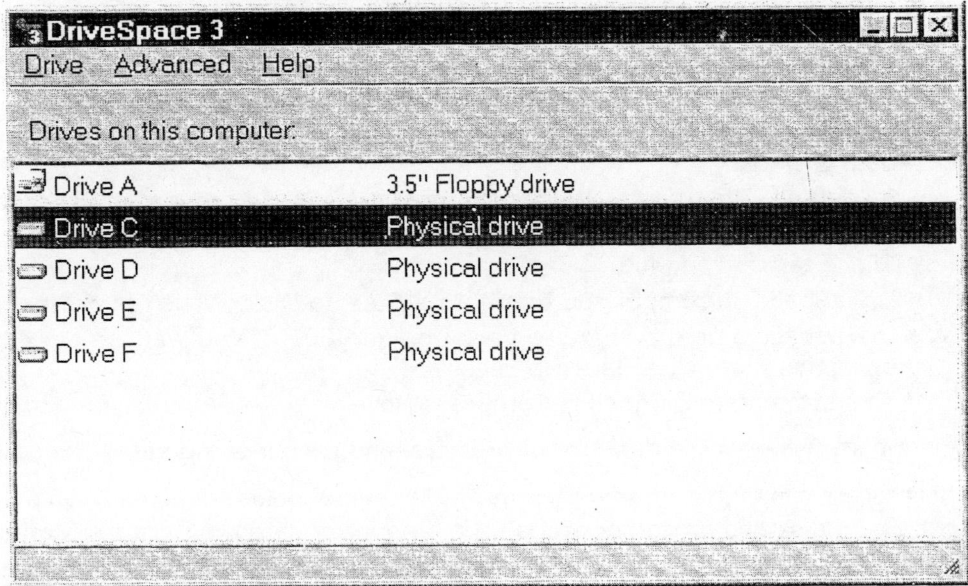

Fig. 10-30 : DriveSpace Compression Program.

There are many products in the market that let you compress the data on the fly, i.e. these software stay memory resident and compress the data as the data is written to the disk and the uncompress the data to its original form when the data is read from the disk.

If you have a 200MB hard disk drive using these software you can increase its effective storage space up to 400MB i.e. you can store up to 400MB of data on a 200MB hard disk drive.

A very common disk compression software is the DriveSpace 3 by the Microsoft Corp. This program is supplied free with the Windows 98.

This program works by creating a hidden read only file in the root directory of the drive on which you want to create a compressed drive. This hidden file is known as Compressed Volume File (CVF).

If your hard disk drive is setup as C: drive then DriveSpace will create a new drive D: as the compressed drive. Any data stored on this new drive will be compressed before writing on the disk.

To compress a drive in Windows-98

- Click Start, click Run, and then type drvspace. Press Enter.
- In DriveSpace 3 main screen, click the drive you want to compress.
- Click the Drive menu, and then click Compress.

- The Compress a Drive dialog box appears, listing the drive about to compress.
- If you want to specify the drive letter or free space to leave available for the host drive, and whether the host will be hidden, click Options.
- Make modifications in the Compression Options dialog box as needed, and then click OK.

  By default, DriveSpace 3 hides the host drive if the amount of free space is 2 MB or less.
- Click Start to continue.
- DriveSpace 3 prompts you to create a Startup Disk. Click Yes or No.
- DriveSpace 3 prompts you to back up your files. If you want to back them up at this time, click Back Up Files.
- To start compression, click Compress Now.

DriveSpace 3 checks the drive for disk errors, and then it compresses the drive.

This process can take from several minutes to several hours, depending on the speed of the hard disk and processor and on the amount of data the hard disk contains.

Using File Compression

Other then compressing the entire drive, another method to increase the effective storage capacity of the disk drive is to compress the files, that are not frequently required, before storing them to the disk drive.

Disadvantage with this method of file compression is, in this method the compression and the uncompression is not done on the fly, i.e. the compression program does not compress and decompress when the file is written and reads from the hard drive. Instead one has to manually compress each file stored on the drive and then whenever the file is required the user need to uncompress them before using.

Two of the most common file compression utilities are WINZIP and WINRAR.

These programs provides many options to the user to compress the file for backup or to transfer to some other computer.

HDD Troubleshooting

The problems with the hard disk drive can be divided into two basic types, one is hard problem i.e. problems with the drive or controller hardware etc. and the other is soft problems or problems related to the software, OS, BIOS etc.

If the hard problem is inside the sealed hard disk assembly then there is not much one can do, but if the problem is with the outside logic board of the drive or the drive controller card then one can replace it with a new working part to make the drive work.

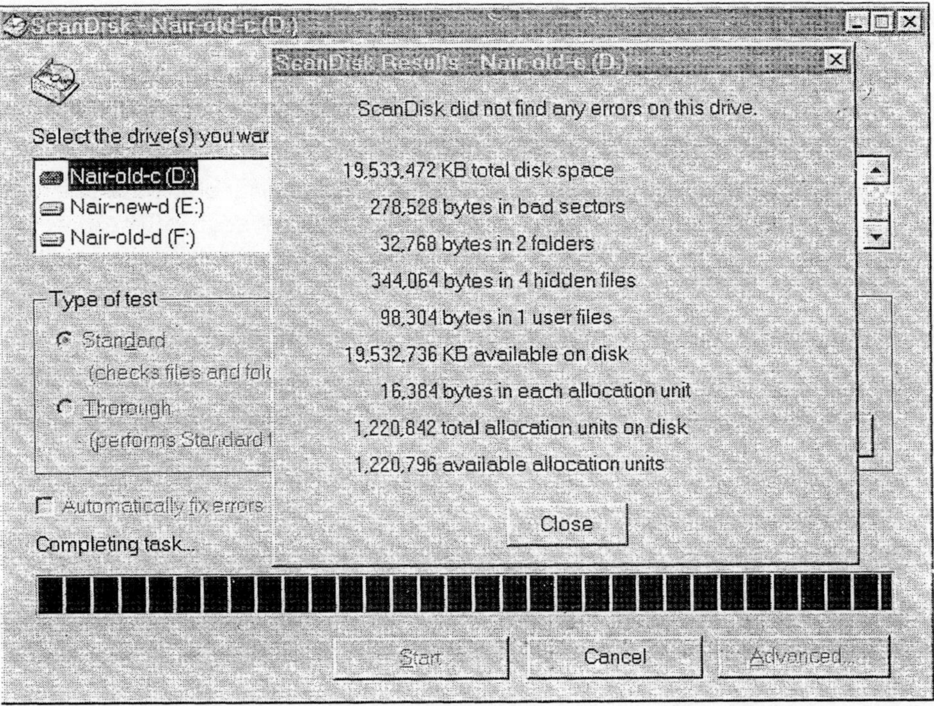

Fig. 10-31 : Scandisk.

A hard problem in a hard disk drive is not very common, instead most of the time the soft problems show a hard problems like symptoms.

If the problem is a soft problem then the sound made by the drive will be normal, if the drive has hard problem, if it is some mechanical trouble then the drive may generate a lot of noise.

Whenever a drive gives any trouble, first you must try to solve the problem thinking that it is a soft problems, but if you are sure that it is a hard problem then try the drive on a different controller, a different machine, try to change the logic board of the drive with a known working logic board.

Many a time the drive cable is main cause of the hard trouble, so try swapping the cables with a working data/control and power cable.

Once the drive start working you must backup the data immediately, as at this stage you cannot be sure about the life of the drive. After the backup low-level, format the drive and then partition and high-level format.

About the soft problems, later we have covered some of the things that you should do in the case of soft errors.

CHKDSK/SCANDISK Errors

CHKDSK and SCANDISK program are used to check the logical structure of the hard disk drive, they can be used to check the FAT and Directory structure for any logical errors such as cross-linked files, lost clusters etc.

The SCANDISK program can also check the physical surface of the drive for any bad areas. The CHKDSK program does not do any physical scan of the disk to find the defects, instead it scans the FAT to report the errors, total free space, total bad areas etc.

These programs CHKDSK & SCANDISK basically do the following things:

- They check the directory entries. They check the size of the file and verify that the number of clusters allocated in FAT chain is enough to save the file.
- They check that the directory structure to verify that the sub-directory entries are in correct format
- It checks the FAT chains to look for any lost clusters, cross-linked clusters etc.
- It also totals the used clusters, available clusters, the bad clusters as specified in the FAT and display these information on screen.

Hardware Failure

A data/control cable fault is one of the most common hardware failure in hard disk drive, some other common problem could be with the controller, drive motor, read/write head getting stuck etc.

Most of these problems generate some type of error message/error beep when the system is switched on, during the POST (Power On Self Test) time.

These errors could be

- "Invalid configuration-press F1 to continue" messages is displayed
- "Invalid configuration-Run SETUP" or "Configuration lost-Run SETUP" messages is displayed
- "0 hard disk(s) found" messages is displayed
- 1701, 1780, 1790 etc. error code is displayed
- "Drive failure" or "Hard disk failure" messages is displayed

Most of these problems can be corrected without using any special tools. One can solve almost 90% of these problems by checking and correcting the following

- Check that the BIOS setup information for the drive is proper, the system has not lost this information or it is not changed.
- Check the BIOS setup to make sure that the primary/secondary IDE ports are enabled in the integrated peripheral setting.

- If the working temperature is very cold then keep the machine on for some time and then reboot the system. Very hot working temperature also generates hard disk faults.
- After you open the system, first thing to check should be the cables, check that the cables are properly connected. Remove and reseat them, if you have another known working cable then swap the cable and try.
- Remove the drive and check that the drive is spinning and the read/write head stepper moves on power-up. If they are stuck then try to release them.
- Check the drive's logic board for any bad chip, chip that is getting very hot, burnt electronic part etc. exchange the board with another board of the same type.

These are some of the steps that you can try when you suspect a hardware failure of your hard disk drive system. Some of the mechanical problems can be solved by reorienting the drive.

Disk Media Error

One of the most common error message faced by the user when a disk media error occur is

```
Sector Not Found or
Data Error Reading Drive X:
```

These error messages indicates some kind of physical error with the disk surface. The "Sector not found reading drive X" error messages is given when the OS cannot find the sector ID placed by the FORMAT program because of fading, loss or corruption of this information from the disk surface.

"Data error reading drive X" error messages is given by the OS when the OS finds that the data read from the drive does not match the ECC (Error Correction Code) stored on the disk surface. The ECC are additional information stored on the disk with the data to find any fault in the data, when the data is read back, the ECC can detect as well as correct small errors in the data.

Once you find a media error, your first objective should be to restore any data on that area.

First check for any virus, check that the drive is not very hot or cold. Make sure that all the device drivers required to access the drive are loaded with proper parameters.

If you find that even after checking all the above specified points the area is still not readable, then you can be sure that you have a disk media error, some area on the disk has developed a hard error.

You can try to fix this problem using some disk surface scanning software such as SCANDISK or NDD from Norton utility.

Some Error Messages

Message by BIOS

`No boot device available Press F1 to retry, F2 for setup`

- Last two signature byte of the MBR is not 55AAh.

`No boot device available Press F1 to retry, F2 for setup`

- No bootable partition entry (80h) byte is found in the MBR

Message by MBR

`Invalid Partition Table`

- In MBR, Partition Table entry is found with other than 80 or 00 as boot indicator byte

`Invalid Partition Table`

- In the MBR, after a bootable partition table entry is found. another entry with other than 00 as boot indicator byte is found

`Error loading operating system`

- The MBR program could not read boot record even after five retries.

`Missing operating system`

- The MBR program has found that the last two bytes of the bootable partition's boot record are not AA55h.

Message by DBR

`Non-System disk or disk error`

`Replace and press any key when ready`

- The DBR program could not reset the drive containing DBR program.

`Non-System disk or disk error`

`Replace and press any key when ready`

- The bootable partition starts after the 32MB * (sectors per track) bytes. For example, if the sectors per track value is 26 then the bootable partition must be within 32MB * 26 = 832MBytes.

`Non-System disk or disk error`

`Replace and press any key when ready`

- The DBR program could not read the 1st directory sector.

`Non-System disk or disk error`

`Replace and press any key when ready`

- The DBR program has found that the first two directory entries are not hidden system files, IO.SYS and MSDOS.SYS.

`Non-System disk or disk error`

`Replace and press any key when ready`

- The DBR program could not read the hidden system file IO.SYS.

Floppy Disk & Disk Drive

Floppy Disk drives are the basic storage device available with almost all the personal computers (the only exception is disk less workstations used in network environment, as these workstations use drives connected on other machine).

Floppy Disk Drives come in 3.5 inch and 5.25 inch sizes. 5.25 inch drives were very common with old computers, but today it is very difficult to find 5.25 inch drives.

Even though the size of 3.5 inch drive is smaller than a 5.25 inch disk, storage capacity of the 3.5 inch drive is higher than 5.25 inch drives, and also the 3.5 inch drives are considered more robust and reliable.

Nowadays most common floppy drive is 1.44MB capacity, 3.5 inch Disk drives.

Drive Components

Major components of a disk drive are

- R/W Head
- Head actuator/Stepper motor
- Spindle motor
- Circuit Board
- Cable connector (Data cable and Power cable)
- Faceplate

R/W Head

This is a magnetic Read/Write head, which reads from and writes to the Disk. All the drives today have two Read/Write heads, one on the top and one at the bottom, to read both sides of the disk.

These drives are called double sided drives.

Some old drives had only one head, at the bottom side of the head assembly, these drives were called single sided drive.

Head moves in and out over the disk surface to read from and to write to the disk. Both upper and lower heads are mounted on a single rack, so they always move together and cannot move independently.

On a floppy drive, during disk read/write operation, head is always in contact with the disk surface. Because of this, slowly, oxide material from the disk starts to attach to the read/write head.

This oxide buildup should be cleaned periodically otherwise drive will start giving read or write error and sometimes when the buildup is large, head starts to scratch the disk surface, damaging the disk permanently.

Head Actuator / Stepper Motor

This motor moves read/write head over the disk surface. This is a stepper motor. The stepper motor as their name suggests, works in steps. It can rotate in any direction but with each step, it rotates a fixed angle.

This motor is connected to the read/write head assembly using a coiled steel band or a lead screw mechanism.

The steel band winds and unwinds around the spindle of the stepper motor, converting motor's rotational motion into heads linear motion.

In the lead screw assembly, motor rotation turns a screw which makes the read/write head assembly connected to the screw move in and out.

Spindle Motor

This motor turns the disk around by clamping the disk at the center. Old drives had a belt assembly to rotate the spindle but newer drives are "direct-drive" drives.

In a direct-drive system, motor is directly connected to the disk spindle. This system is less expensive and more reliable, as in the old belt driven drives, with time, the belt used to become loose.

These drives always maintain a fixed rotation speed of 300-RPM (rotation per minute) or 360-RPM, depending on the drive type.

Circuit Board

Disk drive contain some circuit board for basically two purposes

- to interface outside signal with the disk drive
- to control the stepper and the spindle motors

These circuits also control read/write head, different sensors and other components on the drive.

Cable Connector

A disk drive is connected to the main computer system through following connectors

- Data/Control connector
- Power connector

Data/Control connector

This is a 34-pin edge connector for a 5.25-inch drive or a 34-pin header connector for a 3.5-inch drive.

This connector is used to carry the data and the control signal between the computer and the disk drive.

Power connector

A four in-line connector is used to connect power from the computer power supply to the drive. 5.25 inch drives use a big size male connector known as Molex connector, whereas the 3.5 inch drives use a smaller male connector known as berg connector.

Faceplate

Faceplate, which is also called a "Bezel", is the plastic front cover of a disk drive.

These faceplates are mostly made slightly wider than the disk drive, so that the drive can be pushed into the drive bay from the front of the computer and the faceplate will fit firmly on the front cover of the computer's main system unit.

Floppy Disk Drive Types

There are different types of drive depending on the

- Size
- Drive's storage capacity

Size

The drive can be divided into two types depending on their size

- 5.25 inch
- 3.5 inch

5.25 inch Drives

This was the most common size of the disk drive available with a personal computer. This size 5.25-inch is the diameter of the disk used with these drives. These drives are available in different storage capacities.

5.25 inch Disk/Drive

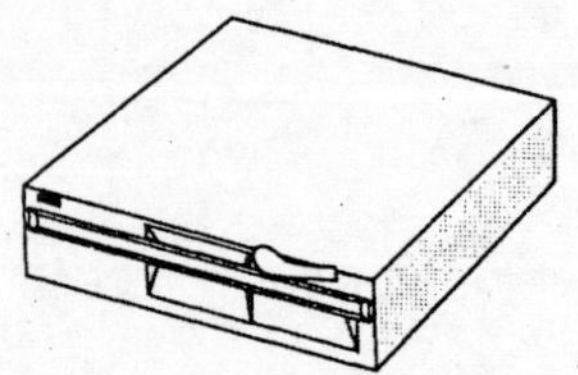

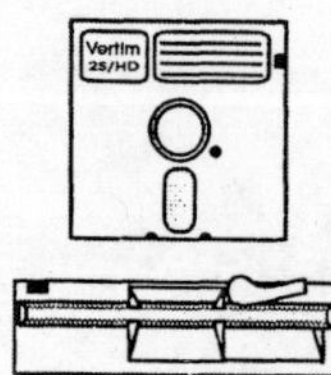

3.5 inch Disk/Drive

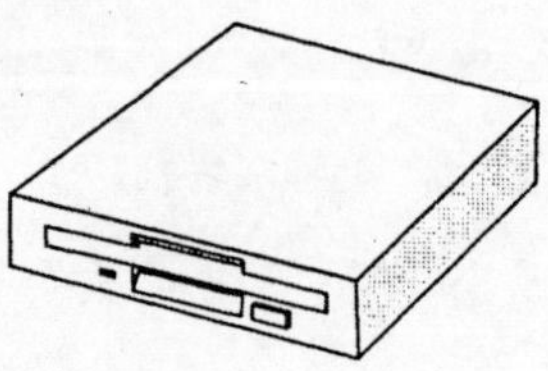

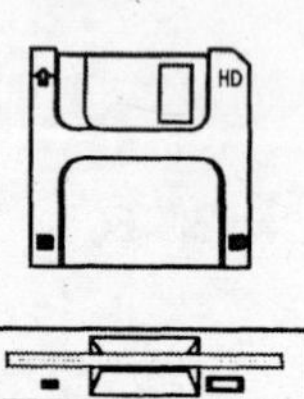

Fig. 11-1 : 5.25 inch and 3.5 inch Floppy Disk Drive.

3.5 inch Drives

IBM has introduced 3.5-inch drives with its PS/2 series of computers. Here also the size 3.5-inch is the diameter of the disk used with this type of drives.

Nowadays, these drives are becoming very common with all the personal computers.

Because of the many advantages that a 3.5-inch disk has over the old 5.25-inch disk, 3.5-inch drive has replaced 5.25-inch drive as the standard drive for the personal computers.

Drive's Storage Capacity

Depending on their storage capacity the disk drives can be divided following types

- 1.2 MB
- 1.44 MB

1.2MB Double Sided High-Capacity or High-Density (DSHD) Drives

The 1.2MB disk drives can read and write to both 1.2MB high-density disk and 360KB double-density disk.

DOS use these drives to store 80 track, 15 sectors per track on each side of the disk.

This drive spins at 360 RPM (rotation per minute) in high-density mode and can transfer data with a PC-AT disk controller at twice the rate of a standard 360KB drive.

1.44MB, 3.5 inch Double Sided High Density (DSHD) Drives

In an AT machine, these drives can work with the existing controller. However, if you connect these drives to a PC or XT machine, it can work only at 720KB capacity.

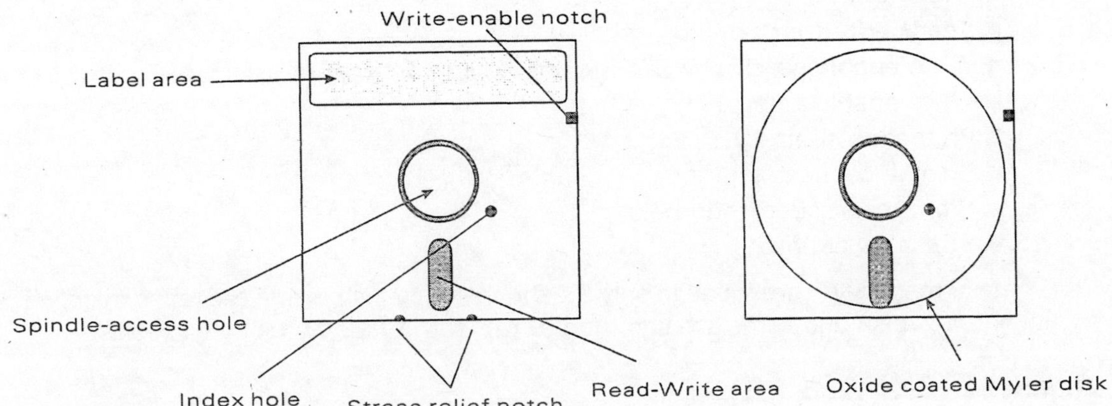

Fig. 11-2 : 5.25 inch Floppy Disk.

This is so because the PC or XT disk controller does not support the higher 500KHz data transfer rate required for the high-density operation.

These drives achieve their storage capacity by using the high-density disk, which can store 80 tracks with 18 sectors per track.

These drives spin at 300 RPM.

Floppy Disk

As one requires a cassette with a cassette player, a floppy drive requires floppy disk as media to store data. The floppy disk is a circular shaped plastic disk, coated with magnetizable coating, enclosed in a protective jacket.

Disk Construction

Both the 5.25″ and the 3.5″ floppy disks are constructed of the same materials with both of them using a plastic base (usually Mylar) coated with some magnetizable compound.

The magnetizable compound is normally an iron-oxide based compound, for the high-density floppy disks normally a cobalt compound is used.

Some of the parts of a floppy disk are

- Jacket
- Recording media
- Label area
- Drive hub hole
- Index hole

- Alignment hole
- Read/Write window
- Write enable notch
- Write enable hole
- Protection shutter
- Spindle connector
- High Density detection hole
- Stress relief notch

Some of these parts are found in only 5.25 inch floppy disk, some are found in only 3.5 inch floppy disk and some are common to the both types of floppy diskettes.

Jacket (3.5 & 5.25)

A floppy disk is mainly made of two parts

- outer jacket
- inner recording media

The jacket of the 3.5-inch floppy disk is made of more rugged plastic shell compared to a 5.25-inch floppy diskette, so, they can withstand any rough handling by the user.

The main job of the outer jacket is to protect the recording media from the dust, touch and other external contamination. It also provides the user with something to hold the floppy safely without affecting the recording medium.

Recording Media (3.5 & 5.25)

The recording medium consists of a flexible Mylar film, coated on both sides with some magnetic compound. Information is stored on it by magnetizing this coating. This recording is done in much the same way as music is recorded on an audiocassette.

A double density floppy disk use ferrite compound coating, a high-density floppy disk usually have cobalt compound coating, and the new 2.88MB storage capacity 3.5 inch floppy disk use special barium compound coating.

Label Area (3.5 & 5.25)

The label is attached to the label area provided on the disk jacket. This label should not in any way interfere with the insertion of the disk in the drive and the disk read/write operation.

When using a ball pen to write on the label of the 5.25-inch floppy disk, it should be written before sticking the label on the disk label area. Otherwise, writing on the label with a ball pen may mark the jacket and may mark the media inside. This may damage the information on the disk.

As the jacket of the 3.5-inch disk is very rigid, you will not have this problem with the 3.5-inch disk.

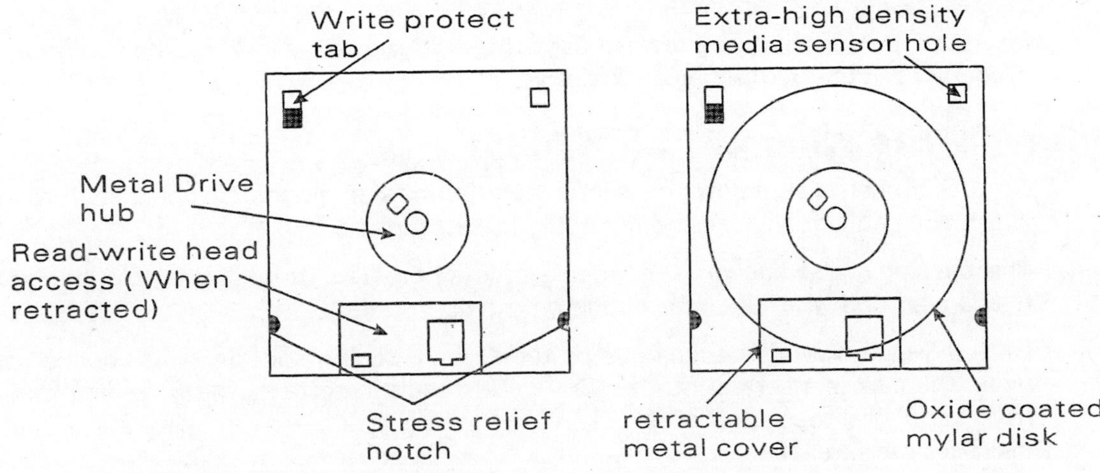

Fig. 11-3 : 3.5 inch Floppy Disk.

Whenever you insert a 5.25-inch disk into the drive, you should hold the disk by the label area and the label side should face up.

Hub Hole (5.25)

A 5.25-inch floppy disk jacket has three openings. The round opening in the center of a 5.25-inch floppy disk is called a hub hole. This opening allows a cone shaped clamp on the disk drive to grab and center the disk.

The recording medium of the floppy disk remains clamped there, so that the motor can spin it inside the jacket.

Index Hole (5.25)

The small circular hole on the recording media and the disk jacket is called an index hole. This index hole is used by the drive as the starting point for all the sectors on the floppy disk or in other words it is used to locate the first sector i.e. sector 0 of a track.

As the disk is rotated inside the jacket, when the index hole on the disk media and on the jacket come together, a sensor will sense this and inform to the drive as start of the sector.

A floppy disk with a single index hole is called a soft-sectored floppy disk. Hard-sectored floppy disks have as many holes as there are sectors on them.

Alignment Hole (3.5)

A 3.5-inch disk uses an alignment hole, rather than an index hole to tell the drive about the first sector of the track.

This alignment hole is located on the metal center hub of the disk. When the disk is inserted into the drive, the drive grasps the disk and this alignment hole is used to properly position the disk inside the drive.

Read/Write Window (3.5 & 5.25)

On a 5.25-inch disk below the center hole is another elongated opening, through which you can actually see the recording media surface.

This opening is also known as the media-access hole. It is through this hole, the drive heads read and write the information on the disk surface.

On a 3.5-inch disk, this opening is protected by a sliding shutter, which opens only when the disk is inserted into the drive. This shutter protects the recording media from accidental touch and other environmental contamination, making the 3.5-inch diskettes more reliable.

Write Enable Notch (5.25)

On the top right side of the 5.25-inch floppy disk jacket is a small rectangular opening. This opening is known as the "write-enable notch".

If this opening is present or open on the floppy disk, the drive can write to the floppy disk, if this opening is closed or not present on the floppy disk then the drive cannot write to the disk.

Floppy disks having this opening covered or with no opening at all are known as the "write-protected floppy disks". You can only read from these write protected floppies but you cannot write any information on them.

These write protected floppies are used to store permanent information, which does not require any correction or change. This opening may not be present on the floppy disk containing software.

Original software/program floppies and the important data floppies should be kept write protected to protect them from computer virus.

Write Enable Hole (3.5)

On a 3.5-inch disk, instead of a write enable notch you have a write enable hole. This hole is at one corner of the 3.5-inch floppy disk with a plastic shutter.

This plastic shutter can be opened or the hole can be made visible to write protect the floppy disk. Closing the hole by sliding the shutter into close position will make the floppy disk a read/write disk.

To make the disk permanently write protected, you can remove this shutter and make the hole permanent.

Protection Shutter (3.5)

On a 3.5-inch disk, the read/write opening is protected with a spring-loaded shutter. This shutter moves to expose the recording media, when the disk is inserted into a disk drive.

This shutter makes it much more difficult to touch the recording surface accidentally. In addition, it protects the disk media from the dust and other environmental contamination.

Spindle Connector (3.5)

Instead of a drive hub opening, the 3.5-inch diskette has a spindle connector to connect the disk to the spindle of the drive motor.

This is a small opening on the hub of the 3.5-inch disk.

High Density Detection Hole (3.5)

The high density 3.5 inch floppy disk (1.44MB) has another aperture on the opposite side of the write enable hole, which enables the drive to distinguish them from the low-density ones (720KB).

Stress Relief Notch (3.5 & 5.25)

This is two small half-circular notches on the bottom center of 5.25-inch disk or on the sides of the 3.25-inch disk.

This notch helps in proper aligning of the disk inside the drive and it also helps in relieving the stress on the disk jacket.

Floppy Disk Types

Like a drive, the disk can also be differentiated based on

- Size
- Disk's Storage capacity

Size

The floppy disk can be divided into different types based on the disk size. The common diskettes are

5.25 inch Disk

The 5.25-inch disk has been most popular disk since the beginning of the personal computer. Some of the early systems had single sided drives installed in them and used single sided single density (SSSD) 5.25 inch disk with a storage capacity of only 180KB.

However, today the 5.25 inch disks is obsolete, you will not find a 5.25 inch disk drive on a new computer system.

3.5 inch Disk

The 3.5-inch floppy disks record at track and data densities greater than the 5.25-inch floppy disks. Therefore, although its size is smaller than a 5.25-inch disk, its storage capacity is more than the 5.25-inch disk.

The outer jacket of these diskettes is made of very rigid plastic material, making these diskettes very rugged.

3.5-inch diskettes use a shutter to protect the media-opening hole. This shutter is opened by the drive when the disk is inserted into them for reading/writing of the data and remains closed when the floppy disk is not in use, i.e., it is outside the drive.

This shutter protection insulates the recording media from the environment contamination and finger touches, this also eliminates the need for a disk cover.

Most common 3.5-inch disk is 1.44MB double side high-density (DSHD) disk.

Disk's Storage Capacity

The floppy disk can be divided into different types based on the storage capacity of the disk. The common diskettes in use are

5.25 inch floppy disk 1.2MB DSHD (Double-sided High-density)

A 1.2MB floppy disk is the most common disk at present, although the 3.5-inch disk is slowly replacing it from the number one position.

3.5 inch diskettes 1.44MB DSHD (Double-sided high-density)

In 3.5-inch disk category, this 1.44 MB floppy disk is the most common disk. A 1.44MB disk drive is backward compatible and can read and write a 3.5-inch DSDD (720KB) disk.

These 1.44MB diskettes have the letter "HD" (High-Density) printed on them.

Physical Working of a Drive

When you insert a floppy disk into the drive and close the drive door, the drive hub clamps the disk to the spindle. Once the door is closed, the head moves into the contact with the recording surface and the drive motor starts to spin the disk inside its jacket.

In the 5.25 inch double density drive and 3.5 inch drives the motor rotates at 300 RPM (Rotation Per Minute), only the 5.25 inch high-density (1.2MB) floppy drive rotates at 360 RPM.

Early drives used a belt to rotate the disk spindle, but modern drives use a direct drive motor i.e. the drive is directly connected to the spindle.

A double-sided drive has two read-write heads, one on the top side and one at the bottom side, to read and write on both the surfaces of the floppy disk. When writing on the floppy disk, the recording head overwrites anything previously recorded on the disk.

As, there could be small difference between the location of the new information being written and the previous information on the disk, when a track is written its outer edges are erased to prevent any interference with the adjustment tracks and to remove traces of the previous information from disk.

This also eliminates the possibility of any interference to the new data. This recording method is called "tunnel erasure recording".

When reading/writing to the floppy disk, the head actuator moves the read/write heads from track to track.

The head actuator motor uses a stepper motor, this is a special type of motor, instead of the normal rotation of other ordinary motors, this motor moves in fixed steps, and with each rotation, it rotates a fixed angle.

The position of the heads at each step determines the position of each track on the floppy disk.

Floppy drives contain several sensors. The write-protect sensor indicates whether the floppy disk in the drive is write protected. It may be a micro-switch, sensing the presence of a write-protect tab on the floppy disks, or could be an LED light source and photocell combination to detect the presence of the write-protecting tab.

Some drives may also have a disk sensor to determine the presence of a floppy disk in the drive.

3.5 inch high-density drives have a media type sensor, similar to the write-protect sensor, used to detect whether the floppy disk used in it is double-density or high-density.

The drive also contains a great deal of circuits on a printed circuit board to controls the read/write and erase heads, head actuator, drive motor and sensors etc. The drives logic board or printed circuit board also provides a standardized interface between the floppy drive and the floppy drive controller.

Floppy Drive SA-450 Interface

To connect a Floppy Disk Drive (FDD) to the computer, a standard interface called Shugart Associates SA-450 interface is used. This interface was developed by Al Shugart, founder of the hard disk drive manufacturer Seagate Technologies.

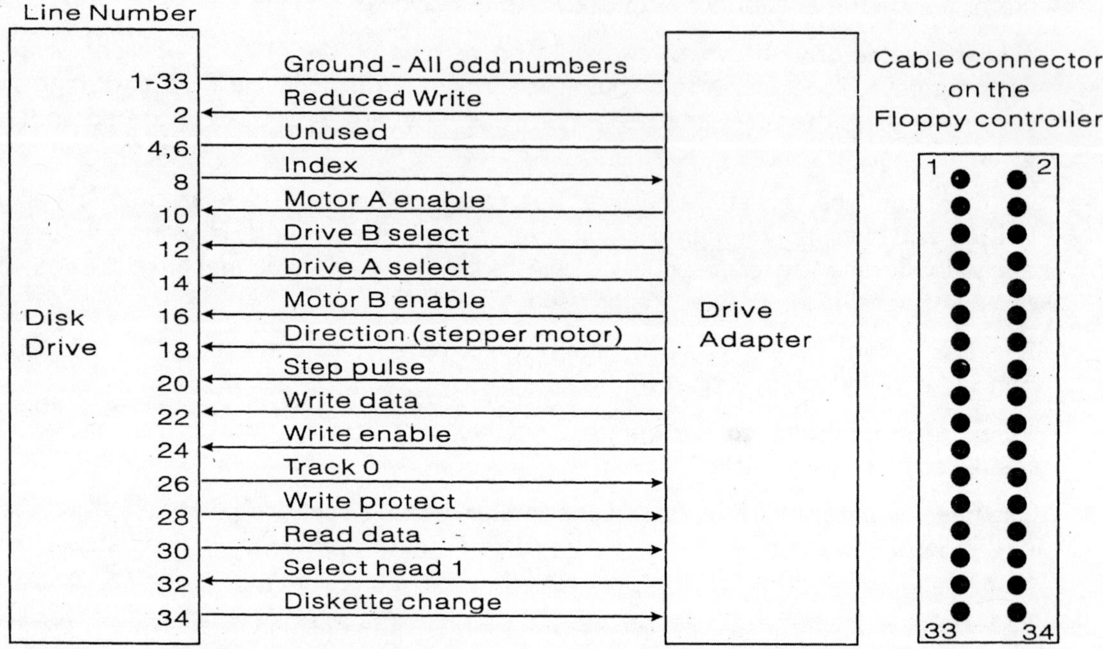

Fig. 11-4 : SA-450 Interface.

On the 5.25-inch drives, connector for this interface is a double-sided printed circuit board edge connector and on the 3.5 inch drives it is a 34-pin IDC connector.

A flat ribbon cable of 34 lines is used to connect the drive with the interface card.

Various signal on this cable are explained next.

Ground (All odd numbered pins)

All odd numbered pins from 1 to 33 are used as ground by the interface.

Reduced Write (pin 2)

When this signal is active, it indicates that a low-density disk (360 KB 5.25 inch) is being used in a high-density (1.2 MB 5.25 inch) disk drive. This signal informs the disk drive to use a reduced write current to write to the disk.

Index (pin 8)

Whenever an index hole is detected by the disk drive circuit, it generates this signal. A signal for about one to eight microseconds is generated on this line.

Motor Enable (pin 10,16)

The drive motor rotates when it receives an active signal at this pin. After the motor started there should be one-second delay before any read or write operation is performed. Pin-10 is used for drive A: and pin-16 is used for drive B:.

Drive Select (pin 12,14)

This signal enables or disables all the other signals except the "motor Enable" signal. If this signal is inactive them all other input signals are disabled. Pin-12 is used to select drive B: and the pin-14 is used to select drive A:.

Direction Select (pin 18)

If this signal is inactive i.e. low, then with each pulse on the step, the head will move away from the center of the spindle or away from the center of the floppy disk.

If this signal is active i.e. high, then with each pulse on the step, the head will move towards the spindle motor or towards the center of the disk.

This signal stays for about one microsecond before and after the step pulse.

Step Pulse (pin 20)

With each one microsecond active pulse on this signal, the read/write head will move one track. The direction of the movement depends on the value of "Direction Select" signal at pin-18.

Write Data (pin 22)

This is a 150 nano-second pulse If the write is in enable stage then the pulse on this signal will get written on the disk as one bit of the data.

If the write enable in not active, then the pulse not appear on this pin.

Write Enable (pin 24)

An active level of this signal enables the write circuit. If this signal is inactive i.e. low, then it removes all the power from the read/write head

Track 0 (pin 26)

Whenever the drive head is at track 0, this is detected by the drive's track 0 sensor circuit and the drive circuit generates this signal.

Write Protect (pin 28)

Whenever a disk with write protect tab (i.e. a read only disk) is used into the drive, this is detected by the drive's write protect sensor circuit and the drive circuit generates this signal.

Read Data (pin 30)

During the disk read operation each bit detected on the disk surface provide a 150 nano-second active pulse on this line.

Head Select (pin 32)

An active signal at this line makes the drive select upper head i.e. head one for the read/write operation, an inactive or low signal on this line selects the lower head i.e. the head 0 is selected.

Disk Changed (pin 34)

This signal is active when the diskette in the disk drive is changed i.e. when the drive door is opened and a new disk is put into the drive after the last disk access.

Tracks & Sectors

A technical understanding of the way data is maintained on the floppy disks will be useful to understand the general principle behind the floppy disk storage.

From the computer's point of view, data on the floppy disks is arranged in tracks and sectors. Tracks are narrow concentric circles that go around the disk and sectors are pie-shaped slices of the disk.

- A 5.25 inch 1.2MB floppy disk has 15 sectors per track at total 80 tracks, and
- A 3.5-inch 1.44MB floppy disk has 18 sectors per track at total 80 tracks.

The capacity differences between different floppy disk formats come from the different numbers of tracks and sectors per track.

Formatting is the process of preparing a blank floppy disk for using on the computer system.

Formatting a floppy disk puts special magnetic marks of tracks and sectors, on the floppy surface. Sectors and tracks do not exists on a floppy disk until and unless it has been formatted.

Formatting a new disk is like adding lines on a blank paper so that you will be able to write properly on it.

When a disk is formatted, other than writing track and sector address on the disk surface, formatting puts some more information that operating system needs to maintain data on the disk.

The track nearest to the outer edge of the floppy disk i.e. track 0 is almost entirely reserved by the operating system for its own use. Track 0, sector 1, contains the "boot record" or the boot sector that the operating system needs to begin its operation.

The next few sectors contain the file allocation table (FAT), which keeps the record of the empty space and about the portions containing information on the floppy disk. It is like an index for the information stored on the disk.

The next few sectors contain the directory, i.e., information about the files stored on the floppy disk. Part of this directory is shown by the operating system, when you use the DOS command DIR, or use Windows Explorer.

Rest of the disk is used to store the user data.

Upgrading/Adding a New Drive

Upgrading a drive or installing a new drive in place of an old drive consist of three steps

- Removing the old drive
- Configuring the new drive
- Installing the new drive

Whereas adding a new drive would require only two steps

- Configuring the new drive
- Installing the new drive

Let us see these steps

Removing Disk Drive

Whenever you want to upgrade your disk drive by installing a new drive, first you may have to remove the old drive from the computer.

To remove a drive from the computer the main steps are

- First and the most important is to switch off the computer's main power supply.
- Open the computer's main case
- Remove the data/control cable (flat ribbon like cable) and the power cable (removing power cable requires some force) from the disk drive you want to remove.
- One should never pull the cables directly, instead pull on the connector.
- Remove the mounting screws of the drive
- Slide the drive towards the front of the computer
- Remove the drive from the mounting bay and keep it in some safe place.

Once the old drive is out of the computer, next step is to configure the new drive to install in your PC.

Configuring the New Drive

When you examine the circuit board of the new drive, you will see several jumpers or small switches. These are used to make the drive work in different environment.

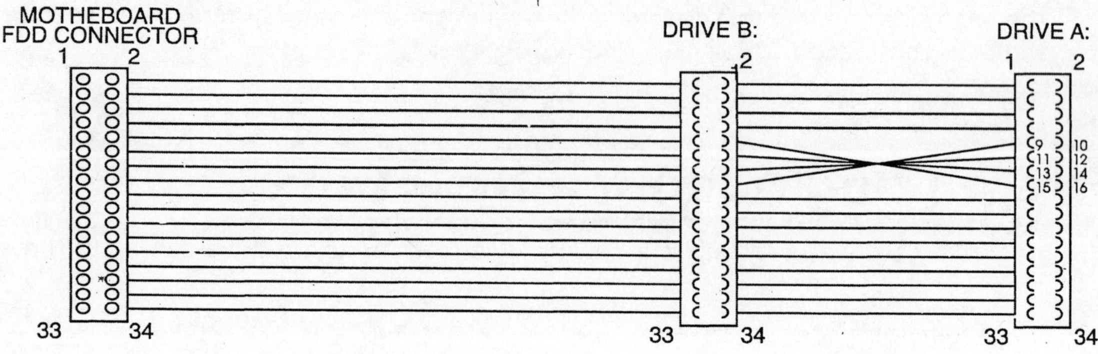

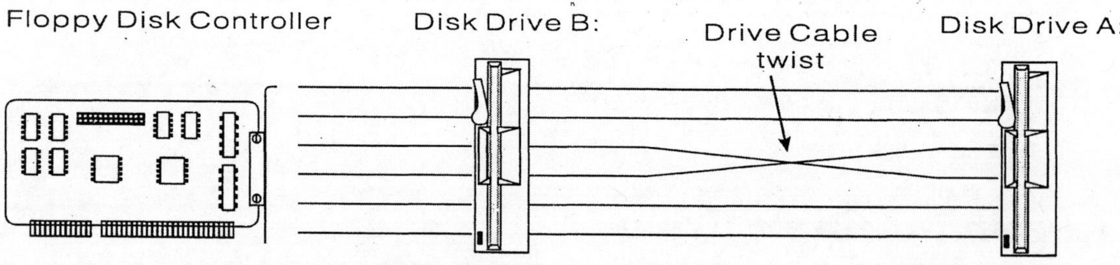

Fig. 11-5 : Data/Control Cable for Floppy Disk Drive.

Usually, these jumpers or switches are identified by a combination of letters and numbers. Some of the most common jumper or switch settings are explained next.

Media Sensor Jumper

High-density 3.5" drives have a media sensor (MS) jumper that enables the drive to sense the disk type being used.

If this option is enabled than the drive can sense the media sensor hole found in the 3.5-inch high-density (1.44 MB) and 3.5 inch extra-high-density (2.88 MB) diskettes.

This option is used so that the drive can find out whether it is writing to a double-density 720KB floppy disk, to a high-density 1.44MB floppy disk or to an extra-high-density 2.88 MB floppy disk, and adjust the write current accordingly.

Data/Control Cable

To make a floppy drive, A: or B:, manufacturers provide DIP switches or jumpers on the main logic board of the disk drive. By selecting the appropriate setting of this Drive select jumpers, most floppy disk drives allow you to select the drive as one of the four drives.

On a PC, all the drives are setup as second drive using these jumpers setting.

A special twist in the data/control cable identifies the drive A: and drive B: on a PC. This twist is given to a group of four lines in the floppy disk data/control cable.

This twist in the cable reverses the drive select and the motor control signals in the cable and rearranges some of the ground wires.

Since all drives are setup as the second drive, this reversal makes the drive attached to the cable after the twist the first drive, i.e., drive A: and the drive attached before the twist as drive B:

In other words, drive A: is attached to the connector at the end of the cable after the cable twist and the drive B: is attached to the connector in the middle of the cable.

The third connector at the other end of the cable with no twist goes to the floppy disk drive connector on the motherboard.

Adding a Disk Drive

Adding a floppy drive is exactly the opposite process of removing a drive.

To add a drive to the computer the main steps are

- First and the most important work is to switch off the computer's main power supply.
- open the computer's main case
- slide the drive into the computer from the front of the computer
- connect the data/control cable and the power cable
- tighten the mounting screws of the drive
- switch on the computer and run BIOS setup to inform the computer about the new drive.

When you switch on the computer, if the floppy drive LED is continuously on, then most probably the drive data cable is connected in wrong way. Switch off the computer and change the cable orientation.

Also, check for any bend pins on the data connector.

Test if the drive is working properly or not.

The drive can be tested by reading an old disk, with some files on it, and also by formatting a new disk and copying some data onto it. The disk formatted on the new drive should be readable on other drives. If not, then the head of the new drive may not be aligned properly, you need to replace the drive.

If everything is working properly, switch off the machine and close the computer case.

Drive Servicing & Maintenance

The disk drive is a complex device containing electronic and mechanical parts. In this section we have given description of common floppy disk/drive problems which could be rectified using general test software, equipment and replacement parts.

Head Cleaning

If your drive starts to give "Data read/write error", one main reason could be a bad or dirty read/write head.

On a floppy disk drive system, the read/write head of the disk drive is in contact with the floppy disk surface during the read/write operation. This makes the oxide coating from the surface of the disk to slowly accumulate on the read/write head of the drive.

Once this accumulation becomes big enough to disturb the read/write process, the drive start to show read/write errors.

Once your drive start to give repeated read/write error, first thing you should try should be cleaning the drive head. Drive head can be cleaned either by

- Opening the computer and directly cleaning the drive head, or by
- Using a head cleaner disk

Cleaning the head directly

For the first method, you need to first open the computer case and remove the disk drive.

Once the drive is out of the computer, take a cotton swab and moisten it with some good quality head cleaner liquid, you can also use medical alcohol or spirit. Rub this swab to the top and bottom head and clear any oxide deposits from the heads.

While rubbing the head you should be careful not to poke or thrust the head as this might make it go out of alignment. Light in-out motion should be used.

When you are satisfied that the head is clean, remove the swab and let the area completely dry. After it is dry, reassemble the system.

Cleaning the head using a head cleaning disk

Second method is more useful for a computer user who does not want to take the computer apart for the head cleaning. For this you need to purchase a floppy disk head cleaning kit from any computer dealer.

This kit consists of a special cleaning disk that should be covered with some cleaning liquid to clean the head. After covering the cleaning disk with the cleaning liquid, place the cleaning disk into the disk drive and rotate the disk using some command such as "DIR", 2 to 3 times.

The spinning action of the drive rubs the disk material and the cleaning liquid against the head. This action rubs off the oxide coating from the head surface.

The disk should be kept in the drive and rotated for about 30 seconds for the head to become clean.

Cleaning and Lubricating the Drive

As the disk drive contains many mechanical parts, if it is being used in a dusty environment, its mechanical part may require cleaning and lubricating after some time.

Door mechanism and the head carriage assembly may require cleaning and lubrication for their easy operation. For lubrication use a silicone or Teflon based lubricant available with the electronic spare parts shops, never use oil as it will collect more dust and jam the complete mechanism.

The disk change sensor, the write protect sensor and the index sensor will require cleaning for the proper functioning of these sensors.

You should also remove any dust etc. from the cable connectors.

Most of the drive problem will disappear after a proper cleaning and lubricating of these parts.

Floppy Disk/Drive Problems and Their Removal

Whenever a drive gives any problem, it could be a software problem or a hardware problem.

Software problems are some problems with the DOS or the Operating System, this could also be a virus problem which makes the drive behave in some unusual ways.

A Hardware problem is mainly problem with the cables. Remove the cables, clean the contacts and reconnect the cables, if this does not clear the problem then replace the cable with another working cable and check.

If the cables are all right then the problem can also be with the power supply of the system.

The disk drive needs both +12V and +5V power supply to work properly. The voltage between +12V and the ground should be within 11.5V to 12.5V and the voltage between +5V and the ground should be within 4.8V to 5.2V for the proper functioning of the drives.

If the problem is with the disk drive then the first thing to try should be the cleaning of the drive head. If this does not solve the problem then try to clean and lubricate the drive.

Many a time, problems related with floppy disk drive are problems with the floppy disk. This can be checked by using a good working disk or a new copy of the DOS disk.

Checking for virus can be done using a latest virus scanning software.

Floppy Disk/Drive Problems

While trying to format a disk, message "Invalid media or Track 0 bad, disk unusable" (or "Write failure, disk unusable" or "Track 0 bad - Media invalid") error is displayed.

This is one of the most common problem with a floppy disk and appears when the outermost track or track 0 of the disk gets damaged. Since this track holds some important information like the BOOT sector and file allocation table (FAT), when this sector gets damaged, DOS refuses to use the floppy disk.

This error can also happen if you try to format a high-density floppy disk (1.2MB) in a low-density drive (360KB) or vice-versa. Try formatting the disk in a proper drive.

If the error message is still displayed, clean the disk drive head and try to format once again, if the problem persists then it would be better to discard that floppy disk.

When booting with a floppy disk, computer displays "Non-system disk or disk error" message.

When the computer is booted from drive A:, it checks for the system files on floppy disk placed in drive A:.

When a disk without the system files is found in drive A:, the above mentioned message is displayed.

Put a bootable disk is drive A:, close the drive door and restart the computer.

A floppy disk copied from one drive, is not readable in the other drive.

Different operating systems format the disk in different ways. Check that the disk is not from some other system such as Unix, Linux etc.

Another reason could be the drive is out of alignment and needs servicing.

Nothing is being read from or written to the disk.

Some basic reasons could be that the disk drive's door is not properly closed. The disk is not properly formatted disk, as the drive cannot read from or write to an unformatted disk.

If none of the above problem is found then the problem could be a bad drive, or bad drive cable.

When formatting a disk, "Attempted write-protect violation" error message is displayed.

The main reason behind this could be that you are trying to format a write-protected floppy disk.

Remove the write-protect tab in case of a 5.25-inch disk or slide the write-protect tab in the 3.5-inch disk to the position so that the hole is not visible.

The other reasons could be that the write protect sensor in the drive is faulty or there may be some problem with the data/control cable.

System displays "No such Drive"

This error is displayed when the drive parameter is not set properly, in the BIOS setup.

System displays "Bad or missing command interpreter"

This error says that the COMMAND.COM file from the boot floppy is missing or the computer cannot read and understand this file.

System displays "Bad command or file name"

The DOS command or the executable file name given at the DOS prompt is misspelled or is not available on the drive.

Internal DOS commands such as DIR, COPY, TYPE etc. can be given without the file being on the current disk in the drive, but an external DOS command such as FORMAT, FDISK, DISKCOPY etc. requires the DOS floppy in the drive, otherwise this error will result.

If the command file is not found in the default directory, then if a path is specified, the path is searched for the specified command.

System displays "Not ready reading drive X:"

If the drive door is not properly closed or the disk is not inserted properly in the drive, this error is displayed by the computer.

System displays "Insufficient disk space"

This error results when you try to write on the disk, and there is not enough space available to safely write the given information.

System displays "General failure reading/writing drive X:"

When the disk is not formatted and the drive is unable to use the given disk this error is displayed. This could also result because of a bad read/write head.

When reading the disk, "Data Error Reading drive X:" error is displayed.

This error message appears when a disk is formatted in one drive and is used in another drive which has a different head alignment. This difference in head alignments makes the drive difficult to locate the data.

Other reasons for this error could be bad read/write head or some bad sectors on the floppy disk.

By using some disk utilities such as PCTOOLS or NORTON UTILITIES or SCANDISK program the surface of the floppy disk can be checked.

When reading the disk, "Sector not found. Error reading drive X:" error is displayed.

Drive cannot find the specified sector on the disk. Try reinserting the disk, cleaning the read/write head. Try the disk on some other drive.

Formatting the disk again rewrites the sector IDs and removes this problem.

When reading the disk, "Bad CRC - Unable to use disk" error is displayed.

The ID field and the DATA field of every sector on the disk contains a 2-byte CRC character, which is used by the system for ensuring its integrity.

This CRC is a special code, which is generated and written every time the ID and DATA is written to the sector. When the data is read back, CRC is again computed and is compared with the already stored CRC value. In case of a mismatch, the message "Bad CRC - Unable to use disk" is displayed.

This message indicates that after the data has been written to the sector, it has somehow got corrupted.

Drive boot sometimes, but refuses to boot some other time

Improper grounding, Check power supply, Check for EMI interference from monitor, power supply etc.

Write protected disk does not boot, unprotected disk can not write to track 0

Track 0 and "Write protect" signal are getting shorted in the drive interface

When monitor is on, error 6xx is displayed on screen, when monitor is off normal booting takes place

Proper shielding of Disk drive and Disk Drive Controller is not provided against the EMI radiation from the monitor.

After installing a new Drive when the system is switched on, drive lights are continuously on

Main reason for this fault is the data cable is not connected properly. Switch off the computer and change the cable orientation. Also, check for any bend pins on the data connector at the back of the floppy disk drive.

Also, check the BIOS setup for proper floppy disk drive type setting.

This fault could be due to some problem with the main logic board on the disk drive, replace the disk drive with a new working disk drive.

Floppy disk drive is completely dead, disk drive lights are off

Check the data and power connections. Remove and reinsert the data and power cables.

Check the power supply connector with a multimeter for proper voltage.

Check/Replace the data cable.

Check the BIOS setup for proper floppy drive type entry.

Check with a new floppy disk drive. If the new drive works without any problem, then the old drive's logic board was faulty.

Finding out which Drive is drive A:

If you are using a two-drive system, to find out which drive is drive A:, one very easy method is to place a disk in any of the drive and give DOS command **DIR A:**.

If the drive with the disk is drive A: then it will read the content of the directory and display it on the screen, otherwise the drive with disk is drive B: and as the A: drive is empty, you will receive DOS error message "Not ready reading drive A:, Abort, Retry, Fail?" on your screen. Press A to abort this operation.

Finding the capacity of the floppy disk drive

As you know that the FORMAT command always tries to format the disk to the maximum capacity of the drive. Place a blank floppy in the drive and give the FORMAT command with the following parameter:

```
FORMAT A: /U
```

If the drive is a 1.2MB, 5.25-inch drive, it will try to format the disk as a 1.2MB disk. FORMAT command tells how it is formatting the disk, so, by reading the message displayed by the FORMAT command you can find out the drive type.

Diskette Care

As a floppy disk is magnetic storage medium, the two main forces that can destroy the data on the floppy disks are magnetism and physical damage.

Extreme temperature can also destroy the data stored on the disk.

- Dirt and fingerprint are cumulative and work slowly, wearing out the disk and the drive mechanism. Even loose disk labels or write-protect tabs can come free and damage the disk or drive mechanism.
- Protect the floppy disk by keeping it in its storage envelope when not in use, specially the 5.25-inch diskettes.

Fig. 11-6 : Floppy Disk Care.

- When using a disk label, write on the label first and then only stick it on the disk.
- Never bend or fold the floppy disk.
- When inserting or removing the floppy disk from the drive, be gentle.
- Never remove a floppy disk from the drive when the drive indicator LED is glowing.
- Check the write-protect tab when in use to see that it is fully sticking to the floppy disk and that it does not snag upon insertion or removal from the drive.
- Never touch the magnetic oxide surface of the floppy disk. Always handle the floppy disk by the edges.
- Avoid Extreme Temperature
- Avoid using the floppy disk in areas where the temperature variation is extreme. The normal range is 10°C-52°C (50°F-125°F). A very high temperature may completely erase the disk content.
- Never place the floppy disk near magnets, magnetic paper clips, on top of monitor or near any other magnet.
- Periodically clean the drive heads with an approved cleaning kit.

Printers

Printers and monitors are two of the most common output devices used with the computer. A monitor provides us with a "Soft Copy" of results, i.e. the result being displayed on the monitor is not permanent, the moment output is changed or the power supply to the monitor is switched off, results being shown is lost.

The printer is used to get a "Hard Copy" of the results, i.e. it provides permanent output (which can be viewed, filed, and used at a later stage) on the paper or some other medium such as the overhead projector (OHP) film.

Today, printers are capable of high-quality monochrome i.e. single color and multicolor printout at very high speed. They are also capable of producing graphic i.e. images other than plain text on the paper.

Printers are often categorized based on the mechanism used by the printer to print the image and they can also be categorized based on the image formation method used by them.

Based on the image formation method printers can be categorized as:

- FULLY FORMED CHARACTER printer and
- BIT IMAGE printer

and based on the printing mechanism, printers are categorized as:

- IMPACT printer and
- NON-IMPACT printer.

Image Formation Method

Different printers use different method to produce the required output on the paper. The quality of the output and different capabilities of the printer such as being able to print graphic image depends on the method used to generate the image by the printer.

Fully Formed Character Printers

Typewriter is a very good example of the fully formed character type printing method. In a typewriter the alphabet shapes are made in advance and provided in the typewriter itself. By pressing any key, one can get the shape (given on that key) printed on the paper.

Just like the typewriter, in a fully formed character type of printer, all the printable characters are made in advance and provided in the printer, as a part of printer hardware itself.

One major drawback of these printers is, one cannot use this type of printer to print a character not provided with the printer.

Almost all fully formed character type printer use impact method to print on the paper. In this method first a hammer strikes the required character shape, this makes the character shape to press an inked ribbon against the paper, which then produce the required shape on the paper.

Some common fully formed character type printers are

- Daisy-Wheel printer,
- Chain printer,
- Drum printer etc.

Bit-Image Printers

Another very common image formation method is known as "Bit-Image" image generation. In this method printer does not contain any specific character shape, instead it prints the required character shape using a matrix of dots.

These dots are arranged to resemble the character or shape that you want to print. In these printers, characters are formed from dots placed within a matrix, this is the reason these printers are also known as "Dot-Matrix printers".

These printers can be used to print text as well as graphic images. By controlling individual dots, computer can make these printers to produce any required pattern.

Some common bit-image printers are

- Dot-Matrix Printer,
- Inkjet Printer,
- Laser Printer etc.

Printing Mechanism

Just as one can categorize printers, based on the image formation method, one can also categorize printers based on their printing mechanism. Printing mechanism refers to the method used by the printer to produce the image on the output media, such as paper, OHP transparency etc.

Based on the printing mechanism, printers can be classified into two groups

- Impact printer
- Non-Impact printer.

Impact Printer

Impact printers, as the name suggests, use impact to create an image on the output media. All impact printers smash a hammer of some kind against an inked ribbon to squeeze ink from the ribbon onto the paper.

Advantage of the impact printers is that they can be used to print on multipart forms. Because the Impact printers strike the media to create an impression, they can print not just through a ribbon but also through several sheets of paper and carbon sheet to print multiple carbon copies in a single pass.

Disadvantage of impact printers is they produce too much noise during operation.

Some common impact type printers are

- Daisy-Wheel Printer,
- Dot-Matrix Printer,
- Chain Printer,
- Drum Printer etc.

In this category, "Dot-Matrix Printer" is the most common printer. A Dot-Matrix printer is an impact printer, which works on bit-image technology.

Non-Impact Printer

Non-Impact printers do not strike any ribbon or paper to produce the image, instead they use ink spraying, electrostatic magnetization or heat process to produce the required image.

Soundless operation and very high quality output of these printers are making them very popular. At the lower price end, InkJet printers are replacing Dot-Matrix printers and at the higher end, Laser printer is the most common printer.

Disadvantage with these printers is they cannot be used to print carbon copies or multiple copies in a single pass.

Some common non-impact type printers are

- Inkjet Printer,
- Laser Printer,
- Thermal Printer etc.

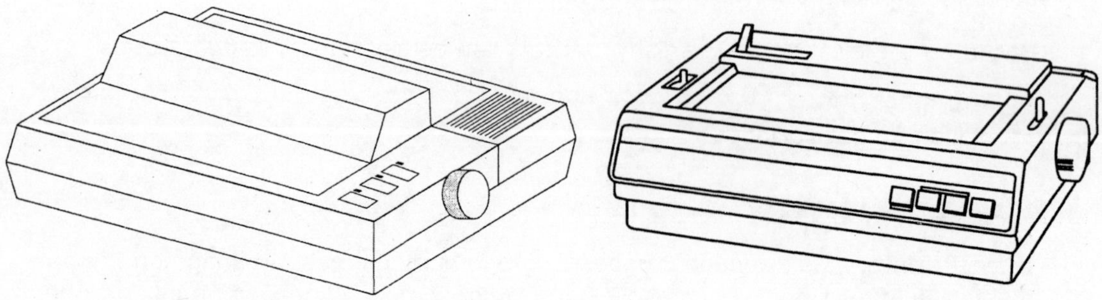

Fig. 12-1 : Dot-Matrix Printers.

Let us see some of the printers that are in use today.

Dot-Matrix Printer

Dot-Matrix printers (also known as matrix printers) are bit-image impact type printers. These printers form characters and images by placing pattern of dots on the paper.

This pattern is placed by striking an inked ribbon with a number of small pins.

These printers use a print head that shuttles back and forth across the width of the paper and a number of thin print wires on the head act as hammers that strike the ribbon and squeeze ink from ribbon to the paper.

These are one of the most common printer in the computer industry because of their simple operation, low-maintenance, low running expense, ruggedness, facility to print on almost any type of paper, and easy serviceability.

As these are impact type printers, one main drawback of these printers is the noise generated by them. The per page printing cost of Dot-Matrix printers are very-very low, because the printer ribbon can be re-inked or refilled at a very cheap price.

The speed of these printers is expressed in Characters Per Second or CPS. Printing speed ranges from 100 CPS to 1000 CPS.

Many of the Dot-Matrix printers offer color-printing option, either using a single multicolor ribbon or using complex multiple color ribbons.

To speed up the printing operation, most of the Dot-Matrix printer print bi-directionally, i.e. they print one row from left to right and then the next row from right to left.

The Dot-Matrix printer available in the market can also be classified according to the number of pins used in their print head.

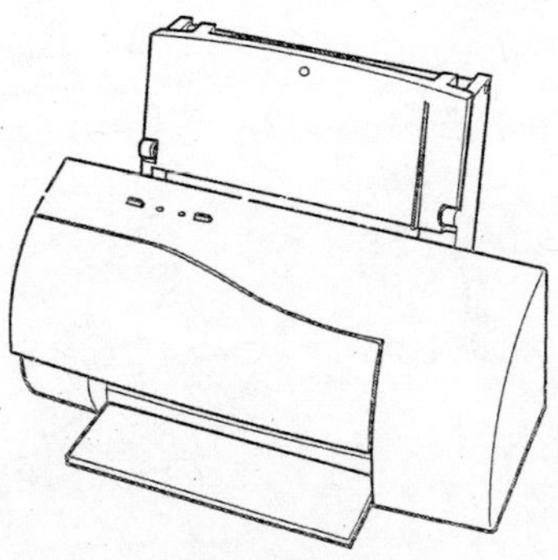
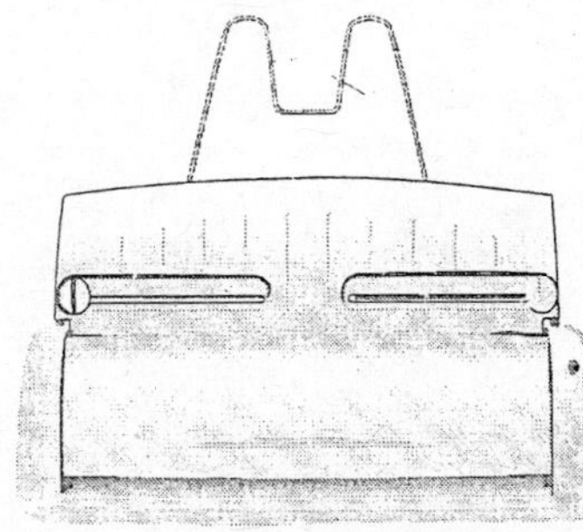

Fig. 12-2 : Inkjet Printers.

- The 9-pin print head is most common and low-cost printers but their print quality is very poor. These printers have nine pins in a single vertical column
- The 24-pin print head is highest quality Dot-Matrix printers. These printers provide very high quality print. The 24-pin heads usually have three offset columns of eight pins each.

InkJet Printer

InkJet printers are bit-image non-impact type of printers. These printers produce character shape and images by spraying ink from tiny nozzles onto the paper. This process places pattern of dots on the paper to generate the required image.

As the InkJets printers do not use any ribbon and the ink is directly released to the paper, the image looks much smoother then the image generate using the Dot-Matrix impact printer.

On these printers the force that drive ink out of the ink cartridge can be a piezoelectric crystal (a thin crystal that bends when electricity is applied across it) or a small resistor (which heats when current is applied to it).

A sharp, digital pulse of electricity causes the piezoelectric crystal to twitch and force ink through the nozzle onto the paper. The same electricity when applied to a resistor makes the resistor hot creating a small air bubble, to force ink out through the nozzle.

These printers are lightweight and small. They produce very good quality print for relatively low price. Because InkJets are non-impact printers, they are much quieter than ordinary Dot-Matrix printers.

For all their advantages, InkJet printers do have a few shortcomings. Unless proper care is taken, the ink in the nozzle can dry out and clog, making the printing very difficult. To avoid such problems, better InkJets have built-in routines that clean the nozzles with each use. Nowadays most InkJets have nozzles that are self-sealing so that when they are not used, air can't get to the ink.

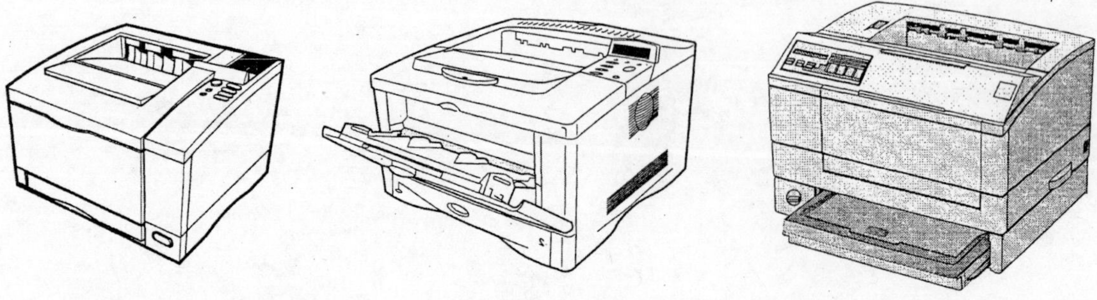

Fig. 12-3 : Laser Printers.

Also, for better results, InkJet printers require special paper with controlled absorbency. If you use cheap paper that is too porous, the ink will run away into a blur. If the paper is too glossy, the wet ink may spread.

For the quality color output, nothing is more cost effective than a color InkJet printer.

Laser Printer

Laser printers are becoming very popular as a high-end printer because of its exceptionally clear and sharp images. Almost all Laser printer have various built-in fonts and also drawing, graphs, charts etc. can be printed very easily and quickly using these printers.

These printers provide very fast output up to 16 PPM (page per minute) without producing any noise associated with the impact Dot-Matrix printers. These printers are very complex precision devices, but the basic idea behind them is simple.

Initially a cylindrical photosensitive drum inside the Laser printer is given an even electrostatic charge all over it's surface. A Laser beam- focused to a tiny spot- scans across the cylindrical drum from left to right.

The Laser beam is switched on and off according to the image to be printed on the paper, as it scans the drum surface. The drum is coated with a special photoconductive layer, which makes the drum to lose its charge from those areas wherever the Laser beam strikes.

The area which are exposed by the Laser beam, attract a black colored toner to the drum's surface, which is then transferred to the paper to form the image.

This sheet of paper is later passed through a fuser roller assembly to melt the toner and permanently fuse the image onto the paper.

Laser printers can produce images with 300 to 1200 DPI or more resolution. This higher resolution allows Laser printers to produce very clear good quality images.

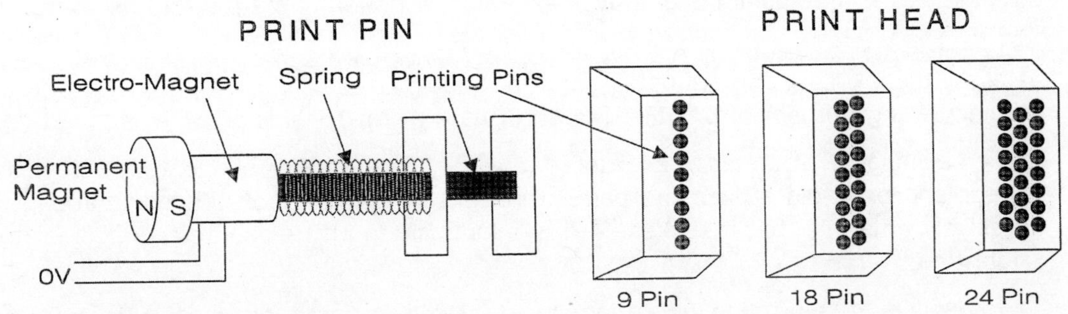

Fig. 12-4 : Dot-Matrix Print Head.

Thermal Printers

Thermal printers use heat to produce image on the printing media. These printers use special heat sensitive paper. Heating elements on its print head are heated by passing current through them and then this heated print head is pressed on the heat sensitive paper.

When the heat is applied to the heat sensitive paper, the paper changes color. Using this process the required image can be drawn as a dot-matrix image by selectively applying the heated print head pins to the paper.

The heat sensitive paper used with the thermal printer will not retain the printed image for longer then six months to one year, as the atmosphere heat will slowly change the paper color.

One should take a photocopy of the thermal printer output to make permanent copy.

How Printers Work

In this section, we shall cover the working principle behind some of the common printers.

Dot-Matrix Printer

The main image formation part of a Dot-Matrix printer is the "print head". On the print head of Dot-Matrix printer there is a number of small print-pin mechanisms.

A print-pin mechanism is a combination of permanent magnet, electromagnet, spring and print pins.

Print head is available in 9-pin, 18-pin and 24-pin models, 9-pin models have one column of nine pins, 18-pin models have two columns of nine pins each, while 24-pin models have three columns of eight pins each, although some printers use different arrangements.

Most of the low cost printers use 9-pin print head, but to produce high quality output, an increasing number of Dot-Matrix printers are using 18-pins or 24-pins.

When a line of character is to be printed, the print head moves horizontally across the paper and print-pin strikes the paper through an inked ribbon. The pins impact is precisely timed so that it strikes on the right position in the character matrix at the right time.

To speed up the printing operation, most of the impact Dot-Matrix printers print bidirectionally, i.e. printing one row from left to right and then the next row from right to left. This saves the time that would ordinarily be wasted to move the carriage to the left side of the page to start the next line.

Most of the impact Dot-Matrix printers generate the character image based on the character shape stored inside its ROM memory.

Let us see step by step printing process of a Dot-Matrix printer

- First, the computer sends a series of ASCII codes that represent characters, punctuation marks etc. to be printed to the printer over the printer cable. With this computer also sends some printer movements information such as tabs, carriage returns and form feeds etc., which controls the position of the print head and print carriage.
- The ASCII codes received by the printer are first stored inside a buffer, which is a small random access memory (RAM) inside the printer. This buffer memory is used because it usually takes longer for a Dot-Matrix printer to print than it takes for a PC to send those characters to the printer, the buffer helps free up the computer to perform other functions during printing. When the buffer gets full, printer informs the computer to stop sending any further character to the printer until some of the characters in the buffer are printed.
- Based on the received ASCII code, the processor inside the printer selects a particular dot pattern from the bit-map table contained in the printer's ROM (read-only memory) chips. This table tells the printer the pattern of dots it should use to produce the character shape represented by the received ASCII code.
- The printer's processor takes the dot pattern information from the bit-map table and sends the signals to the print head. Based on this information the print head fires various pins. The printer processor also controls the movements of the print head and the platen to move paper.
- The print head print-pins are connected to individual solenoid, or electromagnet.
- To fire the print-pins, this electromagnet is energized. This repels the magnet connected at the end of the pin, causing the pin to move with it, towards the paper.

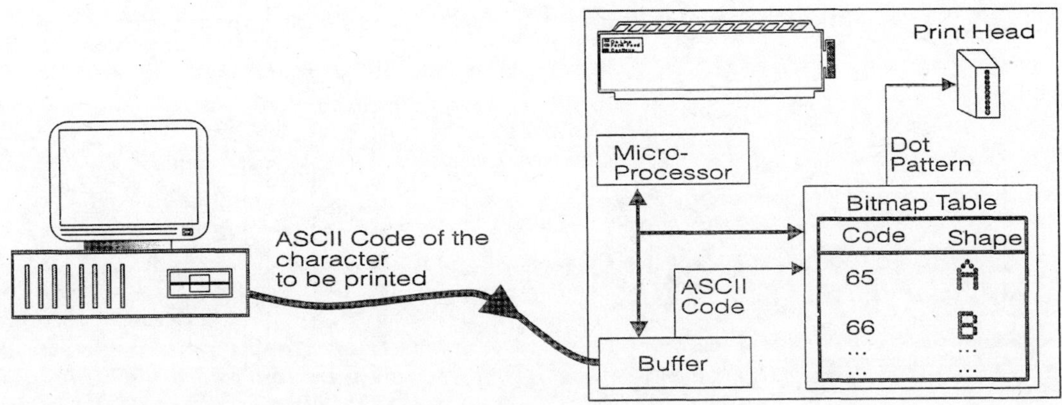

Fig. 12-5 : Printing on a Dot-Matrix Printer.

- The moving pin strikes a ribbon that is coated with ink. The force of the impact transfers ink to the paper, on the other side of the ribbon.
- After the pin fires, the electromagnet is de-energized and the spring pulls back the print-pin into its original position, ready to fire again.
- The print head is mounted on a track so it can slide back and forth across the paper surface. The print head continues firing different combinations of print wires as it moves across the page so that various vertical dot patterns can be printed to produce different character shapes.

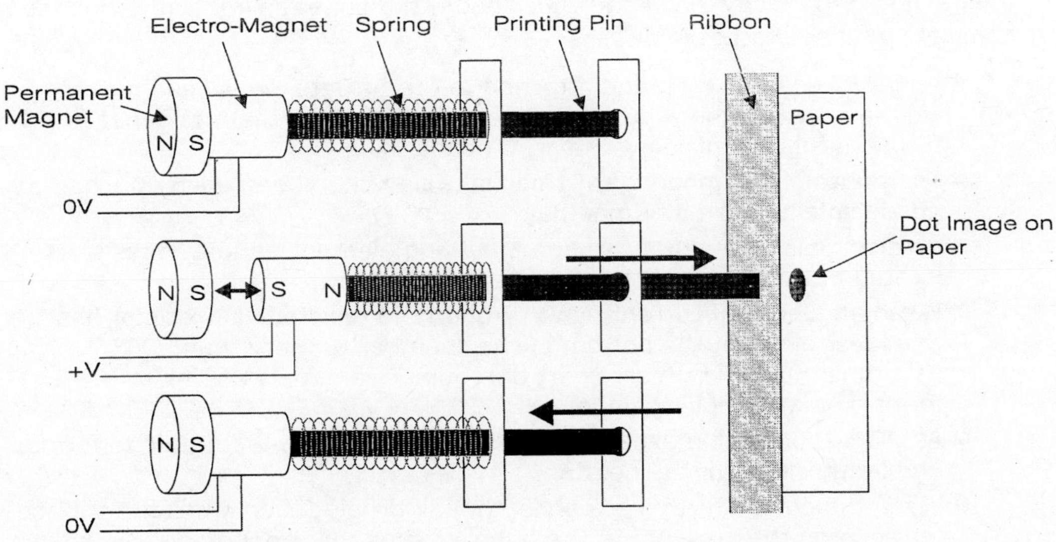

Fig. 12-6 : Process of Firing Print Head.

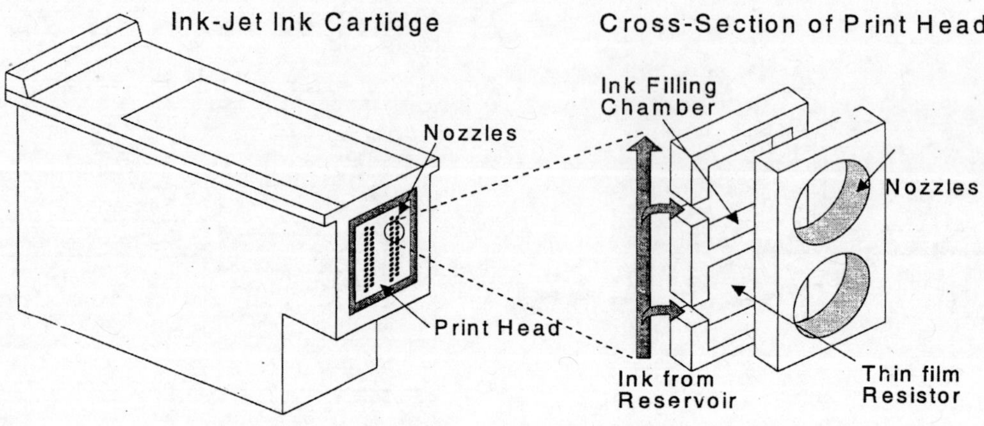

Fig. 12-7 : Inkjet Printer Print Head.

This printing mechanism is designed with one main purpose, i.e. to hold the print-pins away from the paper when no power is supplied to the printer, otherwise the print-pins may stray out of the print head and may get damaged.

Inkjet Printer

The InkJet printers also works like a Dot-Matrix printer. Both of them have print heads that travel across the width of the page, printing an entire line of text with each pass.

The biggest difference between InkJet printer and the Dot-Matrix printer is the InkJet's print head. An InkJet printer spits little drops of ink onto paper to produce an image. It's a technology that works much better than one can imagine, let us see this complete printing process in detail

- An ink-filled print cartridge attached to the InkJet's print head moves sideways across the width of a sheet of paper. This sheet of paper is fed through the printer below the print head.
- The print head is made up of small ink-filled chambers, each attached to a nozzle smaller than a human hair.
- An electrical pulse flows through a heating element i.e. a thin resistors located at the back of the ink chambers.
- When an electrical current flows through the resistor, the resistor heats a thin layer of ink at the bottom of the chamber to more than 900° Fahrenheit for a very-very short duration. This makes the ink to boil and forms a small bubble of vapor.
- As this vapor bubble expands, it pushes ink through the nozzle to form a droplet at the tip of the nozzle.
- When the bubble further expands, the ink droplet overcomes the surface tension and the pressure of the bubble forces the droplet onto the paper forming a small dot.

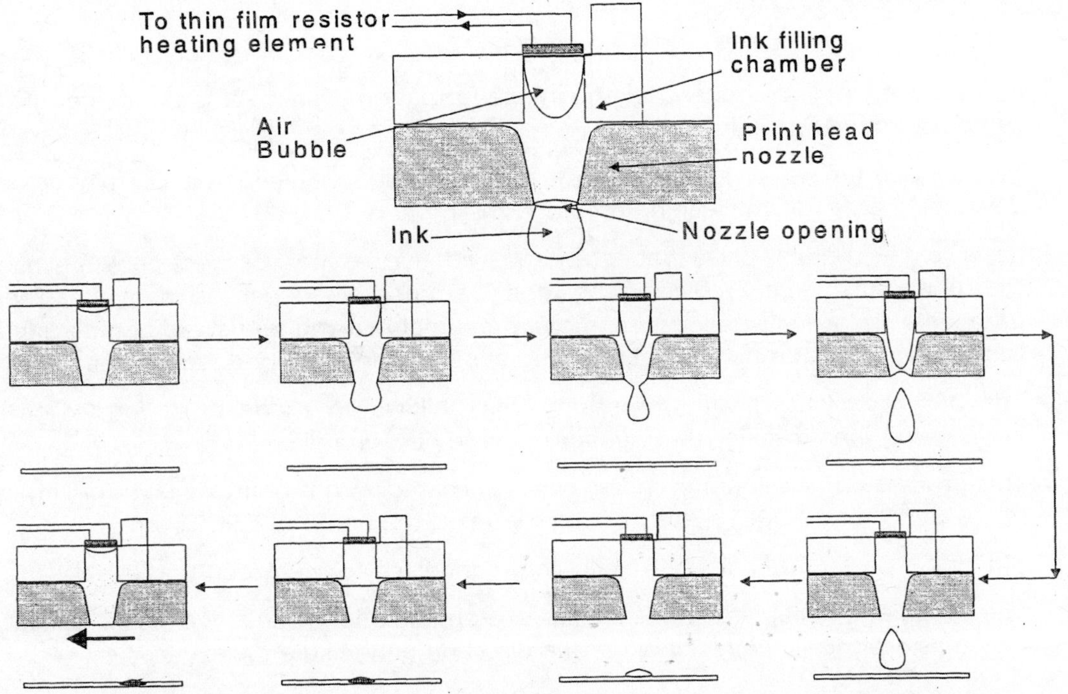

Fig. 12-8 : Printing Process of Inkjet Printer.

- A typical character is formed by a number of these tiny dots.
- As the resistor cools, the bubble collapses and the resulting suction pulls fresh ink from the attached reservoir into the ink chamber.
- For color printing multiple cartridges of three basic colors Cyan, Magenta and Yellow are used. The color output of the InkJet printers are of very high quality because there is no ribbon to fade the color, ink is directly deposited on the paper. In addition, by mixing different colors on the paper InkJet printers can provide millions of colors.
- Most of the good quality InkJet printers provide one additional black cartridge other than three basic color cartridges. This black cartridge is used to print black text or other black color images. Mixing of the three basic colors to produce black gives very faded black color.
- Some InkJet printers use piezoelectric crystal in place of the resistor to force the ink out of the chamber. When the electric current is applied to these crystals, it twitches, forcing the ink out of the chamber.

Laser Printer

In a Laser printer, the Photosensitive Drum or the Organic Photo Conductive (OPC) drum is the main component for the image formation system. It is the center of the complete image formation process.

This OPC drum is contained in a Toner Cartridge, which also contains toner, developing area, drum cleaning area and the primary Corona.

Laser printer contains parts that deteriorate with use, as most of these parts are inside the Toner Cartridge, by replacing the Toner Cartridge-whenever the toner ends-these parts gets replaced. When someone refills an empty cartridge-instead of replacing it-these worn out parts do not get replaced and the print quality deteriorates.

The OPC drum has special properties, which allows an image to be formed on its surface and then transferred to paper or some other media.

This drum is an aluminum cylinder, which is coated with a nontoxic layer of Organic Photo Conductive (OPC) material, which gives it the name of OPC Drum.

Aluminum base of this drum is electrically connected to the ground potential.

The OPC material has properties similar to a photodiode, when it is exposed to light it becomes electrically conductive (in one direction only, like a diode).

When exposed to light, any charge on the surface of the drum, conduct to the aluminum base of the drum (connected to ground i.e. to zero potential). Areas of the drum not exposed to light remain nonconductive and retain the charge.

As the OPC drum is sensitive to the light, it should never be exposed to direct sunlight or any other bright light source; as this could permanently damage the drum.

Let us now see the steps performed by the Laser Printer during the print process.

- Charge

  This step cleans the surface of the cylindrical photosensitive OPC drum and places a uniform negative electrostatic charge.
- Expose

  A data modulated laser beam scans the drum surface, converting selected negative points to positive points.
- Develop

  Dry toner powder gets attached to the positive points of the drum.
- Transfer

  Image made with dry toner powder on the drum surface gets transferred to the piece of paper.
- Detach

  This step removes the piece of paper, along with the dry toner image on the paper surface, from the drum.
- Fusing

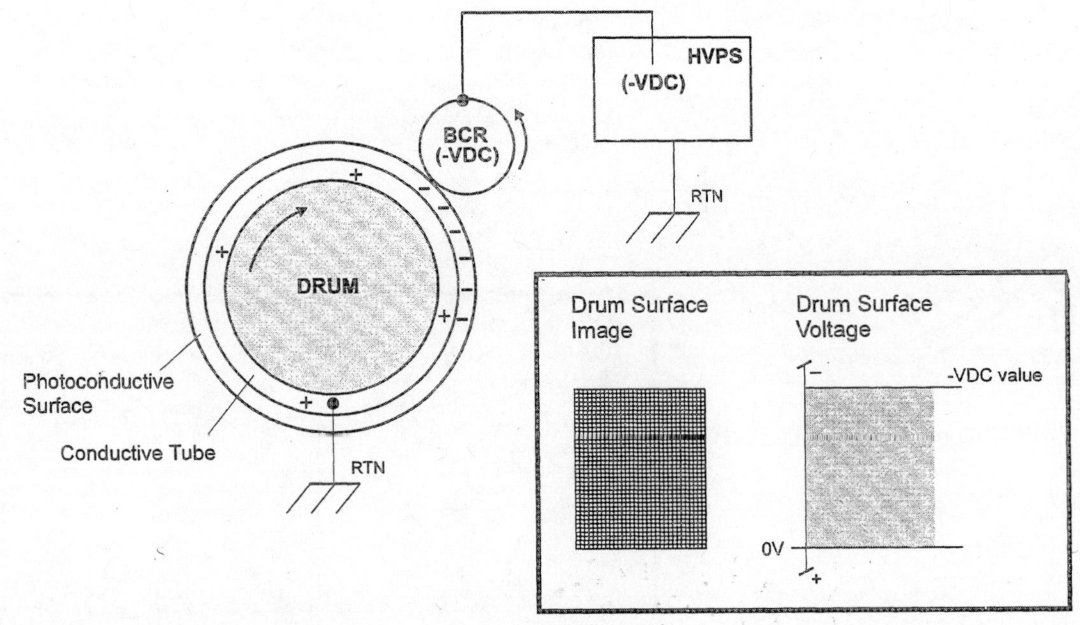

Fig. 12-9 : Charging.

This step fixed the toner image on the paper with heat and pressure.

- Clean

  Cleans any residual toner from the surface of the drum and prepares the drum for the next print cycle.

Charge

The Bias Charge Roller (BCR) places a uniform negative electrostatic charge on the surface of the OPC drum located within the Toner Cartridge. The drum surface is made of a photoconductive material that holds an electrical charge as long as the drum remains in darkness.

The BCR is a conductive roller positioned in contact with the OPC drum.

The high voltage power supply (HVPS) supplies the BCR with two voltages; a negative DC bias voltage (approx. -400VDC) and an AC discharge voltage (apporx. 800uA-850Hz)

AC voltage is used for electrically cleaning the drum of any residual charge left on the OPC drum during the previous print cycle.

DC bias voltage generates a uniform negative charge corresponding to the DC bias voltage level over the entire OPC drum surface.

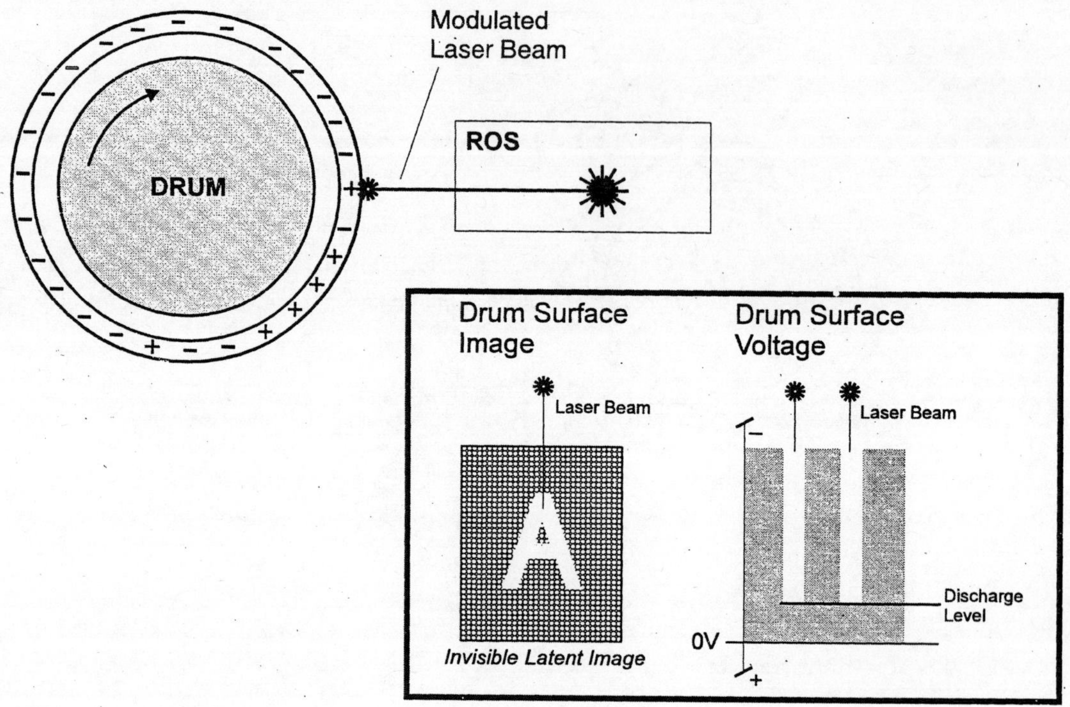

Fig. 12-10 : Expose.

Expose

In this process, the ROS (Raster Output Scanner) ASSY generates the latent image onto the OPC drum surface by scanning the drum with the laser beam.

Image data received from the print controller modulates this beam, turning it on and off according to image information that is received from the host computer.

The scanner motor rotates the polygon mirror within the ROS ASSY. The mirror reflects the laser beam produced by the laser diode so that the beam scans across the drum surface.

Whenever the print controller sends a command to print a dot, the laser switches on long enough to shine onto the drum at a single dot point.

Because of the property of the OPC drum, the areas hit by the laser beam lose its charge and the result is that the negative charge at the areas hit by the laser beam is lower than the negative charge at the non-illuminated areas.

One complete scan by the laser beam from one end of the drum to the other end makes one dot-line of the printed page.

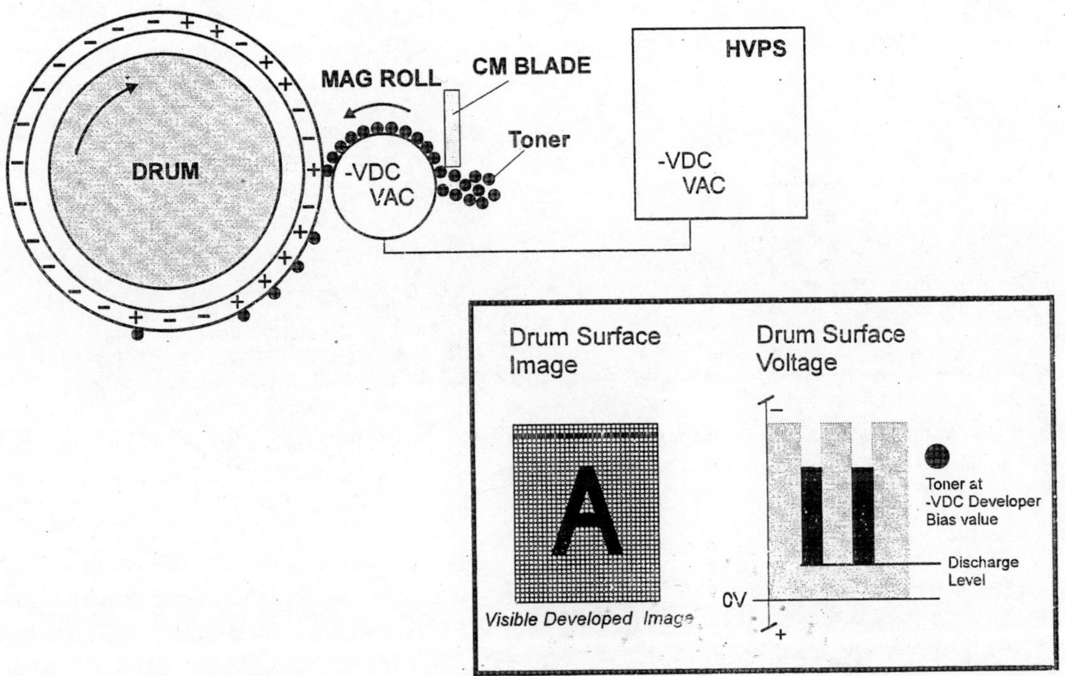

Fig. 12-11 : Develop.

Once one dot-line of image is drawn on the OPC drum, the drum is rotated by 1/600th (in a 600DPI printer) of an inch, and the above process is repeated to write the next dot-line on the drum surface.

This process creates an invisible, electrostatic image on the surface of the OPC drum. This image is called a latent image.

A small beam detect sensor called SOS, or start of scan sensor is placed at the beginning of the Laser beam sweep, before the beam reaches the drum.

This sensor is used to detect the starting point for scanning of each line. It correctly times the switching on/off of the laser diode with the rotation of the polygon mirror.

Develop

This process applies toner to the drum surface to generate the visible image. The toner contained within the Toner Cartridge has a slight magnetic property that causes it to stick to the Magnetic Roll.

The Charge Metering Blade (CM Blade) spreads the toner into a very thin and uniform layer on the Magnetic Roll. Friction between the Magnetic Roll and the CM Blade generates a small electrical charge that is transferred to the toner.

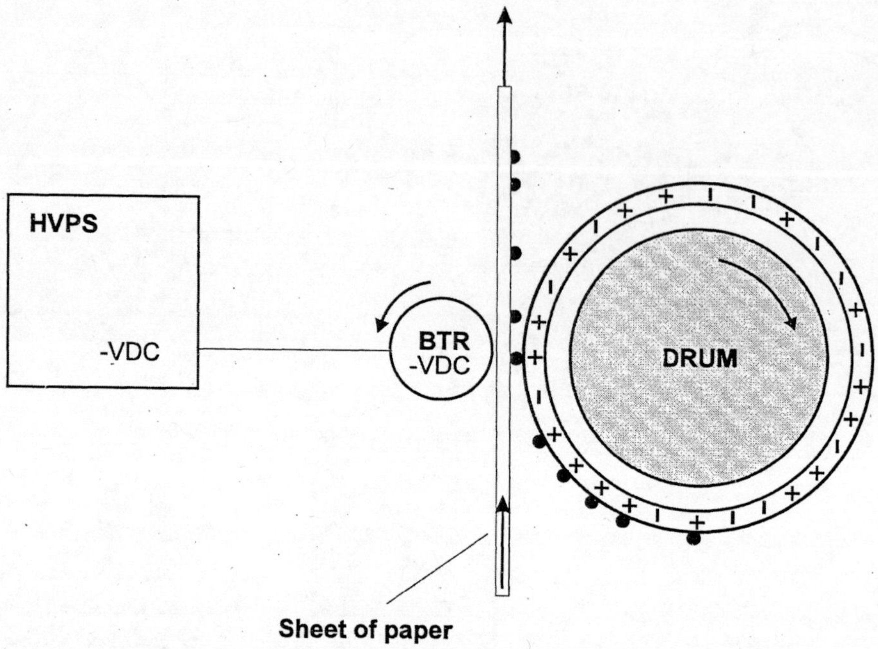

Fig. 12-12 : Transfer.

The surface of the Magnetic Roll is covered with a thin sheet of semiconductive material.

The high voltage power supply (HVPS) supplies this semiconductive sleeve with a negative DC voltage (approx. -315VDC) superposed on an AC voltage (approx. 1.8KVp-p at 3.0KHz), as a developing bias (DB).

The DC voltage keeps the magnetic roll at negative potential with respect to the OPC drum's conductive layer, this helps in transfer of toner from the Magnetic Roll to the drum surface and the AC voltage agitates the toner on the Magnetic Roll, making toner transfer easier.

As a consequence, the parts of the drum surface that were not hit by the laser beam (the areas where the negative charge was not reduced) will have lower potential than the magnetic roll, while the parts that were hit by the laser beam will have higher potential.

Because the toner on the magnetic roll is negatively charged, it will transfer to the OPC drum only at those areas where the potential on the drum is higher than the potential on the magnetic roll, thereby forming the visible image on the drum surface.

This image is called a developed image.

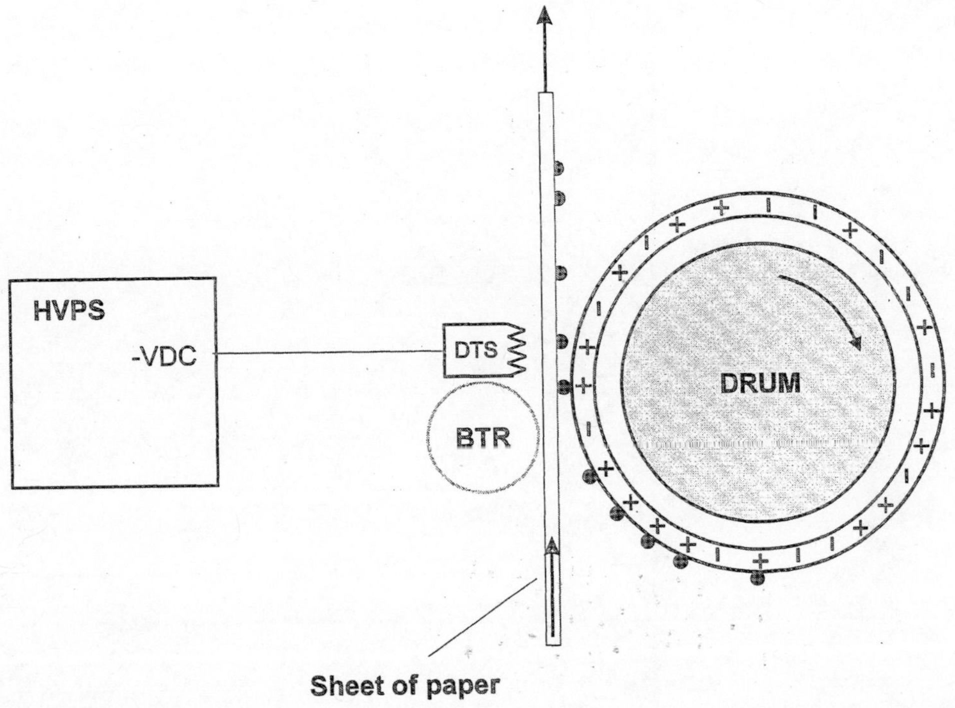

Fig. 12-13 : Detach.

Transfer

This process transfers the visible image formed by a toner on the OPC drum surface, to the paper.

This printer utilizes a BTR (Bias Transfer Roller) to effect the transfer. The BTR is a conductive roller that is positioned in contact with the OPC drum.

When the paper travels between the OPC drum and the BTR, the BTR applies a HVPS-generated positive charge (+700VDC) to the back side of the paper.

This positive charge transfers the negative charged toner image from the drum surface to the paper.

The toner image is now transferred onto the paper.

Detach

Positive charge remained on the paper causes the paper to stick to the drum surface, so, after the toner image transfers to the paper, the Detach Saw (a thin strip of metal that resembles a saw blade) applies a low voltage negative charge to the back of the paper to neutralize the positive voltage that was applied to it by the BTR.

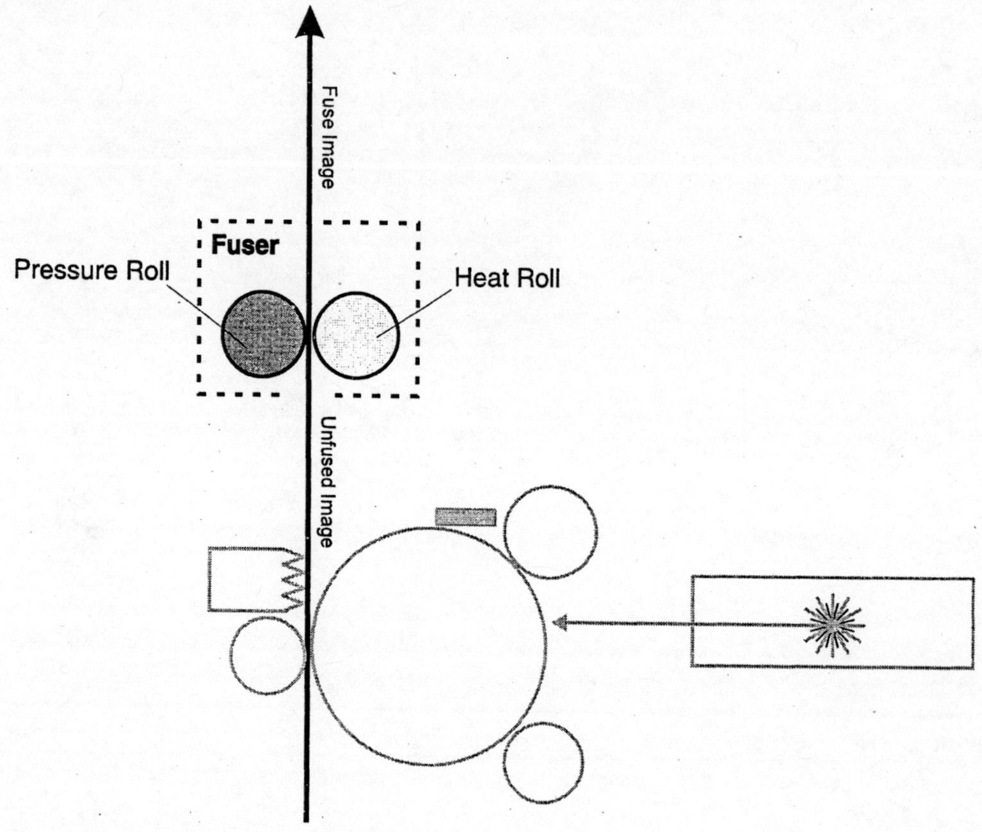

Fig. 12-14 : Fusing.

Once the positive voltage is neutralized, the paper releases easily from the drum surface and continues along the paper path to the Fuser.

Specifically, a HVPS-generated negative voltage (-2.0KVDC) is applied to the Detach Saw.

Fusing

When a sheet of paper leaves the transfer area, static electricity and the force of gravity holds the unfused toner image to the paper.

It is the job of the fusing section to melt the toner and fuse it on the printing media by applying heat and pressure. This makes the image permanent.

Before the fusing process, one can remove the toner image on the paper by just blowing on it.

This section consist of a heat roller, covered with a nonstick Teflon coating. This roller is heated from the inside using a very high intensity heater lamp.

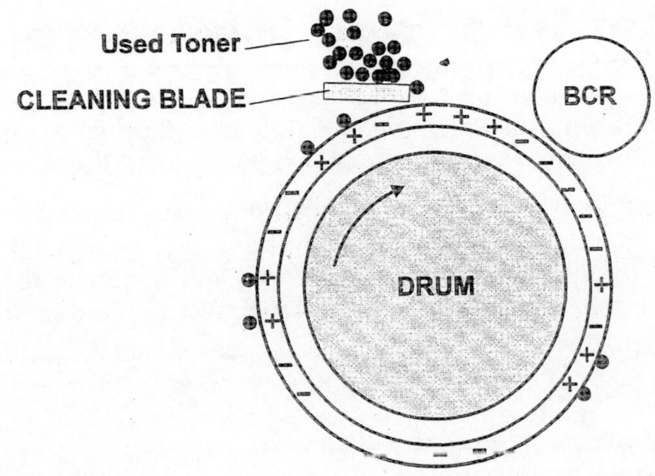

Fig. 12-15 : Cleaning.

The Teflon coating keeps the heat roller away from attracting toner particles, it also keeps the paper or any other printing medium from sticking to the roller.

A cleaning pad applies a thin coat of silicone oil to the surface of the heat roller to further prevent any sticking, this cleaning pad also wipes off toner particle or any other dirt that is on the heat roller.

A pressure roller made of soft rubber is used to apply pressure to the paper and the heat roller.

Combination of heat and pressure melts the toner image and bonds it permanently to the paper. The fused sheet of paper is then transported to the output tray.

Cleaning

In this process, a cleaning plate attached to the OPC drum scrapes residual toner (the toner that not transferred to the paper) off the drum surface. The Cleaning Blade removes any toner that remains on the drum after the transfer process.

The toner that the Cleaning Blade removes is collected in a separate waste-toner compartment within the Toner Cartridge.

Toner that is reclaimed from the drum is not reused by the Toner Cartridge.

Toner collected by cleaning is collected as leftover toner and kept in the different room from that of the unused toner. This, leftover toner is not reused.

In addition to the above cleaning operation, the BTR surface is also cleaned electrically. At the initialization cycle of the printer operation or before starting a print job, a negative charge (approx. -600VDC) is applied to the BTR and the toner sticking on the BTR surface is transferred from the BTR to the drum by this voltage.

PC-Printer Interface (Software)

In this section, we look at how the information is transferred from computer to printer. How the computer makes use of various functions provided by the printer by using control codes. Page description such as PostScript, HP-PCL etc. is also covered.

The printer is connected to the computer through a data cable, the computer sends various information to the printer through these lines. Any information send by the computer to the printer can be interpreted by the printer in many different ways, based on this interpretation, printer acts differently on the received data.

Information send by the computer to the printer can be interpreted as:

- Plain ASCII Data
- Printer Control Code/Escape Code
- Graphic/Bit-Image Data
- Page description language statement

Plain ASCII Data

The plain ASCII data is a byte of information send from the computer to the printer, it contains ASCII (American Standard Code for Information Interchange) code of the character to be printed, it is up to the printer to convert this code into proper character shape and print it.

When a printer receives an ASCII code, it consults its own memory for the shape of the received code, for example when the code 65 is received the printer searches in its own memory for the shape of the character 65 to be printed.

In standard ASCII, code 65 is used for the character "A", so the printer will get the bitmap image of the character "A" from its memory and send it to the printing mechanism. The printing mechanism, based on this information, will print the shape "A" on the paper.

Printer Control Code/Escape Code

ASCII codes are also used to inform the printer about any special function such as printing bold letters, printing underline etc. required by the user. ASCII codes that are used to communicate these special functions to the printer are called printer control codes.

These codes are also referred as embedded commands, as these codes are embedded in the data coming from the computer.

Some of the common function such as backspace, line feed, form feed etc. are included in the standard ASCII character set itself. These functions are assigned specific character value.

To linefeed the printer, computer can just send the ASCII code 10 to the printer. The character 10 is the linefeed character in the standard ASCII code. Upon receiving this character, the printer will move the paper one line up. The entire group of these special ASCII codes is termed control characters.

The number of ASCII characters available for the printer commands are very few and the number of functions that the printer can carry out are many. To allow these additional instructions to be sent to the printer most printers use special combination of characters as printer control codes.

When a combination of ASCII code is used as control code, in most of these codes the first character is always ASCII code 27 (01Bh), commonly known as the Escape character. As most of these control codes start with the escape character these codes are also known as Escape control codes.

In most of these commands, the escape character by itself does nothing. It is only used to inform the printer that the characters that follow the Esc code should be interpreted as control codes and should not be printed as plain ASCII data.

Most of the printers use Epson or IBM compatible control codes, so these codes have become an industry standard in the Dot-Matrix printer segment. Laser and InkJet printers use the Hewlett Packard codes as standard.

Graphic/Bit-Image Data

Sometimes instead of sending ASCII code or control code to the printer, the computer may want to directly control the printing of the image or control the print head of the printer.

In this situation computer sends the bit-image of the required image to the printer and if the printer is a dot-matrix printer, it will generate the image by firing its pins according to the bit-image data being received.

Before sending this type of data to the printer, most of the printer require some type of control code to be send from the computer, to inform the printer that the data being sent by the printer is not ASCII code, instead it is bit-image data, and it should be properly interpreted and printed by the printer.

Page Description Language (PDL)

Some printers especially the page printers such as Laser printer, can generate image according to the page description language statement sent by the computer.

These languages can be used to control any of the printer supporting them. One big advantage of these languages is that they are hardware independent, i.e. when a computer sends output to the printer in this format, the printout can be taken on any printer that supports these languages.

Most of the page description language resemble a high level language such as Pascal or C, with flow control and logic statements etc.

When one uses page description language to send output to the printer it will be the job of the printer to generate the image to be printed based on the instructions received.

This makes it necessary for the printers supporting PDL to have a good deal of computing power and memory capacity, otherwise the printing process by these printers will be very slow.

Two very common industry standard PDL are PostScript and PCL.

PostScript

PostScript is a page description language used to define text, graphics and complete page layout in a high level language like format. This language was developed by the Adobe systems.

One major advantage with the PostScript is it is "device independent", i.e. the same PostScript code when send to different devices produce the same type of image but using the maximum capability such as the resolution available on that particular device, one does not require a different PostScript code for different devices.

For example, when a PostScript file is send to 300-DPI printer, a 300-DPI image is printed, the same file when send to a 1200-DPI PostScript compatible typesetter will print the same image at 1200-DPI resolution.

A printer that has PostScript facility require lot of computing power and memory because the PostScript language is very complex and computer intensive and it is the job of the printer to convert the incoming PostScript instructions into proper image.

PCL (Printer Control Language)

PCL or the Printer Control Language was introduced by the Hewlett Packard to control their ThinkJet printers. This control language was later expanded as PCL3 to control their first laser printer, the original LaserJet printer.

PCL is not a true page description language like the PostScript language, this is more of an expanded printer control command set. To control the printer using the PCL, one need to send long strings of control codes.

Even the PCL5 introduced in 1990 is not a device independent language like the PostScript, It currently works only with laser printers, so its code cannot be used to drive some other device such as a typesetter.

Although, the PCL5 lack many features of the PostScript language, it can produce PostScript quality image on the paper.

HP has currently introduced the PCL6, which has improved the printing speed and provided many new routines to print the scanned images, faster and better.

PC-Printer Interface (Hardware)

After looking at how the data sent from the PC is interpreted by the printer, let us now see how the printer can be physically connected to a computer. Printer can be connected to computer at Serial, Parallel, USB or IrDA (Infrared) port.

Serial Port

The serial port is used for the computer to communicate with a device one bit at a time, the data moves serially one bit at a time from one device to another.

To communicate using the serial communication, two communicating device must use the same communication parameters such as the communication mode, baud rate (bits per second), parity etc.

PC use RS232-C standard interface.

There is basically two type of serial communication

- Synchronous (Controlled by a clock signal)
- Asynchronous (Not controlled by a clock signal)

Because of the use of asynchronous communication method, IBM calls its serial port s asynchronous data communication port or more commonly as async port or comm port.

Serial Interface Connectors

A 25-pin or 9-pin D-shell subminiature male connector is used on the system as connector for the serial interface. The 25-pin connector was introduced with the PC system, but as not all the 25-pins are used for data transmission, IBM introduced 9-pin connectors with the AT system.

The parallel port also uses 25-pin D type connector but it can be distinguished from the serial port because the parallel port connector is female, whereas the connector for the serial port are male connectors (connectors with pin).

Old-style MDA/CGA/EGA video connectors, which use 9-pin D-shell connectors are also female connectors.

If the serial cable for your device contains 25-pin connector and the serial port has only 9-pin connector then many 25-pin to 9-pin converters are available in the market, same is true for connecting 9-pin device to a 25-pin port connector you can get a 9-pin to 25-pin converter.

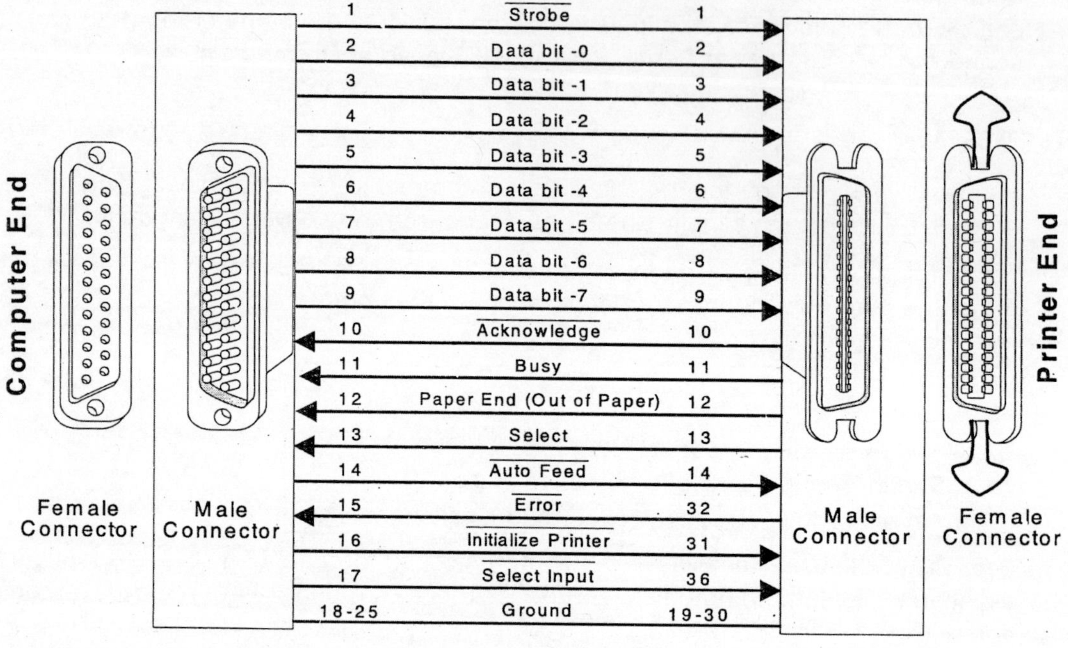

Fig. 12-16 : PC-Printer 25-pin Parallel Interface.

Parallel Port

A parallel port is a fast and trouble free connection you can have on your computer. This port is also known as the "printer port" because it is commonly used for the printer interfacing. Some peripherals other than the printer can also use this port to communicate with the computer.

In this interfacing system, the signals travel through data cable, eight bits at a time. Other than the data, some control signals are also passed through the cable between the printer and the computer.

The parallel interface is one of the simplest communication system available, in this eight different lines are provided for the eight data lines, for each signal required to control the communication process a new wire is provided. This makes the circuitry required to drive the parallel signals very simple.

However, this simplicity has one drawback that is the cable required for the transmission. The increased numbers of lines make the cable required for the parallel transmission very thick. The numbers of lines going together have one more problem of cross-talk. When the electrical signals travel together in a cable, these signals start to affect each other as they travel down the cable. This makes the signal from one wire to change the signal on the other wire or the problem of cross-talk (signal crosses over and start talking with other signals) appears.

To prevent this problem of cross-talk it is recommended to keep the length of the parallel cable limited to maximum 10 feet. If the cable length is more than this, there is a chance of cross-talk appearing in the line.

Uni & Bi-Directional Parallel Port

The original parallel interface provided on the initial IBM computer's were designed as printer output port so they were uni-directional i.e. they could only send the information to the device connected to the port but they could not receive any information from the device.

Later IBM made some change in the design and made the parallel ports capable of the bi-directional operation.

Enhanced Parallel Port (EPP)

Enhanced Parallel Port or the EPP is a new parallel port specification that allows high-speed two-way communication between the computer and the device, other than a printer or scanner.

Extended Capabilities Port (ECP)

Extended Capabilities Port or ECP is also a new high-speed two-way communication parallel port specification. ECP port is mainly used for a printer or scanner.

To connect to a printer to the ECP port you would require

- EPP/ECP port
- ECP capable printer
- EPP/ECP capable printer cable
- Windows 98/2000/ME/XP operating system

Parallel port provided on the motherboard can be setup as EPP/ECP port using the following procedure

- Enter BIOS setup during computer power on by pressing **Del** key.
- In the BIOS setup main menu, select **Peripheral Setup** option.
- Look for **Parallel Port Mode**.
- Change the mode to **EPP/ECP**.
- Save and Exit BIOS setup and restart the system.

Parallel Connectors

IBM has followed the standard developed by the printer manufacturer Centronics when deciding the design of the parallel interface. Although IBM followed the signals of the Centronics, it did not approve of the 36-conductor Amphenol connector used by the Centronics, instead IBM selected 25-pin D-shell subminiature connector for their parallel connection.

Since then, the printer cable for the parallel printer have a 25-pin D-shell connector on one side which is connected to the computer and the other side of the cable will have 36-conductor Amphenol connector, to connect to the printer.

Parallel Port Signal

Computer uses a 25-connector D-Shell miniature connector for the parallel connection. Let us see the function of these lines.

Strobe (pin 1)

This line is used to inform a device connected to the parallel interface that the data is ready at the address line. This signal is a negative active signal.

Data (pin 2-9)

This line is used to send eight bits of data to the device connected to the parallel port.

Acknowledge (pin 10)

This signal is used by the device connected to the parallel port to inform to the computer that the data send is received and taken care properly and the device is now ready for more data.

This signal is also active low signal.

Busy (pin 11)

Even after receiving the acknowledge signal computer will not send data as long as the busy line is high, this line instructs the computer that printer is busy with some job and the computer should not send data to the device.

It stays high when the device connected to the parallel port is unable to receive any more data because of jammed paper, or buffer getting full etc.

Out of paper (pin 12)

This signal is used by the printer to inform the computer that the paper is finished.

Select (pin 13)

This line is used by the device connected to the parallel interface that the device is ready or in on-line condition and selected so that the computer can start sending data to the device.

Auto Feed XT (pin 14)

Using this "Auto Feed XT", line computer can control whether the printer should provide a line feed with the carriage return or not.

By holding this line low, the printer is instructed to automatically feed one line with each carriage return, this line can be made high to instruct the printer that no line feed be provided when carriage return is received.

Error/Fault (pin 15)

This signal is used by the device connected to the parallel port to inform to the computer that there is something wrong with the device and the computer must stop sending of data to it.

This is an active low signal

Initialize Printer (pin 16)

This is another active low signal, used to initialize the printer.

Select Input (pin 17)

This signal is used by the computer to enable or disable the device connected to the parallel interface. Making this line low will turn the device on-line and making this line high will turn the device off-line.

USB (Universal Serial Bus)

The Universal Serial Bus (USB) makes your computer easier to use with advanced plug-and-play capabilities. USB is not a connection only for printers, USB is a bus standard that can be used to connect various external hardware devices, such as keyboards, mouse, speakers, and digital cameras etc. to the computer.

USB devices are hot pluggable, i.e. you can add devices to your computer easily without having to shutdown the computer. External devices can be connected at any time, even when the computer is running.

Because of the USB's Plug and Play capability, computer can identify USB devices when they are plugged in and automatically configure them by loading the appropriate driver.

USB devices can be powered by drawing current directly from the USB cable. If you have a new computer, you will find four/six USB ports on the motherboard. If you have an old system you can connect a PCI USB adapter card, to get USB facility.

Also, one needs to have the latest operating system for the USB support, currently Windows 98/ME/XP/2000 and later versions of Windows operating system support USB port. Older Windows 3.1/95 etc. doses not support USB.

USB port has option to daisy chain the devices connected at its output socket. One can connect a maximum of 127 peripheral devices on a single USB port. Each USB port

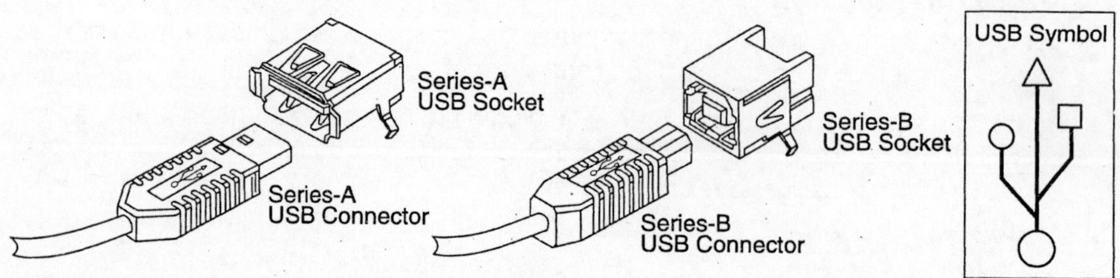

Fig. 12-17 : USB Connectors and Sockets.

connects to a single device, to connect multiple devices one can use hubs. One can connect one hub into other to provide several jacks to connect more devices to a single USB port.

By connecting hubs together, up to 127 total devices, including hubs can be attached to the host computer.

Each device can be located up to five meters from its hub.

USB Cable/Connector

The USB specification defines a standard connector, socket, and cable, which all USB devices can use.

The USB hub uses a type A connector, and the device uses a type B connector.

Type A connector/jack are the thin wide slots provided at the back of the computer to connect a USB device. Type B connector/jack is a small, nearly square hole provided on the USB devices (printer, scanner etc.), into which the mating B plug is connected.

All USB cables will have A plug at one end and B plug at the other end, one end attach to the hub and the other end attach to the device.

There are two types of USB cables: high speed and low speed. Low-speed cables differ primarily in their shielding. Plugging a high-speed device into a low-speed cable can cause signal distortion over long distances. The maximum allowed length of a USB cable is five meters.

Both high speed and low speed USB cable use a four-wire cable. Two wires (+Data and -Data) transfer data as a differential digital data signal, i.e. the voltage on the two wires is of equal magnitude but opposite polarity. When this data signal is subtracted from one another, this results in any noise in the signal getting canceled.

One wire is used as power line, which contains a five-volt DC voltage. This power line is used to provide power for devices connected to the USB cable. Final wire is used as ground return line.

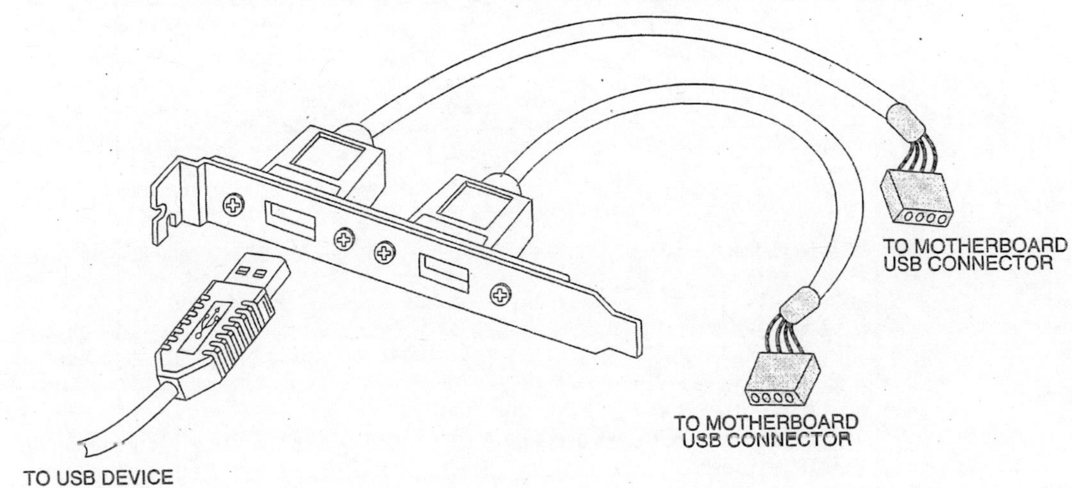

Fig. 12-18 : USB Connector to Motherboard.

On the high-speed line, the two data lines are twisted together.

Following color-coding scheme is used in the USB cable

Color	Signal
Green	+Data
White	-Data
Red	+5V Vcc
Black	Ground

USB Troubleshooting

Check the following to troubleshoot printer connected to the USB port.

Check Window Version

When using USB port to connect a printer, make sure that the operating system supports the USB port. In Windows 3.1, Windows 95 or Windows NT, the USB port would not work. Operating systems Windows 98 onward provide support for USB connection.

If your system has Windows XP or Windows 2000 then the USB port should work without any problem. If your computer system use some older version of operating then upgrade to a new version before installing the USB printer.

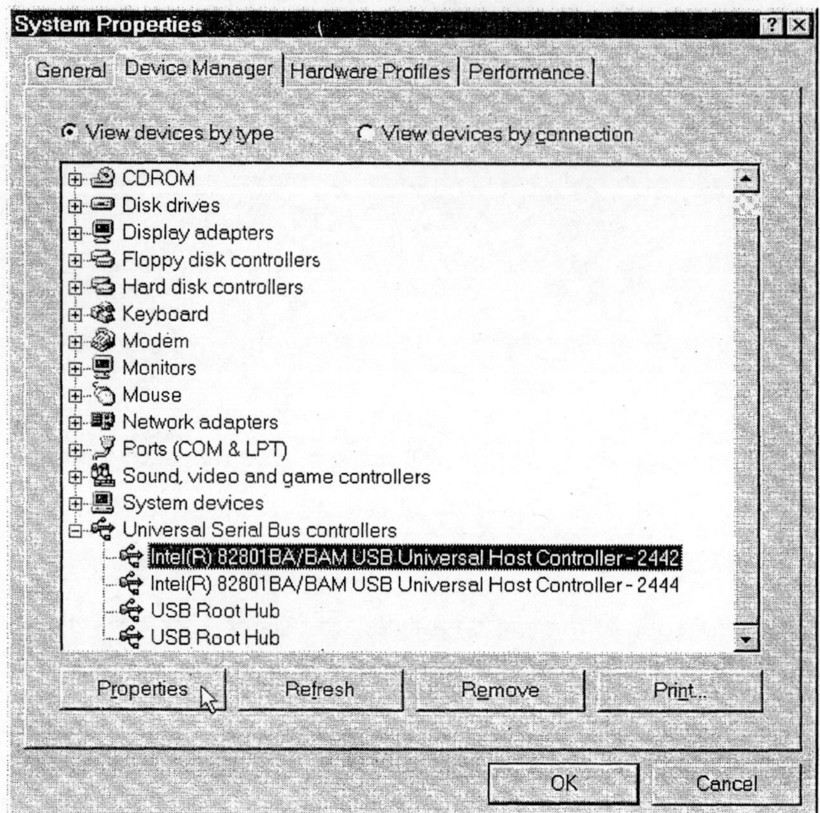

Fig. 12-19 : Checking Version of USB Controller.

Check USB Controller

Some of the initial motherboards with USB support do not provide proper support for the USB port. Therefore, if you have one of those motherboards you need to upgrade the motherboard with a new one.

To check the version of USB controller

- Click on Start, Settings, Control Panel.
- Double Click on System.
- Click on Device Manager tab.
- Double Click on Universal Serial Bus Controllers.
- Double Click on the Intel 82371SB PCI to USB Universal Host Controller entry. If the controller name being shown is different then you have a new controller, you can skip the next step.
- In the General tab check the hardware version, it should not be 000.

If it is 000 then you need to upgrade your motherboard, or disable USB on the motherboard and buy a new PCI USB card.

Read the manual before installing USB printer

Installing a USB printer is not as simple as installing a serial or parallel printer, some printer require that the printer software should be installed before connecting the printer, some require that you connect the printer halfway between installing the software.

If you do not follow these steps exactly, then the printer may not work properly, or may not work at all.

If you made a mistake at the first install then before reinstalling the printer, you cannot just reinstall to correct the problem, you need to first remove the files from the first install. This again is not as easy as just uninstalling the printer from control panel, you can find detailed uninstall procedure in the printer manual or in the printer manufacturers web site.

Printer features are missing

After installing a printer if you find that many of the printers feature are missing in the printer property dialog box then you may be using some old version of the printer driver. Reinstall the printer with latest driver.

IrDA

IrDA (Infrared Data Association) is an international organization that creates and promotes interoperable, low cost, infrared data interconnection standards. However, here by IrDA we mean a group of short-range, high speed, bi-directional wireless infrared port, defined by the IrDA group.

IrDA port allows a variety of devices to communicate with each other. Cameras, printers, portable computers, desktop computers, personal digital assistants (PDAs), and mobile phones can communicate with compatible devices using this technology.

IrDA port supports transmission of data between two devices over short-range at speeds between 9.6 kilobits per second (Kb/s) and 4Mb/s.

IrDA is a small semitransparent red window you may see on your notebook computer, PDA, printers or even on the mobile phones.

Installing an Infrared Device

This section describes how to install infrared devices. If you change the infrared adapter model connected to the computer, you should reinstall it.

The procedure for installing an infrared device depends on whether it is a Plug and Play device or a non-Plug and Play device.

To install a Plug and Play IrDA device

If it is an external device, attach it. The Infrared software loads automatically.

Double-click the Infrared icon in Control Panel to activate the infrared device. If there is no Infrared icon in Control Panel, press F5 to make the icon appear.

To install a non-Plug and Play IrDA device

If it is an external device, attach it.

In Control Panel, double-click the Add New Hardware wizard. Follow the instructions on the screen, making the following choices:

- If asked whether the device you want is in the list, click No.
- When asked whether you want Windows to search for your new hardware, click No.
- When the Hardware Types box appears, click Infrared devices.
- When asked to select a device, accept the default selection Generic Infrared Serial Port or dongle. (The other devices listed are Plug and Play devices.)
- When asked for such information as the communications port that the infrared device is physically connected to, if you are not sure, accept the defaults.

Using the Infrared Monitor

You can use the Infrared Monitor to keep track of your computer's infrared activity. You can activate Infrared Monitor once your infrared device is installed by double-clicking the Infrared icon in Control Panel or by clicking the animated Infrared icon in the system tray on the Taskbar.

Printing with Infrared Transfer

Before attempting to print, make sure the infrared communications driver is properly installed and the infrared devices are enabled.

Make sure the infrared communications driver is installed on the computer.

Bring an infrared-enabled printer within range.

Your computer might automatically detect and install the printer. If not, make sure the printer driver for the infrared-capable printer is installed on the computer.

Try the Print option in a program.

You can make printers without built-in infrared ports infrared-capable by connecting an infrared adapter made for printers into the printer's parallel port.

If a parallel cable is also used to connect the computer to the infrared printer adapter, you can use either the infrared link or the parallel cable to print. The infrared link is used when you select the virtual parallel port; the cable is used when you select the physical parallel port.

To check the infrared link to the printer, make sure the correct printer driver is installed for the infrared-capable printer. (Most printers with built-in infrared ports are

Plug and Play devices, which are installed automatically.) Then use a program to print over the infrared link.

If the program prints on an infrared-capable printer, it confirms that the infrared driver is properly installed.

IrDA Troubleshooting

- Make sure that the IrDA port on the computer and the printer are clean and unblocked.
- Move the computer/printer to one side to bring them in proper line of sight.
- Check that nothing is blocking the infrared ray moving between computer and printer.
- Make sure that the infrared port on the computer is active. Check the BIOS setup.
- Check that no other infrared emitting device is interfering with the communication, such as a TV remote handset.

Printer Sharing

In an organization, one does not need a printer for each computer. To save the cost of the additional printer one can share the printer between two or more computers.

Several printer sharing devices are available in the market, some of them are hardware based and some are software based.

Sharer Switch

One of them is called "Printer Sharer switch" or a "A/B Switch". This device is most commonly used to share the printer between two computers, one can also connect more than two computers to one printer using this type of switch.

This device works like a simple multipole switch, when the switch is in "A" position the information from the computer A is routed to the printer and when the switch is changed to position "B" then the output from the computer B is send to the printer.

This process is almost equal to removing the printer data cable from the computer A and connecting it to the computer B, only difference is one is saved the work of removing and reconnecting the cables every time another computer need the printer.

This type of printer sharer is available for both serial as well as parallel interfaces. One can get them to share one printer with 2, 3 or 4 computers.

Some of these sharers can do autoswitching i.e. they can sense the computer from which the data is coming and can automatically switch it to the printer.

Sharing through Network

If your computer is connected to a network, most of the networks provide printer sharing facility.

If your computer is connected to the local area network and you are using Windows 98 then follow the below given steps to share your printer

- Click Start, point to Settings, and then click Printers.
-
- Click the printer you want to share. Click `Shared As`, type a name you want the others to see for your printer.On the `File` menu, click `Properties`.
- Click the `Sharing` tab, and then

You can only share a printer that is connected to your computer

If the Sharing tab is not visible, you need to enable "file and print sharing services" as explained below.

- Open the Network dialog box by clicking Start, pointing to Settings, clicking Control Panel, and then double-clicking Network.
- Click "`File and Print Sharing`".
- Select the check box for the sharing options you want.
- A check mark indicates the feature is activated.
- Click OK.

Printer Troubleshooting

Ninety percent of the printer problems can be easily rectified by a non-technical person, because most of the time the problem is not because of the electronics inside the printer.

Instead, most of the fault reported about the printer is due to some mechanical fault of the printer, or due to some fault in the printer cable, it could also be due to printer not being setup properly, or even it could be due to some problem in the software being used to print on the printer.

Once you know the working of different printers, you should be able to diagnose and rectify most of the problems. Printers by different manufacturers have some variation in the working and electronic circuit inside them but their basic working principle remains same.

In this section, we shall look at some common problem faced when using a Dot-Matrix printer, InkJet printer and Laser printer. First we start with some preventive maintenance tips.

Preventive Maintenance

Before starting on the troubleshooting let us first see some of the preventive maintenance steps that one should take to keep the printer in good working condition.

When one opens a Dot-Matrix printer, one may find many small pieces of paper inside the printer, especially if continuous stationary is used in the printer. One should periodically vacuum out these paper scraps.

Clean the printer paper path, ribbon path and the head assembly movement path with a dry, soft cloth. You can also use a soft brush for this purpose. Also clean the outer surface of the printer with some soft cloth, damp with warm soap water, do not use cloth that is dripping, instead use a damp cloth.

If you print on self sticking labels and envelops with gum, than the printer rollers may have attracted some glue from these materials. Remove this glue buildup by using alcohol and a clean cloth.

If you periodically clean and lubricate your printer, you can avoid expensive repairs later. Once the cleaning is done, check for any loose belts etc. If any belt is loose then replace it.

Next comes lubricating, lubricating of the head assembly movement mechanism can be done periodically to have a smooth movement of the print head. When applying lubricants one should be careful that they should not be applied to wrong places, otherwise printer damage can occur.

Whenever some lubricant is used it should be silicone or Teflon based. One should apply just enough lubricant so that the extra lubricant will not accumulate dust and create problem for the printer. One can safely lubricate most of the mechanical parts, for smooth working of the printer.

For long life of the printer's print head, keep the print head as cool as possible, do not stack up thing on and around the printer that may stop proper airflow.

Also, for the print head's life you should not use cheap ink to re-ink the ribbon cartridge, the cheap ink used for the re-inking contains acid which corrodes the print head pins and as some necessary lubricant provided in more expensive inks is missing in these inks, after some time, the print head pins start to stick.

One should not turn the printer platen roller when the printer's power is on. The platen roller is turned on by a stepper motor. If you rotate the platen in the power on position, the motor may get damaged. This rule also applies to the ribbon carriage assembly motor, which is moved by another stepper motor.

If your printer has friction feed and tractor feed option then don't engage both the friction feed and tractor feeds at the same time. If you engage both the tractor feed and the friction feed at the same time then the paper feeding will not be proper and the paper may get stuck in the printer.

Troubleshooting Dot-Matrix Printers

Print Quality Poor

Ribbon Worn Out or Damaged

Remove the ribbon and check to see if the ribbon appears to be dried out, damaged or rotation has seized.

Replace the ribbon with the genuine item

Print Head Too Close to the Platen

Adjust the print head lever to ensure that the print head is not too close to the platen and hence paper.

This will cause not only smudging but may lead to paper jamming and in some cases, print head damage

Ribbon Drive Assembly Faulty

Print a self test, or send information to be printed.

While this is happening, observe that the ribbon is turning in both directions.

If the ribbon is not turning or only turning in one direction then the ribbon drive assembly could be at fault and require replacement

Printhead is Faulty

Remove the printhead. Visually inspect the pins. If some are missing or damaged then the printhead is faulty.

Depending upon the brand of your printer, printheads can be repaired for a fraction of the cost of a replacement print head.

Working on printheads is as intricate as working on a watch, be careful when trying to repair.

No Power to Printer

Fuse has Blown

Check the fuse with a meter and replace the fuse. Ensure the correct voltage and amperage

Faulty Power On-Off Switch

Check with a meter and replace the switch.

Ensure the correct voltage and amperage

Internal Power Supply has Failed

Most common fault. Repair yourself only if you know what you are doing.

Chances are there is multiple damage, replacing one or two components will only allow power to circulate temporarily causing greater damage

Main Logic Board is Shutting Down the Power Supply

Repair the logic on the main logic board and in some cases when damage is too extensive or parts are unavailable (custom chipsets), the main logic board will require replacement

Power But Not Printing

Printer Cable Not Installed Properly

Ensure that both ends of the cable are correctly installed

Printer Cable is Faulty

Check for possible pin damage and replace if necessary

No Paper or Paper Not Installed Properly

No paper will result with the printer going into alarm, not coming "on-line" or "ready".

Install some paper. If there is paper, ensure it is correctly installed.

Tractor fed paper needs to be properly aligned and driven up to the start of the platen roller.

Ensure that the "on-line" button has been selected.

There are sensors along the paper path, if these are defective they will cause the printer to not print.

Check the sensors along the paper path and replace if necessary

Printer Port Connection at PC is Faulty

Try printing plain text via DOS (you can even use the "print screen" command on your keyboard while you are in the DOS environment).

If still not printing, refer to you printer's owner's manual and perform a "self test" of your printer.

If the printer prints OK, the fault is more likely with the computer or the printer cable, not with the printer.

Self Test is OK and PC Printer Port is OK

Faulty main logic board. Repair input/output circuit on main logic board.

Extensive damage may require that the main logic board to be replaced

Grinding Noises

Obstruction Along Paper Path

There might be something caught along the paper path or blocking the print head from correctly moving from side to side.

Ribbon Drive Assembly Faulty

If the noise appears to be coming from the ribbon drive assembly, stop the printing, remove the ribbon drive assembly and visually inspect for worn or broken gearing.

Replace if necessary

Ribbon Carriage Assembly Dirty

Inspect the carriage assembly, remove any dust or paper particles.

Lubricate where necessary

Gear Train Assembly Worn Out or Damaged

Inspect the gear train assembly.

If worn out or damaged, replace the gear train assembly

Paper Jamming/Misfeeding

Paper Quality Poor

Ensure that the paper you introduce into your printer meets with the standards of the printer manufacturer and replace if necessary.

Obstruction Along Paper Path

There might be something caught along the paper path.

Sensors Faulty

Faulty sensors along the paper path will not provide the printer with the correct information about the paper's position in the printer and hence the printer will fall into a false paper jam mode.

Inspect and test the sensors and replace if necessary.

Tractors Worn Out

For printers that use tractor fed paper. The tractors may be worn out and can be out of alignment with one another.

Observe the tractors as they feed paper. A good way to test this is to form feed multiple sheets of paper and see what happens.

If the tractors require replacement, always replace both the LHS and RHS tractors at the same time.

Main Logic Board is Faulty

In some cases, the main logic board could be the cause of going into a false paper jam alarm mode.

Repair or replace the main logic board.

Troubleshooting Inkjet Printers

Print Quality Poor

Ink Cartridge Empty or Faulty

Remove the ink cartridge and check to see if the ink cartridge appears to be dried out or damaged.

Replace the cartridge with the genuine item. It's sometimes difficult to tell whether the ink cartridge is empty, as the ink pad still may appear to be damp.

Print Head Faulty

Remove the print head and inspect for blockages.

Replace if necessary.

Purge Unit Assembly Faulty

If your purge unit assembly is damaged, it will cause your ink cartridges to dry up and render them faulty.

Inspect the operation of the purge unit assembly to ensure that the print head is parking itself properly thus sealing itself from the air while not in use.

Replace the purge unit assembly if necessary.

Printer Requires Service

A build up ink, paper dust and residue may occur which will require the printer to be totally serviced, stripped and cleaned.

An alignment of the print head, purge unit and gearing will be required.

Printer Operation Out of Sync

You may have experienced a paper jam and in attempting to retrieve the paper have thrown gearing out of sync.

This will result in the gearing, print head and purge unit assembly to become misaligned.

Dismantle the printer, realign the gearing, print head and purge unit assembly.

Service and clean the printer while you have it dismantled.

No Power to Printer

Fuse Has Blown

Check the fuse with a meter and replace the fuse.

Ensure the correct voltage and amperage

Faulty Power On-Off Switch

Check the switch with a meter and replace the switch.

Ensure the correct voltage and amperage

Internal Power Supply has Failed

Most common fault. Repair yourself only if you know what you are doing.

Chances are there is multiple damage, replacing one or two components will only allow power to circulate temporarily causing greater damage

AC Power Supply has Failed

Most AC adapters are sealed, repair yourself only if you know what you are doing.

Chances are there is multiple damage, replacing one or two components will only allow power to circulate temporarily causing greater damage

Main Logic Board is Shutting Down the Power Supply

Repair the logic on the main logic board and in some cases, when damage is too extensive or parts are unavailable (custom chipsets), the main logic board will require replacement

Power But Not Printing

Printer Cable not Installed Properly

Ensure that both ends of the cable are correctly installed

Printer Cable is Faulty

Check for possible pin damage and replace if necessary

No Paper or Paper Not Installed Properly

No paper will result with the printer going into alarm, not coming "on-line" or "ready".

Install some paper. If there is paper, ensure it is correctly installed.

Ensure that the "on-line" button has been selected.

There are sensors along the paper path, if these are defective they will cause the printer to not print.

Check the sensors along the paper path and replace if necessary

Printer Port Connection at PC is Faulty

Try printing plain text via DOS (you can even use the "print screen" command on your keyboard while you are in the DOS environment).

If still not printing, refer to your printer's owner manual and perform a "self test" of your printer.

If the printer prints OK, the fault is more that likely going to be with the printer cable or computer, not with the printer.

Self Test is OK and PC Printer Port is OK

Faulty main logic board.

Repair input/output circuit on main logic board. Extensive damage may require that the main logic board to be replaced

Grinding Noises

Obstruction Along Paper Path

There might be something caught along the paper path or blocking the print head from correctly moving from side to side.

Purge Unit Assembly Faulty

If the noise appears to be coming from the purge unit assembly, halt the printing, remove the purge unit assembly and visually inspect for worn or broken parts.

Replace if necessary

Gear Train Assembly Worn Out or Damaged

Inspect the gear train assembly.

If worn out or damaged, replace the gear train assembly

Printer Operation Out of Sync

You may have experienced a paper jam and in attempting to retrieve the paper have thrown gearing out of sync.

This will result in the gearing, print head and purge unit assembly to become misaligned.

Dismantle the printer, realign the gearing, print head and clear unit assembly.

Service and clean the printer while you have it dismantled.

Paper Jamming/Misfeeding

Paper Quality Poor

Ensure that the paper you introduce into your printer meets with the standards of the printer manufacturer and replace if necessary

Obstruction Along Paper Path

There might be something caught along the paper path.

Sensors Faulty

Faulty sensors along the paper path will not provide the printer with the correct information about the paper's position in the printer and hence the printer will fall into a false paper jam mode.

Inspect and test the sensors and replace if necessary

Paper Pickup Delivery Assembly Faulty

The paper pickup delivery assembly may be dirty or worn out. Remove the paper pickup delivery assembly and clean the rollers. Reinstall and test.

If the problem reoccurs, replace the assembly

Main Logic Board is Faulty

In some cases, the main logic board could be the cause of going into a false paper jam alarm mode. Repair or replace the main logic board.

Troubleshooting Laser Printers

Print Quality Poor

Toner Cartridge Faulty

Remove the toner cartridge and check to see if the toner cartridge appears to be leaking, damaged or rotation has seized.

Replace the toner cartridge.

Drum Unit Faulty

Some LaserJet printers have a separate drum unit, remove the drum unit being careful not to allow direct sunlight or continuous exposure to daylight and do not touch it even if it appears to have residue of toner on it.

It is probably faulty anyway but if it is not, then touching it will damage it.

Transfer Corona Assembly Faulty

Depending on the brand of your LaserJet, this item will be either a roller assembly or a wire assembly.

Remove, clean thoroughly, replace and test.

If yours is the roller assembly type, make sure that you do not touch the roller, the oil on your skin will damage it.

Fuser Unit Assembly Faulty

Probably the most common place to cause poor print quality and paper jamming.

Inspect the fuser unit assembly for scratches on the fuser roller.

Ensure that the printer has been turned off for at least one hour as extreme temperatures exist within this item.

If scratches are in evidence, replace the entire assembly, you can be sure that the thermistors, thermoswitches, gearing and lamp will fail next.

It is always better to replace the entire assembly.

High Voltage Power Supply Faulty

Classic signs are blank pages, black pages or faint print.

Replace the high voltage power supply

Laser Scanner Unit Assembly & Optical Fiber Cable

Missing print, faint print. Try cleaning the mirror, the front of the scanner unit assembly and then test it.

Most of the time this procedure should work. If this procedure fails to rectify the fault, replace the scanner unit assembly.

It's also good practice to replace the optical fiber cable as well.

No Power to Printer

Fuse Has Blown

Check the fuse with a meter and replace the fuse.

Ensure the correct voltage and amperage

Faulty Power On-Off Switch

Check the switch with a meter and replace the switch.

Ensure the correct voltage and amperage

AC Power Supply has Failed

Replace the AC power supply. Try to repair only if you are sure about what you are doing.

Chances are there is multiple damage, replacing one or two components will only allow power to circulate temporarily causing greater damage

PCA Interface/Main Logic Board is Shutting Down the Power Supply

Repair the logic on the PCA interface/main logic board and in some cases, when damage is too extensive or parts are unavailable (custom chipsets), the PCA interface/main logic board will require replacement

DC Controller is Shutting Down the Power Supply

Repair the logic on the DC controller and in some cases, when damage is too extensive or parts are unavailable (custom chipsets), the DC controller will require replacement

DC Power Supply is Faulty

Repair or replace the DC power supply. DC power supply feeds the DC controller.

Quite often if this is the culprit, then damage to the DC controller could very well have occurred

Power but not Printing

Printer Cable not Installed Properly

Ensure that both ends of the cable are correctly installed.

Printer Cable is Faulty

Check for possible pin damage and replace if necessary.

No Paper or Paper not Installed Properly

No paper will result with the printer going into alarm, not coming "on-line" or "ready". Install some paper. If there is paper, ensure it is correctly installed.

Ensure that the "on-line" button has been selected.

There are sensors along the paper path, if these are defective they will cause the printer to not print.

Check the sensors along the paper path and replace if necessary

Printer Port Connection at PC is Faulty

Try printing plain text via DOS (you can even use the "print screen" command on your keyboard while you are in the DOS environment).

If still not printing, refer to your printer's owner manual and perform a "self test" of your printer.

If the printer prints OK, the fault is more than likely going to be with the printer cable or computer, not with the printer.

Self Test is OK and PC Printer Port is OK

Faulty PCA interface/main logic board.

Repair input/output circuit on PCA interface/main logic board.

Extensive damage may require that the main logic board to be replaced

Grinding Noises

Obstruction Along Paper Path

There might be something caught along the paper path.

Gear Train Assembly Worn Out or Damaged

Inspect the gear train assembly.

If worn out or damaged, replace the gear train assembly

Toner Cartridge is Faulty

Remove the toner cartridge and inspect its gearing and rotation replace if necessary

Main Motor Faulty

Inspect the main motor's gearing and rotation and replace if found to be faulty.

More often than not, damaged gearing attached to the main motor will not be available as a separate entity, meaning that the entire main motor assembly will require replacement

Fuser Unit Assembly Faulty

As with faults with poor print quality and paper jamming, the fuser unit assembly will also cause grinding noises.

Grinding noises coming from the fuser unit assembly is a sure sign of worse things to come.

Replace the fuser unit assembly. It is always better to replace the entire assemblies as well as the meshing gears that it links up with

Cooling Fans

Grinding noises coming from the cooling fans tell you only one thing, it is about to stop.

Seized fans will lead to the printer to overheat and cause possible extensive damage and hence costly repair bills.

Replace the faulty fan immediately when this occurs

Paper Jamming / Misfeeding

Paper Quality Poor

Ensure that the paper you introduce into your printer meets with the standards of the printer manufacturer and replace if necessary.

This is especially important when dealing with transparencies and labels

Obstruction Along Paper Path

There might be something caught along the paper path.

Toner Cartridge is Faulty

Remove the toner cartridge and inspect its gearing and rotation replace if necessary.

Fuser Unit Assembly Faulty

As with faults with poor print quality and paper jamming, the fuser unit assembly is one of the most common faults regarding paper jamming.

It is always better to replace the entire assemblies as well as the meshing gears that it links up with.

Sensors Faulty

Faulty sensors along the paper path will not provide the printer with the correct information about the paper's position in the printer and hence the printer will fall into a false paper jam mode.

Inspect and test the sensors and replace if necessary.

Paper Output Delivery Assembly

This fault will prevent the paper from exiting the printer.

Replace the worn out paper output delivery assembly and don't forget to replace the gear train assembly as well.

Paper Registration Assembly Faulty

This fault will prevent the paper from being "picked up" in the first instance.

Replace the paper registration assembly and it's a good idea to replace the paper path sensors as well.

Clutch Drive Assembly Faulty

Causes internal paper jamming to occur.

Replace both the entire clutch drive assembly and the gear train assembly.

Paper Delivery Assembly Faulty

Causes internal paper jamming to occur.

Replace both the paper delivery assembly and the gear train assembly.

Fuser Malfunction / Error 50

Fuser Unit Assembly Faulty

A Fuser Malfunction or Error 50 means just that - the Fuser Unit Assembly is faulty and requires replacement.

An easy way to tell if your Fuser Unit Assembly is indeed faulty is to feel for any warmth emanating from the Fuser Unit Assembly.

A cold Fuser Unit Assembly will generally inform you that something is wrong with the Fuser Unit Assembly.

It is always better to replace the entire Fuser Unit Assembly along with the Meshing Gears that it links up with.

AC Power Supply Faulty

The AC Power Supply supplies power directly to the Fuser Unit Assembly therefore although you may have power circulating throughout the printer, the circuit responsible in providing voltage to the Fuser Unit Assembly has failed.

Unfortunately faulty AC Power Supplies also cause damage to the Fuser Unit Assembly.

Sometimes both of these devices require replacement.

DC Controller Faulty

The DC Controller is really the heart and soul of control functions within a LaserJet Printer.

The DC Controller to also the cause of Fuser Malfunctions. Repair or replace the DC Controller.

Paper Handling

Any printer must have some mechanism to advance the paper line by line or page by page based on the printing method applied by the printer.

There are many different methods used for this purpose, some of them are useful to print single sheets some or more suited for big jobs where many thousands of sheets are to be printed continuously.

Some of the common paper handling procedures are explained next.

Friction Feed

This is one of the oldest method to move the paper through the printer. Typewriters use friction feed mechanism to feed the paper through its print mechanism.

In this friction feed method the paper is squeezed through a large rubber roller called a platen and a smaller roller.

This type of paper feeding method is suitable to print on the single sheet, which is fed manually into the printer.

Automatic Sheet Feeder

As the use of fraction feed printers increased, need for automatic sheet feeding increased and a device called automatic sheet feeder was introduced.

This devices is also known as the "bin-feed". As its name suggests one can keep a number of sheets inside this feeder and it will automatically feed then one by one to the printer.

Roll Feed

One way to reduce the number of times you have to feed a sheet of paper into the friction-feed mechanism is to make the paper longer. In fact, one can use wrapping the long sheet around a roll to do exactly that.

The printer just pulls the paper through, as it needs it. By firmly setting a roll-holder at the back of the printer, the paper can be kept in reasonable alignment so that the output will not get printed diagonally across the paper.

Pin-feed and Tractor-feed

Although roll-fed paper could be perforated at 11-inch intervals so that you could easily and neatly tear it apart, another problem arises. Most friction mechanisms are not perfect. The paper can slip so that, gradually, the page breaks in the image and the page breaks at the perforations no longer correspond. In effect, the paper and the image will not properly coincide.

By locking perforations in the edge of the paper inside sprockets that prevent slipping, the image and paper breaks can be kept in perfect alignment.

Two different paper-feeding systems use sprocketed paper to avoid slippage.

- Pin-feed uses drive sprockets that are permanently affixed to the edges of the platen roller. Consequently, the pin-feed mechanism can handle only one width of paper, the width corresponding to the sprocket at the edges of the platen.
- Tractor-feed uses adjustable sprockets that can be moved closer together or farther apart to handle nearly any width paper that will fit through the printer.

  Sprocket tractor feed is available as unidirectional tractor and bi-directional tractor. As the names imply,

  - A unidirectional tractor only pulls (or pushes) the paper through, in a single direction normally forward.
  - The bi-directional tractor allows both forward and backward paper motion.

Upgrading The Printer

Let us see how to upgrade your existing printer with a new printer.

Removing Old Printer

Once you have the new printer, you need to remove your old printer to connect the new printer. This is a very simple process, it can be performed in the following steps

- Turn off the printer and the computer. Remove the printer's power cable from the wall.
- Remove all the Accessories/Consumable such as printer ribbon, paper, toner cartridge, ink cartridge etc., from the printer.
- Disconnect the data cable from the rear of the printer.
- Finally, remove the printer away from the computer.

Connecting New Printer

Once the old printer is removed, next step would be to connect the new printer to the computer. Connecting a new printer is one of the easiest upgrade as there is no need to open the computer system.

Make sure that all the packing and protective material inside the printer is removed.

- Once the printer is ready, install all the accessories and the consumable that are required to take out the printout, such as printer ribbon, ink cartridge, Laser toner cartridge, paper etc.
- Connect the power cable from the printer to the mains. Make sure that power cable is properly connected to the printer.
- Switch on the printer and take some self test printouts, almost all the printer provide a self test printing option. For example, on an Epson compatible Dot-Matrix printer model EX-100 this is executed by holding down the Form Feed button when the printer is switched on. Keep this switch down until the printer start printing, once the printer starts printing, you can release the Form Feed button.
- Once the self test is printed, you can switch off the printer.
- Once you find that the printer is working satisfactorily, connect the printer to your computer using proper data cable. If the printer has USB interface than that should be your first choice, connect using a USB cable. Otherwise, use a parallel cable to connect using a parallel interface.
- Before connecting the printer to the computer, make sure that both the computer and the printer are off.

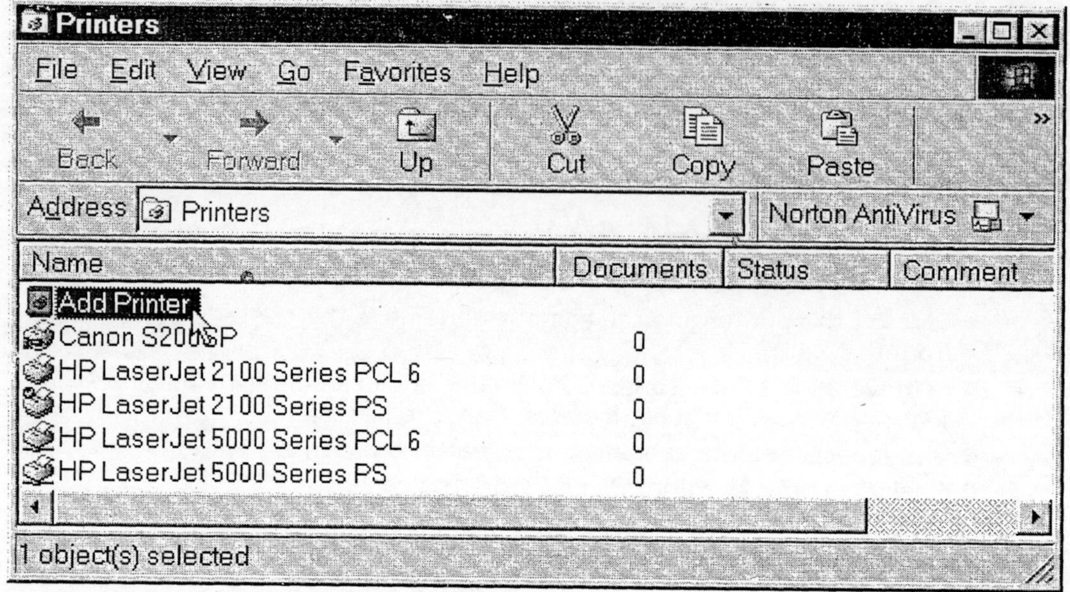

Fig. 12-20 : Adding Printer in Windows-98.

Installing and Configuring Printers in Windows 98

You can install printers in Windows 98 using the Add Printer Wizard.

Using the Add Printer Wizard

Windows 98 provides the Add Printer Wizard to simplify installing printers, and a central place - the Printers folder - for running the wizard and for managing printing processes.

You can open the Printers folder in the following ways

- From the `Start` menu, point to `Settings`, and then click `Printers` or
  In `My Computer`, double-click `Printers` or
  In `Control Panel`, double-click `Printers`.
- In the `Printers` folder, double-click `Add Printer`.
- The Add Printer Wizard leads you though the process of setting up and configuring a printer.

The only difference between installing a network printer and a local printer with the Add Printer Wizard is that you must specify the path to the network printer or browse to find its network location.

Networking

If one has more than one computer under his/her disposal then those computers can be connected together using a network. A network allows Scanner, CD-Writer, HardDisk Drive, printer etc. connected to one computer on the networks to be shared by all other computers connected to the network.

Setting Up a Network

Some times back, network installation was a complex job, but with the arrival of Plug and Play (PnP) devices, PnP operating systems and simple network such as 10Base-T, this process has become quite easy.

With the hardware setup, software setup is a very important part of the network installation. Nearly all networks use software drivers to enable their networking features, giving access to shared resources, passing data through the network adapter, and accessing data from remote computers etc.

When using a network, hardware and software at the sending and receiving end must match. The two ends of the network must speak the same language to understand one another. That is, they must use the same networking protocol.

The protocol defines

- the size of the blocks of bytes transferred between computers,
- the addresses added to each block of bytes
- the means of controlling network access and routing the data, and
- ways to recover when an error appears in the data.

The software for setting up a network ranges from simple to very complex.

For a simple home or small business network, a low end computer network will be more than enough.

If your use is simple sharing of data between computers and sharing of hardware devices, such as printer, scanner, CD-ROM drive etc. then use Windows Operating System (Windows-98 or higher) as your networking software, it will meet all these requirements.

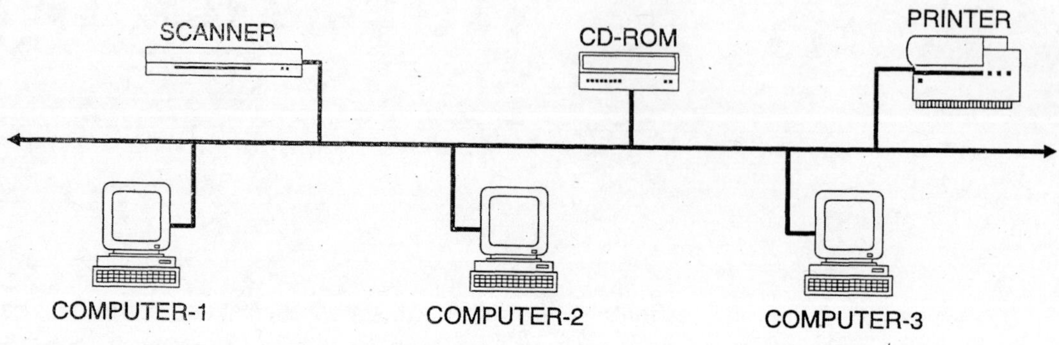

Fig. 13-1 : Network of Computers.

Preparation For Network Installation

The first step in installing any network is planning-deciding exactly what you want the network to do-then you need to find out how to do it.

The hardware for putting together a peer to peer 10Base-T network comprises three parts

- network/host adapters in each computer
- a hub and
- wire/cable that links them together.

Network/Host Adapter

You'll need one 10Base-T network adapter for every computer you want to connect to the network. The network adapter provides the connection between computer and the network cable.

All 10Base-T network adapters provide the same basic functions, although some have more feature than others. Any 10Base-T adapter can be used, provided it is supported directly by the Windows or it has a Windows driver.

Some network adapters have facility for placing optional boot ROMs, which allow computers to boot up from a remote disk drive, but this feature is more applicable to client-server type installation, rather than to the peer to peer type networks.

10base-T network is a peer to peer network system, in this network system every PC is equal. Each computer can share files and other resources (such as printers) among one another. They share equally, each as the peer (equal) of the others, so this scheme is called peer-to-peer networking.

In this peer-to-peer scheme there is no dedicated file server, all computers can have their own, local storage, and each computer can be granted access to the drives and printers connected to the others.

Wiring

A simple 10Base-T network use unshielded twisted pair (UTP) cabling. Ordinary modular telephone cables are unsuitable for 10Base-T because these cables are flat and lack the needed twists.

The twist in the twisted pair cable minimize noise and interference.

Ordinary modular telephone cables use four-wire RJ-11 connectors that will fit into 10Base-T connectors but won't connect with all of the necessary signals. A 10Base-T jack is designed to accept eight-wire RJ-45 connectors even though only four of the connections are active.

If all your PCs are in one room or reasonably close to each other then the best choice is to buy ready-made RJ-45 cables, which are available in standard lengths (for example 10, 25, 50, and 100 feet). After making the connection, any extra cable can be loosely coiled up without any problem.

The only restriction imposed by 10Base-T is that the length of cable between PC and hub cannot exceed 100 meters (328 feet).

Hubs

If you want to network more than two computers then you'll need at least one hub for your network.

A hub is simply a box with circuitry inside and a number of jacks for RJ-45 plugs on the back. The circuitry inside links the 10Base-T cables together.

Hubs are distinguished by the number of features they offer. But most of those features are designed to make the network administrator's job easier and are unnecessary in a small (five or less computers) peer to peer network. For such smaller systems, a simple hub will be all one needs.

The first step in wiring your network is to determine the most convenient location to put the 10Base-T hub. One can always set the hub on or under a desk, adjacent to a PC, or wherever is convenient.

The important consideration with locating the hub is that it should be put in a convenient location, out of the way but easy to reach. Ideally, it should be kept at the exact center of the computers it serves. This will minimize wiring hassles.

As long as one does not violate the 10Base-T wiring limitations, the hub can be placed anywhere.

Cable Installation

Once you've set a location for each computers and the hub, you can start the wiring. You need to take one cable from each computer to the hub. One can use ready-made cables with modular connectors crimped on each ends, or using special crimping tool to crimp modular connectors on the cables, one can make the required cables.

Network Configuration

Once the wiring is done, prepare the network adapter for each computer. Typically, a network adapter requires an interrupt number and base address from your system resources.

If the adapter you choose doesn't follow the Plug-and-Play standard, you can assign resources using DIP switches or jumpers on each network adapter or through the setup software accompanying the adapter.

If you are using a plug and play (PnP) network host adapter then Windows will automatically assign these resource values to the adapter. In a non-PnP adapter card, configure the card to match the settings you've chosen. This could be done with jumpers or switches provided on the card.

- After configuring the card, shut down the computer and install the network adapter in your computer. Unplug the computers power cable, remove the cover, and remove a blank retaining bracket from the empty expansion slot you want to use for the adapter board.
- Now, simply slide the adapter board into the empty expansion slot. Be sure to screw the card tightly to retaining bracket. The screw will prevent board from dislodging when plugging in the network cable, it will also provide a better ground which will improve network reliability.

Before reinstalling system cover, plug it in and switch it on to make sure that the network adapter card doesn't accidentally interfere with some other system function. Once you're sure all is well, shut down and turn off the system and reinstall its cover.

Repeat this process for each computer in your network.

Next step is network software/driver installation.

Under Windows 98, you can install the network adapter in two ways.

- You can step through the Add New Hardware Wizard from Control Panel.
- Or you can use the Network properties sheet, available from the Control Panel.

To use the Network properties sheet, double click on the Network icon under Control Panel. From the next screen, click on **`Add`**, and you'll see a "**`Select Network Component`**" menu.

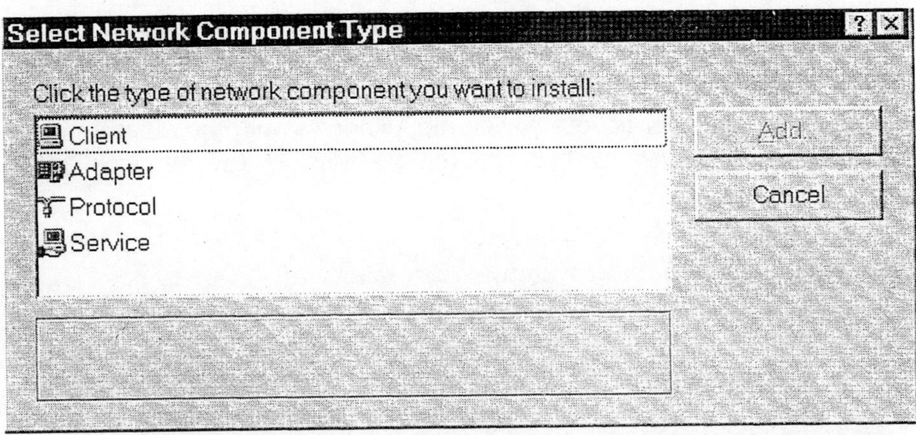
Select Network Component Type
Click the type of network component you want to install:
Client
Adapter
Protocol
Service
Add...
Cancel

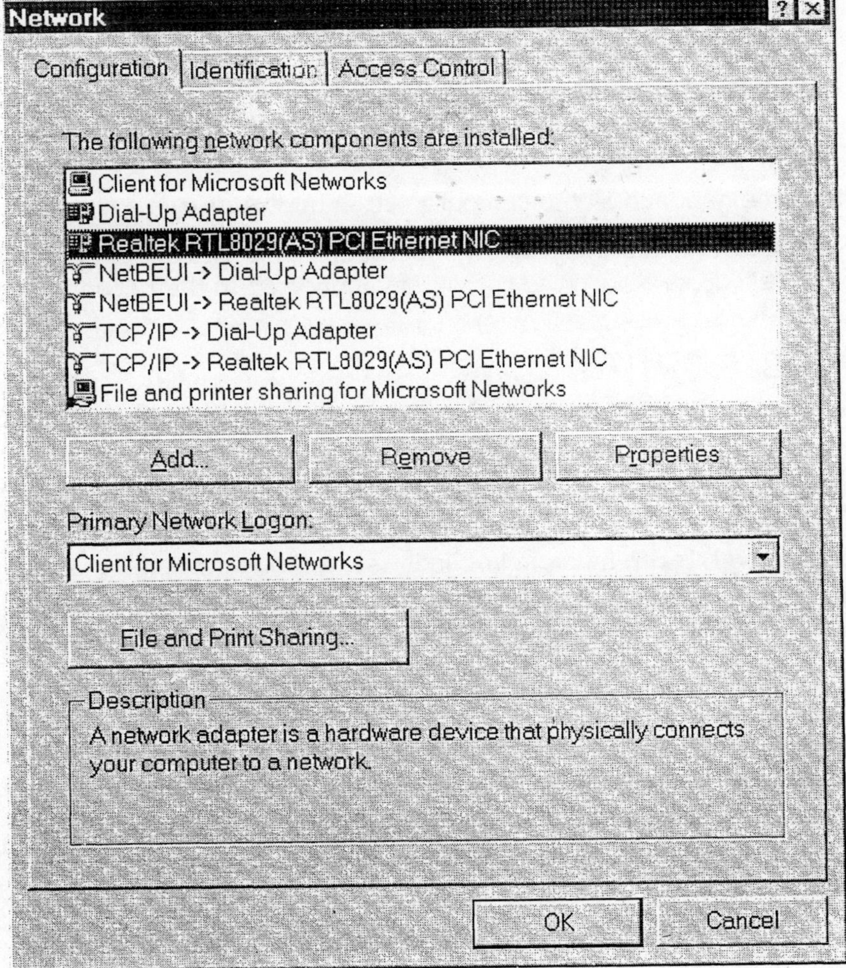
Network
Configuration
Identification
Access Control
The following network components are installed:
Client for Microsoft Networks
Dial-Up Adapter
Realtek RTL8029(AS) PCI Ethernet NIC
NetBEUI -> Dial-Up Adapter
NetBEUI -> Realtek RTL8029(AS) PCI Ethernet NIC
TCP/IP -> Dial-Up Adapter
TCP/IP -> Realtek RTL8029(AS) PCI Ethernet NIC
File and printer sharing for Microsoft Networks
Add...
Remove
Properties
Primary Network Logon:
Client for Microsoft Networks
File and Print Sharing...
Description
A network adapter is a hardware device that physically connects your computer to a network.
OK
Cancel

Click on **Adapter** and click the **Add** button. Windows will then let you choose a manufacturer and model of network adapter to install. Select the board you want to install or choose a suitable compatible board.

Once you've selected an adapter, click **OK**. Windows will immediately install all the drivers required not only by the adapter but also all the services and protocols required to get your network working.

When Windows finishes with the installation, you'll see a revised Network sheet listing everything that the operating system has installed.

If Windows doesn't prompt you for the names you want to use for your computer and the workgroup, then select the **Identification** tab and enter the names.

Choose descriptive names such as Ramesh Computer, Finance, Accounts, DTP Section, and so on.

Once you've finished, click **OK**. Click **OK** on the next screen as well, and Windows will tell you to reboot/restart your system.

Finally you're ready to link your network together. Slide the RJ-45 plug at one end of the cable into the RJ-45 jack at the back of each computer, in your network card. Then plug the other end of each cable into the hub.

Switch on the hub, and all the computers are now a part of the network.

Now you need to setup the Windows operating system to share printer, disk drives and other resources among the computers connected to the network.

Enabling Sharing

Before you can set up your network software for resource sharing, you must have a working network. Once the network hardware is installed you must then configure your networked computers to share various hardware and software installed on different computer connected to the network.

Let us see how this can be done in Windows operating system.

Click on **Start**, point to **Settings** option, in the **Settings** click on the **Control Panel** selection. In the Control Panel, double click on the **Network** icon to open the Network folder.

You'll see a screen that tells you about all the network components that Windows has installed for you.

If your network is operating, you don't have to worry about all the entries in this screen. In this screen our present interest is the "**File and Printer Sharing**" button towards the bottom of the screen.

Clicking on this button will open a small windows giving you the choice of whether to share file and printer on this system.

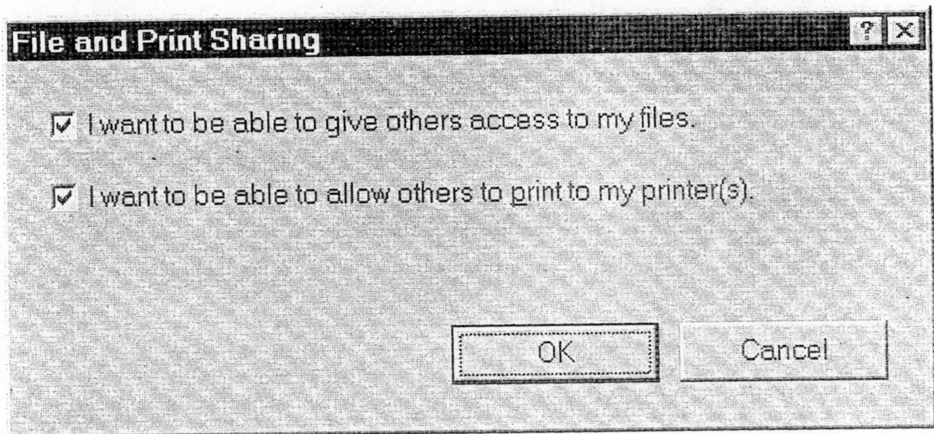

Fig. 13-2 : File/Printer Sharing.

You have two choices, **sharing files** and **sharing printers**. In most cases, you'll want to share files as well share any printer connected to the computer. For this select both the options.

Once you've made your choices, clicking on OK will take you back to the previous screen, the Network folder. Click on OK again to exit back to the Control Panel. Now you need to restart the computer to enable sharing.

Selecting these options will only enable the overall sharing abilities of your computer. But, to make the computer's resources available to other computers. You must alter the properties of each resource you want to share.

Sharing Computer

To enable sharing for a disk drive, be it a hard disk, floppy, or CD drive, highlight the drive's icon in My Computer window. Then choose Sharing from the File menu.

If you do not see the sharing option then sharing abilities of your computer is not properly enabled, you'll have to go back to the Network folder to enable sharing.

Once you've enabled a drive for sharing, its icon will appear in the Network Neighborhood of all the computers that have access to it on the network.

To enable sharing the drive, you only need to click on the "**Shared As**" button and give the drive a name. Other options allow you to limit access so other networked computers cannot alter the content of your drive or can alter it only after giving a password provided by you.

Once you've made all the entries, click OK and your computer is now ready to share its files with all other computers on the network.

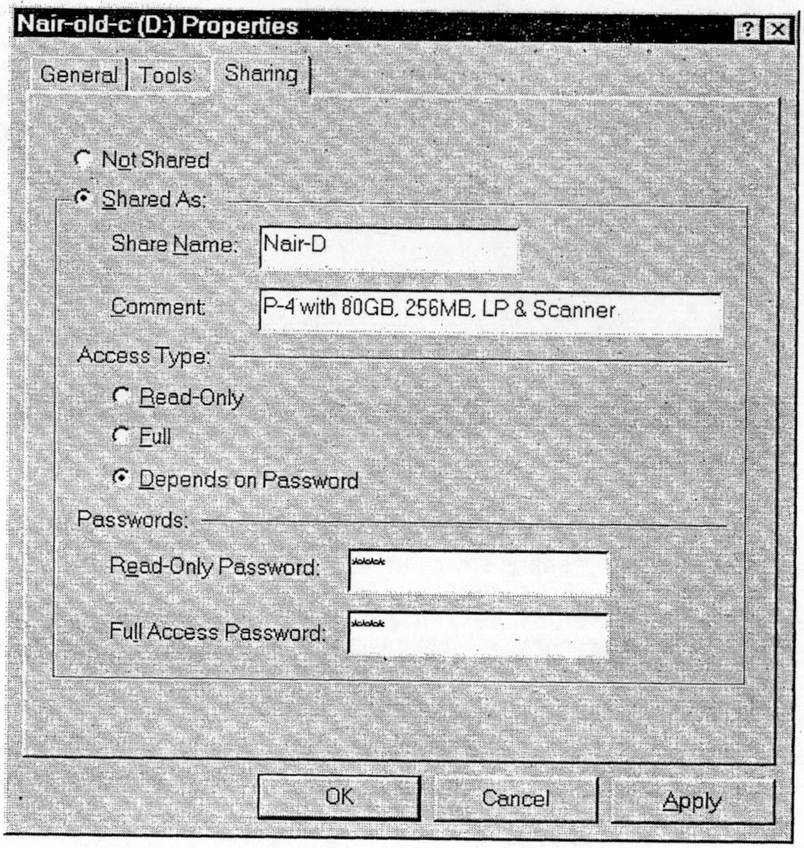

Fig. 13-3 : Drive Sharing Properties.

Mapping Shared Drive

Shared drives automatically appear under Windows, but if you want to use them as drive letters through a DOS box, then you will have to map them to the computer on which you want to use them.

To map a drive on some other networked system as a local drive, first open **Network Neighborhood** and click on the name of the server containing the drive you want to map.

Now, Windows will display the names of the sharable disk drives on the server. Highlight the drive you want to map, then select the **File** menu and select **Map Network Drive** entry.

Windows will assign a drive letter to the selected drive and give you the opportunity to automatically remap the drive every time system boots up. Use the drive letter that Windows has assigned to the remote drive in your DOS box to access the remote drive.

Sharing Printer

Similarly, to share a printer, you have to change the printer's property on the computer to which the printer is connected. For this double click on the `Printers` icon inside the Control Panel.

Windows will display icons for each of the printers installed in your PC, as well as giving you the option to install a new printer.

Now, you can right click on a printer's icon and select `Properties` from the popup menu.

Alternately, double click on the `printer` icon, opening the `printer` menu. From the `Printer` menu, select `properties`.

In either case, you'll have a variety of tabs to choose from. Among them you should see a `Sharing` tab.

If you do not see the sharing option then sharing abilities of your computer is not properly enabled, you'll have to go back to the Network folder to enable sharing.

When this screen initially shows up, "`Not Shared`" option is selected, and the lower part of the screen will be grayed out. Selecting "`Shared As`" will activate other choices.

You must give the printer a name by which other computers in the network will refer to it. You can optionally supply a comment so that later on, you can remember what you've done.

This tab also provides for password protection for printer access. If you want to restrict printer access, you can enter a password here; otherwise, the printer can be used by each and every computer connected to the network.

When you're finished with your entries, click on `OK`, and you are done. Your printer can now be shared with other computers attached to your network.

Installing Network Printer

On each computer that want to share the networked printer, you must install the network printer exactly as you would install a local printer.

Enabling printer sharing on a computer is a bit more complex. Start by double clicking on the `Printer` icon from control panel. This should be done on the computer in which you want to install the networked printer.

Windows will respond by showing a list of already installed printers with the option to add a new printer.

- Double click on "`Add Printer`" option. This will activate the `Add Printer Wizard`, which will step you through the complete printer installation process.

- When the **Add Printer Wizard** starts, your first choice will be whether to install a local or networked printer. The wizard defaults to installing a local printer, so select Network printer option and then click on the **Next** button.
- In order to install a printer, you have to tell the Wizard which printer to use. The Wizard identifies a printer by its assigned name, and it prompts you to type in the name of the printer to install.
- This screen also gives you the choice of routing the print commands from your DOS programs to the networked printer. If you're going to use DOS based programs such as old WordStar, Lotus-123 etc. then select the Yes button to "**Do you print from MS-DOS based programs?**" question.
- If you don't remember the complete name and path of all the printers in your network, you can ask the Wizard to find the available printers for you by clicking on the **Browse** button and looking in the likely places on the network.

The Browse button is a good choice even if you know your network printer's name because by selecting a printer from the names it presents, you can avoid typing errors. Click on the computer that acts as your printer server, and the Wizard will respond by listing the shared printers attached to that server.

- You only need to click on the printer that you want. The Wizard is not finished yet. If you've told it to route your DOS print jobs to print through the network printer, the Wizard will ask you to decide whether you want to capture a printer port.
- Because most DOS applications send their output directly to a printer port, you'll need to enable "**capture printer port**" to allow them to print.
- When you click on the Capture Printer Port button, the Wizard will ask which port to capture.

You'll have to make changes into all your computer's DOS applications to use the port you choose for printing. The Wizard's default choice, LPT1, is a good one.

After you make your choice, click on **OK** to finish the networked printer installation.

The Wizard takes care of all the details for you, automatically copying to your local computer the driver files necessary for your applications and printer.

Your networked printer will now act as if it were locally connected to your computer.

Troubleshooting Networking

Let us now see some basic troubleshooting methods for network components. The following sections describe in more detail how to check individual elements of your network configuration.

Checking user and workgroup names

- In Control Panel, double-click Network, and then click the Identification tab. Check the computer name and workgroup name.

Checking connections to network resources

- Double-click Network Neighborhood on your desktop and check whether workgroups, and computers appear.
- If they appear, try connecting to a computer.
- If they do not appear, check that at least one computer exists on the local network and that client services and protocols are installed.
- If no resources appear in Network Neighborhood but all connectivity appears to be working, attempt to access a network resource by mapping to it using the Map Network Drive dialog box.

You can access the Map Network Drive dialog box either by right-clicking the Network Neighborhood icon and then selecting Map Network Drive, or by selecting Map Network Drive from the Tools menu in Windows Explorer.

You can also make the Map Drive button appear on the Windows Explorer toolbar by clicking the View menu and then clicking Folder Options.

- If you cannot connect to the server or workstation you want, review the error messages.
- At the DOS command prompt, use the `net use` command to verify that you can connect to at least one server and workstation.
- If you cannot connect to any server or workstation, check workgroup assignment, domain assignment, domain logon, and basic network operations.
- If you still cannot connect, check whether you can connect to the server from another computer.
- If this does not work, it probably indicates a problem with the server you are trying to connect to, or with the cabling or hub.

If you are connecting to a printer or drive on a Windows 95 or Windows 98 server running file and printer sharing,

- verify that the file and printer sharing service appears in the list of installed network components on the server to ensure that peer resource sharing is enabled.
- Also verify that the correct settings for the browsing method are configured in the properties for the file and printer sharing service on that server.
- Finally, verify that something is being shared on the server.

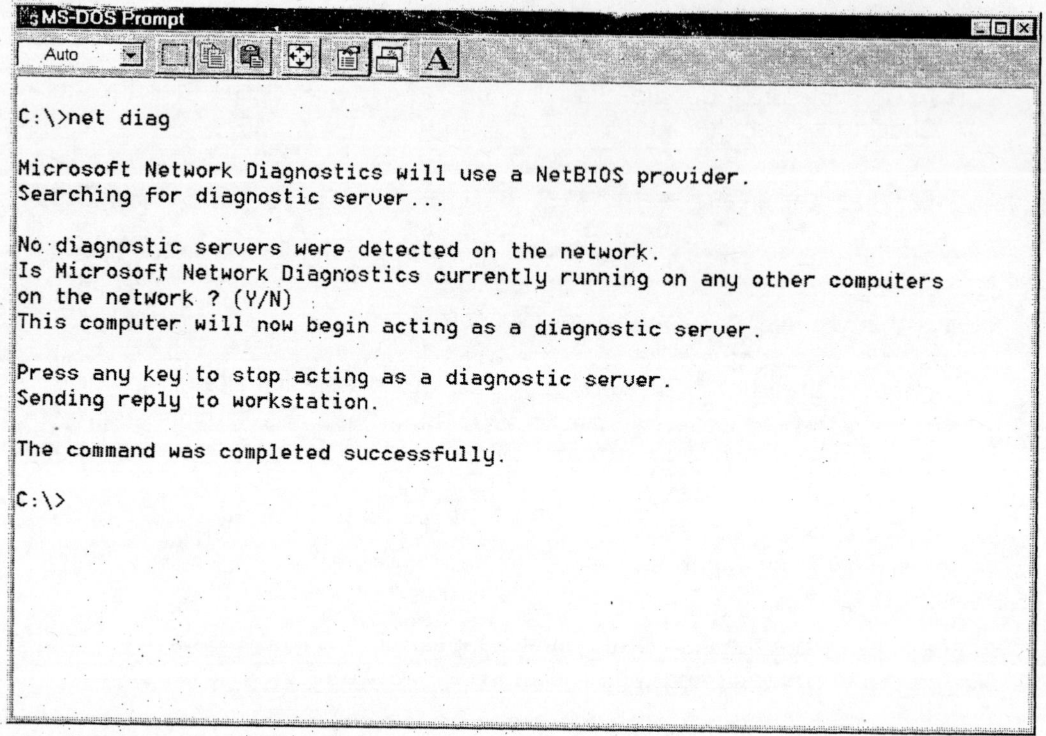

Fig. 13-4 : Use of net diag command.

Checking network adapter settings

- In Control Panel, double-click Network, and then double-click the entry for the network adapter in the list of installed components.
- Click the Advanced tab, and verify that each entry in the Property area has an appropriate value specified in the Value area.
- Click the Driver Type tab, and then verify that the appropriate driver type is selected.
- Click the Bindings tab, and verify that each protocol is checked. If a protocol is not checked, it is not providing network functionality using that adapter.
- In Control Panel, double-click System, and then select the Device Manager tab.
- Expand the Network adapters tree, click the adapter you wish to check, and then click Properties.
- Click the Resources tab, if it exists, and verify that the configuration type, I/O address range, and interrupt request (IRQ) are correct.

Device Manager will also report any device conflicts and enable you to resolve those device conflicts by changing your settings.

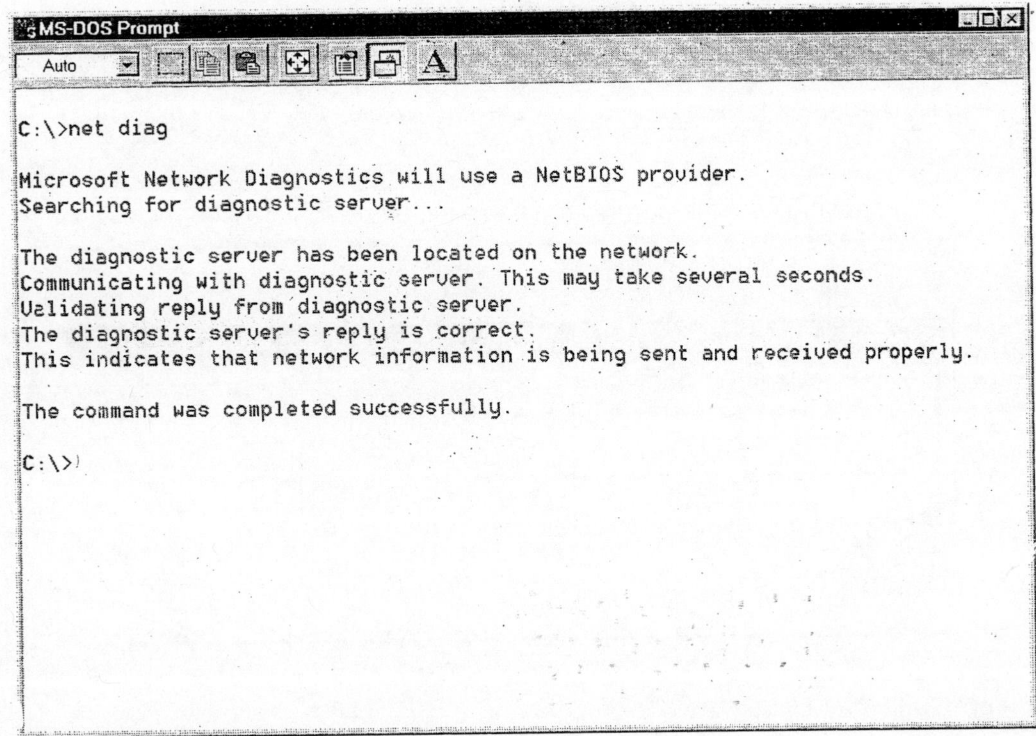

Fig. 13-5 : Use of net diag command.

Checking real-mode network components.

To check basic network communications, at the command prompt you can use the **`net diag`** command with a second computer connected to the same local network segment.

As a diagnostic tool, net diag can assist you in verifying that the local computer can connect to this server. In order for net diag to work, you must be running either the IPX or NetBEUI protocol.

To establish a diagnostic server on a second local computer at the DOS command prompt, type:

```
net diag
```

When a message appears showing you the protocols in use, press the first letter of the protocol indicated in the message to specify the protocol to test.

When a message appears prompting you to specify whether a diagnostic server exists, press N.

To verify that the diagnostic server is detected, on the computer you are trying to troubleshoot, at the DOS command prompt, type:

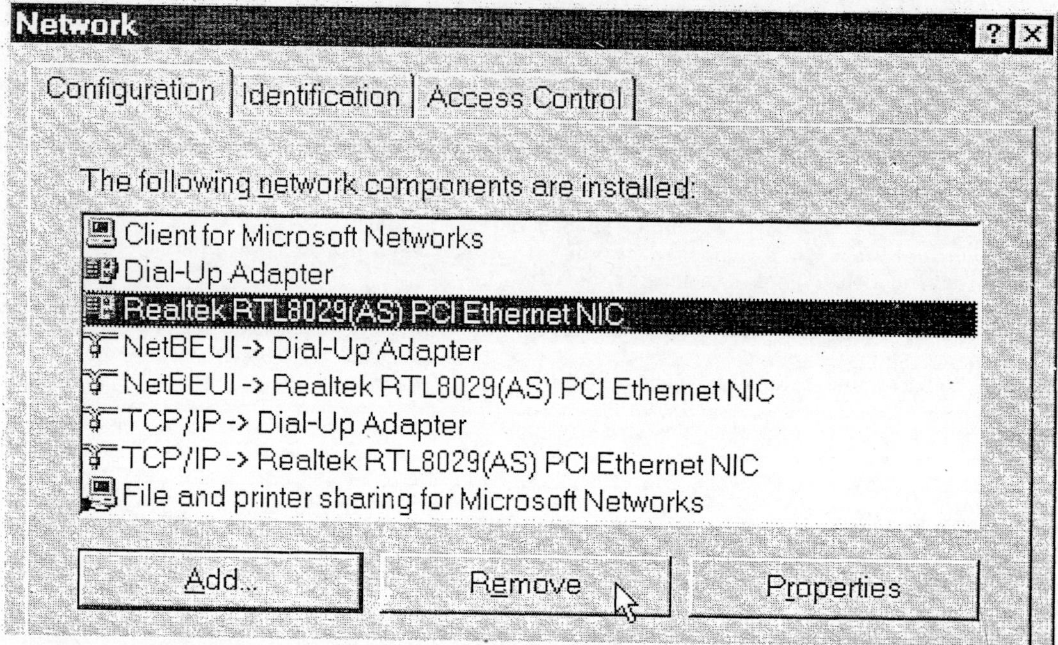

Fig. 13-6 : Removing Network Component.

```
net diag
```

When a message appears showing the protocols in use, specify the same protocol to test as that of the diagnostic server established in the previous procedure.

A message should appear stating that the diagnostic server has been detected. If a message appears stating that no diagnostic servers have been detected, there may be a problem with the network adapter, configuration, hub or cables.

To remove and reinstall drivers in Windows 98

- In Control Panel, double-click Network, and make note of each installed component.
- For each component, click the component, and then click Remove.

Install the components as explained earlier in this chapter.

Once the network components are removed you lose network connectivity. You will not be able to reinstall your network components over the network.

Make sure you have your original installation available on a CD or local hard disk drive before removing your network components.

Understanding Internet

Concept of Internet

The Internet is a world wide network of many small computer networks, that grew out of a 1960 project by American Department of Defense. This project was executed by an Advanced Research Projects Agency (ARPA) and an Internet like system developed by them was called ARPAnet.

This ARPAnet was later joined by other government agencies, research institutions, educational institutions etc. and slowly emerged as today's Internet.

Today the Internet is so large and complex that no one knows exactly how many computers are on it and how many people are actually using it.

There are millions of people connected to tens of thousands of networks in at least 100 countries and any one connected to the Internet can communicate with any other person connected to The Net or the Web.

Internet is also known as network of networks.

In June 1993, the Web had just 130 sites. A year later, the number had risen to nearly 3,000. By April 1998, there were more than 2.2 million sites on the Web and by the year 2001 end the web will have more than a billion sites.

World Wide Web

The www is so large and complex but no one controls it or owns it. But, to keep an eye on the standards of Web technology World Wide Web Consortium or W3C was formed by Berners-Lee in 1994.

In W3C, an international group of industry and university representatives promotes the Web by developing common protocols for transmitting information over the Internet.

The consortium provides information, reference code, and prototype and sample applications to developers and users.

It is hosted by the Massachusetts Institute of Technology's Laboratory for Computer Science in the United States, the Institut National de Recherche en Informatique et en Automatique in Europe, and the Keio University Shonan Fujisawa Campus in Japan.

Applications of Internet

The Internet was started as a military project, but currently Internet's main use is in education/research activities and in business applications.

Some of the uses and advantages of the Internet are

- Information or Marketing material stored in it can reach lots of potential customers quickly and inexpensively.
- It can be used to sell products and services online
- It helps to reduce advertisement and promotion expenses
- It helps to reduce customer service cost
- It helps to streamline information distribution to the employees
- It helps to tap specialized markets
- It helps in providing business information to the customers/ prospective buyers
- It helps to do business round the clock
- It helps quick update of information
- It helps in immediate feedback receiving
- It helps in enhanced customer service

Are the Internet and the Web the same thing?

The Internet and the World Wide Web are closely related but not the same.

- The Internet is a decentralized global network of computers.
- The Web is a collection of documents, or Web sites, that you can access using the Internet and your Web browser software. The Web comprises the vast majority (but not quite all) of the content available over the Internet.

Services on the Internet

Chatting/Internet Relay Chat (IRC)

IRC or Internet Relay Chat allows multiple people to communicate simultaneously over the Internet. This communication is done by typing of message on the computer and reading replies send by other users on the net.

IRC was developed around 1980 as a replacement of UNIX Talk program. IRC is a client/Server application, people who wants to talk to each other need to run IRC client software and they all need to be connected to an IRC server system.

After connecting to the IRC server, clients connect to various channels, often these channels are named on the basis of topics they discuss.

IRC is basically a real time conference system. Unlike a real conference, instead of speaking, here people communicate by typing.

One advantage with IRC conference is no one can take over the conversation by shouting or talking continuously, here every participant will have equal chance to put forward his views.

Newsgroups (UseNet)

Like the IRC, Newsgroups are also online discussions, but instead of doing the discussion in real time, in the newsgroup, the discussion is done by posted messages.

UseNet is short form for User's Network. It is made up of all the machines that receives network newsgroups. A newsgroup is a collection of messages posted by individuals to a news server, a computer that can host thousands of newsgroups.

You can find newsgroups on practically any subject. Although some newsgroups are moderated, most are not. Moderated newsgroups are owned by someone who reviews the postings, can answer questions, delete inappropriate messages, and so on. Anyone can post messages to a newsgroup. Newsgroups do not require any kind of membership or joining fees.

To use newsgroups your Internet service provider must offer links to one or more news servers. To read and post messages in any of the newsgroups stored on that news server, you need to setup an account.

When you find a newsgroup you like, you can subscribe to it. Subscribing provides easy access to your favorite newsgroups, eliminating the need to scroll through the long list on the server each time you want to visit a favorite newsgroup.

NetNews

NetNews is one of the most popular Internet newsgroups, it has more than five thousand discussion groups. NetNews allows you to log on to various other computers such as computer funded by NASA, main library of Munich, archives from Yeshiva University etc.

The news group that will be available to you depends on the news server you have access. Generally, following category of the newsgroup is found on most of the newsgroup services

- Comp - Computer science and related topics
- News - News about NetNews and its administration. This group also includes important information for the new users.
- Talk - This news group provide space for long, unresolved debate on controversial topics such as about religion, child labor etc.

- Rec- Recreational topics on hobbies and arts etc.
- Sci - Scientific topics, related to scientific research, application of established science etc.
- Soc - Social issues, including politics
- Alt - Alternate news group, there are rules for creating a new user group, but anyone can create a new user group in the Alt group
- Misc - This group address anything that incorporates themes from other groups, such as job offering, resume posting etc.

Newsgroup Readers

Newsgroup readers are software tools that is used to read newsgroup articles and to post your own contribution to the discussion. These software usually have search capabilities that help you locate newsgroups of your interest, making it easier to subscribe them.

Subscriptions are simply active links to your favorite newsgroups. The news reader keeps a list of favorite groups and keeps a track of day-to-day activity of each newsgroup.

With the text, the newsgroup can contain images and programs in the form of binary data. These binary files are contained in an encoded form. Two most common encoding formats are called UUEncode and Base64 encoding.

Sometimes if the binary attachment is large, it is often split into smaller parts.

When a news reader reads an article from newsgroup, if it contains binary attachment, the reader will locate the split parts, join them together and decode it back to its original form.

Most of the readers also provide facility to filter the information read from the newsgroup, so that offensive materials, materials unsuitable for children etc. get filtered out.

Some of these filters are

- Bozo List
  It is a list of individuals who routinely post useless or offensive information in newsgroups. This option enables users to ignore such postings
- Kill and Watch Filters
  These filters are user defined rules for screening out unwanted articles. They force the news reader to take a specific action on articles that meet a certain predefined criteria.
- Spam
  Spam is a useless or offensive message broadcast to multiple newsgroups. This can also be filtered out by most of the news readers.

Microsoft Outlook Express provided with Internet Explorer is one of very good news and mail reader software. Some other news reader software are

Fig. 14-1 : E-Mail.

Agent-99, Delrina Cyberjack, Emissary Desktop, Gravity, Internet Chameleon, Internet in a Box, Microsoft Internet News, Netscape Navigator Gold etc.

E-Mail

E-Mail or electronic-mail is one of the fastest and most convenient mail system. One can send an e-mail anywhere in the world, in a fraction of time and cost, compared to the time and cost of the ordinary postal mail.

E-mail involves sending a message from one computer to another computer, on the Internet. It can be used for business as well as for personal communication. With the text mail, graphic images, music files, program files etc. can be sent as attachment.

Mailing List

Mailing list is a way for a group of peoples with common interest to have discussions. For this each member of the mailing list will have a list of all other members of the mailing list. When a person wants to submit a message for discussion, he will send the message to everyone on the list.

Disadvantage of mailing list is everyone on the list need to remember to add or delete members from the list, if there is any change in the membership. Also, the machine of the person sending a message is tied down, while the message is sent to everyone on the list.

There are several programs available to automate the e-mail reading/replying process. E-mail addresses can be kept on a host computer, that runs the mailing list program. All request for information, to subscribe (participate) and unsubscribe (drop out) of the list are handled automatically by the mailing list software.

Most of the mailing list consist of people who have agreed to discuss a particular topic, so there is no need to restrict distribution of mail to each of the subscriber. Some mailing list that discuss controversial subjects keep a moderator, the moderator reads every message to make sure that the content of message is within agreed upon guideline. If the message is not within the guideline then it is deleted, otherwise it is sent to the members.

Using E-Mail

There are many e-mail standards developed for different networks, over a period. These variety of standards make it difficult to have a general purpose application to read and sent E-Mail.

To send and receive E-mail between different standards an e-mail gateway is used. These gateways allow you to send and receive e-mail to the people on these variety of standards as easily as you send e-mail to another Internet user.

E-mail is currently one of the most popular way to conduct business over long distance. Using e-mail to contact a business or personal associate can be better than using telephone, as he can answer it at a convenient time.

Care must be taken when sending sensitive information through Internet, as Internet is not very secure medium.

E-mail client

E-Mail programs are called E-Mail clients because they receive mail from a mail server computers on the Internet.

- Some E-Mail clients can only send and receive e-mail's with text and attachments. Attachments are binary files encoded into alphanumeric character by the sending client and are decoded back into binary format by the receiving client.
- Some clients use filtering rules to check incoming message for specified sender or some specific text in the message and send the message into different folders according to what they find.
- Some client software can respond automatically to the incoming message containing specified text based on some set of rules.
- Some clients that use rules, first file all messages to a central in-box and refile them only after you have viewed them. If you receive only few dozen messages per day then you can manually keep track of them. But, if you receive hundreds of messages then you would want them to be

automatically filed to different folders according to their content, where you don't have to see them unless you wish.

The basic text message send as e-mail reach its destination without any problem. But if you send attachment with the text message, the recipient may not get the attachment in proper form.

The gateway joining your computer and recipient's computer may discard the attachment or it could strip off message header, if it could not recognize it.

Currently the older UUEncode and Mac bin-hex encoding standards are slowly being replaced by more robust MIME standard. MIME is supported by all modern mail clients.

Protecting your e-mail

E-Mail provide a simple and convenient method for sending and receiving mail, but it also provides an easy route to the computer virus to infect the computer system.

Two types of solutions are available to protect the computer from this type of viral attack.

- First one is a server based solution, in which a program scans the e-mail attachments as they pass through the e-mail gateway.
- In the second approach, the e-mail is scanned by an anti-virus software on the client machine.

E-mail Client Program Features

Easy installation and Setup

E-Mail client should be able to install and setup easily. It should permit multiple accounts, allow scheduled retrieval and be able to recognize signature files.

Mail creation option

Should have facility to add a new list and create a mailing list. The package should also accept aliases. It should support MIME and other popular mail attachment formats.

Mail management

The package Should have facility to schedule regular mail check and create folders for sorting and storing your mail. It should have filtering capability and rule based message handling facility to route your mail to proper folder.

Off-line facilities

E-Mail package should have facility to respond to messages without being connected to a server. It should be able to integrate with the address book, while off-line.

How viruses spread by e-mail?

A Trojan horse virus can secretly carry often-damaging software in an e-mail file attachment from someone you may or may not know. The file attachment name itself can also be very misleading.

When you run the attachment, it can do all sorts of things, from erasing files to changing your desktop.

It then sends itself along to other people in your address book so that it can propagate itself.

Telnet

Telnet is used to actually log into other computers on the Internet. Most of the computers on the Internet require you to have and account with then to be able to telnet.

Some computers have facility to telnet as guest account.

The main difference between the FTP and Telnet is, FTP lets you do things related to transferring of files only, such as download, upload etc.

When you connect using telnet, what you see really depends on what the host resource provides. You may see a bulletin board, a menu, or a command line, it all depends on what the resource provides.

World Wide Web (WWW)

World Wide Web (WWW) is a service on the Internet that connects various documents available on the Internet with links to each other and to various other documents. Form one document you can jump to another related document, which in turn may be linked to many other documents.

WWW has information on almost any imaginable subject. It is a client-server based Internet service. A client application can read the information available on various WWW servers.

The documents are stored in a special HTML format on the web. This format puts a tag for each passage of text. This tagging allows various WWW clients to format the HTML text in a way that is suitable for the display, the client computer is using.

HTML also allows you to include in-line graphic in documents, which can be displayed by graphic based client software. One can also insert hypertext links into the WWW document. These links enable one HTML document to load another HTML document on your request, when the user clicks on these links.

A document could contain link to many other related documents, and those related documents can further contain link so many other documents. The linked document could be on the same computer or it could be on a computer halfway around the world.

You can make your own WWW page on many of the WWW servers that provide free space to store a web page. To make your own web page you should know the HTML language or you can make your page on many of the page design software with facility to export into HTML format and then upload the HTML file to server that provide free space.

Gopher

Gopher is a simple menu system that you can use to connect to files on the Internet.

This easy-to-use system introduced many users to the Internet before the World Wide Web became popular.

Using the University of Minnesota's Gopher, which was the first Gopher, you can connect to Gophers worldwide.

You can search Gophers using a program called Veronica.

Internet Protocols

TCP/IP

In Windows, TCP/IP protocol is used to connect computer to the Internet. During Windows 98 installation if you have installed network components then most probably you have installed TCP/IP protocol on your computer.

TCP/IP stands for Transmission Control Protocol/Internet Protocol.

IP Address

IP address is the actual Internet address of any computer on the Internet, its format is 999.999.999.999, where each number 999 is in the range of 0 to 255

Netmask

TCP/IP uses the netmaks to determine the size of the local area network, so that it can broadcast data across the entire local area network, when it needs to.

The netmask indicates what range of IP addresses are on the local area network and therefore, what addresses your computer can receive data from.

- The netmask usually is in the format of 255.255.0.0 or 255.255.255.0. Individual numbers are always in the range of 0-255.

File Transfer Protocol (FTP)

File Transfer Protocol, generally known as FTP is a service that enables you to transfer files to and from other computers on the Internet.

This service allows you to connect to a computer on the Internet, browse through the list of files on that computer and copy files to your computer. FTP can be used to transfer any type of files, programs, text, pictures, sound etc.

FTP also allows you to upload information from your computer to the remote computer on the Internet. For this the remote computer should give you write permission.

FTP is an example of client/server system. You use a program on your computer called client to talk to a program on remote computer, caller server. The server is designed to let you download and upload files.

Initially using FTP often involved giving cryptic UNIX commands, but in Windows, software with Windows Explorer like graphical interface allow one to explore remote computer very easily and allows to copy files to the local computer.

When connected to a remote computer using FTP, you must log into an account on the remote computer. If you have an account on the remote computer then you can log into your account to download/upload from remote computer.

Anonymous FTP

If you have no account on the remote computer then a common method is to use anonymous FTP log in.

In this anonymous log in, the user name is given as anonymous and the your e-mail ID is given as password. Most of the FTP servers allow anonymous FTP log in.

There is a large pool of information available on anonymous FTP servers, often free of charge.

Most of FTP sites do not have a listing of all their available files. So most of the time, to locate the required file, you will have to click on the folders and look through them.

As the format of file and directory name depends on the operating system used on the machine that is being used as FTP server, what you see depends on the type of system you are connected to.

For example, if the server you are connected to is running UNIX operating system then the file names will appear with any combination of upper and lower case letters of any length. If it is a DEC VMS based system then the file name will appear in only uppercase. PC, Mac etc. display files and directory name in their standard format.

Most of the FTP sites contain a README file, you can first download this file and read its content.

Name Server

Name server address is the IP address of the machine that translates textual Internet addresses into their number formats (IP Address).

The Internet uses numeric IP address value because the value of each machine connected to the Internet is unique. People use textual addresses because they are more easier to read and remember.

Time Server

Time server is the IP address of the computer that carries correct time. Most network systems ask a server the time and set your local computer's internal clock to that time.

When your computer is connected to another computer, the two computers often use the date and time for keeping track of messages and files. By insisting that your computer have the same date and time as the network, the time server ensures that the computer carry out transactions accurately.

Domain Suffix

The domain suffix is part of your e-mail address, without the user name, @ symbol and the host name. In the e-mail address lotia@hotmail.com, the .com is domain suffix.

SLIP

SLIP is a protocol that was designed to allow Internet protocol to be run over serial telephone lines.

SLIP stands for Serial Line Internet Protocol.

PPP

PPP stands for Point to Point Protocol.

PPP protocol is a superset of SLIP protocol and is slightly faster.

PPP is generally considered to be a better developed standard than the SLIP protocol.

SLIP and PPP use full TCP/IP protocol, so they actually allow your computer to be part of the Internet network.

Internet Navigation/Surfing/Browsing

The Internet is divided into many conceptual groups, such as educational, commercial, military, government etc. This logical collection is known as domain.

What are domains?

Domains divide World Wide Web sites into categories based on the nature of their owner, and they form part of a site's address, or Uniform Resource Locator (URL). Common top-level domains are:

Some of the major domains names are given below, these domains are knows as top-level domain

- .com - Commercial Organization, business and individuals
- .edu - Educational institutes
- .gov - Nonmilitary government organization
- .mil - Military institute
- .org - Other organization & groups
- .net - Network service provided
- .arts - Cultural groups
- .firm - Businesses firm
- .info - Information services
- .nom - Individuals
- .rec - Recreational sites
- .store - Retailers
- .web - Web-related organizations
- .int - Organizations established by international treaty

Additional three-letter and four-letter top-level domains have been proposed, and some are likely to be implemented.

Each country linked to the Web has a two-letter top-level domain. For example, .in is used for India.

The domain names are also used in E-mail address, for example if an E-mail address is lotia@hotmail.com, then the .com will inform us that the e-mail address is located on a commercial computer.

In an E-mail address such as lotia@vsnl.net.in, the ".in" inform us that this mail address is on an Indian server. ".net" inform us that server is of a network service provider. "vsnl" is the name of the Internet server. "Lotia" is the user name into whose mailbox the mail is deposited.

When an Internet address is given to an Internet browsing software to browse the address, the address is read from right side and proceeded to the left. From a larger

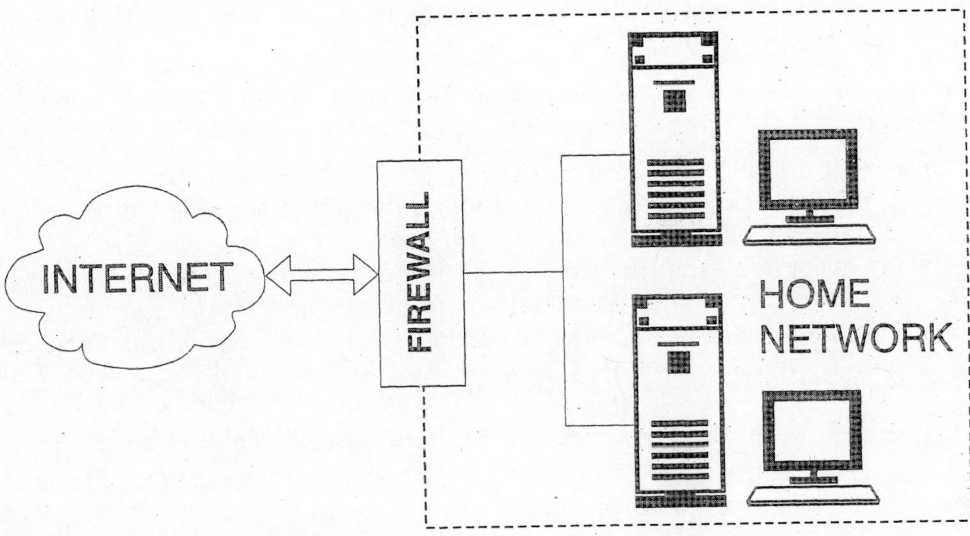

Fig. 14-2 : Concept of Firewall.

domain, it looks for increasingly smaller ones until a particular and unique computer is reached.

As in our above example, only one computer with vsnl.net.in could be there in the entire Internet. The "vsnl" name can be given to another domain such as there could be a vsnl.com or vsnl.edu etc., but there should be only one vsnl.net.in.

FireWall

Basically, a firewall is a barrier to keep destructive forces away from your property. In fact, that's why its called a firewall.

Its job is similar to a physical firewall that keeps a fire from spreading from one area to the next.

A firewall is simply a program or hardware device that filters the information coming through the Internet connection into your private network or computer system.

If you work at a company that has hundreds of computers that all have network cards connecting them together. And, the company has one or more connections to the Internet. Without a firewall in place, all of those hundreds of computers are directly accessible to anyone on the Internet.

A person who knows what he or she is doing can probe those computers, try to make FTP connections to them, try to make telnet connections to them and so on.

If one employee makes a mistake and leaves a security hole, hackers can get to the machine and exploit the hole.

With a firewall in place, at every connection to the Internet. The firewall can implement security rules.

Firewalls use one or more of three methods to control traffic flowing in and out of the network:

- Packet filtering - Packets (small chunks of data) are analyzed against a set of filters. Packets that make it through the filters are sent to the requesting system and all others are discarded.
- Proxy service - Information from the Internet is retrieved by the firewall and then sent to the requesting system and vice versa.
- Stateful inspection - A newer method that doesn't examine the contents of each packet but instead compares certain key parts of the packet to a database of trusted information. If the comparison yields a reasonable match, the information is allowed through. Otherwise it is discarded.

A software firewall, such as Zonealarm, can be installed on the computer in your home that has an Internet connection.

One of the best things about a firewall from a security standpoint is that it stops anyone on the outside from logging onto a computer in your private network.

Proxy Servers and DMZ

A function that is often combined with a firewall is a proxy server. The proxy server is used to access Web pages by the other computers.

When another computer requests a Web page, it is retrieved by the proxy server and then sent to the requesting computer. The net effect of this action is that the remote computer hosting the Web page never comes into direct contact with anything on your home network, other than the proxy server.

Proxy servers can also make your Internet access work more efficiently. If you access a page on a Web site, it is cached (stored) on the proxy server.

This means that the next time you go back to that page, it normally doesn't have to load again from the Web site. Instead it loads instantaneously from the proxy server.

There are times that you may want remote users to have access to items on your network. Some examples are:

- Web site
- Online business
- FTP download and upload area

In cases like this, you may want to create a DMZ (DeMilitarized Zone). It really is just an area that is outside the firewall.

Think of DMZ as the front courtyard of your house. It belongs to you and you may put some things there, but you would put anything valuable inside the house where it can be properly secured.

Setting up a DMZ is very easy. If you have multiple computers, you can choose to simply place one of the computers between the Internet connection and the firewall.

Most of the software firewalls available will allow you to designate a directory on the gateway computer as a DMZ.

Internet addresses/URL

An Internet or Web address (sometimes called a URL, or Uniform Resource Locator) typically is composed of four parts:

- A protocol name (a protocol is a set of rules and standards that enable computers to exchange information)
- The location of the site
- The name of the organization that maintains the site
- A suffix that identifies the kind of organization it is (such as .com for a commercial organization)

For example, the address http://www.rediff.com/ provides the following information:

- http: This Web server uses Hypertext Transfer Protocol (HTTP).
- www This site is on the World Wide Web.
- rediff The Web server is of rediff company.
- .com This is a commercial organizations web site.

When you view a Web page, the page's address appears in the Address bar in Internet Explorer.

What are cookies?

A cookie is a piece of text that a web server can store on a user's hard disk. Cookies allow a web site to store information on a user's machine and later retrieve it.

For example, a web site might generate a unique ID number for each visitor and store the ID number on each user's machine using a cookie file.

These files are basically text files that contain information about you and your preferences.

When you visit a web site and order some product, the site might create a cookie that contains your choices and store it in your computer. This helps the site to customize the views for you, the next time you visit.

If you use Microsoft's Internet Explorer to browse the web, you can see all of the cookies that are stored on your machine. The most common place for them to reside is in a directory called c:\windows\cookies. Each cookie file is a text file that contains name-value pairs.

You can see in the directory that each of these files is a simple, normal text file. You can see which web site placed the file on your machine by looking at the file name. You can open each file up by clicking on it.

For example, when I visit msn.com, the site place a cookie on my machine. The cookie file for msn.com contains the following information:

```
UserID     A4B3BE0E0533972B     www.msn.com/
```

What msn.com has done is, it stored on my machine a single name-value pair. The name of the pair is UserID, and the value is A4B3BE0E0533972B.

Only the information that you provide, or the choices you make while visiting a Web site, can be stored in a cookie. For example, the site cannot determine your e-mail name unless you choose to type it.

Allowing a Web site to create a cookie does not give that or any other site access to the rest of your computer, and only the site that created the cookie can read it.

Internet Explorer is set up to allow the creation of cookies; however, you can specify that you be prompted before a site puts a cookie on your hard disk, so you can choose to allow or disallow the cookie. You can also prevent Internet Explorer from accepting any cookies.

To disable cookies, or to change any other security setting, in Internet Explorer

1. click on the Tools menu
2. click on Internet Options.
3. click on the Security tab.
4. click on Internet in Select a Web content zone.
5. click the Custom Level button. Set different settings in the next Security Settings window.
6. Look for Cookies option in the list.
7. In the following sections:
   - To specify that you want Internet Explorer to accept cookies without prompting you first, click Enable.
   - To specify that you want Internet Explorer to warn you if you are about to receive a cookie from a Web site, click Prompt.
   - To specify that you do not want to allow cookies to be sent to your computer by Web sites, and that existing cookies on your computer cannot be read by Web sites, click Disable.

Using the Internet

Hardware requirement for Internet:

- To use Internet following hardware is required
- a fast computer with enough memory and hard disk space
- a modem and a telephone line

One can use a 386 based computer for Internet access, but to get proper response one should go for a Pentium based computer with at least 64MB RAM and 10GB Hard disk drive. A 56K modem will give good connection speed when using Internet.

As most of the Internet sites have good colorful visual images, it would be better to use a minimum 15 inch size color monitor when using Internet.

A powerful display card (MPEG or AGP) will allow to view movies/3D animation etc. shown on various Internet sites.

Software requirement for Internet:

To connect to Internet, one requires following software

- Windows 95/98 operating system
- Internet Explorer.
- Outlook Express (for E-Mail/New reading etc.)
- Netmeeting (with NetMeeting you can participate in audio and video meetings/conference, collaborate in files using NetMeeting features, and share information over the Internet.)

When buying/using software one should go for the latest version of the software available in the market.

Setting Up a Modem

The modem is a device which allows you to connect your computer to any other computer, anywhere else in the word using a telephone line.

This allows you to communicate with the connected person, transfer data, copy software/programs from the connected computer, sent and receive mail using E-MAIL facility etc.

Currently, the modem can also be used to sent and receives fax, using modem as a fax devices. To connect to the Internet or the WWW (World Wide Web), one requires a modem.

The computer internally works on digital signals, these signals cannot be directly transmitted over the telephone line, which requires analog signals.

A modem does the job of converting the digital signal to the analog signal required to transmit over the telephone line.

Likewise, the modem converts incoming analog signal to digital signal required by the computer.

Modem is available as internal and external device. Physical connection of these internal and external modem was explained in the earlier chapters of this book.

In this section we shall see how to setup the modem to connect to the Internet.

Automatically installing modem driver

After connecting the modem when you switch on the computer system, Windows 95/98 should automatically detect the modem and ask for the modem driver software.

If the auto detection does not work then

1. click on the Start/Settings/Control Panel
2. In the control panel window double click on Add New Hardware icon.
3. In the next Add New Hardware Wizard screen, to automatically detect new hardware click on Next> option.
4. In the next screen select Yes for Do you want Windows to search for your new hardware? question and
5. click on Next> option.
6. click on Modem to select it
7. click on Next> option, this will start the auto detection process, which may take some time.
8. Finally next screen will appear with an option to click on Details... button to see the list of detected hardware.
9. Click on Finish option to install the drivers for the detected hardware.

If your modem was not detected during this process then you need to manually install the modem driver software.

Manually installing modem driver

For this, follow step 1 & 2 of automatic install and in 3rd step, in Add New Hardware Wizard screen

1. click on No, I want to select the hardware for a list, to the `Do you want Windows to search for your new hardware?` question
2. click on Next> option.
3. In the next screen a list of hardware appear, from the list click on **Modem**
4. click on **Next>** option.
   Next Windows will try to automatically detect the modem.

To manually install the modem driver,

1. click on `Don't detect my modem; I will select it from a list`

6. click on `Next>` option.
   Now a list of modem manufacturers and their modem models are shows on the next screen.
   There is also an option called `Have Disk...`, if you have received a modem driver disk or CD with your modem then
7. click on the `Have Disk...` option.
8. Place the driver disk/CD into proper drive and in the next `Install From Disk` screen select proper drive.
   You can also click on `Browse...` option to search for the driver disk/CD.
9. Once the driver is found on disk, click on `OK`, this will install the modem driver into your computer system.
   The driver could be on some sub-directory of the driver disk/CD, check the manual that came with the modem.
10. Restart the computer to make the modem active.

Sometimes the driver disk/CD that comes with the modem contains a SETUP.EXE or INSTALL.EXE program. Running this program will automatically install the modem driver to the Windows.

Once the modem is installed, you can use the Modem icon on the Control Panel to check if the modem is working properly.

Testing the modem

1. click on Start, point to Settings, click on "Control Panel".
2. In the Control Panel window double click on Modem's icon.
3. In the Modem Properties window, select the Diagnostics tab
4. click on the port to which the modem is connected
5. click on "More Info..." button.
6. If the modem is working properly then, after a small duration, a list of modem commands with their response will appear on the next window.
7. If the modem was not setup properly than an error message stating that the Modem Failed to Respond will appear on the screen.

If this error message appear then check the modem setting, cables, connections, driver setup etc.

If the modem pass the diagnostic test then to configure it

1. click on the General tab of Modems Properties window
2. In the General tab click and select the modem you want to configure
3. double click on the Properties... button.
4. In the Properties window, two tabs General and Connection appear. On some modems some additional tabs such as Distinctive Ring, Forwarding etc. may appear.

General Tab can be used to set the

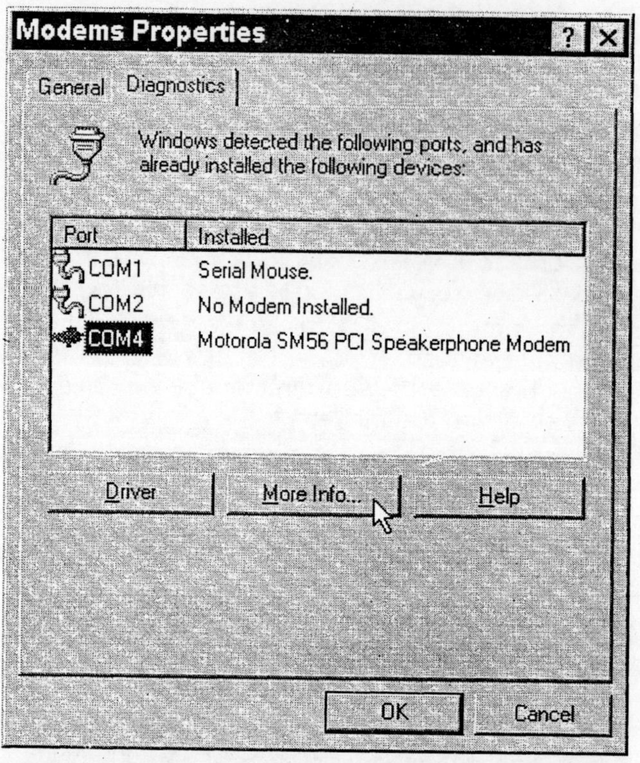
Modems Properties
General
Diagnostics
Windows detected the following ports, and has already installed the following devices:
Port
Installed
COM1
Serial Mouse.
COM2
No Modem Installed.
COM4
Motorola SM56 PCI Speakerphone Modem
Driver
More Info...
Help
OK
Cancel

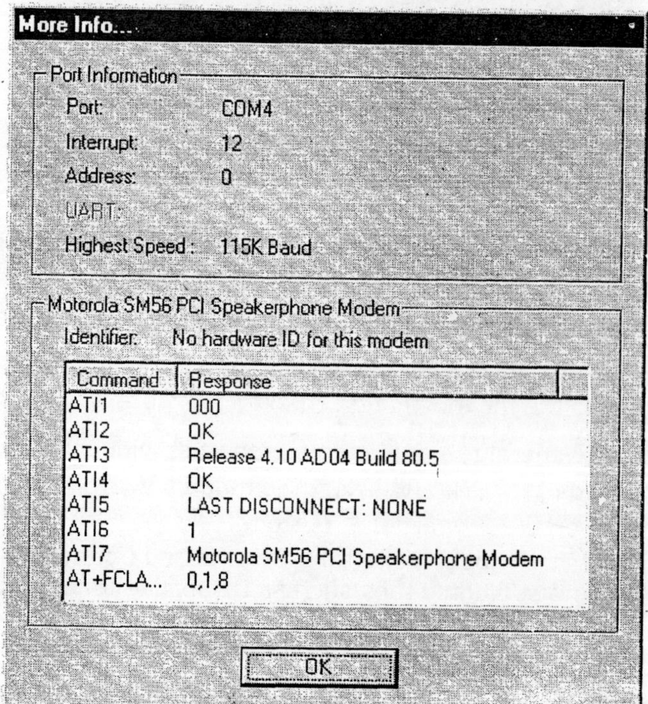
More Info...
Port Information
Port: COM4
Interrupt: 12
Address: 0
UART:
Highest Speed : 115K Baud
Motorola SM56 PCI Speakerphone Modem
Identifier: No hardware ID for this modem
Command
Response
ATI1 000
ATI2 OK
ATI3 Release 4.10 AD04 Build 80.5
ATI4 OK
ATI5 LAST DISCONNECT: NONE
ATI6 1
ATI7 Motorola SM56 PCI Speakerphone Modem
AT+FCLA... 0,1,8
OK

- port to which the modem is connected, do not change this.
- modem speaker volume level, click and drag the slider to increase/reduce the modem speaker volume
- the maximum data transfer speeds the modem can use.
  - This maximum data transfer speed is the speed used in computer-to-modem communication, it is not the maximum speed used by modem during communication with external modem.
  - Not all modems support this function. Generally keep this value to maximum.

The Connection Tab shows

- Connection preference and Call preference
- it also shows Port Settings... and Advanced... setting command buttons.

Connection preference has setting for

- data bit, parity bit and stop bit, generally do not change these values.

Call preference has setting for

- Wait for dial tone before dialing
- Cancel the call if not connected within xx secs
- Disconnect a call if idle for more than xx mins

These Call preference settings can be left as it is without any change.

Generally clear the Wait for dial tone before dialing option.

If this option is not cleared then sometimes "No dial tone detected." error message may appear, even when the telephone line is all right.

Clearing this option could rectify this error.

Port settings... has option to set the receive buffer and transmit buffer size.

"Use FIFO buffers" option should be selected by clicking on it.

Advanced Connection setting has following options

- Use error control and compress data
- Hardware/Software data flow control
- Modulation type selection
- Facility for specifying any extra settings
  - (using AT & ATX commands)
- Facility to make a log file storing modem session information to the modem log file (Modemlog.txt).
- This file is stored in the folder where Windows is installed and is useful for monitoring calls and for troubleshooting.

Setting of this Advanced Connection setting should not be changed, unless required.

- The default values shown work best for Internet connection.
- Click OK twice to go back to the Modem Properties screen.
- In this screen click on Dialing Properties button.
- Select the dialing properties in the Dialing Properties screen.
- In this screen most important setting is the Dial using Tone dial/Pulse dial option. A wrong selection here will not allow modem to dial any number. Use Tone dialing only if your phone has fast dialing option.

Connecting to the Internet

There are many ways you can connect to the Internet. Once you have access to the Internet, you can retrieve information from millions of sources, including school/college libraries, governments records, businesses, and individuals.

To connect to the Internet we use the Dial-Up Networking provided with Windows 98. Following are the steps required for connecting to the Internet using Dial-Up Networking.

- Get an Internet account from an Internet service provider (ISP).
- Set up your communications hardware (i.e. the Modem).
- Make sure Dial-Up Networking is installed.
- Install Windows 98 TCP/IP protocol and bind it to the Dial-Up Networking adapter.
- Setup TCP/IP protocol.
- Setup a connection to your Internet provider in Dial-Up Networking.
- Dial your Internet service provider and type the user name and password at prompts.
- Get connected to the Internet.

Get an Internet Account

To setup an Internet account call an ISP (Internet Service Provider) and sign up for an Internet account. Make sure you get the following information from your ISP:

- User name
- Password
- Access phone number
- Your host name and domain name
- Domain Name System (DNS) server address

The service provider may also supply the following information:

- IP address and subnet mask
- DNS search order (if required)
- Gateway address
- Authentication procedure (whether or not the service provider requires a terminal window to log on, to type user name and password)

- POP3 and SMTP mail server name, port number etc. to access E-mail.

Set up Communications Hardware

You need a modem-28800 bits per second (28.8kbps) or faster is recommended-to connect to the Internet.

Setting up the modem is already explained in the earlier section.

Make sure Dial-Up Networking is installed

Double-click My Computer on your desktop.

If you do not see a Dial-Up Networking icon, then install the dial-up networking. Installing dial-up networking is explained below.

1. click on `Start`
2. point to `Settings`
3. click on `Control Panel`.
4. In the Control Panel screen double click on the `Add/Remove Programs` icon.
5. In the Add/Remove programs Properties screen select `Windows Setup` tab.
6. From the Windows Component list click on `Communications`, and then click on `Details...` command button.
7. In the Communications window click on the `Dial-Up Networking` check box
8. click `OK`.
9. click `OK` in the Add/Remove programs Properties screen.

This will install the Dial-Up Networking component of Windows. Without this component you cannot use modem to connect to the Internet.

Install the Windows 98 TCP/IP protocol

TCP/IP or Transmission Control Protocol/Internet Protocol is the basic communications protocol required for computers to communicate over the Internet.

1. Click on `Start`
2. Point to `Settings`
3. click on `Control Panel`.
4. In the Control Panel screen double click on the `Network` icon.
5. In the Network window, click on the `Configuration` tab.
6. Click on `Add` command button. (If the Windows 98 TCP/IP protocol is already installed, you can skip following steps and directly go to step 9.)
7. Click `Protocol`, and then click `Add`.
8. Click `Microsoft`, and then click `TCP/IP`.
9. Click `OK`.
10. Click `Dial-Up Adapter`, and then click `Properties`.

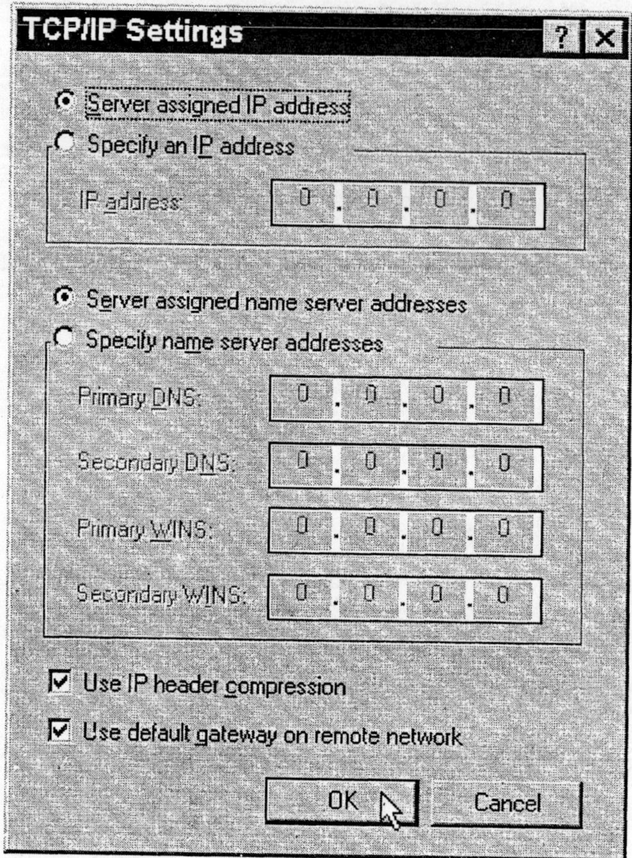

Fig. 14-3 : TCP/IP Setting.

11. Click the **Bindings** tab, and then make sure the TCP/IP check box is selected. Click **OK**.
12. If prompted, restart your computer.

Setup TCP/IP Protocol

1. Click on **Start**
2. Point to **Settings**
3. Click on **Control Panel**.
4. In the Control Panel screen double click on the **Network** icon.
5. In the Network window, click on the **Configuration** tab.
6. Click on **TCP/IP** (if there is more than one TCP/IP entry found, click on TCP/IP->Dial-Up Adapter) and select it,
7. click **Properties**.

8. If your ISP gave you an IP address,click on the IP Address tab, click **Specify an IP address**, and then type your IP address and subnet mask.
9. If your service provider did not give you an IP address, click and select **Obtain an IP address automatically**.
10. On the Bindings tab, it is recommended that you click to clear the File and printer sharing check box.

Setup a connection to your Internet provider

Once the Dial-Up Networking and TCP/IP protocol is installed, you need to setup a dial-up networking connection to your Internet service provider.

1. Click on **Start**,
2. Point to **Programs**,
3. Point to **Accessories**
4. Point to **Communications**, and then
5. Click **Dial-Up Networking**.
   If the dial-up networking is not already setup i.e. if it is your first Dial-Up Networking connection then you'll be prompted to setup a new connection.
   You can also click on **Make New Connection** icon to setup a new dial-up connection.
   Clicking on Make New Connection icon will start the Make New Connection wizard,
6. Type a name for the Internet connection you are setting up, for example VSNL Connection or Mantra Internet etc.
7. Next, select the device i.e. the modem you will use to connect to the Internet.
8. Click on **Next>** on the Make New Connection window.
9. In the next window type the phone number you need to dial to connect to your Internet Service Provider (ISP).
   If required, give the Area code and Country or region code of the number you want to call to.
10. Again click on **Next>** button.
11. On the next window click on **Finish** button to complete making of the new dial up connection.
12. Now this new connection can be double clicked to dial the ISPs telephone number and connect to the Internet.

Before dialing the ISPs number you need to set some properties of this newly created dial-up connection.

Setting Dial-Up Connection Properties

Before you can make use of this new connection, to connect to the Internet, you need to configure it. For this

1. right click on this new connection on the dial up networking.

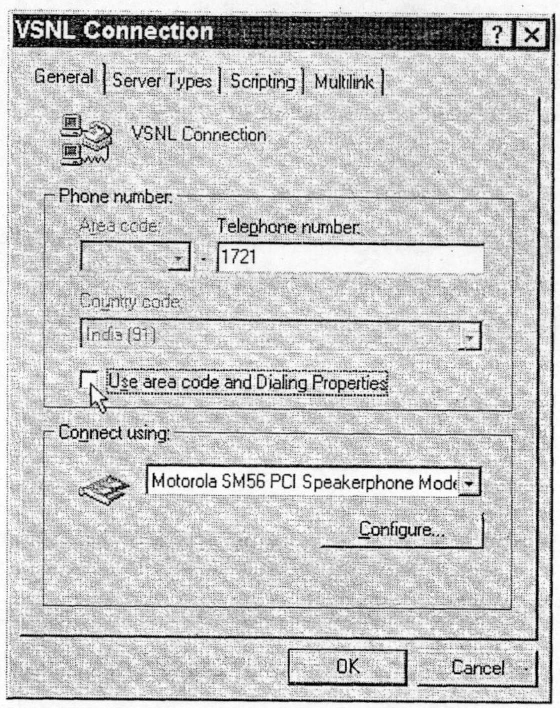
VSNL Connection
General
Server Types
Scripting
Multilink
VSNL Connection
Phone number:
Area code:
Telephone number:
1721
Country code:
India (91)
Use area code and Dialing Properties
Connect using:
Motorola SM56 PCI Speakerphone Mode
Configure...
OK
Cancel

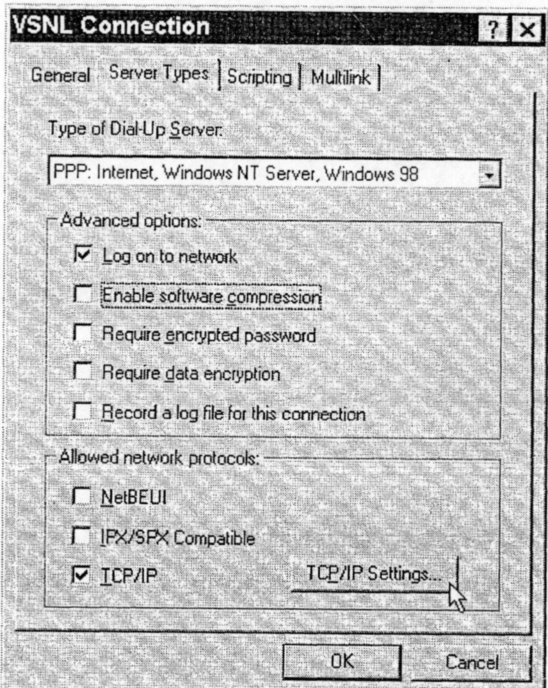
VSNL Connection
General
Server Types
Scripting
Multilink
Type of Dial-Up Server:
PPP: Internet, Windows NT Server, Windows 98
Advanced options:
Log on to network
Enable software compression
Require encrypted password
Require data encryption
Record a log file for this connection
Allowed network protocols:
NetBEUI
IPX/SPX Compatible
TCP/IP
TCP/IP Settings...
OK
Cancel

2. Click on the `Properties` on the pop-up menu.
   In this properties window General, Server Type, Scripting and Multilink tabs are seen.
   In the General tab the `Phone number:` window Provides a space to type or select the area code, phone number, and country code of the computer you want to connect to.
   You can specify that you do not want to dial the area code and country code, when dialing the ISP's number, by clearing the `Use area code and Dialing Properties` check box.
   The `Connect Using:` window lists the devices installed on your system which can be used by Dial-Up Networking to connect to another computer.
   If the device you want isn't in the list, click **Modems** in Control Panel to add a new modem, or click **Network** in Control Panel to add a new network or ISDN adapter.
   At this stage also you can configure the modem by clicking on the `Configure...` button.
3. In the Server Type tab, select the `Type of Dial-Up Server:`, `Advanced options:` and `Allowed network protocols:`
4. In the Type of Dial-up Server: select `PPP: Internet, Windows NT Server, Windows 98` option.
5. In the Advanced options: window set the Log on to network option and clear all other options.
   In the `Allowed network protocols:` window, NetBEUI, IPX/SPX Compatible and TCP/IP protocols are listed.
   - NetBEUI protocol is used to connect to Windows NT, Windows for Workgroups, or LAN Manager servers.
   - IPX/SPX Compatible protocol is used to connect to NetWare and Windows NT servers and Windows 98 computers.
   - TCP/IP protocol is used to connect to the Internet and wide-area networks.
6. To connect to the Internet you require only TCP/IP protocol, check mark on the other two protocols can be cleared here.
7. Now click on `TCP/IP Setting...` command button. This will bring up the TCP/IP settings window.
8. In this TCP/IP setting window keep the settings as Server assigned IP address and Server assigned name server addresses.
   If you have primary and secondary DNS number provided by your Internet Service Provider (ISP) then you can select Specify name server addresses option and give these DNS values in their respective places.
   The DNS address given at this space is used for this particular dial-up connection only. Dial-Up Networking tries to use these addresses first.
   This is useful if you have more than one Internet account and must use different DNS and WINS server addresses for different connections.
9. IP header compression optimizes data transfer between computers. Use default gateway on remote network specifies whether IP traffic is routed to

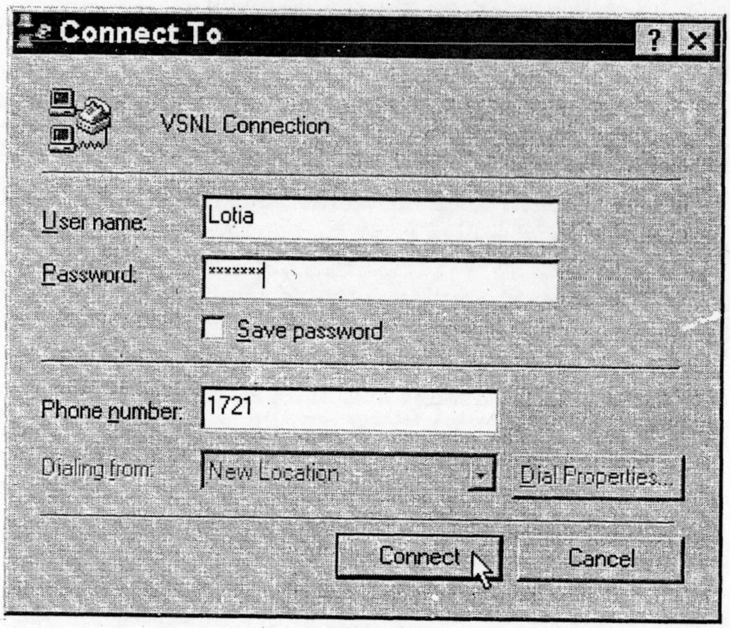

Connect To

VSNL Connection

User name: Lotia

Password: *******

Save password

Phone number: 1721

Dialing from: New Location

Dial Properties...

Connect Cancel

Fig. 14-4 : Dialing Internet Service Provider.

the WAN connection by default. These two options can be kept selected (checked).

10 After specifying these values click on `OK` button.

Next tab in the VSNL Connection, i.e. the **Scripting** Tab, is used to specify a script file name to be used with this connection.

Many ISPs require you to enter information, such as your user name and password, to establish a connection.

You can create a Dial-Up Networking script that provides this information automatically, so you do not have to type it each time you want to get connected to the Internet.

11. Make sure that the **Start terminal screen minimized** option is set.

To create a Dial-Up Networking script, use a simple text editor, such as WordPad or Notepad. In the WordPad, type the file as a text document, without any text formatting.

A script file contains scripting commands, parameters, and expressions that provide and retrieve information to and from the remote computer you are connecting to.

This information includes your user name and password, port information, carriage returns, line feeds, and pauses.

Scripting files are generally given .SCP file name extension.

The last tab of connection property i.e. the **Multilink** tab is used to set up a network connection using multiple modems.

Connecting to VSNL Connection
Status: Dialing...
Cancel

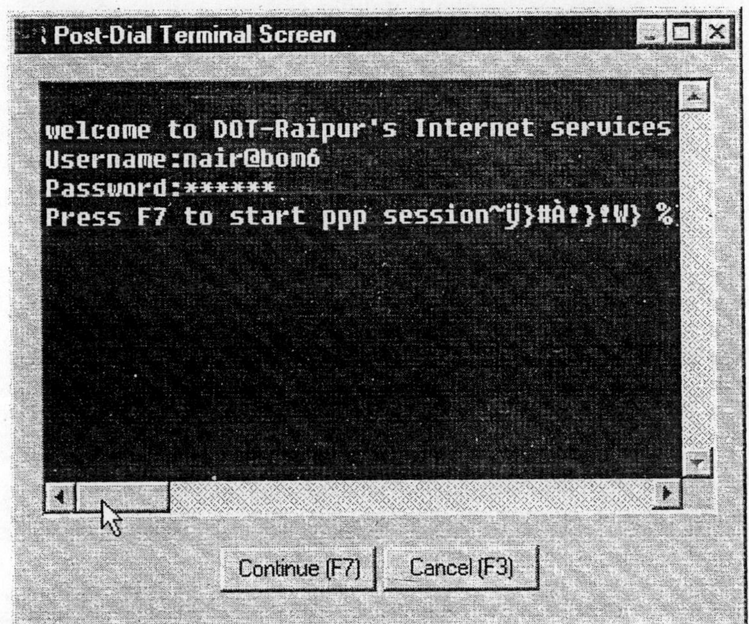
Post-Dial Terminal Screen
welcome to DOT-Raipur's Internet services
Username:nair@bom6
Password:******
Press F7 to start ppp session
Continue (F7)
Cancel (F3)

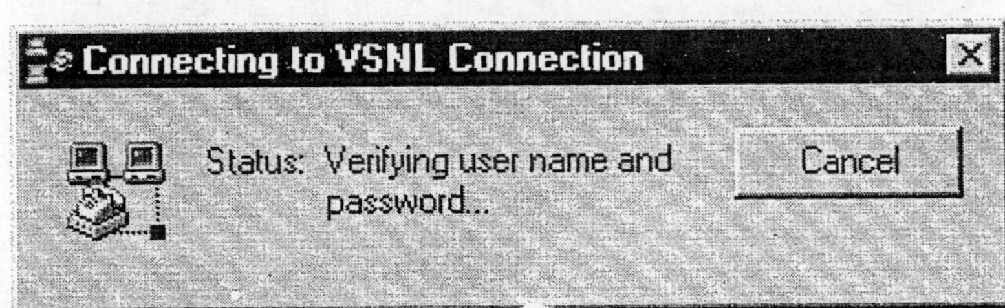
Connecting to VSNL Connection
Status: Verifying user name and password...
Cancel

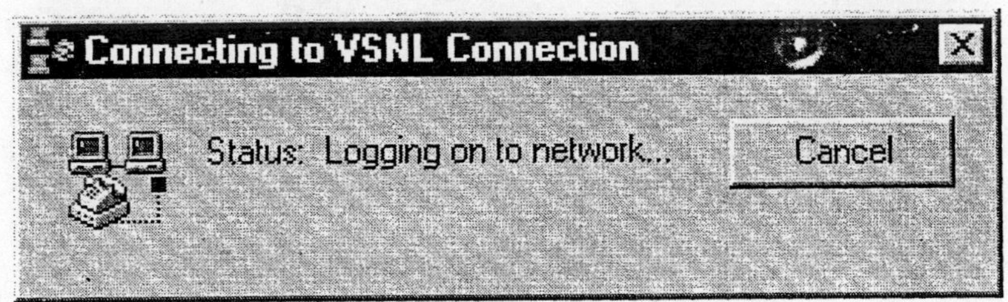
Connecting to VSNL Connection
Status: Logging on to network...
Cancel

To set up a multilink connection, you must have two or more modems installed on your computer, one phone line for each modem, and should have an ISP that supports PPP and Multilink connections.

When trying the multilink operation, if the first modem connects successfully but the second modem fails to connect, multilink is probably not supported by your ISP.

Dialing your Internet service provider

In the Dial-Up Networking window, double click on the connection for your Internet service provider, enter your name and password on the next screen, and then click Connect.

A connecting to VSNL Connection window will appear on the screen with `Status: Dialing` message.

You should be able to hear modem's communication sounds at this time, a lot of high and low pitch beep sounds.

Once you get connected to the Internet, a post-dial terminal screen appears.

In the post-dial terminal screen type User name, press [Enter] key, type Password, press [Enter] key. While typing username and password, take care about the small letters and capital letters.

If the username and password given by you are correct then a message `Press F7 to start PPP session` will appear.

Pressing of F7 key will show Connecting to VSNL Connection screen with `Status: Verifying user name and password...` message.

Next, `Status: Logging on to network...` message will appear.

If the connection to the Internet could be established then given icon will appear at the taskbar indicating that you are connected to the Internet.

Double clicking on this icon will open `Connected to VSNL Connection` window. Indicating connected speed, duration, bytes received and sent during this connection.

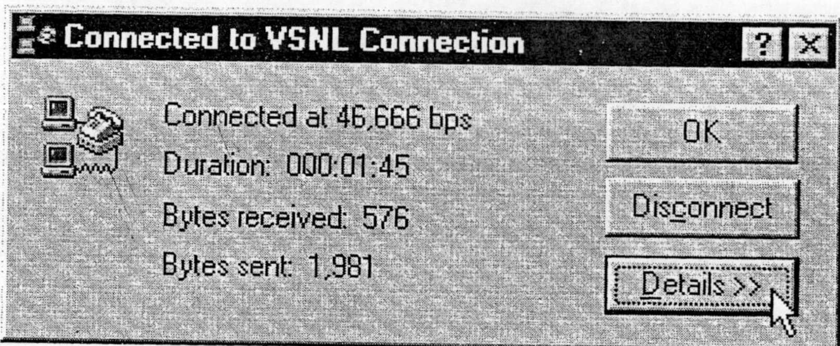

This window has a command button to disconnect the modem from the Internet.

Clicking on **Details>>** button will open a window with some additional information such as the modem, server type, Protocols used etc. about this connection.

Click on **OK** to close this window without disconnecting from the Internet. Now start the Internet Explorer by double clicking on the Internet explorer icon on the desktop and start surfing the WWW.

To surf the WWW type the address of required Internet site at the address bar, and click on **Go** button.

After typing the address you can also press the [Enter] key.

Setting up multilink option

A multilink connection uses multiple modems to create a single connection to the Internet or other computer network.

To set up a multilink connection, you must have two or more modems installed on your computer, one phone line for each modem, and an Internet Service Provider that supports PPP and multilink connections.

To setup the Multilink option

Set up a Dial-Up Networking connection using one modem.

- In the Dial-Up Networking folder, right-click the **connection** icon and click **Properties.**
- On the Multilink tab, click **Use additional devices**, and then click **Add....**
- In Edit Extra Device, select the device you want to add to the connection, and then click **OK.**

Repeat above steps until you have added all the required modems.

Internet Explorer - the web browser

Internet Explorer, the web browser software that comes free with the Windows makes it easier to get the most out of the World Wide Web, whether you are searching for some information or just browsing your favorite Web sites.

Starting Internet Explorer

To start the Internet Explorer

Double click on the explorer icon on the desktop

or you can

1. Click on `Start`
2. Point to `Programs`
3. Click on `Internet Explorer`

Once the explorer starts you will see the following icons on the screen.

Internet Explorer Toolbar Icons

Once the Internet explorer starts, you will see the following icons on the explorer toolbar.

Let us see the use of these icons

Clicking on this will redisplay the previous page you visited.

Clicking on this icon will display next page (this icon enables only after you visit to a previous page.)

This icon can be clicked if the WWW site you want to open is opening very slowly and you want to cancel the loading of that page.

Clicking on this icon reloads the information from the WWW site that you are visiting.

This will take you to your default starting page. This home page could be set up to be any page on any web site.

Click on this icon to search WWW for sites containing information that is of interest to you.

Click on this icon to bookmark your favorite WWW sites, so that you can easily revisit them later on.

Click on this icon to see a list of the WWW pages you've visited in the last few days

Click on this icon to access E-mail and Newsgroup programs

Click on this icon to print the web page displayed on the screen.

Visiting a WWW site

A www site is simply a collection of information stored on a WWW server computer. This data can be easily accessed by people surfing the net.

To access a WWW site you should know the address of that site, in much the same way as if you want to phone someone you have to know his phone number.

The address of a www site is given by something called URL or Uniform Resource Locator. To visit a WWW site, type the site's URL at the address bar of the Internet Explorer and click on the Go button or press the [Enter] key.

If you do not known the URL of the WWW site that you want to visit, you can also use something called search engines to look for the required information

In the search engines you can type a words or a phrase related to the information you want to find.

The search engine will look the entire WWW for your required information and provide you with a list of WWW sites that match the information requested by you.

Home Page

In most of the Internet sites they have a starting page known as the home page of that particular WWW site.

The www sites related to this home site will have a button displaying a word HOME on it, clicking on this will take you to the starting page, i.e. the home page of the site.

Home Page for the Internet Explorer is different. For Internet Explorer the home page is that page which explorer opens by default, every time you start the Internet explorer.

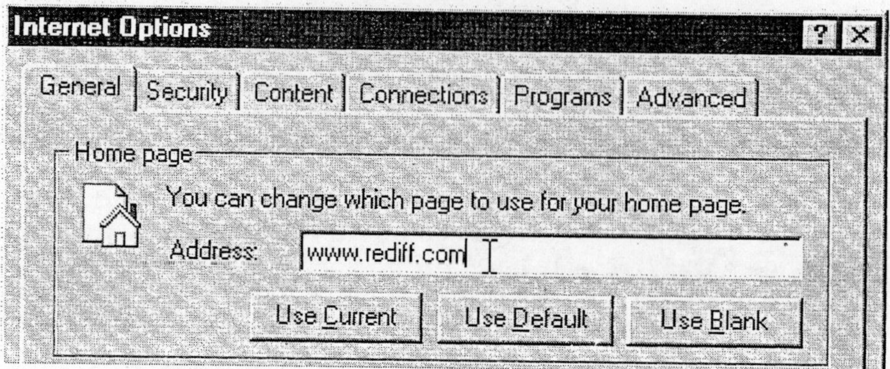

Fig. 14-5 : Changing Default Home Page.

Changing your home page

Home page is the page that is displayed every time you open Internet Explorer. Make sure it is a page that you want to view frequently.

Or use a web site name that you can customize to get quick access to all the information you want, such as the rediff.com home page.

To make a WWW page your home page, go to the page you want to appear every time you start Internet Explorer.

1. On the Tools menu, click on **Internet Options.**
2. Click on the **General** tab.
3. In the Home page area, click on **Use Current.**
4. Click on OK to close the Internet Options dialog box.

To restore your original home page, click on **Use Default.**

If you wish to start the explorer with a blank page click on **Use Blank.**

Saving pictures or text from a Web page

As you view pages on the Web, you'll find information that you'd like to save for future reference or share with other people. You can save the entire Web page or any part of it: text, graphics, or links.

You can print Web pages for people who don't have access to the Web or a computer.

How to save a Web page on your computer?

1. Click on the **File** menu,
2. click on **Save As.**
3. Double-click on the folder you want to save the page in.
4. In the File name box, type a name for the page.

5. In the Save as type box, select a file type.
   - To save all of the files needed to display this page, including graphics, frames, and style sheets, click **Web Page, complete**. This option saves each file in its original format.
   - To save all of the information needed to display this page in a single MIME-encoded file, click **Web Archive**. This option saves a snapshot of the current Web page.

     This option is available only if you have installed Outlook Express 5 or later.
   - To save just the current HTML page, click **Web Page, HTML only**. This option saves the information on the Web page, but it does not save the graphics, sounds, or other files.
   - To save just the text from the current Web page, click **Text Only**. This option saves the information on the Web page in straight text format.

With Web Page, complete and Web Archivc, you can view all of the Web page offline, without adding the page to your Favorites list and marking it for offline viewing.

When you choose Web Page, complete, only the current page is saved. If you want to view Web pages and the pages they link to while offline then make them available for offline viewing.

Making pages available for offline viewing

When you make a Web page available offline, you can read its content even when your computer is not connected to the Internet.

You can specify how much content you want available, such as just a page or a page and all its links, and choose how you want to update that content on your computer.

If you just want to view a Web page offline, and you don't need to update the content, you can save the page on your computer.

There are several ways you can save the Web page, from just saving the text, to saving all of the images and text needed to display that page as it appears on the Web.

In previous versions of Internet Explorer, offline viewing was called subscribing.

If you used channels in a previous version of Internet Explorer, you can find them in the Channels folder in your Favorites list.

Saving a page or picture without opening it

Right-click the link for the item you want, and then click **Save Target As**.

Display/Hide picture/video/sound/animation etc. from web page

To make the loading of WWW pages fast, you can disable the loading of image/animation/video/sound etc. from the web page.

When this option is used, a rectangular box will be displayed in place of the picture, when you view the web page.

To set this option

1. Click on `Tools` menu
2. Click on `Internet Options`
3. Click on `Advanced` Tab
4. Scroll down until you see the option relating to Multimedia.
5. Click on `Show Picture` option to remove the tick next to this option.
6. Close and restart the browser to view the affect of this change.

You can also disable the animation/sound/video by clearing the tick next to these options.

To once again display the images, repeat these steps and place a tick next to `Show Picture` option.

Even when the show picture is disabled, you can make the explorer display the image by right clicking on the image and then clicking on `Show Picture` from the pop-up menu.

Navigating through a web page

When you open a web page, it contains many hyperlinks. Hyperlinks are simply part of the text or some graphic on the web page, that when clicked on will automatically

- take you to another part of the same web page
- take you to a different page on the same web site
- take you to a page on a different web site
- enable you to download a file
- start an application, video or sound

Generally the text is underlined in displayed in a different color to indicate that the text is a hyperlink.

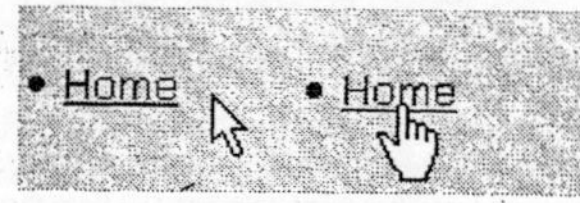

When the mouse cursor is moved over the hyperlink text or graphic, the shape of cursor change to a hand.

When you click on this hyperlink text or graphic, a new page linked to this hyperlink is displayed by the Internet explorer.

From this new web page you can go back to the previous page by clicking on the back button on the toolbar.

Clicking on the down arrow to the right of back button will display a short list of recently visited web pages.

Making the current Web page available offline

- On the Favorites menu, click `Add to Favorites`.
- Select the Make available offline check box.
- To specify a schedule for updating that page, and how much content to download, click `Customize`.
- Follow the instructions on your screen.

Before you go offline, make sure you have the latest version of your pages by clicking the Tools menu and then clicking Synchronize.

Viewing the off-line Web pages

After you mark your favorite pages for viewing offline, you can view them offline by using the following procedure.

- Before you disconnect from the Internet, click the Tools menu, and then click `Synchronize`.
- When you're ready to work offline, click the `File` menu, and then click `Work Offline`.
- In your Favorites list, click the item you want to view.

When you choose to work offline, Internet Explorer will always start in Offline mode until you click Work Offline again to clear the check mark.

Copying information from a Web page

Select the information you want to copy, click the `Edit` menu, and then click `Copy`.

Creating a desktop shortcut to current page

Right-click in the page, and then click `Create Shortcut`. This will place a shortcut of the selected page to the desktop.

Using a Web page image as desktop wallpaper

Right-click the image on the Web page, and then click on `Set as Wallpaper`.

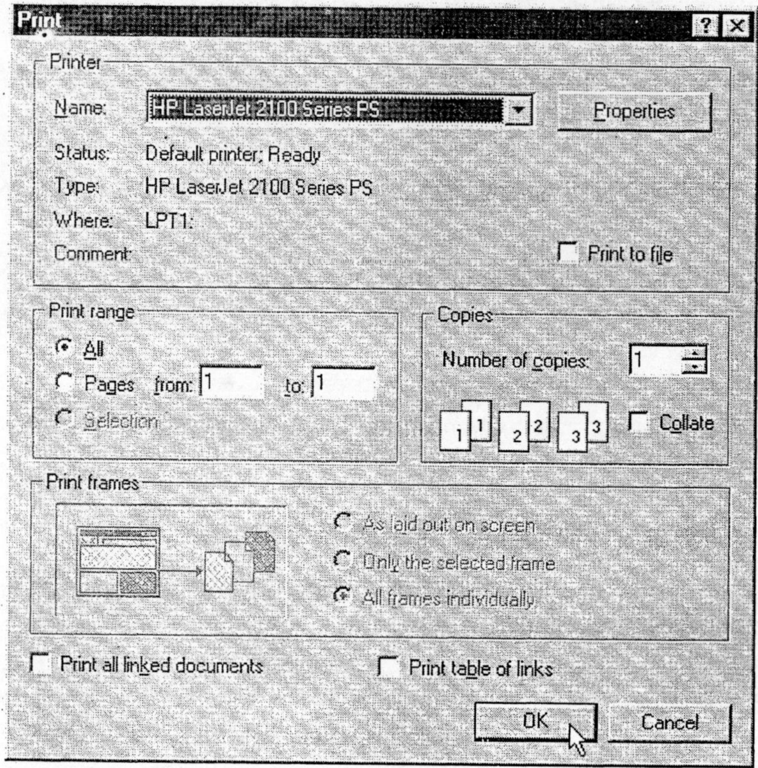

Fig. 14-6 : Printing from Internet Explorer.

Sending a Web page in e-mail

After opening the page, click the `File` menu, point to `Send`, and then click `Page By E-mail...` or `Link By E-mail....` Complete the mail message window, and then send the message.

To complete this process you must have an e-mail account and an e-mail program set up on your computer.

Printing a Web page

Internet explorer provides a print option to print the www page currently being viewed. As a print preview is not provided, you can change the paper size, orientation, margin, header, footer etc. in a page setup option.

On the `File` menu, click `Print.` , Set the printing options you want.

To print a frame or item in a Web page, right-click the frame or item, and then click `Print` or `Print Frame`.

Changing how a page looks when it prints

- On the **File** menu, click **Page Setup**.
- In the Margins boxes, type the margin measurements in inches.
- In the Orientation area, click either **Portrait** or **Landscape** to specify whether you want the page printed vertically or horizontally.
- In the Header and Footer boxes, specify the information to be printed by using the following variables. Variables can be combined with text (for example, Page &p of &P).

To print this	Type this
Window title	&w
Page address (URL)	&u
Date in short format (as specified by Regional Settings in Control Panel)	&d
Date in long format (as specified by Regional Settings in Control Panel)	&D
Time in the format specified by Regional Settings in Control Panel	&t
Time in 24-hour format	&T
Current page number	&p
Total number of pages	&P
Centered text (following &b)	&b
Right-aligned text (following &b&b)	&b&b
A single ampersand (&)	&&

If you want to set margins in millimeters instead of inches, you must change the Regional Settings in Control Panel.

Finding pages you've recently visited/History

There are several ways to find Web sites and pages you've viewed in the last few days, hours, or minutes.

Finding a page you've seen in the last few days

- On the toolbar, click the **History** button.
- The History bar appears, containing links for Web sites and pages visited in previous days and weeks.
- In the History bar, click a **week** or **day**, click a Web site folder to display individual pages, and then click the page icon to display the Web page.
- To sort or search the History bar, click the arrow next to the View button at the top of the History bar.

Finding a page that you just visited

- To return to the last page you viewed, click the Back button on the toolbar.

- To view one of the last nine pages you visited in this session, click the arrow to the side of the Back or Forward button, and then click the page you want from the list.

You can hide the History bar by clicking the History button again.

You can change the number of days that pages are saved in the History list. The more days you specify, the more disk space is used on your computer to save that information.

Specifying how many pages are saved in the History list

- On the Tools menu in Internet Explorer, click Internet Options.
- Click the General tab.
- In the History area, change the number of days that the History list keeps track of your pages.

To empty the History folder, click Clear History. This will temporarily free up disk space on your computer.

Finding information on the Internet

You can find information on the Web in a variety of ways.

- Click the Search button on the toolbar to gain access to a number of search providers. Type the word or term you want to search the net, in the Search box.
- Type go, find, or ? followed by a word or phrase in the Address bar of Internet explorer. Internet Explorer starts a search using its predetermined search provider.
- After you go to a Web page, you can search for specific text on that page by clicking the Edit menu and then clicking Find (on this page).

If a Web address doesn't work, Internet Explorer asks if you want to search for similar Web addresses.

Searching the web from the Address bar

When you search from the Address bar, Internet Explorer can automatically display the Web page that most likely matches what you are searching for and list other likely sites as well.

- Just type the search words in the Address bar, and then click Go. You can view these search results in several ways:
- On the Tools menu in Internet Explorer, click Internet Options.
- Click the Advanced tab.
- In the Search from the Address bar area, select the option you want:

- To view a list of likely matches in the Search bar, and display the most likely Web page in the main window, select Display results, and go to the most likely site.
- To view a list of likely matches in the main window so that you can choose which Web page to display, select Just display the results in the main window.
- To view only the most likely Web page, select Just go to the most likely site.
- To turn off searching from the Address bar, select Do not search from the Address bar.

No matter which option you choose, you can still search for Web sites by clicking the Search button on the toolbar.

To search the Web from the Start menu

Click the Start button, point to Find, and then click On the Internet.

Using Internet Search Engines

Internet search engines are special WWW sites on the Web that are designed to help people find information stored on other sites.

Before a search engine can tell you where a file or document is, it must be found. To find information on the hundreds of millions of Web pages that exist, a search engine employs special software robots, called spiders.

These spider programs build lists of the words found on Web sites. When a spider is building its lists, the process is called Web crawling.

In order to build and maintain a useful list of words, a search engine's spiders have to look at a lot of pages.

Some Common Search Engines

Some commonly used search engines are

```
http://www.google.com
http://www.altavista.com
http://www.hotbot.com
http://www.go.com
http://www.lycos.com
http://www.yahoo.com
http://www.webcrawler.com
http://www.rediff.com
http://www.indiainfo.com
http://www.webduniya.com
```

To use the search engine properly, and to get the information one is looking for requires giving proper search keywords to the search engine.

If you provide some common words to the search engine then the search engine may return more than a million web sites with match.

Normally one should use two or more words or short phrases when using a search engine. Try to use unique words that directly relate to what you are looking for.

For example if you are looking for help on car repair, you should search for "car repair" not just "repair", which could show information on repair of all sort of things.

It would be even better if you could further specify you want information on repair of which part of the car, such as "car engine repair" or "car electrical repair" etc.

Advanced search

Even when you search for car engine repair most of the search engines return all www sites that contain the word "car", "engine" or "repair" and any combination of these words.

To solve this problem and to look for only those WWW sites that contain information about car engine repair you can use something called advanced search options, provided by most of the search engines.

In some search engines if you enclose the search text in quotation marks then the search will be done for exact match. In above example if you search for "car engine repair", then the search engine will search for only those WWW sites that contain information about car engine repair

In some search engines you can put a + (plus) sign before a word that you want to include in the search and a - (minus) sign can be placed before a word that you do not want in the web page.

This + and - sign should be put before the search engine without any space in-between the sign and the search word.

For example, to search for car electrical repair but to exclude battery problems, you can search for

+car +electrical +repair -battery

Use uppercase letters for exact search. If you search for Raipur, the search engine will return all WWW page containing information about raipur, Raipur, RAIPUR etc.

But, if you search for Raipur, then only those www sites that contain information about Raipur will be shown.

To look for multiple form of a word you can use the wildcard character * (star). Typing the word fast* in the search engine will search for fast, faster, fastest, fastener, fasting etc.

Customize the font size, formatting, colors

You can specify the font sizes, styles and colors, and foreground and background colors of Web pages displayed on your computer screen, even if the designer of the Web page has already specified these.

You can also specify the color used to indicate links in Web pages, or a special color for links that is used only when the mouse passes over the link.

This is useful if you need larger fonts, or need high-contrast colors. You can set Internet Explorer to use the colors and fonts you specify, your default Windows colors and fonts, or the settings you specify in your own style sheet.

Changing fonts and colors

When Web designers create Web pages, they often specify particular font colors and sizes, typefaces, and background colors.

These settings are specified for each item, or in a style sheet, which is a type of template for specifying how different styles should appear throughout a Web page or site.

You can specify your font and color preferences for all pages that do not use style sheets, and then you can specify whether to use any or all of your preferences on pages that use style sheets.

To specify which font and color settings to use

- On the Tools menu in Internet Explorer, click **Internet Options.**
- On the General tab, click **Accessibility....**
- Change the settings as needed.

To change how page colors are displayed

- On the Tools menu in Internet Explorer, click **Internet Options.**
- On the General tab, click **Colors....**
- Change the settings as needed.

To display text in a different font

- On the Tools menu in Internet Explorer, click **Internet Options.**
- On the General tab, click **Fonts....**
- In the Web page font and Plain text font lists, click the fonts you want.

Displaying Web pages made in a regional language

Most Web pages contain information that tells the browser what language encoding (the language and character set) to use.

If a page does not include that information, and you have the Language Encoding Auto-Select feature on, Internet Explorer can usually determine the appropriate language encoding.

To turn Auto-Select on

- On the View menu in Internet Explorer, point to `Encoding`, and then make sure Auto-Select has a check mark. If it doesn't, click it.
- If you are prompted to download language support components, click Download.
- If Auto-Select cannot determine the correct language encoding, and you know what language encoding it should be, you can manually select it.

To select the language encoding for a Web page

- On the View menu, point to `Encoding`, point to `More`, and then click the appropriate language.
- If you are prompted to download language support components, click Download.
- If the Auto-Select feature or a specific language pack is not installed on your computer, Internet Explorer will prompt you to download the files as needed.

Adding languages does not guarantee that your computer has a font that can display Web pages in your preferred languages.

If you want to be prompted when fonts need to be added, click the Tools menu, click Internet Options, click the Advanced tab, and then select the Enable Install On Demand check box.

You can add a Language Encoding button to your toolbar to make switching between languages quicker.

How to view a web page in Devnagari (Hindi/Marathi etc.)

When you try to view a web page containing a language other than English, then sometimes the page may appear with strange character as shown in the following figure.

To correct this problem follow the steps given below

- Download Hindi Font from the site which you want to view (most of the web site provide this facility free of cost.)
- Check for a link such as `Click here to download font file (VIGYAPTI.TTF)` or `Download Font` etc.
- Once you click on these options, a window will appear asking to OPEN or to SAVE the selected font. Select SAVE option and click on OK.

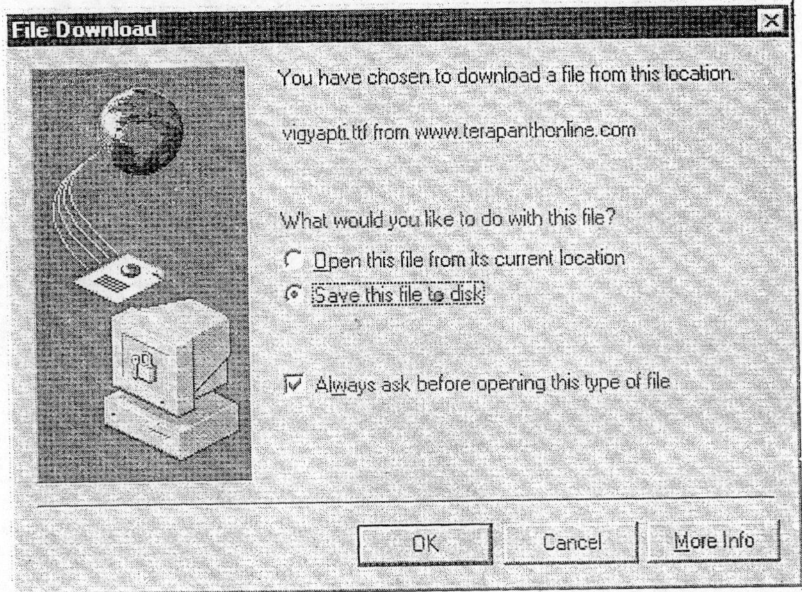

Fig. 14-7 : Downloading Regional Language Font.

- Now it will ask for a location to save the selected font. Specify a temporary directory and press SAVE button (here, do not give the Windows\Font directory name, give some directory such as C:\TEMP.)
- This will automatically start downloading the font file to your specified location.
- Wait for the Download complete message box to appear. In this box click on Close command button.
- Now close your browser i.e. Internet Explorer.

Sometimes in place of TTF font files, an EXE program gets downloaded, in that case you need to execute that file to install the font.

- To execute the downloaded EXE file, switch to Windows Explorer or File Manager and go to the same directory where you have saved the file. Double-click on the downloaded file name.
- Now, to install the font into Windows
- Click on Start/Settings/Control Panel.
- In Control Panel double click on Fonts icon.
- This will open the Fonts Directory. Go to File menu and click on Install New Font option.
- Select the temporary Drive and Directory into which the font is downloaded, from the Add Font dialog box.
- Select the downloaded fonts name from the List of Fonts box, for example select Vigyapti (TRUE TYPE) and Click OK button.

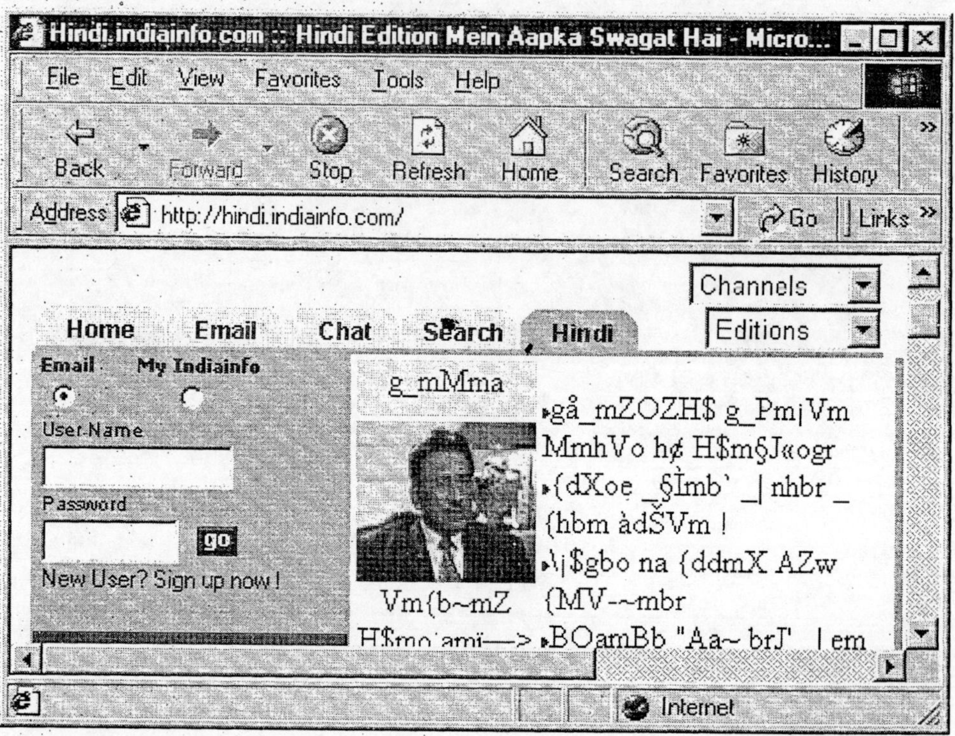
Hindi.indiainfo.com :: Hindi Edition Mein Aapka Swagat Hai - Micro...
File Edit View Favorites Tools Help
Back Forward Stop Refresh Home Search Favorites History
Address http://hindi.indiainfo.com/
Go Links
Channels
Editions
Home Email Chat Search Hindi
Email My Indiainfo
User Name
Password
go
New User? Sign up now !
Internet

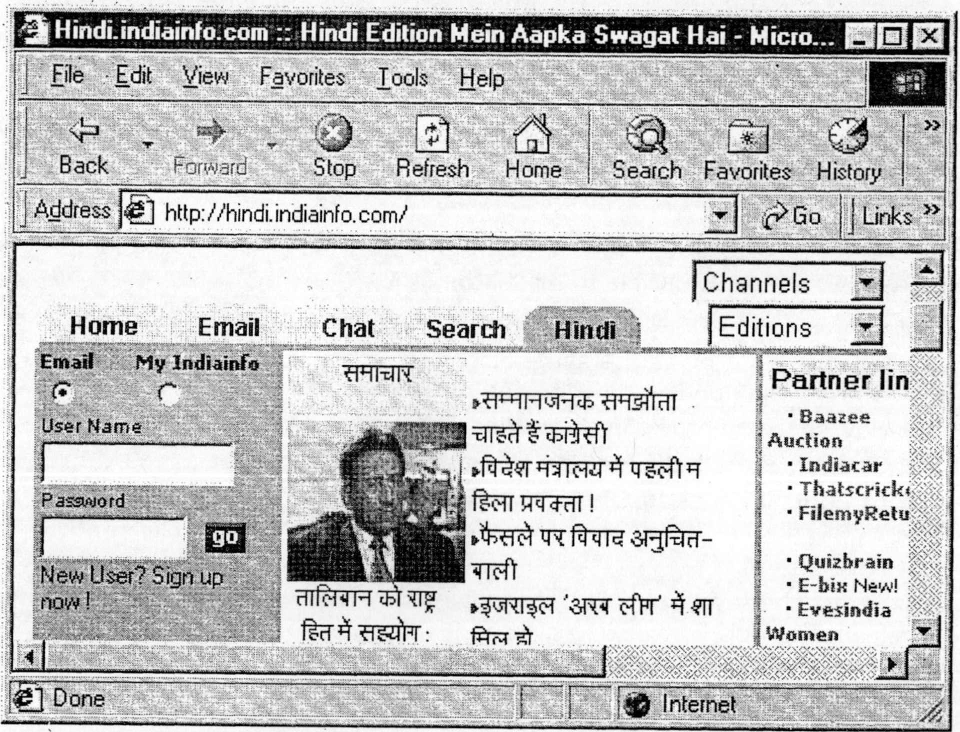
Hindi.indiainfo.com :: Hindi Edition Mein Aapka Swagat Hai - Micro...
File Edit View Favorites Tools Help
Back Forward Stop Refresh Home Search Favorites History
Address http://hindi.indiainfo.com/
Go Links
Channels
Editions
Home Email Chat Search Hindi
Email My Indiainfo
User Name
Password
go
New User? Sign up now !
समाचार
सम्मानजनक समझौता चाहते हैं कांग्रेसी
विदेश मंत्रालय में पहली महिला प्रवक्ता !
फैसले पर विवाद अनुचित- वाली
तालिबान को राष्ट्र हित में सहयोग :
Partner lin
Baazee Auction
Indiacar
Thatscrick
FilemyRetu
Quizbrain
E-bix New!
Evesindia
Women
Done
Internet

- Make sure that the check box in Copy fonts to Font folder is selected.

This will install the selected Hindi Font Vigyapti into your computer.

Restart your Browser i.e. Internet Explorer (You don't need to restart your computer).

Now you can read articles in Hindi.

In some cases Hindi characters might not appear correctly or may appear mixed with some ghost characters.

If this happens, follow the steps given below

If you use Netscape Navigator browser then

- Choose `View` from the Menu bar of your browser.
- Choose Character Set if you are using Ver 4.5 or Encoding if any earlier version.
- Select `User Defined` from the list displayed.

If you use Internet Explorer

- Choose `View` from the Menu bar of your browser.
- Choose `Font` if you are using IE 4.0 or less, otherwise choose `Encoding`.
- Select User Defined from the list displayed.

Above steps should correct the font problem and properly show the pages containing devnagari fonts.

Dynamic Font

Dynamic fonts are one of the latest developments in web page design. Instead of relying on the default fonts that users have in their machines, web authors can now create pages using the fonts they have on their systems.

When the dynamic font is used in web page design, the designer can be assured that the pages will display in any machine with their font formatting intact.

Currently Bitstream provides many fonts and utilities to make dynamic fonts. These can be downloaded from www.bitstream.com.

Based on the security setting of your Internet explorer, you could see the messages shown in the figure when you open a page with dynamic fonts.

Specifying E-mail & other programs you want Internet Explorer to use

You can change the default programs you use for mail, newsgroups, calendar, and Internet calls.

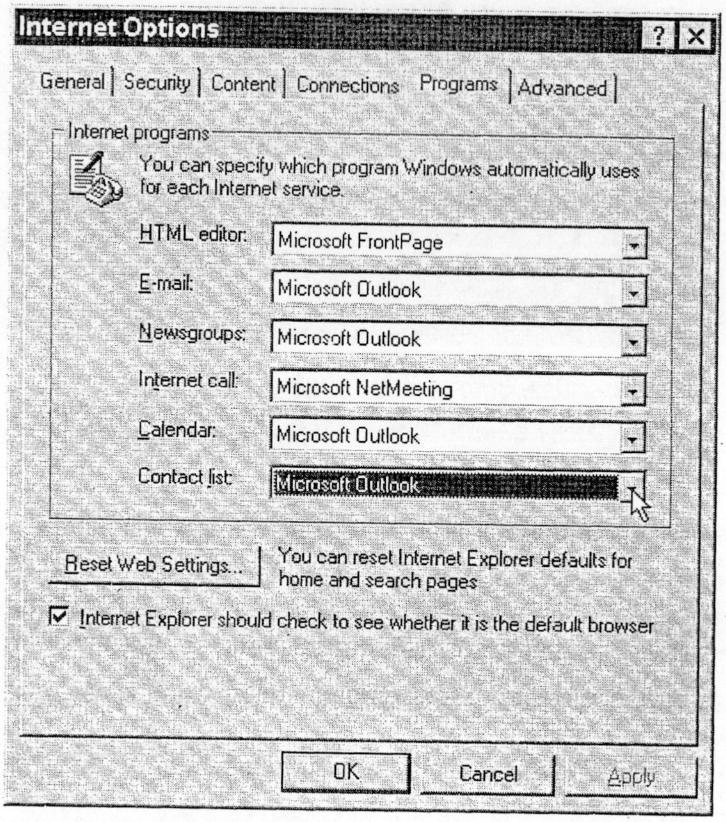

Fig. 14-8 : Internet Explorer Options.

Whenever you click a link on a Web page for these programs, Internet Explorer opens the program you specified.

- On the Tools menu in Internet Explorer, click **`Internet Options`**.
- Click the Programs tab, and then follow the instructions on your screen for specifying default Internet programs.
- To start mail or news program from within Internet Explorer, click the **`Tools`** menu, point to **`Mail & News`**, and then click on required program name.
- To send e-mail messages and place calls from within Internet Explorer, click the **`File`** menu, point to **`New`**, and then click the type of message or communication you want to start.

Resetting Internet Explorer settings

If you installed another Web browser after installing Internet Explorer and Internet Tools, some of your Internet Explorer settings may have changed.

You can reset your Internet Explorer settings to their original defaults, your home page and search pages, and choice of default browser, without changing your other browser's settings.

- On the Tools menu, click `Internet Options`.
- Click the `Programs` tab.
- Click the `Reset Web Settings` button.

Internet based E-mail

With Outlook Express-the Internet Mail extension, and an Internet e-mail account with any Internet service provider, or free e-mail service provider such as rediff.com, sify.com, hotmail.com etc., you can exchange messages with anyone on the Internet.

Messages you send are submitted to an e-mail server that supports the SMTP Internet standard, and then are delivered to the recipient.

Messages you receive are stored in your e-mail account on an e-mail server that supports the POP3 Internet standard.

When you log on to your e-mail account and download your messages, they are stored in your personal folder file in your Inbox folder.

For using Internet e-mail, you need to connect to the Internet and you will need to know the names of your incoming and outgoing e-mail servers (sometimes the same server is used for both incoming and outgoing messages), your account name, and your password.

Your Internet service provider or network system administrator can supply you with these information.

You can connect to the Internet in the following ways:

- Over phone lines, by using a modem. You can manually establish a connection or you can use dial-up networking to automatically connect when you start Outlook. Your Internet service provider can supply you with the phone number, modem settings, and network protocols required.
- Through a local area network (LAN). Your organization might provide external access to the Internet from your computer through a LAN. Your system administrator can provide you with account information and network protocols to gain access to the e-mail servers.

Using Internet based e-mail accounts

IMAP (Internet Message Access Protocol) and HTTP (`Hypertext Transfer Protocol`) are Internet protocols for accessing messages that are stored on an Internet server.

Using IMAP or HTTP, you can access your e-mail from any computer with an Internet connection.

Having an Internet server-based account allows you to save time by downloading only your message headers so that you can choose which messages you want to later download and view in their entirety.

Using Outlook Express, working offline, you can read and respond to e-mail messages just as you would when working online.

The next time you work online (connect to the net), your Internet server-based mail account will synchronize the mail on your computer.

During the synchronization process, the actions you performed in your mail account, in offline state, are carried out on the server.

Adding a new e-mail or news account

You will need the following information from your Internet service provider (ISP) or Local Area Network (LAN) administrator to add a new mail or news account on an Internet server:

For mail accounts, you'll need to know the type of mail server you use (POP3, IMAP, or HTTP), your account name and password, and the name of the incoming mail server and, for POP3 and IMAP, the name of an outgoing mail server.

For a news account, you'll need to know the name of the news server you want to connect to and, if required, your account name and password.

To start the Outlook Express program

1. click on start menu button
2. click on `programs`, to display program submenu
3. click on `Outlook Express`

another option to start Outlook Express would be to double click on the Outlook Express icon on the desktop.

Once the outlook express starts

- On the Tools menu, click on `Accounts`.
- In the Internet Accounts dialog box, click the `Add...` button.
- Select either `Mail` or `News` to open the Internet Connection Wizard, then follow the instructions to establish a connection with a mail or news server.
- Each user can create multiple mail or news accounts by repeating the above given steps for each account.

You can get a free mail account from many Internet sites such as Hotmail.com, Rediff.com, Yahoo.com etc which uses HTTP servers.

- Once an e-mail account is made, select the account and Click on the `Property` command button to make any change to the configuration.
- Click on the Advanced tab and check the Incoming and Outgoing Port Numbers.

Reading E-Mail Message

Once the outlook explorer is properly setup, you can read e-mail messages by clicking on Send/Receive button.

This will send all e-mail's that you have wrote offline, and also this will read new e-mail messages from the Internet.

All new messages read will be shown in the inbox. Double click on the inbox to view these messages.

If the outlook is not connected to the Internet, then it will automatically connect to the Internet using the default dial-up connection.

When a new message is displayed by the outlook express, it shows the various icons to the left of the message. These icons indicate the status of the e-mail.

Opening a E-Mail Message

To check for new message In the Outlook Express

- open the inbox folder by clicking on **send and receive** icon on the standard toolbar

or

- press [F5] key

double click on the message you wish to read to open the Message dialog box.

The message header contains following information

- From - This field contains the name or e-mail address of the person who has sent the message
- To - The names or e-mail address of the recipient of the message are listed here, each address are separated by a semicolon
- Cc - The names and e-mail addresses of persons receiving a copy of the message are listed here, each value separated by semicolon.
- Subject- This header contains a short description of the message topic
- Sent - The date when the message was sent.

Once the message is read, close the message dialog box by

- clicking on the close icon on the top right corner of the message dialog box.

or

- click on the File menu of the message dialog box and
- click on the Close menu option.

or

- Press [Alt]+[F4] keys on the keyboard.

Closing Outlook Express E-mail Program

To close the outlook express program

- click on the close icon on the top right corner of the outlook express screen.

or

- click on the File menu of the message dialog box and
- click on the Exit menu option.

or

- Press [Alt]+[F4] keys on the keyboard.

Reading mail messages offline

When you work offline, Outlook Express downloads mail messages to your local computer. When you choose to work online again, messages you marked for deletion are removed, messages in your Outbox are sent, and all other actions taken offline are completed.

There are two situations where it is beneficial to use Outlook Express offline:

- If your ISP charges you by the hour or if you have only one phone line.
- If you use a laptop to read your messages while you are traveling or any other time you are not connected to the Internet.

Working offline is different from being disconnected. When you are disconnected, Outlook Express tries to reconnect you to the Internet.

When working offline, Outlook Express knows that you want to remain offline until you choose to work online, when it will initiate all actions taken while offline.

Setting up Outlook Express to reduce online time

Use following procedure to set up Outlook Express to automatically disconnect after you select Send and Receive from the Tools menu.

You can then read and compose messages offline without incurring charges or keeping busy your phone line.

- On the Tools menu, click `Options`.
- On the Connection tab, select **`Hang up after sending and receiving`**.
- If you connect to an IMAP or HTTP server, click the server name in the folder list, and then make sure that the items you want to view offline are checked.
- To reconnect to send or receive messages, click the `Tools` menu, point to `Send and Receive`, and then select the option you want.

Reading e-mail messages while away from your Internet connection

- On the `Tools` menu, select `Options`.
- On the `General` tab, find the field labeled If my computer is not connected at this time, and then select Connect only when not working offline.

If you connect to an IMAP or HTTP server, click the server name in the folder list, make sure that the items you want to view offline are checked, and then

- click `Sync Account`.
- On the `File` menu, click `Work Offline`.

To check the type of account you have, click the Tools menu, and then click Accounts. Select your e-mail account and then click Properties. The account type is listed on the Advanced tab.

Specifying which part of E-Mail to download

You can make all messages, only headers, or only new messages available for offline viewing/download by changing the synchronization settings for IMAP, HTTP, or news server folders.

- From the Folders list, select an IMAP server, an HTTP server, or a news server.
- In the main window, select one or more folders or newsgroups.
- Click the Settings button, and then click to change the setting to one of the following:
  - All Messages
  - New Messages Only
  - Headers Only

If you do not want messages from a particular folder or newsgroup to be downloaded, click Don't Synchronize.

Replying to a Message

To replay to the sender of the message

1. Open the Inbox folder
2. Select the message you want to reply
3. Click on the `Reply` icon on the standard toolbar
   The message dialog box will open and the text of the original message appears in the message window.
4. Type your reply above the text of the original message and then click on the Send icon on the message dialog box toolbar.

To reply to the sender of all recipients of a message.

1. Open the Inbox folder

2. select the message you want to reply to
3. Click on the reply to all icon on the Standard toolbar.
   The message dialog box will open and the text of the original message appears in the message window
4. Type your reply above the original message and click on the send icon on the message dialog box toolbar.

Sending an e-mail message

1. On the toolbar, click the New Mail button.
2. In the To and/or Cc boxes, type the e-mail name of each recipient, separating names with a comma or semicolon (;).
3. In Bcc box you can select to send the message to the selected person as a Blind Carbon Copy (Bcc)
   A Bcc is a copy of the message that is sent to someone in secret. Other recipient of the message will not know that the selected person has received the message.

   If this Bcc field is unavailable then click on the View menu and select the Bcc Field command.

   To add e-mail names from the Address Book, click on the book icon in the New Message window next to To, Cc, and Bcc, and then select names.

   To get the Bcc box, click the View menu, and then select All Headers.
4. In the Subject box, type a short message title.
5. Type your message at the place provided at the bottom of screen, below the Subject box, and then click the Send button on the New Message toolbar.

If you have multiple e-mail accounts set up and you want to use one other than your default account, click in the From box, and then click the mail account you want.

If you are composing a message offline, your message will be saved in the Outbox. It will be sent automatically when you go back online.

- To save a draft of your message to work on later, click the File menu, and then click Save.
- You can also click Save as to save a mail message in your file system in mail (.eml), text (.txt), or HTML (.htm) format.

Use of stationery with outgoing messages

With Outlook Express stationery, you can create attractive messages for both e-mail and newsgroups.

Stationery is a template that can include a background image, unique text font, colors, and custom margins.

To apply stationery to all your outgoing messages

- click the Tools menu, click Options, and then click the Compose tab.

- In the Stationery area, select the Mail and/or News check box, and then click Select.

To apply stationery to an individual message, click the Message menu, point to New Message Using, and then select a stationery.

To apply or change stationery after you start a message, click the Format menu, point to Apply Stationery, and then select a stationery.

Inserting items in an E-mail message

You can add the following objects to your mail messages:

- Add a signature to outgoing messages
- Insert a file
- Include a sound
- Insert a picture
- Cut/Paste text from another application such as Notepad, Word etc.

Adding a signature to outgoing messages

You can use a signature to automatically add text to the messages you send. For example, you can create a signature that includes your name, address, and phone number.

1. On the `Tools` menu,
2. click `Options`, and then
3. click the `Signatures` tab.

To create a signature,

1. click the New button and then
2. either enter text in the Edit Signature box or click File, and then find the text or HTML file you'd like to use.
3. Select the Add signatures to all outgoing messages check box.

To use different signatures for different accounts, in the Signatures area

1. select the `signature`,
2. click the `Advanced` button, and then
3. select the account you want to use the signature with.

To use a signature on individual messages only, make sure to clear the Add signatures to all outgoing messages check box.

When you compose the message,

1. click the `Insert` menu,
2. point to `Signatures`, and then

3. click the signature you want.

To insert a file in a message

- Click anywhere in the message window.
- On the Insert menu, click File Attachment, and then find the file you want to attach.
- Select the file, and then click Attach.
- The file is listed in the Attach box in the message header.

You can also add a text file into the body of your mail message by clicking the Insert menu and then clicking Text from File.

To include a sound in a message

- Click anywhere in the message window.
- On the Format menu, point to Background, and then click Sound.

Enter the name of the file you want to include and the number of times you want the sound file to play, when the message is read.

To insert a picture in a message

- In the message, click where you want the image to appear.
- On the Insert menu, click Picture, and then click Browse to find the image file.
- Enter Layout and Spacing information for the image file as needed.

If you cannot select the Picture command, make sure HTML formatting is turned on by clicking the Format menu in the message window and then clicking Rich Text (HTML). A black dot appears by the command when it is selected.

If message recipients are not able to view your inserted images, click the Tools menu, and then click Options. Click the Send tab, click HTML Settings, and then make sure that Send pictures with messages is selected. Then again send your message.

To insert a background picture in your message, in the message window, click the Format menu, point to Background, and then click Picture. Click the Browse button to search for the file you want to use.

Cut/Paste text from another application such as Notepad, Word etc.

If you have typed the message on some other text editing program such as Notepad, Wordpad, MS-Word etc. then you can cut and paste your text from those application into the message area of the Outlook Express

- Open the application in which you have typed the message
- Select the text you want to copy to the message area

- To select the text, click at the beginning of the text, press the [Shift] key, click at the end of selection.
- The selected text will appear highlighted.
- Press [Ctrl]+[C] on the keyboard, this will copy the selection to the Windows clipboard
- Using the taskbar display the message window into which you want to insert the text, of the outlook express.
- Position the insertion point at the location within the message where you want to insert the copied text.
- Press [Ctrl]+[V] to paste the text into the message.

Using Address Book

The Address Book provides a convenient place to store contact information for easy retrieval by programs such as Microsoft Outlook Express.

You'll find that the following features help you organize all your contact information into the most usable form for you.

Store important information about the people and groups who are important to you

With your address book, you have a place to store e-mail addresses, home and work addresses, phone and fax numbers, digital IDs, conferencing information, instant messaging addresses, and personal information such as birthdays, anniversaries, and family members detail.

You can also store individual and business Internet addresses, and link directly to them from your address book.

Adding a mail address to address list

To add an e-mail address to the address list in an address book

1. Open the inbox folder
2. click on the `tools` menu
3. select the `Add Sender To Address Book` by clicking on it.

The address of the open e-mail will be stored in the address book.

This address can be edited by clicking on the Address Book from the tools menu.

- In the address book double click on the name of the contact you want to edit.
- This will open contact properties window, where you can enter additional information such as his/her business, personal etc. information.
- Click on different tabs and type the required information.
- At the end click on `OK` to save the information.

Deleting an address from address list

To delete an address from the address book

1. Click on **Tools** menu and select the **Address Book** option
2. The address book window will be displayed
3. Right click on the e-mail you would like to remove from the address book.
4. From the pop-up menu click on the **Delete** option.
   Are you sure you want to permanently delete the selected item(s)? message will appear, click on **Yes** to remove the address from the address list.

Organizing E-mail messages

Searching for a new message

- Click on the **Edit** menu and select **find**, click on Find Messages in this folder...

or

1. Click on **Find** icon on the standard toolbar and click on **Find Message in this folder...**
2. Type the word you want to search for into the **Look For** text box
3. Click on the **Find Next** button.
4. Outlook will perform a search and list all matches found.
5. Double click on any message to view its content

Creating a new mail folder

1. Open the inbox folder
2. click on **file** menu
3. click on **new** command
4. click on Folder from the sub menu
5. Create new folder dialog box will be displayed
6. type a name for the folder in to the Name text box
7. Click on OK button to close the create new folder dialog box

Once a new folder is made you can make Outlook Express to automatically sort incoming messages into different folders

Deleting a Message

To delete a message

1. select the message you want to delete by clicking on the message entry in the inbox.
2. Press [Delete] key.

Moving Message to a new folder

To move a message from one folder to another folder

1. Select the message you want to move by clicking on it in the message list.
2. Rightclick on the message to open a popup menu.
3. Click on Move to Folder option.
4. The Move dialog box will be displayed
5. Select the folder into which you want to move the selected item, by clicking on it
6. Click on OK button to close the move item dialog box and move the message.

Sorting messages by name/object/date

To sort e-mail messages displayed in the message

- click on the heading of the field you wish to sort the message by, for example to sort the messages by the subject, click on the subject heading
- An arrow will appear on the heading indicating the direction of sort. Clicking once again on the heading will sort the messages in reverse direction.

Internet Connection Sharing

With Internet Connection Sharing, several users can connect to the Internet, at the same time, using only one phone line and dial-up connection.

Each connected computer will have the ability to use all of the Internet services that it could use when connected directly.

With Internet Connection Sharing, one computer on your home network, called the Connection Sharing computer, has an Internet connection and provides private IP addresses and name resolution services for the other computers on the home network.

Then, the other computers on your network can access the Internet through the Connection Sharing computer using private IP addressing translation.

When a computer on your network sends a request to the Internet, its private IP address is transmitted to the Connection Sharing computer, which translates it to the Internet IP address of the Connection Sharing computer, and then sends it on to the Internet.

When the results are returned, the Connection Sharing computer translates the IP address back again and routes it to the correct computer on your network.

The only computer on your home network visible to the Internet is the Connection Sharing computer. None of the other computers on your home network has a direct connection to the Internet.

When automatic addressing is enabled, Internet Connection Sharing uses the Dynamic Host Configuration Protocol (DHCP) to dynamically assign private IP addresses to all computers on the home network.

You can also disable the automatic addressing service and statically assign an IP address to each computer on the network.

To assign a private IP address

1. Open the Network dialog box by clicking `Start`, pointing to `Settings`, clicking `Control Panel`, and clicking `Network`.
2. Select the TCP/IP Ethernet adapter from the list titled The following network components are installed.
3. Click `Properties`.
4. To assign an automatic IP address, click `Obtain an IP address automatically`.
5. To assign a static IP address, click Specify an IP address, and then type in the IP address and subnet mask.
6. Subnet mask is a 32-bit values that allow the recipient of IP packets to distinguish the network ID and host ID portions of the IP address. Typically, subnet masks use the format 255.x.x.x.
7. Most private automatic IP addresses use the LINKLOCAL network IP address in the format 169.254.X.X.

   LINKLOCAL network addresses are used only for private, internal address and are not valid for host computers that are visible on the Internet. They cannot be used for computers linked by Internet Connection Sharing.

   Internet Connection Sharing networks use addresses in the format 192.168.0.xxx

   Before you can use Internet Connection Sharing, all computers on the network must have network adapters installed.
8. Choose the computer that will be the Connection Sharing computer and use it to establish the connection to the Internet.
9. Once your Internet connection is established and known to be working, install Internet Connection Sharing, then configure the Connection Sharing computer and all other computers on the network.
10. You can also configure computers on your network to use file and print sharing, so that they can access these resources from each other.

Installing Internet Connection Sharing

1. Open the `Add/Remove Programs Properties` dialog box at the Windows Setup tab by clicking Start, pointing to `Settings`, clicking `Control Panel`, double-clicking `Add/Remove Programs`, and then clicking the `Windows Setup` tab.
2. Click `Internet Tools`, and then click `Details`.
3. Select `Internet Connection Sharing`, and then click `OK`.

4. Follow the instructions in the `Internet Connection Sharing` wizard.

If you used a CD to install Windows, you will be prompted to insert it into your computer.

To configure Internet Connection Sharing

Run the Internet Connection Sharing wizard by clicking Start, pointing to Settings, clicking Control Panel, double-clicking Internet Options, clicking the Connections tab, and then clicking Sharing under LAN and Internet Sharing Settings.

To edit Internet Sharing settings, click Sharing under LAN and Internet Sharing Settings. Set the following options.

Option	Description
Enable Internet Connection Sharing	Turns Internet Connection Sharing on or off on this computer.
Show icon in taskbar	Adds the Internet Connection Sharing icon to the tray. The icon indicates how many computers are connected at any time, and includes a shortcut menu of Internet Connection Sharing options.
Select the connection you use to connect to the Internet	Choose your preferred option.
Select the network adapter that you use to access your home network	Choose your preferred option.

The Internet Connection Sharing wizard will set the IP address of the Connection Sharing computer to 192.168.0.1. Other computers on your home network can be set statically to any IP address in the range from 192.168.0.2 to 192.168.0.253.

Chatting

In general terms chatting is basically exchange of thoughts and opinions between two or more persons, using speech.

But in Internet CHAT or Conversational Hypertext Access Technology is a method of exchange of thoughts and opinions between two or more person connected to the Internet.

Windows provides two programs for chatting on the Internet one is

- Microsoft chat and the other is
- Microsoft Netmeeting.

In the following section we shall look into these two programs.

Fig. 14-9 : Microsoft Chat Options.

Microsoft Chat

Microsoft Chat is an Internet chat program that gives you the option of conversing inside a comic strip.

With a standard chat program, you can enter a chat room on an Internet server and conduct real-time conversations with other people.

But with Microsoft Chat, you can also pick a cartoon character to represent you, in which case your conversation appears as word balloons inside the frames of a comic strip.

As a cartoon character, you can express a wide range of emotions, send "thoughts," whisper to a single recipient, and save the chat session for offline viewing.

You can also use Microsoft Chat to:

- Send hyperlinks-for e-mail addresses, Web pages, FTP sites, and newsgroups-in your conversation.
- Send and receive requests to play sounds.
- Send and receive files.

- Use another program, such as Microsoft NetMeeting, to communicate using video and audio outside the chat room with a chat room member, while also conversing in the chat room with them.
- Save or print your chat conversation for publication or offline viewing.
- Filter which chat rooms are displayed on your computer by size, content, or ratings.
- Host your own chat rooms, and control access, size, and content.
- Create rules that automate Chat's response to certain events.

Getting started with Microsoft Chat

Microsoft Chat provides a place for you to talk with other people on the Internet, using either text or cartoon characters to convey your thoughts. To get started, you must have an Internet connection, which links you to a computer (that is, a server) that contains chat rooms. You follow these basic steps to enter into a chat:

- Log onto a chat server.
- Select the room you want to go to on that server.
- Start typing a chat message.

The following topics explain how you get started using cartoon characters to talk in a comic strip.

Basic setup

- Provide information about yourself
- Choose a character
- Choose a comic background
- Connect to a chat server

Chatting with someone

- Finding a chat room to join
- Enter a chat room

Exiting a chat room

- Leave a chat room
- Save a conversation

Provide information about yourself

1. On the View menu, click Options.
2. In the Nickname box, type a name you'd like to be known by.
3. In the Brief description of yourself box, type something that you'd like other people to know about you. This information appears when other people request your profile.

Others can to send you e-mail or visit your WWW home page if you include your e-mail address and home page address in your personal information.

Choose a character

- Make sure you are in comics mode. (On the View menu, Comic Strip must be marked.)
- On the View menu, click Options, and then click the Character tab.
- In the Character list, click the character you want. Your character appears in the Preview area.

To see characters show different emotions, drag the black dot in the center of the emotion wheel to different positions.

Choose a comic background

1 Make sure you are in comics mode. (On the View menu, Comic Strip must be marked.)

2 On the View menu, click Options, and then click the Background tab.

3 In the Background list, click the background you want. The background you select appears in the Preview area.

Connect to a chat server

1 Connect to the Internet.

2 On the Start menu, point to Programs, point to Internet Explorer, and then click Microsoft Chat.

3 In the Chat Connection dialog box, type or select the name of the chat server or chat network in the Server box.

4 Choose the way you want to connect to the server:

- To go directly to a chat room, click Go to chat room, and type the name of the chat room.
- To select from a list of rooms on the server, click Show all available chat rooms.
- To connect to a server but join a room later, click Just connect to server.

If you are using Chat for first time, you should indicate your personal information, your character choice, and a comic background as explained earlier.

Finding a chat room to join

You can find chat rooms to join on a chat server by looking through the room list for a chat room or by typing the name of a specific chat room.

You can even look for a specific person on the server and join them in the room they are in. And when you find a chat room you'd like to return to, you can add it to your Favorites list.

If you don't find anything you like on your current chat server, you can disconnect from it and connect to a different chat server to check out its chat rooms. Or, depending on the chat server, you may be able to start and host your own chat room.

Entering a chat room

To enter a chat room

1. On the File menu, click New Connection.
2. In the Server box, type or select the name of the server that contains the chat room you want to enter (for example, mschat.msn.com).
3. If you know the name of the chat room you want to go to, click Go to chat room, and then type the name of the chat room you want to enter.

If you type the name of a chat room that does not exist, Microsoft Chat creates a new chat room with that name.

If you want to pick a chat room from the room list, click Show all available chat rooms. You may be able to screen out chat rooms that contain inappropriate or offensive names or topics by selecting the Show only registered rooms check box.

The Internet service provider or system administrator registers the rooms, so whether inappropriate material slips through depends on how closely they monitor names and topics.

To find a specific chat room by room name, type a word or a portion of a word in the Display chat rooms that contain box, attempting to match all or part of the room name you are looking for.

If you also want to search chat room topics, select the Also search in room topics check box.

Leave a chat room

To leave a chat room

- On the Room menu, click Leave Room.

After you leave a room, you are still connected to the chat server.

Save a conversation

To save a conversation

1. On the File menu, click Save.
2. Double-click the folder you want to save the conversation in.
3. In the File name box, type a name for the conversation, and then click Save.

When you are in Plain Text view, you can save a conversation as an .rtf (Rich Text Format) file.

All character formatting is saved, including font, color, size, and style.

By saving conversation files offline, you can view and print chat-room sessions and share them with your friends.

Add a chat room to your Favorites list

To add a chat room to your Favorites list

- While in the chat room, click the Favorites menu, and then click Add to Favorites.

Netmeeting

Windows NetMeeting provides people around the world with a whole new way of communicating.

With NetMeeting you can participate in meetings, collaborate in files using NetMeeting features, and share information over the Internet or your corporate intranet.

NetMeeting features

- NetMeeting allow you to place calls using directory servers, conferencing servers, and Web pages.
- NetMeeting makes it easier to place calls over the Internet, your organization's intranet, and with telephones.
- You can work easily with other meeting participants by sharing programs.
- Only one computer needs to have the program, and all participants can work on the document simultaneously.
- In addition, people can send and receive files to work on.
- NetMeeting's audio and video let you see and hear other people. Even if you are unable to transmit video, you can still receive video calls in the NetMeeting video window.
- With the Chat feature, you can talk with multiple people. In addition, Chat calls can be encrypted, ensuring that your meetings are private.
- Using the Whiteboard, you can explain concepts by diagramming information, using a sketch, or displaying graphics.
- You can also copy areas of your desktop or windows and paste them to the Whiteboard.

Placing calls

You can use NetMeeting to call people over the Internet, a corporate intranet, or directly, using a modem connection.

The person you call does not have to be using NetMeeting. Many other software can receive NetMeeting calls.

To place a call

- In the Address bar, type one of the following:
  - e-mail address
  - computer name
  - telephone number

- IP address
- Click the Place Call button.

If NetMeeting can determine how to place the call, it does so automatically. Otherwise, the Place A Call dialog box opens. Then, in Using, click the appropriate connection type.

If you select security on a call-by-call basis, place your calls through the Place Call button rather than the Address bar or a SpeedDial.

The Address bar and SpeedDial do not give you the Place A Call dialog box, which displays the Require security for this call check box.

To display a list of people you called recently, click the arrow next to the Address bar.

You can create a SpeedDial list for people you call frequently.

To place calls to a telephone

1. On the Tools menu, click Options.
2. On the General tab, click Advanced Calling.
3. In the Advanced Calling Options dialog box, under Gateway settings, select the Use a gateway to call telephones and videoconferencing systems check box.
4. In Gateway, type the computer name.

To place calls to an automated telephone system

1. On the View menu, click Dial Pad.
2. Enter the main telephone number by clicking dial pad buttons or using your computer keyboard, and then click the Place Call button.
3. After the call is answered by the automated telephone system, use the dial pad to enter the extension number or menu option.

If the Place A Call dialog box opens, in Using, select Phone number.

Extension or menu items are sent to the automated telephone system as you type them.

Do not click the Place Call button again after entering the numbers on the dial pad.

You cannot enter letters using the dial pad.

To use a directory server to place calls

1 On the Tools menu, click Options.
2. On the General tab, under Directory Settings, in Directory, type or click the name of the directory server you want to use.

If you want to log on automatically, select the Log on to the directory server when NetMeeting starts check box.

If you do not want your name and e-mail address to appear in the directory list when you are logged on to the directory, select the Do not list my name in the directory check box.

To accept or reject a call

When someone calls you, the Incoming Calls dialog box appears. Click Accept or Ignore.

If this is a secure call, a Details button also appears. Click it to see the type of security and certificate being used.

To stay logged on to the directory server, but be unavailable for calls, on the Call menu, click Do Not Disturb.

You also can set NetMeeting to accept calls automatically.

To end a call

Click the End Call button.

Finding People

Using the Find Someone dialog box, you can view directory servers and address lists that provide the names and addresses of people you want to call.

You can find names from address books, directory servers, and the Internet.

To find an address using directories or address books

- Click the Find Someone in a Directory button.
- In Select a directory, click an address book or directory.
- Type the name of the person you want to call, or select it from the list.
- Click Call.

To change the default directory server

- On the Tools menu, click Options.
- On the General tab, under Directory Settings, in Directory, type or click the new directory server name.

To log on or off a directory server

- On the Call menu, click Log Off from <directory server name> or Log On to <directory server name>.

By default, you are logged on to a directory server when NetMeeting starts.

To remove your name from the directory server list

1. On the Tools menu, click Options.

2. On the General tab, under Directory Settings, select the Do not list my name in the directory check box.

Hosting & Joining Meetings

NetMeeting allows you to exchange information with friends and colleagues, to collaborate on projects, teach a class, and give presentations.

During meetings, you can jointly create documents, spreadsheets, or other files without having the software on each computer.

Also, you can send files to one or all meeting participants.

Meetings can be hosted from your computer or a computer called the conferencing server. When hosting a meeting, you choose a meeting name, password, security, and who can be invited to the meeting.

When hosting a meeting from a conferencing server, you can access the server and then select a meeting from a list. If a meeting is not named, you can use the default name, Personal Conference, or provide a name of your own.

During your meeting you can communicate using Chat, audio, and video; illustrate using the Whiteboard; transfer files; and access remote computers using Remote Desktop Sharing.

To host a meeting

1. On the Call menu, click Host Meeting.
2. In Meeting Name, type the meeting name or leave it set to Personal Conference.
3. In Password, type the meeting password, and then click OK to start the meeting.

Notify meeting participants of the time of your meeting, the meeting password, and whether this will be a secure meeting.

To monitor who joins the meeting, click the Only you can accept incoming calls check box.

To restrict participants from inviting other people, click the Only you can place outgoing calls check box.

You can activate and deactivate tools at any time during the meeting.

To join a meeting

Call the meeting host or any meeting participant.

If you call a meeting participant who is not the host, the call may fail. If so, call the meeting host to join the meeting.

When you call a participant, you can remain connected as long as the person you called remains connected. When that person leaves or is disconnected from the meeting, you are disconnected also.

To remove a caller from a meeting

- Right-click the name of the meeting participant and then click Remove from Meeting.
- You can also press [SHIFT]+[F10] to remove a meeting participant.

Only the meeting host or the person who initiated the call can remove a meeting participant.

Communicating with Audio

NetMeeting provides full audio capabilities. The audio feature supports microphones, speakers, and telephones.

If you are using a microphone and speakers, your audio can be either half-duplex or full-duplex.

- Half-duplex audio allows one person to speak at a time.
- Full-duplex audio allows two people to speak simultaneously.

Check your sound card to determine your sound card capabilities.

To adjust your audio settings

1. On the Tools menu, click Options.
2. On the Audio tab, make the desired changes.

If your computer does not have a sound card, the Audio tab is not visible.

If the Enable full-duplex audio so I can speak while receiving audio check box appears dimmed, your sound card does not support full-duplex audio.

Auto-gain is a sound card and driver feature that automatically adjusts the microphone volume. Auto-gain is not available with all sound cards.

The Automatically adjust microphone volume while in a call option achieves similar results for people whose sound cards do not have the auto-gain feature.

DirectSound improves audio performance by shortening the time between when audio is sent and received.

To manually configure compression settings, click Advanced, and then click the Manually configure compression settings check box. In Preferred codec for audio compression, click an available setting.

To adjust the microphone and speaker volume

1. Click the Adjust Audio Volume button.

2. Move the microphone or audio slider to increase or decrease volume.

To mute the microphone or speakers, clear the respective check box next to the microphone and speaker icons.

NetMeeting automatically filters out background noise.

To disable full-duplex audio

If your computer has full-duplex capabilities, NetMeeting automatically uses it. If you experience poor audio, you can disable it.

1. On the Tools menu, click Options.
2. On the Audio tab, clear the Enable full-duplex audio so I can speak while receiving audio check box.

If your sound card supports full-duplex mode, but the Enable full-duplex audio so I can speak while receiving audio check box is not available, then install or reinstall the full-duplex driver.

To run the Audio Tuning Wizard

- On the Tools menu, click Audio Tuning Wizard, and then follow the instructions on the screen.

The wizard cannot run while you are in a call. If the Audio Tuning Wizard command is not available, click the End Call button.

If you use full-duplex audio and experience poor audio quality, try switching to half-duplex.

Communicating with Video

You can use NetMeeting to send other meeting participants a video image of yourself or an item under discussion.

To send a video image you need either a video-capture card and camera or a camera that supports Video for Windows.

You can receive and view video images even if you do not have video equipment.

Although several people may be in a meeting, you can exchange video images with only one person.

To send video

- Click the Start Video button.
- You can also send video by clicking the Tools menu, pointing to Video, and then clicking Send.
- After starting the video, the button changes to Stop Video. To stop the video, click the Stop Video button.

To receive video

- On the Tools menu, point to Video, and then click Receive.

To automatically send video

1. On the Tools menu, click Options.
2. On the Video tab, select the Automatically send video at the start of each call check box.

If you do not send video automatically, you can start video during a call by clicking the Start Video button to start sending video.

Although several people may be in a meeting, you can exchange video with only one person.

To adjust your video settings

1. On the Tools menu, click Options.
2. On the Video tab, make the desired changes.

To change your video camera properties, click Source. The Source button is available only if you are viewing your video image.

To view the video image you are sending

- Click the Picture-in-Picture button. The image you are sending appears in a small video window within the main video window.
- If you are viewing your video image before a call, NetMeeting starts sending the image as soon a connection is made.
- If you want to view the image you are sending in its own video window, on the View menu, click My Video.

To enlarge or reduce your video window

On the Tools menu, point to Video, point to Window Size, and then select the desired size.

Using Chat

Meeting participants can talk to each other simultaneously using Chat function of NetMeeting.

Since only two people can have an audio or video connection, Chat is useful in a group meeting because everyone can participate.

When someone sends you a Chat message, the message appears in the Chat window.

To send a message

1. Click the Chat button to open Chat.
2. In Message, type the message you want to send, then do one of the following:

- To send a message to everyone, in Send To, click Everyone In Chat.
- To send a message to just one person, in Send To, click the person's name.

3. Click the Send Message button.

You can also press [Ctrl]+[Enter] to send a Chat message.

To change the fonts used in Chat

1. Click the Chat button to open Chat.
2. On the View menu, click Options.
3. Under Fonts, click the appropriate button, and make the desired changes.

To change the information display

1. Click the Chat button to open Chat.
2. On the View menu, click Options.
3. Under Information display, make the desired changes.

To change the message format

1. Click the Chat button to open Chat.
2. On the View menu, click Options.
3. Under Message format, click one of the following:
   Entire message is on one line.

Wrap (message appears next to information display).

Wrap (message appears below information display).

If you choose Entire message is on one line, your message may run beyond the visible area of the screen.

A horizontal scroll bar appears so you can scroll to the end of the message.

Using Whiteboard

Whiteboard allows everyone in a meeting to draw and type simultaneously. You can add and delete Whiteboard pages, draw shapes, type text, and emphasize an item using the Highlighter or the Remote Pointer.

You can copy and paste items between the Whiteboard and other programs, and from windows and areas of your desktop to the Whiteboard.

Then, you can use Whiteboard's tools to further illustrate the objects. Other meeting participants can see your work without having access to your desktop.

Synchronization allows everyone to automatically view the same Whiteboard page.

To open Whiteboard

On the NetMeeting Tools menu, click Whiteboard.

If all meeting participants are using NetMeeting 3.0, the standard version of Whiteboard is used by default.

To add pages to the Whiteboard

1. Click the Whiteboard button to open Whiteboard.
2. Click the Insert New Page button.

To type text

1. Click the Whiteboard button to open Whiteboard.
2. In the Whiteboard toolbox, click the Text tool.
3. Click the Whiteboard to display the text box, and then begin typing.

To specify the font, size, and color of the text, on the Tools menu, click Font.

To draw a shape

1. Click the Whiteboard button to open Whiteboard.
2. In the Whiteboard toolbox, click one of the following shape tools:
   - Unfilled/Filled Rectangle
   - Unfilled/Filled Ellipse
   - Line
   - Pen
3. Drag the tool to draw a shape.

To highlight text or graphics

1. Click the Whiteboard button to open Whiteboard.
2. In the Whiteboard toolbox, click the Highlighter tool.
3. Drag the tool to highlight.

You can choose a color for the highlighter by clicking the color box.

To erase an object

1. Click the Whiteboard button to open Whiteboard.
2. On the Tools menu, click Eraser.
3. Click anywhere on the object.

The entire object you click with the eraser disappears. Objects inside, in front of, or in back of that object remain. To delete individual letters in a text block, click the Text tool, and then delete the text.

To use the remote pointer

1. Click the Whiteboard button to open Whiteboard.
2. In the Whiteboard toolbox, click the Remote Pointer tool.
3. Drag the remote pointer to the item you want to point out.

■ To turn off the remote pointer, click the Remote Pointer tool again.

Sharing Program in Meeting

Shared programs allows meeting participants to view and work on files simultaneously.

For example, you may have a PowerPoint presentation that several peopie need to work on. You can open the presentation on your computer, share it, and then everyone can provide their contributions directly in the presentation.

Only the person who has opened the file is required to have the program on their computer. Other participants can work on the document without having the program.

Only one person can be in control of a shared program at a time. If controllable appears in the title bar of the shared program window, the person who shared the program has control and is allowing others to work in the program.

If the mouse pointer has a box with initials, then another meeting participant has control of the program.

All meeting participants can share programs during a meeting. The shared programs of each participant appear in separate shared program windows on the other participant's desktops.

Remote Desktop Sharing

Remote Desktop Sharing allows you to access a computer at one location from a computer at another location.

You can share your work computer and access it from your home computer.

Remote Desktop Sharing allows you to work on the computer's desktop and files from another location.

You can also use Remote Desktop Sharing for technical support. If you have a computer problem, a technical support person can access your computer and then fix the problem as you watch.

To use Remote Dcsktop Sharing, you activate it in NetMeeting, and then close NetMeeting.

Remote Desktop Sharing does not work if NetMeeting is running on the computer. Once you set up Remote Desktop Sharing, and close NetMeeting, you can access it from any remote location.

Exchanging Files in a Meeting

To send a file

1. Click the Transfer Files button.

2. In the File Transfer dialog box, click the Add File button, and select the files you want to send.
3. Click the name of the person you want to send the file to, or click Send All to send it to everyone in the meeting.

To cancel a file transfer before it is complete, click the Cancel Transfer button.

To remove a file from the list, click the Remove File button.

You can send a listed file only once. To resound it, click the Add Files button and select the file again.

If you are accessing the computer from a remote location, on the desktop of the computer being accessed, right-click the NetMeeting icon in the status area, and then click Send Files.

To receive a file

Click Accept to receive the file and close the dialog box.

If the Accept button is not clicked during file transmission, it changes to Close after the file is received. Click Close to close the dialog box.

To reject the file, click Delete.

NetMeeting places the file in the NetMeeting\Received Files folder on your hard disk.

To start a meeting using Microsoft Office 2000

Open the file you want to share.

On the Tools menu of the program running the file, point to Online Collaboration, and then do one of the following:

To start a meeting immediately, click Meet Now.

To schedule a meeting for later, click Schedule Meeting.

Some Interesting World Wide Web Sites

To open any of the following WWW sites, type their address in the Address bar of Internet Explorer, and then press enter key or click on the Go button.

If a page you are trying to view is taking too long to open, click the Stop button.

Search Sites

The following site can be used to search for any information available on the web. Once the site comes on the screen, type the search word into the place provided on the screen and press the Enter key.

Yahoo! - http://www.yahoo.com
MSN - http://www.msn.com
Lycos - http://www.lycos.com
Netscape - http://www.netscape.com
Google - http://www.google.com
All the web - http://www.alltheweb.com
HotBot - http://www.hotbot.com

Indian Search Sites

Following are some Indian WWW sites, that have search facility

www.webdunia.com
www.bhaskar.com
www.netjaal.com
www.rediff.com
www.indiatimes.com
www.hinduonline.com
www.khoj.com
www.indiaworld.com

News

CNN - http://www.cnn.com/
MSNBC - http://www.msnbc.com/
Washington Post - http://www.washingtonpost.com/
New York Times - http://www.nytimes.com/
USA Today - http://www.usatoday.com/

Indian News Sites

www.timesofindia.com
www.indianexpress.net
www.expressindia.com
www.rediff.com
ww.indiatimes.com

Astrology

www.bubble.com
www.jadoo.com
www.panditji.com
www.astroadvice.com

Cancer

www.cancer.org
www.nci.nih.gov
www.cancercareinc.org
www.iarc.fr
www.4cancer.com
www.cancerguide.org

Sports

Sportsline - http://www.sportsline.com/
ESPN - http://www.espn.com/
CNN/SI - http://www.cnnsi.com
Sports Slueth - http://www.sportssleuth.com/
SportingNews - http://www.sportingnews.com/

Stocks

Yahoo! - http://finance.yahoo.com/
CNBC - http://www.cnbc.com/
Nasdaq - http://www.nasdaq.com/
Super Star - http://www.superstarinvestor.com/

Finance

Quickwen - http://www.quicken.com/
BankRate - http://www.bankrate.com/
Money Central - http://moneycentral.msn.com/home.asp
INS - http://www.insweb.com/

Weather

Weather.com - http://www.weather.com/
Yahoo! - http://weather.yahoo.com/
AccuWeather - http://www.accuweather.com/

Health

WebMD - http://www.WebMD.com/
Health Watch - http://www.cbshealthwatch.com/
Dr. Koop - http://www.drkoop.com/
onHealth - http://www.onhealth.com/

Education

BigChalk - http://www.bigchalk.com/
Study Web - http://www.studyweb.com/
Discovery - http://school.discovery.com/
Britannica - http://www.britannica.com/

Books

Amazon - http://www.amazon.com/
Barnes & Noble - http://www.bn.com/
Books - http://www.baazee.com/
Best Book Buys - http://www.bestbookbuys.com/

Music

Top 20 Music Link - http://www.top20musiclinks.com/
Billboard - http://www.billboard.com/
Napster - http://www.napster.com/
MP3 - http://www.mp3.com/

Games

iWin - http://www.iwin.com/
FreeFunGames - http://www.freefungames.com/
Yahoo! - http://games.yahoo.com/
Gamesville - http://www.gamesville.com/

Travel

Yahoo! - http://travel.yahoo.com/
Expedia - http://travel.yahoo.com/
Travelocity - http://www.travelocity.com/
BizTravel - http://www.biztravel.com/
MapQuest - http://www.mapquest.com/

Kids

Nickelodean - http://www.nick.com/
Cartoon Network - http://www.cartoonnetworkindia.com/
Fox Kids - http://www.foxkids.com/
LycosZone - http://www.lycoszone.com/
Nick Jr. - http://www.nickjr.com

Computers

CNet - http://www.cnet.com/
ZDNet - http://www.zdnet.com/
PC Magazine - http://www.pcmag.com/
PC World - http://www.pcworld.com
Tom's Hardware - http://www.tomshardware.com/

Autos

Autobytel - http://www.autobytel.com/
Cars - http://www.cars.com/
MSN Carpoint - http://carpoint.msn.com/
CarsDirect - http://www.carsdirect.com/
Autoweb - http://www.autoweb.com/

Free/Shareware Software

Shareware - www.shareware.com
Download - www.download.com

Indian food

www.sanjeevkapoor.com
www.truefoods.com
www.indiamart.com/nirulas/
www.karimhoteldelhi.com

Indian Hotels

www.travel.indiamart.com
www.india-travel.com
www.indianhotels.net
www.oberoy.to
www.taj.to

Indian Films

www.indianfilm.net
www.filmindia.com
www.filmfare.com
www.indianbollywood.com
www.shammikapoor.com

Indian Television

mtvindia.com

channelv.com

starplus.com

starsports.com

espnstar.com

Some More Web Sites

Indian site of world famous computer book/magazine publisher ziff davis.

www.zdnetindia.com

Web site of Chip-India magazine, English edition.

www.chip-india.com

site for online help on computing problems, run by chip india magazine.

www.drchip.com

site to provide online visa and passport forms.

www.visaonnet.com

site of surbhi program on television.

www.indiasurabhi.com

site on shri Atal Bihari Bajpai.

www.atalji.com

online news paper by India Today group.

www.thenewspapertoday.com

History of many Indian languages with a comprehensive list of newspaper, magazzine, websites etc. on these languages

www.indianlanguages.com

complete information about indian democracy, election, indian gov. etc.

www.sansad.com

On line shopping site.

www.namaste.com

detailed list of tample and religious places of India. List of various festivals, their importance, celebration method etc.

www.blessingsonthenet.com

information about media and advertising.

www.media2k.com

information about hospitals, clinic, doctors labs, etc. in various cities.

www.meditimes.com

list off schools in delhi area

www.delhischools.com

complete information about indian constitution

www.alfa.nic.in/const/const.htm

children education and entertainment site
www.appukids.com

information about films and tv programs
www.filmtvinfdia.com

complete information about cricket
www.cricmania.com

web site on cricket
www.cricinfo.com

information about IT developments in India.
www.indianitonline.com

complete portal providing free e-mail, with information on various indian cities, classified, entertainment, sports, music, matrimonial, current news, education, health, festivals etc.
www.sify.com

official site of CDAC India, developer of various indian language fonts and software.
www.cdacindia.com

History & culture of Punjab. Pujnabi food & matrimonial section. You can also download punjabi songs and videos.
www.punjabonline.com

Official site of Bombay Stock Exchange.
www.bseindia.com

Electronic greeting cards, e-mail to your friends and relatives.
www.egreetings.com

Site on health information. First-aid, investigation, childcare, yoge etc.
www.eeseehealth.com

A complete site providing information about health, auto, astrology, sports, TV guide, ymovie information, tutorials, news, jobs, finance etc.
www.inda.com

wecomplete information about income tax, with facility to download various income tax forms. You can also online filss these forms.

b site on information about all type of taxes,sales tax, income tex etc.
www.taxationindia.com

this site helps in calculating your income tax.
www.taxhelpcenter.com

Indian governments site on income tax.
www.incometaxdelhi.nic.in

Indian airlines official site
nic.in/indian-airlines/

Make Your Own Computer

In this section we shall see how one can assemble a perfect computer. Assembling a computer is a very easy job, one just need to select proper components and then connect them properly.

Let us see how to build your dream PC.

First, buy the components required to make the PC and keep them ready.

- Monitor, Main case with Power Supply, Keyboard, Mouse
- Motherboard, Processor, RAM
- Display card, Scund card, Modem card, LAN card
- Floppy drive, Hard Disk drive, CD/DVD drive
- Speaker/Microphone, External Modem

Keep the following tools handy

- Star/Philips screwdriver set, nose pliers

Before starting the assembly process, touch some metallic grounded object, to make sure that you are free from any static charge. Also, handle the Motherboard, CPU, RAM etc. static sensitive components only from its edges.

Following is a step-by-step procedure to assemble a computer.

1 - Remove Cover of the Main Unit

1. Open the four screws at the back of the system's main unit.

2. Slide the top cover off the main unit.

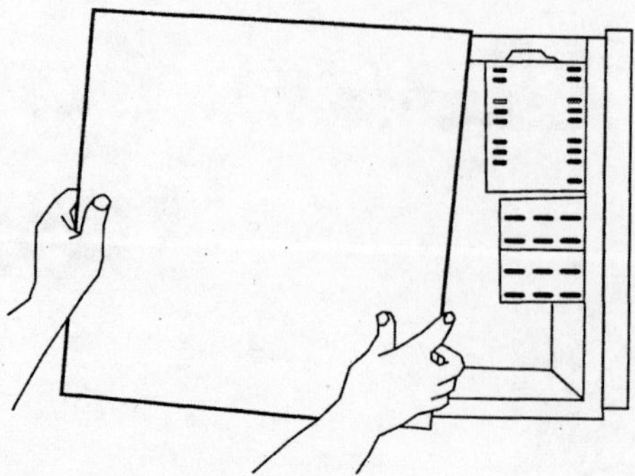

2 - Remove Base Plate from the Main Unit

1. Remove the screws holding the base plate to the main unit
2. Lift the base plate out of the main unit

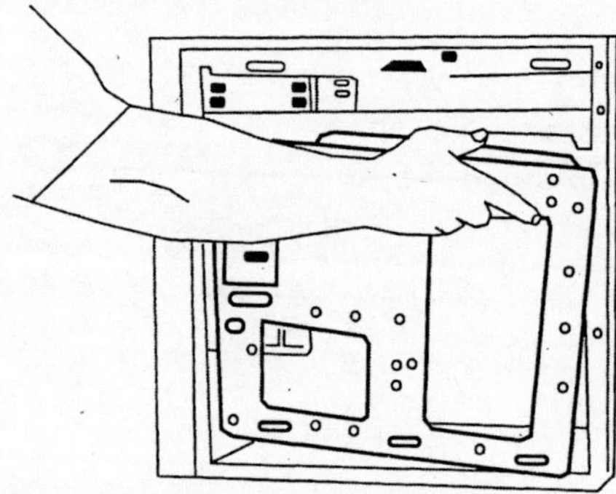

3 - Mount the Motherboard to the Base Plate.

1. Place the Motherboard on the base plate using the spacers and screws provided (this process is explained later).
2. Tighten the screws provided to fix the Motherboard to the base plate. Do not completely tighten the screws, leave a little room to make any adjustments when some new expansion card is installed.

   Tighten the screws only after you mount all the cards to the Motherboard.

   One can place foam pieces or old newspaper between Motherboard and base plate, so that Motherboard components will not touch the base plate and short circuit.

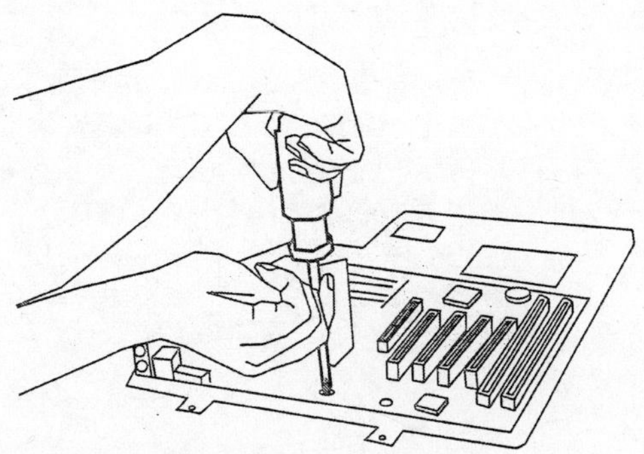

4 - Attach the Processor to the Motherboard

1. Attach the CPU to the Motherboard
   Based on the CPU used, you may use Socket-370 or SEC slot socket.
2. Attach CPU fan to the power connector (this is very important, as excessive heat build up may permanently damage the processor)
3. Set any jumpers to configure the Motherboard for the CPU type, this information should be available in the Motherboard manual.
   On most of the new Motherboards, the board automatically detects the processor clock speed and core voltage, without any need for setting up the jumpers

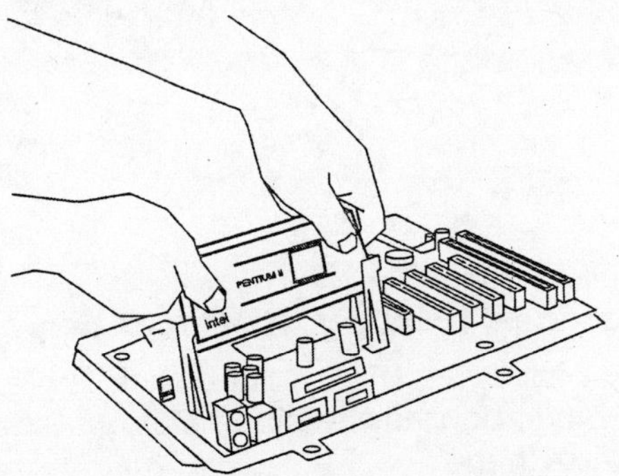

5 - Attach the RAM modules to the Motherboard

1. To attach RAM module, properly align both ends of the module with the slot given on the Motherboard and push the module into the slot with a smooth push.
   Based on the Motherboard, you may need to install SIMM or DIMM type memory module.

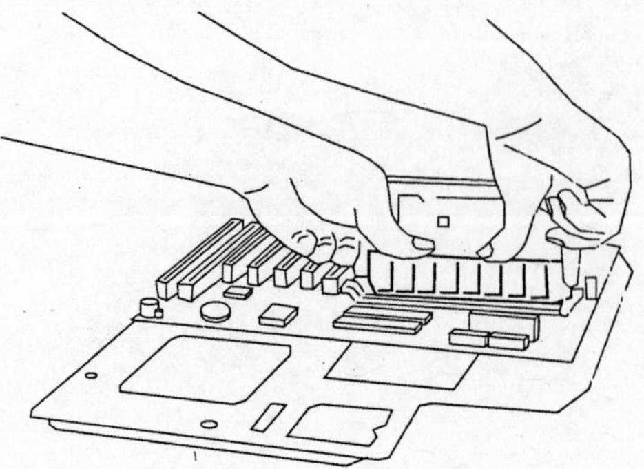

6- Mount the Motherboard into the computer Unit

1. Once the CPU and Memory is attached to the Motherboard you can mount the back plate (with the Motherboard) into the main system unit.
   Remember to tighten the screws only lightly. You can fully tighten them after the expansion cards are mounted on the Motherboard.

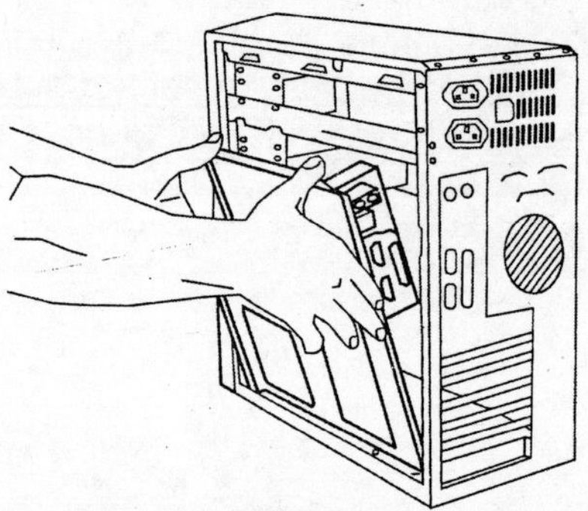

7 - Attach Storage Devices (Floppy /HDD /CD drive etc.) to the Main Unit

1. Place the Floppy Disk Drive (FDD), Hard Disk Drive (HDD) and CD/DVD etc. to their respective bays, tighten the side holding screws only after power and data cables are attached.
   CD/DVD and floppy drive need to be inserted into their bays from the opening at the front of the system unit.
   If your Motherboard and HDD support ATA/66, then use new ATA/66 cable. Connect Blue Connector of ATA/66 cable to the IDE channel on the Motherboard. Black Connector of this cable should be connected to the master IDE drive, connect White Connector to the slave device.

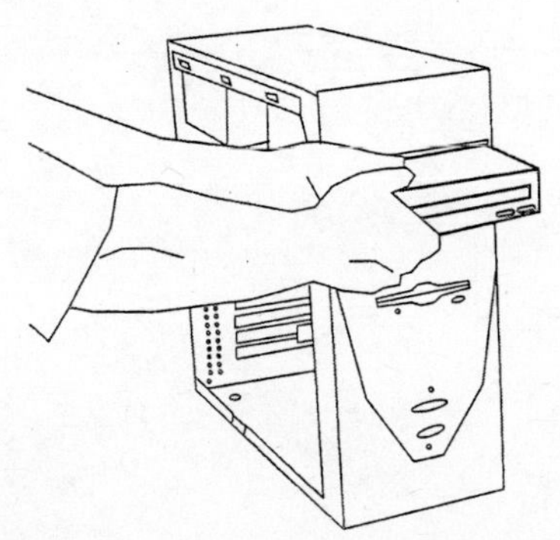

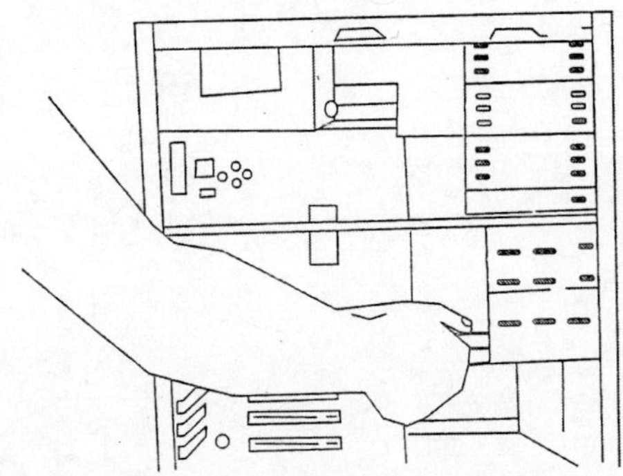

8 - Connect Cables (Reset, Speaker, Power Indicator LED etc.) to the Motherboard

1. Connect power cable to the Motherboard. If you have ATX Power Supply then the connector will fit in only one direction.
   When connecting AT power cable, make sure that black ground lines on both connector are placed next to each other.
2. Attach various front panel connectors to the Motherboard (reset, power/HDD indicator LED, speaker etc.). As a rule attach red wire to pin 1 and black wire to pin 2.
   Information for attaching the front panel connectors to the Motherboard are given in the Motherboard manual.

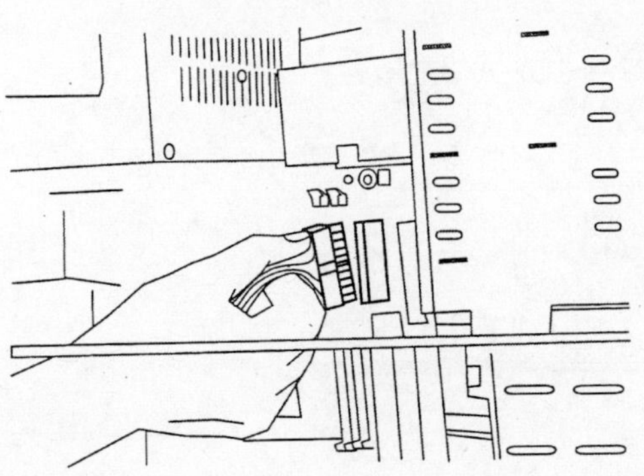

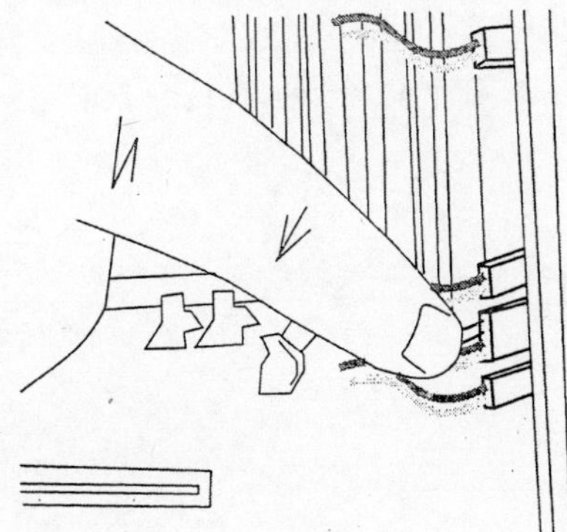

9 - Attach drive data cable and power connectors to the Storage devices

1. Connect primary IDE channel to the master/boot hard disk drive.
   Primary IDE channel is indicated as Pri-Master, or IDE0 on the Motherboard.
   When attaching data cable, red/dotted wire on the cable should align with pin-0 on the connector.

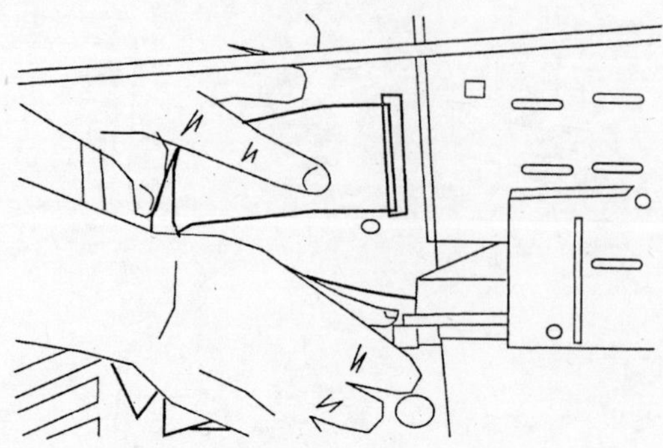

2. Attach power connector to the hard disk drive

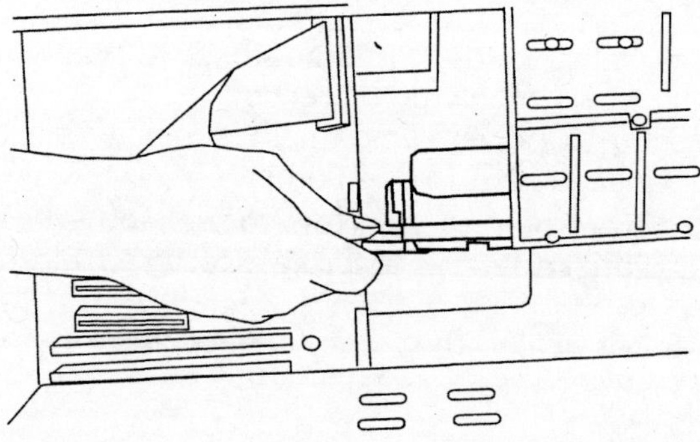

3. Connect secondary IDE channel to the CD/DVD drive.

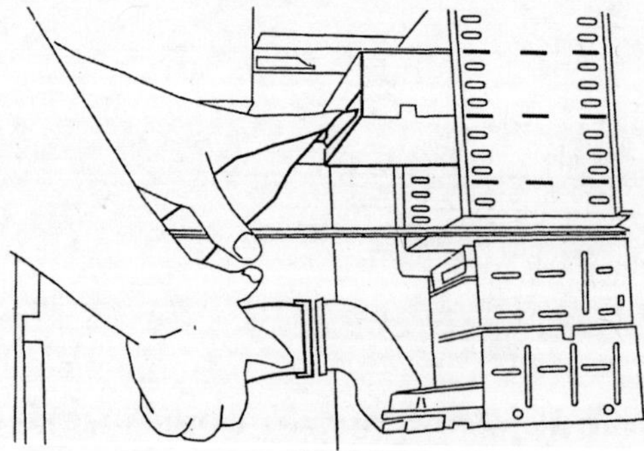

4. Attach power connector to the CD/DVD drive

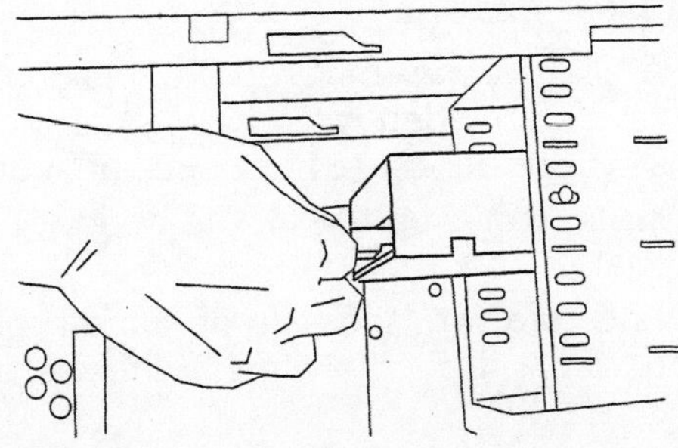

5. Connect floppy drive to the Motherboard connector.

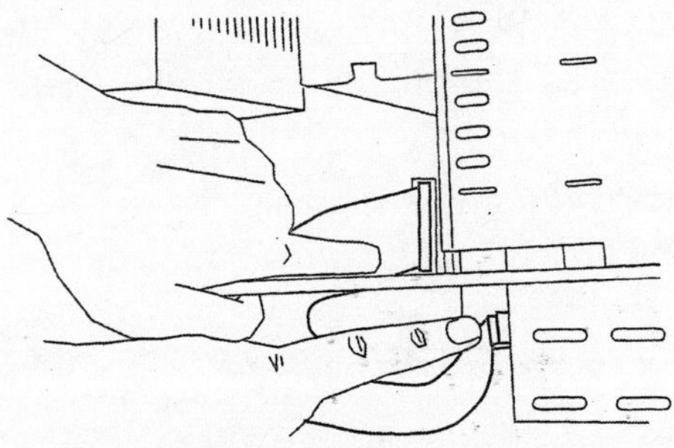

6. Attach power connector to the floppy drive.

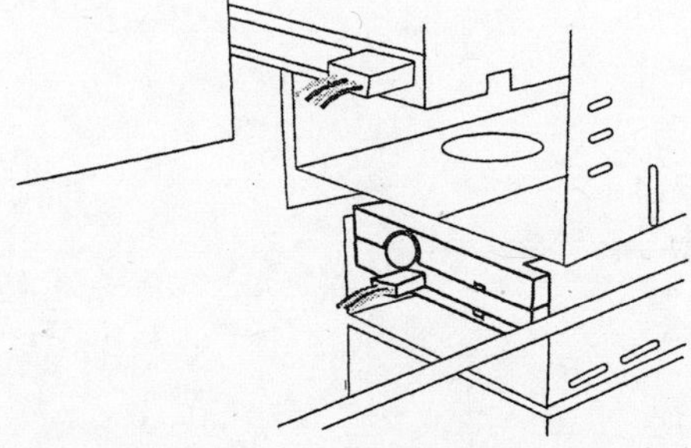

Connecting CD/DVD drive to Secondary IDE channel will improve the speed of the Primary IDE Hard disk drive, compared to connecting the CD/DVD as slave to the Primary IDE channel hard disk drive.

A HDD/CD/DVD can be made master/slave by changing the position of jumper provided on its back.

Once the data cable and power cable is connected to the hard disk and floppy disk drives, use some rubber band or tie-wrap to arrange the data and power cable, so that the air flow inside the system is not blocked.

10 - Connect external port cables

1. Connect Serial, Parallel, Game, Infrared etc. ports to the Motherboard. Connectors for this are provided with the Motherboard. ATX Motherboard does not require this, as these ports are built into the Motherboard itself.
   Position of these connectors, on the Motherboard, is generally provided in the Motherboard manual.
   Arrange these connectors with the help of some rubber band or tie-wrap so that they do not obstruct the airflow inside the system case and keep the system cool.

11 - Connect Display Card and Sound Card

If your Motherboard does not have integrated Display/Sound card then you need to connect these cards to your system.

When handling these cards remember to handle them by edges to prevent any damage due to static charge.

1. To connect the cards find an empty slot
2. Insert the card by first aligning card's edge connectors to the slot on the Motherboard.
3. Slide in the card into the slot by gently rocking the card back and forth and pushing down
   Never try to force a card into the slot
   Make sure that the card is firmly seated in the slot
4. Tighten the screw to fix the card to the Motherboard.

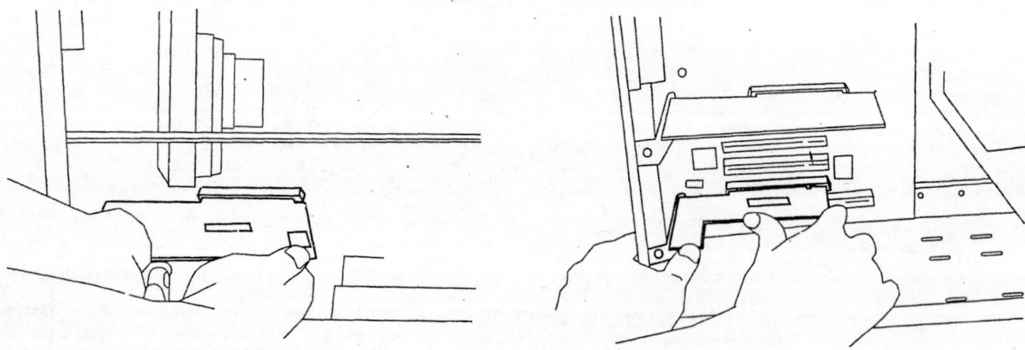

12 - Connect CD Audio cable

1. To use you CD drive to hear Audio CDs, connect Audio Out socket on the CD/DVD drive to the CD-in connector on the Soundcard/Motherboard (if the Motherboard has built in Soundcard)
   The cable required to make this connection is generally provided with the CD/DVD drive.

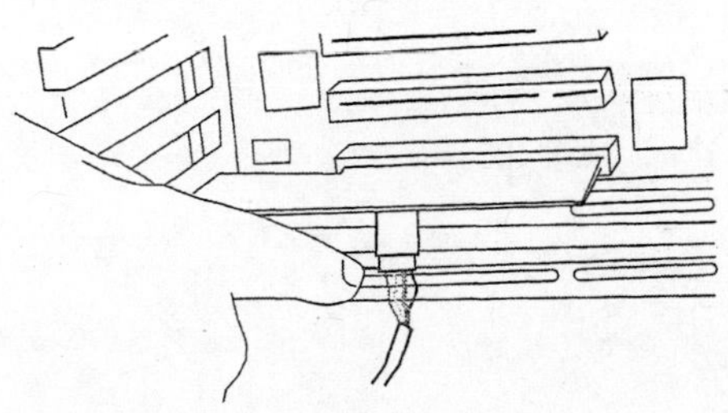

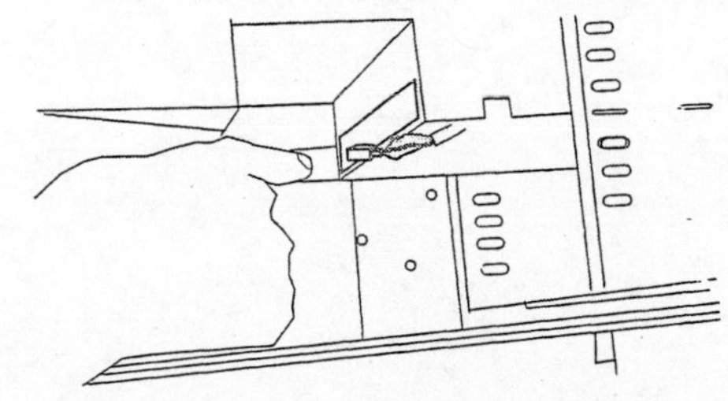

13 - Connect Peripherals

1. Connect keyboard to the round opening provided at the back of the system.
2. Connect mouse to the serial port connector provided at the back of the system.

If you have PS/2 keyboard then connect it to the lower PS/2 port (port closer to the surface of the Motherboard), upper PS/2 port is used to connect a PS/2 mouse.

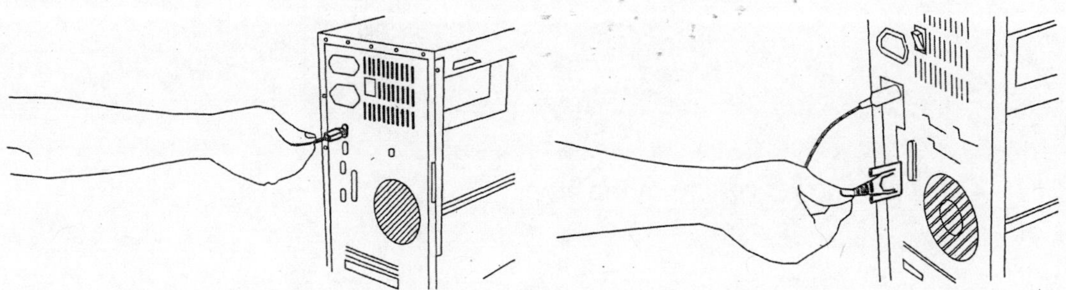

14 - Connect external cables

1. Connect Data cable from the monitor to the connector at the back of the display card.

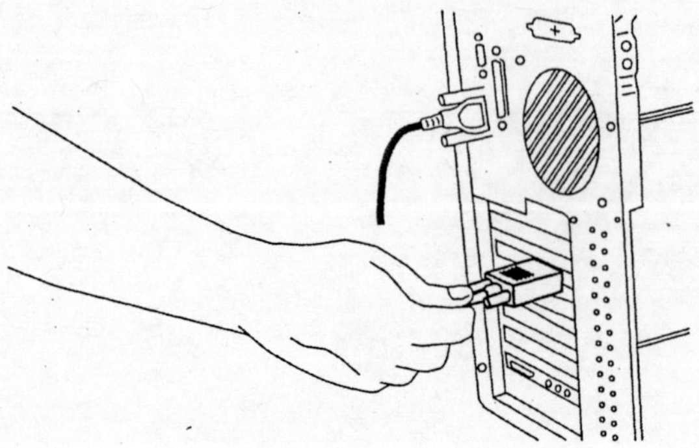

2. Connect mains power cord to the system's power supply.

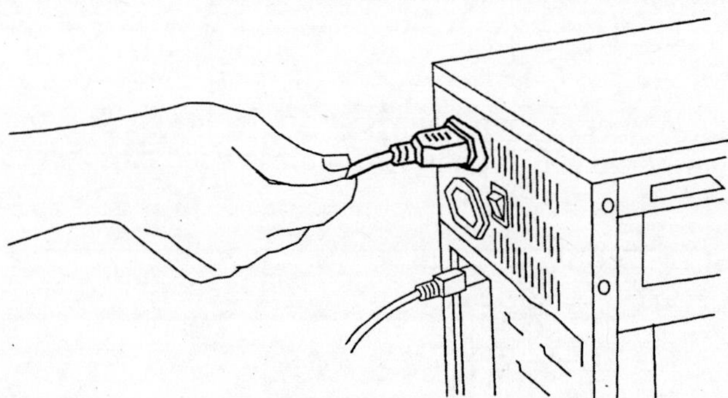

3. Connect power cord from the monitor to the power supply.

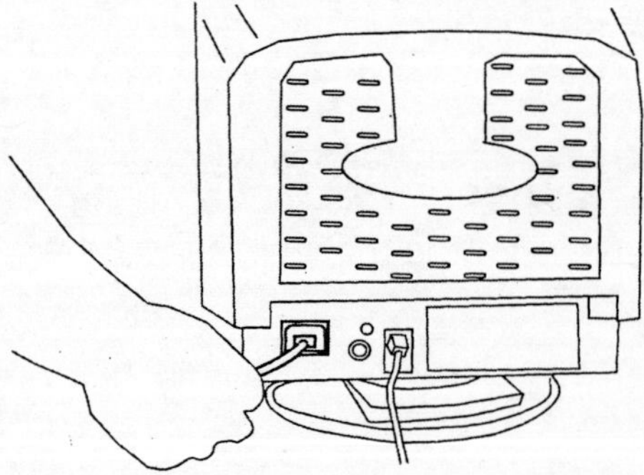

Depending on the type of monitor power cord, the cord may be connected directly to the mains power supply or to a connector provided on the system unit power supply near the mains power connector.

Before connecting computer to a mains power outlet, make sure that the power outlet has proper earthing. This is very important, as improper earthing could permanently damage the computer.

Get the earthing checked by an electrician, without proper earthing, floating voltages on the power line could damage the electronics inside the computer.

15 - Check Connections

Now you are ready to switch on the system, but before switching on the system, check all connections; make sure that there is no loose contact anywhere. Check that all cards are seated properly into their sockets.

This is a very important step before switching on the system. One should carefully check all the cards and connectors.

16 - Switch on the System

1. Turn the mains power on
2. Switch on the power supply/UPS etc. if you are using any.
3. Press the power on button on the front panel of the main system unit.

You should hear the hard disk drive spinning and a single beep sound will be heard from the system. This indicates that everything is functioning properly.

Make sure that the CPU fan and the power supply fan are spinning

Check for any abnormal system behavior such as system stopping frequently, this could mean that there is some problem with the system setup, or some card may be configured incorrectly, or some card could be loose.

Make sure that the CPU speed indicated during the system startup matches with the original CPU speed, if there is some mismatch then check the Motherboard jumper setting.

Current generation Motherboards do not require jumper setup they can be setup from the BIOS setup program.

Also, most of these Motherboards are auto-jumper type, which do not require any jumper setting. Based on the processor being used the Motherboard automatically makes required changes in the setup.

17 - Configure BIOS

Ones things are working properly you can make changes in the BIOS Setup to make the system function in a better way.

A detailed discussing on various options provided in the BIOS Setup is given in a separate chapter.

18 - Switch off System and Close System Unit's Cover

Ones your system is running without any problem, the system cover can be closed.

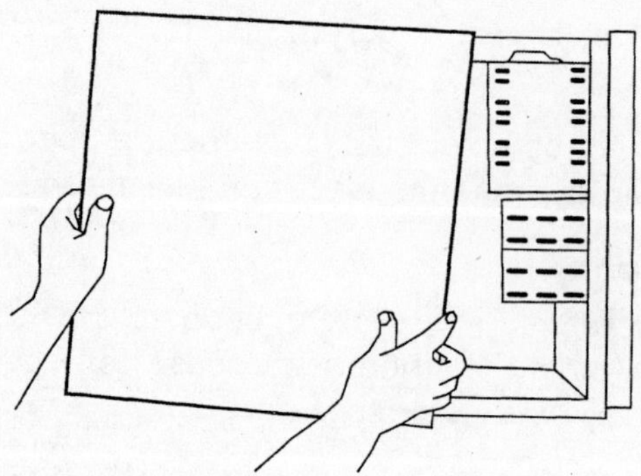

1. Before closing the cover, switch off the system.
2. Slide the cover on the system unit and fasten the screws at the back of the unit.

19 - Install the required Software/Programs

Ones your machine is ready, you need to install the operating system (Windows 98/NT/2000/XP, Linux etc.) into your system.

Ones the operating system is installed, install the software required for your work, such as the Microsoft Office, Tally, DTP software such as CorelDraw, PageMaker, Ventura etc.

You can also install various regional fonts and their keyboard, if your job requires it.

Windows 98 Setup

This section provides step-by-step information on the installation process for installing Windows 98 on a computer with a new or reformatted hard disk.

Running Setup

To install Windows 98 on a computer with a new or reformatted hard disk, you start Setup from MS-DOS.

- Start your computer with the Windows 98 Setup CD in the drive. CD should be a bootable CD.
- When the Microsoft Windows 98 Startup menu is displayed, select the "`Start computer out CD-ROM support`" menu option, and then press ENTER.
- When a command prompt is displayed, type
  SETUP
- and then press ENTER.
- This command will start the Windows 98 setup.
- After starting, setup performs a routine check on your computer.
- It runs the real-mode version of ScanDisk. It creates the Scandisk.log file and checks for errors in the directory structure, file allocation table, and file system.
- A surface scan is not performed, the disk is not checked for physical errors.
- If ScanDisk finds errors, it will let you know. You can view the log file by selecting `View Log` from the ScanDisk screen; otherwise, select `Exit`.
- Next, setup program initializes your system and copies the necessary files for installing Windows 98.
- Afterwards, setup displays the Windows 98 Setup screen. This screen has an information bar on the left-hand side that displays the five steps that Setup will perform and a timer that shows the estimated time remaining to complete the installation.
- To begin the Setup process, click `Continue`.
- Setup prepares the Windows 98 Setup Wizard. Then, Setup starts its five-step installation process:

- Preparing to run Windows 98 Setup.
- Collecting information about your computer.
- Copying Windows 98 files to your computer.
- Restarting your computer.
- Setting up hardware and finalizing settings.

The following sections describe each of these steps.

Step One: Preparing to Run Windows 98 Setup

During this step, Setup prepares the Windows 98 Setup Wizard, which guides you through the installation process.

- Next, Setup displays the Windows 98 Setup dialog box.
- Creates the Setuplog.txt file in the root directory (C:\).
- Identifies the drive where Windows 98 is being installed and the source drive where the Windows 98 installation files are located (drive assignment).
- Creates the C:\Wininst0.400 temporary directory and copies Mini.cab to it. Mini.cab contains the mini-Windows program files required by Setup.
- Extracts all files in Precopy1.cab and Precopy2.cab to C:\Wininst0.400. These are the files necessary to run Setup Wizard.

Step Two: Collecting Information About Your Computer

During this step, Setup collects information about your computer and prepares it for copying the Windows 98 files through the following phases, where Setup:

- Presents the License Agreement (License Agreement dialog box).
- Prompts you to enter the Product Key (Product Key dialog box).
- Prompts you to select a directory for installing Windows 98 (Select Directory dialog box).
- Informs you that it is preparing the directory where it will install Windows 98 and verifying that there is enough space to install it (Preparing Directory dialog box).
- Lets you choose the type of Setup you want - Typical, Portable, Compact, or Custom (Setup Options dialog box).
- Prompts you to enter your name and company name (User Information dialog box).
- Lets you install the most common components or customize your selection (Windows Components dialog box).

- Lets you add or remove components (Select Components dialog box).
- Prompts you to identify your computer on the network (Identification dialog box).
- Lets you select the location for getting region-specific information from the Internet (Establishing Your Location dialog box).
- Prompts you to create the Startup Disk (Startup Disk dialog box).
- Starts copying files (Start Copying Files dialog box).

The License Agreement

After Setup Wizard is loaded, the License Agreement is displayed. You must accept the License Agreement to continue.

Product Key

Setup prompts you to enter the **Product Key**.

Type the Product Key in the spaces provided. The Product Key is located either on the Certificate of Authenticity (COA) or on the backliner of your Windows 98 compact disc. If the number you type is not accepted, check the following:

- Make sure the Caps Lock key is not on.
- If you are using the keypad to the right of your keyboard, make sure the Num Lock key is on.

The Product Key dialog box might not appear if you are installing Windows 98 from the network, depending on the requirements at your site.

Select Directory

After you enter your Product Key, the Select Directory dialog box appears.

The default directory is `C:\Windows`. If you want to install Windows in a directory other than C:\Windows, follow these steps.

To install Windows 98 in a new directory

- In the Select Directory dialog box, click **Other directory**, and then click **Next**.
- The Change Directory dialog box appears.
- Type a new directory name, and then click **Next**. If you specify a directory that does not exist, Setup creates one for you.

Preparing Directory

After you select a directory, the Preparing Directory dialog box appears.

Setup checks for installed components and then checks whether there is adequate disk space for the files. It creates the Windows 98 directory structure, including all required folders under the \Windows (or \Your_InstallDirectory) and \Program Files folders.

If there is not enough disk space, Setup Wizard prompts you to free some hard-disk space and then restart Setup.

Setup Options

Once Setup finishes setting up the directory structure, it prompts you to select the type of Setup you want through the Setup Options dialog box.

Each Setup option contains a specific set of components to install. When you choose a Setup option, Setup selects by default a set of appropriate components based on your choice. Later, through the Select Components dialog box, Setup gives you the choice to either accept the default selection or select your own components.

To choose a Setup option

In the Setup Options dialog box, click the Setup option you want, then click **Next.** The **Typical** Setup option is selected as the default.

Click following option

If you want

Typical

All of the components that are usually installed with Windows 98. Most users should select this Setup option.

Portable

To install the options generally required for portable computers.

Compact

The smallest possible installation of Windows 98. For example, you may want to perform a Compact installation if your hard disk does not have much free space. Setup then installs no optional components.

If you later want to use an optional component, such as Games or WebTV for Windows, then you have to install it using **Add/Remove Programs** in Control Panel.

Custom

To choose which optional components are installed. If you do not select a Custom installation, then Setup installs only the optional components that are selected by default. If you know you are going to need certain Windows components, you may want to select a Custom installation and ensure that those components are included during Setup.

User Information

After the Setup Options phase, Windows 98 Setup asks you to type your name and company name, which Windows 98 uses to identify you for various operations.

You must enter this information for Setup to continue.

Windows Components

After you provide the user information, Setup displays the Windows Components dialog box.

If you select Install the most common components, Setup continues the installation. If you select `Show me the list of components so I can choose`, the Select Components dialog box appears.

Select Components

The Select Components dialog box lets you customize your installation by choosing the components you want to install.

To select which components are installed

In the Components list, click a component set (for example, Communications), and then click Details. A shaded box means that only part of the component will be installed.

A dialog box appears, listing the components in the category.

Select or deselect the component you want to add or remove, and then click `OK`.

- To add a component, make sure the component is checked.
- To remove a component, clear its check box.
- To prevent a component from being installed, make sure the component is not checked.

Repeat this procedure for each category in the Components list in the Select Components dialog box.

When you are satisfied with your selections, click `Next`. If you want to reset the list of components to the default, click `Reset`.

Note

`You can install or remove any of these components after Windows 98 is installed by using Add/Remove Programs in Control Panel.`

Identification

After you have selected which components you want to install, Setup prompts you to identify how you want your computer to be identified on your network by displaying the Identification dialog box.

The computer name must be unique on the network, and can be up to 15 characters long with no spaces (no blank characters). The name can contain only alphanumeric characters and the following special characters:

! @ # $ % ^ & ( ) - _ ' { } . ~

The workgroup name can be up to 15 characters long and uses the same naming convention as the computer name. The workgroup is used to associate groups of computers together for more efficient browsing.

The computer description can be up to 48 characters long, but it cannot contain any commas (,). This text appears as a comment next to the computer name when users are browsing the network, so you can use it to describe the department or location of the computer.

Establishing Your Location

Next, Setup prompts you to establish your location by displaying the **Establishing Your Location** dialog box.

Select the location for getting region-specific news and other information through media such as channels - Web sites designed to deliver content from the Internet to your computer.

To establish a location for receiving region-specific Internet information

- From the Select your country or region from the list below list, click the country or region you want. For example, India.
- Click **Next.**

Startup Disk

After establishing your location, Setup prompts you to create a Windows 98 Startup Disk by displaying the Startup Disk dialog box.

The Startup Disk is a bootable system disk with a collection of real-mode Windows 98 commands and utilities that you can use to restart your computer if you have trouble starting Windows 98 or to run diagnostic programs.

It is recommended that you create several Startup Disks. You can create a Startup Disk during Setup and you can create extra copies by using Add/Remove Programs in Control Panel as explained below.

To make a Startup Disk, you need one 1.44 MB floppy disk or two 1.2 MB floppy disks.

To create a Startup Disk during Setup

- Click `Next` on the Startup Disk dialog box.
- Setup starts creating the Startup Disk.
- Label a floppy disk "Windows 98 Startup Disk" and insert it into drive A.
- Click `OK` to create the disk.

If you cancel creating a startup disk now, you can make the startup disk later by using Add/Remove Programs in Control Panel

- In Control Panel, double-click `Add/Remove Programs`.
- Click the `Startup Disk` tab.
- Click `Create Disk`.
- Follow the instructions on the screen.

Start Copying Files

After Setup finishes creating the Startup Disk, the Start Copying Files dialog box appears. Click `Next` to start copying Windows 98 files to your computer.

Step Three: Copying Windows 98 Files to Your Computer

After Setup has collected the information it needs, it begins copying the Windows 98 files to your computer. During this phase, Windows 98 Setup does not require any input.

Caution

> Do not interrupt file copying. If Setup is interrupted during the file-copying phase, Windows 98 may not run when you restart your computer because Windows 98 will not have all of the necessary files to start.
>
> If you interrupt Setup during this phase, you must run Setup again.

Step Four: Restarting Your Computer

After Setup finishes copying the Windows 98 files to your computer, you are prompted to restart your computer. You can click the `Restart Now` button to restart your computer immediately.

If you do not click the button or wait more than 15 seconds to click it, Setup restarts your computer automatically.

After Setup restarts your computer, the following message appears on your screen:

`Getting ready to start Windows 98 for the first time.`

Step Five: Setting Up Hardware and Finalizing Settings

During this phase, Setup configures the following:

- Control Panel
- Programs on the Start menu
- Windows Help
- MS-DOS program settings
- Tuning Up Application Start
- Time zone
- System Configuration

When Setup finishes setting up hardware and configuring settings, Setup restarts your computer and asks you to log on. If your computer is connected to the network, you may be asked for a domain name and a network password. After you log on, Setup:

- Builds a driver information database.
- Updates system settings.
- Sets up personalized settings such as settings for the Internet Explorer browsing software, Start menu, Online services, Volume Control, and Channels.

Then, Setup displays the **`Welcome to Windows 98`** dialog box.

This completes the Windows 98 Setup.

Introduction to Windows 98

Windows 98 is the next version of Windows by Microsoft, after the Windows 3.1, Windows 3.11 and Windows 95. It was officially released on June 25th 1998.

The Windows 98

- provides many options for better Internet connection
- It makes computer work faster
- It provides increased storage space on a storage devices such as the hard disk drive.

Minimum system requirement for Windows 98 is

- a 486DX / 66 Mhz Computer with
- 16 MB of memory
- approximately 200 MB of free hard disk space,
- CD-ROM or DVD-ROM drive
- VGA or higher-resolution monitor.
- Microsoft Mouse or compatible pointing device.

Starting Windows 98

You do not need to specifically start the Windows 98, if you have Windows 98 installed in your computer, when the computer is switched on, Windows 98 will automatically start.

Windows Desktop

Once the Windows 98 starts, you will see a screen with many icons on the screen, this screen is called `Windows 98 desktop`.

Icons are small pictures on the desktop, each icon represents an object, such as a file, a folder or directory or a program.

You can double click on these icons to run/execute the programs associated with them.

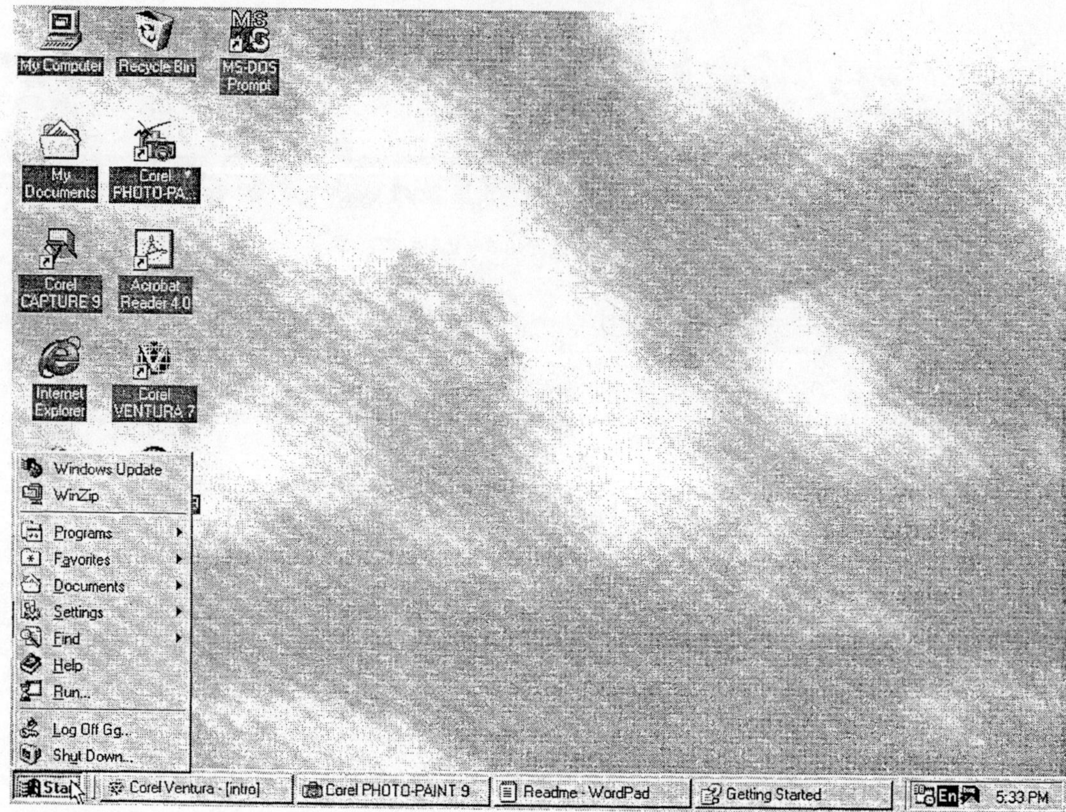

Fig. 17-1 : Windows 98 Desktop.

The bottom most area off the desktop is known as **Taskbar**. The Taskbar can be used to start applications, open documents, manage running applications, etc.

Right edge of the Taskbar is called **tray**, it shows the current time, when mouse point is moved to this time, a pop-up screen shows current date.

The tray also shows Volume Control icon (a speaker) and icons of various program which are currently running in Windows 98.

Leftmost edge of taskbar contains the **Start** button, a command button with Start word on it.

Moving the mouse pointer to this **Start** button and clicking on this will open the Start Menu.

Start Menu is used to start various applications, open documents, etc. It also contains many other options to use the Windows 98.

Some of the options shown on the Start Menu are Run, Help, Find, Settings, Documents, Favorites, Programs, etc.

Start Menu Options

Programs

This menu option is selected from the Start Menu to start various applications/programs. The program menu shows a list of program groups such as Startup, Corel, Adobe, etc.

To open a program from this menu, one need to select proper program group and then click on the required program from the sub-menu.

Favorites

This menu option is used to keep links to various web pages visited by you. Any object added to favorite will appear here.

You can easily open objects in Favorites from the Start Menu.

Documents

This menu option keeps a list of recently used document files. To open a file shown in this menu, click on the file name.

This menu keeps track of the last 15 documents you opened.

Settings

This menu option gives access to the Control Panel, Printer Folder and Taskbar Setup.

Clicking on Control Panel will open the control panel options.

Clicking on "Printers" menu will open printer folder containing list of all the installed printers with an option to Add Printer.

Using "Taskbar and Start Menu..." option will open a dialog box which can be used to customize the start menu and the taskbar.

Find

This menu option can be used to look for a specific file/folder on the current computer. It can also be used to look for a specific computer on the network.

Using Find one can search the Internet for some specific information or person.

Help

Windows 98 provides a comprehensive help to the user.

Click on this menu option to start the help screen. help screen provides table of contents, index and a search option. One can use any of these options to look for the required information.

Run

This menu option is used to execute any application that does not appear on the desktop or the program menu.

After selecting this menu option, one need to give the program name, or one can use the `Browse...` option to find and execute the required program.

Shut Down...

In Windows 98, one need to shut down the system before switching off the computers power supply. This menu option can be used to shut down the system.

During the shut down process Windows closes all open programs and your computer gets ready for power down.

During shut down if any file is open, i.e. if you have not saved your work, then you're prompted to do so.

Starting/Closing Programs

Let us now see how to start and exit programs using the Start Menu. For example, let us see how to start the Calculator program provided with Windows 98.

This calculator has facility to do simple as well as advanced scientific calculation.

The scientific calculator provides many mathematical and statistical functions.

To start the calculator program

1. click on the "`Start`" button
2. point mouse pointer to `Programs` menu item
3. point to `Accessories` sub-menu item
4. click on the **Calculator** option.

This will start the Calculator program.

Once a program starts, a button corresponding to this program will appear on the Taskbar.

To close this calculator program

Click on the `close` button, on the top, right corner of the calculator window.

You can also double click on the calculator icon on the top, left corner of the calculator window.

Switching off (Shutting Down) the Computer

Before continuing, let us see what one should do to properly switch off a computer running the Windows 98.

Before switching off a Windows 98 computer, one should Shut Down the computer using the following procedure..

1. Click on the `Start` button.
2. Click on `Shut Down` menu option.
   A `Shut Down` window will appear on the screen.
   This screen will have an options to `Shut Down` the Windows. Other options on this screen are Restart the Windows 98, Restart computer in MS-DOS mode and make the Windows go in Standby Mode.
3. Click on the `Shut Down` option and click on `OK`.
4. Click on `Cancel`, if you do not want to shut down the computer.

After giving shut down command wait for some time, as it takes Windows some time to properly shut down the computer.

After some time a message `It is now safe to turn off your computer` appears on the screen. Once this message comes, you can safely switch off the computer.

My Computer

One of the first icon on the desktop is called `My Computer`. Clicking on this icon runs a computer program, which can be used for various file management operations such as

- File Copying, Changing name of a file, Deleting a file, Viewing disk content, etc.

Double click on this icon to start My Computer program.

Viewing Content of a Disk

Here we look at how to view the content of the floppy disk using the My Computer.

1. Place a floppy disk in drive A:
2. Double click on the A: drive icon in My Computer

This will show the contents of Drive A: on a new window.

Renaming a File

To rename a file on Drive A:

1. Click on the file or folder that you wish to rename.
2. Click on `File` on the main menu.
3. Click on `Rename` from the sub-menu options.

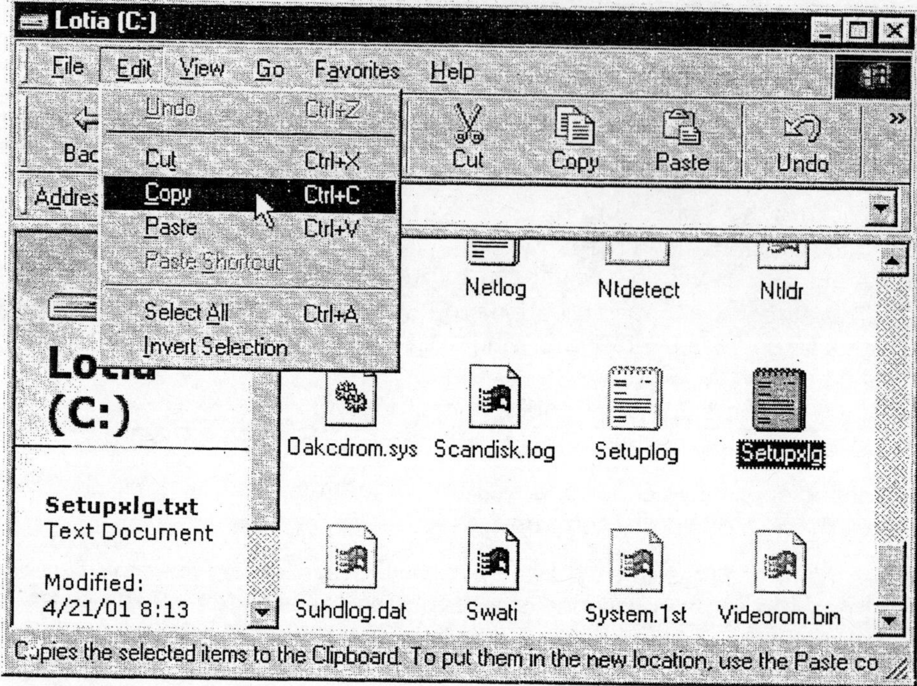

Fig. 17-2 : Copying a File.

4. Now, the old name will get highlighted and the cursor will wait there to type a new name.
5. Type a new name and press the [Enter] key.

Undoing last activity

After renaming a file, or deleting a file, if you want to undo this operation, i.e. keep the old name of files or undelete the deleted file, then follow the below given process

1. Click on **Edit** menu item
2. Click on **Undo operation**, such as Undo Rename or Undo Delete, etc.

Copying a File

1. Select the file you want to copy by clicking on the file names list in My Computer window.
2. Click on **Edit** on the main menu
3. Click on **Copy** on the sub-menu

Now a copy of the selected file is in the Windows memory, you can paste it on a new drive or folder/sub-directory using the following process.

In My Computer

1. Select the new drive and folder, where you want to copy the selected file. This can be done by clicking on proper drive/folder on the My Computer window
2. Click on `Edit` on the main menu
3. Click on `Paste` on the sub-menu

Deleting a File

To delete a file on Drive A:

1. Select the file you want to delete by clicking on the file name icon.
2. Click on `File` on the main menu
3. Click on `Delete` on the sub-menu
4. Windows will confirm the file delete operation, by showing Are you sure you want to delete "File Name"?
5. Click on `Yes` to delete the file, click on `No` if you do not want to delete the selected file.

Another method to delete a file is to select the file and press the [Delete] key on the keyboard.

Windows Explorer

As you can use My Computer to copy, delete, rename files, you can use another Windows 98 program "Windows Explorer" for these file management operations.

Using Windows Explorer you can

- Copy, Delete, Rename, Move and View files/folders
- Run/Execute a program
- Undo the last operation
- Find and View files

Starting Windows Explorer

To start Windows Explorer

1. Click on `Start`
2. Point to `Programs`
3. Click on Windows Explorer

After the Explorer starts, on the Explorer screen

- Left side of Explorer shows the disk drives and folders
- Right side of the Explorer screen shows the content of item, drive or folder selected on the left side.

Looking at the content of a folder

In Explorer, to look into the content of a folder, click on the folder on the left side of the Explorer window.

Creating a new folder

In Windows Explorer, to create a new folder

1. Click on **`File`** on the main menu of Explorer
2. Point to **`New`**
3. Click on **`Folder`**

A folder icon with New Folder name on it, appears on the Screen.

This New Folder name stays selected so that you can type another name for this newly created folder and press the [Enter] key.

Renaming a File

To rename or change the name of a file in Windows Explorer use the following method

1. Click on the file or folder that you want to rename.
2. Click on **`File`** on the main menu.
3. Click on **`Rename`** from the sub-menu options.
4. Now, the old name will get highlighted and the cursor will wait there to type a new name.
5. Type a new name and press the [Enter] key.

Another method to rename a file is

1. Click on the file/folder name you want to rename. The file/folder becomes highlighted
2. Click once again on the highlighted file/folder name
3. Now, type a new name and press [Enter] key.

Deleting File/Folder

To delete a file/folder in Windows Explorer use the following method

1. Click on the file or folder that you want to delete.
2. Click on **`File`** on the main menu.
3. Click on **`Delete`** on the sub-menu options.

Now, the selected file/folder will get deleted..

After selecting the file/folder, you can also delete it by pressing the [Delete] key on the keyboard.

After the Delete command is given, you will be asked "**`Are you sure you want to send file to the recycle bin?`**", confirm it by clicking on **`Yes`** button.

Copying/Moving Files and Folders

Copying a files keeps the original files and makes a new copy of the file at the copied location.

Whereas, when a file/folder is moved, it is removed from the original location and is placed at the new location.

So, moving is equivalent to copying the file/folder to a new location and deleting the original.

Let us copy/move files and folders in Windows Explorer

Copying a file

1. Select the file or folder you want to copy by clicking on it
2. Click on `Edit` on the main menu
3. Click on `Copy` on the sub-menu.
4. Select the new folder/drive where you want to copy the selected file/folder.
5. Click on `Edit` on the main menu.
6. Click on `Paste` on the sub-menu.

Moving a File

1. Select the file or folder you want to move by clicking on it
2. Click on `Edit` on the main menu
3. Click on `Cut` on the sub-menu.
4. Select the new folder/drive where you want to move the selected file/folder.
5. Click on `Edit` on the main menu.
6. Click on `Paste` on the sub-menu.

Copying using Drag/Drop method

Other than using the menu commands to copy file/folder, one can also use the drag/drop method as explained below

1. Hold down the control [Ctrl] key on the keyboard.
2. Click on the file/folder to be copied, after clicking, keep the mouse button depressed.
3. Drag the file over to the destination folder and release the mouse button.
4. Release the control [Ctrl] key.

Moving using Drag/Drop method

Procedure to move a file/folder using the drag/drop method is similar to the procedure used for copying a file/folder.

The difference between copying and moving is when moving a file or folder, the control [Ctrl] key is not kept pressed.

Running Programs/Viewing Documents with Explorer

By double clicking on program names, one can run these programs from the Explorer, also by double clicking on any document file, these files can be opened in the programs associated with that document.

For example, when you double click on a text document file, Explorer will start MS Word program and open that document in Word.

Finding File/Folder

Explorer can also be used to look for some specific file or folder on the computer.

To find a file or folder

1. Click on the `Tools` on the main menu
2. Point to `Find`
3. Click on `Files or Folders....`
4. In the Find window type the name of the file you want to find
5. select the drive to look for the search file and
6. click on `Find Now` button

Once the search operation finishes, a small window at the bottom of Find Screen will list the matches found for your search.

You can double click on these matches found to start these programs or to view the document files.

Close the Find window by clicking on File on the main menu and then by clicking on Close option.

Windows Help

Windows 98 provides a comprehensive help explaining almost everything one would want to know about the Windows 98.

Starting Help

To start Windows 98 help

1. Click on `Start`
2. Click on `Help`

This will open the Windows 98 help screen.

There are three sections in help, Contents, Index and Search

- The `Content` Tab shows the help in a table of content like layout, where topics are arranged in chapters. One can go through these chapters by clicking on them.
- `Index` Tab shows the help in a books index like layout. You can type in a topic of your interest, and search for it. If the search topic is found then Help will provide you with some options. You can also click on the topics shown at the bottom window.
- The `Search` Tab provides facility to search the complete help file for some specific text. The search tab is not organized in topics, like the index tab, so it will look through all of the help file for the word you type.

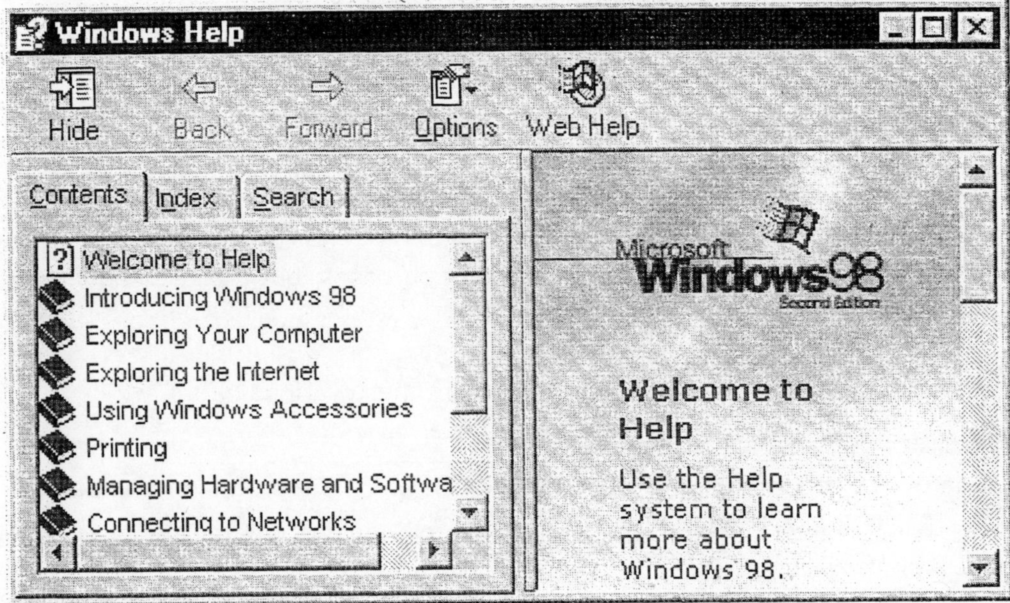

Fig. 17-3 : Windows Help.

On-line Help

Other than the windows Help explained earlier, almost all Windows application program come with their own on-line help.

This on-line help is generally like a very detailed built-in user manual, explaining almost everything you want to know about the software.

On almost all the applications the Help is last item on the main menu bar.

To start the help click on Help on the main menu and select Help Topics, User Guide or Tutorial or some similar option by clicking on it.

Almost all Windows application open on-line help when the [F1] function key is pressed on the keyboard.

Window Application

Windows provides many small applications for general jobs such as

- WordPad/NotePad for typing simple letter,
- Paint for drawing some simple image,
- calculator for doing calculation,
- address book for keeping record of your friends and relatives, etc.

These applications are known as Windows Accessories.

Starting a Windows application

To start a Windows Application/Accessory

1. Click on `Start`
2. Point to `Programs`
3. Point to `Accessories`
4. Click on the required application from the available options such as the Notepad, Paint, Calculator, Address Book, etc.

All these accessories are made for different purposes, but their screen look almost same, all of them have Title Bar, Menu Bar, Tool Bar, Scroll Bar, Status Bar and Program Area.

In the following section we shall see what are these various bars.

Title Bar

Title Bar is the topmost area of the window in which the program is running.

This bar contains the name of program, and the name of any document file currently open in that program.

Other than this, the left corner of the title bar show a small icon indicating the program being run. Right corner of Title Bar has minimize, maximize and close buttons.

Minimize/Maximize/Restore/Close Buttons

The Minimize Button is on the top right corner of the Title Bar. When this button is clicked, the Window is minimized, it is removed from the screen and placed on the taskbar, as an icon.

In minimized state program will still be running, click on the program icon button on the Taskbar to restore the program to normal state.

When the Maximize Button is clicked, the program window will fill the entire screen.

Clicking on the Close Button will close down the application.

After maximizing a window, Restore Button can be clicked to revert the window back to non-maximized normal state.

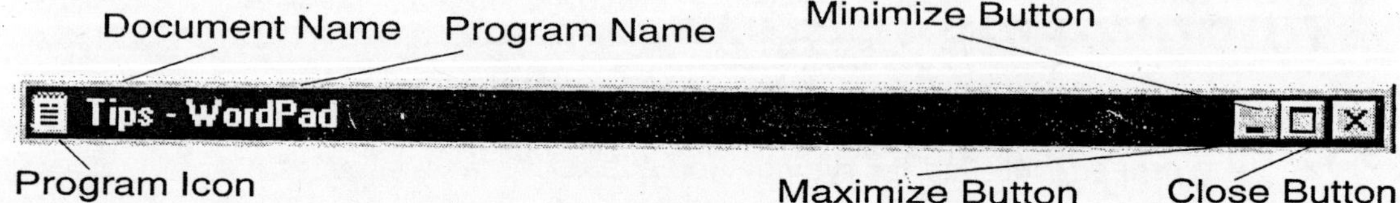

Menu Bar

File Edit View Insert Format Help

The Menu Bar gives a list of options available in the program. Clicking on any option on this menu bar will show a number of sub-menu options.

Characters with underline show that they can be pressed with the [Alt] key to select that particular menu item. For example, when the [Alt]+[E] key is pressed, the Edit Menu is selected.

Tool Bar

Toolbars are usually located below the menu bar.

Toolbars are provided to make working with frequently used program options faster. Instead of going to menu bar and looking for the required action, one can access the required action with one click of the mouse on the tool bar.

Toolbar is a set of icons, you can click on them to perform the task associated with that particular icon. Common tasks such as copying, pasting, and deleting items; changing views, etc. are shown as icon on the ToolBar.

Scroll Bar

If the document you are working on is too large to fit in the program window then Scrollbars, Scroll Boxes and Scroll Arrows allow you to view portions of your workspace in the current window.

You can click on the Scroll Arrows to scroll through different areas of your document.

The Scroll Box can be dragged up/down of left/right for the same purpose.

Clicking on the Scroll Bar at different points will also allow you to move to different parts of your document.

Status Bar

For Help, press F1 CAP NUM

Status bar is generally located at the very bottom of the program window. As the name suggests Status Bar indicates current status of the program.

Position of some of the keys on the keyboard such as Caps Lock, Num Lock, etc. are also shown here.

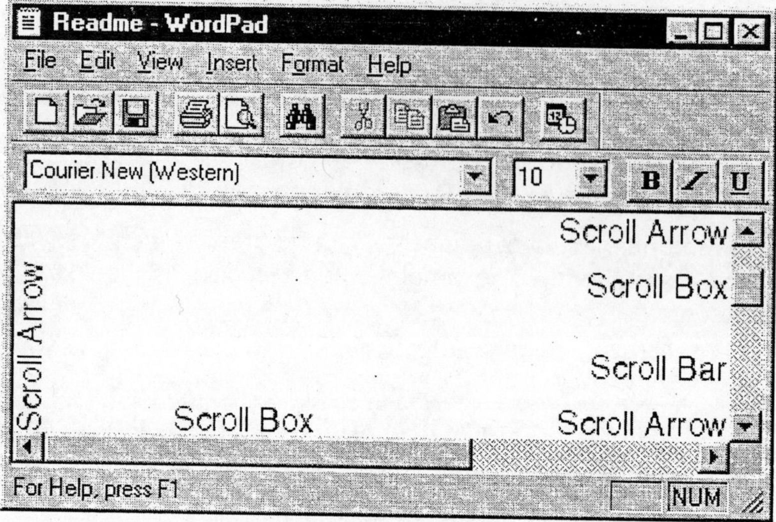

Fig. 17-4 : Scroll Bar, Scroll Arrow and Scroll Box.

Windows Accessories

In the following section we shall take detailed look at many of the accessories/application programs provided with Windows 98.

Calculator

Calculator can be used to perform simple and advanced arithmetic operations by simply entering the digits and selecting the required operation.

Calculator provides a simple calculator for general arithmetic operations and an advanced scientific calculator is provided for advanced scientific, mathematical and statistical functions.

Starting Calculator

To start the calculator program

1. click on the `Start` button
2. point to `Programs`
3. point to `Accessories`
4. click on the `Calculator` option.

This will start the Calculator program.

Once a program starts, a button corresponding to this program will appear on the Taskbar.

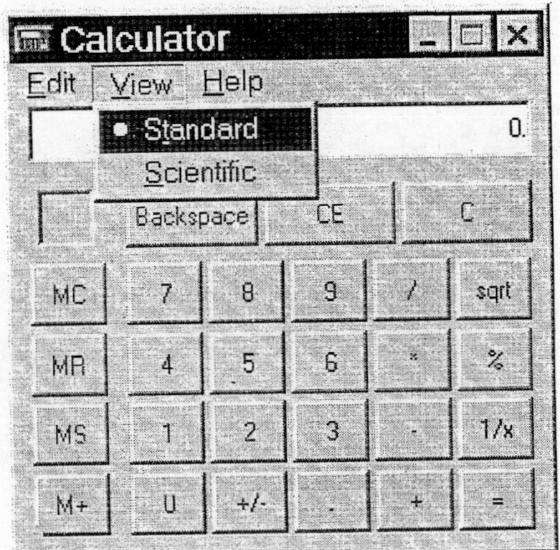

Fig. 17-5 : Calculator - Standard View.

Closing Calculator

To close this calculator program

Click on the **close** button, on the top, right corner of the calculator window.

You can also double click on the calculator icon on the top, left corner of the calculator window.

Using Calculator

This calculator can be used as you would use a hand held calculator.

For example to multiply 123 and 456

1. Type [1], [2], and [3] on the numeric keypad. (make sure that the [Num Lock] key is on)
2. Type [*] (for multiplication)
3. Type [4], [5] and [6]
4. Type [=] button for result, or press the [Enter] key.

The result 56088 will appear on the Calculator display. Instead of entering the digit using the keyboard one can also click on the digits on the calculator screen.

While using the calculator, the following buttons can be used

- Click on Backspace button, or press [Backspace] on keyboard to erase last digit you have entered.
- Click on CE (Clear Entry) button, or press [Delete] on keyboard to clear the most recent number entered

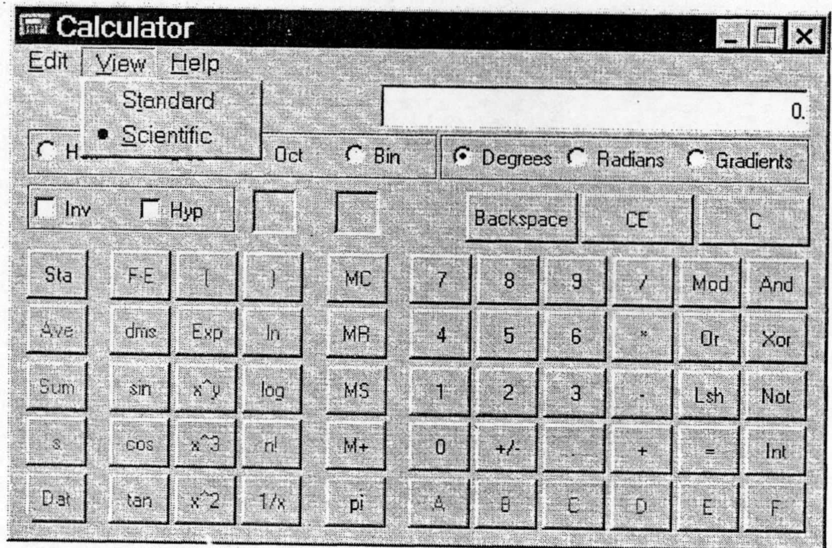

Fig. 17-6 : Calculator - Scientific View.

- Click on C (Clear All) button, or press [Escape] on keyboard to clear the entire calculation.

This calculator also provides memory buttons for storing and reusing intermediate results in a multi-step calculation

- To store a displayed number into memory, click MS.
- When you store a number, an M appears in the box above the memory options. If you store another number, it replaces the one currently in memory.
- To recall a stored number, click MR.
- To clear the memory, click MC.
- To add a displayed number to the number already in memory, click M+. To see the result of this addition, click MR.

The result of any calculation can be copied to the Windows clipboard to use the result in any other Windows application.

For this

1. Click on the **Edit** menu
2. Click on **Copy** menu option

You can also press [Ctrl]+[C] for this

To change the calculator from simple to scientific mode. In the calculator program

1. click on the **view** menu
2. click on either **scientific** or **standard** calculator mode.

Games

Four games are included with Windows 98. They are FreeCell, Hearts, Minesweeper, and Solitaire. Most of these games i.e. FreeCell, Hearts and Solitaire are card based games.

To start these games:

1. Click on the `Start` button, at the lower left corner of the screen. The Start menu will appear.
2. Point to `Programs`.
3. Point to `Accessories`.
4. Point to `Games`. A list of games will appear.
5. Click on the game `FreeCell`, you can click on any game you want to play.

FreeCell

The object of FreeCell game is to move all the 52 cards to the home cells in the upper right corner of playing area.

To move these cards, the free cells in the upper right corner can be used as intermediate placeholders.

To win, you make four stacks of cards on the home cells, one for each suit, stacked in order of rank, from lowest to highest.

Starting New Game

If you selected FreeCell game, the game opens on the desktop. To start a new game,

1. click the `Game` menu option
2. click on `New Game`

As an alternative, you can press the [F2] key on your keyboard to begin a new game.

Game Rules

The game area consists of four Home Cells and four Free Cells and a deck of cards, which is dealt face up in eight columns at the beginning of the game.

To move a card, click the card you want to move, and then click where you want to move it. You can move cards according to following rules

A card from the bottom of a column can move to a Free Cell.

A card from a Free Cell or from the bottom of a column can move to a Home Cell. Moves to a Home Cell must be made in order of lowest to highest, of the same suit.

Aces can move to an empty Home Cell.

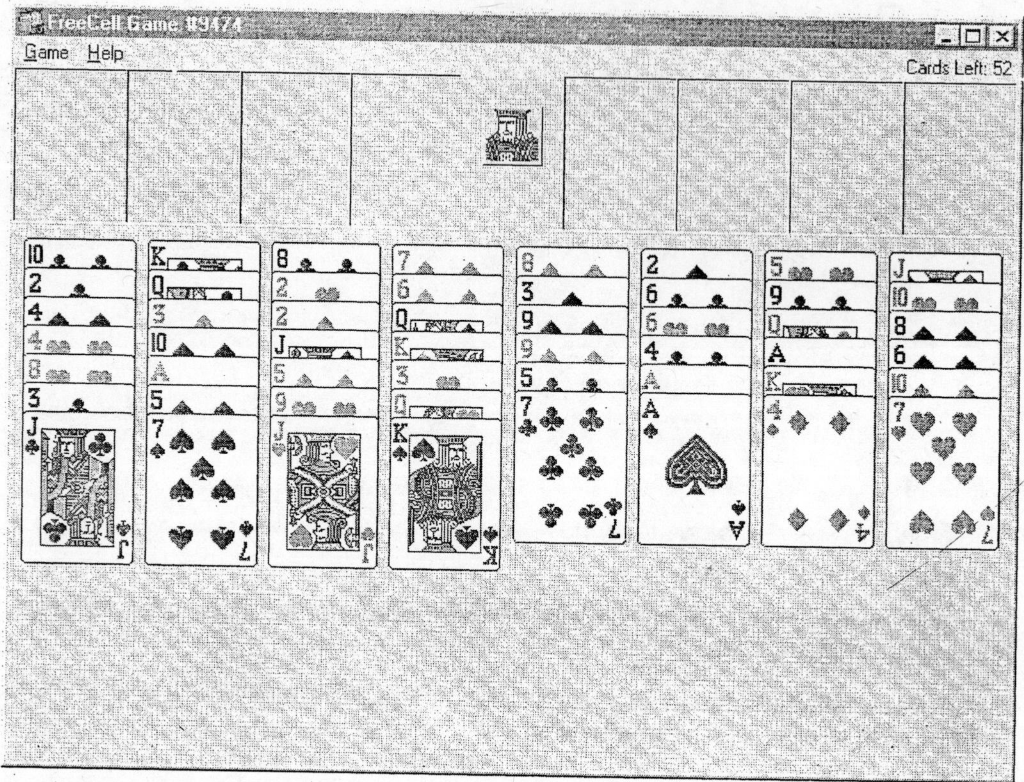

Fig. 17-7 : Free Cell Game.

A card from a Free Cell or from the bottom of a column can move to the bottom of another column. Moves to a column must be made in order of highest to lowest, alternating suit colors.

Playing Game

Begin the game by rearranging cards within the same column. Move card from the bottom of one column to the bottom of another, in rank order (king to ace), in alternating suit colors (black and Red).

For example, move a Red 5 to a Black 6.

If required move a card to Free Cell to help you in rearranging the columns in order. Each Free Cell can hold a single card.

When possible, move a card to its home cell, from the bottom of any column or from any free cell.

If you remove all the cards from a given column, cards from other columns or Free Cells can be moved to the empty column.

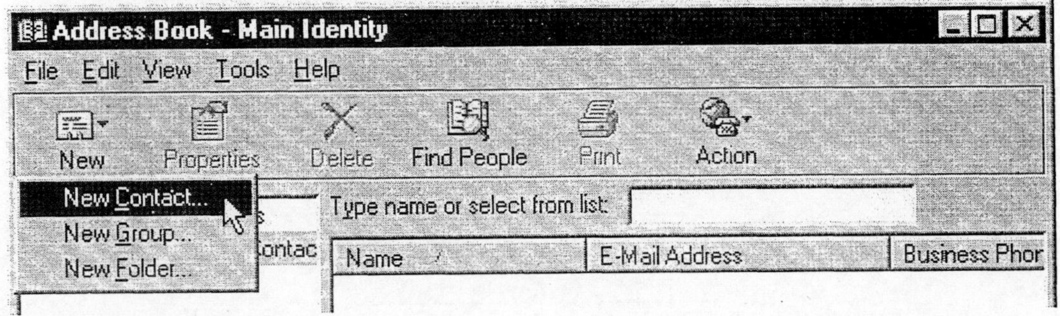

Fig. 17-8 : Address Book.

You win the game when you successfully move all the four suits of cards to their respective Home Cells.

At the end of game FreeCell show a Game Over screen, with an option to try another round of game.

If you need some additional help in learning how to play the game, click the Help menu option or press [F1] key any time during the game.

Starting any of Windows 98's built-in games is pretty much the same as starting FreeCell, except that when you want to start a new game of Solitaire, you select the Deal option in the Game menu.

Address Book

Address book provided with Windows 98 can be used to store all kind of personal data, such as home and business address, phone and fax numbers, and miscellaneous notes about ones friends, relatives and business associates.

Starting Address Book

To start Address Book program

1. click on the `Start` button
2. point to `Programs`
3. point to `Accessories`
4. click on the `Address Book` option.

This will start the Address Book program.

Once the Address Book is open it will display a list of all the people currently stored in you address file.

Adding New Contact

To add a new contact in the address book

Properties

Name | Home | Business | Personal | Other | NetMeeting | Digital IDs

Enter name and e-mail information about this contact here.

First: Middle: Last:

Title: Display: Nickname:

E-Mail Addresses: Add

Edit

Remove

Set as Default

Send E-Mail using plain text only.

OK Cancel

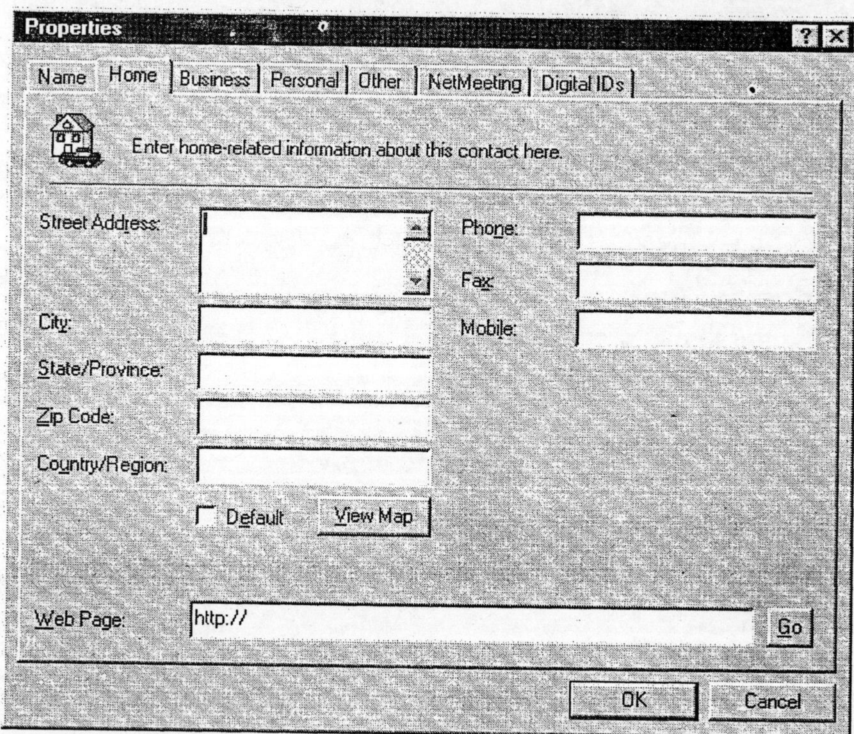

1. Click on `File` on the main menu
2. Click on `New Contact...`

Alternatively, you can press [Ctrl]+[N] on the keyboard,

or you can click on `New` button and click on `New Contact...`

This will start a new contact property window, with many tabs such as Name, Home, Business, Personal, other, NetMeeting and Digital Ids.

Select each one of these tabs and type the required information. Of these tabs, information in the Name, Home, Business and Personal are important.

Once all the required information is fed into the Address Book, return to main window. In this main window, moving the mouse pointer over a line containing persons name will show a pop-up box showing all the information entered for this person.

Notepad

Notepad is a small word processing program using which you can create, edit and read small text files.

Notepad can be used for simple editing of text files.

Starting Notepad

To start Notepad program

1. click on the `Start` button
2. point to `Programs`
3. point to `Accessories`
4. click on the `Notepad` option.

This will start the Notepad program.

Opening an Existing Text File

To open an existing text file in Notepad

1. click on the `File` on main menu
2. click on `Open...`
3. this will open a `File Open` Dialog Window
4. choose proper drive and folder
5. click on the required file from the file list
6. click on `Open` button

Saving a Text File

To save a text file in Notepad

1. click on the `File` on main menu
2. click on `Save`

3. this will open a `File Save` Dialog Window
4. choose proper drive and folder
5. type a proper file name for the file
6. click on `Save` button

Printing a Text File

To print a text file in Notepad

1. click on the `File` on main menu
2. click on `Print`

This will start printing the text file to a printer attached to the computer.. Make sure that the printer is online and there is enough paper available.

Starting a New Text File

To start a new blank text file in Notepad

1. click on the `File` on main menu
2. click on `New`

This will open a blank text file. You can start typing on this new file. At the end save/print this file as explained earlier.

Using word-wrap

If the text file contains long lines of text then to see it on the Notepad window, without using the scroll bars, choose the word-wrap option.

word-wrap breaks long lines into smaller lines that can be viewed within the current notepad window.

This option affects only the display of the text file, no actual line break is added to the file.

WordPad

The notepad can be used to open or type only small size files, also the notepad does not provide any facility to format the text, such as changing the size, font, color, etc.

If one wants to do ali this on a text file, or if the file one wants to open is a large text file then one can used the Wordpad program provided with Windows 98.

Starting Wordpad

To start Wordpad program

1. click on the `Start` button
2. point mouse pointer to `Programs` menu item
3. point to `Accessories` sub-menu item
4. click on the `Wordpad` option.

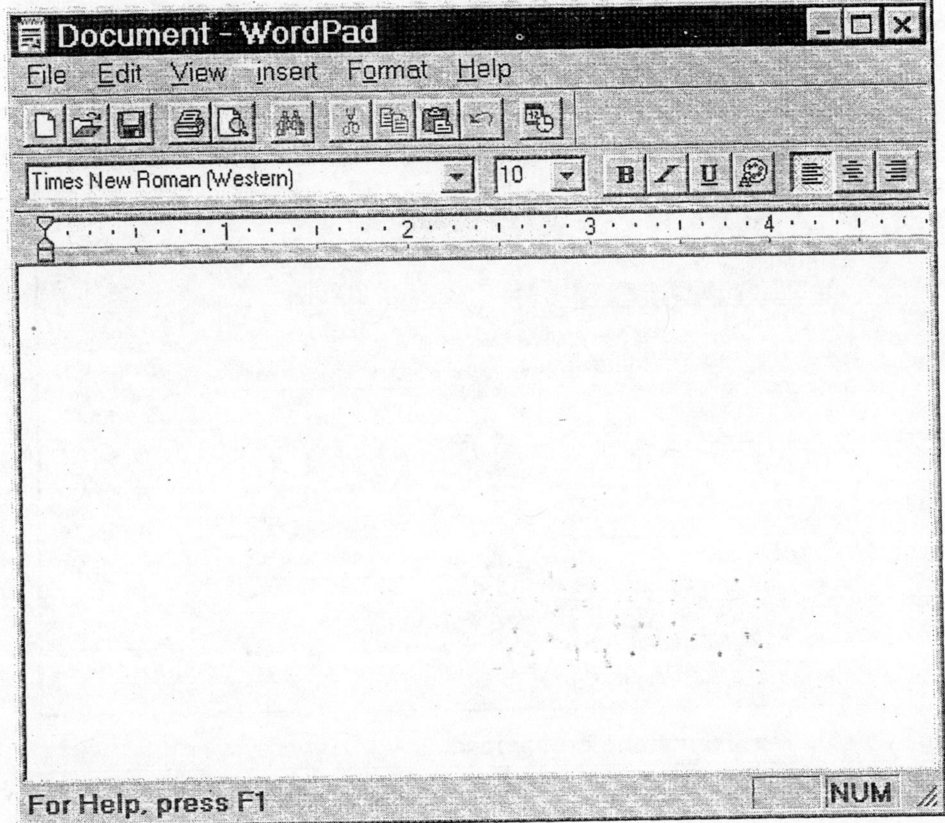

Fig. 17-9 : Wordpad Main Screen.

This will start the Wordpad program.

Opening a Text File

To open an existing text file in Wordpad

1. click on the **File** on main menu
2. click on **Open...**
3. this will open a **File Open** Dialog Window
4. choose proper drive and folder
5. click on the required file from the file list
6. click on **Open** button

Alternatively, you can also press [Ctrl]+[O] to start the File Open Dialog Window. Or, you can click on the Open button on the toolbar.

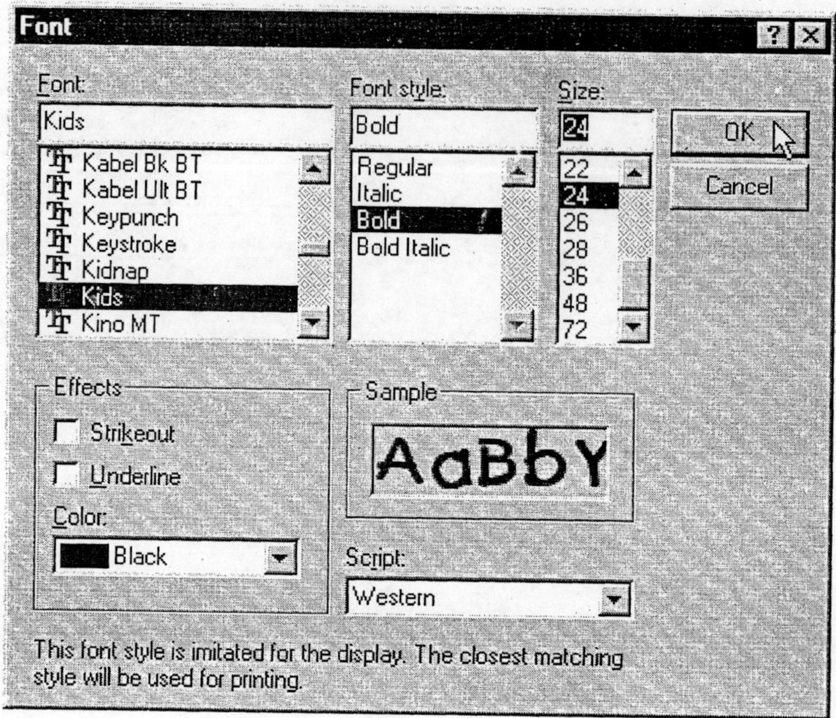

Fig. 17-10 : Text Formatting in Wordpad.

Formatting Text in Wordpad

Compared to Notepad, Wordpad provides many text formatting facility. One can change the shape, size and color of text.

The following formatting can be done on the selected text

- Change in font type, style, size, or color
- Paragraph alignment and indentation setup
- Creating a bulleted list

Changing font type, style, size, or color

1. Select the text whose format you want to change.
   (To select the text Click at the beginning of the text you want to copy.) Press and hold down the [SHIFT] key, and then click at the end of the text you want to copy.)
2. Point to the `Format` menu, click on `Font...`.
3. A Font Selection Window comes up, select Font, Font Style, Size, Color , etc. from the given options.
4. After selecting proper font type, font style, size and color, click on `OK` button

To change the font of an entire document

1. click on the `Edit` menu and then click `Select All`.
2. click on the `Format` menu and then click on `Font`.

This will bring up the Font Selection Window.

Formatting a paragraph

1. click anywhere in the paragraph you want to format
2. click on the `Format` menu
3. click on the `Paragraph ...` menu option
4. Enter the Left, Right and First line indentation and choose from Left, Right or Center alignment options.

Creating a bulleted list

1. Click where you want the bulleted list to start.
2. Click on the `Format` menu
3. click on Bullet Style, and then type your text. When you press [Enter] key, another bullet appears on the next line.
4. To end the bulleted list, click on `Format` menu and click on Bullet Style again.

Saving changes to a document

1. click on the `File` menu
2. click on `Save`

You can save an existing document with a new name by clicking on `Save As` and then typing a new name in File name.

Printing a document

Once you have typed a document, and made all formatting, you can take a print out of the document.

Before printing a Wordpad document, `Print Preview` command can be used to see how it will look on a printed sheet

Print Preview

1. click on the `File` menu
2. click on `Print Preview`.

In Print Preview, you can click Close to return to the previous view.

Setting Margin

If the preview does not appear in proper size, then set page margins as explained below

1. click on the `File` menu
2. click on `Page Setup`
3. enter proper values under Margins.

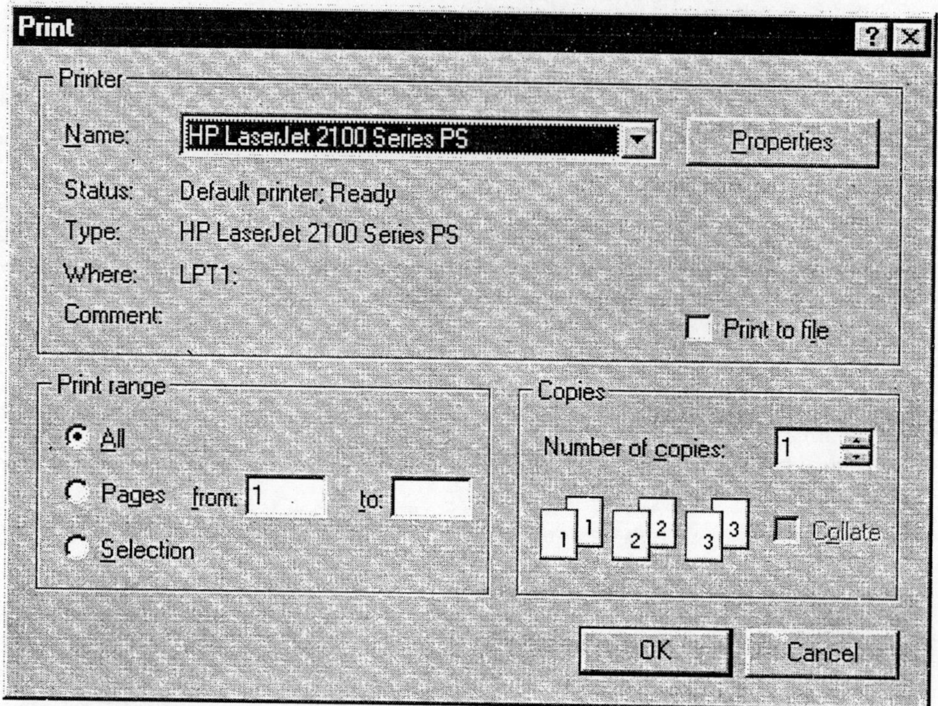

Fig. 17-11 : Printing in Wordpad.

4. Click on **OK**

Printing

Finally when the Print Preview appear all right, you can take the printout by

1. click on **File** menu
2. Select **Print Range** (pages to print) and **Number of Copies** to print in the Print Window
3. Click on **OK** to start printing.

Paint

Paint program provided with Windows 98 can be used to draw simple drawings, one can also apply various colors to these drawings.

Starting Paint

To start Paint program

1. click on the **Start** button
2. point mouse pointer to **Programs** menu item
3. point to **Accessories** sub-menu item

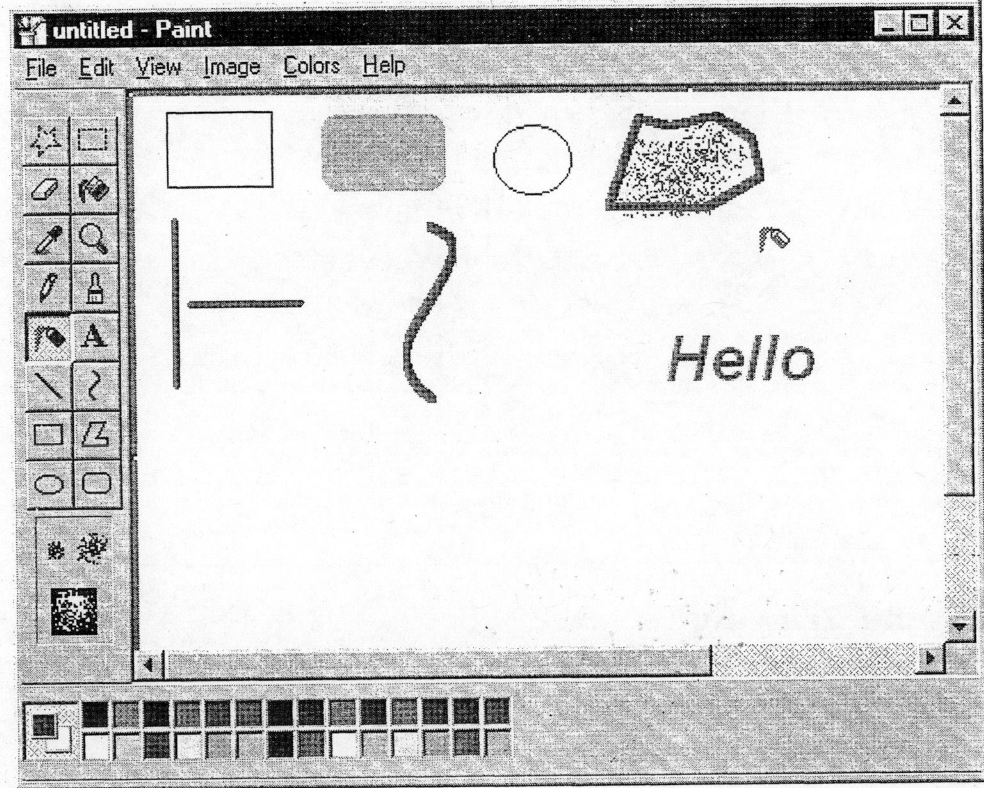

Fig. 17-12 : Paint Main Screen.

4. click on the `Paint` option.

This will start the drawing program Paint.

Opening a Drawing

To open an existing drawing file in Paint

1. click on the `File` on main menu
2. click on `Open...`
3. this will open a File Open Dialog Window
4. select the file type you want to open (BMP, JPG, etc.)
5. choose proper drive and folder
6. click on the required file from the file list
7. click on `Open` button

Alternatively, you can also press [Ctrl]+[O] to start the File Open Dialog Window.

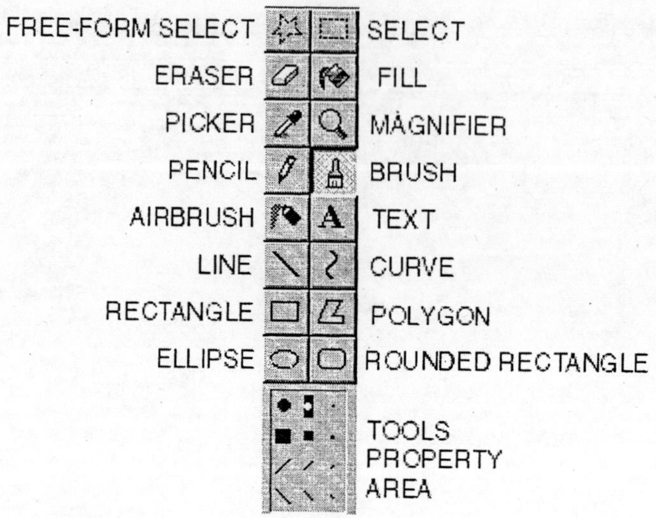

Fig. 17-13 : Paint ToolBox.

A Simple Drawing

Let us now see how to use Paint to make a simple drawing.

To start with, select a new drawing

1. click on the **File** on main menu
2. click on **New**
3. this will open an empty drawing file.

Before continuing, make sure that the Tool Box and Color Box are available on Paint's screen, if not then

click the View menu make sure a check mark appears next to **Tool Box** and **Color Box**, click to set the check mark.

To hide these boxes, click to clear the check mark.

Select Drawing Tool

Select drawing tools by clicking on proper tool from the Tool Box. Available options are Pencil, Brush, Airbrush, Text, Line, Curve, Rectangle, Polygon, Ellipse and Rounded Rectangle.

Select Tool Option/Property

Once a tool is selected, Options/Properties related to that tool will appear on the Tools Property Area.

Select a property by clicking on it

Select Color

Color is shown at a separate Color Box

- To set the foreground color click on a color in the color box.
- To set the background color right-click on a color in the color box.
- The foreground color is used for lines, borders of shapes, and text.
- The background color is used to fill the inside of enclosed shapes and the background of text frames. It also appears when you use the eraser.

The default background and foreground colors appear at the left of color box. The top color chip represents the foreground color. The bottom color chip represents the background color.

Start Drawing

After selecting foreground and background colors you can start your drawing. For this move the mouse pointer to the drawing area.

In drawing area, shape of mouse pointer will change based on the currently selected tool.

Hold down the left mouse button and drag the mouse to draw on screen, when done, release the mouse button.

Saving a Drawing

To save a drawing

1. click on the `File` on main menu
2. click on `Save`
3. this will open a `File Save` Dialog Window
4. choose proper drive and folder
5. type a proper file name for the drawing file
6. Select the drawing type, monochrome, 16 color, 256 color or 24-bit color
7. click on `Save` button

Printing a Drawing

To print a picture

1. Click on the `File` menu
2. click on `Print`, you can see how the printed picture will look before you print by clicking on `Print Preview`.

To set picture margins or to change picture orientation

1. click on the `File` menu and then
2. click on the `Page Setup`.

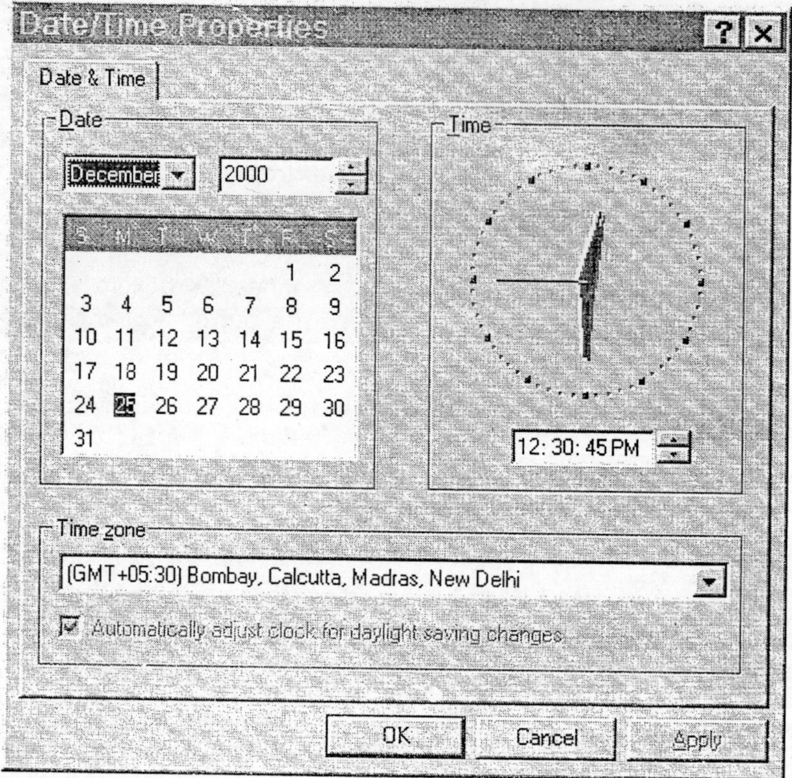

Fig. 17-14 : Setting Date/Time.

Changing the date and/or time

Computers internal clock and calendar provides correct date and time for many important operations.

Sometimes you might need to adjust the date and time to keep them accurate.

To change the date and/or time:

1. Click on the `Start` button, at lower left corner of the screen. The Start menu will appear.
2. Click on `Settings`. A sub-menu will appear.
3. Click on `Control Panel`. The Control Panel will open.
4. Click on `Date/Time` icon. The Date/Time Properties dialog box will appear.
5. In the Date frame, select the month and year.
6. In the Month field, click to open the drop-down menu and select the current month.
7. Type the year in the Year field or use the arrows next to the field to move forward or backward until you get to the current year.

8. The Time field is divided into four segments: hour, minutes, seconds, and AM and PM. To make an adjustment:
   Click in the segment and either type in the correct information or use the arrow keys on the right side to select the correct hour, minute, second or AM or PM.
9. To change the Time Zone, click on the Time Zone tab. Select the correct time zone from the drop-down menu.
   India requires (GMT+5.30) Setting.
10. If you want the clock to automatically adjust to daylight saving time, check the box on the screen.
11. Click on the `Apply` button.
12. Click on `OK`.

Selecting a screen saver

Computer monitors display images by firing electron beams at a phosphor-coated screen. If the same image stays on the screen for too long, there is a danger that the image will leave a permanent imprint on the screen.

Screen savers help prevent this possibility by providing a constantly changing image.

To select a screen saver:

1. Right-click anywhere on the Windows desktop. A menu will appear.
2. Select Active Desktop.
3. Click on **`Customize My Desktop`**.
   You can also click on Properties on the pop-up menu.
4. Click on the **`Screen Saver`** tab.
5. The Screen Saver field provides the list of available screen savers. Select the screen saver you want from the list.
6. Click on **`Settings`** to set the display options associated with the screen saver.
7. Checkmark Password Protected to set a password for your screen saver. Password protection prevents the screen saver from being turned off unless a password is entered.
8. Click on **`Change`** to set the password.
9. Set the number of minutes of inactivity before the screen saver starts in the Wait field.
10. Click on `OK`.
11. You can see a preview of the screen saver you have selected by clicking on the **`Preview`** button.

Desktop shortcut

A desktop shortcut, usually represented by an icon, is a small file that points to a program, folder, document, or Internet location on the desktop.

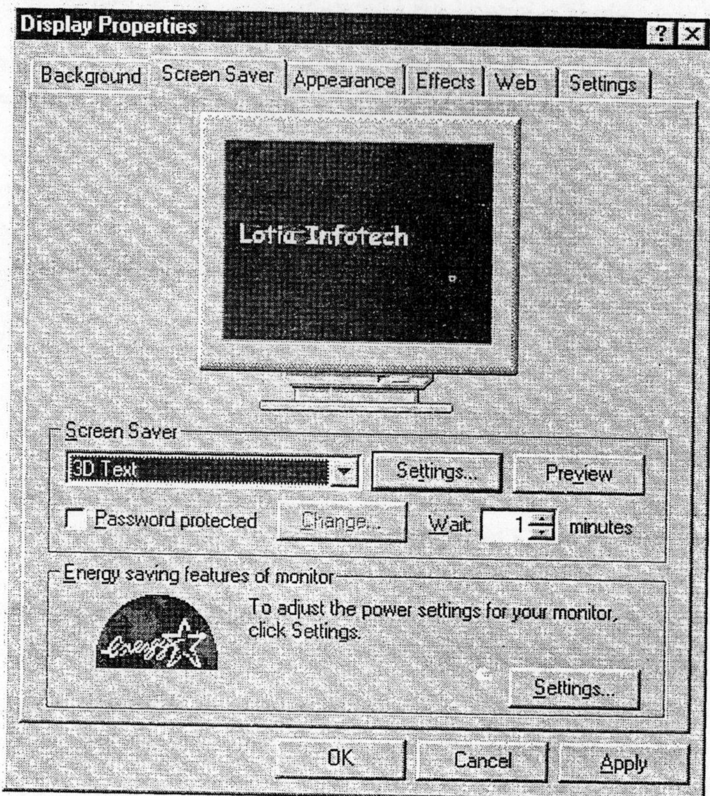

Fig. 17-15 : Setting Up Screen Saver.

Clicking on a shortcut icon takes you directly to the object to which the shortcut points. Shortcut icons contain a small arrow in their lower left corner.

Shortcuts are just pointers-deleting a shortcut will not delete the item to which the shortcut points.

Creating a desktop shortcut

To create a shortcut to an item located on the Start menu:

1. Click on `Start`. The Start menu will appear.
2. Locate the item to which you want to create a shortcut. If the item is located on a sub-menu, go to the sub-menu.
3. Right-click on item and drag it to your desktop.

To create a shortcut in Windows Explorer:

1. Open Windows Explorer.
2. Reduce the Windows Explorer window from full screen.
3. Locate in Windows Explorer the item to which you want to create a shortcut.

4. Hold down the right mouse button and drag the item onto the desktop.
5. Release the right mouse button. A pop-up menu will appear.
6. Click on Create Shortcut(s) Here option in the menu.

How to rename a desktop shortcut?

To rename a shortcut:

1. Right-click on the shortcut.
2. Click on `Rename`.
3. Type the new name.

How to delete a desktop shortcut?

To delete a shortcut:

1. Click on the shortcut.
2. Press the `delete` key.

How to change icon associated with object?

To change the icon associated with an object on the desktop:

1. Right-click on the icon. The pop-up menu will appear.
2. Click on `Properties`.
3. Click on the `Change Icon` button.
4. Click on the icon of your choice.
5. Click on `OK`.

Not all icons on the desktop can be changed. If you do not see the Change Icon button, the icon cannot be changed.

Wallpaper

Wallpaper is the background that displays on your desktop. If you have your desktop set to View as a Web Page, your wallpaper can be an image or a HTML file. If your desktop is not set to View as a Web page, wallpaper can only be an image file.

How to set my desktop to view as Web page?

To set your desktop to view as a Web page.

1. Right-click on your desktop. A menu will appear.
2. Point to **`Active Desktop`**.
3. If **`View As Web Page`** has a checkmark next to it, your desktop is already being viewed as a Web page.

If View As Web Page does not have a checkmark next to it, click on **`View As a Web Page`**.

How to change my wallpaper?

To change your wallpaper:

1. Right-click on your desktop.
2. Click on `Properties`.
3. Click on the `Background` tab.
4. Select the wallpaper you want from the list that appears, Select a HTML Document or a Picture.

If you would like to display an image you created, you can click on Browse to find the image.

If you have your desktop set to view as a Web page, you can display any file with a .bmp, .dib, .rle, .gif, or .jpeg extension. If not, you can display any image with a .bmp, .dib, or .rle extension only.

Select how you want your image to appear on the screen. Choose from the following:

- Center- Place the image in the center of the screen.
- Tile- Have the image display as tiles across and down the screen.
- Stretch- Stretch the image so the image covers the entire screen.

Font

A font is a set of characters represented in a single typeface. Each character within a font is created by using the same basic style.

Font size

Fonts are measured in points. There are 72 points to an inch. The number of points assigned to a font is based on the distance from the top to the bottom of its longest character.

How to install a new font?

To install a new font:

1. Click on the `Start` button.
2. Point to `Settings`.
3. Click on `Control Panel`.
4. Click on `Fonts` in the control panel window. The Fonts window opens.
5. Click on `File`, which is located on the menu bar.
6. Click on `Install New Font...`.
7. Specify the drive and folder where the font you want to install is currently located.
8. Select the font you want to install from the fonts listed in the List of Fonts box.

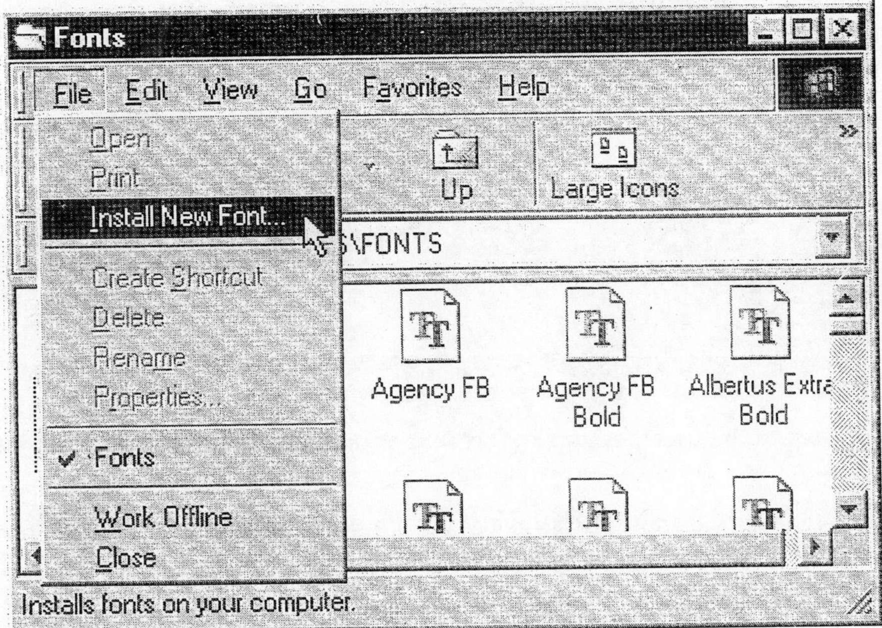

Fig. 17-16 : Installing New Fonts.

9. Select **Copy Fonts to Fonts Folder** (this will put a copy of the font, you are installing, in the Fonts folder).
10. Click on **OK**.

Character Map

The Character Map displays the characters available in a selected font. To view the Character Map dialog box:

1. Click on the **Start** button.
2. Click on **Programs**.
3. Click on **Accessories**.
4. Click on **System Tools**.
5. Click on **Character Map**.
6. The Character Map window will open on the desktop.

Select a font from the Font field drop-down menu. Click on a character box to display an enlarged version of the character.

The keystroke necessary to produce the character is displayed in the lower left corner of the screen.

Double-click on a character or click on the character and click on the `Select` button to send the character to the `Characters to Copy` field. You can send multiple characters to the `Characters to Copy` field.

Click on the `Copy` button to move the `Characters to Copy` field contents to the Clipboard.

Moving, Sizing, and Organizing Windows

In Windows 98, one can run different applications on different windows at once to accomplish more than one thing at a time.

You can search the Internet and import text or pictures into a Word document; or, you can write memos in Word Pad while you are reading your e-mail.

The following are some tips for moving, sizing, and organizing windows that you have open on your desktop at the same time:

Move

Use the Title Bar to move a window around on the desktop.

Click on the title bar, and while holding down the mouse button, drag the window to a new location on the desktop.

This is helpful when you are using more than one program at a time and need to see them both simultaneously, such as when you are editing a picture in Paint and then want to import the picture into a Word document.

Resize

Customize the size of a window with the resize pointers.

You can drag the window's borders to make the window larger or smaller.

To try this, open Notepad from the Accessories sub-menu (on the Programs menu). Move the pointer over to the right edge of the window.

The pointer will change to a Resize Pointer, a short line with arrows at both ends. Hold down the left mouse button and drag any part of the window's edge to change the windows size.

Or, drag the window from the corner to resize the height and width at the same time.

Organize

When you right-click on the Taskbar, a menu appears. This handy menu contains commands for cascading and tiling windows, and for minimizing all open windows.

To try out these features, open a few accessory programs such as Word Pad, the calculator, and Paint, and then right-click an open space on the taskbar and click to choose Cascade Windows or Tile Windows Horizontally.

Adjusting Mouse Settings

1. Click `Start` to display the Start menu.
2. Point to `Settings` and then click `Control Panel` from the sub-menu.
3. Double-click the Mouse icon to open the Mouse Properties dialog box.
4. Click either the `Buttons` tab, `Pointers` tab, or `Motion` tab. Adjust the settings and then click Apply.
5. Click `OK` to close the dialog box.

Button Tab

This tab has option to change the mouse button for left-handed users.

One can also adjusts the amount of time that can pass between clicks when you double-click your mouse button.

If you are an inexperienced mouse user, keep double-clicking speed slow by dragging the slider to the left.

You can test the double-click speed by double-clicking on the image provided in the test area.

Pointers Tab

This tab has options to change the look of mouse pointers. Make them larger for easier visibility.

Motion Tab

This tab has option to show pointer trails and to adjust mouse pointer speed.

Pointer Speed

Adjusts the speed at which the mouse pointer moves on your screen.

Click on the speed indicator and, while holding down the mouse button, drag it to the left or right.

Pointer Trail

Adds a trail to the mouse pointer, which makes it easier to see on Liquid Crystal Display (LCD) screens.

To adjust the length of the pointer trail, drag the slider to short or long.

Finding a File/Folder

If you need a file or program located on your computer or network, but you cannot remember its name or location, use the Find File command.

1. click the `Start` button
2. point to `Find`,
3. click `Files` or `Folders`.

When you choose this command from the Start menu, the Find Dialog Box opens.

From this dialog box, you can find the file or program based on several types of search criteria, such as

- the file type, such as text, graphic etc.,
- a partial file name, or
- words in a file, etc.

The more specific you can make the search criteria, the faster the search results are displayed.

For example, if you know the document you are looking for is a text file, it contains the word "Welcome", and it is on your computer

Then in the search criteria you could choose

- "*.TXT" from the dropdown list for the Named field,
- type "Welcome" in the Containing text field, and
- select your hard drive in the Look in field

before pressing Find Now to start the search.

When the search is completed, a list of files and folders matching your criteria appears in the field at the bottom of the Find dialog box.

Open the files or folders in this field by double clicking on the file or folder.

You can also right-click the file or folder for more options, such as printing it (for files), moving or copying it, or deleting it, etc.

The following options are also available from the Find command on the Start menu:

Computer

search for another computer on the network by name.

On the Internet

launches the Web browser so that you can search the Internet.

People

Opens your personal address book if available.

Starting Programs Automatically

You can have your computer automatically run programs whenever Windows starts. For this put a shortcut for that program in the StartUp menu.

You can have virus checking software scan your computer every time it starts, or you can open Outlook Express e-mail first thing every morning when you turn on your computer.

Too many programs running at startup can slow your computer's performance.

Adding a shortcut to StartUp

- Move the pointer over the shortcut icon and press and hold the left mouse button.
- Drag the icon to the StartUp menu and release the mouse button.

Removing a shortcut from StartUp

- Drag the shortcut to the Recycle Bin, or.
- Right-click the shortcut icon and then click Delete from the shortcut menu.

Restart Windows 98 to test your new StartUp shortcut.

Desktop Themes

Windows 98 provides many desktop themes to make the use of Windows entertaining and fun.

Themes included with Windows 98 are Underwater, Jungle, Baseball, Space and the entire Microsoft Plus! for Windows 95 themes package.

You can dramatically change the look and sound of your desktop by applying a theme.

Each desktop theme includes wallpaper, screen savers, icons, sounds, fonts, color schemes, and mouse pointers.

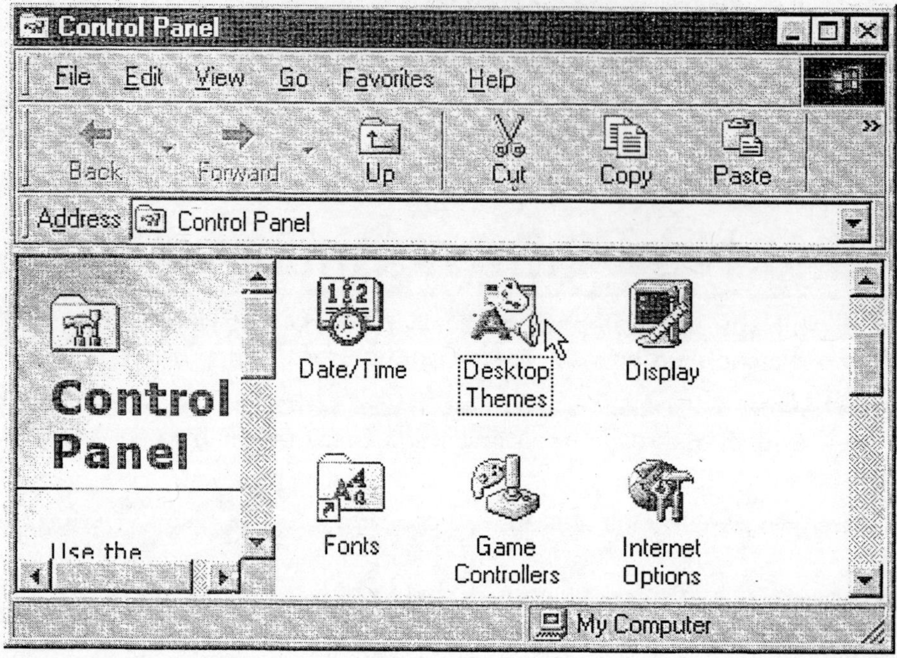

Fig. 17-17 : Starting Desktop Themes.

Installing Desktop Themes

To install desktop themes

1. click on `Start`,
2. point to `Settings`,
3. click on `Control Panel`,
4. double-click on `Add/Remove Programs`,
5. click on the `Windows Setup` tab,
6. click on `Desktop Themes`, and then
7. click on `Details`.
8. select all options from the shown list
9. click `OK`

Changing Desktop Themes

1. Click on `Start`,
2. point to `Settings`,
3. click `Control Panel`, and then
4. double-click on `Desktop Themes`.

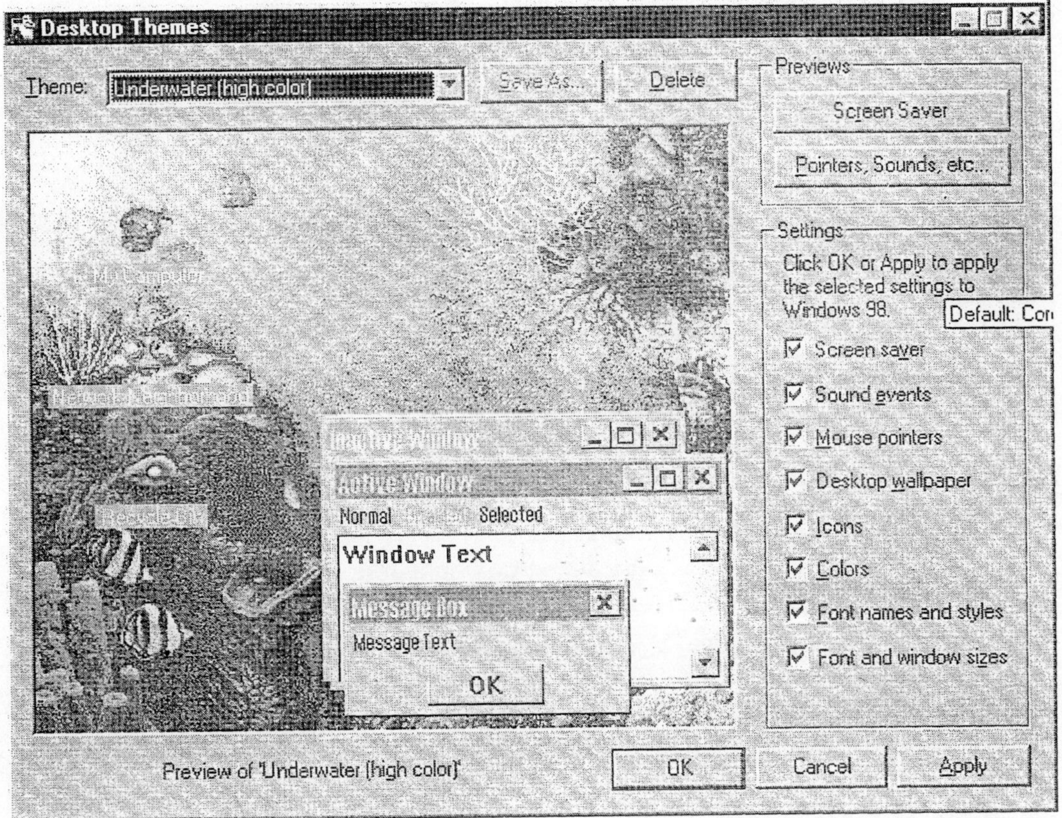

Fig. 17-18 : Changing Desktop Themes.

5. In the Desktop Themes dialog box, click on the theme you want in Themes drop down list
6. click on OK.

If you don't want to use one of the theme's desktop items, make sure its check box is clear in the Settings box.

If Desktop Themes is missing from Control Panel, install it as explained earlier.

You can also customize an existing theme by changing different desktop elements and create a new theme by saving your changes to an existing theme under a new name.

Recycle Bin

Whenever you delete a file, it is temporarily moved to the Recycle Bin on your desktop. If you change your mind, you can restore the file.

However, when you empty the Recycle Bin, all of the items in it are permanently deleted from your computer.

Empty and full recycle bin icons look different as shown in the adjoining figure.

To delete files and folders

1. On the desktop, double-click **My Computer.**
2. The My Computer window appears.
3. Select the file or folder you want to delete.
4. On the **File** menu, click **Delete.**
5. The **Confirm File Delete** dialog box appears.
6. Click **Yes.**

The file is moved to the Recycle Bin.

To permanently delete files and folders

1. On the desktop, double-click Recycle Bin.
2. The Recycle Bin opens.
3. On the **File** menu, click on **Empty Recycle Bin.**

CD Player

You can use CD Player accessory of Windows 98 to play Audio Compact Discs (Audio CD) on a CD-ROM drive connected to your computer.

To listen to an audio CD, you can use headphones that are plugged in to the CD-ROM. Or, if you have a sound card installed, you can listen to audio CD over your speaker system.

Starting CD Player

1. click on **Start,**
2. point to **Programs,**
3. point to **Accessories,**
4. point to **Entertainment**, and then
5. click on **CD Player.**

Fig. 17-19 : Playing Audio CD.

This will open the audio CD player program.

Paying Audio CD

To play an audio CD

Make sure the CD is in the CD-ROM drive, and then click on **play** button

To stop playing CD, click on **stop** button .

To eject CD from the drive, click on **eject** button .

To pause and resume a CD, click on **pause** button , and then click on **play** button to resume playing.

To change to a different track Click on to **move to the next track**, or click on to **move to the previous track.**

You can move forward or backward within a track by clicking on **forward** or **backward** button.

To play tracks in random order on the Options menu, click on **Random Order** or click on **Random** Button on the toolbar.

For continuous play click on the **Continuous Play** Button on the toolbar

You can click on **Intro Play** button to listen to 10 seconds of each tracks on the CD.

Automatic CDs play

If you want the computer to start playing the CD inserted in the CD drive, automatically, then follow the steps given below

1. click on **Start**
2. point to **Settings**
3. click on **Control Panel**
4. double-click on **System.**
5. In System window click on the plus sign next to CD-ROM
6. right-click on the CD-ROM device you want to use
7. click on **Properties.**
8. Click the **Settings** tab.
9. Set the **Auto Insert Notification** check box.
10. To prevent CDs from playing automatically, click to clear the **Auto Insert Notification** check box.

This setting applies to all CDs, including games, multimedia, and audio CDs.

You can also press the [SHIFT] key while inserting a CD to stop it from playing automatically. Keep the shift key pressed for about 10 seconds.

To enable/disable automatic play of only Audio CDs use the following method . To disable automatic play

1. Double-click on My Computer.
2. On the **View** menu, click **Folder Options**, and then click the File Types tab.
3. Click on AudioCD, and then click **Edit.**
4. In Actions box, click on **Play**, and then click **Set Default.**

Repeating the above procedure will enable automatic play.

You can temporarily disable AutoPlay by pressing [SHIFT] key while you insert an audio CD.

Volume Control

To adjust the playback volume open the Multimedia Properties dialog box. To open this dialog box

1. click on **Start,**
2. point to **Settings,**
3. click on **Control Panel**
4. double-click on **Multimedia.**
5. Click on **Audio** tab
6. In Playback, click the **Speaker Volume** icon to display the Master Out dialog box.

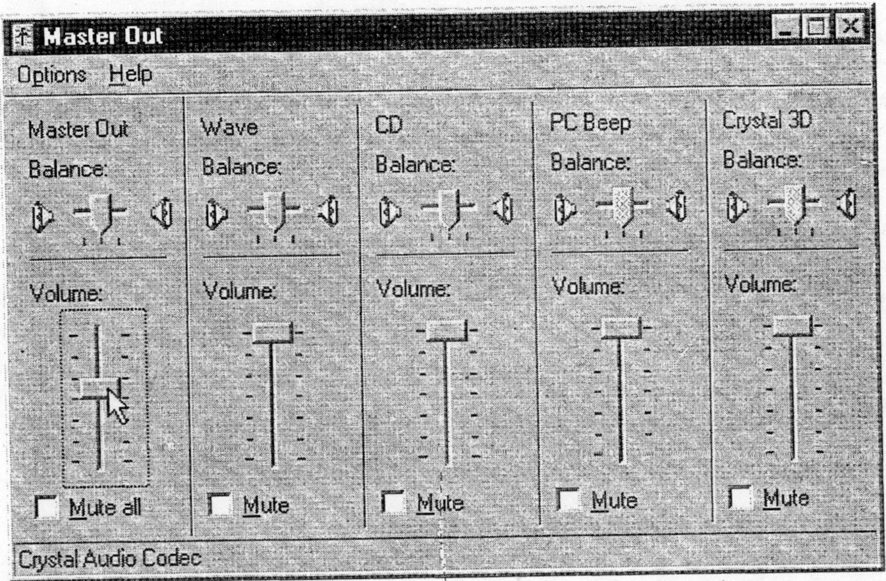

Fig. 17-20 : Volume Control.

7. Adjust the volume for the appropriate device by dragging the control sliders

If the Show volume control on the taskbar check box is selected and your sound card volume can be changed using software, a speaker icon appears on the taskbar.

You can then change the volume by clicking on that speaker icon and dragging the control slider.

Using Volume Control

If you have a sound card, you can use Volume Control to adjust the volume and speaker balance when you play audio files.

To start Volume Control.

1. click on `Start`
2. point to `Program`
3. point to `Accessories`
4. point to `Entertainment`
5. click on `Volume Control`

To turn off sound

In the above Volume Control window Under Master Out, click and set **`Mute All`**.

One can also click on the speaker icon on the taskbar and click to set the Mute option box shown there.

Sound Recording

Using Sound Recorder you can record, play, and edit sound files. To use Sound Recorder, you must have a sound card and speakers installed on your computer.

To record live sound, you also need a microphone.

To start Sound Recorder.

1. click on `Start`
2. point to `Programs`
3. point to `Accessories`
4. point to `Entertainment`
5. click on `Sound Recorder`.

This will open the Sound Recorder accessory of Windows 98.

Changing the sound quality of recordings

You can also open the Multimedia Properties dialog box at the Audio tab by clicking Start, pointing to Settings, clicking Control Panel, and then double-clicking Multimedia. Open the Multimedia Properties dialog box at the Audio tab.

In Recording, click the Microphone icon to display Recording Control to adjust the recording volume.

Recording a Sound

Make sure you have an audio input device such as a microphones or a CD-ROM player connected to your computer.

1. click on the `File` menu
2. click on `New`
3. To begin recording, click on `record` button.
4. Once the recording is done, to stop recording, click on `stop` button.
5. Click on the `File` menu
6. click on `Save`

In the `Save As` dialog Box, select proper drive and folder and give a name to the recorded sound.

This recorded sound file can be later played back from the Sound Recorder or in the Media Player.

To Play a Sound in Sound Recorder

1. Click on the `File` menu

2. click on `Open`
   An open file dialog box opens on the screen, open the folder containing the sound file you want to play,
3. click on the required file
4. click on `Open` button.
5. Click on `play` button to start playing the sound.
6. Click on `stop` button to stop playing the sound.

You can move to the beginning of a sound file by clicking on << and to the end by clicking on >> buttons.

DVD Player

Windows 98 provides a DVD Player accessory to play DVD discs from a DVD drive connected to your computer. You can also use your DVD drive to play software and music CDs.

To open DVD Player after you have inserted a disc,

- click `Start`, point to `Programs`, point to `Accessories`, point to `Entertainment`, and then click on `DVD Player`.

DVD player provided with Windows 98 is not of very good quality, so one should use the software that comes with the player to play DVD discs.

Adding Fonts Under Windows

In this section, we will see how additional fonts can be added to your computer system working under the Microsoft Windows. This upgrade does not involve any type of hardware, it is one of the easiest upgrade that you can do for the printer.

Adding new fonts to the your system will not improve your printer's speed or the quality of its output, but this will help you to get better looking outputs from your printer.

Window uses two type of outline fonts, TrueType and Adobe Type-1, for adding TrueType fonts control panel's fonts option is used and to add Type-1 fonts you need to use the Adobe Type Manager (ATM) software.

Adding TrueType fonts

Microsoft provides various TrueType fonts in a variety of shapes and styles. Useful for body text, headline fonts, decorative fonts and symbol fonts.

To install TTF fonts from disks or a network location

- In Control Panel, double-click `Fonts`.

- Click the **File** menu, and then click **Install New Font.**
- Click **Start**, point to **Settings**, click **Control Panel**, and then double-click **Fonts.**
- On the **File** menu, click **Install New Font.**
- In the **Add Fonts** dialog box, use the Folders and Drives boxes to specify the drive and folder containing the fonts you want to install.
- In the List of fonts, select the fonts you want to install, and then click **OK.** To select more than one font to add, hold down the **CTRL** key, and then click each of the fonts you want.

To copy the font to the Windows directory click on the **Copy Fonts to Windows directory** check box.

Verify that the copied font is available by looking on the list of Installed Fonts in the Fonts dialog box.

Once you have completed the installation process, any Windows applications that support multiple fonts will list your new fonts and you can begin to use them immediately to give your documents and presentations a more professional look.

Adding Type-1 fonts

Type-1 fonts are available from more sources than the TrueType fonts, the main reason for this is type-1 fonts are a very old typeface format, it has been in the market for a long time. The main source of type-1 font is its creators Adobe systems.

To add new type-1 fonts to the window environment will require a type-1 font manager such as the Adobe Type Manager (ATM) software.

Using the ATM software one can add type-1 fonts to the already existing type-1 fonts.

- To add font double click on the ATM Control Panel icon, once this icon is double clicked you will get the ATM control panel, in this panel there is an option to add more fonts.
- Click on this option, another Add ATM Fonts screen will appear. On this screen, type the source of the font and the place where these Type-1 fonts are to be copied.
- Type-1 fonts are made of two parts the actual outline font (with .PFB extension) and the font description (with .PFM extension).
- These .PFB and .PFM files (also called font matrix files) are sometime stored in separate directories, these directory names can be given separately.

Next, select the fonts to be copied and choose OK, ATM will copy the required fonts into proper directories.

Computer Virus

Many of the virus infection produce a symptom, as if there is some software/hardware problem with the computer. In this section we have given introduction about virus, how to detect virus infection, precautions that one should take to prevent a virus infection etc. is covered in detail.

What is Computer Virus?

Let us start with what is a computer virus, a computer virus is nothing but a small program written by someone to corrupt or damage the information stored in the computer system, and to replicate itself from one computer system to another.

The term virus is used for this type of programs because as the biological virus spread disease from one person to another, these virus programs also spread from one computer to another.

These viruses spread when someone copies a virus infected program from one computer and runs it on some other computer. This infects the new computer system. Again, when someone copies from this newly infected system, the virus will again spread and the spreading of the virus continues.

A virus cannot spread by using any data file such as text file, image file, sound file etc. A virus needs some kind of executable program such as, .EXE, .COM, .SYS, Window Macro etc. to become active, infect a system and to spread.

Based on its working principle and the spreading method used, a virus can be divided into different types.

Types of Computer Virus

Worm

Worms were one of the first computer viruses. A program written as worm virus normally do not do any destructive work, a worm's main work is to replicate itself, i.e.

to keep-on copying itself to any new disk used in the system, or in the network copying to new systems, and keep spreading.

The original worm programs were made as experimental programs in computer labs to test if a program can be made to replicate itself.

Most of the current viruses contain a worm program in them to manage the replication part of the virus.

To spread, these worms stay resident in the computer's memory and keep a watch on disk access activities. Whenever a new disk is put in the drive and a disk access command such as DIR is given, these programs immediately copy themselves to some .EXE, .COM etc. executable program on the new disk.

Later when this infected disk is taken on some other machine and the infected program is executed, the virus becomes active in the new computer's memory, again waiting for some disk to copy itself.

These viruses also spread by copying themselves to the boot sector of the floppy, after this when the infected floppy is used to boot on some machine these virus become active.

If the machine, where the virus becomes active contains a hard disk drive, then the virus also copies itself to the hard disk drive be writing itself to the MBR (Master Boot Record), DBR (DOS Boot Record) or the executable programs on the hard disk drive.

Trojan

Trojan is a name given to those programs that appear as some useful utility, but they contain some hidden destructive parts. A virus that has infected a useful .COM or .EXE program makes that executable program a Trojan because the moment someone executes them, the virus will become active and starts doing its job.

For example, your word processing program WS.EXE may become infected by some virus and when you are doing some typing work in the WS, the virus active in memory, may be destroying some data on your hard disk drive.

Therefore, hiding some destructive program in a legitimate appearing program is called Trojan program. A pure Trojan virus does not replicate itself, but currently most of the virus contain a Trojan, as well as worm, so a useful looking program can destroy the data as well as can replicate itself.

Bomb

Another type of virus programs is known as bombs. These are programs that waits for some specific event to occur and when that particular event occurs the bomb becomes active destroying or corrupting the information inside the computer.

The event could be anything defined by the programmer writing this type of programs, it could be a particular date, a particular day coming on some specific date such as Friday coming on 13th, it could be some event such as after virus had made 10 copies of itself it may format the hard disk drive, some programmer may write a bomb program to delete the complete FAT table, if his name is removed from the payroll file.

A virus may contain bomb, worm and the Trojan horse all the three parts, to effectively replicate and destroy data.

MBR (Partition Table) Infector

Other than their working method, a virus can also be classified based on the area infected by a virus. A MBR or Partition table infector viruses infects the Master Boot Record (MBR) of the hard disk drive, (floppy disk does not contain any MBR).

These viruses become active every time the machine is booted from the hard disk drive, because during booting, first thing the BIOS does is to execute the program located in the MBR.

Removing a MBR virus is very, easy as one needs to just overwrite the infected MBR code with a good MBR code, taking care that the partition table information is not overwritten and become corrupted.

DBR (Boot Sector) Infector

Another virus type based on the area infected by them is DBR or DOS Boot Record infector viruses. These viruses very commonly spread through infected floppy disks. Every time a boot sector infected floppy is used to boot a system the virus becomes active in memory and starts spreading and destroying.

These viruses also infect the hard disk drive's DOS partition's boot sector and every time the machine is switched on and booted from the hard disk drive the virus becomes active in the memory.

Even if a disk is not bootable, if the disk contains a boot sector virus and by mistake if you try to boot from this disk, the virus in the DBR will become active in memory.

If you are booting from a hard disk drive, and if the A: drive of your system contains a floppy disk, then make sure that the drive door is open, so that the computer will not try to read the DBR of the floppy disk and make any DBR virus active.

Program/File Infector (Parasitic Virus)

Another type of virus do not infect the MBR or the DBR, instead they attach themselves to some executable program such as .EXE, .COM, .SYS, .OVL, .BIN, .DLL, .DRV, .VXD etc.

These viruses turn the useful program which they infect into Trojan programs, anytime these infected programs are executed, the virus becomes active in memory and starts its work of replication and destruction.

Multipartite Viruses

A virus can contain all the above three infectors, MBR, DBR and the program infector part in its program. This type of virus program is called multipartite virus.

Stealth Viruses

Stealth viruses are special type of virus, once they become active in memory they conceal themselves from detection. These viruses hide themselves from detection by a virus scanner, by constantly changing their code. The code can be changed by either using encryption or by inserting NOP (No OPeration) instruction at random places in the virus program.

A virus scanner program scans and finds a virus by comparing the information on the hard disk drive with some predefined 8-10 character codes unique to each virus (known as virus strain). Once the virus changes its code, comparing of the code with the predefined strain may not work and the scanner may prove to be ineffective.

Another method used by these viruses is they copy the original part of the infected portion of the disk or program, into some other part and when the virus is active in memory, every time a scanning program checks, the uninfected part is shown to the scanner program.

For example, a MBR infector may copy the original MBR to some other sector and every time a scanner or any other program asks for the MBR, the virus program will show the original MBR not the infected MBR.

If you try to check the MBR using the Norton's Diskedit program, the virus active in memory will show you the original MBR sector. Only when the virus is not active in memory you will be able to see the virus infected MBR. This is the reason, after a virus infection, a virus scanner program requires you to boot from a write-protected, uninfected system disk.

Polymorphic Viruses

Viruses that change their appearance by using the encryption method to avoid detection are known as polymorphic viruses. These viruses change their code with each run by using some encryption code and also they change their encryption method with each run making it very difficult to detect this type of viruses by using the simple virus scanning method.

Currently, the "dark avenger" virus writer has made a mutation engine, which can make any virus a polymorphic virus. His mutation engine causes the virus program to which it is attached, to continually change its appearance, This makes detection of virus using scanning method a very difficult job.

Macro Virus

Macro viruses appeared after the introduction of macros in the various applications such as spreadsheet, word processor etc. Most of the macro viruses are written to infect Microsoft Word and Microsoft Excel documents.

Macro viruses generally spread through Internet, and e-mail.

If a Word or Excel file containing macro is send as attachment with the e-mail, when the document is opened by the recipient, the macro gets executed and the virus becomes active in his computer and starts spreading further.

Many of these viruses look in the user's address book and send themselves as e-mail with attachment to all available e-mail address, spreading even further.

To protect from macro virus one should never open a document with attachment, without scanning it first with latest virus scanner.

Web Applet Virus

A new type of virus can be made in the web scripting language such as Active X, Javascript, Java etc. When a web page containing infected Active X, Javascript or Java code is opened, the virus will infect your system.

Once the virus becomes active it can do all the works done by a virus such as destroying data, spreading itself etc.

How Does a Virus Work?

Now that we have seen the different types of the viruses, let us see how these viruses infect a system.

A virus comes to a system from another infected system, may be by copying a program from the infected system, or booting an infected floppy, or from opening any infected file over the network.

Once a virus infects a system it becomes memory resident, every time the infected part of the system is used.

For example, a virus that has infected MBR, DBR, or the system files, will become active every time the system is switched on or a virus that has infected a .COM or .EXE program will become active when that particular infected program is run.

After becoming active in the memory, virus starts to monitor different activities of the system, such as the disk read/write operation, keyboard operation, system clock etc.

The worm part of the virus starts to replicate the virus to new programs and disks. The bomb part of the virus waits for some specific event to make the bomb active and does the destruction for which it is programmed.

When you suspect a virus, press reset key or turn the machine off and then boot from a protected floppy disk or CD-ROM and clean virus using some good anti-virus software.

Where Do Viruses Live?

We have already said that a computer virus is an executable program code. Because a virus is a computer program, it cannot do anything unless it is executed, for this reason the virus program writers makes these virus programs to infect some executable program, or some executable part of the drive such as MBR, DBR etc.

When the infected program or the infected MBR, DBR etc, is executed the virus will also be executed with it, providing a chance for the virus to become active.

A virus can never spread if you copy the data file from one infected floppy or hard disk drive and use it on some other clean system. On this type of situation only chance of infection comes if the data file contain some macro and is infected with a macro virus.

Keeping Virus Away

Let us see some of the things that you should follow to keep the virus away from infecting your system.

To prevent a virus infection one method could be to never to use the floppy disk, network, modem etc., but this is not possible in the real life, without an exchange of data and program a computer will not be of much use.

Therefore, to prevent a virus infection one can take some precautions such as

Keep the floppy disk drive door open

Whenever the system is booted from a hard disk drive, if you have some disk in the floppy drive then keep the drives door open.

Keeping the door closed will give the boot sector virus from the floppy disk to become active. One can use a boot sector infected floppy disk to read and write data, but only when the system is booted using the infected floppy, even if it is not a bootable floppy, the virus will get a chance to become active.

Do not use pirated software

Pirated software, specially games and demonstration packages are one of the main carriers of the viruses.

Buy original software from the known dealers, this will keep your system virus free.

Get shareware for some reputed company/BBS

Shareware software should be obtained from some reputed dealer, well known BBS operator or directly from the program author. This again will reduce the chance of virus infecting your system.

Run virus scanner/checker program regularly

One should run the latest available virus scanner program regularly. DOS provides MSAV (Microsoft Anti Virus) program with the current version of DOS. This can be used to regularly check the system for any infection.

Also some other good virus scanning programs such as Nashot from Nash Systems, IAVT, SCAN from McAfee Associates, Norton Anti Virus from Norton etc. are available.

Use a memory resident anti virus program

Use some memory resident, TSR (terminate and stay resident) program, that can monitor different activities on the system and inform the user if any program tries a virus like activity such as directly writing to the FAT table, writing on track 0, formatting hard disk, trying to be memory resident etc.

Current version of DOS provides a TSR program for this purpose known as VSAFE. This program can be made memory resident and made to alert the user on different virus like activities.

Use write protect tab on the floppy disks

Always the floppy disks containing programs must have read only tabs on them. Also, if you are taking your data files on floppy to some other place for reading then put the read-only tabs on them because even if there is no executable program in them the boot sector of the floppy could become infected.

Always Keep current version of Anti-virus software

Everyday some new virus is made so, you cannot get a virus scanner, install it and forget about it. The old virus scanner may not recognize new viruses so always try to get the latest version of the scanner software. Keep the software uptodate by getting current version.

Backup the data regularly

Finally, even after all this precautions you may get infected. Therefore, whatever protection you follow, you must back up your important data regularly. This will help in the worst virus infection. You can always reformat and restore the data.

Watch out when you get a Service Engineer's visit

One main source of virus infection on many computers is the computer Service Engineers. These SE's carry diagnostic diskettes with them and uses it on many different systems. Most of the time these disks are not write protected. Even if these disks are write protected, sometime when they see some good utility on a system they copy it on their diskette. This gives the virus in the system a chance to infect these disks.

Later these infected diskettes spread the infection from one system to the next systems, wherever these disks are used.

Do not open e-mail attachments from unknown address

In this Internet era, the e-mail attachments are one of the biggest medium of virus infection. One should never open an e-mail attachment coming from unknown address. Even attachments from known addresses should be scanned with latest anti-virus software before opening it.

Take care when downloading files from Internet

When downloading files from the Internet is should be scanned properly. Download files from reputable web sites such as shareware.com, download.com, tucows.com etc.

Virus Infection Symptoms

Some of the very common symptoms shown by a system infected by a virus are given next.

Unexplained slowdown of the System

This is one main symptom of the virus infection. If the system without any apparent reason starts to take more time to load programs from the disk or starts to operate slower than its normal speed then you can suspect a virus infection.

Decrease in the amount of available memory

This is another symptom of virus infection. When checked with the CHKDSK, the system shows some KB of memory missing from the main memory or when checked with the MEM/D/P command, the memory module list shows some program resident in the memory without any proper module name.

Increase in Bad Sectors/Lost clusters etc.

When the number of bad sectors start increasing, or when the number of lost clusters reported by the SCANDISK or CHKDSK start increasing without any special reason them one main reason behind this could be a virus infection

Cannot Execute Executable Files

If you find that the executable files (.EXE, COM etc) which you were able to execute till yesterday start missing from the directories or when executing them you start getting some error messages then this again could be one major indication of the virus attack.

Screen Shows Some Unusual Outputs

Getting of some message such as "legalize marijuana" or dropping of letters to the bottom of the screen or some special character appearing or moving around on the screen or blank spots on the screen etc. could also be a symptom of virus infection.

Another indication could be some music being played by the computer without running any specific music program.

Drive's Light Turns On

The drive's light may turn on indicating that a read or write is taking place even when you have not given any read or write command, or when you have put a read only disk in the drive the system tries to write to the disk without any write command being issued are some other symptoms of virus infection.

Some software such as Windows keep temporary data on the disk and read and write to them periodically.

New ".COM" files appear for the ".EXE" files

This shows a companion type virus where the virus stays as a .COM file for and .EXE file. This gives the virus a chance to get executed because the DOS always executes the .COM file before executing a .EXE file if both the files are of same name.

Some DOS program and utility programs contain both .COM and .EXE file with the same name. For example, the DOS program MSD (Microsoft Diagnostic) contains both MSD.COM and MSD.EXE.

Anti-Virus Software

There are basically four type of anti-virus software, they are

- Checksum (CRC) Type
- TSR (Activity Monitor) Type and
- Scanner Type
- Program Screeners

Checksum Type

Viruses live in MBR, DBR or in executable files. Normally these MBR, DBR and executable files do not change, so an anti-virus program can check these places for virus infection by periodically checking for any change.

To check these places for a change, the virus checker program (for example the MSAV program) calculate CRC of each executable program and the MBR and DBR location and store them in some place on the hard disk drive.

CRC is a checksum calculated by the virus scanner by reading each character of the file and then returning a unique 16-bit or 32-bit number for that file.

Every time the file is checked by the scanner the CRC is again calculated and checked with the original CRC value, any change in the file will produce a different CRC and some virus program can be suspected for this change.

Some program such as WS, Norton Editor (NE) etc. keep the configuration information in themselves, in this type of programs whenever the configuration is changed the CRC value also changes. Therefore, a changed CRC does not always mean that a program has become infected

TSR (Activity Monitor) Type

TSRs anti-virus programs monitor system activity and flag any suspicious program behavior. This virus scanner stays memory resident and checks all the program being executed for a virus like activity, such as directly writing into FAT table, writing on track 0, formatting hard disk, trying to be memory resident by a program etc.

Any such activity is immediately informed to the user by these monitor programs and normally user is provided with the option to let the offending program continue, if it is a valid activity such as formatting a disk by the user, or to stop the offending program from continuing the operation.

Scanner Type

These anti-virus programs contain information about the virus-strain (special 10- to 16- bytes long character patterns specific to each virus) of all the known viruses.

A virus scanner searches for a virus by matching this character pattern string with the programs on the disk being scanned. Any match found could indicate a virus infection.

This method has two drawbacks:

- One is the special character pattern being used to look for the virus could also exist on some legitimate software code, this will give a false virus infection message, although the chance of this is very-very small.
- Another drawback of this method is, one must always keep the virus signature file uptodate. Otherwise, the scanner will not be able to detect the new viruses that keep on appearing.

Program Screeners (Intelligent Rule Based)

To overcome the second problem faced with the virus scanners an intelligent rule based program screeners are used in many of the current virus scanners. These scanning programs look for some virus like piece of code in the programs being scanned. By virus like code, we mean piece of program code to reformat the hard disk, write to sector 0, corrupt the FAT, display "formatting", "Killing" etc. on the screen etc.

If any of virus like code is found in the program being scanned, these scanners inform the user and wait for the user response to take proper action.

What to do After Infection?

Once the system becomes infected with virus, your first aim should be to recover as much as important data as possible. Next, you should try to remove the infection from the system.

If the virus cannot be removed them you can delete the infected file, format the drive unconditionally, so that no undelete information is saved or you can low-level format the drive to remove any trace of the virus.

If the virus has infected MBR, DBR or some executable programs then you can recover from this by using the methods explained below

Before doing any of these procedures turn the machine off, to remove any trace of the virus from the memory. Do not do a warm boot by pressing Ctrl+Alt+Del keys, some of the viruses can remain active in the memory after this warm boot.

Recovering from a Boot Sector or MBR Virus

The Boot sector and the MBR viruses are easy to remove as you can overwrite their code with the original MBR or DBR code.

To overwrite the virus infected DBR code, boot from a clean DOS disk in A: drive and using a write protected, clean DOS disk, give

```
SYS C:
```

command. This command will copy the system to C: drives DBR and overwrite the COMMAND.COM on the C: drives root drive with a clean copy.

You can also use the Norton DISKTOOL program's make a disk bootable option to overwrite the infected DBR with a clean DBR.

The virus from the MBR can be removed using the

```
FDISK/MBR
```

command after booting the system with a clean write protected DOS diskette. This command will overwrite the infected MBR code with a clean MBR code.

Recovering from a .COM or .EXE File Virus

Best way to recover from the file infector viruses is to boot the system from a clean write protected DOS diskette and then overwrite the infected program with the programs on the original program disks. Make sure that these original diskettes are write protected before you use them.

Many of the virus scanner programs can also remove some of the viruses from a .COM or .EXE program.

Check the entire executable program thoroughly using the latest version of a good virus scanner utility, any program with virus will again spread the infection to all the programs.

Keep One or More Emergency Disk Ready

To recover from a virus infection you will require a clean boot disk with all the drivers used to access your drive and a good set of anti-virus software.

Also, keep a backup of the MBR, DBR and the CMOS information of your system on a floppy disk, it could be useful to return the system to "before infection" status.

Keep the DOS commands such as AUTOEXEC.BAT, CONFIG.SYS, FDISK, FORMAT, SYS, DEBUG, SCANDISK, DEFRAG, MSAV, VSAFE, MSD, UNDELETE, UNFORMAT etc. on some write-protected floppy disk.

Keep another write-protected disk with a low-level format and setup program such as Disk Manager, utility programs such as Norton utilities, PCTools etc.

After Recovery

Once the virus is removed from the system, you need to do some data recovery. The virus might have destroyed some data, deleted some files, or corrupted the FAT (File Allocation Table) etc.

Run the SCANDISK or CHKDSK program to find out if any lost clusters or some other logical error exists on the drive. Convert any lost cluster into file and check these files (FILExxxx.CHK) for any useful data.

Some Common Virus Myths

- Virus Can Destroy all data on the disk
- If a file is damaged it must be some virus infection
- Virus can hide in data file
- Data Backup after virus infection is useless
- Read/Only files are safe from virus
- Write protected floppies can be infected by virus
- Anti-virus software or hardware can protect from all viruses

MultiMedia

Currently one of the main use of computer is in the field of multimedia. Especially in the home segment computer is mainly used to play video games, watch CD/DVD movies, play MP3 and other audio files etc. In this section we look at some of the components of a multimedia computer.

To qualify as a multimedia computer, a basic computer configuration needs the following additional components

- Sound Card, Speakers
- CD-ROM/DVD
- One can also add a TV tuner card, and a video capture board.

A Multimedia computer is mainly used for the following applications:

- Playing Video Games, with the complex, realistic graphics and audio.
- For Education, with full-screen video, interactive animation, and so on.
- For communications through multimedia e-mail, Internet audio phone, video phone etc.
- Interactive, high-resolution television and movie viewing.
- For fast and easy capture, editing, and playback of audio/video.
- For connection with consumer-electronics devices for providing surround audio such as Dolby Digital for games and DVD movies.

Multimedia Computer

The following sections provide guidelines for what to look for in a multimedia system. A multimedia computer should consist of the following:

- At least 2GHz Pentium-4 processor, or equivalent CPU. The CPU should support the demands of rich multimedia and Internet access requirement.
- Minimum 256-KB Level 2 (L2) cache.
- System memory (RAM) minimum 128MB, 256MB or higher is recommended.
- Memory should be high speed SDRAM or better.
- System bus (FSB) speed 400MHz, 800MHz recommended.

- 7200-RPM 80GB HDD, Serial ATA or Ultra ATA-133 interface recommended.
- 64MB, AGP-4X, 3D Graphics adapter.
- Adapter/Monitor should support screen resolutions 640 x 480, 800 x 600, and 1024 x 768 x [8, 15, 16] bpp, 1280 x 1024, 1600 x 1200, 1920x1080, 1920 x 1200,1920 x 1440,2048 x 1536 at 32 bpp color depth.
- Monitor at least 17inch, 19inch is better.
- Two USB ports to support connection of auxiliary input devices, such as game pads, joysticks, track balls etc.
- Two IEEE 1394/FireWire ports to support camcorders and other digital consumer electronics devices.
- CD-R/RW, or DVD/CD combo writer.
- Keyboards, pointing devices, and game pads and their connections compliant with the USB Device version 1.0 or higher.
- 56K V.90 Data/fax/voice modem.

Audio Support

Following are some key features to look for when purchasing a multimedia computer with high-quality audio :

- A sound card with a minimum 16-bit digital-to-analog converter (DAC) for playback and a 16-bit analog-to-digital converter (ADC) for recording.
- Full-duplex support to record and play sounds at the same time.
- Audio hardware supporting CD-ROM and DVD media playback.
- Audio hardware featuring the acceleration supporting 3-D games.
- Speaker with separate subwoofer.

Audio system providing support for basic data formats. The audio system must provide full-duplex support of the following audio formats:

- Mono/stereo
- 8-bit unsigned
- 16-bit signed

Audio system support for recording and playback at 8, 11.025, 16, 22.05, 44.1, and 48 kHz waveforms. CD quality sound uses 44 kHz.

Audio system with sufficient externally accessible inputs and outputs. At a minimum, the audio system must have the following features:

- A microphone input, stereo line input, or both
- Stereo line-level output

Currently you get very good quality 24-bit, 96kHz, 3D, 5.1 channel "surround sound" sound cards at a very affordable prices.

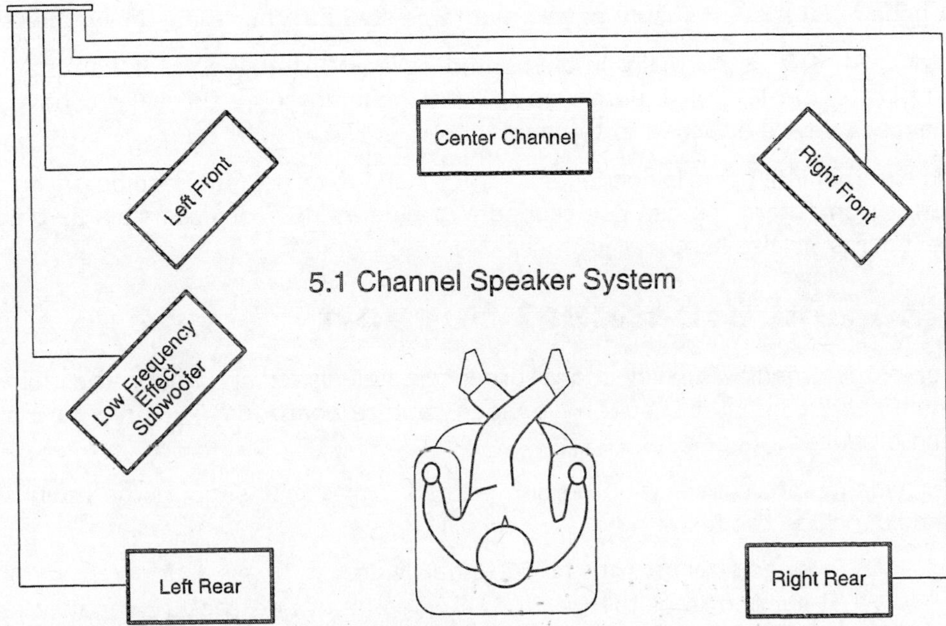

Fig. 19-1 : 5.1 Channel Speaker System.

5.1 Channel Speaker System

5.1 is a generic description of a multi-channel sound system. All of these surround sound types use 5.1 channel decoding to provide surround sound. The 5.1 channels are as follows:

- Left Front
- Right Front
- Center Channel
- Left Rear
- Right Rear
- Low Frequency Effect Subwoofer

MIDI Support

A multimedia computer's sound card should include general MIDI support.

General MIDI system assigns numbers to each kind of instrument, so that, for example, instrument 10 on one computer is the same as instrument 10 on all others.

Support for at least 32-voice polyphony (Polyphony is the ability to play multiple sounds at the same time.) Support for more simultaneous sounds provides a fuller sounding playback.

A good MIDI system should have wave table sound rather than FM synthesis.

Standard MIDI is normally implemented as an MPU-401 port. If you play a MIDI stream to the MPU-401 port, you will not hear anything unless you have a MIDI playback device attached to the port.

An external MIDI port is needed only if you have external MIDI equipment to connect to the computer. You can use this port to plug in MIDI devices such as piano-style keyboards; it also supports joysticks.

Video and Broadcast Support

For a multimedia PC, video and broadcast television are important elements. A multimedia computer should have video capture board and TV tuner card for video and broadcast support.

For video capture, television output, and DVD playback support the multimedia PC should include the following:

- DVD-Video support with MPEG-2 hardware.
- WDM support implemented for all video input and capture capabilities.
- Support for NTSC/PAL, or both types of television output.
- Hardware-assisted DirectDraw acceleration, Direct3D acceleration, and video playback.

Connecting Soundcard

- Connecting a soundcard to the computer system is like connecting any other PCI card, which is explained in detail, in previous sections.
- Once the card is installed, start the system and install proper drivers.
- Connect the speaker and microphone to their respective connectors.
- If you want, you can connect sound board output into your stereo system. Just connect an unused input of your stereo system to the output of your sound board, auxiliary output is best, but the speaker output will also work.

File Name Ext. of Some Multimedia Files

File Format	File Name Extension
Video for Windows	.avi
Waveform-audio	.wav
Moving Picture (MPEG)	.mpg
Quick Time for Windows	.mov
Musical Instrument Digital Interface (MIDI)	.mid
MP3 Audio File	.mp3

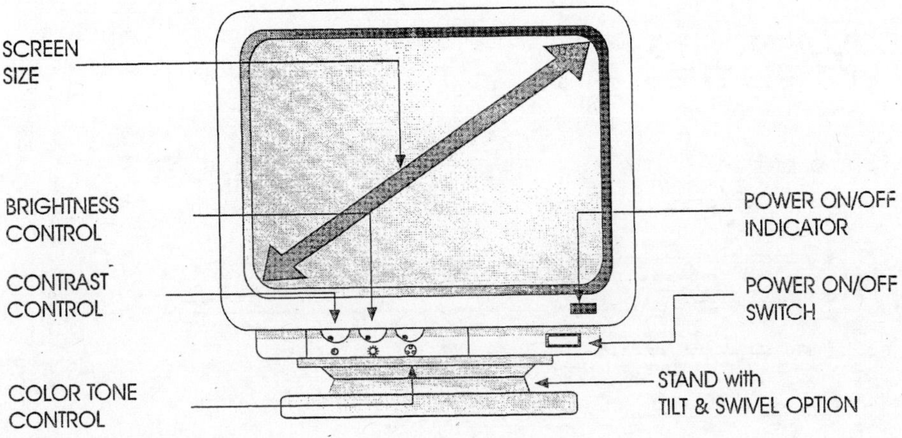

Fig. 19-2 : Monitor.

Monitor

Monitor or the VDU (Visual Display Unit), a Television like output device is used to show the result of any processing done by the computer. Result of an operation can be shown as text, numbers, or graphic image such as a charts, graphs, figures etc.

The monitor is available in many different sizes. Like B&W and Color TVs, monitors are available in multicolor and in single-color (Monochrome).

The size of the monitor is measured diagonally , a common monitor size is 15 inch, but for designing and desktop publishing (DTP) purposes 17 inch or bigger monitor is preferred.

A good quality monitor should have anti-glare coating, to reduce the reflection which makes the viewing difficult in brightly lit room, it must also have stand with tilt and swivel option to adjust the viewing angle.

Most of the monitors provide control on the front panel or as OSD (On Screen Display) to adjust the brightness, contrast, color, horizontal and vertical size of the image, horizontal and vertical position of the image, and to correct pincushion or barrel distortions.

How Monitor Works?

Characters and images appear on screen by illuminating small dots on the display screen. These dots are called picture elements or pixels. On a color monitor each pixel is made up of a red green and blue color phosphor dots.

The coating inside a color monitor consists of tiny dots of different phosphors that emit red, green or blue light when hit and energized by the electron beam.

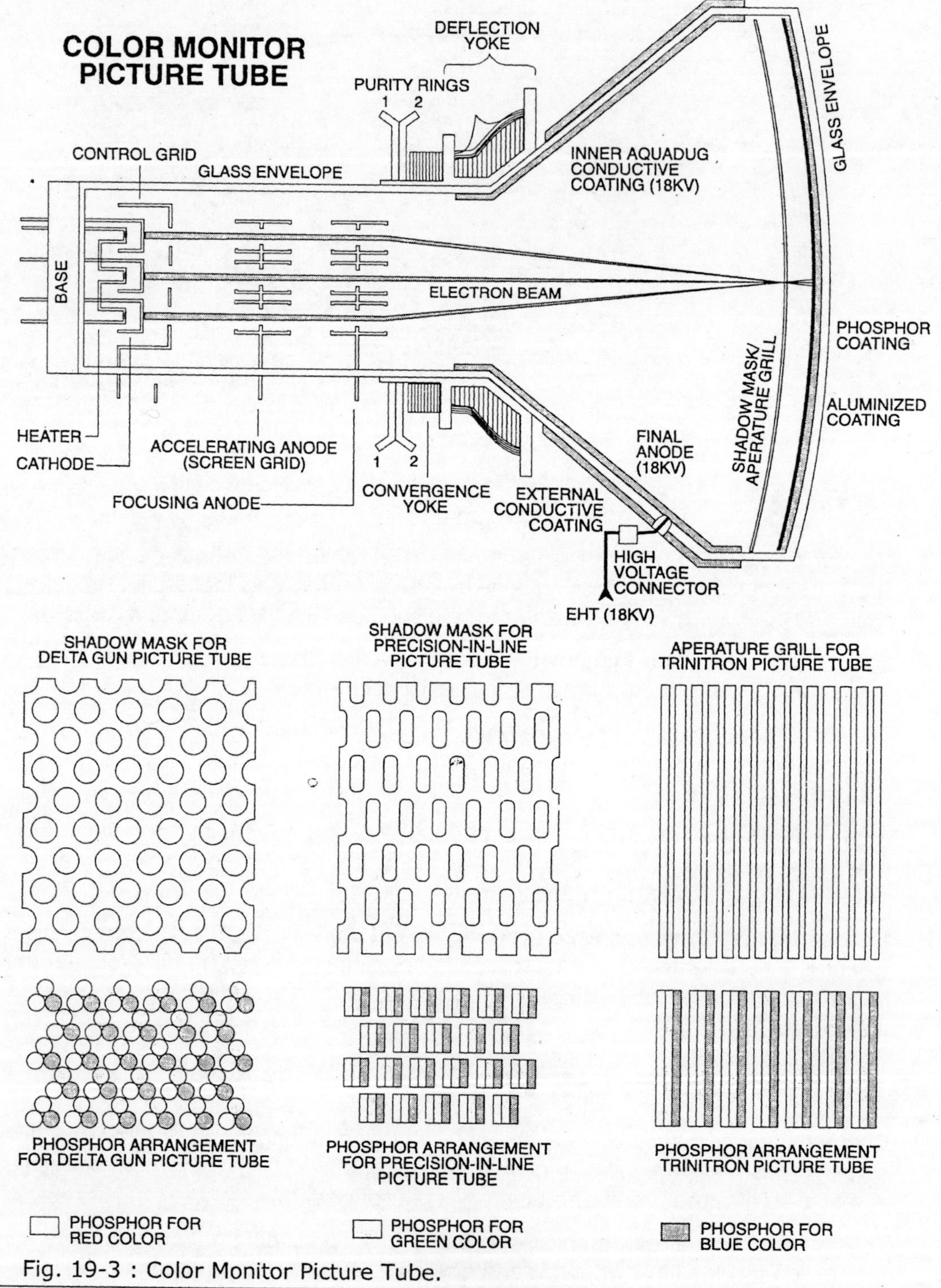

Fig. 19-3 : Color Monitor Picture Tube.

These red green and blue dots are illuminated in different intensities to get a color pixel on the screen. The color monitor contains three electron guns, one for each dot. When the beam strikes a dot, based on the beam intensity, the dot glows in various intensity.

The phosphor has "persistence", which means it keeps radiating light after the electron beam has moved on. The scan rate and persistence together make the user sees a steady, flicker-free image.

To display an entire screen image, the electron gun repeatedly scans the monitor surface, illuminating the pixels. This scanning takes place across and down the screen.

With each scan, different intensity beams strike red,green and blue phosphor dots of a pixel and generate a complete picture by scanning the complete screen surface.

To maintain the screen image, the phosphor dots are continuously refreshed by the electron beams. The speed at which the monitor screen is refreshed is known as "vertical refresh rate". Common vertical refresh rate range from 50 - 120 Hertz.

Hertz is a unit of number of times an operation is performed per second. If the screen is refreshed 80 times per second then the refresh rate is 80 Hertz or 80Hz.

Monitor resolution is the number of pixels (rows and columns) the monitor can display on the screen. The higher the screen resolution, the sharper the screen image will appear.

The image sharpness also depends on the dot pitch of the monitor. Dot pitch is the distance between successive pixels. The smaller the dot pitch, the sharper the image will appear. A good monitor should have 0.28mm or less dot pitch.

A monochrome monitor needs three signals to produce a display, horizontal synchronization (HSYNC) to tell it when a scan line is about to begin, vertical synchronization (VSYNC) to tell when the display is going to start at the top of the screen and VIDEO which switches the electron beam ON and OFF. In practice, a fourth signal (intensity) selects whether the displayed dots are dim or bright.

In a color monitor instead of a single VIDEO signal, three different signals RED, GREEN and BLUE switch on/off three different electron beams to generate a color image.

These signals are generated by the display adapter.

How image is displayed on monitor?

CPU sends the text or image that is to be displayed to the monitor to the video adapter. The video adapter converts this information into a format that can be displayed on the monitor and sends this to the monitor.

On a color monitor this signal coming from adapter is given to the three electron guns located at the back of monitor picture tube.

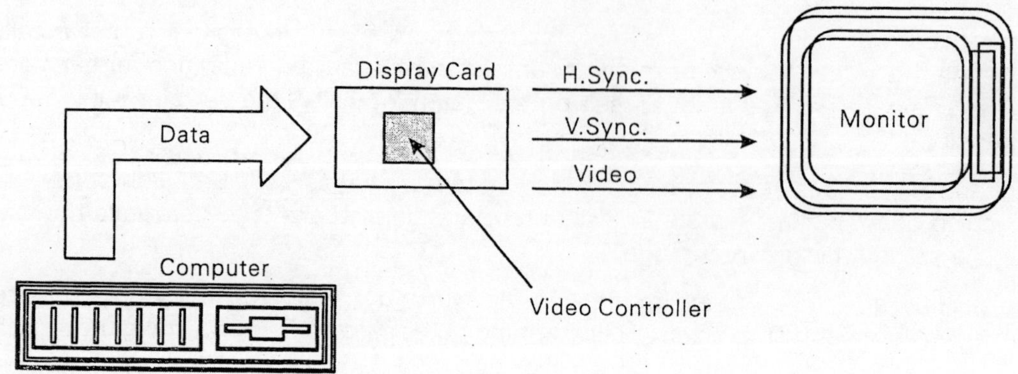

Fig. 19-4 : Image from Computer to Monitor.

These electron gun shoot out a stream of electron beams, one beam for each of the read, green and blue phosphor dots. The intensity of each beam is controlled by the signal from the display adapter.

The adapter also sends signal to the focus and aim mechanism at the neck of picture tube. This mechanism sweep the electron beam across the display screen and also focus them to their respective phosphor dots.

The electron beam sweeps the screen surface from top to bottom, from left to right.

When this electron beam strike the phosphor coating, inside the screen, based on the intensity of beams these phosphor emit different intensity of light.

By changing the electron beam intensity, the intensity of light emitted by these phosphors can be changed. A combination of different intensity of red, green and blue color can create different colors on the display.

The screen resolution, number of colors displayed on screen and display speed depends on the video adapter being used.

Display Memory

A video board's memory requirements are determined by two things: its resolution and the number of colors that it can display.

The math for finding the amount of memory required to display a color graphics screen is straightforward. Simply multiply the number of pixels on the screen—that is, the resolution—by the bit-depth of each pixel, then divide the result by eight to translate bits into bytes.

For example, a VGA graphics screen (640 x 480 pixels) comprises of total 307,200 pixels (that's 640 pixels times 480 pixels). With a bit depth of four (allowing 2^4 = 16 colors on the screen), the minimum memory required is 307,200 x 4 = 1,228,800 bits. Divided by eight, that equates to 153,600 bytes.

The next highest standard increment of memory is 256K, so you'd need 256K of RAM to store a 16-color 640 x 400 pixel VGA image.

Display Memory Required for Given Resolution and Color Depth (in Bytes)

Resolution	Mono	16 colors	256 colors	High Color	TrueColor
Bits per pixel	1	4	8	16	24
Bytes per pixel	0.125	0.5	1	2	3
640x480	38,400	153,600	307,200	614,400	921,600
800x600	60,000	240,000	480,000	960,000	1,440,000
1024x768	98,304	393,216	786,432	1,572,864	2,359,296
1280x1024	163,840	655,360	1,310,720	2,621,440	3,932,160
1600x1200	240,000	960,000	1,920,000	3,840,000	5,760,000
1920x1440	345,600	1,382,400	2,764,800	5,529,600	8,294,400
2048x1536	393,216	1,572,864	3,145,728	6,291,456	9,437,184

Current motherboards contain the display adapter on the motherboard itself. For example, motherboard using Intel 810 chipset contains AGP graphics controller on the motherboard.

This board also allows the display adapter to use the system's main memory (RAM) as display memory.

Interlacing

Information on a monitor is displayed by an electron gun scanning the phosphor inside of the display. The gun scans from top to bottom, left to right with each complete scan displaying a "frame".

The gun works like a thin beam of spray paint, coating the inside of your monitor.

In order to avoid a flickering image, some display adapters force the monitor to create an interlaced image. Instead of the electron gun scanning from top to bottom in a continuous manner, on the first pass it will skip every next line. On the second pass, it will scan the lines it missed during the first time, thus creating the full image in two scans instead of one.

Non-interlaced Display

It is the opposite of interlaced display, i.e., all the lines are scanned or displayed in one pass instead of the two passes required in the interlaced display.

Video Bandwidth

It is the highest input frequency a monitor can handle and helps in determining the resolution capabilities of the monitor. It is measured in megahertz (MHz, one million cycles per second). If the bandwidth of input signal exceeds the given range of a monitor, it may cause compatibility problems and you may not get proper image on screen.

The higher the value, the better is the image. This frequency range is factor determining the resolution of the monitor.

The bandwidth does not represent the exact frequency at which the data is transferred instead it indicates the range in which the monitor can operate most optimally.

In order to find out the minimum bandwidth required by a monitor to achieve a resolution, you must know the number of pixels and the frame rate related with that particular standard of display.

Bandwidth is the product of the total number of horizontal and vertical pixels and the frame rate, assuming each pixel is produced by a single signal pulse.

Bandwidth = horizontal pixel x vertical pixel x frame rate

for a 600 by 400 display if the frame rate is 25, bandwidth will be 5,760,000 or 5.7 MHz., actual bandwidth may slightly be higher than this (allowing for retrace time).

Synchronizing Signals

The electron beam in the monitor is spread across the screen by a combination of magnetic fields. One of the field moves the electron beam horizontally while the other moves it vertically.

Circuitry in the monitor supplies a steadily increasing voltage to two sets of deflection coils to control the spreading of electron beam.

These coils are electromagnets and the increasing voltage causes the field strength of the coils to increase and deflect the electron beam farther.

At the end of line, the field that controls the horizontal spreading of electron beam is instantly switched OFF, returning the beam to the starting side of the screen.

Similarly, when the beam reaches the bottom of the screen, the field controlling the vertical spreading of electron beam is switched OFF, returning the beam to the top of the screen.

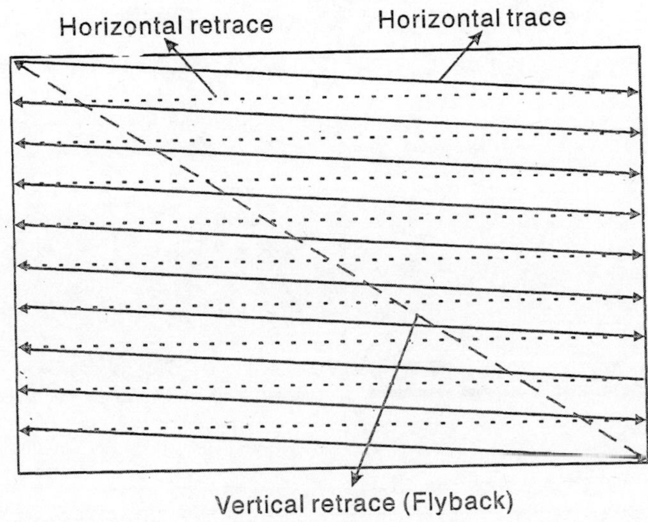

Fig. 19-5 : Horizontal and Vertical Scanning.

The result is that the electron beam follows a tightly packed zigzag path from the top of the screen to the bottom and again to top to repeat this path.

Horizontal Scanning Frequency

The frequency at which the monitor repaints the horizontal lines that make up a single line of the image is called horizontal scanning frequency.

Horizontal scanning frequency is measured in kHz and is standardized at 31.5kHz for a VGA. For SuperVGA, this frequency ranges from 35kHz to 48kHz, depending on the refresh rate of the video adapter.

If your resolution is 800 x 600 i.e. if you have 600 lines per screen, and to avoid flicker if you show 30 frames per second (frame rate is 30). You will be showing 18,000 lines per second or you can say your horizontal scanning frequency is 18,000 Hz (Hertz) or 18 kHz (Kilo Hertz, one thousand cycles per second).

Vertical Scanning Frequency

The frequency at which the monitor repaints the whole screen, sometimes also known as the vertical refresh rate, is called the vertical scanning frequency.

This is measured in Hz (numbers of cycles per second), and higher rates associate with less flicker. VGA has a vertical scanning frequency of 60 to 70Hz and SuperVGA vary from the VESA guidelines of 56Hz (which is about the minimum tolerable) and 60Hz, to the official recommended standard of 72Hz (it means that screen should be redrawn 72 times per second).

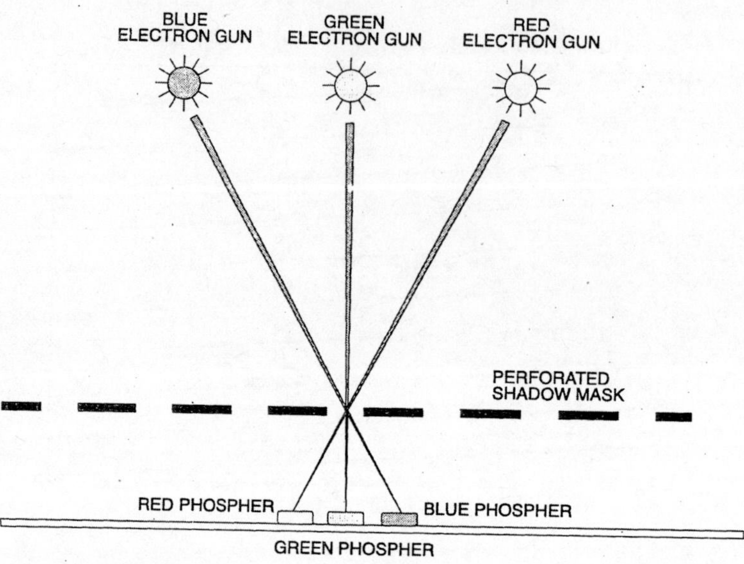

Fig. 19-6 : Shadow Mask.

Several hundred horizontal lines are drawn for each vertical frame. vertical frequency is also known as frame rate of the system because, one complete image frame is created every time the beam spreads from top to bottom.

The electronics generating the spreading frequencies used by a monitor are inside the monitor itself. However, signals themselves must be synchronized with the data coming from the computer so that the characters appear at their proper positions on the screen.

In order to keep things organized, the video controller sends out special synchronizing signals, i.e., horizontal sync before each line is send to display and similarly vertical sync before each frame is send.

Shadow Mask

A finely perforated metal grid called a shadow mask or aperture grill is placed inside picture tube, just in front of the phosphor. It ensures that the electrons from each beam hit only the dots for which they are intended. Thus the red beam energizes only red dots and so on.

To produce a color pixel just pointing the electron beam at the right dots is not enough because part of the beam will spill over and hit the other dots in the triad. The result of this spillover is a loss of color purity (bright hues become muddied).

To prevent this effect and make images as sharp and colorful as possible, all color CRTs use a shadow mask (a metal sheet with fine perforations in it). It is located inside the display tube at a small distance behind the phosphor coating of the screen.

The shadow mask and the phosphor coating on the CRT screen are critically arranged so that through the shadow mask the red electron beam can hit red color phosphor only. The other two colors of dots are in "shadow" of the mask and cannot be seen by the electron beam i.e. why we call it shadow mask.

The spacing of holes in the shadow mask, to a great degree determines the quality of the displayed image. For the spacing of the system to work properly, phosphor dots on the CRT screen must be spaced at the same distance as the holes in mask.

Since the hole spacing determine the dot spacing, it is often termed the dot-pitch of the CRT, the term for slotted tubes is slot-pitch. (CRTs with in-line gun or Trinitron gun use slots rather than holes in the mask to achieve the same result).

The dot-pitch or slot-pitch of a CRT is simply a measurement of the distance between dots or slots. This measurement is independent of the size of the tube or the size of the displayed image.

Closely looking at the screen of a color monitor, you can see the shadow mask behind it. If you can see the holes in the mask, they are most likely .40mm or larger. On the other hand, if you cannot see the holes on the mask then they are likely .30mm or smaller.

Slot Mask (Aperture Grille)

Also known as aperture grille, it is a series of vertical wires held tightly in a frame to align the electron beams. They have the same function as shadow mask but achieve it in a better way. This technology was introduced by Sony Corporation. Aperture grille based monitor produce brighter and sharper image.

Screen Size and Image Size

Most computer displays are rated by their screen size. As with television sets, measurement of the cathode ray tube (CRT or picture tube) in a computer monitor is made diagonally across its face.

Two monitors with the same size of screen may have entirely different on-screen image sizes. Actual image size that is displayed rather than screen size should be taken into account when comparing monitors.

Aspect Ratio

In computer graphics the width-to-height ratio of an image or computer screen is known as the "aspect ratio". A ratio of 2:1 indicate that the width is twice the height.

Aspect ratio become important in preventing distortion when an image is resized or incorporated into another software. Standard television has an aspect ration of 4:3, where width is 4 and height is 3.

Video Cards / Display Card

A computer and a monitor without any video display card attached to it is of no use for you. A display adapter or a video card is a must for transferring data that is to be displayed on the screen, from the CPU to the monitor.

VGA (Video Graphics Array) display card and AGP based display card are the standard display for current computers.

VGA (Video Graphics Array)

VGA stands for Video Graphics Array, it was a high-color and high-resolution graphics adapter built into IBM's PS/2 computers, introduced in 1987.

With the introduction of VGA, one could still run applications written for earlier display standards, however, you could not use the same monitor. The only monitor capable of handling the vertical and horizontal frequencies set by the new VGA standard is the multiscanning monitor and VGA monitor.

VGA offers more graphics, more colors and highest resolution of any graphics adapter before it. It has a lot of features and flexibility. As far as graphics mode is concerned, VGA is very versatile. It is fully compatible with MDA, CGA, EGA etc.

Pin Configuration of VGA Display Adapter Cable

(Female 15-Pin D-Subminiature, Cable requires male)

Pin No.	Function
1	Red Video
2	Green Video
3	Blue Video
4	Monitor ID bit-2
5	Ground
6	Red Return (Ground)
7	Green Return (Ground)
8	Blue Return (Ground)
9	Composite Sync.
10	Sync. Return (Ground)
11	Monitor ID bit-0
12	Monitor ID bit-1
13	Horiz. Sync.
14	Vert. Sync.
15	Reserved

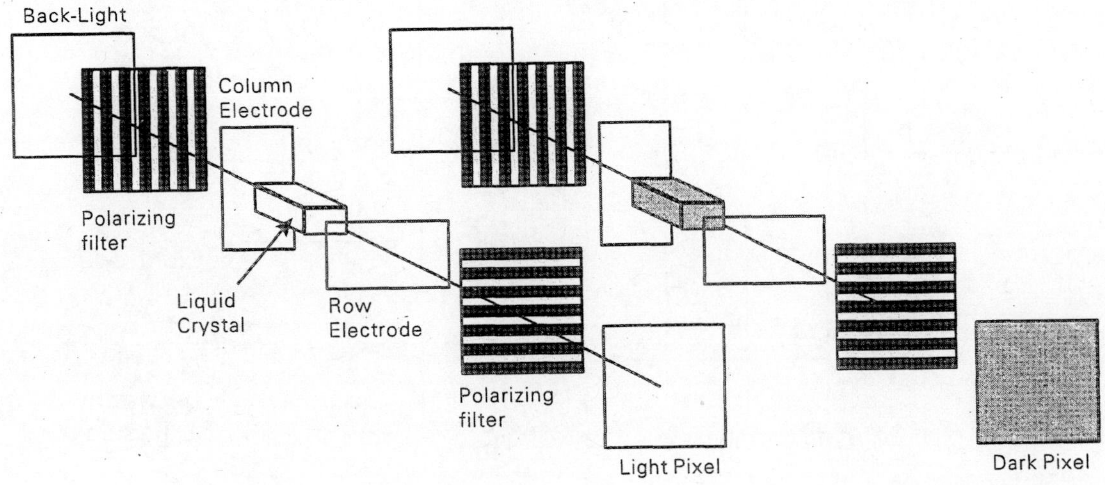

Fig. 19-7 : Working of LCD Display.

Special Purpose Monitors

CRT monitors are too big and heavy and consume too much current for laptop computers. Therefore, laptops use liquid crystal display (LCD) or gas plasma display that are light and draw little current.

LCD Display

LCD's are familiar from there use in digital watch and calculators.

In it each pixel is an individual solid-state device, addressable by row and column coordinates.

In an LCD display each pixel is filled with a transparent material called liquid crystal, when energy is supplied, the liquid crystal material becomes polarized (i.e., it will pass/reflect light of a certain polarity only) and appear darker than its background or becomes opaque. In order to improve the contrast LCD's are usually back-lit or edge-lit. Still they are sometimes difficult to read at an angle or in bright sunlight.

Working of LCD

In an LCD panel a light source is used to produce light at the background.

That light is passed through a polarizing filter (polarizing filter allows light vibrating in only one direction to pass).

Polarized light passes through a liquid crystal sandwiched between transparent column and row electrodes.

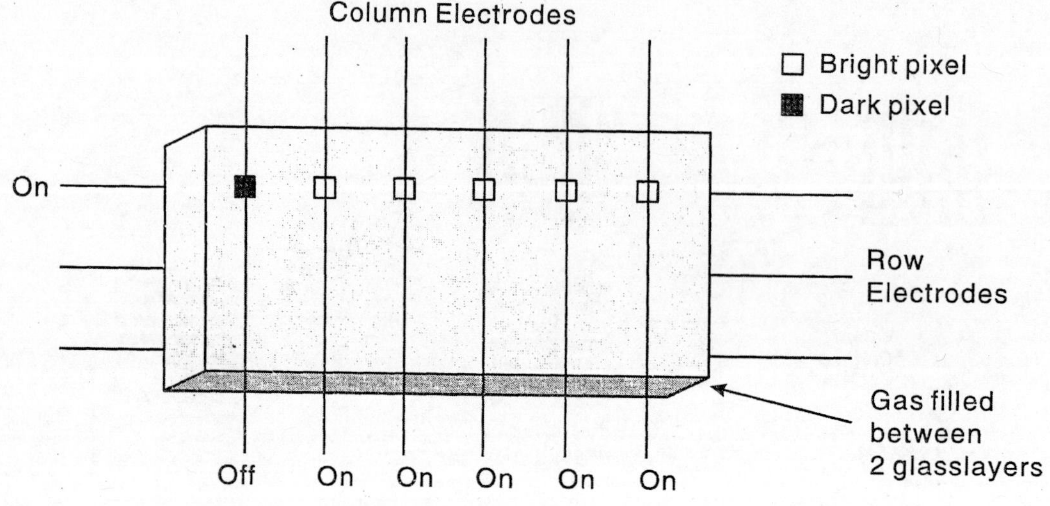

Fig. 19-8 : Gas Plasma Display Panel.

When current is passing through electrodes the molecules of the liquid crystal twist and they rotate incoming light by 90 degree.

Next we have another polarizing filter which is in 90 degree to the first filter.

So, if light coming out of first filter is turned by 90 degree then only they can pass through second filter and show on display as a bright pixel.

If you do not apply any current to electrode, liquid crystal would not rotate incoming light and pass them as it is.

The second filter will block that light and you get a dark or black pixel on display.

Gas-Plasma Display

Gas-plasma display also use individually addressable pixels. Each element is infect a tiny fluorescent light containing a neon or neon-argon mixture gas between sandwich of glass, which glows when it is energized by applying sufficient voltage at the intersection of electrodes.

Gas-plasma displays produce an orange-red, brighter and sharper picture in comparison to the LCD's, but, require much more current and hence they are mainly used in portable computers which run on AC power.

Being solid state, LCD and plasma display are reliable and rugged. Sometimes when a display driver circuit fails, makes horizontal and vertical row of pixels either dark or light permanently. The only solution to this is replacing the screen.

Installing Display Adapter

The method of installing a new display card or replacing the old display card is as given below.

1. Switch off the system and remove PC's cover.
2. Remove the monitor cable attached with the display card and remove old card if you are upgrading.
3. Set dip switch, jumper etc. of new card.
4. Press down the new card in a proper slot (PCI, AGP etc.).
5. Attach monitor cable to the display card.
6. Switch on the system and test the display card.

   If nothing is seen on the monitor, check whether the monitor is properly plugged in and is switched on, as most of the monitor have a power switch of their own. Also make sure that the brightness/contrast on the monitor is set to proper value.

   If you hear some squeaking sound or smell or see smoke, switch off the monitor immediately.
7. If everything is OK, close the case.
8. Setup Computer and all the software you have, for the new card.

Monitor Care

Monitors attract a lot of dust, and you may find finger prints and other mess on the display. To clean the monitor

- Switch off your monitor and computer.
- To clean your monitor, dip a towel into some soap water. Squeeze water from the towel or the water may drip inside monitor and short-circuit its circuits.
- Now softly clean monitor surface.

Preventing Phosphor Burn-In In Monitors

Leaving your monitor on all the time leads to something called phosphor burn-in and after sometime, the same image becomes "etched" on the screen. This happens because displaying the same image for a period of time burns up the phosphor lining inside your display. To avoid phosphor burn-in, turnoff your monitor when you are not using the PC.

Another way to avoid phosphor burn-in is to use a screen saver software. These special programs blank the screen after a given amount of time, usually when you haven't touched the keyboard or mouse for a predefined time.

Windows contains its own screen saver. You can find it by clicking on Start, Settings, Control Panel and double clicking on Display Properties.

CD-ROM Drive

This acronym CD-ROM stands for Compact Disk Read Only Memory and it is pronounced "See Dee Rom". A CD-ROM drive can read an optical read-only CD-ROM disk. The CD-ROM disk is a very high capacity disk which can store about 600 million characters or roughly 300,000 pages of text.

A CD-ROM disk is mainly used to store permanent information that does not require any change, such as encyclopedia, dictionary, graphic image etc.

Currently many of the software packages are also being distributed on the CD-ROM disks. This saves the user from keeping a large number of floppy disk and also reduces the time required to shuffle 30-40 disk when copying/installing the software from the floppy disk to the hard disk.

The original CD-ROM were read only media i.e. they can be used only for reading purpose, no changes can be made on the stored data, but recently many different technologies have come up to make CD-R and CR-RW media and device, using which one can write the data as well as read the data from these optical storage devices.

If one has a CD Drive in his computer system, then that drive can be used to play music by putting normal Audio CDs in them and also one can watch movies by putting Video CDs in the same CD Drive.

How CD-ROM Drive Works?

CD-ROM are small, mirror like disk, just like audio compact discs. From the CD-ROM, data is retrieved using laser beam. A CD-ROM can store about 640MB of data in digital format.

A CD-ROM is read only medium, one cannot erase or change the data stored on a CD-ROM. Let us now see how is the data stored on a CD is read.

When the CD is placed on the tray and the tray is closed, the CD drive starts rotating CD. A laser beam optical assembly moves in and out under the CD, reading the data stored on the CD surface.

To read the information stored on the CD surface, the optical assembly sends a concentrated beam of laser light to the CD surface. This laser light is focused on the CD surface by a focusing coil on the optical assembly.

This laser beam pass through the clear plastic coating on the CD surface and strike the layer that has the data stored on it.

Data is stored on the CD in a form of flat areas called "Land" and small depressions called "Pit". These Land and Pit are used to store binary 1 and 0.

Light that strike a land is reflected directly back to the optical assembly. Light that hit the pit gets scattered and will not be received back by the optical assembly.

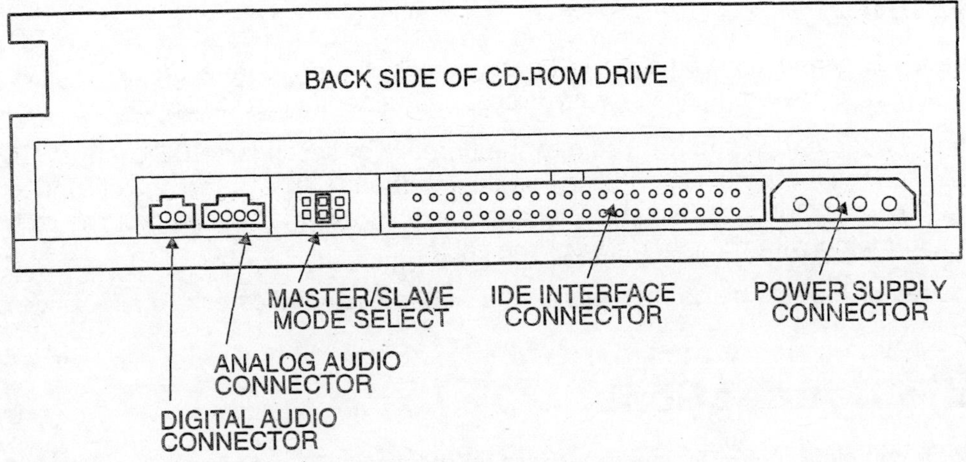

Fig. 19-9 : Connectors at the back of CD-ROM Drive.

The light received back by the optical assembly is given to a light sensing diode inside the assembly.

Each pulse of light that strike the light sensing diode generates a small eiectrical voltage. These voltages are matched against a timing signal to generate a stream of 1s and 0s. These 1s and 0s are then given to the computer for further processing

CD-ROM Installation

The CD ROM players is mainly connected to the IDE (actually the AT Attachment Packet Interface, ATAPI) connector on the motherboard, the same connector to which the Hard Disk Drive is connected. Some external CD-ROM models use the parallel or USB interface.

Some older CD-ROM models, had proprietary connections, but currently only IDE or SCSI based players are available.

IDE or ATAPI is now the main interface for both CD and DVD drives. The IDE-based CD drives are the easiest to install and are also very cheap.

Most CD-ROM players require three connections:

- one for control and data,
- one for audio, and
- one for power.

For control and data, CD drives use the same interfaces as the hard disk drives.

ATAPI/IDE

The ATAPI connection combines low cost and easy wiring. Connecting a CD drive using the ATA/IDE system is a very easy process. One needs just a IDE cable.

Connect one end of the IDE cable to the primary or secondary IDE channel (IDE1 or IDE2) on the motherboard and connect the other end to the data/control connector on the CD drive. Only one thing you need to make sure is that he pin-1 of the connector should match with the pin-1 side of the cable.

The red or blue stripe on the edge of the ribbon cable indicates the pin-1 side of the cable.

Audio Connections

When you play audio CD the digital data on the audio CD get transformed by digital to analog conversion circuitry built into the CD drive itself.

To transport this analog signal to the sound board, CD drives provide a separate shielded audio cable.

Connect one end of this audio cable to the audio out connector provided at the back of the CD drive and connect the other end of the cable to the CD-in connector provided on your sound board or the motherboard (if the audio is built in the motherboard).

If this cable is not connected then one would not be able to hear output from audio CDs, MP3 CDs and audio from video CDs which is processed by the CPU will provide audio output without any problem, even if this cable is not connected.

Power Connections

CD ROM drive requires an electrical connection to power its circuitry and motors. The same four-pin Molex connector, which is used to provide power to the hard disk drive is used to provide power to the CD-ROM drive.

This connector is keyed so that one can plug it in only the right way.

This connector provides +5V, +12V and ground connection.

If a free power connector is not available then one can use a Y-cable and get an additional power connector.

Drivers

Once the CD drive is connected to the system and the system is switched on, the BIOS will automatically recognize the drive. If the BIOS does not detect the drive then there is some problem with the master/slave setting of the drive, or the cable is faulty or there is some other hardware problem.

Correct the problem and make sure that the BIOS recognizes the CD-ROM drive.

If you are using Windows operating system, then Windows will automatically recognize the CD drive, and load appropriate drivers, for other operating system such as DOS you may need to manually install the required drivers, then only DOS will recognize the CD drive.

To make the DOS recognize CD drive, in the DOS bootable disk the CONFIG.SYS file should contain the following line.

```
device=c:\cdromdrv.sys /d:MSCD001
```

where the cdromdrv.sys is the driver program for the CD drive, and this file is located in the root directory of the C: drive. Next, the AUTOEXEC.BAT file should contain the following line.

```
c:\mscdex.exe /d:MSCD001
```

Where mscdex.exe is Microsoft CD extension program, located in the root directory of the C: drive. MSCD001 is the drive identifier for your CD-ROM drive, it should be same in the config.sys and Autoexec.bat file.

DVD Drive

What is DVD?

DVD, which stands for digital video disc or digital versatile disc, is the next generation of optical disc storage technology. It's a bigger, faster CD that can hold cinema-like video, better-than-CD audio, and computer data.

Using a DVD you can have home entertainment, computers, and business information with a single digital format. The DVD will eventually replace audio/video CD, videotape, laserdisc, CD-ROM, and video game cartridges.

There are various variations of DVD. DVD-ROM or DVD-R are physical formats and DVD-Video or DVD-Audio are application formats. DVD-ROM is the base format that holds data.

Physical format DVD-ROM includes recordable variations DVD-R, DVD-RAM, DVD-RW, and DVD+RW. The application formats include DVD-Video, DVD-Video Recording, DVD-Audio, DVD-Audio Recording, DVD Stream Recording, and SACD.

There are also special application formats for game consoles such as Sony PlayStation-2.

DVD Data Storage Capacity

DVDs are of the same diameter and thickness as CDs, and they are made using some of the same materials and manufacturing methods. Like a CD, the data on a DVD is encoded in the form of small pits and bumps in the track of the disc.

A DVD is composed of several layers of plastic, totaling about 1.2 millimeters thick. Each layer is created by injection molding polycarbonate plastic. This process forms a disc that has microscopic bumps arranged as a single, continuous and extremely long spiral track of data.

Once the clear pieces of polycarbonate are formed, a thin reflective layer is sputtered onto the disc, covering the bumps. Aluminum is used behind the inner layers, but a semi-reflective gold layer is used for the outer layers, allowing the laser to focus through the outer and onto the inner layers.

After all of the layers are made, each one is coated with lacquer, squeezed together and cured under infrared light.

For single-sided discs, the label is silk-screened onto the nonreadable side. Double-sided discs are printed only on the nonreadable area near the hole in the middle.

If you could lift the data track off a single layer of a DVD, and stretch it out into a straight line, it would be almost 7.5 miles long. A double-sided, double-layer DVD would have 30 miles of data.

Multi-Layer Storage

To increase the storage capacity, a DVD can have up to four layers, two on each side. The laser that reads the disc can actually focus on the second layer through the first layer.

Here is a list of the capacities of different forms of DVDs:

Format	Capacity	Approx. Movie Length
Single Sided/Single Layer	4.38GB	2 hours
Single Sided/Double Layer	7.95GB	4 hours
Double Sided/Single Layer	8.75GB	4.5 hours
Double Sided/Double Layer	15.9GB	Over 8 hrs

The capacity of a DVD doesn't double when you add a whole second layer to the disc, because when a disc is made with two layers, the pits have to be a little longer, on both layers, than when a single layer is used.

This helps to avoid interference between the layers, which would cause errors when the disc is played.

Single-sided, single layer (4.7GB)

Single-sided, double layer (8.5GB)

Double-sided, double layer (17GB)

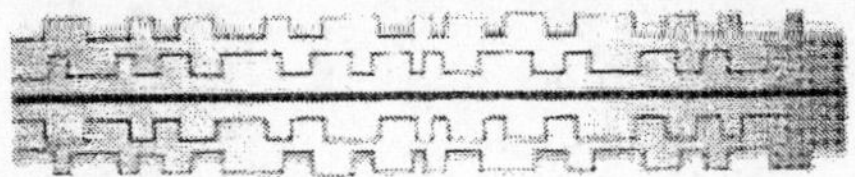

Fig. 19-10 : Various Types of DVD.

Recordable DVD: DVD-R, DVD-RAM, DVD-RW, and DVD+RW

There are five recordable versions of DVD-ROM: DVD-R for General, DVD-R for Authoring, DVD-RAM, DVD-RW, and DVD+RW. All recordable drives can read DVD-ROM discs, but each uses a different type of disc for recording.

DVD-R can record data once (sequentially only), while DVD-RAM, DVD-RW, and DVD+RW can be rewritten thousands of times.

A big problem is that none of the writable formats are fully compatible with each other or even with existing drives and players.

DVD-R

DVD-R uses organic dye technology, like CD-R, and is compatible with most DVD players. First-generation capacity was 3.95 billion bytes, later extended to 4.7 billion bytes. In early 2000 the format was split into an "authoring" version and a "general" version.

DVD-RW

DVD-RW (formerly DVD-R/W and also briefly known as DVD-ER) is a phase-change erasable format. DVD-RW is playable in most DVD drives and players.

Capacity is 4.7 billion bytes. DVD-RW can be rewritten about 1,000 times.

DVD-RAM

DVD-RAM, with storage capacity of. 4.7billion bytes, uses phase-change (PD) technology with some MO features mixed in. DVD-RAM is the best suited of the writable DVD formats for use in computers.

It is not compatible with most drives and players. DVD-RAM can be rewritten more than 100,000 times, and the discs are expected to last at least at least 30 years.

DVD+RW

DVD+RW is an erasable format based on CD-RW technology. DVD+RW drives will read DVD-ROMs and CDs, and probably DVD-Rs and DVD-RWs, but will not read or write DVD-RAM discs.

The drives are expected to write CD-Rs and CD-RWs. DVD+RW discs hold 4.7 billion bytes per side. It should be readable in about 70% of the existing DVD-Video players and DVD-ROM drives.

DVD+RW media can be rewritten about 1,000 times.

How long do DVDs last?

- Mass-market pressed discs will last anywhere from 50 to 300 years.
- DVD-R discs are expected to last anywhere from 40 to 250 years, about as long as CD-R discs.
- The erasable formats (DVD-RAM, DVD-RW, and DVD+RW) are expected to last from 25 to 100 years.

In comparison, a magnetic media such as tapes and disks lasts only 10 to 30 years.

What are "Regional Code", "Country Code", or "Zone Lock" ?

Motion picture studios want to control the home release of movies in different countries because theater releases aren't simultaneous (a movie may come out on video in the U.S. when it's just hitting theaters in India). Therefore they required that the DVD standard include codes that can be used to prevent playback of certain discs in certain geographical regions.

Each player is given a code for the region in which it's sold. The player will refuse to play discs that are not coded for its region. This means that discs bought in one country may not play on players bought in another country.

Some people believe that region codes are an illegal restraint of trade, but there have been no legal cases to establish this.

Regional codes are entirely optional for the maker of a disc. Discs without region locks will play on any player in any country. It's not an encryption system, it's just one byte of information on the disc that the player checks.

Region codes do not apply to DVD-Audio.

There are 8 regions (also called "Locales"). Players and discs are often identified by the region number superimposed on a world globe. If a disc plays in more than one region it will have more than one number on the globe.

1: U.S., Canada, U.S. Territories

2: Japan, Europe, South Africa, and Middle East (including Egypt)

3: Southeast Asia and East Asia (including Hong Kong)

4: Australia, New Zealand, Pacific Islands, Central America, Mexico, South America, and the Caribbean

5: Eastern Europe (Former Soviet Union), Indian subcontinent, Africa, North Korea, and Mongolia

6: China

7: Reserved

8: Special international venues (airplanes, cruise ships, etc.)

How to Clean and Care for DVDs?

Since DVDs are read by a laser, they do not get affected by play. However, surface contaminants and scratches can cause data errors. On a DVD drive, the effect of data errors ranges from minor video noise to frame skipping to complete unplayability.

So it's a good idea to take care of your DVDs. It's best to keep your discs clean, which will also keep the inside of your DVD drive clean. Never attempt to play a cracked disc, as it could shatter and damage the drive.

In general, there's no need to clean the lens on your drive, since the air moved by the rotating disc keeps it clean. However, if you commonly use a lens cleaning disc in your CD drive, you may want to do the same with your DVD drive.

It is better to use a cleaning disc designed for DVD drives, since there are minor differences in lens positioning.

Handle the DVD disc only at the hub or outer edge. Don't touch the shiny surface with your fingers. Store the disc in a protective case when not in use.

Do not bend the disc when taking it out of the case, and be careful not to scratch the disc when placing it in the case or in the drive tray.

Make certain the disc is properly seated in the drive tray before you close it.

Keep away from radiators/heaters, hot equipment surfaces, direct sunlight (near a window or in a car during hot weather), pets, small children, and other destructive forces.

Magnetic fields have no effect on DVDs.

The DVD specification recommends that discs be stored at a temperature between -20 to 50 °C (-4 to 122 °F) with less than 15 °C (59 °F) variation per hour, at relative humidity of 5% to 90%.

Cleaning DVD Discs

If you notice problems when playing a disc, you may be able to correct them with a simple cleaning.

Do not use strong cleaners, abrasives, solvents, or acids.

With a soft, lint-free cloth, wipe gently in a radial direction (a straight line from center to the edge of DVD, between the hub and the rim).

Since the data is arranged circularly on the disc, the micro scratches you create when cleaning the disc in circular direction will create more error than correcting them.

Don't use canned or compressed air, which can be very cold and may thermally stress the disc. For stubborn dirt or gummy adhesive, use water, water with mild soap, or isopropyl alcohol.

There are commercial products that clean discs and provide some protection from dust, fingerprints, and scratches.

Cleaning products labeled for use on CDs work as well as those that say they are for DVDs.

If you continue to have problems after cleaning the disc, you may need to attempt to repair one or more scratches.

Sometimes even hairline scratches can cause errors. There are essentially two methods of repairing scratches:

- fill or coat the scratch with an optical material
- polish down the scratch.

There are many commercial products that do one or both of these, or you may wish to buy polishing compounds or toothpaste and do it yourself.

The trick is to polish out the scratch without causing new ones. A mess of small polishing scratches can cause more damage than a big scratch.

As with cleaning, polish only in the radial direction, from center to edge.

The data layer on a DVD is only half as deep as on a CD, so a DVD can only be re-polished about half as many times.

Troubleshooting Multimedia

This section describes how to identify and resolve multimedia software problems.

Correcting Problems with Playing WAV Files

When a multimedia application is unable to play waveform-audio (WAV) files, it is usually caused by one or more of the following problems.

- The sound card is not installed properly.
  - Try to run the test program that come with the sound card. If the sound card does not work with these programs, it will not work with Windows 98.
  - Check that the sound card settings do not conflict with other hardware. Check in the System Properties. Verify port and IRQ settings.
  - Use the Add New Hardware icon in Control Panel to detect any new hardware for which the proper driver is not yet installed.
  - If the sound card can play MIDI files, the card is probably properly installed.
- The volume is muted or too low.
  - Check to see that the volume in Volume Control is not muted or set at too low.
  - To check the volume, click the Volume Control icon on the system tray, and make sure the Mute all check box and mute check box for Wave is not enabled. Raise the volume slider for Wave if it is too low.
  - If the Volume Control icon is not on the system tray, click Start and point to Programs, Accessories, and Entertainment, and then click Volume Control.
- A waveform-audio driver is not installed.
  - When running Sound Recorder if there is no waveform-audio driver installed, you will receive an error message. In this case, make sure that the waveform-audio driver is listed in the Multimedia devices list. To check this click on the Devices tab in the Multimedia option in Control Panel.
  - Check with the manufacturer of the sound card to ensure you have the proper drivers. If you cannot find the correct driver for the sound card in the list, try connecting to the manufacturer's Web site and downloading current driver.
  - You should also make sure the correct codec is installed. You can check the codec by clicking Multimedia in the Control Panel and then clicking the Devices tab. The codecs are listed under Audio Compression Codecs.
- A waveform-audio MCI driver is not enabled.
  - If you are running Media Player and cannot play WAV files, enable the waveform-audio MCI driver using the following procedure.
  - In Control Panel, double-click Multimedia, and then click the Devices tab.

- In the Multimedia devices list, click the plus (+) sign next to Media Control Devices.
- If Wave Audio Device (Media Control) does not appear in the list, the driver is not installed.
- Click Wave Audio Device (Media Control), and then click Properties.
- In the Properties dialog box, click Use this Media Control device.

Correcting Problems with Playing MIDI Files

A multimedia application's inability to play MIDI files is commonly caused by one or more of the following problems.

- The sound card is not installed properly.
  - Check the sound card as explained earlier
  - If the sound card can play WAV files, the card is probably properly installed.
- The volume is muted or too low.
  - Check to see that the volume in Volume Control is not muted or set too low.
  - Click the Volume Control icon on the system tray, and make sure the Mute all check box for MIDI is not enabled, or raise the volume slider for MIDI if it is too low.
  - Make sure the Mute all check box and mute check box for MIDI is not enabled. Raise the volume slider for Wave if it is too low.
  - If the Volume Control icon is not on the system tray, click Start and point to Programs, Accessories, and Entertainment, and then click Volume Control.
- A MIDI driver is not installed.
  - If you are using Media Player and cannot play a MIDI file, it might be because there is no MIDI driver installed. Try installing the driver that came with the sound card.
- A MIDI MCI driver is not installed or enabled.
  - In Media Player, make sure that the option named MIDI Sequencer appears in the Device menu. If not, the MIDI MCI driver is not installed or not enabled.
  - To verify that the MIDI MCI driver is enabled, in Control Panel, double-click Multimedia, and then click the Devices tab.
  - In the Multimedia devices list, click the plus (+) sign next to Media Control Devices.
  - If MIDI Sequencer Device (Media Control) does not appear in the list, the driver is not installed. See the following procedure for instructions.
  - Click MIDI Sequencer Device (Media Control), and then click Properties.
  - In the Properties dialog box, click Use this Media Control device.
  - To install the MIDI MCI driver, in Control Panel, double-click Add New Hardware, click "No, I want to select the hardware from a list" when

prompted to have Windows 98 search for your hardware, and then click Next.

- In the Hardware Types list, click Sound, click "Video And Game Controllers", and then click Next.
- Click "Microsoft MCI" in the Manufacturers list, and then click "MIDI Sequencer Device (Media Control)" in the Models list.
- Click Next.
- To complete the installation, click Finish.

■ The incorrect MIDI output device is selected.

- If the selected midi device is incorrect, you hear no MIDI output. Choose only External MIDI or MIDI OUT for an add-on MIDI daughter card or if an external MIDI device (for example, a synthesizer) is connected to the MIDI port of a sound card.
- For example, if you do not have an MPU-401 compatible synthesizer plugged into the MIDI port, make sure that MPU-401 is not selected as your default MIDI device.
- To select the correct MIDI output device, in Control Panel, double-click Multimedia.
- Select the MIDI tab.
- Choose the proper MIDI playback device under MIDI output so that it appears in the box under Single Instrument.
- Click OK.

■ Correcting Problems with Playing a DVD Disc

- Make sure that the DVD drive is displayed as functioning correctly in Device Manager.
- Make sure that Windows 98 can read the data on the CD by using Windows Explorer to see the contents of the DVD disc.

Correcting Problems with Playing Audio CD

When a you are unable to hear an audio CD being played, it is commonly caused by one or more of the following problems:

■ The CD-ROM drive is not properly installed.

- Place a data CD in the CD-ROM drive, and make sure you can view the files in Windows Explorer or list the files at the command prompt. If you can, the CD-ROM drive is properly installed. If not, verify your disk drivers, and make the proper changes so that you can view the files on a data CD.

■ The volume is muted or too low.

- Check to see that the volume in Volume Control is not muted or too low.
- To check the "CD Audio" volume, click the Volume Control icon on the system tray, and make sure the Mute all check box and Mute check box for CD Audio is not enabled.
- Raise the volume slider for CD Audio if it is too low.

- The CD audio MCI driver is not installed.
  - In Media Player, make sure that the option "CD Audio" appears in the Device menu. If not, the "CD audio MCI driver" is not installed or not enabled.
- To verify the "CD audio MCI driver" is enabled
  - In Control Panel, double-click Multimedia, and then click the Devices tab.
  - In the Multimedia devices list, click the plus (+) sign next to Media Control Devices.
  - If "CD Audio Device (Media Control)" does not appear in the list, the driver is not installed. See the following instructions.
  - Click "CD Audio Device (Media Control)", and then click Properties.
  - In the Properties dialog box, click "Use this Media Control device".
  - To install the CD audio MCI driver, in Control Panel, double-click "Add New Hardware", click "No, I want to select the hardware from a list" when prompted to have Windows 98 search for your hardware, and then click "Next".
  - In the Hardware Types list, click "Sound", click "Video And Game Controllers", and then click Next.
  - Click "Microsoft MCI" in the Manufacturers list, and then click "CD Audio Device (Media Control)" in the Models list.
  - Click Next.
  - To complete the installation, click Finish.
- The CD-ROM is not connected to the sound card.
  - If the CD-ROM is playing and there is no sound coming from the sound card speakers, try plugging the speakers or headphones into the audio jack on the face of the CD-ROM drive.
  - If you get sound, check the internal or external audio connection between the CD-ROM drive and the sound card.
- Correcting Problems with Hearing from Headphones
  - Verify that the sound card is correctly installed by reviewing the card's properties.
  - To view your sound card's properties, in Control Panel, double-click Multimedia, and then click the "CD Music" tab.
  - Make sure that the volume level is set to produce sound from the headphones.
  - If not, use the slider to adjust the "CD Music Volume".

If you have "Digital Playback" enabled on the CD Music tab, the headphone output for the CD-ROM drive is disabled.

Troubleshooting Video/Display Problem

Whenever there is a display problem, the first step is to find out what could be the cause of the problem, is it due to incompatible display card and monitor or is it incorrect configuration information or is it due to faulty monitor or faulty display adapter card.

The display card and monitor are quite reliable but a gradual appearance of faults with age is very common. Many display related problems are caused by incorrect configuration and cable fault. Another common reason of blank display could be monitor's power switch being OFF or the brightness being turned down.

There are many thing that can cause display problems. Some of the most common faults are listed below:

Monitor dead

- Monitor's fuse blown.
- Monitor's power supply section faulty.
- Fault in horizontal section.

On Power-On system beeps but no display appears

- Setup information incorrect.
- Display adapter not seated properly in expansion slot.

Power on LED glows but no raster

- Power Supply voltage abnormal.
- Some loose connection in power supply circuit.
- Brightness control is in extreme OFF position.

Abnormal brightness in display

- Power supply voltage output high.
- Screen voltage (G2) high.

Bright spot on screen

Note: decrease brightness to minimum

Warning: This may damage the CRT permanently.

- Monitor cable broken or loose-connected.
- Faulty monitor deflection circuits (Vertical and Horizontal).
- Display adapter fault, try another adapter.
- CRT defective.

After switching on the system, raster appears after sometime and defocused display

- CRT weakening or CRT aging.

Display intermittent

- Loose contact in video circuit.
- Display cable loose.
- Loose contact in CRT base.

Small or stamp type raster

- Power supply voltage output low.
- No regulation in power supply.
- Fault in bridge rectifier circuit .
- Main filter capacitor in power supply dry.

Only one horizontal line appears

Note: decrease brightness to minimum

Warning: This may damage the CRT permanently.

- Deflection yoke's vertical winding is loose or open.
- Loose contact in vertical section or print open.
- Vertical circuit fault.

Only one vertical line appears

Note: decrease brightness to minimum

Warning: This may damage the CRT permanently.

- Deflection yoke's horizontal winding is loose or open.
- Circuit fault between EHT and horizontal winding.

Improper height of the display

- Check circuit of vertical output section.
- Supply to vertical section low.
- Supply resistance of vertical section has increased.
- Fault in feedback circuit (output to input).
- Vertical height preset misadjusted.

Vertical non-linearity in character size from top to bottom in a column

- Fault in feedback circuit (output to input).
- Vertical linearity preset misadjusted.
- Coupling capacitor dry.

Horizontal non-linearity in character size from left to right in a row

- Linearity coil - if provided - misadjusted.
- Capacitor value between EHT and horizontal winding not proper.

Display shaking

- Open diode in power supply - bridge rectifier circuit.

- Main filter capacitor dry.
- Power supply regulation not proper.
- Electromagnetic interference.

Unsteady display, moving band on screen

- Interference in supply line.
- Power supply voltage very low
- Power supply circuit faulty.

Display out of sync

- Cable not connected properly.
- Vertical/horizontal hold misadjusted.
- Monitor synchronization circuits needs adjustment.
- Display mode not supported by monitor.
- Wrong software driver for display adapter.

Display rolling in horizontal direction

- Horizontal hold control misadjusted.
- Cable loose contact.

Display rolling in vertical direction

- Vertical hold not adjusted properly.
- Cable loose contact.

Fold-over in the beginning or end of scan line

- Phase control preset misadjusted.
- Fault in vertical output or horizontal output section (component value deviated).

Brightness control not working, abnormal or no change in brightness

- Brightness control defective.
- Abnormal grid voltage (G2).

Spot seen when switching off

- CRT weakening.
- CRT aging.

Black vertical bar on the screen

- Control grid (G1) voltage not proper.
- Control grid (G1) circuit defective.

Defocusing of dots

- Improper focus voltage.
- CRT deterioration.

Weak contrast

- Fault in video circuit.
- Fault in contrast control circuit.

Raster OK, no video

- Video cable contact not proper.
- Fault in video circuit.

Noisy display

- Problem in grounding.
- Video cable loose contact.

Fine noise on the screen (white spot)

- Contact problem in connectors.
- Leakage in high voltage protection.

Corrupt display

- Software corrupts display adapter memory.
- Display adapter memory (RAM) faulty.

Distorted characters on screen

- Display adapter fault.

No cursor

- Software fault.
- Adapter not fully IBM-compatible.

"CMOS Display Type Mismatch" Error On power on

- CMOS setup incorrect for type of display, run SETUP.

Corners of the display are improper

- Adjust ring magnets located on deflection yoke.

Display on the screen is displaced to one side

- Centering magnet of deflection yoke misadjusted.

Display tilted towards one direction

- Deflection yoke tilted due to loose fitting.

Motherboard/Cabinet Form Factors

Form Factor term describes the physical dimensions and various types of the motherboard and cabinet available in the market. A motherboard or cabinet can be any size or shape as long as its connectors are at standard places and it has standard size expansion slot connectors.

The motherboard or cabinet can be of any size, but most of the motherboards and cabinets are based on standard sizes. One main advantage of standard size is the users can easily replace an old motherboard or cabinet without going for any major change in the computer setup.

Let us now see some common motherboard and cabinets, first we start with some common motherboard form factors.

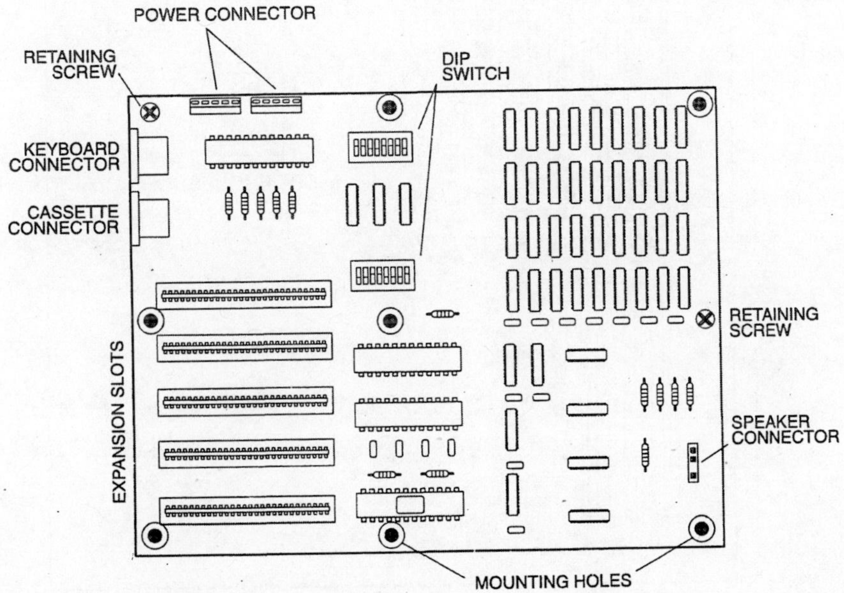

Fig. 20-1 : First IBM PC Motherboard.

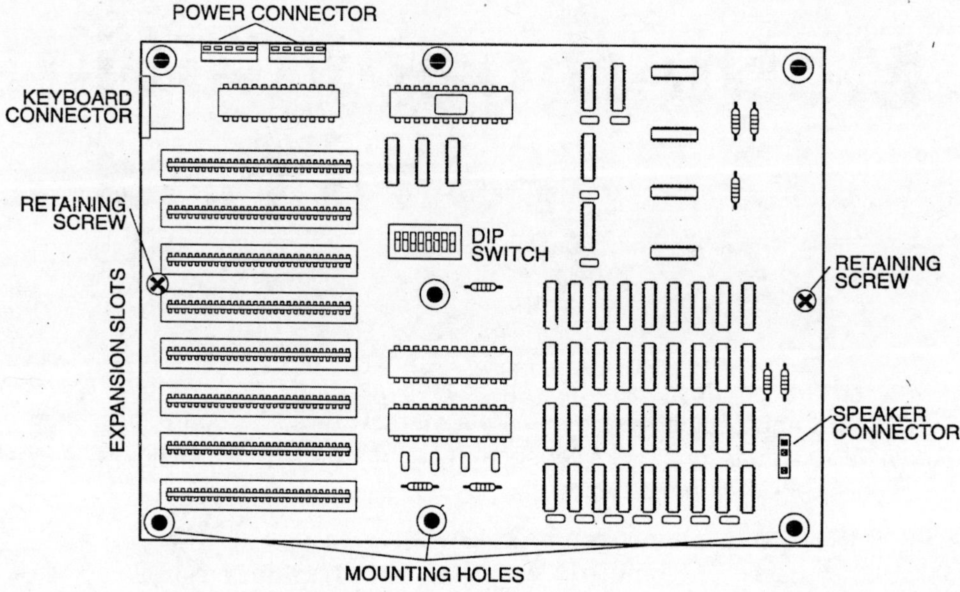

Fig. 20-2 : PC-XT Motherboard.

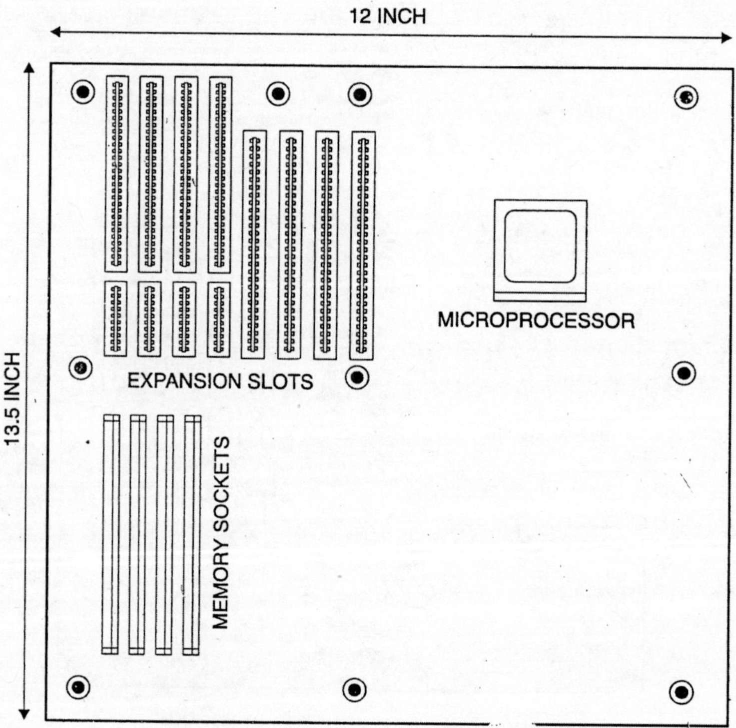

Fig. 20-3 : PC-AT Motherboard.

Older motherboard specification was limited to the size of the motherboard but current specifications such as ATX specify not only dimensions and mounting holes but also connector placement and designs as well.

Initial IBM PC Motherboard

The motherboard used in the initial IBM PC measured about 8-1/2 by 11 inches. This board had five expansion slots spaced one inch apart in the left rear corner of the board.

PC-XT Motherboard

Next motherboard standard was IBM's PC-XT motherboard. In this motherboard the size was changed to 8.5 by 12 inches.

In this motherboard, the number of slots were increased from five to eight. This was done by placing the expansion slots closer.

This slot spacing has since become the standard among nearly all PC compatibles.

PC-AT Motherboard

PC-AT motherboard was the most popular motherboard layout.

The original AT motherboard measured about 12 by 13 1/2 inches, and this size is still used for motherboards that require the large area for its circuit components.

Mini-AT Motherboard

As the number of chips used on the motherboard reduced, the motherboard size also reduced. By making the motherboard size smaller, manufacturers could reduce the cost of the motherboard.

Because the placement of mounting holes and the spacing of expansion slots of the AT motherboard have become industry standards, engineers have designed smaller motherboard that retain these features of AT Motherboards.

These smaller AT-compatible boards were called Mini-AT motherboards.

A Mini-AT motherboard measures about 13 inches by 8.7 inches.

As the mini-AT motherboards are designed to fit a variety of cabinets and connector arrangements, only the keyboard connector is directly placed on the printed circuit board.

Other ports are provided as headers, and short ribbon cables connect these headers to the external connectors mounted on the PC chassis.

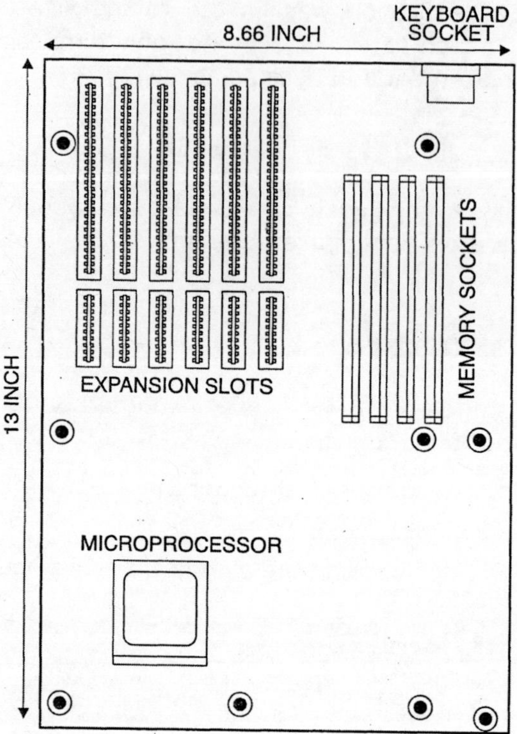

Fig. 20-4 : Mini AT Motherboard.

LPX Motherboard

LPX is Low Profile Motherboard Specification.

The standard low profile Motherboard measures 8.66 by 13 inches (or 220 by 330 millimeters), this is almost same as the dimensions of a mini-AT board.

The main difference between an LPX motherboard and a mini-AT board is the form and placement of the expansion connectors

To make the motherboard low profile, the LPX motherboard does not contain any expansion slots, instead it has a single master expansion connector near the rear of the board.

A small daughtercard plugs into this slot and hold one or more standard expansion connectors. These expansion slots could be ISA or PCI or both.

The keyboard connector on an LPX motherboard is at the same location as that of the mini-AT design.

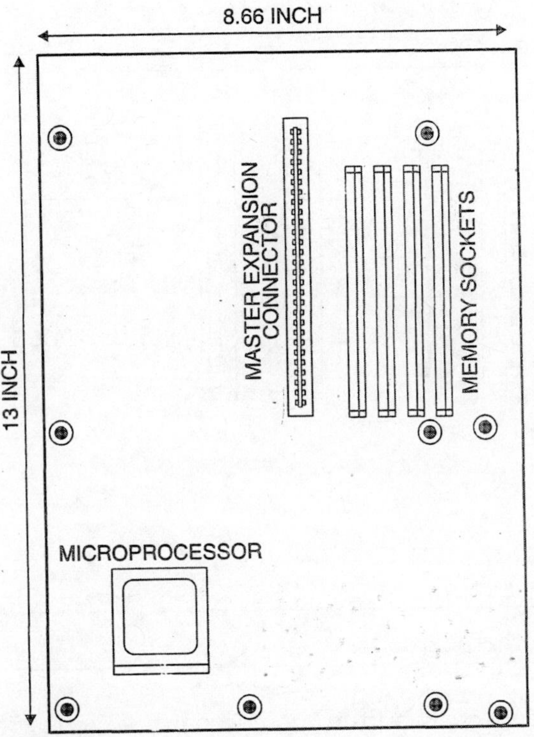

Fig. 20-5 : LPX Motherboard.

ATX Motherboard

ATX is a new motherboard specification introduced by Intel. This standard is roughly same as the mini-AT board size but with a few changes that result in lower cost.

ATX board is basically the AT board with a 90 degree turn. This orientation provides the maximum space for expansion boards and port connectors at the rear.

The ATX specification defines the number and position of the mounting holes and gives recommendations about component, expansion board, and port connector placement.

The specification recommends that the microprocessor be located near the right edge of the board where it will be in close to the power supply and cooling fan. Also the memory sockets can be placed between the microprocessor and expansion slots.

The ATX board measures about 12 by 9.6 inches. This size was selected to allow manufacturers to cut two boards from a standard size printed circuit board.

This motherboard has space for about seven expansion slots. Other than specifying board dimensions, this ATX specification also specifies a new ATX power connector. This new power supply helps to run the PC cooler and quieter.

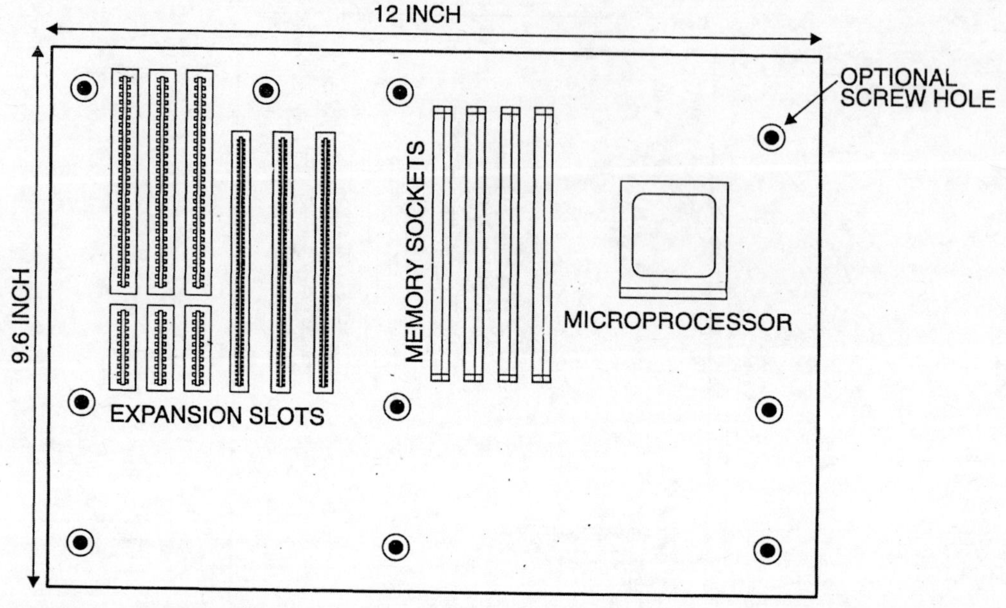

Fig. 20-6 : ATX Motherboard.

By putting port connectors on the motherboard, ATX design eliminates the cost of connecting cables as well as the labor required for assembly, thus reducing the costs for PC makers.

Mini-ATX

As with the improvement in technology, the AT board was reduced to mini-AT size, it become possible to reduce the ATX size to a mini-ATX size.

Compared to a full-size ATX board, the Mini-ATX design reduces the material costs for a motherboard by about 30%.

The Mini-ATX design motherboard measures around 11.2 by 8.2 inches.

When installed in a computer cabinet, this Mini-ATX motherboard is placed at the rear edge of the chassis so that port connectors can be mounted directly to it without cables.

Because of its smaller size, the Mini-ATX motherboard cuts off one row of ATX mounting holes. As a result, the lower row of mounting holes are displaced on the Mini-ATX design.

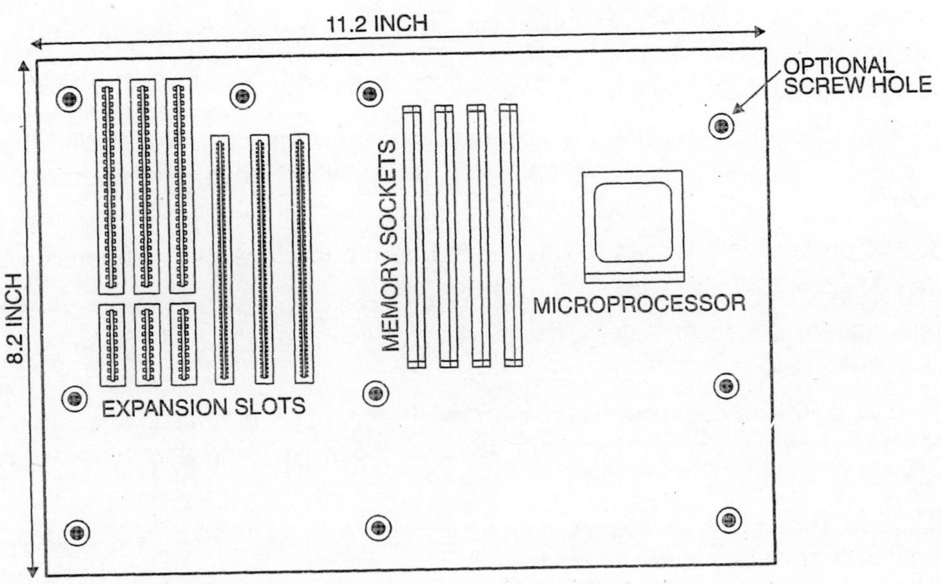

Fig. 20-7 : Mini ATX Motherboard.

Micro-ATX

Micro-ATX is another small size motherboard following the ATX specification. A micro-ATX motherboard measures 9.6 inch by 9.6 inch.

This micro-ATX is a bit larger than the mini-ATX but it uses nearly same mounting scheme as the full ATX board. So, it can fit neatly into a full size ATX board chassis. Even the screw holes used for mounting the micro-ATX board match the position of those on the full size ATX board.

Because of its reduced size the micro-ATX board has fewer expansion slots, generally three PCI and one AGP slot.

Flex-ATX

Intel engineers reduced the micro-ATX board further and introduced a new specification Flex-ATX. A flex-ATX board measures 9 inch by 7.5 inch.

Flex-ATX board retains the same area (in size and position) for various ports and connectors, as used in the ATX and micro-ATX boards.

NLX

NLX is new low profile motherboard specification. This specification was introduced to overcome the drawbacks of the older LPX and mini-LPX designs.

NLX was designed to support all current generation of Intel processors, memory technologies and the AGP port.

Main component of the NLX design is the raiser board. In the LPX design the raiser board was used to connect various expansion boards, but in the NLX design the raiser board works as a backplane which is permanently attached to the chassis of the computer.

NLX motherboard is attached to this raiser board backplane as an expansion board.

The NLX specification reserves the area on the left side of the motherboard , opposite the riser board, for an AGP slot. The AGP board slides into the AGP slot parallel to the riser board.

NLX uses 340-pin connector between motherboard and riser board, this single connector carries signal for ISA and PCI bus, IDE drives and various other system functions.

NLX specification gives a freedom to its designers as far as its size is concerned. A NLX board's width can be between 8 and 9 inch and its length can be between 10 and 13.6 inch.

The smallest NLX beard is of the size of mini-LPX board and the largest NLX board is of the size of an LPX board.

NLX specification specifies three different mounting screw patterns, so a NLX chassis must accommodate all three patterns.

WTX

WTX is a new specification introduced by the Intel for workstation computers.

Under this specification the motherboard could measure up to 14 inch by 16.75 inches. Intel no longer promote this specification.

Cabinet Form Factor

It has to be large enough to accommodate the expansion boards you want to plug in as well as provide adequate space for all the floppy and hard disks, optical, and tape drives your PC and life would not be complete without.

The case also has to provide a place for such mandatory system components as power supplies and loudspeakers.

In addition, everything must be arranged to allow air to freely flow around to bring your PC's circuitry and peripherals a breath of cooling fresh air.

PC and PC-XT Cabinet

Original IBM PC and PC-XT cabinet size has become an industry standard called XT size. Although these two cabinets look identical, the cases of IBM's PC and XT computers were different in expansion slot spacing and number (one-inch spacing of five slots for the PC and 0.8-inch spacing of eight slots for the XT).

The original design had space at the front for two 5.25 inch disk drives, a power supply behind the drives, and a motherboard at the base of the cabinet to the left.

The height of the case was set by the need to use the full height drives and the expansion boards.

The desk space needed by the XT cabinet was 21 inches wide by 17 inches deep. Its height measures 5.5 inches.

The bottom of the cabinet formed the computer's chassis, the foundation to which all mechanical components of the system are bolted.

AT Cabinet

To accommodate the larger motherboard required by the AT, the PC-XT cabinet size was broadened by two inches (to 23 by 17 inches) and its height was increased by nearly an inch

Increased height allowed both taller expansion boards and accommodation for a stack of three half height storage devices in the mass storage bay.

A taller power supply with greater power was also fitted inside the cabinet.

As in the PC-XT cabinet, two side by side bays were installed for floppy disk drive, and the inner, left side bay was reserved for hard disk drives that required no access to their front panels.

The AT cabinet also added an access control system by introducing a keylock using a cylindrical key that physically locked the cabinet lid on the case and electrically disabled the keyboard.

The front panel introduced a power on indicator and a hard disk activity indicator LED.

ATX Cabinet

ATX refers to a motherboard form factor, not to a cabinet design, as the ATX mother board requires a specific type of cabinet, the cabinet which can accommodate the ATX motherboard is known as the ATX cabinet.

In any ATX motherboard, the port connectors are in the same position, this is very useful for a cabinet designer as any ATX cabinet can accept any ATX motherboard and will allow access to all of its port connectors without any problem.

MAIN SYSTEM UNIT

DESKTOP

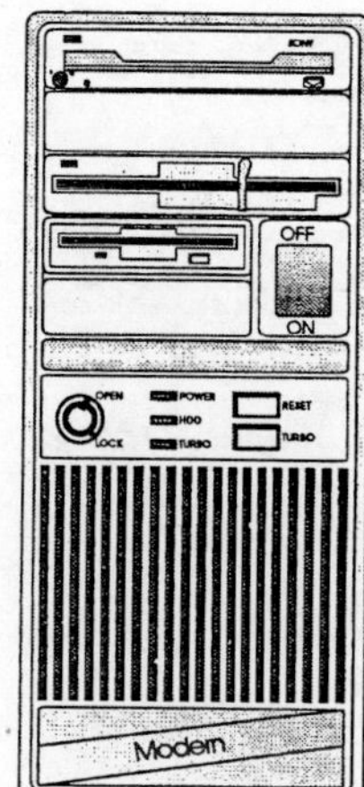

TOWER

Fig. 20-8 : Tower and Desktop Model of the Cabinet.

The ATX specification does not require a case of a particular size or layout as long as an ATX motherboard will properly fit inside.

You can find both desktop and tower style ATX cabinet with various external dimensions and drive mounting systems.

Tower/Desktop Cabinet

The initial Personal Computer (PC) had desktop style case, but currently the tower style case is more common with the PCs.

The shape of the case has no special advantage or disadvantage, one can decide the case style based on the place where the computer is going to be used, and according to the expansion facility available in the computer to add any additional devices in the future. For example, there should be place for a CD-writer, if you plan to purchase a CD-writer in near future.

Towers type cabinets come in various sizes:

- Mini-tower cabinet are the most compact and usually accommodate only mini-AT and smaller motherboards and a few drives.
- Full-size-tower cases can hold full size motherboards and provide more drive bays than most people require.
- Recently midi-tower cases, with accommodation falling in between mini and full-size, have become a popular option.

These terms are not standardized. One manufacturer's mini could be another's midi.

Complete Boot Process

The complete boot process of a PC is explained next. Later parts of this process, after the operating system is loaded mainly refers to the DOS operating system based computer.

Windows 98 files used during the system startup is given at the end of this chapter.

- After the machine is switched on, the power supply performs a self check and once the output becomes stable, it sends a powergood signal to the computer's motherboard.
- After the timer chip on the motherboard receives the powergood signal, it stops sending reset signal to the CPU. CPU starts executing the BIOS program from location FFFF:0000 onwards.
- The BIOS program at location FFFF:0000h starts checking all the main devices like CPU, DMA controller, RAM etc., any error is displayed on the screen and indicated by the error-beep.
- Next, BIOS looks for the video ROM. If a video ROM is found, its checksum is tested. If the checksum test fails "ROM Error" message is displayed, otherwise the video ROM is executed. The video ROM initializes the display system and the cursor appears on the screen.
- If no video ROM is found then motherboard ROM's video driver initialize the display system and the cursor appears on the screen.
- BIOS checks memory C800:0000 to DF80:0000 in 2K increment for any other ROM, if any ROM is found, its checksum is tested and after a successful test the ROM program is executed.
- A checksum test failure is displayed by "XXXX ROM Error" error message on the screen, where XXXX is the segment value of the failed ROM.
- BIOS checks the word at location 0000:0472, if this word is 1234 then a warm boot is done, any other value indicates a cold boot.
- A warm boot makes the memory test to be skipped during the POST process.
- Next the Power On Self Test (POST) is done. Any error is displayed on the screen and indicated by the error-beep sound.
- A POST without any error is indicated by a single beep sound.

- BIOS looks for DOS volume Boot Sector at track/Cylinder 0, head 0, sector 1, i.e. the first sector of the disk A:.
- This sector is loaded into memory location 0000:7C00 and checked.
- If the first sector cannot be read or if the drive is empty and there is no hard disk present then "DRIVE NOT READY, Insert boot diskette in A:, Press any key when ready" error message is displayed and the system stops.
- If the first byte of the loaded boot sector is less than 6h or if the first byte is equal to or more than 6h and the first nine words contain same data pattern then

  "602: Diskette Boot Record Error"

  message is displayed and system stops. Otherwise the sector loaded at 0000:7C00 is executed.
- If the DOS diskette was formatted with version earlier to 3.3 then if the boot sector is corrupt, the following message is displayed

  "Disk Boot Failure" and system stops.
- This Boot Sector program checks for the two system files (IBMBIO.COM and IBMDOS.COM on PC-DOS systems, IO.SYS and MSDOS.SYS on MS-DOS systems).
- If the boot sector is corrupt, or if these two files are not in the root directory, or if a problem is encountered in loading them then

  Non-System disk or disk error,

  Replace and press any key when ready

  error message is displayed.
- If the DOS volume boot sector cannot be read from the drive then BIOS tries to read the MBR (master boot record) from cylinder 0, head 0, sector 1 of the hard disk drive.
- If this sector is found then it is loaded into the memory address 0000:7C00 and the signature (55h AAh) of this sector is checked.
- If the signature byte (i.e. the last two byte of the sector) is not 55AAh the BIOS invokes a software interrupt INT 18h. On most of the machines this will either bring ROM based BASIC interpreter on screen or display the following message

  No Boot Device Available

  Press F1 to retry, F2 to run setup
- If the signature byte of the master boot record (MBR) is correct then the program at the MBR is given the control. This program looks at the partition table entry for an entry with system indicator byte indicating an extended partition.
- If an extended partition is found then the program loads the extended partition boot sector. Next this extended partition boot sector's partition table is searched for any more extended partition.
- If another extended partition is found then that extended partition is loaded and the above process of searching for more extended partition is again repeated.

- This process continues until no more extended partitions are found or the total number of partition reaches 24.
- Once all the partition table are loaded into the memory they are searched for a bootable partition (with boot indicator on).
- If none of the partition is marked bootable or if more than one partition is marked bootable then this will either bring ROM based BASIC interpreter on screen or display the following message

  "Invalid partition table"

  is displayed and the system stops.
- If the MBR finds an active (bootable) partition in the partition table, then the boot sector from that partition is loaded and tested for the signature byte (last two digit of sector are 55AAh).
- If the bootable volume/partition's boot sector could not be read successfully in five retries then following message appears and the system stops.

  "Error Loading Operating System"
- After successful loading of the bootable volume's boot sector, if the signature i.e. the last two bytes of the sector is not 55AAh then the following message appears and the system stops.

  "Missing operating system"
- Once the bootable volume's boot sector is successfully loaded, the program at the boot sector is executed. If this is a DOS Boot sector then this program checks for the two systems files IBMBIO.COM and IBMDOS.COM in PC-DOS or for files IO.SYS and MSDOS.SYS when using the MS-DOS.
- If these two files are not present or if they could not be loaded properly then in DOS 3.3 or earlier version the following message appears.

  Non-System Disk or Disk Error

  Replace and strike any key when ready.
- But, if the boot sector is corrupt the DOS3.3 and earlier will display the following message.

  "Disk Boot Failure"
- If the disk is using DOS 4.0 or later version then if the system files are not first two files in the directory or if they could not be loaded properly or if the boot sector is corrupt then all this condition will display the following message on the screen.

  Non-System Disk or Disk Error

  Replace and strike any key when ready.
- Once the IO.SYS (or IBMBIO.COM) can be read, this program is loaded into the main memory (RAM) and executed. On execution the first thing this program does is to move itself into the highest memory available.
- Next, IO.SYS (or IBMBIO.COM) loads the MSDOS.SYS (or IBMDOS.COM) into the main memory and executes it.
- The MSDOS.SYS (or IBMDOS.COM) initializes device drivers, resets the disk status, determines the status of devices connected to the system and sets default parameters for system operation.

- Now the complete DOS is active, as next step, IO.SYS (IBMBIO.COM) is again given the control and it reads the CONFIG.SYS and process it. To process the commands given in CONFIG.SYS files, it is read four times.
- During the 1st pass, IO.SYS (IBMBIO.COM) reads all the CONFIG.SYS statements except DEVICE, INSTALL and SHELL statement.
- During the 2nd pass all the DEVICE statements are executed in the order in which they are given in the CONFIG.SYS files. This makes all the device drivers specified in the CONFIG.SYS to be loaded and executed.
- During the 3rd pass all the INSTALL statements are executed in the order in which they appear in the CONFIG.SYS files. This makes all the programs specified in the INSTALL statement of CONFIG.SYS to be loaded and executed.
- During the 4th pass if CONFIG.SYS contains any SHELL command then the command processor specified in the SHELL is loaded and executed, otherwise \COMMAND.COM is loaded as the default command processor.
- COMMAND.COM checks for AUTOEXEC.BAT, if present then each command in the AUTOEXEC.BAT is executed and finally DOS prompt appears on the screen.
- If AUTOEXEC.BAT is not present then COMMAND.COM executes DATE and TIME command and shows the DOS prompt after displaying a copyright message.

When the system has Windows 98 operating system installed, this boot operation will process the following files.

- IO.SYS

  In Windows 98, the IO.SYS system file replaces the MS-DOS system files IO.SYS and MSDOS.SYS. This file contains the information needed to start the computer. Your system no longer needs CONFIG.SYS and AUTOEXEC.BAT files to start the Windows 98 operating system.

  The values in IO.SYS file cannot be edited. So, to override any default values in IO.SYS one can place an entry in CONFIG.SYS file with the required value. CONFIG.SYS entries override the IO.SYS defaults.
- MSDOS.SYS

  Windows 98 Setup creates a hidden, read-only system file named MSDOS.SYS in the root of the computer's boot drive. This file contains important paths used to locate other Windows files, including the registry. MSDOS.SYS also has an [Options] section, where you can add to instruction to change the startup process.
- CONFIG.SYS

  In Windows 98, CONFIG.SYS defaults are implemented by IO.SYS file, as described in the previous section. However, CONFIG.SYS can contain application-specific entries, these entries are processed in the sequence they are listed.

After the base CONFIG.SYS file has been read, all devices are loaded, and COMMAND.COM is started.

If you want to edit Config.sys in Windows 98, observe the following basic guidelines:

- Do not include the smartdrv command. Windows 98 includes built-in disk caching, and double-buffering is now provided by Dblbuff.sys.
- Remove any device=mouse.sys lines or similar lines. Windows 98 includes built-in mouse support.

■ AUTOEXEC.BAT.

AUTOEXEC.BAT is not required for Windows 95 or Windows 98, but it is included for compatibility purposes. If the computer has an AUTOEXEC.BAT file, each line is processed in sequence during system startup.

If you want to edit Autoexec.bat in Windows 98, observe the following guidelines:

- Do not include other versions of Windows in your path.
- Start the path with C:\Windows;C:\Windows\Command (using the name for the Windows 98 directory on your hard disk if it is not \Windows).
- Windows 98 Setup leaves your previous MS-DOS directory in the path. Do not change this.
- Do not add SMARTDrive or other disk caches. Windows 98 includes built-in caching.
- Do not include any statements for loading mouse support software. Windows 98 includes built-in mouse support.
- If it is necessary to connect to a network server when you start Windows 98, create a batch file, and run it from the STARTUP directory, rather than placing an entry in Autoexec.bat.

■ SYSTEM.INI and WIN.INI.

Most of these options for Windows 98 are now stored in the registry and are no longer required.

■ BOOTLOG.TXT

The BOOTLOG.TXT file contains a record of the current startup process. This file is created during Setup when the Windows 98 operating system is first started from Windows 98 Setup. This file shows the Windows 98 components and drivers loaded and initialized, with their status.

OTHER TITLES OF INTEREST

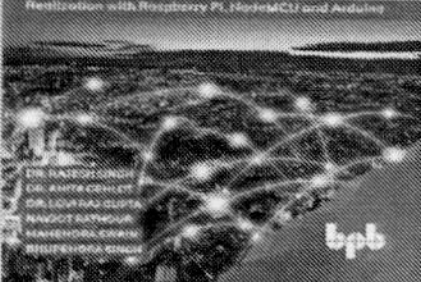

IoT Based Projects
ISBN: 9789389328523

Internet of Things (IoT)
A Quick Start Guide
ISBN: 9789389845860

Fundamentals of **IoT**
ISBN: 9789355518644

IoT for **Beginners**
ISBN: 9789355510068

21 **Internet Of Things (IOT)**
Experiments
ISBN: 9789386551832

Internet of Things
Theory and Practice
ISBN: 9789355512437

Learn **IoT Programming**
Using **Node-RED**
ISBN: 9789391392383

Internet of Things (**IoT**)
ISBN: 9789389423365

IoT Data Analytics
using **Python**
ISBN: 9789355515759

The Today & Future of **WSN,**
AI and **IOT**
ISBN: 9789389845167

IOT and Smart Cities
ISBN: 9789388511322

Internet of Things with
Arduino & Bolt
ISBN: 9789387284265

Fundamentals of
Software Engineering
ISBN: 9789388511773

Applied Quantum
Computers
ISBN: [illegible]

Foundations of
Computing – 5th Edition
ISBN: 9789355512550

Enhancing **IoT Security**
ISBN: 9789355515506

Windows XP Setup/ Installation

To install Windows XP (Home or Professional Edition), you can use this section as a guideline to make yourself familiar with the process. This procedure is not valid for installation of Windows XP via a "Recovery CD-ROM".

To start with, your system should be able to boot from a CD-ROM. This should not be an issue, because if your system is not able to boot from a CD-ROM, it is most probably already a few years old and not powerful enough to run Windows XP.

If your system is NOT able to boot from CD-ROM and you insist on installing Windows XP, you can download "Boot Floppies" from the Microsoft Website.

Check in your PC-BIOS setup, that "boot from CD-ROM" is enabled and that the system will first try to boot from the CD-ROM, before attempting to boot from harddisk or some other device.

Insert your Windows XP installation CD-ROM in the CD-Drive and power-on/restart your system, system will show the PC-BIOS startup message, like: memory test, memory installed etc.

```
PhoenixBIOS 4.0 Release 6.0
Copyright 1985-2000 Phoenix Technologies Ltd.
All Rights Reserved
Copyright 2000-2001 VMware, Inc.
VMware BIOS build 212

CPU = Pentium III  733 MHz
640K System RAM Passed
159M Extended RAM Passed
256K Cache SRAM Passed
Mouse initialized
Fixed Disk 0: VMware Virtual IDE Hard Drive
ATAPI CD-ROM: VMware Virtual IDE CDROM Drive




Press <F2> to enter SETUP
```

When you get the message to "press any key to boot from CD...", press any key.

```
Press any key to boot from CD..._
```

This is new on Microsoft Windows 2000 and XP CD's, if you do not press any key, it will NOT boot from CD-ROM, but boot from harddisk, so if you forget to take out bootable CD-ROM, you will not get confused by the CD-ROM installation procedure.

Once the boot from CD-ROM has started, it will display at the top of the screen:

"Setup is inspecting your computer's hardware configuration. . ."

```
Setup is inspecting your computer's hardware configuration...
```

After a brief delay, the typical Microsoft "blue Installation screen" is displayed, with "Windows Setup" displayed at the top and at the bottom of the screen the information, that "Setup is loading Files" (loading all type of device drivers):

```
Windows Setup

Setup is loading files (Windows Executive)...
```

It will finally display : "Setup is starting Windows" and will display after a short delay the "Windows XP Professional Setup" or "Windows XP Home Setup" screen:

```
Windows XP Professional Setup

  Welcome to Setup.

  This portion of the Setup program prepares Microsoft(R)
  Windows(R) XP to run on your computer.

     •  To set up Windows XP now, press ENTER.

     •  To repair a Windows XP installation using
        Recovery Console, press R.

     •  To quit Setup without installing Windows XP, press F3.

ENTER=Continue   R=Repair   F3=Quit
```

Select "to set up Windows XP now" and press the ENTER-key. The "Windows XP Licensing Agreement" is displayed, accept it by pressing the F8-key. (as indicated on the bottom of the screen).

```
Windows XP Licensing Agreement

  Microsoft Windows XP Professional

  END-USER LICENSE AGREEMENT

  IMPORTANT-READ CAREFULLY: This End-User
  License Agreement ("EULA") is a legal agreement between you
  (either an individual or a single entity) and Microsoft
  Corporation for the Microsoft software product identified above,
  which includes computer software and may include associated
  media, printed materials, "online" or electronic documentation,
  and Internet-based services ("Product").    An amendment or
  addendum to this EULA may accompany the Product.  YOU AGREE TO BE
  BOUND BY THE TERMS OF THIS EULA BY
  INSTALLING, COPYING, OR OTHERWISE USING THE
  PRODUCT. IF YOU DO NOT AGREE, DO NOT INSTALL
  OR USE THE PRODUCT; YOU MAY RETURN IT TO YOUR
  PLACE OF PURCHASE FOR A FULL REFUND.

   1. GRANT OF LICENSE. Microsoft grants you the following rights
      provided that you comply with all terms and conditions of
      this EULA:

      * Installation and use.  You may install, use, access,
        display and run one copy of the Product on a single
        computer, such as a workstation, terminal or other device
        ("Workstation Computer").  The Product may not be used
        by more than two (2) processors at  any one time on any

 F8=I agree  ESC=I do not agree  PAGE DOWN=Next Page
```

Setup will now display the partitions on your disk:

If your system has already an operating system installed, you will see them listed. You can now create or delete partitions.

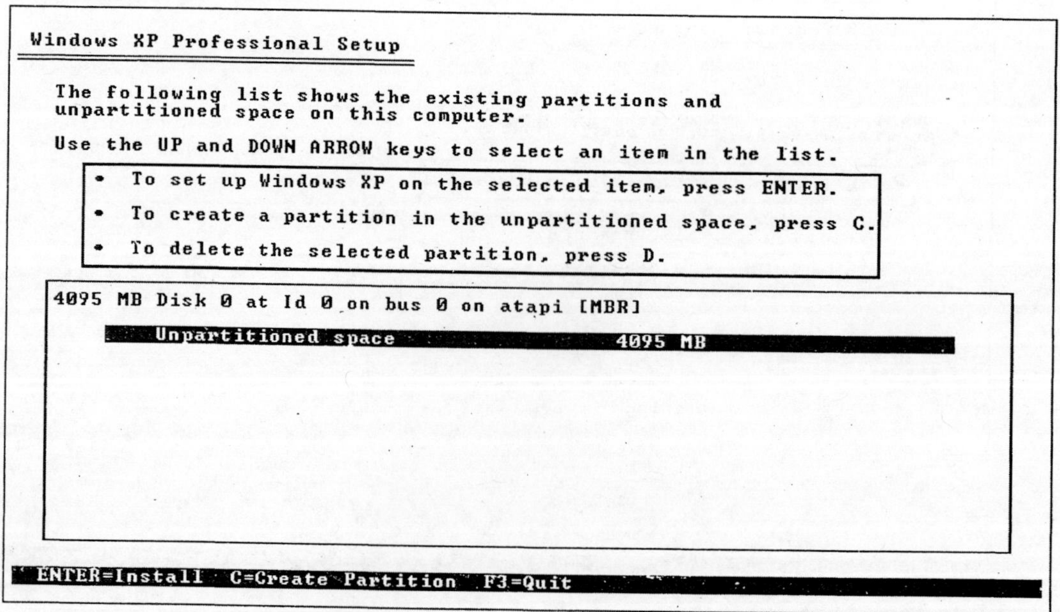

```
Windows XP Professional Setup

   The following list shows the existing partitions and
   unpartitioned space on this computer.

   Use the UP and DOWN ARROW keys to select an item in the list.

     •  To set up Windows XP on the selected item, press ENTER.

     •  To create a partition in the unpartitioned space, press C.

     •  To delete the selected partition, press D.

   4095 MB Disk 0 at Id 0 on bus 0 on atapi [MBR]

        Unpartitioned space                    4095 MB

 ENTER=Install  C=Create Partition  F3=Quit
```

You will need to select either an existing partition or "Unpartitioned space" (if available) to define the partition to install Windows XP, then press ENTER.

The next screen asks for the type of disk formatting to be used:

(if you install XP into an already existing partition, you have additional options to leave the current disk formatting intact). Select the type of disk formatting : FAT or NTFS

- FAT :
  Possible to access from a DOS-boot floppy, but limited to max. 4 GByte with very inefficient file-storage and no Security features.
- NTFS :
  Not accessible from a DOS-boot floppy, but NOT limited in size and use an efficient file-storage, able to use File-System Security features.

Windows XP requires a lot of disk-space for itself, you should use at least a 4 GByte partition to install XP.

We suggest to use NTFS : make your choice (highlight it) and select it by pressing ENTER.

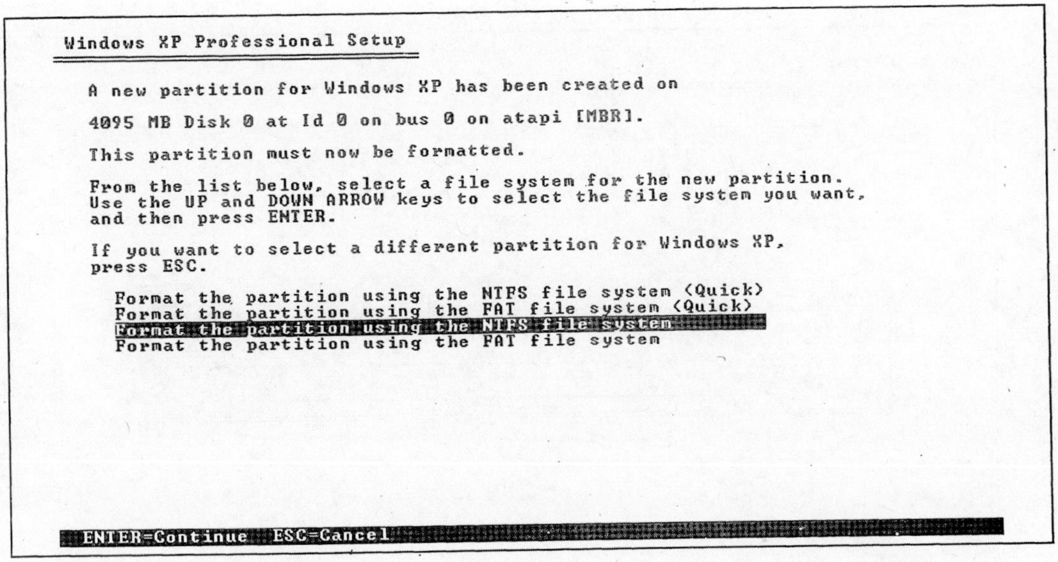

```
Windows XP Professional Setup

  A new partition for Windows XP has been created on

  4095 MB Disk 0 at Id 0 on bus 0 on atapi [MBR].

  This partition must now be formatted.

  From the list below, select a file system for the new partition.
  Use the UP and DOWN ARROW keys to select the file system you want,
  and then press ENTER.

  If you want to select a different partition for Windows XP,
  press ESC.

    Format the partition using the NTFS file system (Quick)
    Format the partition using the FAT file system (Quick)
    Format the partition using the NTFS file system
    Format the partition using the FAT file system

 ENTER=Continue  ESC=Cancel
```

Setup will start formatting the disk:

```
Windows XP Professional Setup

              Please wait while Setup formats the partition
     C:  Partition1 [New (Raw)]                4087 MB (  4086 MB free)
            on 4095 MB Disk 0 at Id 0 on bus 0 on atapi [MBR].

       Setup is formatting...
                                    20%
```

and will then start copying files from the CD-ROM to the disk:

```
Windows XP Professional Setup

                  Please wait while Setup copies files
                  to the Windows installation folders.
                This might take several minutes to complete.

       Setup is copying files...
                                    4%

                                              Copying: symbole.fon
```

The system will then need to reboot:

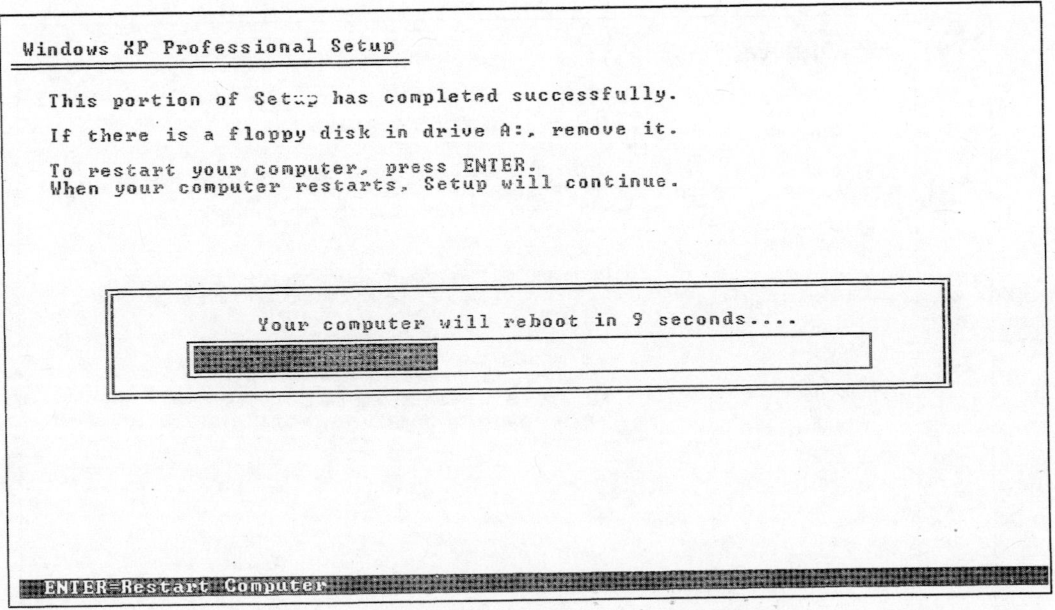

(you can press ENTER here to shorten the delay in restarting)

After the restart, Windows XP starts the first time with the Graphical User Interface (GUI):

Setup will continue to copy files and to install devices:

Collecting information

Dynamic Update

Preparing installation

Installing Windows

Finalizing installation

Setup will complete in approximately:
39 minutes

An exciting new look

Windows® XP Professional sports a brand-new visual design that combines a sleek look, clean lines, and appealing colors with a task-oriented design and exceptionally streamlined navigation.

The redesigned Start menu makes it easier to find important information and to access the programs you use most frequently.

By automatically cleaning up the notification area of the taskbar and grouping related taskbar items, Windows XP makes it easier to switch between programs and to open, view, or close multiple items at the same time.

Microsoft Windows XP

Collecting information

Dynamic Update

Preparing installation

Installing Windows

Finalizing installation

Setup will complete in approximately:
37 minutes

Installing Devices

Get support for the latest hardware and software

Windows® XP Professional supports a large number of programs and has built-in support for the latest hardware, including DirectX® 8 for great multimedia support.

When you insert a floppy disk, ZIP® disk, CD, or memory card from your digital camera, Windows XP identifies the content (such as pictures, music, or video), and automatically starts the appropriate program. Windows XP Professional also supports DVD-RAM drives.

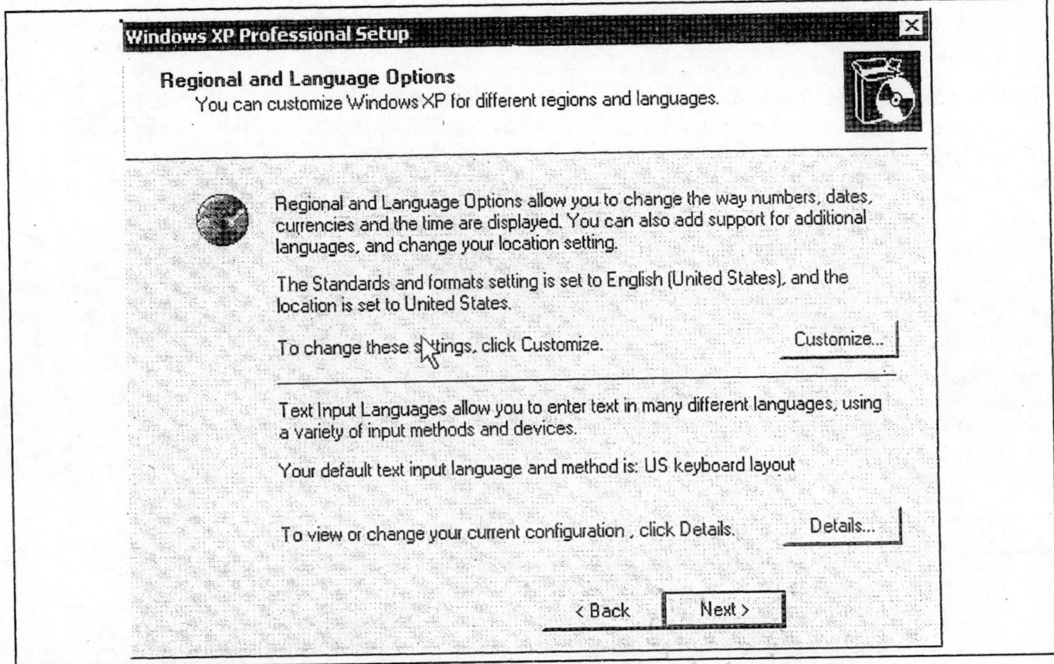

You can adjust regional settings using the "Customize.." option:

Personalize your system by entering your name and organization:

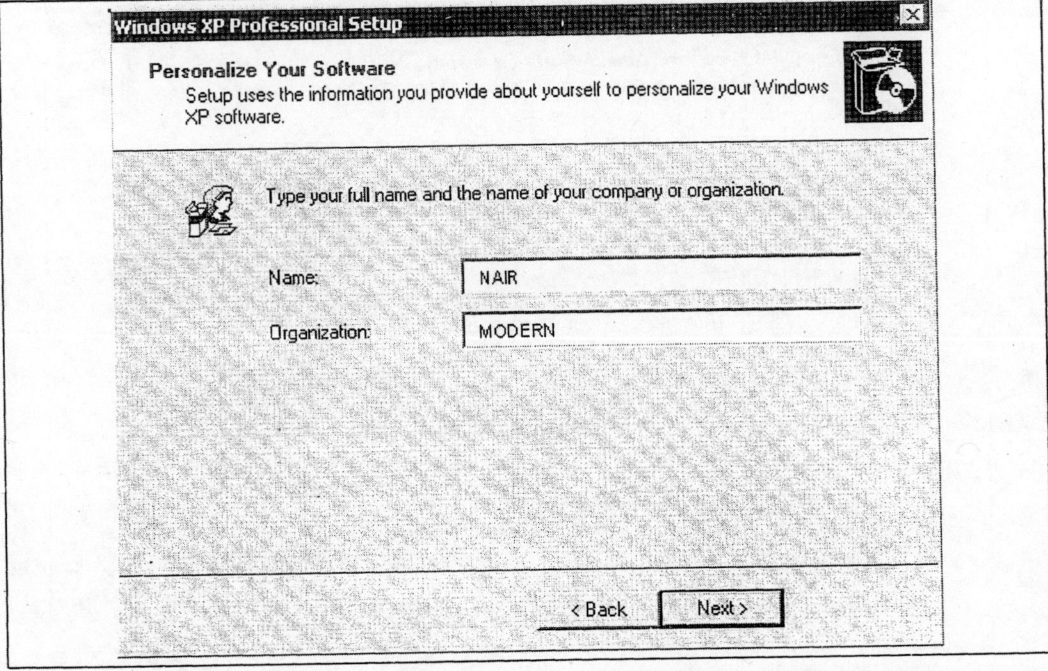

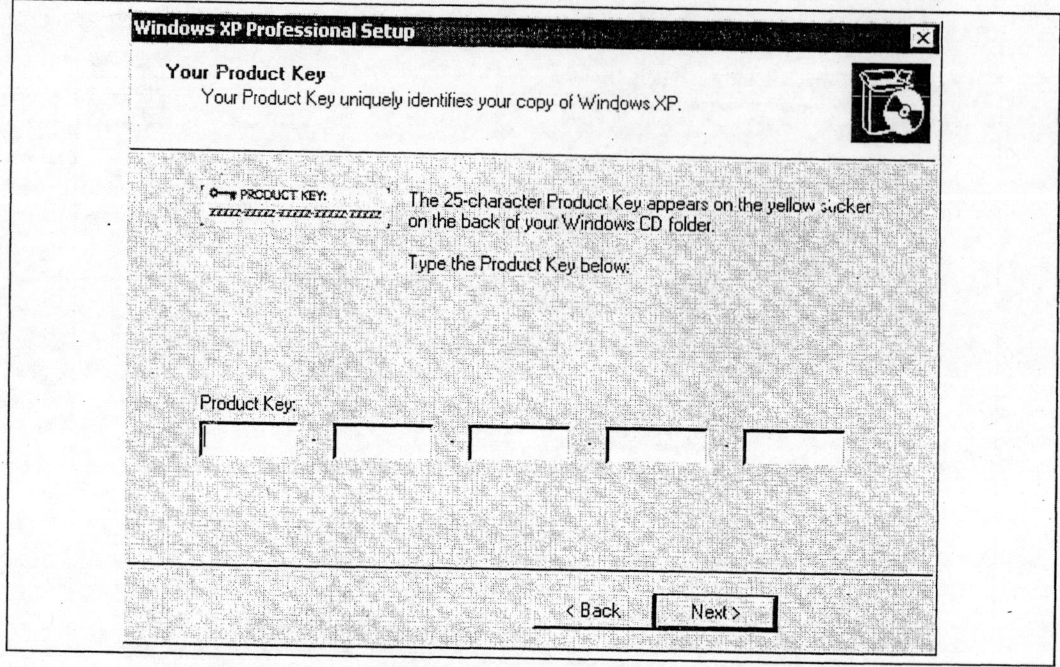

Enter your 25 character Product key (as given on your Windows XP CD-ROM):

Define name for your computer and the password for Administrator account:

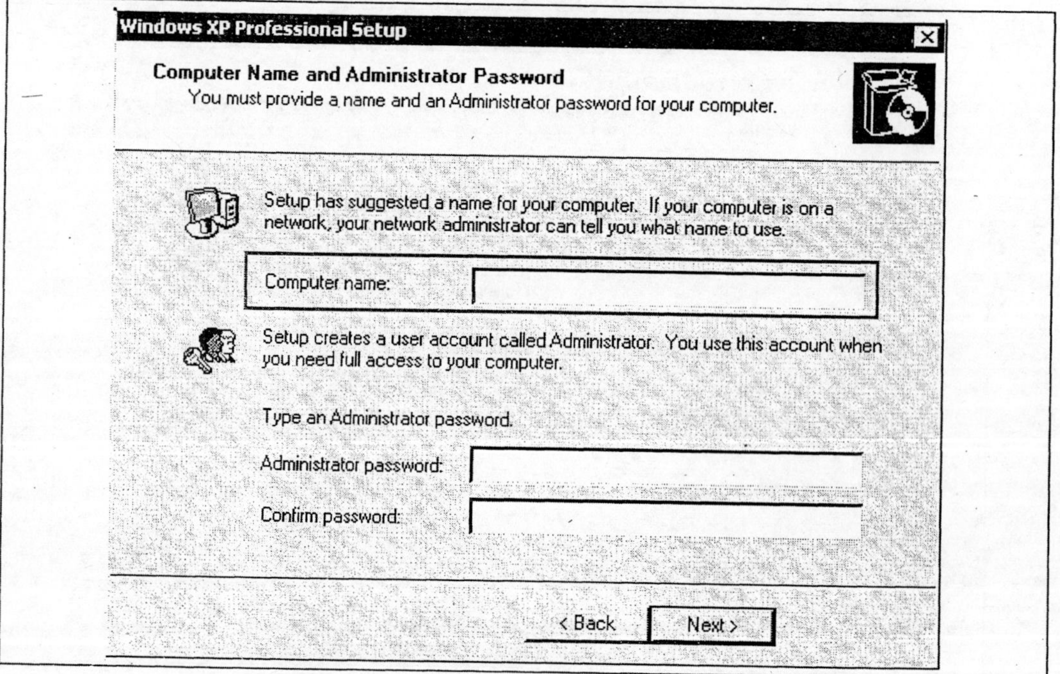

Based on the organization (defined above), Setup creates a name for your computer, which will be unique in the network configuration.

Since this name will be used later inside the "Network Neighborhood" / "My Network places", change it to an easy to understand, but unique name.

If you enter a password for the Administrator Account, make sure that you remember it (to be safe, write it down).

Check the "Date and Time Settings", allowing to check/define/correct the date, time and timezone:

If you have a network card in your system, which was detected by Setup, you will be asked to select whether to install

- a typical configuration (which you can always change later) or
- if you like to make now already special settings (like: defining your IP-address) .

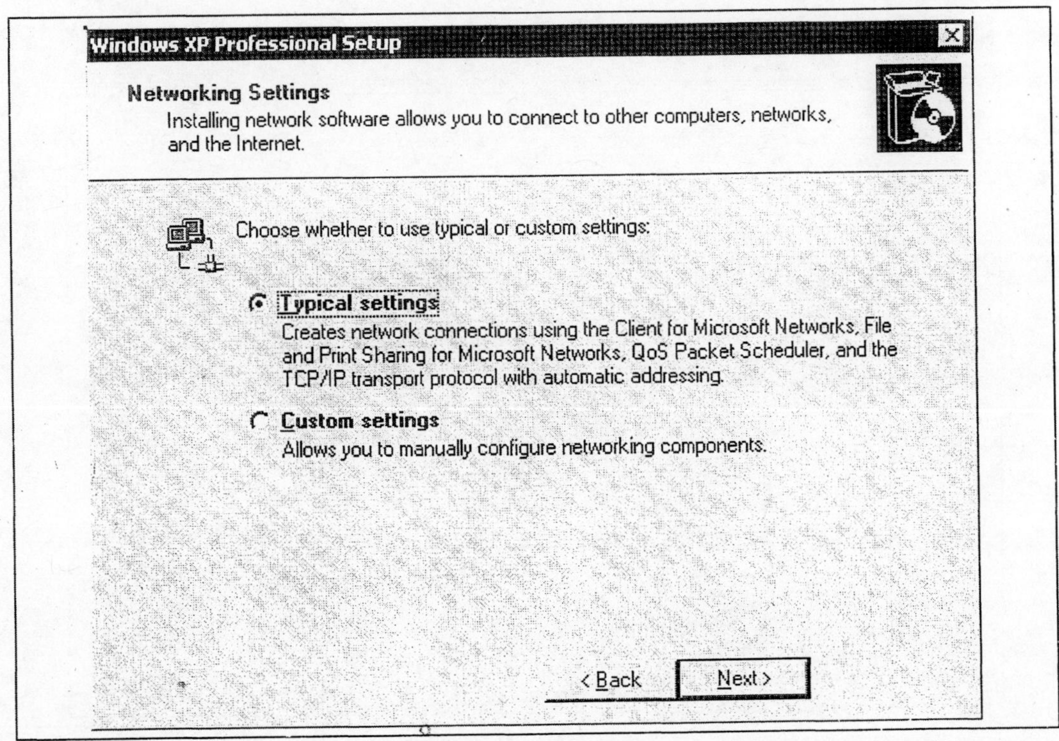

Setup continues with "Finalizing installation ":

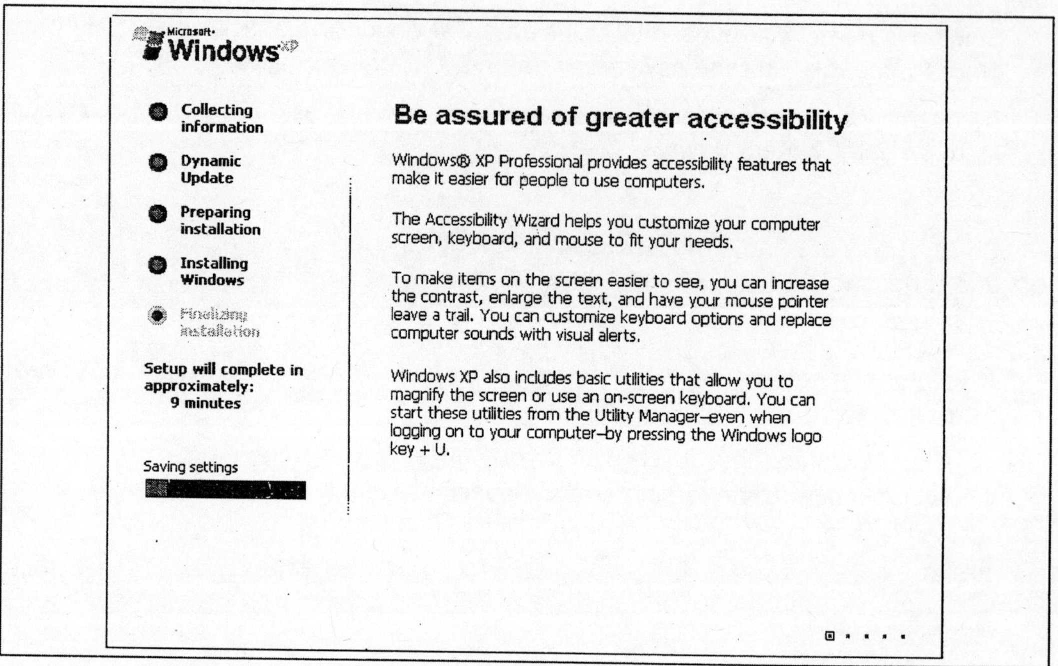

The system will reboot again.

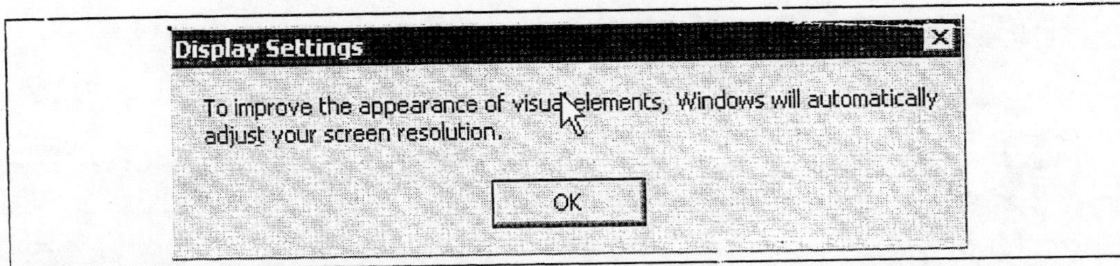

Setup will then configure your screen resolution.

The system will try to connect via the Internet to the Microsoft Website, you can select to "Skip" this step.

You will be prompted to enter the first Usernames (which will be defined as Administrators) and you will get the new XP Welcome screen:

(note : if only one user was defined during setup and no password was defined, the system will skip the Welcome screen and continue to display the new Windows XP desktop).

You are now ready to use the new improved and colorful Windows XP.

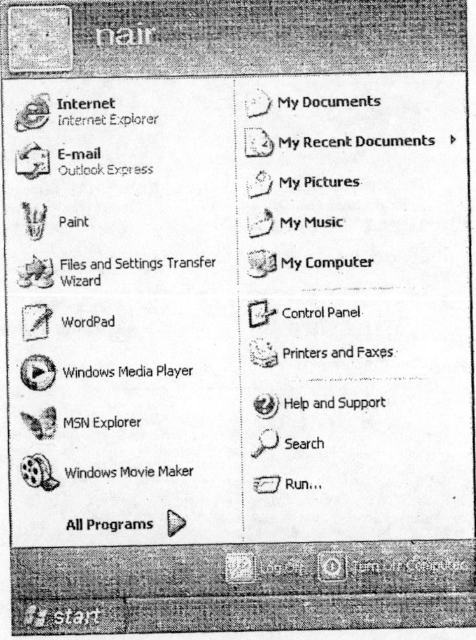

Latest Technology in Computer Hardware

In this section we shall take a look at current trends in computer hardware field, such as Intel P4 processor based on HT technology, Motherboard based on 915 chipset, computer memory based on dual channel DDR2 RAM, Serial ATA (SATA) interface for storage devices, RAID, PCI Express expansion slot etc.

Pentium 4 with Hyper Threading (HT) Technology

Intel Pentium-4 processor with Hyper-Threading (HT) technology is based on the Intel NetBurst microarchitecture.

These processors are binary-compatible with previous generation Intel architecture-based processors.

This processor is best suited for Internet audio and streaming video, image processing, video content creation, speech, 3D, CAD, games, multimedia, and multitasking user environments.

The Pentium 4 processor is available with 1-MB L2 cache and 2-MB L2 cache plus advanced technologies to improve system utilization.

Pentium 4 processor Extreme Edition (EE) supporting HT Technology features 3.46 GHz with 2 MB of L3 cache and 3.73 GHz with 2 M of L2 cache to offer high levels of performance for high-end gamers and computing power users.

With Hyper-Threading Technology, desktop users can experience greater system responsiveness and performance when multitasking.

The Pentium 4 processor 6xx and 3.73 GHz Extreme Edition provide Intel Extended Memory 64 Technology (Intel EM64T) support for 64-bit computing.

Additionally, the Pentium 4 processor 6xx also provides power saving capabilities with Enhanced Intel SpeedStep technology, and is available with an advanced 1066 MHz system bus.

The Pentium 4 processor 5xx is supported by the Intel 925X, Intel 925XE, 915 Express chipset family, Intel 875P and Intel 865 Express chipset family.

The Pentium 4 processor 6xx is supported by the, Intel 925X, Intel 925XE, and Intel 915 Express chipset family.

The Pentium 4 processor Extreme Edition 3.73 GHz is supported by the Intel 925XE Express chipset.

Intel Express chipsets enabled for HT Technology and currently supported by their respective Pentium 4 processor are: Intel 925XE, 925X, 915G, 915GV, 915GL, 915P, 915PL, 875P, 865G, 865PE, 865P, 850E, 845GE, 845PE, 845GV, 845G2 and 845E Express chipsets.

Intel Pentium 4 Processor Family

Speed	Cache size	HT	Speed Step	EM64TF	System Bus	Package	Product Name
2.40 GHz	512 KB	No	No	No	400 MHz	mPGA478	Pentium 4 processor 2.40 GHz
2.40A GHz	1MB L2	No	No	No	533 MHz	mPGA478	Pentium 4 processor 2.40A GHz
2.40B GHz	512 KB	No	No	No	533 MHz	mPGA478	Pentium 4 processor 2.40B GHz
2.40C GHz	512 KB	Yes	No	No	800 MHz	mPGA478	Pentium 4 processor with HT 2.40C GHz
2.60 GHz	512 KB	No	No	No	400 MHz	mPGA478	Pentium 4 processor 2.60 GHz
2.60C GHz	512 KB	Yes	No	No	800 MHz	mPGA478	Pentium 4 processor with HT 2.60C GHz
2.66 GHz	512 KB	No	No	No	533 MHz	mPGA478	Pentium 4 processor 2.66 GHz
2.80 GHz	1MB	Yes	No	No	800 MHz	FCLGA775	Pentium 4 processor 520 with HT
2.80 GHz	512 KB	No	No	No	533 MHz	mPGA478	Pentium 4 processor 2.80 GHz

Speed	Cache size	HT	Speed Step	EM64TF	System Bus	Package	Product Name
2.80A GHz	1MB	No	No	No	533 MHz	mPGA478	Pentium 4 processor 2.80A GHz
2.80C GHz	512 KB	Yes	No	No	800 MHz	mPGA478	Pentium 4 processor with HT 2.80C GHz
2.80E GHz	1MB	Yes	No	No	800 MHz	mPGA478	Pentium 4 processor with HT 2.80E GHz
3.00 GHz	1MB	Yes	No	No	800 MHz	FCLGA775	Pentium 4 processor 530 with HT
3.00 GHz	2 MB	Yes	Yes	Yes	800 MHz	FCLGA775	Pentium 4 processor 630 with HT
3.00 GHz	512 KB	Yes	No	No	800 MHz	mPGA478	Pentium 4 processor with HT 3 GHz
3.00E GHz	1MB	Yes	No	No	800 MHz	mPGA478	Pentium 4 processor with HT 3E GHz
3.06 GHz	512 KB	Yes	No	No	533 MHz	mPGA478	Pentium 4 processor with HT 3.06 GHz
3.20 GHz	1MB	Yes	No	No	800 MHz	FCLGA775	Pentium 4 processor 540 with HT
3.20 GHz	2 MB	Yes	Yes	Yes	800 MHz	FCLGA775	Pentium 4 processor 640 with HT
3.20 GHz	512 KB	Yes	No	No	800 MHz	mPGA478	Pentium 4 processor with HT 3.20 GHz
3.20E GHz	1MB	Yes	No	No	800 MHz	mPGA478	Pentium 4 processor with HT 3.20E GHz
3.40 GHz	1MB	Yes	No	No	800 MHz	FCLGA775	Pentium 4 processor 550 with HT
3.40 GHz	2 MB	Yes	Yes	Yes	800 MHz	FCLGA775	Pentium 4 processor 650 with HT

Speed	Cache size	HT	Speed Step	EM64TF	System Bus	Package	Product Name
3.40 GHz	512 KB	Yes	No	No	800 MHz	mPGA478	Pentium 4 processor with HT 3.40 GHz
3.40 GHz	512-KB L2 cache 2-MB L3 cache	Yes	No	No	800 MHz	FCLGA775	Pentium 4 processor with HT, Extreme Edition 3.40 GHz
3.40E GHz	1MB	Yes	No	No	800 MHz	mPGA478	Pentium 4 processor with HT 3.40E GHz
3.46 GHz	512-KB L2 cache 2-MB L3 cache	Yes	No	No	1066 MHz	FCLGA775	Pentium 4 processor with HT, Extreme Edition 3.46 GHz
3.60 GHz	1MB	Yes	No	No	800 MHz	FCLGA775	Pentium 4 processor 560 with HT
3.60 GHz	2 MB	Yes	Yes	Yes	800 MHz	FCLGA775	Pentium 4 processor 660? with HT
3.73 GHz	2 MB	Yes	No	Yes	1066 MHz	FCLGA775	Pentium 4 processor with HT, Extreme Edition 3.73 GHz
3.80 GHz	1 MB	Yes	No	No	800 MHz	FCLGA775	Pentium 4 processor 570 with HT

Intel NetBurst Microarchitecture

Intel NetBurst microarchitecture delivers a number of innovative features including Hyper-Threading Technology, hyper-pipelined technology, 1066, 800, 533 or 400 MHz system bus, and Execution Trace Cache.

It also provides a number of enhanced features such as Advanced Transfer Cache, Advanced Dynamic Execution, enhanced floating-point and multimedia unit, and Streaming SIMD Extensions 2 (SSE2).

Further enhancements in the 90 nm process-based Pentium 4 processor include Streaming SIMD Extensions 3 (SSE3).

Many of these innovations and advances were made possible with improvements in processor technology, process technology, and circuit design and could not previously be implemented in high-volume, manufacturable solutions.

The features and resulting benefits of the microarchitecture are defined below.

Hyper-Threading Technology

Hyper-Threading Technology (HT Technology) is a groundbreaking technology to improve processor performance.

It allows software programs to "see" two processors and work more efficiently. This new technology enables the processor to execute two series, or threads, of instructions at the same time, thereby improving performance and system responsiveness.

Hyper-Threading Technology requires a computer system with an Intel Pentium 4 processor supporting HT Technology and a HT Technology enabled chipset, BIOS and operating system.

Hyper-Pipelined Technology

The hyper-pipelined technology of the Intel NetBurst microarchitecture increases the pipeline depth delivering increased performance, frequency, and scalability of the processor.

1066MHz, 800 MHz, 533 MHz or 400 MHz System Bus

In the Pentium 4 processor with 1066 MHz system bus, the bus supports high performance by delivering up to 8.5 GB of data-per-second into and out of the processor.

This is accomplished through a physical signaling scheme of quad-pumping the data transfers over a 266 MHz clocked system bus and a buffering scheme allowing for sustained 1066 MHz data transfers.

The same quad-pumping of data is true for Pentium 4 processors with 800 MHz system bus (6.4 GB data-per-second with a 200 MHz clocked system bus), 533 MHz system bus (4.2 GB data-per-second with a 133 MHz clocked system bus) and 400 MHz system bus (3.2 GB data-per-second with a 100 MHz clocked system bus).

Level 1 Execution Trace Cache

The 90 nm Pentium 4 processor features 16-KB data cache compared to 8-KB on the 0.13 micron Pentium 4 processor.

In addition to the data cache, the Pentium 4 processor includes an Execution Trace Cache that stores up to 12-K decoded micro-ops in the order of program execution.

This increases performance by removing the decoder from the main execution loop and makes more efficient usage of the cache storage space since instructions that are branched around are not stored.

The result is a means to deliver a high volume of instructions to the processor's execution units and a reduction in the overall time required to recover from branches that have been mis-predicted.

Enhanced Intel SpeedStep Technology

Enhanced Intel SpeedStep technology can enable power savings and acoustics improvement benefit. When running applications that demand less processor power, the operating system will adjust the processor clock down.

Enabling of Enhanced Intel SpeedStep technology can lead to power efficient systems that can run quieter and cooler.

Intel Enhanced Memory 64 Technology (Intel EM64T)

Intel EM64T provides an enhancement to Intel's 32-bit architecture by enabling the desktop processor platform to access larger amounts of memory.

With appropriate 64-bit supporting hardware and software, platforms based on an Intel processor supporting Intel EM64T can enable use of extended virtual and physical memory.

EM64T requires a computer system with a processor, chipset, BIOS, operating system, device drivers and applications enabled for Intel EM64T. Processor will not operate (including 32-bit operation) without an Intel EM64T-enabled BIOS.

1-MB or 512-KB Level 2 Advanced Transfer Cache

The 90 nm process-based Pentium 4 processor features 1MB (5xx) or 2-MB (6xx) L2 Advanced Transfer Cache (ATC) compared to 512-KB on the 0.13 micron process-based Pentium 4 processor.

The Level 2 ATC delivers a much higher data throughput channel between the Level 2 cache and the processor core.

The Advanced Transfer Cache consists of a 256-bit (32-byte) interface that transfers data on each core clock.

As a result, the Pentium 4 processor with 1MB L2 cache at 3.80 GHz can deliver a data transfer rate of 122 GB/s.

Non-Blocking, full speed, on-die level 2 cache

8-way set associativity, 256-bit data bus to the level 2 cache.

Integrated 2MB Level 3 Cache on Intel Pentium 4 Processor Extreme Edition 3.46 GHz

The 2-MB L3 cache is available only with the Pentium 4 processor Extreme Edition.

The additional third level of cache is located on the processor die and is designed specifically to meet the compute needs of high-end gamers and other power users.

The Integrated L3 cache is available in 2 MB and when coupled with either the 1066 MHz or 800 MHz system bus provides a high bandwidth path to memory.

The efficient design of the integrated L3 cache provides a faster path to large data sets stored in cache on the processor. This results in reduced average memory latency and increased throughput for larger workloads.

Integrated 2MB Level 2 Cache on Intel Pentium 4 Processor Extreme Edition 3.73 GHz and 6xx

The 2-MB Advanced Transfer Cache (on-die, full-speed Level 2 cache) with 8-way associative and Error Correcting Code (ECC) can improve overall performance by allowing the processor to have faster access to a larger amount of the most often used data.

Advanced Dynamic Execution

The Advance Dynamic Execution engine is a very deep, out-of-order speculative execution engine that keeps the execution units executing instructions.

It also includes an enhanced branch prediction algorithm that has the net effect of reducing the number of branch mis-predictions.

Enhanced Floating-Point and Multimedia Unit

The Pentium 4 processor expands the floating-point registers to a full 128-bit and adds an additional register for data movement which helps improve performance on both floating-point and multimedia applications.

Streaming SIMD Extensions 3 (SSE3) Instructions

With the introduction of SSE2, the Intel NetBurst microarchitecture extended the SIMD capabilities that Intel MMX technology and SSE technology delivered by adding 144 instructions.

The next generation 90 nm process-based Pentium 4 processor introduces the Streaming SIMD Extensions 3 (SSE3), which includes 13 additional SIMD instructions over SSE2.

The 13 new instructions in SSE3 are primarily designed to improve thread synchronization and specific application areas such as media and gaming.

Features Used for Testing and Performance/Thermal Monitoring

Built-in Self Test (BIST) provides single stuck-at fault coverage of the microcode and large logic arrays, as well as testing of the instruction cache, data cache, Translation Lookaside Buffers (TLBs), and ROMs.

IEEE 1149.1 Standard Test Access Port and Boundary Scan mechanism enables testing of the Pentium 4 processor and system connections through a standard interface.

Internal performance counters for performance monitoring and event counting.

Includes a Thermal Monitor feature that allows motherboards to be more cost effective.

Intel 915 Chipset

Intel 915G Chipset is designed for the Intel Pentium 4 processor with Hyper-Threading (HT) Technology in the LGA775 package. This chipset brings compelling new capabilities to the mainstream desktop PC.

Third generation Intel graphics with Intel Graphics Media Accelerator (GMA) 900, supports widescreen LCD displays, accelerated DirectX 9, dual independent display, enhanced display modes for widescreen flat panels, and optimized 3D support.

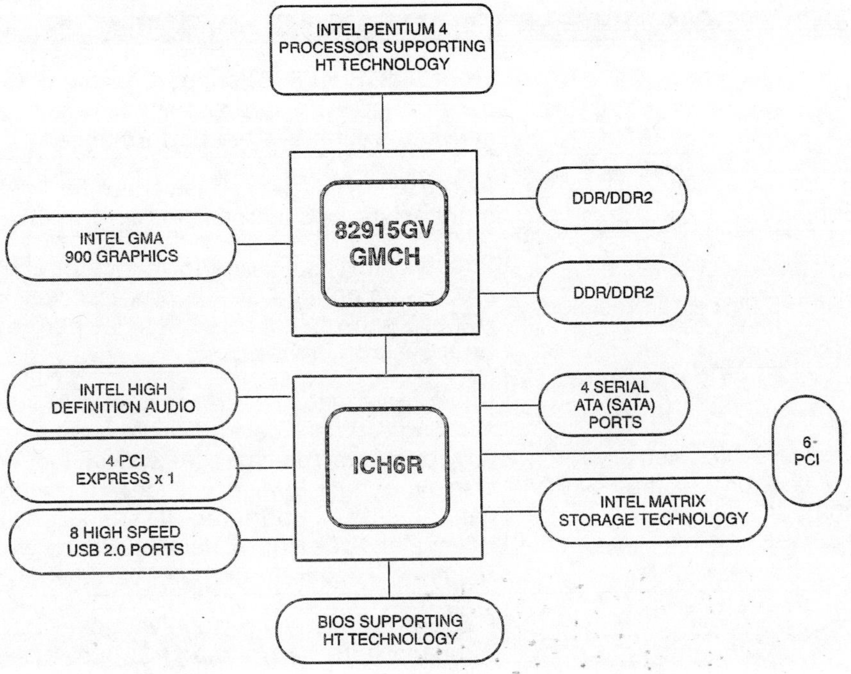

Fig. 23-1 : 915 Chipset.

Platforms based on the Intel 915G Express Chipset can deliver an intense and realistic visual experience without requiring a separate graphics card.

The new graphics core, combined with Intel's high-performance dual-channel memory interface, can deliver up to twice the graphics performance of previous Intel platforms.

Advanced features such as Intel High Definition Audio (Intel HD Audio) technology, features eight independent DMA audio engines that support multiple simultaneous and separate audio input and output streams. This enables high quality integrated audio that rivals the performance of high end discrete solutions.

Intel HD Audio is also capable of supporting major consumer entertainment industry formats, such as 7.1 surround sound, Dolby Digital*, and DTS*.

Intel Matrix Storage Technology integrated into the chipset provides Enhanced RAID support, which allows critical data to be stored on one array that is designed for high reliability (RAID1), while performance intensive applications like games can reside on separate array designed for maximum performance (RAID0).

Flexible memory support for both dual channel DDR2 533 memory, which can deliver up to 8.5 GB/s bandwidth, and dual channel DDR memory allows for a range of memory configurations.

Features	Benefits
800-/533-MHz System Bus	Front Side Bus (FSB) support for high-performance Intel processor frequencies and delivers greater system performance.
Hyper-Threading Technology Support	Increased system responsiveness for multitasking and increase in performance.
LGA775 Processor Package	Supports the highest performance Intel desktop processors on the LGA775 processor package. LGA775 socket supports the high- performance Intel desktop processors.
Intel Graphics Media Accelerator 900(Intel GMA 900)	Incorporates latest Microsoft DirectX9 support, allowing software developers to create real-life environments and characters. Dual independent display, enhanced display modes for widescreen flat panels, and optimized 3D support deliver an intense and realistic visual experience without requiring a separate graphics card.
PCI Express	PCI Express x 1 I/O bus delivers over 3.5 times the bandwidth for I/O than PCI bus. Designed for bandwidth-intensive applications. PCI Express x 16 graphics delivers up to 4 GB/s per direction, more than three and a half times the bandwidth of previous high-end discrete graphics solutions. PCI Express x 1 I/O offers 500 MB/s concurrently, over three and a half times the bandwidth of traditional PCI architecture.
Dual-channel DDR2 or DDR	Flexible memory support for both dual channel DDR2 533 memory, which can deliver up to 8.5 GB/s bandwidth, and dual channel DDR memory allows for a range of memory configurations of up to 4 GB RAM.
Direct Media Interface (DMI)	For I/O intensive applications, new serial point-to-point bus delivers up to 2.0 GB/s concurrent bandwidth between the memory and I/O controllers, compared to 266 MB/s with previous generation Intel Hub Architecture.
Intel High Definition Audio	Support for new consumer audio entertainment formats such as 7.1 surround sound, Dolby Digital, and DTS. Audio codec support for 192 kHz quality, multiple streams, and better voice input for speech recognition and voice-over-IP.

Features	Benefits
Intel Matrix Storage Technology with ICH6R only	Boosts storage performance with RAID 0, while helping to protect your digital memories with RAID 1, on the same disks. Advanced Host Controller Interface (AHCI) further boosts performance with Native Command Queuing (NCQ), and provides native hot plug for drive swaps.
Integrated 4 Serial ATA Ports (SATA/150)	Facilitates high-speed storage and data transfers at up to 150 MB/s for each of 4 ports. Allows easier hard drive upgrades and expansion for new SATA optical drive.
Ultra ATA/100	Supports legacy hard drives and optical drives.
Integrated Hi-Speed USB 2.0	Eight ports offer up to 40X greater bandwidth over USB 1.1, for high-speed I/O peripherals such as digital video cameras.
Intel Serial Digital Video Output (SDVO)	Dual SDVO ports offer maximum display (digital CRT or TV) flexibility through the existing PCI Express x16 connector.

Motherboard Based on Intel 915 Chipset

This Intel 915 chipset based motherboard explained in this sections is in Micro ATX form factor (9.6-in x 8.6-in or 24.4 cm x 21.8 cm).

Specifications

CPU

This board supports Intel 775-Pin Socket supporting Intel Pentium 4/Celeron processor in 775-land LGA package

Chipsets

North Bridge: Intel 915GL chipset, FSB 800 / 533MHz, supports Hyper-Threading Technology. South Bridge: Intel ICH6, supports SATA 1.5Gb/s

Memory

2 DDR DIMM slots: DDR1 and DDR2 supports PC3200 (DDR400) / PC2700 (DDR333), Max. 2GB Dual Channel Memory support

Layout of Intel 915 Chipset Based Motherboard for P4

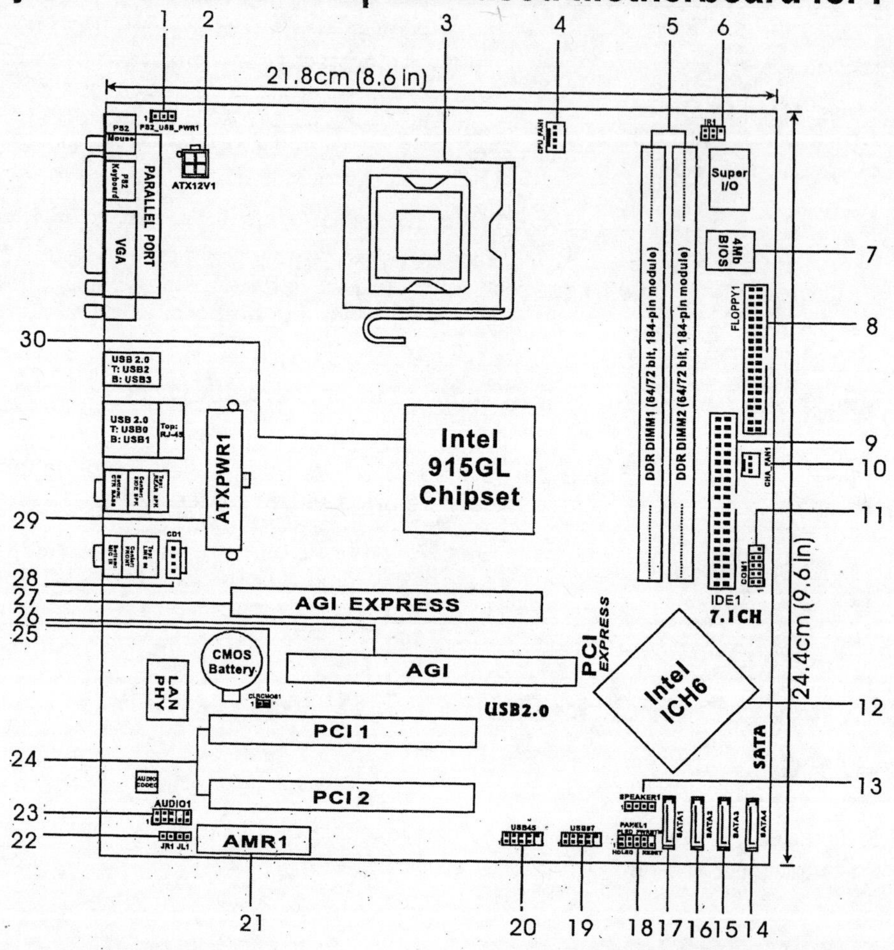

1 PS2_USB_PWR1 Jumper
2 ATX 12V Connector (ATX12V1)
3 775-Pin CPU Socket
4 CPU Fan Connector (CPU_FAN1)
5 184-pin DDR DIMM Slots (DDR1-2, Dual Channel)
6 Infrared Module Connector (IR1)
7 BIOS FWH Chip
8 Floppy Connector (FLOPPY1)
9 Primary IDE Connector (IDE1, Black)
10 Chassis Fan Connector (CHA_FAN1)
11 COM Port Header (COM1)
12 South Bridge Controller
13 Chassis Speaker Header (SPEAKER 1)
14 Fourth Serial ATA Connector (SATA4, black)
15 Third Serial ATA Connector (SATA3, black)
16 Secondary Serial ATA Connector (SATA2, blue)
17 Primary Serial ATA Connector (SATA1, blue)
18 System Panel Header (PANEL1)
19 USB 2.0 Header (USB67, Blue)
20 USB 2.0 Header (USB45, Blue)
21 AMR Slot (AMR1)
22 JR1 / JL1 Jumpers
23 Front Panel Audio Header (AUDIO1)
24 PCI Slots (PCI1-2)
25 Clear CMOS Jumper (CLRCMOS1)
26 Graphics Interface Slot (AGI)
27 AGI Express Slot (PCI Express x 4)
28 Internal Audio Connector: CD1 (Black)
29 ATX Power Connector (ATXPWR1)
30 North Bridge Controller

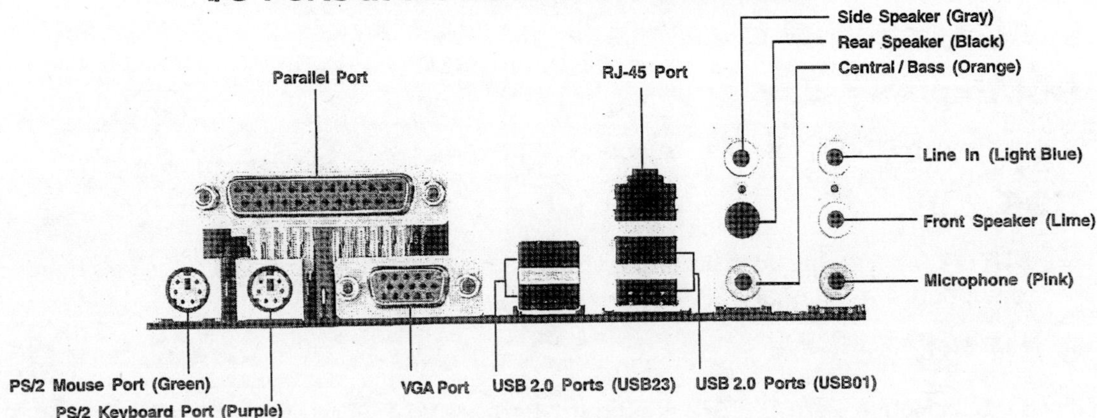

IDE

ATA 100 / Ultra DMA Mode 5, supports up to 2 IDE devices.

Serial ATA (SATA)

Supports up to 4 SATA devices at 1.5Gb/s data transfer rate.

Floppy Port

Supports up to 2 floppy disk drives.

Audio

7.1 channels AC'97 Audio

PCI LAN

Speed: 802.3u (10/100 Ethernet), supports Wake-On-LAN

Hardware Monitor

CPU temperature sensing, Chassis temperature sensing, CPU overheat shutdown to protect CPU life, CPU fan tachometer, Chassis fan tachometer, Voltage monitoring: +12V, +5V, +3.3V, Vcore

PCI slots

2 PCI slots with PCI Specification 2.3

MR slot

1 slot, supports modem riser (MR) card.

AGP slot

1 AGP slot for Grapic Card.

PCI Express slot

1 slot with PCI Express x 4 , supports PCI Express x 16 Graphic Card.

USB 2.0

8 USB 2.0 ports: includes 4 default USB 2.0 ports on the rear panel, plus two headers to support 4 additional USB 2.0 ports.

8 CH I/O

1 PS/2 Mouse Port, 1 PS/2 Keyboard Port, 1 VGA Port, 1 Parallel Port (ECP/EPP Support), 4 Ready-to-Use USB 2.0 Ports, 1 RJ-45 Port.

Audio Jack: Side Speaker / Rear Speaker / Central/Bass / Line In / Front Speaker / Microphone.

COM Port

1 COM Port Header to support a COM port module.

BIOS

AMI BIOS, with support for "Plug and Play", ACPI 1.1 compliance wake up events, Supports jumperfree, SMBIOS 2.3.1 support, CPU frequency stepless control.

This motherboard supports Dual Channel Memory Technology.

For microphone input, this motherboard supports both stereo and mono modes. For audio output, this motherboard supports 2-channel, 4-channel, 6-channel, and 8-channel modes.

If you use 2-channel speaker, connect the speaker's plug into "Front Speaker Jack". See the following table for connection details in accordance with the type of speaker you use.

Audio Output Connection

Audio Output Channels	Front Speaker	Rear Speaker	Central / Bass	Side Speaker
2	V			
4	V	V		
6	V	V	V	
8	V	V	V	V

Installation

Take note of the following precautions before you install motherboard components or change any motherboard settings.

1. Unplug the power cord from the wall socket before touching any component.
2. To avoid damaging the motherboard components due to static electricity, NEVER place your motherboard directly on the carpet or the like. Also remember to use a grounded wrist strap or touch a safety grounded object before you handle components.
3. Hold components by the edges and do not touch the ICs.
4. Whenever you uninstall any component, place it on a grounded antistatic pad or in the bag that comes with the component.

Secure the motherboard to the chassis. Do not over-tighten the screws, doing so may damage the motherboard.

CPU Installation

For the installation of Intel 775-LAND CPU, please follow the steps below.

Before you insert the 775-LAND CPU into the socket, please check if the CPU surface is unclean or if there is any bent pin on the socket.

Do not force to insert the CPU into the socket if above situation is found. Otherwise, the CPU will be seriously damaged.

Open the socket:

Disengage the lever by depressing down and out on the hook to clear retention tab.

Rotate the load lever to fully open position at approximately 135 degrees.

Rotate the load plate to fully open position at approximately 100 degrees.

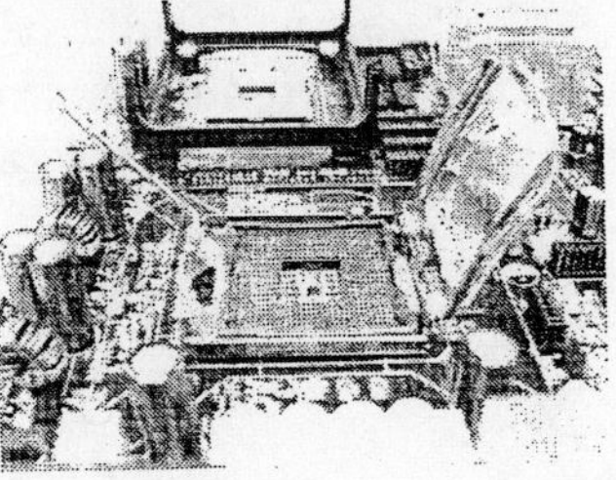

Insert the 775-LAND CPU:

Hold the CPU by the edges where are marked with black lines.

Orient the CPU with IHS (Integrated Heat Sink) up. Locate Pin1 and the two orientation key notches.

For proper inserting, please ensure to match the two orientation key notches of the CPU with the two alignment keys of the socket.

Carefully place the CPU into the socket by using a purely vertical motion.

Verify that the CPU is within the socket and properly mated to the orient keys.

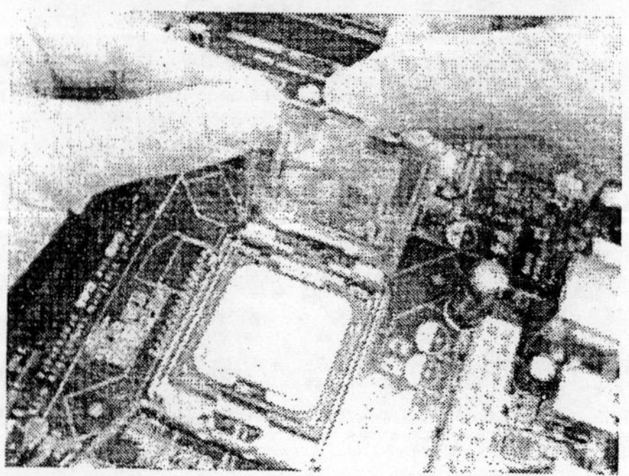

Remove PnP Cap (Pick and Place Cap), use your left hand index finger and thumb to support the load plate edge, engage PnP cap with right hand thumb and peel the cap from the socket while pressing on center of PnP cap to assist in removal.

It is recommended to use the cap tab to handle and avoid kicking off the PnP cap.

Close the socket:

Rotate the load plate onto the IHS.

While pressing down lightly on load plate, engage the load lever.

Secure load lever with load plate tab under retention tab of load lever.

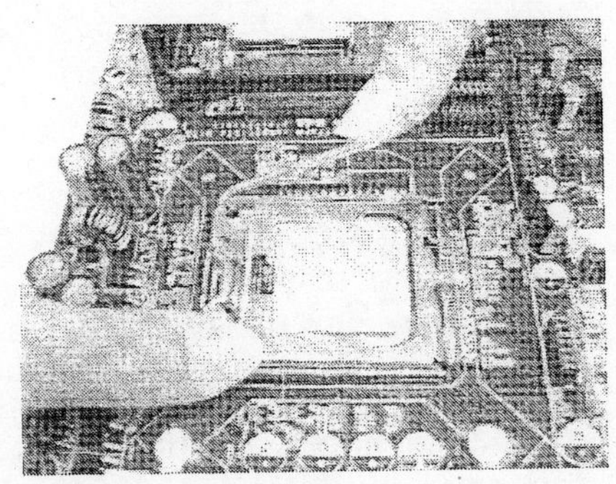

Installation of CPU Fan and Heatsink

This motherboard has 775-Pin socket that supports Intel 775-LAND CPU. Use a heatsink and cooling fan compliant with Intel 775-LAND CPU. Before installing the heatsink, use thermal grease between the CPU and the heatsink to improve heat dissipation.

Once the CPU and heatsink are securely fastened and in good contact with each other, connect the CPU fan to the CPU_FAN connector on motherboard.

Apply thermal grease onto center of IHS on the socket surface.

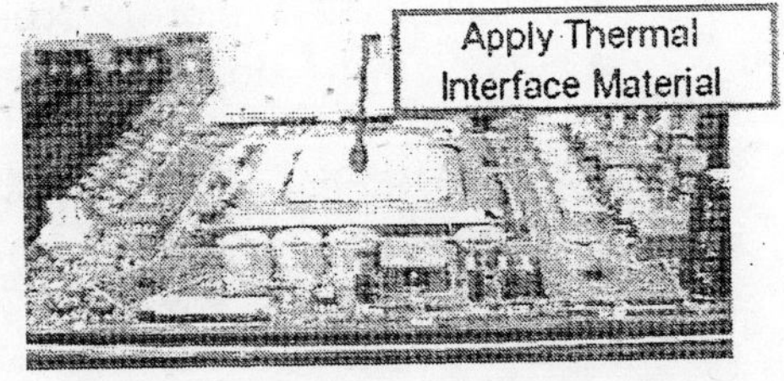

Place the heatsink onto the socket. Ensure fan cables are oriented on side closest to the CPU fan connector on the motherboard.

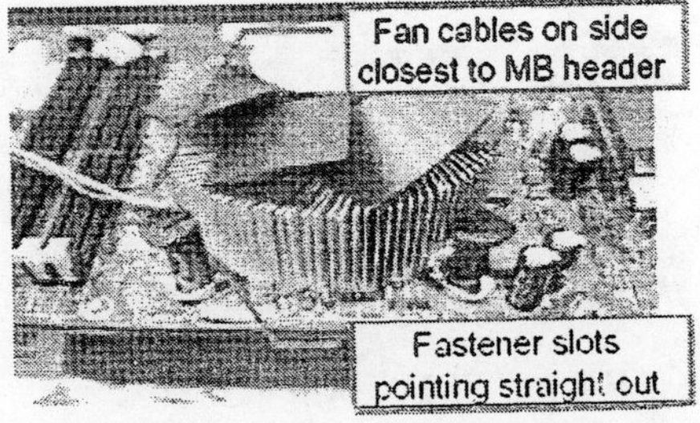

Align fasteners with the motherboard throughholes.

Rotate the fastener clockwise, then press down on fastener caps with thumb to install and lock. Repeat with remaining fasteners.

If you press down the fasteners without rotating them clockwise, the heatsink cannot be secured on the motherboard.

Connect fan header with the CPU fan connector on the motherboard.

Installation of Memory Modules (DIMM)

This motherboard has two 184-pin DDR (Double Data Rate) DIMM slots, and supports Dual Channel Memory Technology.

For dual channel configuration, you always need to install two identical (the same brand, speed, size and chip-type) memory modules in the DDR DIMM slots, otherwise, it will operate at single channel mode.

If you install only one memory module or two non-identical memory modules, Dual Channel Memory is not activated.

Installing a DIMM

- Disconnect power supply before adding or removing DIMMs.
- Unlock a DIMM slot by pressing the retaining clips outward.
- DIMM on the slot such that the notch on the DIMM matches the break on the slot.
- The DIMM only fits in one correct orientation. It will cause permanent damage to the motherboard and the DIMM if you force the DIMM into the slot at incorrect orientation.
- Firmly insert the DIMM into the slot until the retaining clips at both ends fully snap back in place and the DIMM is properly seated.

Onboard Headers and Connectors

Make sure the red-striped side of the cable is plugged into Pin1 side of the connector.

FDD connector

34-pin FDD Connector.

Primary and Secondary IDE connector

40-pin IDE connector(IDE1 & IDE2) for HDD and CD Drives. Use 80-conductor ATA 66/100 ribbon cable.

Serial ATA Connectors

SATA1, SATA2, SATA3 & SATA4

These four Serial ATA (SATA) connectors support SATA data cables for internal storage devices. The current SATA interface allows up to 1.5 Gb/s data transfer rate.

Serial ATA (SATA) Data Cable

Either end of the SATA data cable can be connected to the SATA hard disk or the SATA connector on the motherboard.

Serial ATA (SATA) Power Cable

Connect the black end of SATA power cable to the power connector on each drive. Then connect the white end of SATA power cable to the power connector of the power supply.

USB 2.0 Header

This board has 4 USB 2.0 ports at the back I/O panel, if those USB 2.0 ports are not sufficient, USB 2.0 header is available to support 2 additional USB 2.0 ports.

Infrared Module Header

This header supports an optional wireless transmitting and receiving infrared module.

Internal Audio Connectors

These connectors allow you to receive stereo audio input from sound sources such as a CD-ROM, DVD-ROM, TV tuner card, or MPEG card.

Front Panel Audio Header

This is an interface for front panel audio cable that allows convenient connection and control of audio devices.

System Panel Header

This header accommodates several system front panel functions.

Chassis Speaker Header

Connect the chassis speaker to this header.

Chassis Fan Connector

Connect a chassis fan cable to this connector and match the black wire to the ground pin.

CPU Fan Connector

Connect a CPU fan cable to this connector and match the black wire to the ground pin.

ATX Power Connector

Connect an ATX power supply to this connector.

COM Port Header

This COM port header is used to support a COM port module.

ATX 12V Connector

Connect an ATX 12V power supply to this connector.

Serial ATA (SATA) Hard Disks Installation

This section will guide you to install the SATA hard disks.

- Install the SATA hard disks into the drive bays of your chassis.
- Connect the SATA power cable to the SATA hard disk.
- Connect one end of the SATA data cable to the motherboard's SATA connector.
- Connect the other end of the SATA data cable to the SATA hard disk.

Before you install OS into the SATA hard disk, you need to check and ensure the configuration of the OnBoard IDE Operate Mode" option in BIOS setup is correct according to the condition of your system.

BIOS Setup

This section explains how to use the BIOS setup to configure your system. To run the BIOS SETUP UTILITY when you start up the computer, please press <F2> during the Power-On-Self-Test (POST).

If you wish to enter the BIOS SETUP UTILITY after POST, restart the system and press <F2> key during POST.

BIOS Setup Main Screen

When you enter the BIOS SETUP UTILITY, the Main screen will appear and display the system overview

System Time [Hour:Minute:Second] :

Use this item to specify the system time.

System Date [Day Month/Date/Year] :

Use this item to specify the system date.

Advanced Screen

In this section, you may set the configurations for the following items:

CPU Configuration, Chipset Configuration, ACPI Configuration, IDE Configuration, PCI PnP Configuration, Floppy Configuration, Super I/O Configuration, and USB Configuration.

Setting wrong values in this section may cause the system to malfunction.

CPU Configuration

CPU Host Frequency

While entering setup, BIOS auto detects the present CPU host frequency of this motherboard. The actual CPU host frequency will show in the following item.

Boot Failure Guard

Enable or disable the feature of Boot Failure Guard.

Spread Spectrum

This item should always be [Auto] for better system stability.

Ratio Status

This is a read-only item, which displays whether the ratio status of this motherboard is "Locked" or "Unlocked".

- If it shows "Unlocked", you will find an item Ratio CMOS Setting appears to allow you changing the ratio value of this motherboard.
- If it shows "Locked", then the item Ratio CMOS Setting will be hidden.

If you use the ratio value to time the CPU frequency, it will be equal to the core speed of the installed processor.

Ratio Actual Value

This is a read-only item, which displays the ratio actual value of this motherboard.

CPU Thermal Throttling

You may select [Enabled] to enable P4 CPU internal thermal control mechanism to keep the CPU from overheated.

Hyper Threading Technology

To enable this feature, it requires a computer system with an Intel Pentium4 processor that supports Hyper-Threading technology and an operating system that includes optimization for this technology, such as Microsoft Windows XP.

Set to [Auto] if using Microsoft Windows XP, or Linux kernel version 2.4.18 or higher. This option will be hidden if the installed CPU does not support Hyper-Threading technology.

Max CPUID Value Limit

For Prescott CPU only, some OSes (ex. NT4.0) cannot handle the function with disable. This should be enabled in order to boot legacy OSes that cannot support CPUs with extended CPUID functions.

No-Excute Memory Protection

No-Execution (NX) Memory Protection Technology is an enhancement to the IA-32 Intel Architecture. An IA-32 processor with "No Execute (NX) Memory Protection" can prevent data pages from being used by malicious software to execute code. This option will be hidden if the current CPU does not support No-Excute Memory Protection.

Enhanced Halt State

All processors support the Halt State (C1). The C1 state is supported through the native processor instructions HLT and MWAIT and requires no hardware support from the chipset. In the C1 power state, the processor maintains the context of the system caches.

Intel SpeedStep Tech.

Intel SpeedStep tech. is Intel's new power saving technology. Processor can switch between multiple frequency and voltage points to enable power savings.

If you select [Enabled], you need to set the "Power Schemes" as "Portable/Laptop" to enable this function.

Chipset Configuration

DRAM Frequency

If [Auto] is selected, the motherboard will detect the memory module(s) inserted and assigns appropriate frequency automatically.

You may also select other value as operating frequency: [166MHz (DDR 333)], [200MHz (DDR 400)].

Flexibility Option

The default value of this option is [Disabled]. It will allow better tolerance for memory compatibility when it is set to [Enabled].

Configure DRAM Timing by SPD

Select [Enabled] will configure the following items by the contents in the SPD (Serial Presence Detect) device.

If you select [Disabled], you will find the items "DRAM RAS# Precharge", and "DRAM RAS# Activate to Precharge" appear to allow you adjusting them.

DRAM CAS# Latency

Use this item to adjust the means of memory accessing. Configuration options: [3], [2.5], [2], and [Auto].

DRAM RAS# to CAS# Delay

This controls the latency between the DRAM active command and the read / write command.

Configuration options: [2 DRAM Clocks], [3 DRAM Clocks], [4 DRAM Clocks], and [5 DRAM Clocks].

DRAM RAS# Precharge

This controls the idle clocks after a precharge command is issued. Configuration options: [2 DRAM Clocks], [3 DRAM Clocks], [4 DRAM Clocks], and [5 DRAM Clocks].

DRAM RAS# Activate to Precharge

This controls the number of DRAM clocks for TRAS. Configuration options: [4 DRAM Clocks], [5 DRAM Clocks], [6 DRAM Clocks], [7 DRAM Clocks], [8 DRAM Clocks], [9 DRAM Clocks], [10 DRAM Clocks], [11 DRAM Clocks], [12 DRAM Clocks], [13 DRAM Clocks], [14 DRAM Clocks], and [15 DRAM Clocks].

Onboard VGA Selection

This allows you to enjoy the benefits of Surround Display feature. If you select [Auto], the onboard VGA will be automatically disabled when you install AGP 8X or PCI Express X 16 VGA card; the onboard VGA will be enabled without the installation of any add-on VGA card.

If you select [Enabled], the onboard VGA will be enabled, and your first screen will always be onboard VGA.

Aperture Size Select

You may select [256MB] or [128MB] as the aperture size select. The default value of this option is [256MB].

OnBoard LAN

This allows you to enable or disable the "OnBoard LAN" feature.

OnBoard AC'97 Audio

Select [Auto], [Enabled] or [Disabled] for the onboard AC'97 Audio feature.

OnBoard MC'97 Modem

Select [Auto] or [Disabled] for the onboard MC'97 Modem feature.

ACPI Configuration

Restore on AC/Power Loss

This allows you to set the power state after an unexpected AC/ Power loss. If [Power Off] is selected, the AC/Power remains off when the power recovers.

If [Power On] is selected, the AC/Power resumes and the system starts to boot up when the power recovers.

Ring-In Power On

Use this item to enable or disable Ring-In signals to turn on the system from the power-soft-off mode.

PCI Devices Power On

Use this item to enable or disable PCI devices to turn on the system from the power-soft-off mode.

PS/2 Keyboard Power On

Use this item to enable or disable PS/2 keyboard to turn on the system from the power-soft-off mode.

RTC Alarm Power On

Use this item to enable or disable RTC (Real Time Clock) to power on the system.

IDE Configuration

ATA/IDE Configuration

Select [Compatible] when you install legacy OS (Windows ME / 98SE / NT). If native OS (Windows 2000 / XP) is installed, please select [Enhanced].

Note that the following options will be varied depending on the "Onboard IDE Operate Mode" ([Compatible] or [Enhanced]) that you selected. When [Compatible] is selected Combined Option

It allows you to select between [SATA 1, SATA 2, SATA 3, SATA 4], [SATA 1, SATA 3, IDE 1], and [IDE 1, SATA 2, SATA 4].

If it is set to [SATA 1, SATA 3, IDE 1], then SATA2, SATA4 will not work. Likewise, if it is set to [IDE 1, SATA 2, SATA 4], then SATA1, SATA3 will not work.

Because Intel ICH6 south bridge only supports four IDE devices under legacy OS (Windows ME / 98SE / NT), you have to choose [SATA 1, SATA 2, SATA 3, SATA 4], [SATA 1, SATA 3, IDE 1], or [IDE 1, SATA 2, SATA 4] when the installed device is used with legacy OS.

IDE Device Configuration

You may set the IDE configuration for the device that you specify. Let us use the "Primary IDE Master" as the example in the following instruction. Use this item to configure the type of the IDE device that you specify.

Configuration options: [Not Installed], [Auto], [CD/DVD], and [ARMD].

- [Not Installed]: Select [Not Installed] to disable the use of IDE device.
- [Auto]: Select [Auto] to automatically detect the hard disk drive.
  After selecting the hard disk information into BIOS, use a disk utility, such as FDISK, to partition and format the new IDE hard disk drives.
  This is necessary so that you can write or read data from the hard disk.
  Make sure to set the partition of the Primary IDE hard disk drives to active.
- [CD/DVD]: This is used for IDE CD/DVD drives.
- [ARMD]: This is used for IDE ARMD (ATAPI Removable Media Device), such as MO.

LBA/Large Mode

Use this item to select the LBA/Large mode for a hard disk > 512 MB under DOS and Windows; for Netware and UNIX user, select [Disabled] to disable the LBA/Large mode.

Block (Multi-Sector Transfer)

The default value of this item is [Auto]. If this feature is enabled, it will enhance hard disk performance by reading or writing more data during each transfer.

PIO Mode

Use this item to set the PIO mode to enhance hard disk performance by optimizing the hard disk timing.

DMA Mode

DMA capability allows the improved transfer-speed and data-integrity for compatible IDE devices.

S.M.A.R.T.

Use this item to enable or disable the S.M.A.R.T. (Self-Monitoring, Analysis, and Reporting Technology) feature. Configuration options: [Disabled], [Auto], [Enabled].

32-Bit Data Transfer

Use this item to enable 32-bit access to maximize the IDE hard disk data transfer rate.

PCI/PnP Configuration

PCI Latency Timer

The default value is 32. It is recommended to keep the default value unless the installed PCI expansion cards' specifications require other settings.

PCI/IDE BusMaster

Use this item to enable or disable the PCI/IDE BusMaster feature.

Floppy Configuration

In this section, you may configure the type of your floppy drive.

Super I/O Configuration

OnBoard Floppy Controller

Use this item to enable or disable floppy drive controller.

Serial Port Address

Use this item to set the address for the onboard serial port or disable it. Configuration options: [Disabled], [3F8 / IRQ4], [2F8 / IRQ3], [3E8 / IRQ4], [2E8 / IRQ3].

Infrared Port Address

Use this item to set the address for the onboard infrared port or disable it. Configuration options: [Disabled], [2F8 / IRQ3], and [2E8 / IRQ3].

Parallel Port Address

Use this item to set the address for the onboard parallel port or disable it.

Configuration options: [Disabled], [378], and [278].

Parallel Port Mode

Use this item to set the operation mode of the parallel port. The default value is [ECP+EPP]. If this option is set to [ECP+EPP], it will show the EPP version in the following item, "EPP Version". Configuration options:

- [Normal]
- [Bi-Directional], and
- [ECP+EPP].

EPP Version

Use this item to set the EPP version. Configuration options: [1.9] and [1.7]. ECP Mode DMA Channel Use this item,to set the ECP mode DMA channel. Configuration options: [DMA0], [DMA1], and [DMA3].

Parallel Port IRQ

Use this item to set the IRQ for the parallel port. Configuration options:

[IRQ5] and [IRQ7].

USB Configuration

USB Controller

Use this item to enable or disable the use of USB controller.

USB 2.0 Support

Use this item to enable or disable the USB 2.0 support.

Legacy USB Support

Use this item to enable or disable the support to emulate legacy I/O devices such as mouse, keyboard,... etc. Or you may select [Auto] so that the system will start to auto-detect; if there is no USB device connected, "Auto" option will disable the legacy USB support.

Hardware Health Event Monitoring Screen

In this section, it allows you to monitor the status of the hardware on your system, including the parameters of the CPU temperature, motherboard temperature, CPU fan speed, chassis fan speed, and the critical voltage.

Boot Screen

In this section, it will display the available devices on your system for you to configure the boot settings and the boot priority.

Boot Settings Configuration

Boot From Network-Use this item to enable or disable the Boot From Network feature.

Boot Up Num-Lock

If this item is set to [On], it will automatically activate the Numeric Lock function after boot-up.

Security Screen

In this section, you may set or change the supervisor/user password for the system. For the user password, you may also clear it.

Exit Screen

Save Changes and Exit

When this option is selected, it shows following message, "Save configuration changes and exit setup?" Select [OK] to save the changes and exit the BIOS SETUP UTILITY.

Discard Changes and Exit

When you select this option, following message, "Discard changes and exit setup?" is shown. Select [OK] to exit the BIOS SETUP UTILITY without saving any changes.

Discard Changes

When you select this option, it will pop-out the following message, "Discard changes?" Select [OK] to discard all changes.

Load Optimal Defaults

When you select this option, it will pop-out the following message, "Load optimal defaults?" Select [OK] to load the default values for all the setup configurations.

DDR Memory

Double Data Rate (DDR) SDRAM provides speed almost equal to the RDRAM. DDR SDRAM doubles the rate at which SDRAM process data.

SDRAM carries information only on the rising edge of clock signal, whereas the DDR RAM is able to read data on the rising as well as falling edge of the clock signal. This results in double performance by the DDR RAM.

DDR SDRAM is costlier than standard SDRAM but it is much cheaper than the RDRAM. This resulted in most of the Pentium 4 based system going for DDR DIMM, instead of going for costlier RIMM.

DDR DIMM use a connector with 184-pins. This connector contains a single notch near the center of the connector.

Some of the variations of the DDR RAM available in the market are

- DDR 266
- DDR 333
- DDR 400 and above
- DDR2 533

DDR 266

This is one of the cheapest DDR memories available. This is the minimum one should get for a P4 motherboard.

Even if the motherboard does not support dual channel DDR memory, one should install the maximum DDR 266 memory that one can afford.

DDR 333

DDR 333 is required for those users who use powerful applications such as video processing software, latest games etc. Also, a good quality DDR 333 can be overclocked.

To use DDR 333 memory your motherboard should support it.

DDR 400 and higher

This DDR 400 memory is recommended for some of the latest motherboards with at least P4 2.8 GHz or above or Athlon 64 processor.

With the DDR 400 memory and a good board and processor combination one can easily overclock the system. To get the best performance it should be run in the dual channel mode.

DDR2 533

This is a new DDR memory standard and boards that support this new memory standard are gradually beginning to show up in the market.

Once its price becomes competitive one should go for it, provided the motherboard supports it.

DDR2 Memory

DDR SDRAM or Double Data Rate Synchronous DRAM is a special type of memory which can transfer data on the rising and falling edges of a clock cycle.

Unlike the normal SDRAM which carries information only on the rising edge of a clock signal, DDR is able to read data on both the rising and falling edges.

This property of DDR memory effectively doubles the memory chip's data throughput.

DDR2, the newer DDR memory standard, which uses the 240-pin FBGA (Fine Ball Grid Array) packaging, compared to the TSOP packaging used by DDR. This packaging offers higher scalability as it has lower resistance. However, manufacturing memory in this package costs a bit more than TSOP.

DDR2-SDRAM, also consumes less power-it requires a 1.8 V power supply, while DDR needs 2.5 V.

One drawback with DDR2 is, it is not backward compatible with DDR, you will not be able to insert DDR2 memory modules into DDR slot.

DDR vs DDR2

	DDR	DDR2
Data Bus	64 bits	64 bits
Data Rate	200/266/333/400 MHz	400/533/667 MHz
Packaging	TSOP / BGA	BGA
DRAM Frequency	100/133/166/200 MHz	200/266/333 MHz
Densities	128 MB to 1 GB	256 MB to 4 GB
Voltage	2.5 V	1.8 V

The memory chips which run at 333 MHz DDR has effective throughput of 667 MHz. This translates into a bandwidth of 5,333 MBps-in single channel mode.

In dual channel mode, the bandwidth will go up to l0666 MBps, that is 10 GB per second.

DDR2 chips are available for 400 MHz, 533 MHz and 667 MHz. These speeds are possible because of additional features such as a larger prefetch and improvised registers.

The bus width (64-bit), is the same for DDR and DDR2.

One issue that needs to be resolved is that the motherboards need to be compatible with memory modules working at this speed. Intel's 925XE chipset is said to have this compatibility. SiS SiS5656 chipset, also has support for the DDR2 specification.

Memory	Clock (MHz) DDR	Type	Single Channel (MBps)	Dual Channel (MBps)
DDR400	200 MHz DDR	PC3200	3,200	6,400
DDR2-400	200 MHz DDR	PC2-3200	3,200	6,400
DDR2-533	266 MHz DDR	PC2-4300	4,266	8,533
DDR2-667	333 MHz DDR	PC2-5300	5,333	10,666

What is Dual-channel Mode Memory?

A motherboard can have a maximum of two memory channels controlled by the memory controller, and each of the memory channels can handle two or three slots on the motherboard.

Now in single channel memory systems there is only a single route for the memory to access the memory controller. But with dual-channel memory, double the bandwidth can be achieved as the memory modules are inserted in two separate channels.

Each of these channels has its own separate lane to access the memory controller and therefore the bandwidth is doubled.

For instance, there are four memory slots on the motherboard: A, B and C, D. Now if you want to run the memory in the dual channel mode, you will need to insert the memory sticks in slot A and C or B and D if you are using two memory sticks.

Any normal DDR memory can be used to work under the dual channel mode, provided

- the motherboard chipset supports it
- both the memory modules are of the same density
- both the memory modules are running at the same speed and are inserted in different channels (alternating slots).

If you plan to use four memory sticks, you can utilize all four slots, provided all the memory sticks are of the same speed and density For instance, 256 MB x 4.

RAID (Redundant Arrays of Inexpensive Disks)

Just as one would use DDR2 memory to increase memory speed, one can use the RAID or "Redundant Arrays of Inexpensive Disks" to improve the disk i/o speed. RAID is also used to increase fault tolerance of the disk drive system.

Different types of RAID implementation is available for different application.

RAID 0 and RAID 1 are two of the common RAID implementations that one can easily implement on a PC system. Of these implementations, RAID 0 can raise disk I/O speed and RAID 1 can enhance fault-tolerant ability. One can get both the benefits of increased disk i/o speed and fault tolerance using RAID 0+1 implementation.

RAID 0

RAID 0 is also called stripe array, it implements a striped disk array and the data is broken down into blocks in which each block is written to a separate disk drive.

I/O performance is greatly improved by spreading the I/O load across many channels and drives. Best performance is achieved when data is striped across multiple channels with only one drive per channel.

RAID 0 is not a "True" RAID because it is NOT fault-tolerant. The failure of just one drive will result in all data in an array being lost.

RAID 0 should never be used in mission critical environments.

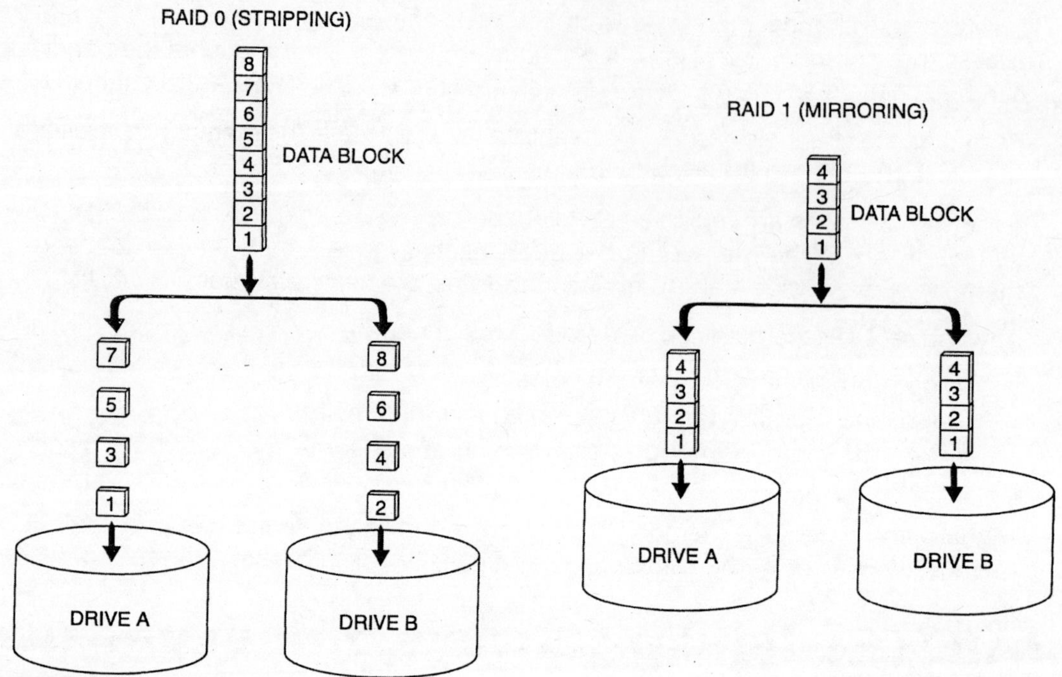

RAID 1

RAID 1 is also called mirror array, it provides 100% data redundancy. No rebuild is necessary in case of a disk failure, simply copy data from the remaining healthy disk to the replacement disk.

You can specify a disk as the auto-selected replacement disk for a Mirror Array, this replacement disk is called Spare Disk.

RAID 0+1

RAID 0+1 is implemented as a mirrored array whose segments are RAID 0 arrays. It has the advantages both provided by RAID 0 (high I/O performance) and RAID 1 (fault tolerance). At least four disks are needed to create a RAID 0+1 disk array.

Span Array

Span Array is also called JBOD (just A Bunch Of Disks), which uses a bunch of disks as a larger disk. Span provides no fault tolerance and no I/O performance enhancement, it's just a measure to enlarge disk capacity.

Pen Drive/Thumb Drive/Memory Cards

At the beginning, when the file sizes were small, people used 1.44MB floppy disk for backup/storage and data transfer purpose. As the file sizes stand today, one cannot use the floppy disk for backup or storage purpose.

Currently most of the files are above 30~40MB size and to take backup of a 40MB file on a floppy disk, one would require around 35 floppy disks. Backing-up and restoring 35 disks is an impossible task.

One can use a CD for this purpose, but CDs are generally considered more appropriate for backup/storage than as a portable media.

On a normal CD-R you can't delete or change any data. A CD-RWs (rewritables) allow one to change the data, but they rewrite data at very slow speeds

Another problem with these devices is they are not very reliable. Floppy disk is a very unreliable media, but the CD is also prone to damage. Mishandling by the user may make the data stored on the CD surface disappear.

One can use a thumb drive for backup/storage and as a portable media without worrying about the problems associated with floppy disk or the CD. With a thumb drive, you can add, change or remove data as if it were a folder in your computer.

A thumb drive, also known as flash drive, pen drive or USB drive is a small portable device in the shape of the thumb, which can be connected to the USB port of a computer.

Main component of a thumb drives is Flash memory. Flash memory is a special type of memory which can retain data even when there's no current passing through it.

It is somewhat like an external hard drive, without any motor or moving part.

Information stored on a Flash drive can last for around 10 years, after which, they will become corrupted and you'll have to delete them.

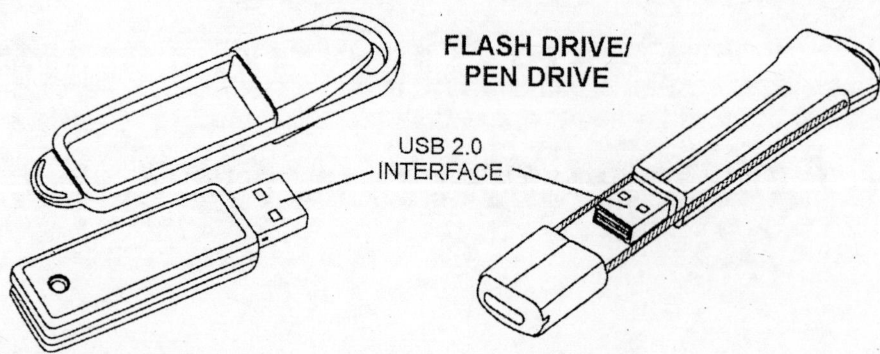

Today the use of flash memory is very common in the electronic industry. One will find flash memory in, mobile phone, digital camera, PDA (personal digital Assistant) etc.

Flash memory is basically a type of Electrically Erasable Programmable Read Only Memory (EEPROM), the only difference being that Flash memory can delete a chunk of data at a time, which makes the job of reading and writing much faster as compared to EEPROM, which can only erase data byte by byte.

As the data stored in the flash memory is changed by a sudden 'flash' of voltage, it is known as flash memory.

Motherboard BIOS programs are also stored in flash memory. This is why one says 'flashing a BIOS' when BIOS program is updated.

Flash Memory

Basic element of a flash memory is a flash memory cell. This cell consists of two transistors that are separated by a thin layer of oxide.

- Data is stored as a value of 0 by exciting the electrons on introducing a low voltage.
- When the electrons return back to normal via an electric field applied to the cell, state 1 is induced.

Flash memory can be of two types,

- NOR and
- NAND.

This classification is based on the logic gates used to construct the Flash memory cells.

NOR was invented by Intel in 1988 and is used in devices that require program storage, cell phones, PDAs, etc.

NAND was invented by Toshiba in 1989 and is used in thumb drives and memory cards such as Compact Flash (CF) Multi-Media Card (MMC) etc.

Advantage/Disadvantage

Flash memory being a solid-state device, data is stored in them in electronic format. Unlike hard drives, which are mechanical and consist of moving parts, Flash-based memory does not consist of any moving parts.

The advantage of having a Flash- based memory is that it is generally free from the problems associated with mechanical storage devices.

Disadvantage with Flash- based memory is its limited transfer speed and low storage capacity, compared to mechanical storage devices. Flash-based memory cards cannot store as much as their mechanical counterparts, such as a hard disk drive.

Compared to mechanical storage devices, a thumb drive, being an electronic device, is portable and damage resistance.

Since Flash drives have no movable parts, they are much more resistant to damage as opposed to hard drives which can develop bad sectors with physical shocks.

They are also resistant to magnetic fields, high temperatures and even water. Only one needs to make sure not to insert a wet thumb drive into the USB port.

As the thumb drive is connected to the USB port, it is also known as USB drive. Since it works through a USB interface, it is compatible with any computer that has a USB port.

Because it draws power from the computer, through the USB interface, it is independent of any wires or batteries.

Newer operating systems such as Windows 2000 and XP have embedded drivers, which make Flash drives truly plug and play. All one need to do is insert the drive into the USB port and watch your computer do all the setting ups automatically.

Older OS such as Windows 95/98 require drivers to be installed, which the Flash drive manufacturers provide on a CD along with the Flash drive.

Features

Currently thumb drive is available with the following features:

- Sizes range from 32 MB to 2 GB.
- With USB 2.0 technology. A USB 2.0 compliant device can have data transfer rates of up to 15 MBps, which is much faster than what CD-writers offer nowadays.
- Multifunction devices are also available, that are also MP3 players, voice recorders, low resolution digital cameras or even fingerprint analyzers.
- Write protect feature on USB drives can lock the drive, blocking any write access.

- You can even set up a public or private partition/drive. The public part is always accessible, while the private part is secured through passwords and/or encryption technology. When using this feature one must be careful, as losing the password/key may prevent one from accessing ones own files.

When buying a thumb drive, one should look for the following points:

- Size:
  Look for a small size that is both rugged and convenient to handle. Check to see whether a cap is provided to protect the USB head of the device. Some thumb drive manufacturers offer swivel caps for safety against loss.
- Capacity:
  There are a variety of sizes in the market. If you want to carry music and/or videos files then go for a 512 MB+ device. Documents and photos take up less space. Here 128-256 MB should do just fine.
- Compatibility:
  Check to see whether the device is USB 2.0 compliant and has compatibility with several operating systems, not just Windows 2000/XP.
- Multi-functionality:
  Many thumb drives come with additional features such as bundled MP3 players or even digital cameras. Look in this area as well, if you find them useful.

Memory Cards

Currently most of the portable devices such as latest mobile phones, MP3 player, digital camera and PDA provide a built-in memory card slot. One can connect memory cards of various capacities into these slots to increase the storage capacity.

Memory card is equivalent of a hard drive for these portable devices. Memory cards are most popular method to store, transfer and carry all kinds of digital data.

As these memory cards are used on almost all portable devices, one finds a variety of them in the market.

In the following section we take a look at some of the common type of memory cards available in the market.

Compact Flash Memory Cards

Compact Flash Card or CF Card was introduced by SanDisk in 1994. It is mainly used in digital cameras, because of their higher capacities and faster transfer speeds.

There are two kinds of CF Cards

- Type I and
- Type II.

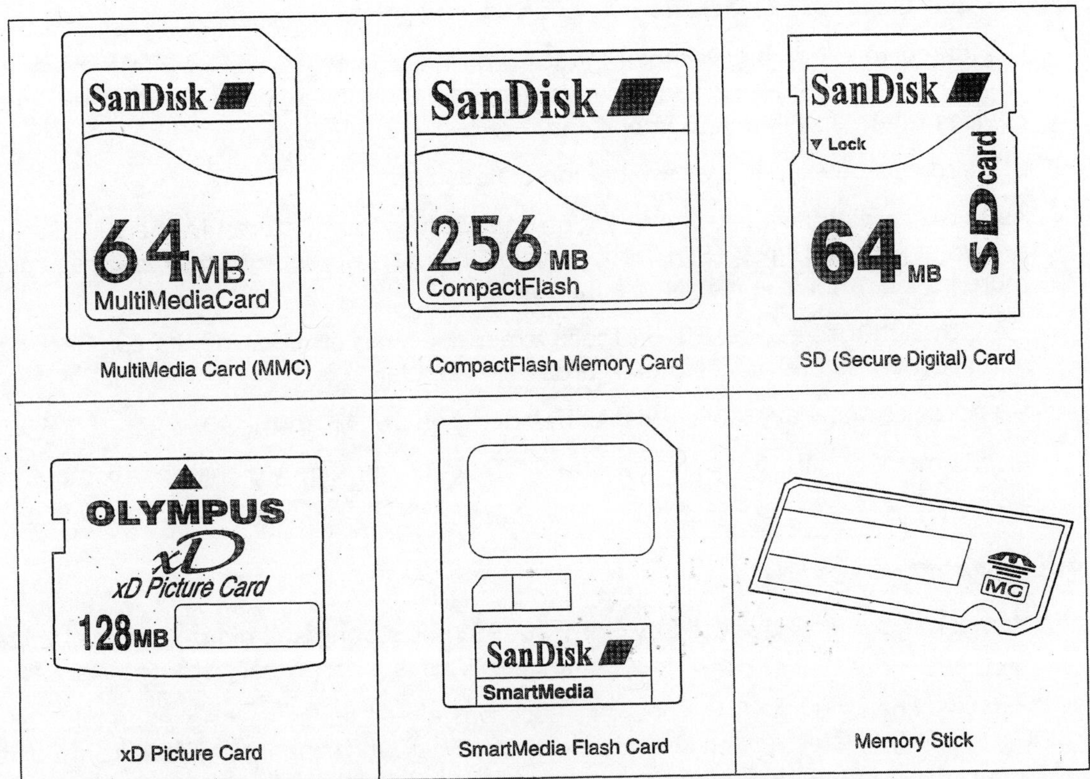

MultiMedia Card (MMC) — CompactFlash Memory Card — SD (Secure Digital) Card

xD Picture Card — SmartMedia Flash Card — Memory Stick

Type II cards typically allow higher storage capacities but are also physically thicker. When buying a CF Card, it is important to check the type of CF Card your device supports.

Capacity of a CF card will range from 64 MB to a maximum of 4GB. The most common cards come in 128, 256 and 512 MB, and offer good value per MB of data stored.

If one goes for higher than 512 MB CF cards then the value per MB increase very much because the cost of producing a higher-capacity CF card is very high.

The write speed of the CF Card is the speed at which it records data on the card. The read speed is the speed at which data can be transferred from the card to another device.

Speed is often given as a multiplier, such as 4x, 24x, 40x and 80x. There is no indication what 1x represents, but it's generally defined as a write speed of 150 kilobytes of data per second (KBps).

With a 80x card one should be able to write at a speed of 12 MBps. The read speeds are usually similar to the write speeds.

SD (Secure Digital) Cards

Compared to CF cards, Secure Digital Cards (also known as SD cards), are much smaller. These cards were mainly developed for mobile phones and other small devices where size is a very important criteria.

SD card was developed by Toshiba and Matsushita.

As these cards offer built-in encryption-to safeguard data stored in them-these are known as Secure Digital (SD) cards. This built-in security feature makes these cards more popular than the MultiMedia Cards.

Even though these cards are bit more expensive than other cards, its compact size and security feature makes these cards very popular.

SD Cards are now available in capacities between 16 MB and 1 GB.

An SD memory card typically measures 32x 24x2 mm and weighs approximately 2 grams.

Memory Stick

Memory stick was introduced by Sony in 1998 for storing still digital images, video, music files and other type of electronic data. This is a proprietary storage standard.

Initially, when launched, the memory stick was almost twice as long as a MultiMedia Card (MMC), a later version known as Memory Stick Duo is about half the weight of its predecessor and is backward-compatible when used with an adapter.

To launch the Memory Stick Duo, Sony tied up with the Flash memory card giant SanDisk. Memory Stick Pro supports higher speeds and capacities (256 MB and above).

Latest development is this format is known as Memory Stick Duo Pro, which supports higher capacities while retaining the small size of the original Duo.

Sony Provides its own proprietary security feature for the memory stick, known as the Magic Gate. One problem with this security is, any content written on the Memory Stick using the Magic Gate software cannot be copied or transferred to other computers or devices.

Magic Gate is Sony's proprietary data encryption and authentication technology specifically made for their storage formats, including the Memory Stick Duo Pro.

Currently you can buy Memory Sticks is available in the capacities ranging from 128 MB to 512 MB.

When buying a memory stick, one need to be aware of the exact type of Memory Stick required, because the multiple formats and revisions in the Memory Stick family makes very easy to confuse one with the other.

MultiMedia Cards (MMC)

MultiMedia Card or the MMC was introduced by the Flash memory card giant SanDisk and Siemens in 1997.

These are small stamp sized cards, based on the flash memory. It is a cheaper alternative of the SD cards, and are commonly used in mobile phones.

These are cheaper than the SD Cards because it does not contain the security feature found in the SD Cards. Also, the read/write speed of the MMC are not as fast as the SD cards.

These cards can easily fit into the standard SD card slots, but the SD cards cannot be used in the MMC slots.

Advantage with the MMC is its smaller size and cheaper cost. It is one of the cheapest flash based memory card.

MMC cards are available in capacities ranging from 64 MB to 512 MB.

SmartMedia Flash Cards

SmartMedia Flash Cards, also known as SSFDC (Solid State Floppy Disk Card), were introduced by Toshiba in 1995.

At that time they were very popular because of their small size and super-thin architecture. With the arrival of MMC and SD Cards, only a few old devices use this type of storage.

Because of its limited storage capacity and slow transfer speeds it is being rapidly replaced by MMC and SD storage.

xD Picture Card

xD Picture Card was developed by Fuji and Olympus companies for use in their cameras. As xD Cards are often sold under license, one may find different brand on the packaging.

xD Picture Cards have a distinctive, shield-style design and are roughly the size of thumb.

xD picture cards are not used as a generic storage solution, Olympus and Fuji companies use the cards predominantly for their digital cameras.

Storage capacity of the xD Picture card can vary from 8 MB to 512 MB.

OTHER TITLES OF INTEREST

Machine Learning for **Finance**
ISBN: 9789389328622

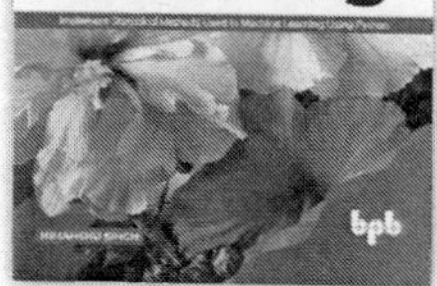

Statistics for **Machine Learning**
ISBN: 9789388511971

Machine Learning
ISBN: 9789391392352

Machine Learning for **Education**
ISBN: 9789355511133

Machine Learning with **Python**
ISBN: 9789386551931

Building Machine Learning Systems Using **Python**
ISBN: 9789389423617

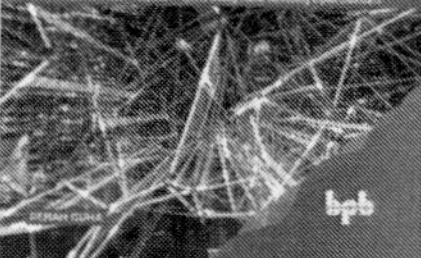

Machine Learning Cookbook with **Python**
ISBN: 9789389898002

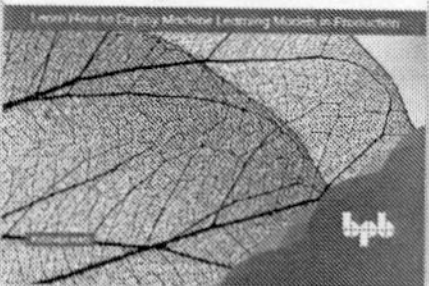

Pragmatic **Machine Learning** with **Python**
ISBN: 9789389845365

Operationalizing **Machine Learning Pipelines**
ISBN: 9789355510235

Practical **Machine Learning** with **Spark**
ISBN: 9789391392086

AI & **ML** – Powering the Agents of Automation
ISBN: 9789388511636

Fun with **Machine Learning**
ISBN: 9789355517852

IBM Watson Solutions for **Machine Learning**
ISBN: 9789390684700

Continuous Machine Learning with **Kubeflow**
ISBN: 9789389898507

Cloud Native AI and **Machine Learning** on **AWS**
ISBN: 9789355513267

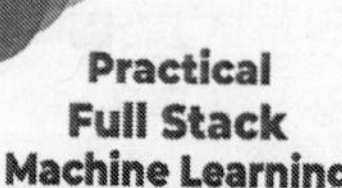

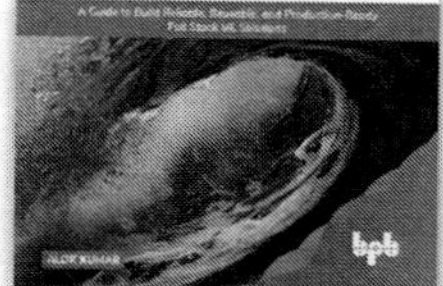

Practical Full Stack **Machine Learning**
ISBN: 9789391030421

CD-ROM/DVD Troubleshooting Guide

Problem	Possible causes
CD is totally dead.	■ Check Power connectors/socket. ■ Damage to power wire. ■ Bad connections or faulty component in power supply (including blown fuse). ■ Defective mainboard on CD/DVD.
Front Panel Buttons do not Operate.	■ Bad connections to one or more buttons or sets of buttons. ■ Microcontroller failed to reset properly. ■ Missing/bad voltages from power supply. ■ Defective microcontroller or other logic.
Tray does not open or close.	■ Worn, stretched, oily, flabby, belt. ■ Dirty mechanism or gummed up lubrication. ■ Stripped gear or other mechanical damage. ■ Defective motor or bad connections to motor. ■ Bad drawer/eject button. ■ Missing/bad voltages from power supply. ■ Defective microcontroller or other logic.
Tray operation is erratic.	■ Dirty sense switch contracts or bad connections. ■ Worn, stretched, oily, flabby, belt. ■ Dirty mechanism or gummed up lubrication. ■ Defective motor or bad connections to motor. ■ Stripped gear or other mechanical damage. ■ Missing/bad voltages from power supply. ■ Defective microcontroller or other logic.

Problem	Possible causes
Tray does not close (or open) completely.	■ Worn, stretched, oily, flabby, belt. ■ Dirty mechanism or gummed up lubrication. ■ Foreign object blocking drawer. ■ Stripped gear or other mechanical damage. ■ Gear timing is messed up.
CDROM drive damages CDs.	■ Broken, bent, or missing part. ■ Messed up gear timing (mainly cartridge changers). ■ Other mechanical fault. ■ Lens hitting CD/DVD due to electronic fault or need to adjust focus servo.
Spindle table loose or sticks to clamper upon eject.	■ Set screw loosened or glue failed holding spindle to motor shaft. ■ Parts of spindle table broke.
Intermittent or erratic operation.	■ Dirty, scratched, or defective disc. ■ Dirty lens. ■ Extended length discs too long for player. ■ Loading (mechanical) not completed reliably. ■ Bad connections including missing/erratic optical deck shield. ■ Cracks in ribbon cable to optical pickup. ■ Dirty drawer or limit switches. ■ Power supply or logic problems. ■ External interference. ■ Internal damage (e.g., loose parts) in optical pickup.
CDROM drive overheats.	■ Excessive room temperature. ■ Failing/marginal part in power supply, logic, or optical pickup.
Operation is poor or erratic when cold.	■ Gummed up grease or dirt inhibiting movement until warm. ■ Condensation on optical components due to temperature change. ■ Bad connections or dirty contacts affected by temperature.
Disc spins in wrong direction or overspeeds and is never recognized.	■ Disc loaded upside-down. ■ Dirty, scratched, or defective disc. ■ Dirty or damaged objective lens. ■ Tracking or CLV servo out of adjustment or faulty. ■ Bad component in optical pickup. ■ Microcontroller or control logic problems. ■ Bad connections or defective ribbon cable to optical pickup. ■ Defective spindle motor including worn bearings.

Problem	Possible causes
Disc is not recognized.	■ Disc loaded upside-down. ■ Transportation lock engaged. ■ Dirty, scratched, or defective disc. ■ Dirty or damaged objective lens. ■ Loading (mechanical) not completed reliably. ■ Damaged lens suspension or damaged lens cover preventing free movement. ■ Dirt, gummed up lubrication, or damage in sled drive mechanism. ■ Dirty/defective limit switch or sensor. ■ Defective spindle motor. ■ Spindle table height incorrectly set. ■ Bad component in optical pickup. ■ Cracks in ribbon cable to optical pickup. ■ Need to adjust servo (or less likely, optical) alignment. ■ Faulty power supply, electronics, or control logic. ■ Bad connections including missing/erratic optical deck shield. ■ External interference.
Pickup attempts to reset past inner track.	■ Dirty or defective limit switch, bad connections to it, or its electronics. ■ Broken parts preventing limit switch from being activated. ■ Tracking servo out of adjustment or faulty. ■ Microcontroller or logic problems.
Seek operations take too long or fail to complete.	■ Dirty, scratched, or defective disc. ■ Transportation lock engaged. ■ Dirty or damaged objective lens, suspension, obstruction, etc. ■ Tracking or CLV servo out of adjustment or faulty. ■ Mechanical problems with sled movement. ■ Faulty sled motor or drive IC. ■ Faulty control logic. ■ Bad ribbon cable to optical pickup.
Search, seek, or play starts correctly, then loses time or position.	■ Dirty, scratched, or defective disc. ■ Dirty or damaged objective lens, suspension, obstruction etc. ■ Tracking or PLL servo out of adjustment or faulty. ■ Stuck button. ■ Defective sled motor drive IC. ■ Faulty control logic.
Short distance skipping.	■ Dirty, scratched, or defective disc. ■ Dirty or damaged objective lens, suspension, obstruction etc. ■ Fine tracking servo out of adjustment or faulty. ■ Weak laser or other defective part in the optical pickup.

Problem	Possible causes
Playback gets stuck (continuos repeat).	■ Dirty, scratched, or defective disc. ■ Dirty or damaged objective lens, suspension, obstruction etc. ■ Dirt, gummed up lubrication, or damage in sled drive mechanism. ■ Transportation lock engaged. ■ Need for servo alignment.
Occasional long distance skipping or repeating.	■ Dirty, scratched, or defective disc. ■ Dirty or damaged objective lens, suspension, obstruction, etc. ■ Dirt, gummed up lubrication, bad belt, or damage in sled drive mechanism. ■ Transportation lock engaged. ■ Need for servo alignment.
Player gets stuck at approximately same time on multiple discs.	■ Dirt, gummed up lubrication, or damage in sled drive mechanism. ■ Sled reaching mechanical stop with extended length (>74 minute) disc. ■ Transportation lock engaged. ■ Need for servo alignment. ■ Defective spindle motor.
Various tracking problems on parts of discs.	■ Dirty, scratched, or defective disc. ■ Faulty spindle motor. ■ Misalignment of spindle table and sled track. ■ Need for CLV adjustment.
Repetitive noise at disc rotation rate.	■ Dirty, scratched, or defective (possibly warped) disc. ■ Dirty or damaged objective lens, suspension, obstruction etc. ■ Loose spindle or foreign material on spindle table. ■ Disc not firmly clamped. ■ Bent spindle. ■ Excessive spindle runout due to worn bearing. ■ Need for servo alignment.

General Inspection, Cleaning, and Lubrication

One should perform the following as a general preventive maintenance on a CD-ROM/DVD drive. These procedures can also be performed when one detects erratic behavior of CD-ROM/DVD drive.

As a preventive step the lens and its suspension, turning mirror, drawer mechanism, spindle, and sled drive should be checked, and cleaned and/or lubricated if necessary.

Objective Lens

When cleaning the objective lens, one should be very careful. The lens is suspended by a voice coil actuated positioner which is very delicate.

One can also use a lens cleaner disc, but these discs are not of much use except for the most minor dust. These cleaning discs will not completely remove grease, grime, etc.

To clean the objective lens, first, gently blow out any dust or dirt which may have collected inside the lens assembly. An air bulb with a brush, generally used by photographers for cleaning their lens, is very good for this.

One should not use compressed air source.

Once the dust particles are removed, clean the lens. As the lens is made of plastic, never use any strong solvents.

Some special cleaner are available for his, but one can use isopropyl alcohol or a lens cleaning liquid. Use a soft cotton bud and clean gently. Once the lens is cleaned, dry everything.

One should never lubricate the optical assembly.

Never use strong solvents or anything with abrasives - you will destroy the lens surface rendering the entire optical assembly worthless.

Once the lens is clean, it should be perfectly shiny with a blue tinge uniform over the central surface.

Drawer Mechanism

Check the drawer mechanism for free movement. If the mechanism has belt, then check the belt for life - it should be firm, reasonably tight, and should return to its original length instantly if stretched by 25% or so.

If the belt fails these tests then one should immediately replace it, as it may give problems in the future.

Clean the belt and pulleys with isopropyl alcohol (dry quickly to avoid damaging the rubber) or soap and water. When the isopropyl alcohol is used, dry it immediately, otherwise the rubber parts may get damaged.

Also, check the gears and motor for lubrication and damage and correct as necessary.

Clean and lubricate other parts that help the mechanism. For lubrication use very high quality silicone based grease. One can also use silicone based oil for lubricating most of the parts.

A drop of oil in the motor bearings may cure a noisy or dry bearing.

Sled Drive

During the preventive maintenance, check the components which move the pickup including belt, worm gear, other gears, slide bearings etc.

All these mechanism should move freely.

If any damage is found, repair or replace as appropriate.

If the there is dirty or hardened grease, clean the gears and track thoroughly with the isopropyl alcohol, as this may interfere with free movement of mechanism.

One can use a sharpened toothpick or a pin to get in between each of the gear teeth.

Clean and lubricate the mechanism. For lubrication use very high quality silicone based grease. One can also use silicone based oil for lubricating most of the parts.

A drop of oil in the motor bearings may cure a noisy or dry bearing.

Comparison of CD and DVD Specifications

Parameter	Compact Disc/CD-R	Digital Versatile Disc (DVD)
Disk diameter	120 mm	120 mm
Disk thickness	1.2 mm	1.2 mm
Disk structure	Single substrate	Two bonded 0.6 mm substrates
Laser wavelength	780 nm	650 to 635 nm
Numerical aperture	0.45	0.60
Track pitch	1.6 um	0.74 um
Minimum pit/land length	0.83 um	0.4 um
1X speed (CLV)	1.2 m/sec	4.0 m/sec
Number of data layers	One	One or Two
Number of sides	One	One or two
Data capacity	680 Mbyte	4.7 Gbyte (one layer) 8.5 Gbyte (two layer) 17 Gbyte (two layer, two sides)
User data rate (1X)	153.6 K/sec (mode 1) 176.4 K/sec (mode 2)	1,108 K/sec (mode 1)

Power Supply

In electronic, two kinds of Power Supplies are used. Linear Supplies and Switching Power Supplies. Switch Mode Power Supply (SMPS) is very commonly used type.

Low cost, Small size and high efficiency are the major features of SMPS that has replaced the conventional Linear Power Supply used in electronic equipment.

Following section describes the design and construction of a Switch Mode Power Supply (SMPS) for the Personal Computers.

Operating Characteristics

The Power Supply Unit (PSU) described here is capable of providing continuous operation at over 110W. It is suitable for IBM compatible PC configuration supporting two floppy drives (360KB or 1.2MB) and one hard disk drive.

Various PC configurations demand different Power Supply requirements depending upon the add-on cards used in the expansion slots of the computer type and number of drives used.

The latest version of PCs utilizing advanced low current devices/components consume much less power as compared to their predecessor. In general, PSU capable of providing continuous power of over 300W is adequate up to a normal Pentium4 Configuration.

The PSU supplies various voltages and "power good" signal necessary for the operation of PC's system board, keyboard and other installable optional cards.

It can be operated over an input voltage range of 160V to 260V AC and provides regulated DC output voltages of +3.3V, +5V,-5V, +5VSB (standby), +12V, -12V.

AT supply also output a power good signal which is used by the SMPS to indicate the motherboard that all the outputs from power supply are at the correct level and safe for use by the computer.

ATX power supply adds two new signals PW_ON (power on) and +5V SB (Standby) for the new generation of computers.

"Power ON" signal is used by the motherboard to switch on/off the power supply. This signal allows the motherboard to control the power supply. Motherboard can put the

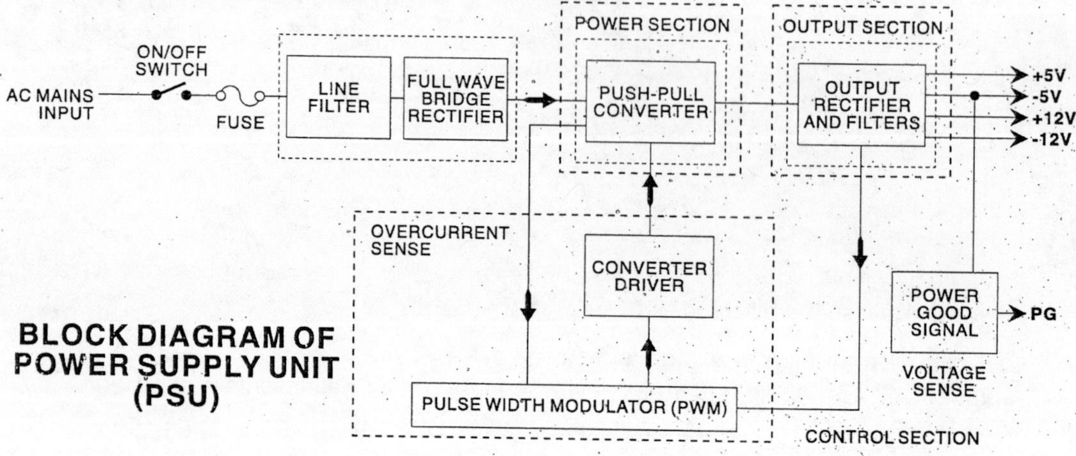

BLOCK DIAGRAM OF POWER SUPPLY UNIT (PSU)

system in standby by switching off the power supply, and shift back to normal operation by restoring the power.

"+5V standby" is not controlled by the "power on" signal, it is used to provide power to the motherboard when the system is in standby mode and the main voltages from the power supply has been switched off.

The input portion of PSU is protected by a fuse of suitable rating. The +5V DC powers the logic ICs on the system board, the disk drives and adapters in the system expansion slots.

The +12V is used for the system's dynamic memory and disk drive motors. The -5V DC levels is designed for dynamic memory bus voltage and has a longer decay on power than of +5V and +12V outputs.

When Power Supply is turned on, it generates a power good signal which indicates that there is adequate power for processing. When the output voltages are above the minimum sense level, a TTL compatible high level (2.4V DC to 5V DC) is generated on the power good line.

This power good signal has a turn-on delay of about 100 ms after the output voltages have reached their respective levels.

The input AC supply is first filtered to suppress any spikes/surges entering the power supply circuit. This is an important part of the circuit and helps in preventing data loss or erroneous working during power line disturbances.

Filtered mains supply is then rectified by a full-wave bridge rectifier to produce +150V DC for the power converter section. The input supply is switched with the help of this power converter and the energy transferred to the output through a high frequency ferrite transformer.

The power converter consists of two external driver transistors operating in push-pull configuration these are driven by converter driver.

The power converter transformer produces low voltage switched waveforms on the secondary side which are rectified and filtered to produce well regulated output DC voltages.

The +5V DC output voltage is sensed by control section of the PSU which essentially consists of a pulse width modulator (PWM) controller IC. This PWM produces suitable drive pulses at about 22KHz of the converter driver.

The width of these pulses is controlled by the modulator depending upon the output sense voltages and over current voltages, thus ensuring correct operating voltages at the output and providing necessary protection to the PSU.

In an AT Power Supply, two 6-pin connectors (or one 12-pins connector) are used for connection PSU to the motherboard of the PC and many 4-pin connectors are provided for connecting hard disk drive, floppy disk drive, CD-ROM etc.

ATX power supply use a single 20-pin connector to connect to the motherboard.

Input supply is given through mains connector or directly through a 3-core mains cable from the rear panel of the PC.

Circuit Description

Following are the basic SMPS components:

- Control IC
- High Frequency Power Transistor
- Fast recovery switching power diode
- Low ESR capacitor
- Low loss & high frequency ferrite cores transformers
- Cooling fan.

The input mains supply is applied to the circuit via an on-off switch to fuse F1. Resistor R1 limits the inrush of current. Power converters operating directly " off-line " like this one draw heavy current when switched on.

This inrush of current causes great stress on input components, switches, rectifiers and capacitors. For low power applications, simple series resistor is used to limit the initial high voltage and high current.

Special high current surge rated resistors are best suited for this application. However adequately rated wirewound resistor also serves the purpose and is frequently used.

SMPS FOR PC USING IC TL494

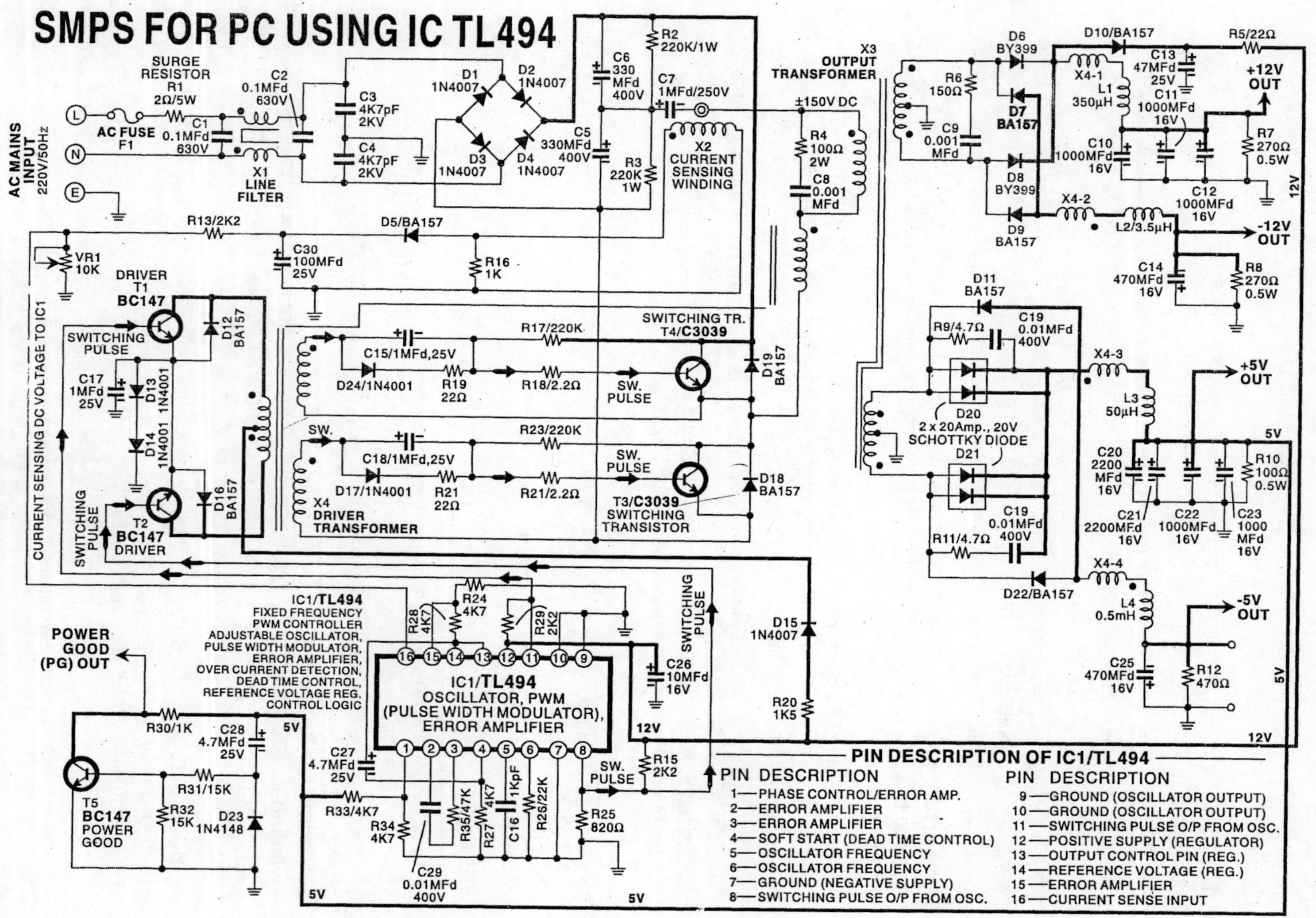

Capacitors C1, C2, C3, C4 & transformer X1 form a balanced input line filter. X1 has two separate inductors wound on a single core. Such that the two windings are in antiphase.

When the two windings are connected in this way the magnetic field that results from the normal supply currents is canceled. Hence the low frequency line current will not saturate the core and a high permeability material may be used without the need for an air gap.

However, for noise which appears on both the lines at the same time with respect to ground, the two windings are in parallel and in phase.

Also, a very high inductance is presented to common mode currents.

This arrangement prevents any significant interference circuits from being conducted back to the input supply lines. Filtered AC mains lines are then connected to diodes D1 through D4 acting as a full-wave rectifier.

C5 and C6 are the smoothing capacitors.

This arrangement provides approximately +/-150V DC to the power converter transformer with respect to the center point i.e. junction of C5 and C6.

The power converter has been configured in half-bridge push-pull configuration. This is preferred topology for direct off-line switch mode supplies because it causes reduced voltage stress on switching devices.

Switching transistors T3 and T4 form only one side of the bridge circuit, the remaining half being formed by capacitors C5 and C6.

The major difference between this card full-bridge is that the primary of transformer X3 will take only half supply voltage into consideration i.e. 150V DC approximately.

T3 and T4 are power switching transistors connected across the input supply, the center point being connected to the second end of primary winding of X3 when transistor T4 turns on half the input supply voltage is applied across the primary winding of X4 with the start going positive.

After a time duration defined by the control circuit of IC1, T4 is turned off. As a result of primary and leakage inductance, current will continue to flow into the primary winding.

The junction of T3 and T4 will swing negative and if the energy stored in the primary leakage inductance is sufficiently large, diode D18 will conduct to clamp any further negative excursion and return the remaining flyback energy to the supply.

The voltage at the center of T3 and T4 will eventually return to its original central value with a damped oscillatory action. After a period defined by the control circuit T3 will turn on making the primary winding negative.

The former process will repeat but with primary current in the opposite direction. The difference is that at the end of the on period, the junction of T3 & T4 will go positive, bringing D19 into conduction and returning the leakage inductance energy to the supply line.

The junction of T3 & T4 will eventually return to the central voltage with a damped oscillatory motion. The cycle of operation is now complete and will continue.

As C5 and C6 are the main reservoir capacitors for the input filter, their value is very large consequently the voltage at the junction point of the capacitors C5 & C6 will not change significantly during a cycle of operations.

Let us now consider the operation of secondary side of the switching transformer X3. When T4 turns on, the start of all the secondary windings (for 5V and 12V) will go positive.

For 5V secondary D20 will conduct the current will flow from X4-3 and L3 into the capacitor bank C20 through C23 and external load.

When T4 turns will continue to flow in the secondary diodes as a result of forcing action of chock X4-3 and L3.

When the secondary voltage has fallen to zero diodes D20 and D21 share the inductor current almost equally, acting as flywheel diodes and damping the secondary voltage at zero. When the opposite transistor T3 turns on similar operations result.

Under steady state conditions, the current will increase in X4-3 and L3 during on period and decrease during off; period with a mean value equal to the output current. The output voltage can be maintained at a constant by controlling on and off times.

This is done in the circuit with the help of PWM IC TL494 which forms the heart of the controller section of PSU.

TL494 is a fixed frequency, pulse width modulation controller.

TL494 incorporates an error amplifier, Additional functions include over current detection, dead time control, a precision 5V reference regulator and control logic which allows push-pull operation of the two switching transistors.

Description of TL494

Oscillator

The TL494 oscillator frequency is controlled by connecting an external timing circuit consisting of a capacitor and resistor to pins 5 and 6 the oscillator is set to operate, at about 22KHz using the component value calculated by the following equation

$f = 1 / (2 RC)$

for push-pull operation where R is value of timing resistance R26 and C the value of timing capacitor C16.

Error Amplifier

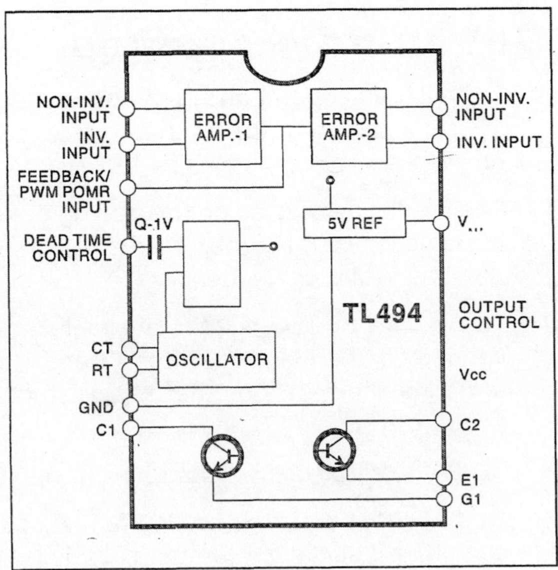

The error amplifier compares a sample of the 5V output to a reference and adjust the pulse width modulator to maintain a constant output.

The internal 5V reference of TL494 (pin 14) is reduced to 2.5V by R28 and R24 and the output voltage is also reduced to 2.5V by R33 and R34 to increase the stability of the error amplifier circuit, the output of error amplifier is fed back to the inverting input through R35, reducing the AC gain to 10.

Soft-start

To reduce the stress on the switching transistors at starting, the start up surge which occurs as the output fitter capacitor charges, must be reduced.

The availability of the dead time control makes implementation of a softstart circuit relatively simple. The soft-start circuit allows the pulse width at the output to increase slowly by applying a negative sloped waveform to the dead time control pin 4, initially, capacitor C27 forces the dead time control input to follow the 5V reference which disable the outputs (100 percent dead time).

As the capacitor charges through R27, the output pulse width slowly increase until the control loop takes command. This helps to eliminate any false signals which might be created by the control circuit as power is applied.

Current Limit Circuit

The PSU has been designed to operate continuously at over 110W output load. The converter supply current is monitored by current transformer X2.

The induced pulses are rectified by diode D5 and filtered by C30 to produce a DC voltage proportional to the converter supply current. Potential divider formed by resistors R13 and VR1 produces a voltage of 2.5V at the maximum allowed load of 110W.

As the output load current increases the converter supply current also increases, inducing more voltage in the current sense, winding of transformer X2.

This reduces the output pulse width thus limiting the output load power up to a predetermined limit. By using a variable resistance the over current limit of their circuit can be set accordingly.

Output driver stages

For push-pull operation (each output stage conducting alternately) output control pin 13 is connected to the internal reference voltage pin 14, enabling the pulse steering flip-flop.

The flip-flop is toggled on the trailing edge of the pulse width modulated signal gating it to each output alternately, thereby making the switching frequency of each output half the oscillator frequency.

The output of TL494 PWM available at pins 11 and 8 for push-pull operation are connected to driver transistors T1 and T2. Primary of center tapped transformer X4 is switched alternately by these transistors producing suitable base drive pulses for the power transistors T3 and T4.

TL494 gets its supply voltage from the 12V output through D10, C13, R5 and C26.

In the PSU chassis the cooling fan is mounted on the top cover with its face oriented such that it sucks air into the chassis.

The exit for the air is provided on the back cover behind the transistor and diode heatsinks.

Precautions

The following precautions should be observed during checking of the PSU.

- It is strongly recommended that an isolation transformer be used on the mains input side of the PSU or oscilloscope.
- PCB contains un-isolated mains supply voltages. Hence due care should be taken while checking its operation.
- You must be fully satisfied with working of PSU before interfacing it with your PC.

Power-Supply Sizes

Just as you can buy replacement cases for your PC, you can also buy replacement power supplies. The specifications of your new power supply must be suitable for your computer.

For the latest Pentium4 processor based computers one should go for at least a 300W power supply (SMPS).

Additionally, when buying a new SMPS, the physical size and mounting holes of the power supply must match your current cabinet.

Monitor

Computer Display System

Computer display system is made up of two different parts

- a video card or video adapter and
- a monitor

These parts work together to show any output or display on the monitor. The information that is displayed on the monitor is provided and controlled by the video card and the crispness and quality of display depends on the monitor used.

Without a good video card, a good monitor will not provide satisfying results. Conversely, without a good monitor, the capabilities of a good video card will be of no use.

It is important that both elements be matched in capability and features so that the user can get the best possible display.

Monitor

Picture Tube

Monitor is the most common device used with a computer to display results. And the most common display unit for the past several years is based on Cathode Ray Tube (CRT). This display is also called a VDU (Visual Display Unit) or a Screen.

The main unit in the CRT monitor is a picture tube. This tube is an evacuated glass tube with a phosphor coating (Phosphors are materials that glow when they are struck by electrons) on the inner front surface.

Electron Gun

An electron gun from the opposite end (neck) of the tube emits an electron beam. This beam is directed towards the inner front surface. When the beam strikes the surface, the phosphor coating on the screen produces illumination at the spot where the electron beam strikes.

Horizontal / Vertical Deflection

An electromagnetic deflection deflects the electron beam in order to produce the illumination at various spots on the screen. Horizontal deflection coils deflect the beam in the horizontal direction and the vertical deflection coils deflect the beam in the vertical direction.

Together these two horizontal and vertical deflection coils can deflect the beam to any spot on the screen.

Persistence

After being struck by the electron beam, when the beam moves to next dot the illumination of the dot stays for a few milliseconds this is called persistence. After which the dot loses it illumination.

Scanning

As the dot loses its illumination after a few millisecond, to create a permanent image on the screen, it is necessary to illuminate the dots repeatedly. This is done by repeatedly scanning the CRT screen with the electron beam.

Raster Scanning

The common method of scanning is called Raster scan. In this method, the electron beam is moved back and forth across the screen from top to the bottom of the screen.

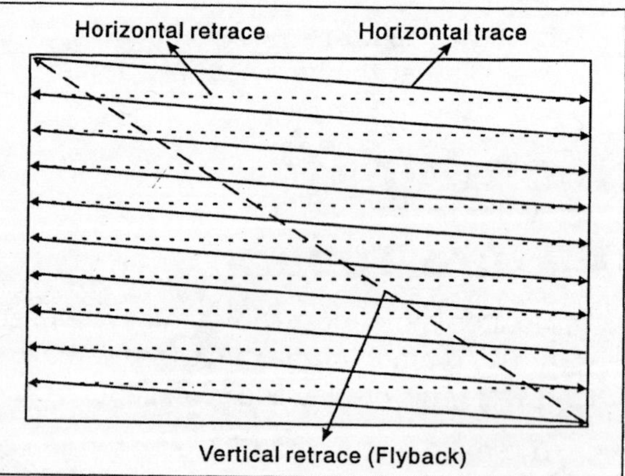

First the scanning starts from the top left corner, on reaching the extreme right, the beam is brought back to the left, to the next scan line and again the scanned to the extreme right.

This process is repeated until the bottom of the screen is reached. On reaching the bottom, the beam is brought back to the top left of the screen and the whole process from the beginning is repeated.

A complete scan of the screen is called a field. Upon completing a field, the beams return to the upper-left corner to begin a new field. The screen is normally redrawn, or refreshed, about 60 times a second.

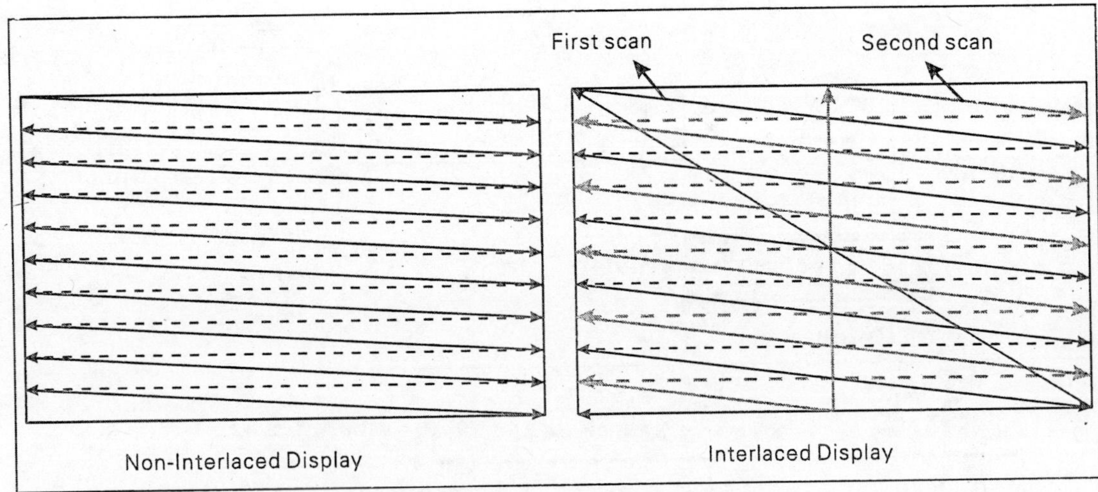

Interlacing/ Non-interlacing

Some display adapters scan only every other line with each field, a process called interlacing. Interlacing allows the adapter to create higher resolutions-that is, to scan more lines-with less expensive components. But the fading of the phosphors between each pass can be more noticeable, causing the screen to flicker.

Image Generation

To produce an image, the beam is turned on or off while scanning. The video information from the computer is used for turning the beam on or off at appropriate places when the beam scans the screen.

The HSYNC from the computer provides horizontal synchronization. VSYNC from the computer is used for vertical synchronization. Color information is also provided by the computer to produce a color image on the color monitor.

Monitor Interfacing

There are two methods of interfacing a Monitor to a computer:

- TTL video interface
- Composite video interface.

In the TTL video interface, the computer sends video, HSYNC and VSYNC signals on separate wires. In the composite video interface, all the three signals, video, HSYNC and VSYNC are mixed and sent as a composite video waveform on a single wire.

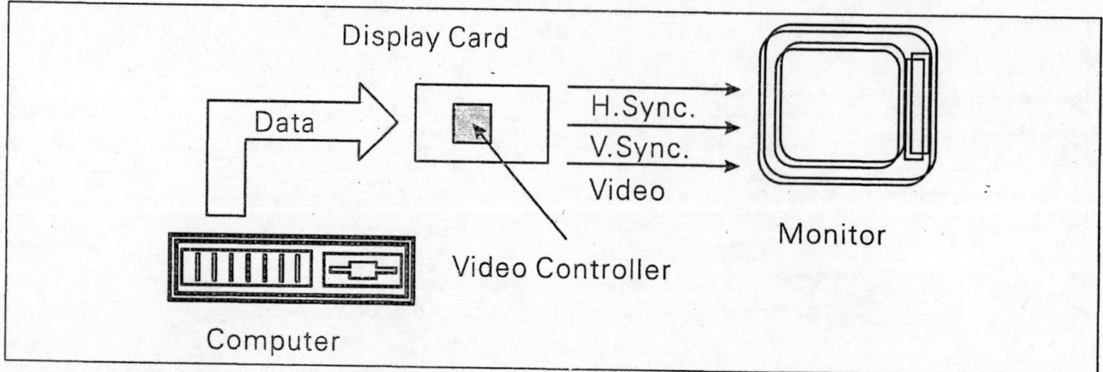

Working of a VGA Color Display

VGA color monitor is the most common color monitor in use today. Older monitors used digital signal that could be only on or off, making it difficult to achieve subtle difference in displayed colors.

A VGA monitor uses analog signal to work i.e. a digital signal from computer is converted into different voltage levels and these voltage levels are used to vary the brightness of the spot on the screen.

This makes it easy to produce a number of shades on the screen.

In next few paragraphs we have tried to briefly explain the working of a VGA color display system.

Computer to Display card

In this display system first the computer sends the required color to be displayed on the screen as a digital signal to the VGA display card. The card sends these signals through a circuit called a digital-to-analog converter (DAC).

This DAC circuit is usually contained within one single specialized chip. This special DAC chip actually contains three DACs-one for each of the primary colors red, green and blue.

The job of this DAC circuit is to compare the value sent by the computer with a table inside its circuit. This table contains the voltage levels for the three primary colors (red, green and blue) needed to create the required color on the screen.

The table contains values for 262,144 possible colors, of which 256 values can be stored in the VGA card's memory. Super VGA displays, with more memory, can handle more colors with more dots on the screen.

Display card to Monitor

The display card then sends signals to three electron guns located at the back of the monitor's cathode-ray tube (CRT) or picture tube. Each electron gun emits electrons and the intensity of each stream is controlled by the signals from the display card.

The adapter also sends signals to the neck of CRT that focuses and aims the electron beams. The assembly which is fitted in the neck of CRT is called as "Magnetic Deflection Yoke". It uses electromagnetic field to band the path of the electronic streams. The signal which are send to the yoke help determine the resolution of the monitor.

These beams pass through holes in a metal plate called a shadow mask. The shadow mask is situated inside the picture tube just before the inner front surface. The purpose of this mask is to keep the electron beams precisely aligned with their dots on the inside of the CRT's screen.

The CRT's "dot pitch" is the measurement of how close the holes are to each other; the closer the holes, the smaller the dot pitch. This, in turn, creates a sharper image. The smallest dot that can be display on the screen is called a "pixel".

The holes in most shadow masks are arranged in triangles, with one exception of the Sony Trinitron CRT used by many monitor manufacturers. The Trinitron's holes are arranged as parallel slots called "aperture grille".

Inside the picture tube three different phosphor materials are used-one each for red, blue and green. When the electrons strike this phosphors coating the stronger is the electron beam that hits a phosphor, the more light the phosphor emits.

If each red, green and blue dot in an arrangement or single pixel is struck by equally intense electron beams, the result is a dot of white light. To create different colors, the intensity of each of the three beams is changed.

After the beams make one horizontal sweep across the screen, the electron streams are turned off as the electron guns refocus the paths of the beams back to the left edge of the screen at a point just below the previous scan line. The process is called raster scanning.

The magnetic deflection yoke continually changes the angels at which the electron beams are bent so that they sweep across the entire screen surface from the upper-left corner of the screen to the lower-right corner. A complete sweep of the screen is called a "Field". Upon completing a field, the beams return to the upper-left corner to begin a new field. The screen is normally redrawn, or refreshed, about 50 times a second.

Some display adapters can scan only every other line with each field, a process called "Interlacing". Interlacing allows the adapter to create higher resolutions - that is, to scan more lines - with less expensive components. But the fading of the phosphors between each pass can be more noticeable, causing the screen to flicker.

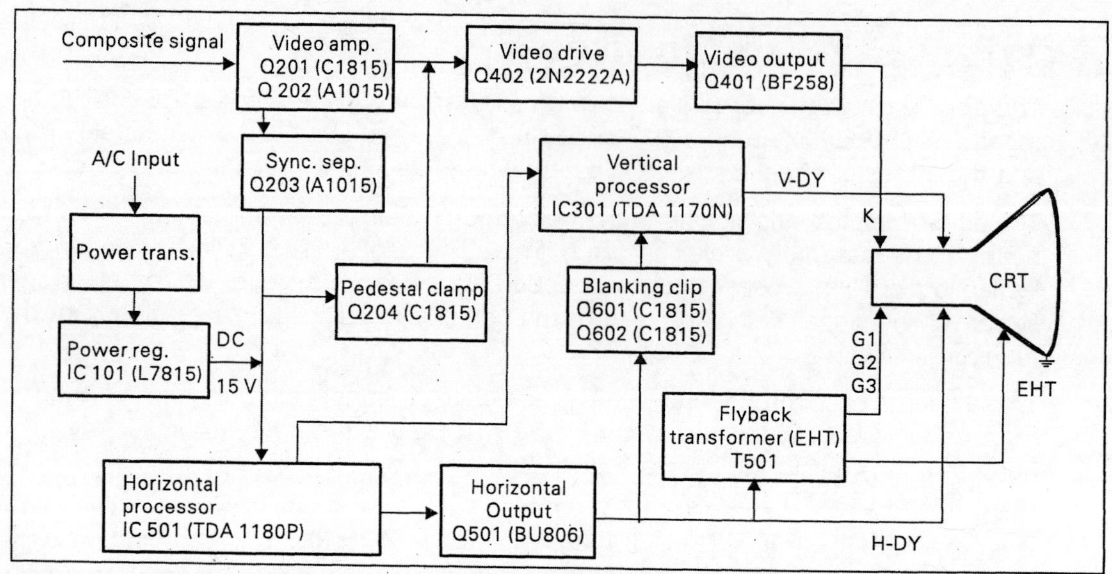

Block Diagram of a Mono Monitor

Video Amplifier Drive And Output

Video amplifier consists of four stages, Q201 (2SC1815) is the first amplifier, Q202 (2SA1015) is the second amplifier, Q601 (2SC1815) and Q602 (2SC1815) are connected in a cascade configuration. Composite video signal given at the base of Q201 (2SC1815) is developed across collector load.

This is amplified and given to drive transistor Q402 (2N2222A) through contrast volume VR201 (500K). The finally obtained signal is given to the CRT cathode through the output amplifier Q401 (BF258).

Q401 (BF258) and Q402 (2N2222A) are cascade configuration. Q402 (2N2222A) operates as a common emitter configuration and Q401 (BF258) operates in common base configuration.

Sync Separation

This circuit consists of one stage, Q203 (2SA1015). This circuit separates synchronous signal from the composite signal which is composed of video and synchronous signal. This separated synchronous signal is supplied to IC501 (TDA1180P).

Pedestal Clamp Circuit

The pedestal clamp circuit is employed in this character display in order to stabilize the brightness of the picture. Q204 (2SC1815) is switched by means of the pulse produced by time-delayed horizontal signal from the collector of transistor Q203 (2SA1015).

The base potential of video exciting transistor Q402 (2N2222A) is clamped to the emitter potential of Q204 (2SC1815). While transistor Q204 is activated, the pedestal level of the video signal applied to the base of Q402 (2N2222A) is kept constant.

Horizontal Processor Circuit

Horizontal processor circuit consists of one stage, IC501 (TDA1180P). The synchronous pulse from transistor Q203 (A1015) is applied to pin no. 8 of IC501 (TDA1180P). The applied pulse separates vertical and horizontal signal from the synchronous pulse.

Separated vertical synchronous pulse is applied to IC301 (TDA1170N) through pin no. 10 of IC501 (TDA1180P). Horizontal synchronous pulse is applied to the oscillator stage and the oscillator output is applied to the base of Q501 (BU806) through pin no. 2 of IC501 (TDA1180P). The free running frequency is held by VR501 (22K).

Vertical Processor Circuit

Vertical processor circuit consists of one stage, of IC301 (TDA1170N) and it accomplishes all the active vertical sync function. Vertical input pulses are differentiated by C520 (0.0015MFd) and R310 (3.9K).

The sync input performs several functions. It removes any random noise that may be present on the input line and conditions the vertical pulses for processing.

It also converts the input voltage pulses to current which controls the internal oscillator. A non-symmetric square wave is generated by the oscillator with a short duty cycle of approximately 50Hz. VR302 (100K), R312 (120K) and C308 (0.15MFd) determines the frequency.

This square wave frequency is given to a ramp generator whose slope and amplitude is determined by VR303 (100K) and R311 (120K).

The ramp voltage signal is applied to a buffer stage which isolates the ramp generator from the output stages and reduces any loading effect on the previous stages. Components R303 (820K), VR301 (220K), C301 (0.1MFd) and C302 (0.1MFd) reshapes the ramp voltage to make it extremely linear.

The output signal from the buffer stage is applied to a preamplifier for amplification and then to a power ramp stage which drives the vertical deflection coils directly through the coupling capacitor C305 (1000MFd/16V), R304 (100K), R305 (100K), R306 (56K), R302 (470K), R309 (1.8W), C307 (10MFd/25V) and C306 (0.1MFd/100V) provide AC and DC feedback for the output stage to maintain proper gain and linearity.

Horizontal Output/Transformer

The horizontal output transistor Q501 (BU806) is simply a switch which is turned on and off at the horizontal scan rate by the driving signal applied at its base.

A sawtooth current through the deflection coil is required to sweep the beam linearly across the CRT screen. This happens when Q501 (BU806) is turned on and its collector voltage drops to nearly zero.

C516 (0.039MFd/400V) begins discharging through the deflection coil which deflect the beam to the right edge of the CRT.

At that time, Q501 (BU806) cuts off and C516 causes to supply current to the deflection coil. However an induced voltage appears across the deflection yoke coil as the magnetic field collapses and an oscillation then takes place between the deflection coils and C516.

During the first half cycle of this oscillation the induced voltage is felt across the collector of now cut Q501 (BU806), C516 and the primary of fly-back transformer T501. This voltage is stepped up by T501 and is rectified to produce high voltage that is applied to the 2nd anode of the CRT.

During the second half cycle of the deflection coil/C516 oscillation, the voltage on the collector is still cut if Q501 (BU806) becomes negative.

At this time, the damper diode D504 (RGP30G) becomes DC operating voltages for the CRT with the exception of the heater voltage being obtained by rectifying and filtering the horizontal flyback pulse.

D507 (MR818) and C515 (0.047MFd/630V) rectify and filter the flyback pulse across Q501 (BU806) to produce a G2 voltage. This voltage also feeds to the flyback pulse rectified and filtered by D505 (IN4003) and C519 (10MFd/160V) to produce voltage which is used as the source voltage for G1 to control raster brightness.

T501 also generates the CRT anode voltage and for a typical 12" CRT it is 13.0KV.

Blanking Clip

Blanking clip circuit consists of two transistors, Q601 (2SC1815) and Q602 (2SC1815). The vertical blanking signal received from the vertical output stage is applied to the base of Q601 (2SC1815) through R601 (2.2K) and C601 (1MFd/50V).

Also, the horizontal blanking signal from the horizontal output stage is applied to the base of Q602 (2SC1815) through R605 (56K), C605 (47Pf) and C603 (0.0056MFd).

These applied signals appear at the collector (Q601-Q602) with phase reverse, amplification and composition. These signals are applied to the brightness grid of CRT through C524 (0.22MFd/100V).

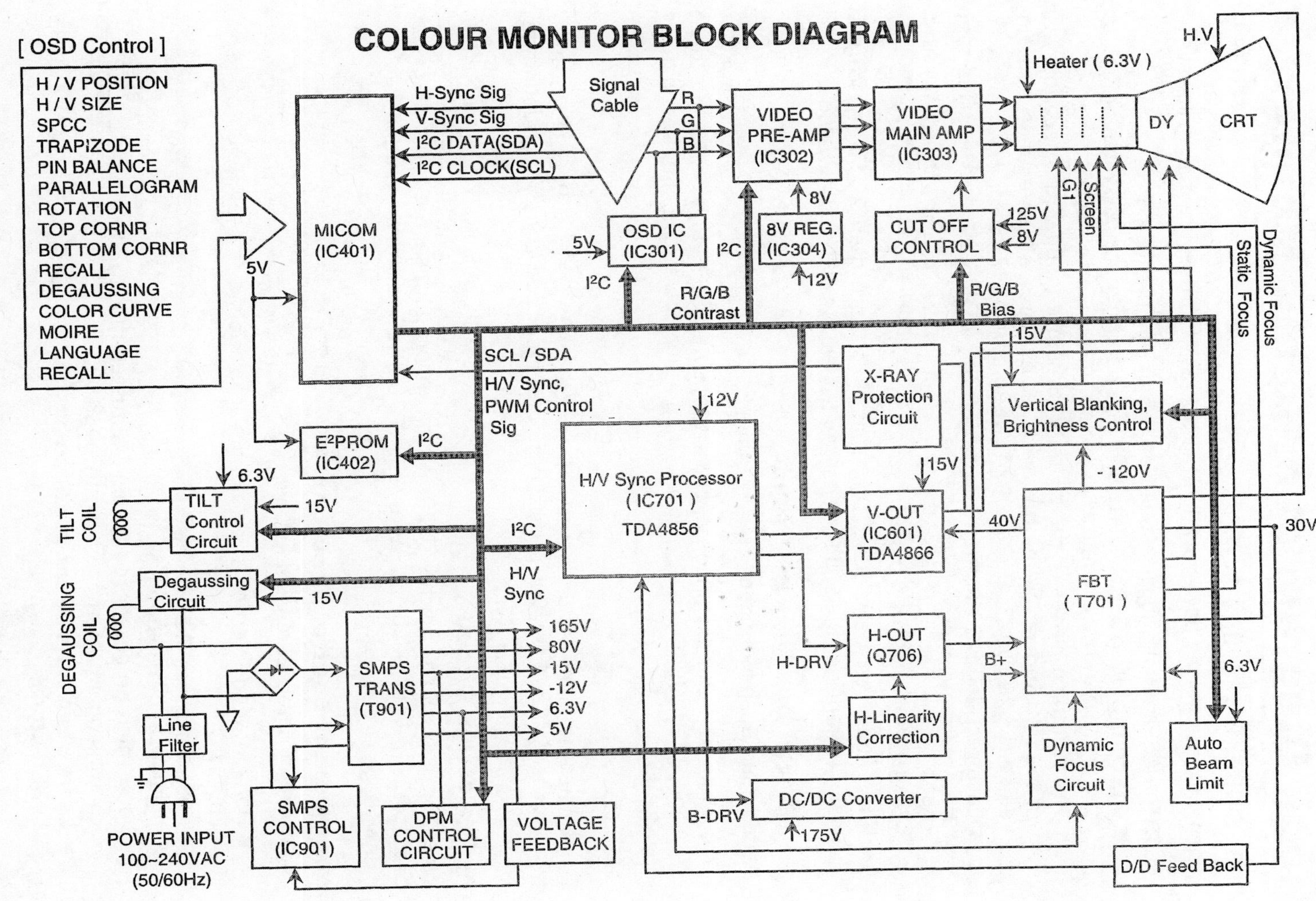
COLOUR MONITOR BLOCK DIAGRAM
[OSD Control]
H / V POSITION
H / V SIZE
SPCC
TRAPIZODE
PIN BALANCE
PARALLELOGRAM
ROTATION
TOP CORNR
BOTTOM CORNR
RECALL
DEGAUSSING
COLOR CURVE
MOIRE
LANGUAGE
RECALL
MICOM (IC401)
5V
H-Sync Sig
V-Sync Sig
I²C DATA(SDA)
I²C CLOCK(SCL)
Signal Cable
R
G
B
OSD IC (IC301)
5V
I²C
VIDEO PRE-AMP (IC302)
8V
8V REG. (IC304)
12V
VIDEO MAIN AMP (IC303)
CUT OFF CONTROL
125V
8V
R/G/B Contrast
R/G/B Bias
I²C
Heater (6.3V)
H.V
DY
CRT
G1
Screen
Static Focus
Dynamic Focus
SCL / SDA
H/V Sync, PWM Control Sig
15V
X-RAY Protection Circuit
Vertical Blanking, Brightness Control
- 120V
12V
H/V Sync Processor (IC701) TDA4856
15V
V-OUT (IC601) TDA4866
40V
30V
FBT (T701)
E²PROM (IC402)
I²C
6.3V
TILT Control Circuit
15V
TILT COIL
I²C
H/V Sync
Degaussing Circuit
15V
DEGAUSSING COIL
SMPS TRANS (T901)
165V
80V
15V
-12V
6.3V
5V
H-DRV
H-OUT (Q706)
B+
H-Linearity Correction
6.3V
Dynamic Focus Circuit
Auto Beam Limit
Line Filter
POWER INPUT 100~240VAC (50/60Hz)
SMPS CONTROL (IC901)
DPM CONTROL CIRCUIT
VOLTAGE FEEDBACK
B-DRV
DC/DC Converter
175V
D/D Feed Back

Block Diagram of a Colour Monitor

SMPS (Switching Mode Power Supply)

When you turn on the power switch, the operating procedure is as follows:

- The AC line voltage is rectified by the bridge diodes D900.
- The control IC (IC901) starts switching and generates switching pulses in the primary turns of the SMPS transformer (T901).
- The switching pulses of the primary turns are induced the secondary turns of the transformer by the turn ratio. These pulses are rectified by each diode (D920, D922, D923, D924, D926 and D937) .
- Each rectified DC voltage (75V, 165V, 5V, 15V, 6.3V, and -12V) is supplied to the main circuit.

Over Voltage Protection Circuit

When the input voltage of IC901 Vin (pin 4) is more than 22.5V (typical), all the secondary voltages of the SMPS transformer (T901) down to low value.

Display Power Management Circuit

Standby and Suspend mode.

- When no input of horizontal or vertical sync, Q923 and Q930, are turned on and Q920, Q926 are turned off. Then input power consumption is below 15 watts.

OFF mode

- When no input of horizontal and vertical sync, Q923, Q926, Q930 are turned off and Q920 is turned on. Then input power consumption is below 5 watts.

X-ray Protection Circuit

When the high voltage reaches to 29kV in an abnormal case, the high voltage detector circuit, R734, R717, R718, R719, R785, VR701, IC701 start operation to shut down high voltage circuit.

Microprocessor Control Circuit.

The operating procedure is as follows :

- Horizontal and Vertical sync signals are supplied to the microprocessor (IC401).
- Microprocessor (IC401) discriminates the operating mode from the sync polarity and resolution.
- After microprocessor reads these adjusted mode data stored at EEPROM, it controls operating mode data through IIC.
- Users can control screen condition by the OSD, SET, UP, DOWN, RIGHT and LEFT buttons.

D/D Convert Circuit.

To obtain constant high voltage, this circuit supplies controlled DC voltage for FBT and horizontal deflection circuit according to the horizontal sync frequency.

Horizontal and Vertical Sync Processor Circuit.

The horizontal and vertical sync processor IC (IC701) has a sync detector, a saw-tooth generator, and drive function.

So output horizontal and vertical drive signal control screen distortions.

Horizontal linearity Circuit.

This circuit corrects the horizontal linearity for each horizontal sync frequency.

Horizontal drive and Output Circuit.

This circuit is a horizontal deflection amplifier for raster scan.

ABL Circuit.

This circuit limits the beam-current for the reliability of the CRT.

Vertical Output Circuit.

This circuit takes the vertical ramp wave from the TDA4856 (IC701) and performs the vertical deflection by supplying the saw-tooth wave current to the vertical deflection yoke.

Blanking and Brightness Control Circuit.

Blanking circuit eliminates the retrace line by supplying a negative pulse wave to the G1 of the CRT.

Brightness control circuit is used for control of the screen brightness by changing the DC level of the G1.

Video Processor Circuit.

Video processor circuit consists of the video drive output block. The video drive IC (IC302) receives the video signal from PC. The gain of each channel is controlled by the voltage of contrast pin.

The cutoff circuit compensate different voltage of each channel between the cathode and the G1 of the CRT.

OSD (On-Screen-Display) Circuit.

This circuit displays on the screen information of the monitor's status.

Front View and Control

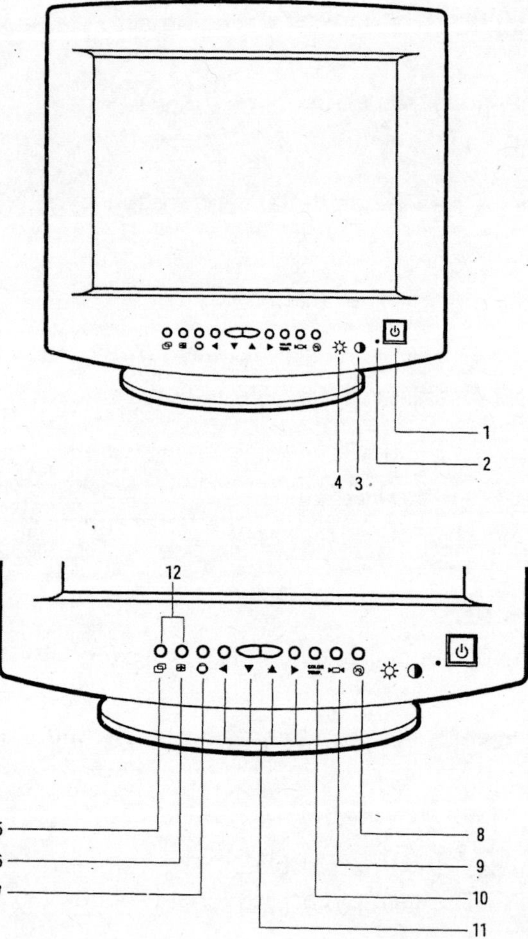

Location	Symbol	Description
1		Power Button
2	●	Power Indicator LED (Dual Color)
3		Contrast Control
4		Brightness Control
5		Position and Modes Push once: Position (Horizontal/Vertical) Push twice: User and Preset Modes
6		Size (Horizontal/Vertical)
7		G/D (Geometric Distortion) Push once: Pincushion/Trapezoid Push twice: Parallelogram/Tilt
8		Degauss Button
9		Recall Button
10	COLOR TEMP	Color Temperature Control
11	◀▶▼▲	Adjustment Buttons
12	+	Pinbalance and Vertical Linearity

On Screen Display

This monitor features an On-Screen Display (OSD) that shows information about the display setting. The OSD appears on the screen when you select a function button. The OSD shows the name, range and current setting of the control function. In addition, the OSD shows the current input signal frequency and the list of user and factory preset timings. The OSD remains active for approximately 8 seconds after the completion of any adjustment.

TFT LCD Monitor

LCD or Liquid Crystal Displays are non-emissive type display devices. A non-emissive display do not produce any form of light like a Cathode Ray Tube (CRT) or picture tube.

Liquid crystal was discovered by the Austrian botanist Fredreich Rheinizer in 1888. "Liquid crystal" is neither solid nor liquid.

In the mid-1960s, scientists showed that liquid crystals when stimulated by an external electrical charge could change the property of light passing through the crystals. This property of the LCD crystal is used in LCD display.

LCDs either pass or block light that is reflected from an external light source or provided by a back/side lighting system.

There are two modes of operation for LCDs during the absence of an electric field (applied Power)

- Normal White mode: the display is white or clear and allows light to pass through and
- Normal Black Mode: the display is dark and all light is diffused.

Virtually all LCD displays in use currently are normal white mode type to optimize contrast and speed.

LCD Fundamental

Following is a simplified description of how a dot matrix LCD display works.

A twisted nematic (TN) Liquid Crystal (LC) display consists of two polarizers, two pieces of glass, some form of switching element or electrode to define pixels, and driver Integrated Circuits (ICs) to address the rows and columns of pixels.

To define a pixel (or subpixel element for a color display), a rectangle is constructed out of Indium Tin Oxide - a semi-transparent metal oxide (ITO) and charge is applied to this area in order to change the orientation of the LC material.

The method utilized to form a pixel in passive and active matrix displays differs.

Following figure illustrates a cross sectional view of a simple TN LC display.

Polarizers are an integral part of an LCD display, possessing the unique property of only passing light if it is oriented in a specific (orientation) direction.

- To utilize this phenomena in TN LC displays, the bottom polarizer pass the light from the back-light oriented in one specific direction.
- The light passes through the LC material and is either unaltered or "bent" 90 degrees.
- Depending on the orientation of the top polarizer, this unaltered or bent light will either pass through or be diffused.

Viewer **LCD DISPLAY**

Polarizer
Glass
Row Electrode
Liquid Crystal
Column Electrode
Glass
Polarizer

Backlight

- If the light is diffused, it will appear as a dark area.
- If the light pass through the top polarizer, it will appear as a bright area.

Instead of bending the light 90 degree, one can control the polarization direction changes. This allows more or less of the light to be able to pass through the polarizing layer to generate different level of grays.

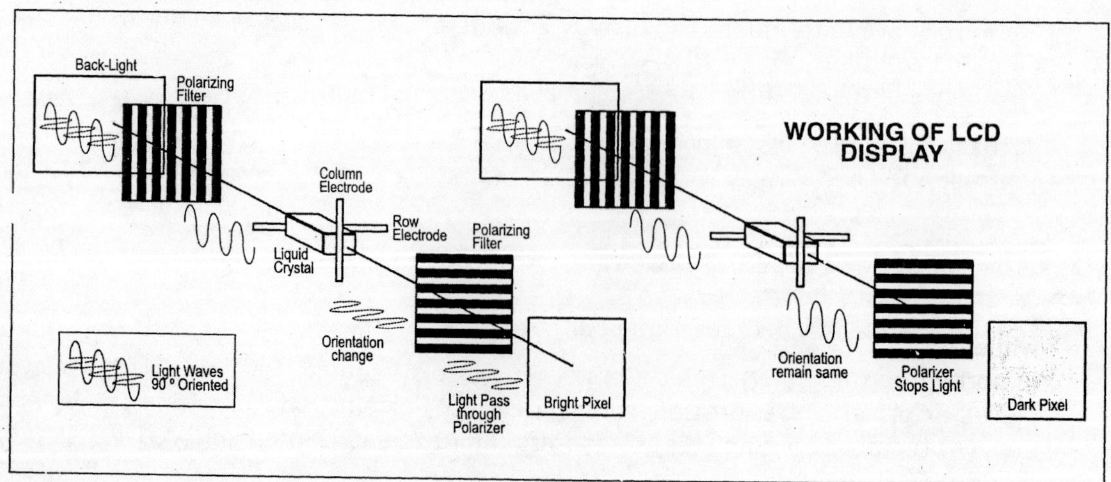

So, change the voltage applied to row/column electrodes, and the amount of light coming out of the top layer is changed.

Given figure shows a simple illustration of the sequence of events that occur when light passes through polarizer and Liquid Crystal.

Segment Driving / Matrix Driving LCD

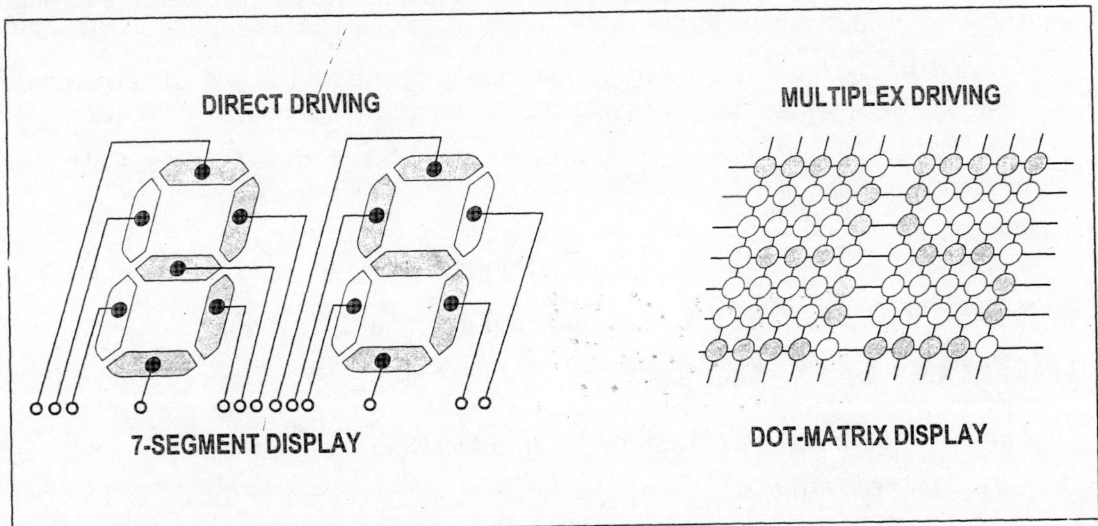

The most common liquid-crystal displays (LCDs) in use today rely on picture elements, or pixels, formed by liquid-crystal (LC) cells that change the polarization direction of light passing through them in response to an electrical voltage.

As the polarization direction changes, more or less of the light is able to pass through a polarizing layer on the face of the display.

Change the voltage, and the amount of light is changed.

There are two ways to produce a liquid-crystal image with such cells: the segment driving method and the matrix driving method.

- The segment driving method displays characters and pictures with cells defined by patterned electrodes.
- The matrix driving method displays characters and pictures in sets of dots.

The segment drive method is used for simple displays, such as those in calculators, while the dot-matrix drive method is used for high-resolution displays, such as those in portable computers and TFT monitors.

Direct Driving / Multiplex Driving LCD

Two types of drive method are used for matrix displays. In the static, or direct, drive method, each pixel is individually wired to a driver.

This is a simple driving method, but, as the number of pixels increase, the wiring becomes very complex.

An alternative method is the multiplex drive method, in which the pixels are arranged and wired in a matrix format.

To drive the pixels of a dot-matrix LCD, a voltage can be applied at the intersections of specific vertical signal electrodes and specific horizontal scanning electrodes.

This method involves driving several pixels at the same time by time-division in a pulse drive.

Therefore, it is also called a multiplex, or dynamic, drive method.

Passive Matrix LCD and Active Matrix/TFT LCD

Dot-matrix LCDs can be further divided into following categories.

- Passive-matrix LCD
- Active-matrix LCD/ TFT LCD

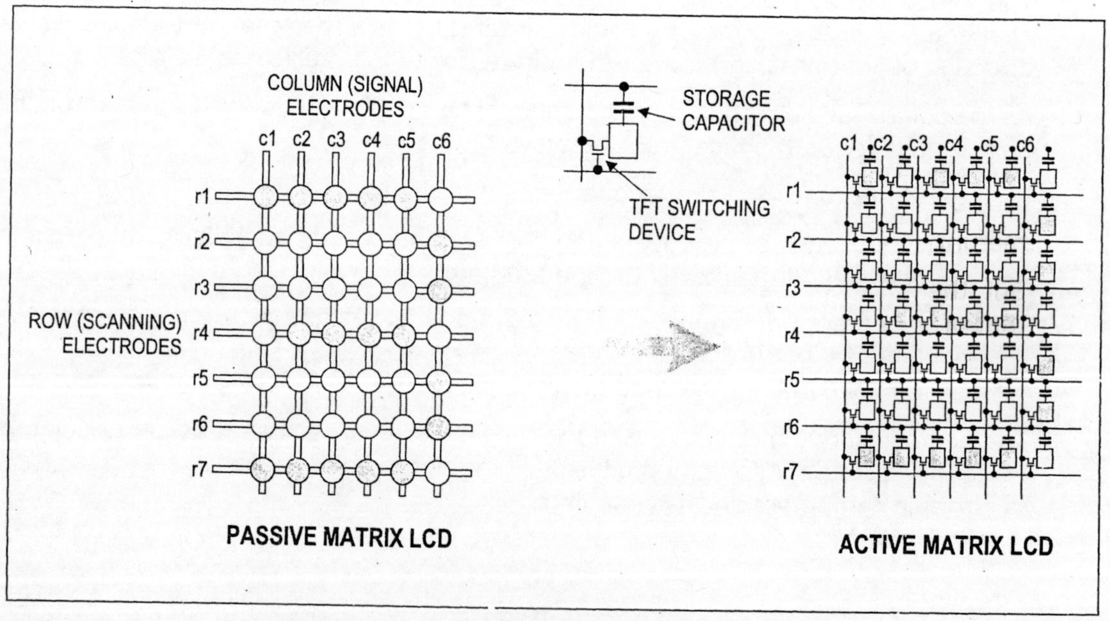

Passive-matrix LCD

In passive-matrix LCDs there are no switching devices, and each pixel is addressed for more than one frame time.

The effective voltage applied to the LC must average the signal voltage pulses over several frame times, which results in a slow response time of greater than 150 msec and a reduction of the maximum contrast ratio.

The addressing of a passive-matrix LCD also produces a kind of crosstalk that produces blurred images because non-selected pixels are driven through a secondary signal-voltage path.

Active-matrix LCD/ TFT LCD

In active-matrix LCDs, on the other hand, a switching device and a storage capacitor are integrated at the each cross point of the electrodes.

The active addressing removes the multiplexing limitations by incorporating an active switching element.

In contrast to passive-matrix LCDs, active-matrix LCDs have no inherent limitation in the number of scan lines, and they present fewer cross-talk issues.

There are many kinds of active-matrix LCD. For their integrated switching devices most use transistors made of deposited thin films, which are therefore called thin-film transistors (TFTs).

The most common semiconducting layer is made of amorphous silicon (a-Si).

a-Si TFTs can be used for large-area fabrication using glass substrates in a low-temperature (300°C to 400°C) process.

An alternative TFT technology, polycrystalline silicon - or polysilicon or p-Si is costly to produce and especially difficult to fabricate when manufacturing large-area displays.

Nearly all TFT LCDs are made from a-Si because of the technology's economy and maturity.

But, the electron mobility of a p-Si TFT is one or two orders of magnitude greater than that of an a-Si TFT.

This makes the p-Si TFT a good option for an TFT array containing integrated drivers, which is likely to be an attractive choice for small, high definition displays such as view finders and projection displays.

Structure of a color TFT LCD Panel

A TFT LCD module consists of TFT LCD Panel, Driving Circuit Unit, and Backlight & Chassis Unit.

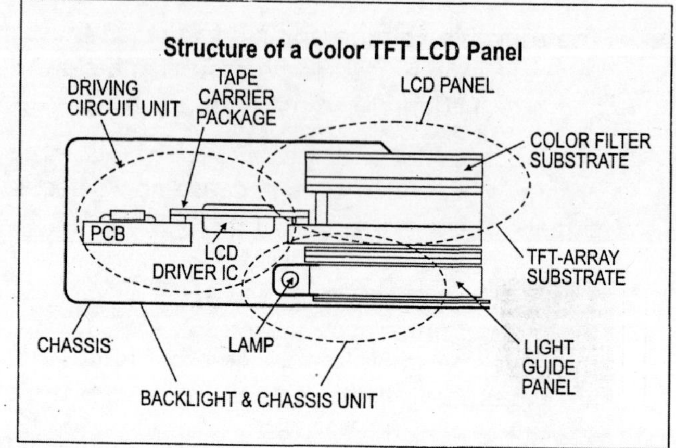

TFT LCD Panel

- TFT-Array Substrate
- Color Filter Substrate

Driving Circuit Unit

- LCD Driver IC (LDI) Chips
- Multi-layer PCBs
- Driving Circuits

Backlight & Chassis Unit

- Backlight Unit
- Chassis Assembly

TFT LCD Panel

The TFT-Array substrate contains the TFTs, storage capacitors, pixel electrodes, and interconnect wiring.

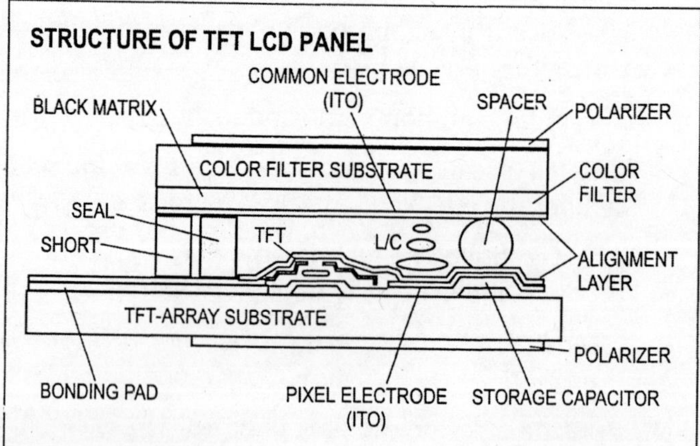

The color filter contains the black matrix and resin film containing three primary-color - red, green, and blue - dyes or pigments.

The two glass substrates are assembled with a sealant, the gap between them is maintained by spacers, and Liquid Crystal material is injected into the gap between the substrates.

Two sheets of polarizer film are attached to the outer faces of the sandwich formed by the glass substrates.

A set of bonding pads are fabricated on each end of the gate and data-signal bus-lines to attach LCD Driver IC (LDI) chips.

Driving Circuit Unit

Driving an a-Si TFT LCD requires a driving circuit unit consisting of a set of LCD driving IC (LDI) chips and printed-circuit-boards (PCBs).

To reduce the footprint of the LCD module, the drive circuit unit can be placed on the backside of the LCD module by using bent Tape Carrier Packages (TCPs) and a tapered light-guide panel (LGP).

The assembly of LCD driving circuits.

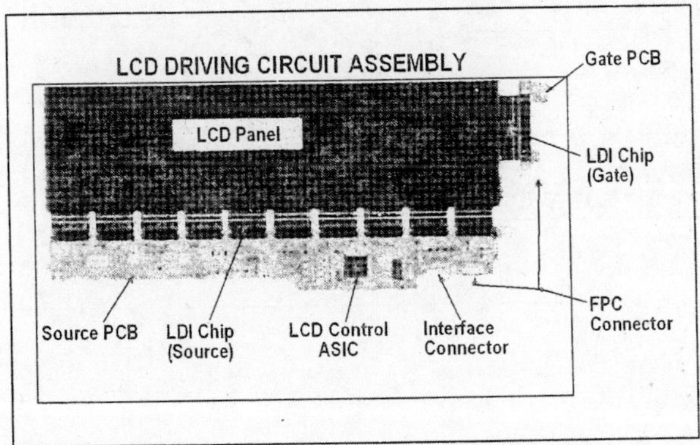

Following is a block diagram showing the driving of an LCD panel.

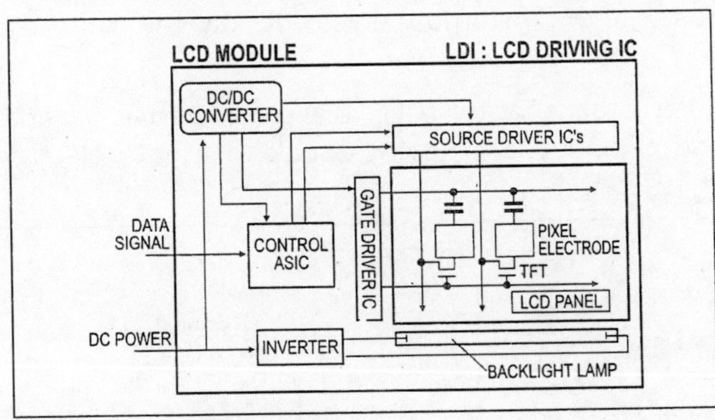

To reduce the footprint of the LCD module, the drive circuit unit is generally placed on the backside of the LCD module by using bent Tape Carrier Packages (TCPs) and a tapered light-guide panel (LGP).

How TFT LCD Pixels Work

A TFT LCD panel contains a specific number of unit pixels often called subpixels.

Each unit pixel has a TFT, a pixel electrode (ITO), and a storage capacitor (Cs).

For example, an SVGA color TFT LCD panel has total of 800 x 600 x 3 (one each for R, G, & B colors), or 1,440,000, unit pixels.

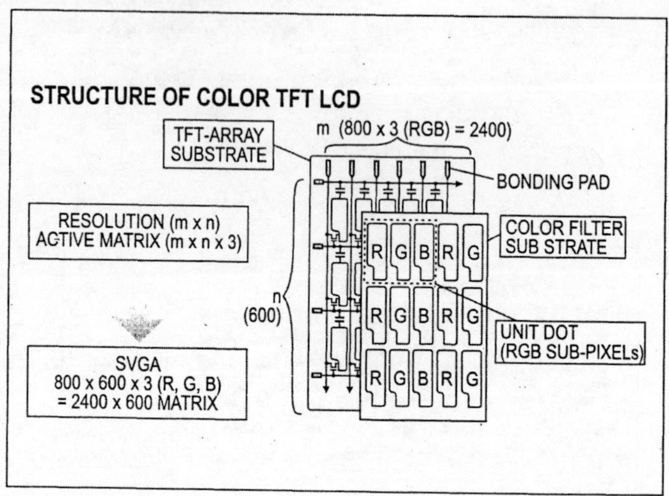

Each unit pixel is connected to one of the gate bus-lines and one of the data bus-lines in a "3 x m x n" matrix format.

For SVGA this matrix is "800 x 3 x 600".

Because each unit pixel is connected through the matrix, each is individually addressable from the bonding pads at the ends of the rows and columns.

In a TFT LCD's unit pixel, the liquid crystal layer on the ITO pixel electrode forms a capacitor whose counter electrode is the common electrode on the color-filter substrate.

A storage capacitor (Cs) and liquid-crystal capacitor (CLC) are connected as a load on the TFT. Applying a positive pulse of about 20V peak-to-peak to a gate electrode through a gate bus-line turns the TFT on.

Clc and Cs are charged and the voltage level on the pixel electrode rises to the signal voltage level (+8 V) applied to the data bus-line.

The voltage on the pixel electrode is subjected to a level shift, resulting from a parasitic capacitance between the gate and drain electrodes when the gate voltage turns from the ON to OFF state.

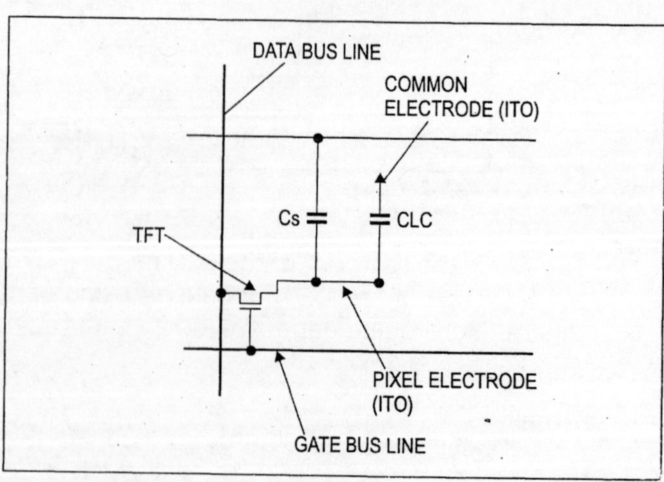

After the level shift, this charged state can be maintained as the gate voltage goes to -5 V, at the time, the TFT turns off.

The main function of the Cs is to maintain the voltage on the pixel electrode until the next signal voltage is applied.

Liquid crystal must be driven with an alternating current to prevent any deterioration of image quality resulting from dc stress.

This is usually implemented with a frame-reversal drive method, in which the voltage applied to each pixel varies from frame to frame.

If the LC voltage changes unevenly between frames, the result would be a 30-Hz flicker.

(One frame period is normally 1/60 of a second.) Other drive methods are available that prevent this flicker problem.

Polarity-Inversion Driving Methods

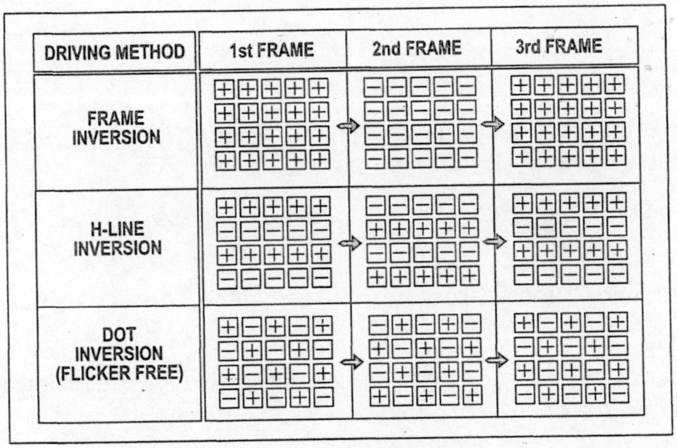

DRIVING METHOD	1st FRAME	2nd FRAME	3rd FRAME
FRAME INVERSION	+ + + + + + + + + + + + + + + + + + + +	− − − − − − − − − − − − − − − − − − − −	+ + + + + + + + + + + + + + + + + + + +
H-LINE INVERSION	+ + + + + − − − − − + + + + + − − − − −	− − − − − + + + + + − − − − − + + + + +	+ + + + + − − − − − + + + + + − − − − −
DOT INVERSION (FLICKER FREE)	+ − + − + − + − + − + − + − + − + − + −	− + − + − + − + − + − + − + − + − + − +	+ − + − + − + − + − + − + − + − + − + −

In an active-matrix panel, the gate and source electrodes are used on a shared basis, but each unit pixel is individually addressable by selecting the appropriate two contact pads at the ends of the rows and columns.

Active Addressing of a 3x3 Matrix

By scanning the gate bus-lines sequentially, and by applying signal voltages to all source bus-lines in a specified sequence, we can address all pixels.

One result of all this is that the addressing of an AMLCD is done line by line.

Virtually all AMLCDs are designed to produce gray levels - intermediate brightness levels between the brightest white and the darkest black a unit pixel can generate.

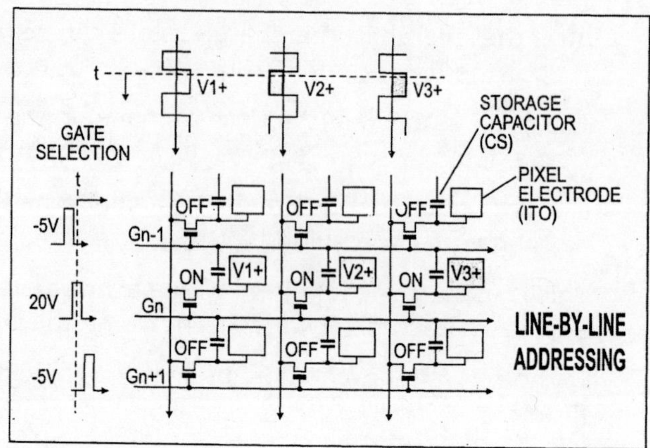

There can be either a discrete numbers of levels - such as 8, 16, 64, or 256 - or a continuous gradation of levels, depending on the LDI.

The optical transmittance of a TN-mode LC changes continuously as a function of the applied voltage.

An analog LDI is capable of producing a continuous voltage signal so that a continuous range of gray levels can be displayed.

The digital LDI produces discrete voltage amplitudes, which permits on a discrete numbers of shades to be displayed.

The number of gray levels is determined by the number of data bits produced by the digital driver.

Generating Colors

The color filter of a TFT LCD TV consists of three primary colors - red (R), green (G), and blue (B) - which are included on the color-filter substrate.

The elements of this color filter line up one-to-one with the unit pixels on the TFT-array substrate.

Each pixel in a color LCD is subdivided into three subpixels, where one set of RGB subpixels is equal to one pixel.

Because the subpixels are too small to distinguish independently, the RGB elements appear to the human eye as a mixture of the three colors.

Any color, can be produced by mixing these three primary colors.

CCFL - Cold Cathode Fluorescent Lamp

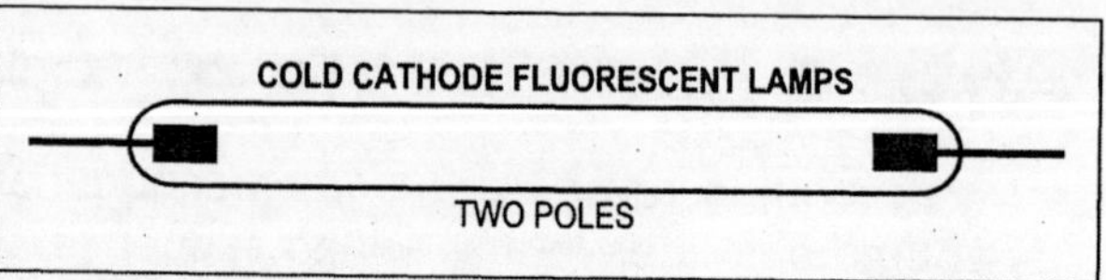

The CCFL or Cold Cathode Fluorescent Lamp is a light source used in TFT LCD monitors as backlight source. CCFL light up the display from behind/side.

The CCFL in basically a gas-discharge light source, which produces its output from a stimulated phosphor coating inside the glass lamp envelope.

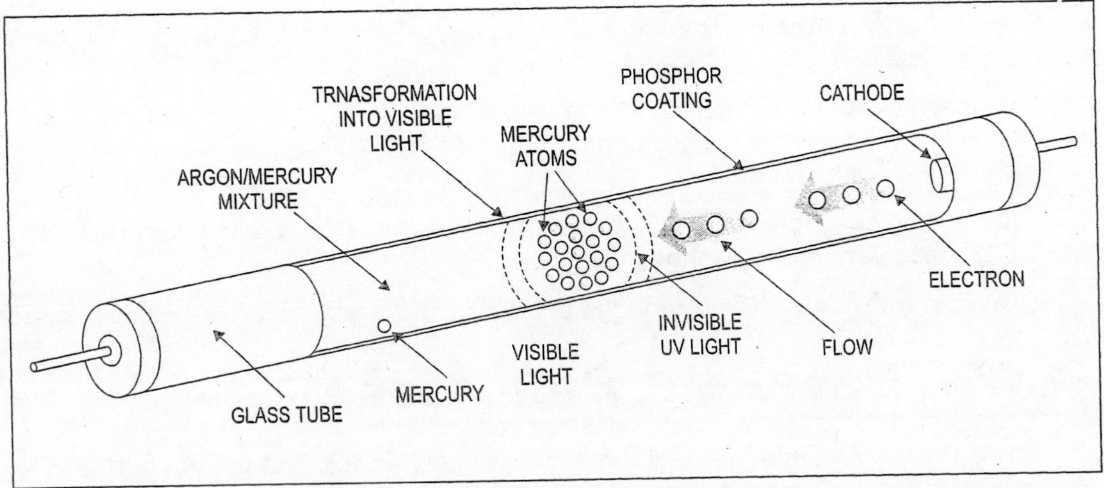

CCFLs are called "Cold" Cathode Fluorescent Lamps because they are not heated like the standard neon lamps.

The heating of electrodes of common neon tubes leads to a highly reduced startup and working voltage.

On the contrary CCFLs need high startup and working voltages and therefore special inverters are used to provide supply to them.

Additionally CCFLs need external excitation by free electrons in the air, thus it may happen that your CCFL based notebook-display may refuses to work in a deep cave.

Inside a CCFL a very small portion of Mercury (Hg) and a mixture of different gas are used.

The basic lighting process results from a constant excitation of the gaseous molecules by acceleration and crashing against each other in the electric field of high voltage.

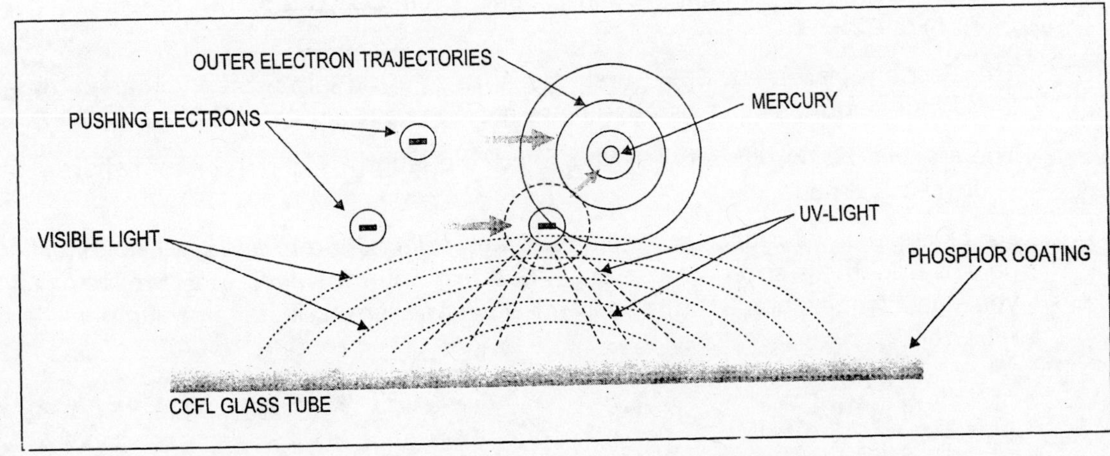

Around 60% of the emitted light is invisible UV-light, 2% visible light and the rest simply heat.

Inside the CCFL is covered with a white varnish like phosphor substance. This substance is the most important part of a CCFL as it transforms the invisible UV-light into visible white light.

Depending on different compounds used in this substance, the color produced by the CCFL may vary in a big range.

One can also make colored lighting CCFL by use of certain mixtures in this substance.

CCFL Backlight Reflector

This CCFL is mounted inside a reflector assembly on top and bottom of the TFT LCD display panel. Some smaller size display panel may have the lamp on both sides mounted vertically.

Backlight reflector is special polyester film with outstanding optical, mechanical and thermal properties sputter-coated with silver.

The CCFL Lamp is mounted inside this reflector. Each reflector can install 1-3 CCFL Lamps.

Usually two reflector are used on TFT panel, mounted on the top and bottom of TFT display panel.

Selecting Replacement CCFL

When selecting a replacement CCFL to replace a defective lamp, the length and diameter of the lamp is an important criteria.

Unfortunately, there is no standard length of LCD Backlight (CCFL lamp) on each size of LCD Panels. For Example, 15 inch panel could use the length of CCFL between 297mm to 325mm.

To select a replacement CCFL, first, measure your old lamp, then you need to get a lamp with length as close as possible to the original CCFL lamp's length.

There would be no difference if you select the length is about 2-8mm shorter then your measurement.

For Example, if your measurement is 310mm, select 306mm and it will not affect LCD panel's Brightness and Contrast at all. Besides, 306mm will fit in the reflector and if you select longer then 310mm, you will have problem to install new lamp inside the reflector.

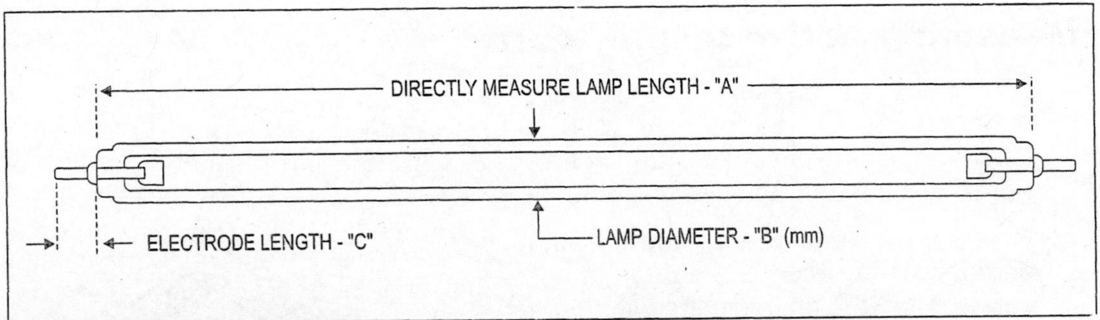

Measuring the Length of LCD Backlight

Direct Measurement

This is the best way to measure the length of CCFL lamp.

To measure the length :

- Carefully remove CCFL from Backlight reflector,
- Slowly pull out rubber cap at both ends of the lamp.
- Measure the length of CCFL lamp.

Once the length of the original lamp is measured, select a CCFL whose length is slightly shorter then your measurement.

For Example: Your old lamp measurement is 320mm, You should use the length of 316mm

Indirect Measurement

LCD Backlight (CCFL Lamps) are hold on inside of reflector. There are Silicone rubber cap on both ends of CCFL Lamps.

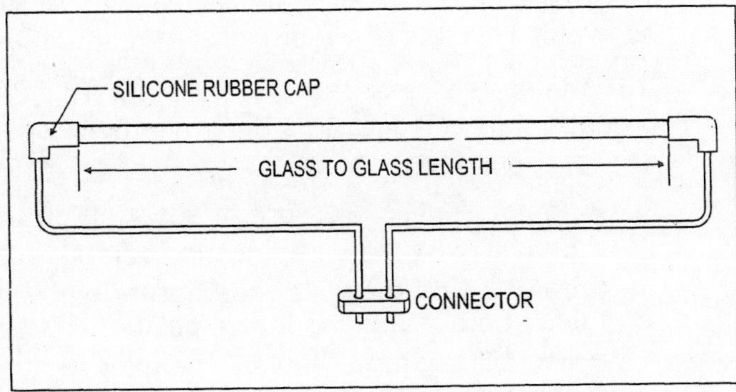

The measurement should be from glass to glass (as shown in the given figure). On this measurement add the length of one of the Silicone rubber caps.

For example, if the measurement from glass to glass is 310mm, and rubber cap measurement is 5mm (measure only one), add these two values, 310+5 = 315mm.

Add 5mm to this total, i.e. 315+5 = 320mm. Select the lamp with slightly shorter length than this 320mm.

Measuring Active Display Area

One can also measure the active display area, i.e. the display width (View Area) from left to right Horizontally) to find the lamp length.

Measure the display area width and add/deduct between 1-3mm on this value to find the approximate width of the CCFL lamp.

For example, if your measurement is 308mm for 15 inch laptop screen, you should used 305mm lamp.

As a rule always select a slightly shorter lamp, as that would easily fit into the CCFL assembly.

Handling of CCFL

CCFL is an extremely small Fluorescent lamp made of lead glass, which is easily broken, you must handle them with extra caution.

Replacing CCFL lamp requires only good soldering technique. However, replacing CCFL on laptop screen is a lot difficult because the way CCFL is mounted.

Laptop screen usually does not have metal reflector separately like LCD monitor.

Shock of any kind should not be applied to the lamps tube, otherwise, this may result in damage and electrode deformation. Unnecessary heating of the lamps tube should be avoided for it is easily broken.

If the lamp is stressed at their sealing ends, though invisible from outside, it may produce slow leakage. This destroys the vacuum state inside and makes the lamp useless. Therefore

- do not impose pressure of any kind on wire ends directly.
- do not twist the wire ends in radial direction.
- do not wind the wire ends at the joint ends. If necessary, please fix the wire before winding it at a position 10 mm or more from the ends.
- The CCFL-lamps shouldn't be exposed to temperatures at or below 0 °C, constantly. Low temperature shortens the average lifetime and decreases brightness.
- If low temperature situations can't be avoided make sure to heat the area of the CCFL-lamp before starting to at least 15°C.
- The CCFL-inverters startup voltage should be 2.5-3.0 times higher than working voltage.

- Due to the high voltage the lamp is started-up with, keep the lamp during startup away from combustibles and explosive material.
- Other light sources are needed to assist starting the lamp in dark places (e.g. caves) due to a need of free electrons to activate the lamp.
- Do not watch into the bare shining lamp directly for a long time as the lamps high brightness is harmful for your eyes once it shines.

Description of Different Blocks of TFT LCD Monitor

Power Supply-Block Diagram Description

230V AC mains supply entering the TFT LCD monitor first reaches the AC filtration and protection section of power supply.

a. AC Filtration and Protection Section

F101 fuse in this section protects the circuit from flow of excess current. NTC/TH101 is used to limit any sudden increase in the AC mains supply.

Filter circuit made using line filter LF101 and CX101, CY101, and CY102 filters out any irregularities in the AC mains supply.

Filter section also stops the switching noise generated by the power supply from entering into the AC mains supply. Filtered supply from this section is next sent to the input rectifier and filter section.

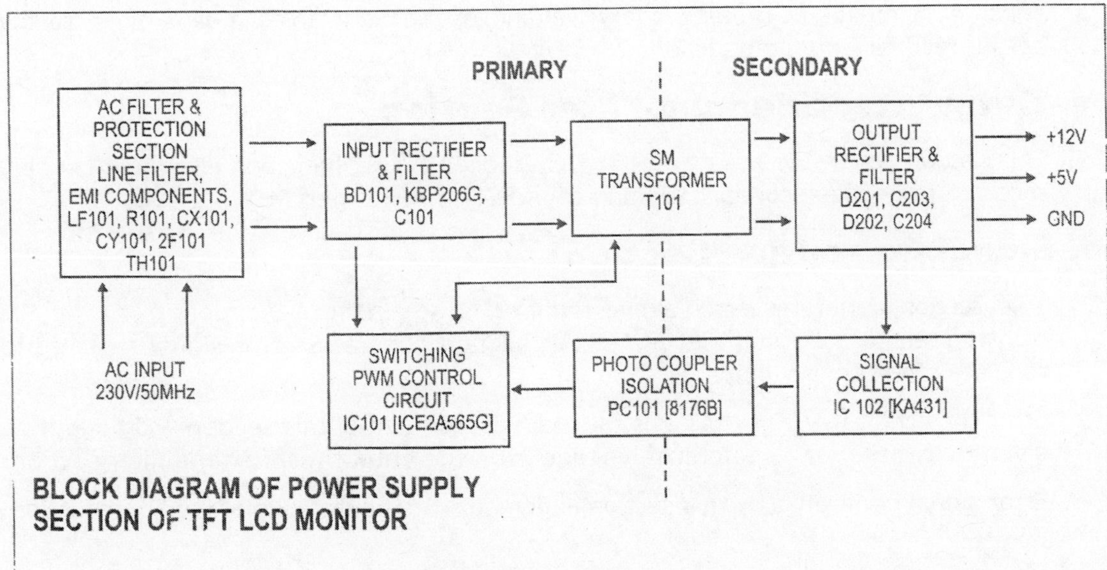

BLOCK DIAGRAM OF POWER SUPPLY SECTION OF TFT LCD MONITOR

b. Input Rectifier and Filter Section

This section converts the AC supply received from AC filtration and protection section into DC supply. This DC supply is filtered by the main filter capacitor C101.

This rectified and filtered DC supply is given to the PWM controller and switching section through primary winding of the SM transformer T101.

This DC supply is given to pin-4 and 5 of IC 101 in the PWM controller and switching section.

c. PWM Controller and Switching Section

Main component of this section is a PWM controller and switching IC 101 (ICE2A565G). This IC contains an oscillator, PWM controller and switching circuit.

Using the switching process, with the help of oscillating signal, this section converts the DC supply received through the primary winding of the SM transformer into AC supply. AC supply generated by this process is then given to the primary winding of the SM transformer.

d. SM Transformer Section

To be able to operate at high frequency, this section uses a ferrite core transformer.

AC supply generated by the PWM controller and switching section is given to the primary winding of this SM transformer.

Flow of AC current in the primary winding of SM transformer generates various AC supplies at its secondary windings.

These AC supplies at the secondary winding of the SM transformer is given to the output rectifier and filter section.

e. Output Rectifier and Filter Section

This section generates +12V and +5V DC supplies by rectifying and filtering AC supply received from the secondary winding of the SM transformer/T101.

f. Signal Correction Section

This section generates error signal required to keep the DC supply from the SM transformer, to a constant level, i.e. this section generates error-signal required to regulate the output supply.

Error correction IC 102 (KA431) is the main component of this section. +5V supply is given to this section as reference voltage from the output rectifier and filter section.

Error signal generated by this section is given to the photo coupler isolation section.

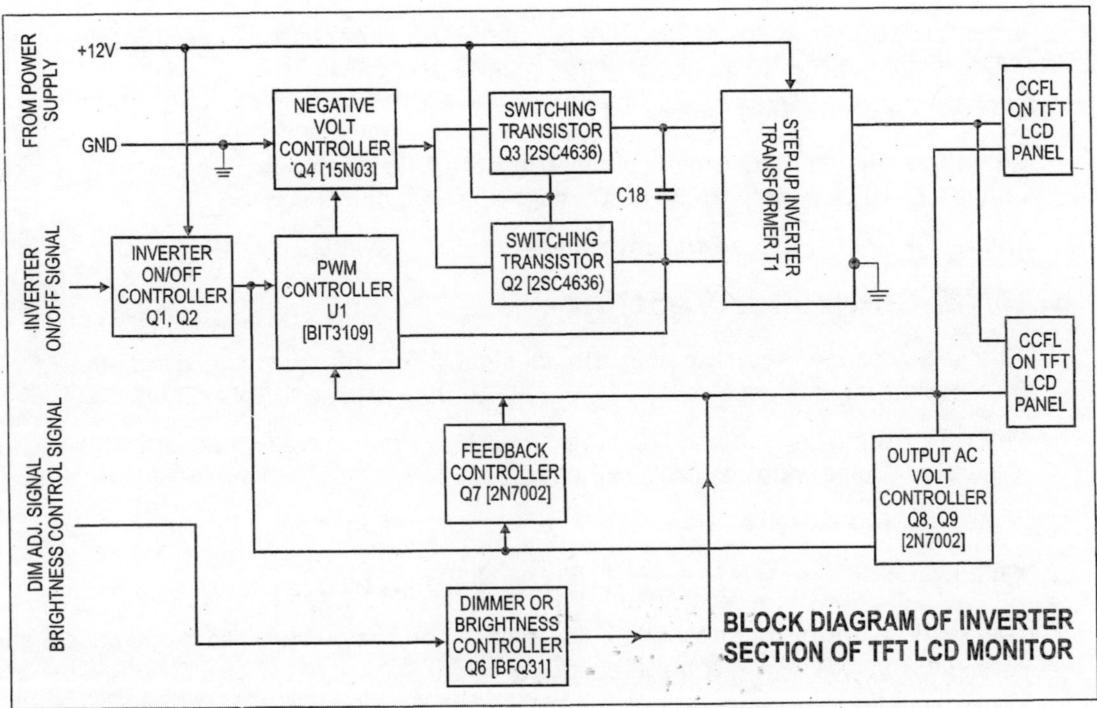

BLOCK DIAGRAM OF INVERTER SECTION OF TFT LCD MONITOR

g. Photo Coupler and Isolation Section

This section sends error-signal from the "signal correction section" in electrically insulated form to the "PWM controller and switching section" at the error winding of the SM transformer.

Based on the error-signal received, the "PWM controller and switching section" controls its switching process and regulates the output supply.

Inverter-Block Diagram Description

Inverter section is used in the TFT monitor to generate high voltage AC supply for proper operation of the CCFL. CCFL or the Cold Cathode Fluorescent Lamp is used as back-light for the TFT display.

12V DC supply from the power supply section is given to the inverter section. This 12V supply is given to the step-up transformer T1 and "inverter on/off controller section" in the inverter section.

a. Inverter on/off Controller Section

Based on the control signal from the "monitor controller section", this section turn on/off the inverter section. Two transistors Q1 and Q5 are used in this section to switch on/off the inverter.

When this section receives high signal from the "monitor controller section", it outputs +12V supply to the IC U1 at the "PWM control section".

This will switch on the Inverter.

When this section receives low signal from the "monitor controller section", it stops outputs of +12V supply to the IC U1 at the "PWM control section".

This in turn will switch off the Inverter.

b. PWM Controller Section

This section generates switching control signals for the switching transistors. PWM (pulse width modulation) control IC U1/BIT 3109G is used in this circuit.

When 12V supply is received from the "inverter on/off controller section", this section generates "pulse width control" signal.

This "pulse width control" signal is sent to the "DC negative voltage control section".

c. DC Negative Voltage Control Section

This section controls the negative voltage based on the pulse width modulation signal received from the "PWM control" section.

This controlled -Ve voltage is given to switching transistors Q2 and Q3 in the switching section. Transistor Q4 is used in this section for negative supply to Q2 and Q3.

d. Switching Section

This section consists of step-up inverter transformer T1, capacitor C18, switching transistors Q2 and Q3 and 12 volt positive and negative supplies. Based on the switching signal from the PWM control section, this section converts 12V DC into AC supply.

e. Inverter Transformer

This AC supply generated by the switching section, flows through the primary winding of the step-up inverter transformer T1.

Flow of high frequency AC supply through the primary winding of the step-up transformer T1 will induce high frequency, high value AC supply at the secondary of the transformer T1.

f. CCFL

This high frequency, high value AC supply at the secondary winding of the transformer T1 is given to the CCFL lamp. This will turn on the CCFL lamp and the TFT LCD monitor will start to glow.

g. Output AC Voltage Controller Section

To regulate the AC supply received at the secondary winding of the step-up transformer T1, this section is used. MOSFET Q7, Q8 and Q9 are main components of this section.

AC voltage returning from the CCFL is converted into DC voltage and fed to this "output AC voltage controller section". Based on the value of the returning AC voltage, this section generates a control voltage.

This control voltage is used to regulate the AC supply received at the secondary winding of the step-up transformer T1. For this purpose, this generated control voltage is given to the feedback controller section.

h. Feedback Controller Section

Based on the control voltage received from the "output AC voltage controller section" this section generates an error signal.

This error signal is then given to Q7 in the PWM controller section.

i. PWM Controller Section

Based on the error signal received from the "feedback controller section" this section makes required changes in its switching process so that the output AC supply at the step-up transformer gets regulated.

j. Brightness Controller Section

This section increase/reduce the brightness of the TFT LCD monitor based on the dimmer control signal received from the monitor control section.

Dimmer control signal from the monitor control section is given to this brightness control section.

Based on this control signal, the brightness control section sends a control voltage to the PWM controller section.

Based on this control signal the PWM control section makes changes in its switching process.

This change in the switching process will increase/reduce the current from the output of the step-up transformer, which in turn will increase/reduce the brightness of the CCFL lamp and the TFT LCD monitor.

TFT LCD Monitor Block Diagram- Description

Primary job of the main PCB on the TFT LCD monitor is to process the video signal coming from the computer system and send it to the TFT module in a proper manner so that the information can be viewed on the display screen.

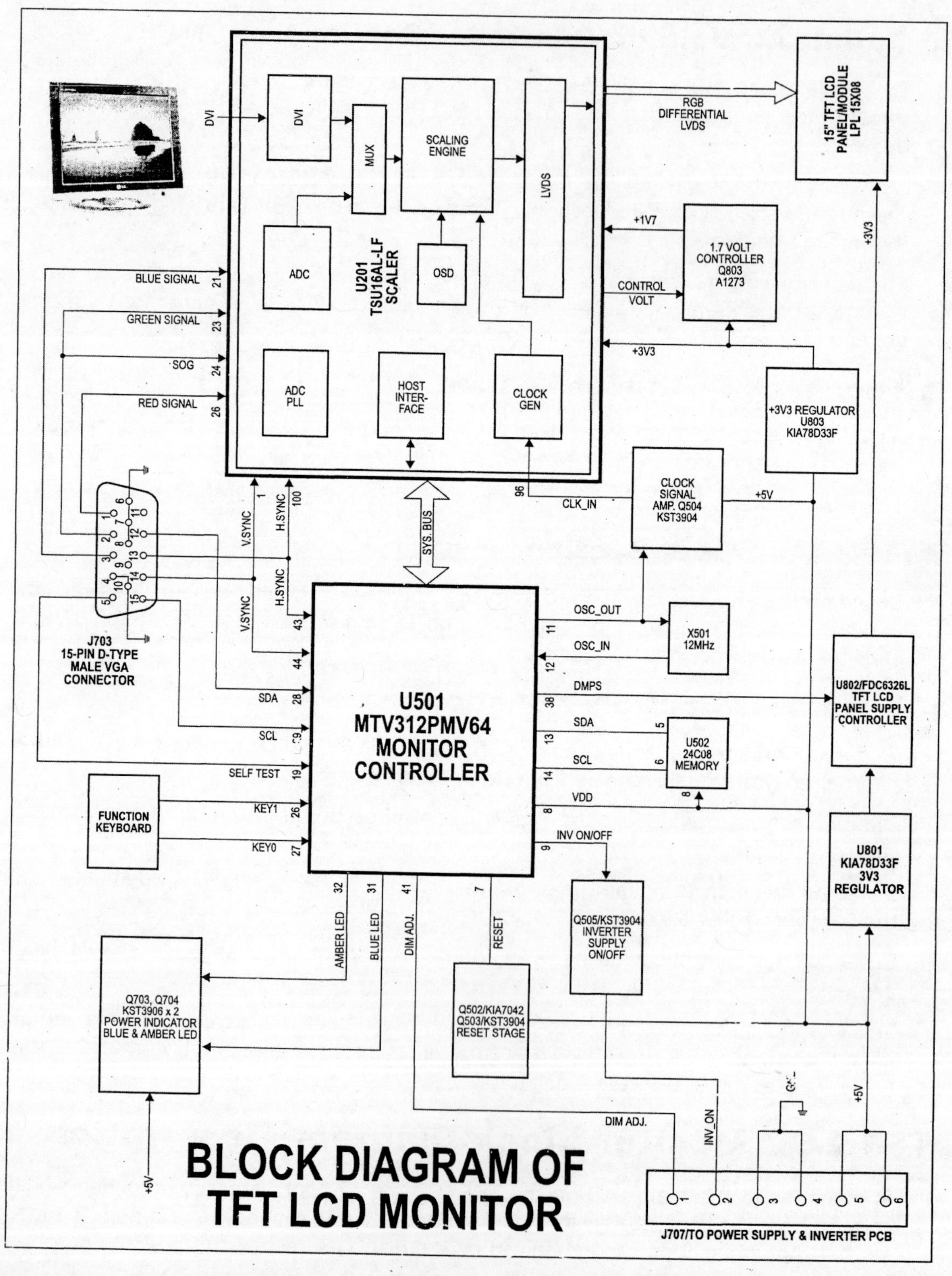

BLOCK DIAGRAM OF TFT LCD MONITOR

+5V supply from the power supply section reach main PCB of the TFT monitor through pin-5 and 6 of connector J707.

This +5V supply reaching the main PCB is given to the monitor control section, memory section, 3V3 regulator section, reset generator section, clock signal amplifier section, and power indicator section.

3V3 Regulator Section regulates the 5V supply to 3.3 volts using the regulator IC U803. This 3V3 supply is given to IC U201 and 1V7 control transistor Q803 in the scalar section.

Based on the control signal received from the scalar IC U201, transistor Q803 regulates 3.3 volts supply to generate 1.7V. This 1.7 volts supply is given to various pins of scalar IC U201.

IC U801 in the "3.3V Regulator Section" regulates +5V supply received from the power supply section and generates 3.3V regulated supply.

This regulated supply is given to the IC 802 in the TFT LCD panel supply controller section. Based on the Display Power Management Signal (DPMS) from pin-38 of monitor controller IC U501, IC 802 delivers 3.3V regulated supply.

This supply is given to the TFT LCD module. In this manner all the section of the TFT LCD monitor receive the required supplies.

IC 802 in the TFT LCD monitor circuit is used to control the supply going to the TFT LCD module. Transistor Q505 controls the inverter section by supplying on/off signal.

Horizontal sync signal from the pin-13 of VGA connector J703, reach pin-43 of monitor control IC U501 and pin-100 of scalar IC U201.

Based on the horizontal sync signal reaching its pin-43, IC 501 controls the standby mode. Also, horizontal sync signal at pin-100 of IC 201 is used to keep the screen image horizontally stable.

Vertical sync signal from pin-14 of VGA connector J703, reach pin-44 of monitor control IC U501 and pin-1 of scalar IC U201.

Based on the vertical sync signal reaching its pin-44, IC 501 controls the standby mode. Also, vertical sync signal at pin-1 of IC 201 is used to keep the screen image vertically stable.

Monitor control circuit will function only when pin-43 and 44 of monitor control IC U501 receive horizontal and vertical sync signals, otherwise the circuit will go into standby mode and the supply to the inverter section and TFT LCD panel will be switched off.

Control signals generated by the monitor control section reach the horizontal and vertical scalar section of IC U201, through the system bus.

These control signals are used to shift the picture in horizontal and vertical direction and to control the picture brightness, contrast and gamma values.

To store the values of various functions set by the monitor controller section, pin-13 and 14 of the monitor controller IC U501 is connected to pin-5 and 6 of 8-pin memory IC U502.

Inverter on/off switching signal from pin-9 of monitor controller IC U501 is processed by transistor Q505 and given to inverter section through pin-2 of connector J707. This control signal is used to switch on/off the inverter section.

Dimmer (brightness) control signal is received from pin-41 of monitor controller IC U501. This signal is given to inverter section through pin-1 of connector J707.

This signal is used to control the brightness of the CCFL lamp, which in turn controls the TFT display brightness.

12MHz crystal oscillator is connected between pin-11 & 12 of monitor controller IC U501. This 12MHz clock signal is amplified by clock signal amplifier transistor Q504 and given to pin-96 of scalar IC U201 as CLK_IN signal.

This clock signal at pin-96 of U201 is given to scaling engine section inside U201, through the clock generator section of scalar IC U201.

A low-level self-test signal reach pin-19 of monitor controller IC U501, from pin-5 of VGA connector J703. If this signal is missing then the monitor will display "Check Signal Cable" message.

Serial data SDA and serial clock SCL signal reach pin-28 and 29 of monitor controller IC U501, from pin-12 and 15 of VGA connector J703, respectively.

Pin-26 and 27 of monitor controller IC U501 receive menu, light-view, brightness, auto-select etc. control signals from the operating function keyboard to control the monitor OSD function.

When the power supply is switched on, reset circuit consisting of Q502 and Q503 provide reset signal to pin-7 of IC U501.

This will reset the monitor controller IC U501, and make it ready for further operation.

When the monitor is on, a Blue LED on signal is output from pin-31 of IC U501. This signal is given to Blue LED controller Q704, which turn on the Blue LED on the monitor front panel.

When the monitor is in standby mode, i.e. in the power saving mode, pin-32 of IC U501 outputs Amber LED-on signal. This signal is given to Amber LED controller Q703, which turn on the Amber LED on the monitor front panel.

Red, Green and Blue color analog video signals coming from the computer at pin-1, 2, and 3 of the VGA connector is given to pin-26, 23 and 21 of scalar IC U201, respectively.

These analog signal reach the analog to digital converter section inside the IC U201. This section converts these signals into 8-bit digital video data. This 8-bit digital data is given to the scaling engine section through multiplexer section.

The scaling engine scales the digital video data according to the TFT LCD panel. After scaling, this digital data, which is in parallel format is given to parallel to LVDS (Low Voltage Differential Signal) section.

Parallel to LVDS (Low Voltage Differential Signal) section converts this parallel video data signal into LVDS signal. This LVDS signal reach the TFT module through connector J704.

OSD signal reach the OSD section inside the scalar IC U201, from the system controller IC U501 through system bus. OSD signal is processed by the OSD section and given to the scaling engine section. Scaling section scales the OSD signal according to the TFT display panel.

This OSD signal is displayed with the main image on the display panel. SOG (Sync On Green) signal is extracted from the Green analog video signal received from the VGA connector and given to the pin-24 of scalar IC U201.

TFT LCD Monitor Functional Block Diagram-Description

Connector J704 of the monitor's main PCB is connected through a cable to the TFT LCD panel. This connector is used to send various control signals (H Sync, V Sync, Clock, Data, Enable, etc.), and supply to the TFT LCD panel.

As the RGB data and control signals reaching the TFT LCD panel are in LVDS format, this data is first given to the LVDS receiver section.

LVDS section process this incoming data and convert it into parallel data format. This parallel data is given to the timing controller section for further processing.

Based on the parallel RGB data and control signals received from the LVDS receiver section, the timing controller section sets timing of the TFT LCD data.

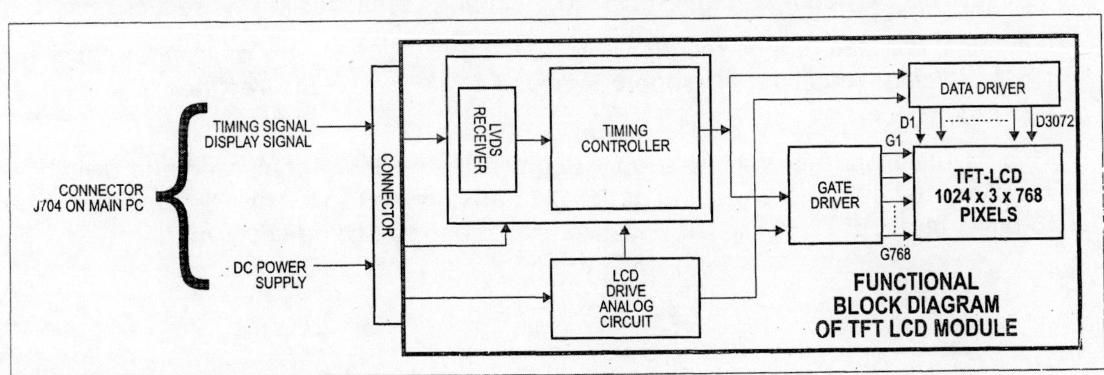

FUNCTIONAL BLOCK DIAGRAM OF TFT LCD MODULE

Value of the timing depends on the pixel resolution of the TFT LCD panel.

Once the timing is set by the timing controller section, the signal is sent to gate driver section and data driver section on the TFT LCD panel.

Gate driver IC provides horizontal supply signal to the gate data line. One gate driver IC controls 128 horizontal lines of the TFT LCD display panel.

Data driver IC provides vertical supply signal. One data driver IC controls 154 vertical lines of the TFT LCD display panel. Based on the display signals received from the timing controller section, the gate driver and data driver ICs control pixels on the TFT LCD panel.

This results in displaying of the required image on the display panel. The image being displayed on the display panel is illuminated by the CCFL lamp behind the display panel.

TFT LCD Monitor Power Supply-Description

230V AC mains supply entering the monitor first reaches the AC filtration and protection section of power supply.

a. AC Filtration & Protection Section

F101 fuse in this section protects the circuit from flow of excess current. NTC/TH101 is used to limit the sudden increase in the AC mains supply.

Filter circuit using line filter LF101 and CX101, CY101, CY102 filters out any irregularities in the AC mains supply.

Filter section also stops the switching noise generated by the power supply from entering into the AC mains supply. Filtered supply from this section is next sent to the input rectifier and filter section.

b. Input Rectifier & Filter Section

This section converts AC received from AC filtration & protection section into DC supply. This DC supply is filtered by the main filter capacitor in this section.

For this a compact bridge rectifier unit BD101 (KBP 206G) and main filter capacitor C101 is used. Negative DC supply received from the bridge rectifier is known as floating ground.

This rectified and filtered DC supply is given to the PWM controller and switching section through primary winding of the SM transformer T101. This DC supply is given to pin-4 and 5 of IC 101 in the PWM controller and switching section.

c. PWM Controller and Switching Section

Main component of this section is a PWM controller and switching IC 101 (ICE2A565G). This IC contains an oscillator, PWM controller and switching circuit.

Pin Description of IC 101 (IEC 2A565G)

Pin-1 : Soft start controller section pin. Connected to ground through C104.

Pin-2 : Feedback pin, connected to PWM controller inside the IC. Receives feedback from pin-4 of photo coupler IC PC 101. Connected to ground through ZD102, C106.

Pin-3 : Current sense pin, source pin of MOSFET inside the switching section of IC. Receives negative supply through R105.

Pin-4 & 5 : Drain pins of MOSFET inside the switching section of IC.This pin is connected to positive supply through primary winding of T101.

Pin-6 : N/C

Pin-7 : Positive supply pin. Receives starting positive supply from positive end of mains filter capacitor C101, through R102.

To filter and store this supply, C103 is connected to ground, to bring down the positive supply at this pin, negative supply is given through R106. ZD101 is used for the safety. This pin receives feedback supply from feedback winding of SM transformer, through R104, and D102.

Pin-8 : This is negative supply pin. It is connected to the floating negative in the circuit. Using the switching process, with the help of oscillating signal, this section converts the DC supply received through the primary winding of the SM transformer into AC supply.

AC supply generated by this process is then given to the primary winding of the SM transformer. Positive supply at pin-7 and negative supply at pin-8 of PWM controller IC 101 will generate 100KHz switching frequency inside the IC's oscillator section.

This switching frequency is given to the switching MOSFET gate inside the IC 101. Drain of the switching MOSFET receives high voltage DC supply through pin-4 and 5. Source of the switching MOSFET receives negative supply at pin-3 through R105.

Switching signals at the gate of the MOSFET inside the PWM controller IC 101 will start high speed switching process. This switching process will start flow of AC current through drain pin, pin-4 and 5, primary winding of SM transformer, source pin and pin-3 of IC.

To balance the flow of AC current through primary winding of the SM transformer, a circuit made of diode D101, capacitor C102, and resistance R103 is made parallel to the primary winding.

d. SM Transformer Section

To be able to operate at high frequency, this section uses a ferrite core transformer. AC supply generated by the PWM controller and switching section is given to the primary winding of this SM transformer.

Flow of AC current in the primary winding of SM transformer generates various AC supplies at its secondary windings. These AC supplies at the secondary winding of the SM transformer is given to the output rectifier and filter section.

e. Feed Back Section

This SM transformer also contain a feedback winding, AC voltage at this feedback winding is rectified by diode D102 and filtered by C103. This resulting DC supply is given to pin-7 of IC 101 as regulator supply to regulate the oscillator output.

f. Output Rectifier & Filter Section

This section generates +12V and +5V DC supplies by rectifying and filtering AC supply received from the secondary winding of the SM transformer/T101.

AC supply from the 12V secondary winding of the SM transformer is rectified by D201 and converted into DC supply. This DC supply is filtered by C203. This filtered 12V DC supply is given to the inverter section of the TFT LCD monitor.

AC supply from the 5V secondary winding of the SM transformer is rectified by D202 and converted into DC supply.

C202 and R202 parallel to the D202 protects the diode from any sudden high voltage supply.

Rectified 5V DC supply is filtered by C204 and given to the monitor control section on the main PCB.

g. Signal Correction Section

This section generates error signal required to keep the AC supply received from the SM transformer, to a constant level, i.e. this section generates error-signal required to regulate the output supply.

Error correction IC 102 (KA431) is the main component of this section. +5V supply is given to this section as reference voltage from the output rectifier and filter section.

Error signal generated by this section is given to the photo coupler isolation section.

5V supply parallel to the C204 is given to pin-1 of photo coupler IC PC101, through R204. This 5V supply is also given to pin-2 of IC PC101, through R206 and cathode pin of error correction IC 102.

Anode of IC 102 is connected to the ground. Reference pin of IC 102 is given positive supply from voltage divider circuit made of R207 and R208.

If due to any reason, the value of the output from the SM transformer change, then the value of the reference voltage reaching the reference pin of the error correction IC 102 also change.

Change in the reference voltage reaching the reference pin of error correction IC 102 will output error signal from cathode pin of this IC.

This error signal corresponds to the change in the output of the SM transformer. This error signal is given to pin-2 of the photo-coupler IC PC101.

h. Photo Coupler & Isolation Section

This section sends the error-signal from the "signal correction section" in electrically insulated form to the "PWM controller and switching section" at the primary winding of the SM transformer.

Error signal reaching pin-2 of photo-coupler IC PC101 is output in electrically insulated form from pin-4 of this IC. This output from pin-4 reach pin-2 of the PWM controller IC U101.

This error signal reaching pin-2 of the PWM controller make changes in the output from the PWM controller IC.

These changes in the switching pulses from the PWM controller IC make the required correction in the switching operation so that the output supply once again gets regulated to a constant value.

DVI Connector/Cable

DVI stands for (D)igital (V)ideo (I)nterface. After VGA, DVI is appearing as a popular form of video interface technology.

This interface is specially made to maximize the quality of flat panel LCD monitors and modern video graphics cards.

Most of the popular DVI video cards include both a VGA and a DVI output port.

In addition to being used as the new computer interface, DVI is also coming out as the digital transfer method of choice for HDTV, EDTV, Plasma Display, and other ultra-high-end video displays for TV, movies, and DVDs.

DVI Formats

There are three types of DVI connections: DVI-D (Digital), DVI-A (Analog), and DVI-I (Integrated-Digital & Analog)

Following is a brief introduction to these formats.

DVI-A (Analog only)	DVI-I (Digital and Analog)	DVI-D (Digital only)
DVI-A Male	DVI-I Male Single-Link	DVI-D Male Single-Link
DVI-A Female	DVI-I Female Single-Link	DVI-D Female Single-Link
	DVI-I Male Dual-Link	DVI-D Male Dual-Link
	DVI-I Female Dual-Link	DVI-D Female Dual-Link

DVI-D (Digital)

DVI-D cables are used for direct digital connections between computer and digital LCD/CRT monitors.

Digital interface provides a faster, higher-quality image than with analog.

All video cards initially produce a digital video signal, which is converted into analog at the VGA output.

If an LCD monitor is used, then this analog display is reconverted back into a digital signal by the monitor circuit.

DVI-D eliminates this conversion process and improves the connection between source and display.

DVI-A (Analog)

DVI-A cables are used to carry a DVI signal to an analog display, such as a VGA CRT monitor.

When DVI-A is used, some signal quality is lost due to digital to analog conversion. But still it transmits a higher quality picture than standard VGA.

DVI-I (Integrated-Digital & Analog)

DVI-I cables are integrated cables with option to transmit either digital-to-digital signal or an analog-to-analog signal. This makes it usable in either digital or analog situations.

DVI digital and analog formats are non-interchangeable. A DVI-D cable will not work on an analog system, nor a DVI-A on a digital system.

Only equipment with a DVI port labeled 'DVI-I' will accept both a DVI-D and DVI-A source signal.

Single and Dual Link DVI

The Digital formats are available in DVI-D Single-Link and Dual-Link as well as DVI-I Single-Link and Dual-Link format connectors.

These DVI cables send information using a digital format known as TMDS (Transition Minimized Differential Signaling).

Single link cables use one TMDS 165MHz transmitter, while dual links use two.

The dual link DVI pins effectively double the power of transmission and provide an increase of speed and signal quality.

A DVI single link 60-Hz LCD can display a resolution of 1920 x 1080, while a DVI dual link can display a resolution of 2048 x 1536.

DVI Cable Length

The official DVI specification says that DVI cable can be maximum 5 meters or 16 feet in length. Cable with longer length generally results in signal loss and an unusable image on the display.

When using DVI-I cables at extensive lengths, you may not be seeing a digitally-clear image on your screen.

To make sure you're getting the best digital image, use DVI-D cables and make sure that your display is set to digital input.

Using Right DVI Cable

Determining the type of DVI cable to use for your products is very important for getting best output from your display device.

Check both of the female DVI plugs (on computer and on monitor) to determine what signals they are compatible with.

- If one or both connections are DVI-D, you need a DVI-D cable.
- If one or both connections are DVI-A, you need a DVI-A cable.
- If one connection is DVI and the other is VGA, and the DVI is analog-compatible, you need a DVI to VGA cable or a DVI/VGA adapter.
- If both connections are DVI-I, you may use any DVI cable, but a DVI-I cable is recommended.
- If one connection is analog and the other connection is digital, there is no way to connect them.

Pin assignment of 24-Pin DVI-D (TMDS) Signal Cable Connector

Pin	Function	Pin	Function
1	TMDS Data2-	13	No Connection
2	TMDS Data2+	14	+5V Power
3	TMDS Data2 Shield	15	Ground (for +5V)
4	No Connection	16	Hot Plug Detect
5	No Connection	17	TMDS Data0-
6	DDC Clock	18	TMDS Data0+
7	DDC Data	19	TMDS Data0 Shield
8	No Connection	20	No Connection
9	TMDS Data1-	21	No Connection
10	TMDS Data1+	22	TMDS Clock Shield
11	TMDS Data1 Shield	23	TMDS Clock+
12	No Connection	24	TMDS Clock-

Recognizing DVI Cable

There are two parts in every DVI connector, and each represents one attribute.

The flat pin on one side denotes whether the cable is digital or analog:

- A flat pin with four surrounding pins is either DVI-I or DVI-A
- A flat pin alone denotes DVI-D

The pinsets vary depending on whether the cable is single-link, dual-link, or analog:

- Two separated 9-pin sets (rows of 6) for a single-link cable
- A solid 24-pin set (rows of 8) for a dual-link cable

A separated 8-pin and 4-pin set is for DVI-A.

External Connectors Pin Assignment

PS/2 Keyboard Connector

Connector	Pin	Signal
	1	Data
	2	Unused
	3	Ground
	4	+5 VDC
	5	Clock
	6	Unused

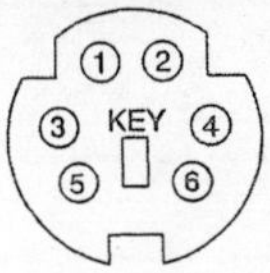

PS/2 Mouse Connector

Connector	Pin	Signal
	1	Data
	2	Unused
	3	Ground
	4	+5 VDC
	5	Clock
	6	Unused

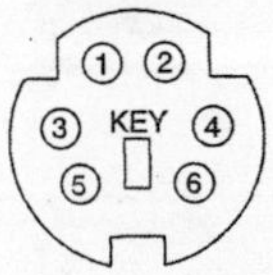

MIDI/Game Port

Pin	Signal	Pin	Signal
1	+5 V	9	+5 V
2	Joystick Button	10	Joystick Button
3	Joystick Direction	11	Joystick Direction
4	Ground	12	MIDI Out
5	Ground	13	Joystick Direction
6	Joystick Direction	14	Joystick Button
7	Joystick Button	15	MIDI In
8	+5 V		

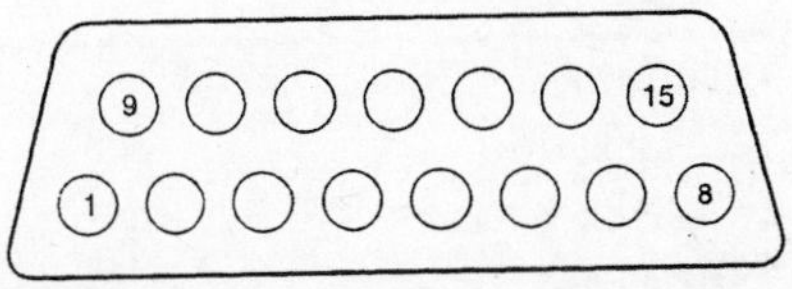

Ethernet RJ-45

Connector	Pin	Signal
	1	(+) Transmit Data
	2	(-) Transmit Data
	3	(+) Receive Data
	4	Unused
	5	Unused
	6	(-) Receive Data
	7	Unused
	8	Unused

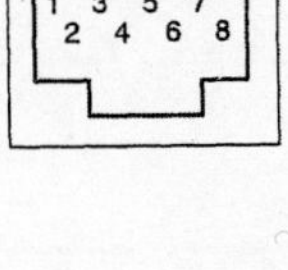

Monitor (VGA)

Pin	Signal	Pin	Signal
1	Red Analog	9	Blank
2	Green Analog	10	Ground
3	Blue Analog	11	Blank
4	Blank	12	Monitor ID (DD)
5	Ground	13	Horizontal Sync
6	Ground	14	Vertical Sync
7	Ground	15	Monitor ID (CC)
8	Ground		

Serial Port

Pin	Signal	Pin	Signal
1	Carrier Detect	6	Data Set Ready
2	Receive Data	7	Ready to Send
3	Transmit Data	8	Clear to Send
4	Data Terminal Ready	9	Ring Indicator
5	Ground		

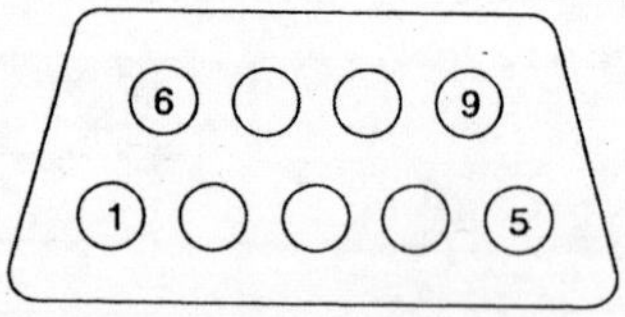

Parallel Port

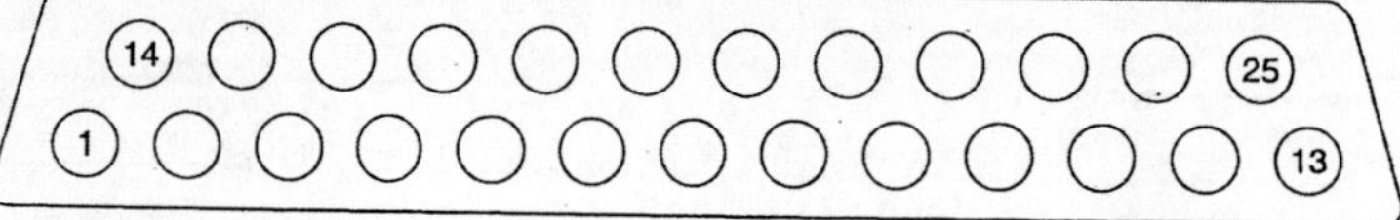

Pin	Signal	Pin	Signal
1	Strobe	14	Auto Linefeed
2	Data Bit 0	15	Error
3	Data Bit 1	16	Initialize Printer
4	Data Bit 2	17	Select In
5	Data Bit 3	18	Ground
6	Data Bit 4	19	Ground
7	Data Bit 5	20	Ground
8	Data Bit 6	21	Ground
9	Data Bit 7	22	Ground
10	Acknowledge	23	Ground
11	Busy	24	Ground
12	Paper End	25	Ground
13	Select		

AT Power Connector

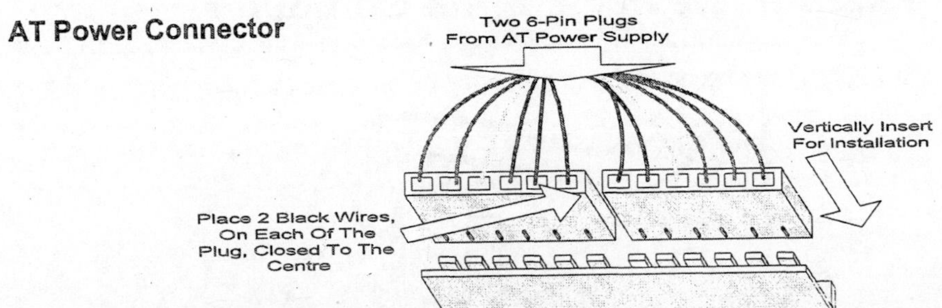

Pin	Signal Name	Pin	Signal Name
1	Power Good Signal	7	Ground
2	+5V	8	Ground
3	+12V	9	-5V
4	-12V	10	+5V
5	Ground	11	+5V
6	Ground	12	+5V

ATX Power Connector

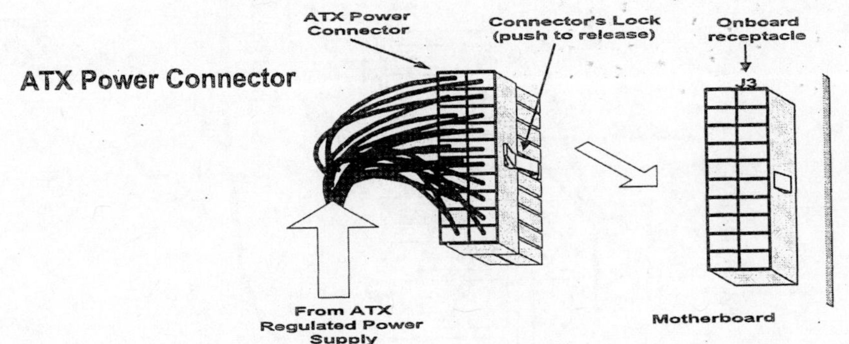

Pin	Signal Name	Pin	Signal Name
1	+3.3V	11	+3.3V
2	+3.3V	12	-12V
3	Ground	13	Ground
4	+5V	14	PW_ON
5	Ground	15	Ground
6	+5V	16	Ground
7	Ground	17	Ground
8	PWRGOOD	18	-5V
9	+5VSB	19	+5V
10	+12V	20	+5V

Connecting Various Devices to the Computer

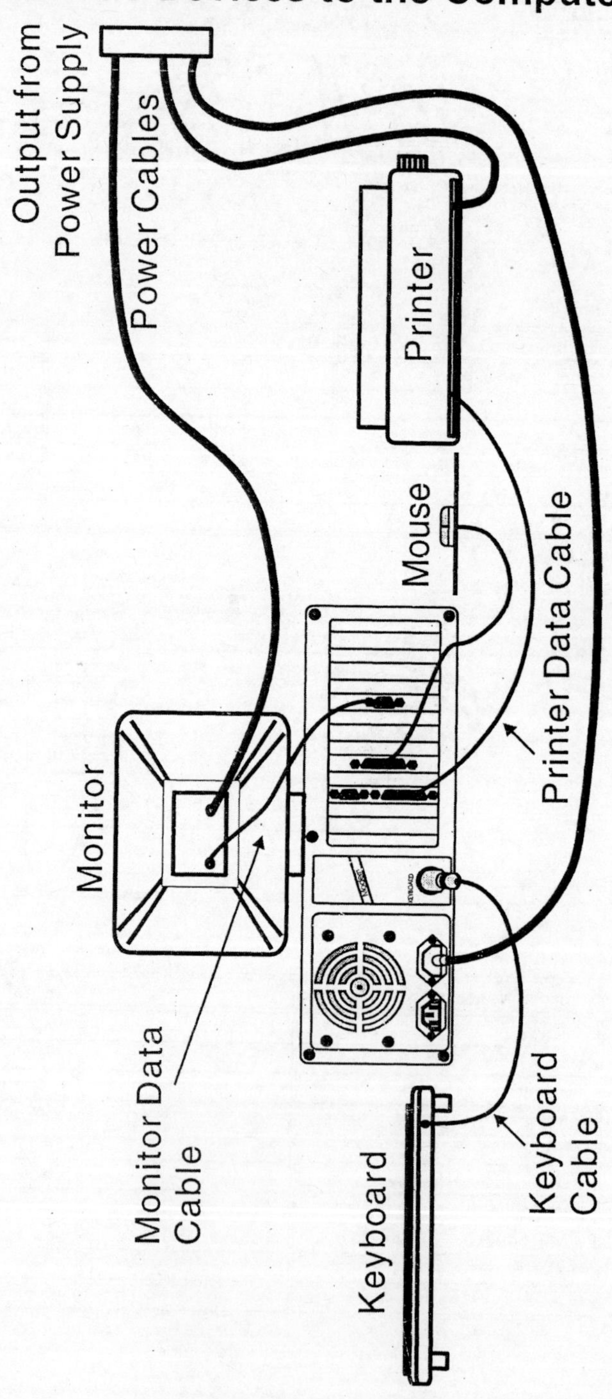

Index

B

C

N

O

P

T

U

V

W

X

Y

Z